I0022786

POST ARAB SPRING:
MIDDLE EAST REVIEWS

POST ARAB SPRING: MIDDLE EAST REVIEWS

Edited by

Mohammed M. Aman, PhD
Mary Jo Aman, MLIS

Westphalia Press

An Imprint of the Policy Studies Organization
Washington, DC
2015

Post Arab Spring: Middle East Reviews
All Rights Reserved 2015 by
Mohammed M. Aman and Mary Jo Aman, Editors
Copyright © 2015

CIP
Aman, Mohamed M.
Middle East Reviews, Mohammed M. Aman and Mary Jo Aman, Editors
Washington, DC: Westphalia Press, 2015

Middle East & North Africa-Policy and politics
1. Middle East and North Africa-Study and Book Reviews
2. Middle East and North Africa-Media Reviews 3. Arab Spring
i Aman, Mary Jo, Jt. Editor

ISBN-10: 1633912159
ISBN-13: 978-1-63391-215-1
Printed in the United States of America

Book cover and interior design
by Jeffrey Barnes
jbarnesbook.design

Westphalia Press
An imprint of Policy Studies Organization
1527 New Hampshire Ave., NW
Washington, DC. 20036
info@ipsonet.org

Updated material on this edition
can be found at the Westphalia Press website:
www.westphaliapress.org

Contents

INTRODUCTION

This monograph *Post Arab Spring: Middle East Reviews* brings together detailed reviews of the most recently published print and nonprint sources dealing with issues and events in and about the countries of the Middle East and North Africa (MENA). The signed and detailed review essays presented in this book and published on the Middle East Media & Book Reviews (MEMBR) website are detailed, descriptive, informative, and analytical. The reviews are written by experts in their respective fields of MENA studies and who are affiliated with major academic and research institutions and organizations around the world. The reviews are designed to inform and enrich the knowledge of readers, experts as well as novices, about new print and electronic publications on most important strategic and economic, yet volatile regions of the globe.

The books and media reviewed in this book cover wide-ranging subjects that range from humanities, philosophy and religion, broad areas of social sciences, history, arts, and literature published by major American and European publishers. Books dealing with scientific and technical subjects are not included, as they are outside the primary scope and intended subject coverage of this book. The reviews should also be of value to librarians, and area studies specialists in particular as well as decision makers with the important task of selecting book and media titles to be added to their library collections and resources in order to provide the best library services to their readers and the community of scholars and students they serve.

The reviews are grouped in alphabetical order by the titles of books under broad subject headings in alpha order, such as Arab Spring, Arts & Culture, Economics, Ethnic Minorities, History, Politics, Islam & Muslims, Judaism and Jews, Christianity and missionaries, Women, U.S. policy and intervention in the MENA region, and other related topics. Full bibliographic information is given for each listed title: authors(s) or editor(s) names(s), title, subtitle (if any), and place of publication, publisher, and year of publication, number of pages, price and the ISBN number, followed by the reviewer's initials. Reviewers' initials are arranged in alphabetical order at the end of the book and full names, terminal degrees, and present institutional affiliation are listed to correspond with the initials that appear under each review.

Future current reviews on MENA will continue to be published on a regular basis on the website of the Middle East Media & Book Reviews (MEMBR).

The editors wish to thank the publishers and authors of the reviewed books for making them available to MEMBR's panel of reviewers who also deserve our sincere thanks for the timely submission of their reviews.

Mohammed M. Aman, Ph.D.   **Mary Jo Aman, MLIS**

ARAB SPRING

*

REVIEW ESSAY

Sonia L. Alianak. *The Transition Towards Revolution and Reform: The Arab Spring Realized?* Edinburgh, UK: Edinburgh University Press, 224 pp. $56.42. ISBN: 978-0748692712. ISBN: 978-0748692729. (webready PDF)

Dalal Ghandour, et al. Revolution by Love: Emerging Arab Youth Voices. Philadelphia, PA: New City Community Press, 2014, 194 pp. $19.82 ISBN: 978-0984042999.

David Govrin. *The Journey to the Arab Spring: The Ideological Roots of the Middle East Upheaval in Arab Liberal Thought.* Portland, OR: Vallentine Mitchell, 2014. 334 pp. ISBN: 978-0853039174. Ebk: ISBN: 978-0863039273.

Edward Webb. *Media in Egypt and Tunisia: From Control to Transition.* New York, NY: Palgrave/Pivot, 2014. 128 pp. $62.42. ISBN: 978-1137409973. Ebk: ISBN: 978-113740996-6.

This review essay examines four books published on the topic of the Arab Spring that swept across the Middle East and North Africa and gained worldwide attention when it began in late 2010 and, with the exception of Tunisia, collapsed into dismal failure by the unexpected turn of events that befell others by the mid-2014. While Tunisia, thanks to its peaceful Jasmin revolution, enjoyed success with fair and peaceful elections and no intervention by its military, Egypt saw the military bring down the first democratically elected president since the army overthrew King Farouq of Egypt in July, 1952. Libya saw its colonel turned dictator Mu'ammar

1

al-Qadhafi killed by one of the rebels, and the ensuing civil war among various factions with no clear peaceful end in sight. Yemen's latest president is under house arrest at the time of this writing and battles are raging between the Houthi rebels and government forces around the Presidential Palace in San͏a. His predecessor Saleh, joined his Tunisian counterpart as political refugees in Saudi Arabia. Syria's situation is the worse in the lot, with the army fighting Western-backed rebels and the intrusion of ISIS/IS/Daʿish, or by whatever name they are known in the media, in the civil and ethnic war, not only in Syria, but also in parts of Iraq.

The oil-producing monarchies of the Arab Gulf States and members of the Gulf Cooperation Council (GIC) first feared the spread of the Arab Spring into their countries and reacted with the usual promises of introducing a semblance of democratic reforms and increasing the salaries of government employees and increasing food and fuel subsidies. The Bahraini Shiʿa uprising was met with joint Gulf military force led by Saudi Arabia. Other mini Arab Spring demonstrations in Qatar, UAE, and Oman were brought under control. The long-lasting monarchs of Jordan and Morocco kept up with the rising tide by temporarily acting on their promises for introducing some tolerable elements of democratic reforms in their kingdoms and affecting some unobjectionable political reforms, but also reminding their subjects of their historic religious standing as the descendants of the Prophet Muhammad and hence as legitimate commanders of the faithful. However, with the change of events in the affected countries and the demise of the Muslim Brotherhood and other opposition parties, we are now witnessing a return to political oppression and curtailment of freedom of speech and expression as evidenced by the imprisonment and flogging of bloggers and "netizens" in Arab countries.

The Arab Spring from 2010 to 2014 was mainly about jobs for the many unemployed but educated Arab Youth, rising prices, corruption at political and other levels, presidents and their families, and political cronies who enriched themselves to no end and manipulated elections and media so they could stay in power forever. One cannot ignore the impact of the new infosphere (Internet, mobile phones, social media, and satellite television such as Al-Jazeera) that also played a major role in broadcasting the revolutions calling for the uprising and to organize the massive demonstrations that forced unwanted rulers such as Ben Ali of Tunis, Mubarak of Egypt, and Saleh of Yemen to abandon their posts as presidents and find refuge in Saudi Arabia (as in the case of Ben Ali and Saleh) or to be brought to trial (Mubarak, which was aborted with the ascendance of the military to power in 2014).

The Arab Spring and uprisings produced numerous books dealing with various aspects of the Arab people's revolts to get rid of their long presiding rulers. Some of these books are reviewed separately in this book, but others are examined in this review essay on this important milestone in the history of MENA countries.

Sonia L. Alianak's book, *The Transition towards Revolution and Reform: The Arab Spring Realized?* is a valuable academic contribution to the literature on the Arab Spring. As a professor of political science at the University of Texas-Rio Grande

Valley, Dr. Alianak gives her readers a comparative perspective on the Arab Spring people in the affected countries transitioning to a democratic system of government. Her study attempts to evaluate the relative success or failure of the move to democracy of the four countries of Tunisia, Egypt, Morocco, and Jordan. She addressed these issues as they pertain to the 2011 uprisings especially in these four countries as her four case studies.

Dr. Alianak uses a theoretical approach to analyzing, in particular, the revolutions in Tunisia and Egypt which can also be applied to potentially similar revolutions in the Middle East and North Africa. Her study compares the methods used by the secular leaders of Tunisia and Egypt in dealing with people demanding political and economic reforms, with those resorted to by the monarchs of Morocco and Jordan in accommodating their people's priority of reform. While the revolutions in both Egypt and Tunisia were secular, the attempts for reform in Morocco and Jordan took on religious overtones by the monarchs in both countries as they consider themselves descendants of the Prophet Muhammad and hence, commanders of the faithful, and retained and commanded the loyalty and support of their militaries as well as prominent Muslim leaders.

After a very informative introduction, Dr. Alianak deals with the issues of the transitions toward revolution: Jasmine Revolution in Tunisia; the transition toward reform; reforming the Moroccan monarchy; and reforming the Jordanian monarchy, followed by a detailed conclusion and a comprehensive bibliography (pp. 169-203). Professor Alianak meticulously and extensively documented her study, which is major contribution to understanding the forces behind the Arab Spring. The book should be a valuable source for students and writers on the short-lived Arab Spring.

The Journey to the Arab Spring: The Ideological Roots of the Middle East, by David Govrin provides an in-depth treatment of the new liberal discourse on attempts for democratization and political discourse in the Arab world over the last three decades. The book is divided into two parts: first, the definition and importance of terms that have originated in the West, and later adopted by the Arab world and entered into the Arab vocabulary. The second part deals with the principal approaches to the analysis of the democratization attempts in the Arab world as reflected in the research literature and the various explanations given by writers about the absence of democratization in the Arab countries. The explanations are varied and they include historical, economic, cultural, cultural, and social aspects and influences.

Govrin focuses on a broad diverse range of new liberals, including heads of research institutes, editors of periodicals, writers, intellectuals, policies, publicists, academics, public activists, business leaders, and economists, among others. The writings and opinions of these liberal activists provide excellent analysis of the new Arab liberal discourse from the 1990s in attempt to answer several principal questions, mainly: What is the historic and ideological background of the growth of the new liberal currents, which circles belong to it and what is their world view? What is the impact of regional and international events and the weight of the media in creating ideological pluralism related to the discourse and its events? What is the new liberal's democratic vision of their way to realize democracy in their countries and what are the main obstacles to it? What are the status in and the influence of the new liberals on the state, society, and central regime in comparison with other ideological currents, in particular Islamists and Arab nationalists. The book's six chapters address these and other vital issues relating to the broad topic of "Arab liberals," the approach to democratization as reflected in the research literature, and the various explanations for the absence of democracy in the Arab world.

In his book, Media in Egypt and Tunisia: From Control to Transition, Dr. Webb, who teaches Middle East politics at Dickinson College in Pennsylvania and was previously media officer at the British Embassy in Cairo, provides an informed discussion of the two case studies of the Internet and media systems using a comparative analytical approach to address theoretical questions about the relation between media systems and their social and political contexts, to understand change over time in media systems, and to deepen our understanding of particular national media institutions. Building on this approach, Dr. Webb's book explains "how the pre-uprising regimes in Egypt and Tunisia managed or resisted change in media, and what the consequences of their strategies may be for the transitional and future political regimes." (p. 5).

The author divided his book into four chapters: "Egyptian and Tunisian Systems in Global Context;" "Egypt;" "Tunisia;" "After the Uprisings;" and "After the Revolution." In Chapter 1, the author argues that, even with the globalization of media, national media systems continue to be work studying. Webb discusses various schemas for categorizing media systems and explains and justifies the interview-based research methods he used for this book. In Chapters 2 and 3, Webb describes and analyzes the media systems of Mubarak's Egypt and Ben Ali's Tunisia, respectively, based mainly on interviews with media professionals. In Chapter 4, he considers some examples of emerging media such as YouTUBE and online-only news operations, as well as emerging collaboration between social and traditional media.

The book concludes with a useful list of references which lists Arabic and English sources that are useful for further research on the subject. While social media played a role in spreading the news about the Arab demonstrations against these Arab regimes, the established Arab media became part of the news coverage supplementing the nonestablished new media run mostly by amateurs and nonestablished news conveyers like young Arab bloggers and netizens. Drawing on a comparison with the experiences of other transitional systems, Webb advances some preliminary projections about unlikely future developments, and concludes with some tentative policy recommendations. Among these recommendations are how hard it is with the new government—as with Dr. Morsi before General El-Sisi—to have a pluralistic media to emerge as once hoped in the aftermath of toppling Mubarak. In Tunisia, the hope is for the transfer of media from government ownership to genuine autonomous or independent public institutions.

The common thread that runs through the book's essays are: (1) New media; (2) Education; and (3) Demographic transitions. As discussed in great length in Webb's book, the new and social media played a major role in the most recent Arab uprising.

Revolution by Love is a collection of brief essays by 17 young Arabs from various Arab countries with various education and professional backgrounds that had lived the Arab Spring that ended before what they inked had dried. To many the turn of events in 2014 that saw the Arab Spring fade into a bloody counter revolution—especially in Egypt, Libya, Syria, Yemen, and Bahrain—must have been a major disappointment to these young people's hopes and dreams for a better future for their native lands.

The common thread that runs through the book's essays are: (1) New media; (2) Education; and (3) Demographic transitions. As with Webb's book reviewed above, the new and social media is also a major topic of discussion in Revolution by Love, albeit with less academic fervor than in Webb's book, but with a more personal and autobiographical touch from each young contributor. Topics like education, family and parental influence, community activism, and individual idealism come through the writings of these young educated people. The book concludes with background information about each writer, and it is interesting to read how many of them are or have been involved with nongovernmental organizations (NGOs) such as BRAVO in Bahrain; INJAZ in Jordan; AMIDEAST; UNDP; UNOPS; EU; ACT-Think & Decide; UNRWA; Carnegie Endowment for International Peace. **MMA**

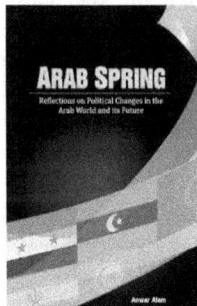

Anwar Alam, Ed. *Arab Spring: Reflections on Political Changes in the Arab World and its Future.* **New Delhi, IN: New Century Publications, 2014. 433 pp. $87.50 ISBN: 978-8177083958.**

Most of the 19 chapters of this book were originally papers read at an international conference held on February 15–17, 2012 at Jamia Millia Islamia in New Delhi, India, and organized by the Center for West Asian Studies, then edited for this volume; other chapters were later added to complete the plan of the book.

It begins with a magisterial Introduction by Anwar Alam entitled "Making Sense of Arab Spring," followed by an essay by M. K. Bhadrakumar entitled "Arab Spring is in Great Distress," which could have been better placed at the end of the book as an Afterword. The 19 chapters come next and are neatly divided into five thematic parts. Their authors deal with various aspects of the Arab Spring, including the social and political forces that led to it; and they examine the contending ideas that eventually brought it about in various forms in different Arab countries.

Western colonialism had been ousted from the Arab world for some time before the Arab Spring, but it had been replaced by indigenous autocratic and authoritarian rule. Democracy, freedom, individual dignity, and fulfillment of aspirations were still a far cry when, on December 17, 2010, the self-immolation of a fruit vendor, Mohammed Bouazizi, happened in Sidi Bouzid in Tunisia in an exasperated protest against authorities harassing him. This simple but horrible act heralded what came to be called "the Arab Spring," for it was followed by riots and a revolt that brought down the Tunisian government structure in favor of democratic principles. It was succeeded by similar and mostly spontaneous riots and revolts in Egypt, Yemen, Libya, and other Arab countries and, likewise, it prompted democratic change and promises of better life conditions.

It is not only the details and results of how, for example, Gaddafi was removed from power and killed by the people in Libya, or how Hosni Mubarak was deposed, imprisoned, and brought to trial in Egypt that are interesting, but also larger issues such as the place of Islam in the Arab Spring (Part 4) or the responses of the international community to it (Part 5).

Regarding the place of Islam in the Arab Spring, Shajahan Madampat's article, "Islamism and Democracy: Between Tactical and Pragmatic Imperatives and Doctrinal Inflexibility," argues that Islamism contravenes the idea of equal citizenship irrespective of religious affiliation and says that an Islamic state contradicts the essential elements of democracy, based as it is on the idea of the Muslim majority coming to power without internalizing democratic values, including secularism in public life. Democracy would necessitate doctrinal flexibility and tactical pragmatism in the political give-and-take of governance. It is not that Islam is anti-democratic but it is the ideological construction of Islam—or Islamism—that is undemocratic.

As demonstrated in this book, the Arab Spring succeeded in bringing about certain democratic changes in the Arab world, but not all that the Arab people wanted; nor was it similar in all Arab countries—in some, its successes were muted or followed by dissensions. Institutional transformations and stability are bound to eventually emerge, and this book helps in understanding what is happening and what may still be expected to happen. **IJB**

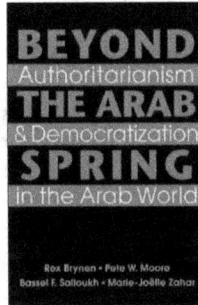

Rex Brynen, Pete W. Moore, Bassel Salloukh Salloukh. *Beyond the Arab Spring: Authoritarianism and Democratization in the Arab World.* Boulder, CO: Lynne Reiner, 2012. 349 pp. $27.50. ISBN: 978-1588268785.

The events of the "Arab Spring" of 2011 generally came as a surprise to scholars. For much of the past 20 years, analysts of Middle Eastern politics had been preoccupied with explaining the unique persistence of authoritarianism in the region in contrast with widespread democratization throughout Africa, Latin America, and other portions of Asia. In this book, the authors seek to explain the Arab Spring amid theoretical debates that have dominated the discipline of political science, including political culture, the spread of political Islam, institutional change, and political economy. In so doing, they create a sense of the continuity of theory for understanding both past authoritarianism and present transition to democratic forms.

Brynen, Moore, Salloukh, and Zahar are researchers associated with the Interuniversity Consortium for Arab and Middle Eastern Studies (ICAMES) and linked through their shared experiences as faculty and former doctoral students at McGill University in Montreal. They collaborated on a prior project, the two-volume Political Liberalization and Democratization in the Arab World edited by Brynen, Bahgat Korany, and Paul Noble in the mid-1990s. At the time, the notion of political liberalization and democratization in the Middle East was not much more than a dream, encapsulated in essays that highlighted pressures for democratic reform coming from nascent civil societies, tentative legislative initiatives, and popular demands for change. Almost 20 years later, the authors return to the themes of their prior work to write up a sort of report card. They conclude that any explanation one might give for the extensive political change embodied in the Arab Spring must hang on multiple causes and multiple levels of analysis, stressing "catalytic and synergistic effects different variables and levels have on each other" (p. 288, stress in original). Hence they pursue a comprehensive analysis of theories of authoritarianism and democracy in the region.

The book opens with an extensive survey of the history and events of the Arab Spring. This overview is comprehensive and fast-paced. It first turns to North Africa, where revolutionary movements arose and found their greatest successes. The links and similarities between the Tunisian and Egyptian revolutions are highlighted and contrasted with the cases of Libya, Algeria, and Morocco, where "institutional settings and historical legacies" served as barriers to change (p. 37). Moving to the Arab Mashreq, the authors conclude that the absence of regime change so far is rooted in the more complex array of domestic societal cleavages, tighter relations between the militaries and the regimes, and the shadow of regional and international crises such as the Iraq War and the ongoing Israeli occupation of Palestinian lands (pp. 62-63). Closing off the section, the authors turn to the reactionary and conservative monarchies of the Arabian Peninsula, where, with the notable exceptions of Bahrain and Yemen, the Arab Spring had little impact. In this region, oil rents, external supports, and cooptation of societal groups have perpetuated autocratic rule, but not without some stirrings of political opposition.

After this introductory survey of the Arab Spring, the authors turn to theoretical and methodological considerations that played a role in the process of change across the region. Through a series of essays, they deal ably with the scholarly debates that have dominated causal inference with regard to authoritarianism in the region. The first theme is political culture, which is largely dismissed by the authors for its tendency to lean in the direction of essentialism, even among scholars who seek to contextualize their understandings of cultural factors. The second theme is the significance of political Islam, a topic which is covered by guest writer Janine Clark, who cautions the reader to understand Islamists based less upon their public rhetoric and more on their practical choices. Third and fourth come installments on institutional issues, specifically electoral politics and the efforts of monarchies aimed at maintaining their position in spite of pressures for change.

More substantial chapters follow on the political economies of rentier states and economic liberalization, the new Arab media, and regional and international influences on authoritarianism and democracy. The authors argue against the overdetermination of oil revenues as a factor encouraging authoritarianism and make the case that economic liberalization has not favored democratization, rather that it has reinforced the rule of a coterie of military and political clients of Arab regimes. The authors assess the development of new media as a political influence through the lens of state ownership and rightly point out that outside social media platforms, much of the electronic media follows the dictates of state owners. At the same time, they admit that where the media is concerned, "[n]othing compares to Al Jazeera's coverage of the popular uprisings that swept across the Arab world in 2011" (p. 238). Finally, they deal with the persistence of external attention to the region which allows many regimes to stay in power without needing to pursue serious efforts at reform. They conclude that a troika of external alliances, rents, and coercive apparatus is essential to resisting democratic change in these states: "where one or more have been wanting, they have faced challenges" (p. 278).

This book is a timely summary of the fount of wisdom coming out of studies of

Middle East politics in the run-up to the Arab Spring. It does particularly well at updating the reader on the state of knowledge in the discipline of Middle East politics. Indeed, it would thus serve as an excellent summary for graduate students preparing for comprehensive exams. As an assessment of the roots of the Arab Spring, it does not do quite as well. There are times when the work reads like an extended literature review rather than a causal contribution to our understanding of the Arab Spring. Indeed, in some chapters the Arab Spring is something of an afterthought. As a result, the promise of the title, going beyond the Arab Spring, is not entirely fulfilled, paralleling the expectations of many reform-minded Arabs.

The authors are particularly tentative about what can be gained through political–cultural analysis. Nonetheless, political–cultural developments clearly help us to understand the more proximate changes that took place on the ground in the early 2011. In one parenthetical remark, the authors dismiss the relevance of interactive reality television, which did not enhance democratic participation but instead allowed "regimes to mobilize their publics around parochial national sentiments and cloak their authoritarianism with a veneer of participation" (pp. 247-248). This seems to ignore the extent to which such participatory media reinforced the kind of Internet organizing, Facebook postings, and media feeds that flowed out of Tahrir Square in January and February that year. Cultural developments in the liberalized media of Egypt would also go a long way to reinforcing the authors' argument that the "imagination of the possible" contributed to the Arab Spring. For example, it is strange that there is no mention of the publication of the damning critique leveled by Alaa al-Aswany's 2002 novel The Yacoubian Building, considering the book's astonishing popularity as a novel and a motion picture amid the storm of discontent in Egypt following the 2005 elections.

Furthermore, despite concentrating on the complexity of institutional and economic influences on change in the Middle East, the authors give relatively short shrift to the real challenge of developing a pluralist model in the wake of each revolution. It is stated that such societal complexity is a problem that hinders change in the Mashreq, but the truth is that cultural pluralism is an obvious impediment even in those countries that seem to be most homogeneous, such as Egypt. Demonstrators in Tahrir Square in early 2011 emphasized national unity, chanting the slogan of "Christians and Muslims, one hand." This went a long way toward reassuring foreign audiences and defusing any attempts by the regime to marshal sectarian resentments against the popular movement. In the wake of the revolution, the politics of cultural pluralism have become far more problematic. Enshrining constitutions that take into account the desire for change while maintaining openings for cultural pluralism has arisen as the single most divisive challenge.

The strengths of this book include the authors' deep insights into political theories of authoritarianism and democracy as well as their excellent summaries of the Arab Spring movement. Indeed, as a report on the state of the discipline in the midst of the Arab Spring, this book is a rare accomplishment. For a more fulsome understanding of political developments beyond the Arab Spring, this book merely provides an introduction. **PSR**

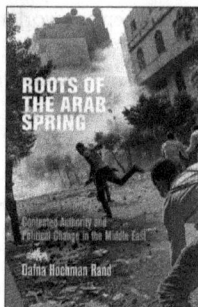

Dafna Hochman Rand. *Roots of the Arab Spring: Contested Authority and Political Change in the Middle East.* **Philadelphia, PA: University of Pennsylvania Press, 2013. 171 pp. $47.50. ISBN: 978-0812245301.**

The conventional wisdom that saw Middle Eastern governments as stable prior to 2011 was wrong, as it did not understand the political changes that saw popular frustration build until it exploded following the Tunisian vegetable street trader's self-immolation. Dafna Hochman Rand offers the Roots of the Arab Spring: Contested Authority and Political Change in the Middle East, a book that presents an important first glance at the events that led to the Arab Spring. According to the author, the 2011 uprisings were not random, but were the long-term outcome of transformations that took place in the region over the previous two decades.

Rand points to three political changes dating from the 1990s to 2000s as the source of the widespread indignation that drove the Arab Spring. First, a desire for free expression, aided by new technology, made it possible to hold public conversations that the state could not prevent or regulate which allowed people to read and openly discuss subjects that were previously forbidden. Second, several Middle Eastern leaders modified the government institutions to de-democratize and restrict personal freedoms. Third, new leaders came to power, around the millennium, who sought to prevent liberal reforms. These factors altered the relationship between the government and the public in a way that saw massive resentment, dissention, and rage grow; and this supported the passionate protests that emerged in 2011. American policymakers failed to recognize these tensions or the possibility for massive collective action against leaders who appeared to have secure control over their societies. Rand offers these three changes as the main factors that led to the Arab Spring and presents three case studies to support her proposal.

The author took several trips to the region before the uprisings in 2011 and was surprised to find authoritarian governments struggling to control their people, and saw the danger of a political miscalculation by rulers. Rand perceived the potential for political instability as the regimes were discredited and new independent journalists and bloggers emerged in Morocco, Algeria, Egypt, Jordan, Kuwait, Yemen, and Bahrain challenging the limits to free speech. The global governance liberal norms reached a critical level; Arab leaders needed to speak the language of democracy while maintaining authoritarian institutions. Expectations were raised, followed by disappointment, which contributed to the anger against the regimes.

When press censorship weakened and readers could freely encounter and participate in open discussions in subjects that had previously been taboo, Middle Eastern governments did not foresee the long-term consequences. In the 1990s, there was a movement in several Arab states to attempt to slightly liberalize speech and permit an independent media. This opportunity saw debates appearing in newspapers and online addressing previously forbidden topics. Arab societies changed during this time as literacy rates grew and the population with Internet access increased, thus giving people a desire for free communication. Local governments failed to see how this openness could produce negative consequences that would weaken their ability to maintain censorship. Technological changes made it difficult, if not impossible, for authorities to control speech and soon people challenged the limits they experienced in their daily lives. Once the public had a desire for open discussion, the governments could not prevent it and leaders were no longer able to impose absolute censorship. Nevertheless, governments tried to target free speech and started to arrest bloggers and journalists. Egypt, Bahrain, Morocco, Tunisia, and Jordan all changed their laws to inhibit discourse. This failed as anonymous bloggers continued to write and did not consent to the restrictions. This weakened the impediments to collective action and contributed to the broad support for protests that emerged in the Arab Spring.

Another approach Middle Eastern regimes used to consolidate dictatorships was to institute constitutional reforms that increased the dictator's control, but were strategic in that the government could frame the change so that it sounded democratic to outsiders. From 1990 to 2010, there were 16 instances where a regional government made anti-liberal constitutional revisions. The most common form was to create an upper legislative chamber staffed by the leader's men or to change election laws. While this tactic had the short-term benefit of reinforcing the rulers' control over society, it also weakened support for gradual democratic reforms as people saw that only a radical change that completely broke from the current government could bring freedom. Governments implementing these changes were spared international criticism, as foreign states fell victim to the rhetoric and misunderstood constitutional revisions. The unintended consequence was the growing dissatisfaction with the regime that would erupt in the intense protests that affected every area government.

The final focus Rand presents is the vulnerability new leaders faced as they emerged to succeed their father or half-brother. This caused them to initially take steps to expand limited freedoms and, after they solidified their control, they would then move to curtail the new liberties. From 1995 to 2006, leadership changes took place in Morocco, Jordan, Qatar, Syria, Bahrain, Kuwait, and Saudi Arabia. The reforms that were initiated were designed to find new patrons that would be used to consolidate the dictatorship. The new rulers introduced reforms to help economic growth and to attract members of the opposition, so that it would then be further divided, thus solidifying the ruler's control. The new rights would also deflect international criticism that would otherwise arise to condemn the handing over of power to a family member, and Rand argues, leaders would also be able to attract foreign aid. The difficulty was that once reforms started, their momentum was difficult to control, and this generated unintended consequences that threatened rulers' legitimacy. Once leaders saw the dangers and perceived the threat to their interests, the liberalizing policies were reversed and governments moved to reintroduce social restrictions, thereby intensifying popular frustration and anti-authoritarian sentiments.

What were Washington's policies toward Arab governments in democracy and human rights promotion? The United States has provided minimal support to liberal reform initiatives in the region, but failed to recognize the tensions and vulnerabilities that would confront the region in 2011. The 2003 Iraq War was one path used to promote democracy, but, tragically, this made reforms even less likely in surrounding states. In the mid-2000s, Rand points out that the Bush Administration used its "Freedom Agenda" to promote democracy, but this was dismissed in 2006, as Washington saw Islamists come to power through the initiatives it encouraged. When the new Arab leaders undertook reforms that weakened representation and took away rights, the United States consented without protest. Rand points out that the United States also misunderstood the leadership changes in Bahrain, Jordan, Morocco, and Syria, and that its general efforts to promote democracy were inadequate because these policies were based on false assumptions concerning governmental stability and popular support.

What lessons does the Arab Awakening present to evaluate the U.S. policy to the region? The United States did not understand the domestic consequences leadership changes produced in Middle Eastern states and has only weakly worked to promote democracy in the region. Rand argues that Washington should change its approach to the Middle East and promote democratic reforms, but in a case-by-case basis rather than through a region-wide project. The local demands for freedom of speech should be promoted diplomatically and the institutional reforms that make governments less democratic should be challenged. The regimes supporting continuous gradual reforms should be rewarded and the United States needs to recognize the unique opportunity provided by leadership changes and be present to offer help in bringing about liberal governmental reforms.

This work suffers from one important weakness: selection bias in Rand's case studies. She presents her theory, so that it appears to apply to all Arab States and then goes on to offer examples that are not representative of the entire region. In other words, she illustrates each theoretical proposal with a case the most clearly fits it. This weakens her claims as the subjects she highlights were not present in all the states where she claims they apply. This is a common problem in case study research as scholars tend to focus on areas with which they are familiar rather than on subjects more representative of the population they wish to understand. Nevertheless, Rand's work presents important ideas that create a compelling narrative recounting the events that led to the massive protests in the countries where the Arab Spring produced the strongest changes.

In some ways, the Arab Spring is like the nonviolent revolution of 1989 which was not predicted by the scholars most familiar with the region; after the event, it was possible to piece together the changes that made the iron curtain fall. The same can be said for the Arab Spring; while it is still too early to understand and offer a definitive account, the author contributes a valuable work that offers an initial explanation for the 2011 events that led to uprisings and leadership changes in the Middle East and North Africa. Because of this, her work will benefit policymakers, academics, and field workers. **GDD**

Hamid Dabashi. *The Arab Spring: The End of Postcolonialism*. New York, NY: Zed Books, 2012. 296 pp. $ 19.95. ISBN: 9781780322230.

From the outset it is important to underscore the fact that The Arab Spring: The End of Postcolonialism represents a gesture of solidarity with, and endorsement of the Arab Spring. On the other hand, this book should be placed within the context of Dabashi's earlier arguments; it should be conceived as a continuation in its fundamental process of argumentation of the author's earlier analysis of the civil rights movement in Iran of 2009 and the Green Movement and the U.S. (2010). The Arab Spring, on this account, is yet another chapter in the author's thinking that stresses the fact of substantive and consistent movements for change, which have been carving out a new "liberation geography" in the Islamic world at large. There is of course a degree of unknowability about this new and unfolding horizon, yet Dabashi insists that we need to continue to imagine it and theorize it even in its most precarious and perhaps cryptic and premature stages. The need to theorize this post ideological moment must also come from Dabashi's positioning in the U.S. academia marred by an institutionalized racism against Islamic and Arab ideas (real or sublime). U.S. academia, having limited the study of the Middle East to national interests, and security concerns, has only promoted the politics of despair and fatalism about the Arab world. The Arab Spring has continued to challenge the myopic hermeneutics of many so-called experts on the Middle East, who, like Bernard Lewis and others, continue to rehearse what is not only unreliable knowledge, but also shamelessly oppressive imagining. The current spin-doctors, or as Dabashi categorizes them, the analysts and the annalists exhibited little trust in the very possibility of democratic thinking and agency among Arabs and Muslims.

This exigency for theorization inevitably inspired and enhanced by revealing events on the grounds, means that the relationship between all movements of civil rights and liberation in the larger Islamic world are "variations on the same theme of delayed defiance of both European colonialism and its extended shadow of post-colonial aftermath." For Dabashi, the Arab Spring announces a new consciousness whose drive and even raison d'être is not only to overthrow corrupt, self-colonized and self-imperialized regimes, but to declare the birth of a new knowledge—an epistemology of liberation that must suspend the persistent old fashioned binaries and clichéd ideas of Orientalism. The Arab Spring marks an ecstatic moment for self-fashioning; it unravels a double bind in its resistance of both domestic and global structures of tyranny. The Arab Spring advances a new perspective that emphasizes cosmopolitan worldliness. Of greater significance, this moment reclaims history; it develops a democratic vocabulary, and even mobilizes European and American centers to revise their own structures and institutions of democratic practice. The Arab Spring, for Dabashi, ultimately announces the self-exhaustion of all regressive, authoritarian and imperialistic projects of Islamism, "new American Century" and colonial Zionism.

In the final analysis, Dabashi's strongest point is to see these revolts not as ideological constructions, but as a "retrieval" of a dormant and innate cosmopolitan worldliness characteristic of many Arab and Islamic cultures. The idea of "liberation geography" consists of freeing one's space from within the context of one's historical connection with that geography of worldliness, and thus, inclusion of other perspectives and other possibilities. Imagining the Arab and the Muslim, in his and her full capacity to retrieve history, to renew it, to make it, is what proclaims the end of distorted Western imagination, and Israeli propaganda. This new theory of history, this "revolutionary dispensation" is what provincializes the west, what terminates its self-declared and enforced auto normativity. The Arab Spring remaps a new geography based more on a new configuration of ethos rather than ethnos. On this account the driving slogan, al-Sha'b Yurid Isqat al-Nizam, is more than a will-to-overthrow, but it is a will-to-know differently.

Since this book was written in the midst of the Arab Spring, Dabashi is clearly caught up in the excitement of these radical transformations in many Arab nation states. The real exuberance on the ground finds its expressions in the metaphors, turns of phrase, paradoxes and at times sublime language that haunt the book. In fact, according to Dabashi's analysis "we are moving—almost imperceptibly but nevertheless consistently—towards the discovery of a new world" (p. 9). This new world predicts the erasure of postcolonial condition, and the irrelevance of its ruling protagonists; in other words, European and U.S. imperialistic habits and deeply seated structures of control, discipline, enframing, and museumizing of its others have begun to shutter by the sheer fearlessness of ordinary people demanding dignity and freedom. Dabashi has maintained the fervor of the Arab moment by framing the materialization of such ending of postcoloniality in one syncretic and synthesizing concept, that of exhaustion. Exhaustion is the moment when an idea becomes extinct, self-defeating, and self-negating by the sheer measure of its many repetitions, its many ideological pronouncements; and by very fact that the idea had been overtaken by the internal logic of historical processes. For the first time, postcolonial critics may bring the debate of postcoloniality to a close; the idea of postcolonialism can be pronounced dead; "The epistemic condition of that state of coloniality has finally exhausted itself."

Yet, even as we take Dabashi's optimism seriously and the potential for the idea of postcoloniality to have exhausted itself, aren't we simplifying the latent ideological sediments of global capitalism; its slippery capacity to remain invisible and suspiciously quiescent in the emerging new structures of domestic and global discourses as we see in the most prominent case of Egypt in its attempt to further resolve the mandate of the democratically elected new president? Is the postcolonial condition truly and completely over or "overcome?" Isn't this "overcomeness" not necessarily total, totalizing or complete as yet? How do we know the completeness of epistemic exhaustion if we continue to also see its returns—usually hidden in national and global capitalist subconscious as the White House itself becomes black, yet continues to perform white supremacy? The two adjectives that have occurred consistently in Dabashi's analysis (exhaustion and finality) may be too premature at times considering the unfinality of both operations and therefore the need for waiting and more patience to allow more realistic time and its many contingencies to subvert postcoloniality's procedures of persistence. Dabashi's insightful, thought-provoking and progressive reading is punctuated by a sneaky certitude that may be unsettling and at times more wishful than real.

This audacious elevation of the Arab Spring to the level of epistemic breakthrough, of radical discontinuation with discourses of imperialism and postcoloniality is necessary, but should remain un-circumscribable. The strength of Dabashi's argument is paradoxically his deferral of any potential faux pas in articulating the new knowledge of Arab self-liberating modernity; the Arab has indeed woken up from a deep slumber for good, and as a result he will circumvent the restrictions of his postcolonial condition of political and cultural malaise. This is indeed just the "outdated ethnos" that will be overcome by the Arab's ethos of inclusion that will undermine the production of repressive knowledge from ethnographic museums, the National Geographic, the academic discipline of anthropology and their modes of "auto-normative superiority" and its ultimate metaphysics of discipline, control, and enframing.

No doubt, the strength of such argument lies more in what can be attributed to Dabashi's work in general, as a work of the public intellectual. Dabashi insists that we need to push the boundaries of our thinking; he alerts us to be one step ahead of history by learning and inventing conceptual frameworks that are capable of grasping and theorizing such history. A public and humanist intellectual is the one who does not settle for less than seeing a light at the end of that very decadent and dehumanizing tunnel called postcoloniality. In this sense, I read Dabashi's use of a seemingly deterministic lexicon describing a resolved, fully fledged Arab Spring more as a cognitive and political strategy for responsible deconstructive hermeneutics that must begin now at this very moment.

Dabashi's assessment of Arab revolts is a refreshingly forward-looking perspective that places the Muslim and the Arab at the heart of worldliness. The Arab subject should be perceived more through his and her sheer acts-in-history whose purpose is to concretize his delayed, deferred aspirations and ideas, and to turn them into realities that can—over time—bring the theoretically exigent anxiety for a final and exhaustive closure of postcolonial condition.

NB: On page 23 "Major oppositional rallies in Morocco in February forced Hassan II" should be corrected instead, to a reference to the current king Mohammed VI, who succeeds Hassan II in 1999. **YY**

ARTS & CULTURE

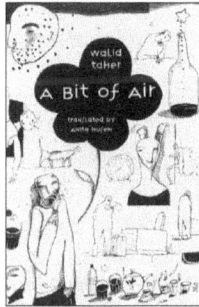

Walid Taher. Translated by Anita Husen. *A Bit of Air.* **Austin, TX: The Center for Middle Eastern Studies. University of Texas at Austin, 2012. 136 pp. $16.00. ISBN: 978-0292742383.**

This delightful little book in the series of "Emerging Voices from the Middle East" edited by Tarek el-Ariss was originally published in Arabic in Egypt in 2008 as *Habbet Hawa.* Its author, Walid Taher (born in Cairo, 1969) is a well-known illustrator and writer of children's books who has won several awards. This is his first book that goes beyond children's literature; it has received wide acclaim in the Arab world, as much for its novelty as for it pointed political, social, and existential views, accompanied by illustrations, and virtually creating a new literary genre.

The book consists of a succession of brief and independent observations on life, each with a cartoon-like illustration. Simple but profound, they are written in the Egyptian dialect. They sometimes have allusions to well-known Egyptian songs or famous sayings, but they always stir reflection. They are presented in hand-written Arabic on the page and each has its succinct translation in English, the illustration being integral to both adjacent texts.

The English translation has successfully tried to preserve the spirit of the colloquial Egyptian Arabic by using conversational English except where the Arabic sometimes rises to a more formal register, and so the English follows suit. The effect is invariably a happy one in conveying the message of Walid Taher, despite cultural differences between speakers of the two languages, differences which have been dealt with creatively by the translator. Perhaps a few examples might be sufficient to bring home the delicacy of the translation.

On page 42 is the following Arabic text with an illustration showing a man with a sheep's face and ears: *kân nifsî/ ashûf nafsî/ mish kharûf...../ ....qabli mâandibih!*

On page 43 is the following English translation: I have always wished/I could see myself/As something other than a sheep...../ ....before my slaughter!

This is an image of an Egyptian human being who knows he will be sacrificed like a sheep by those in authority, but who wishes he could see himself as a real person with human and civil rights before that.

On page 78 is the following Arabic text with an illustration showing a man running and looking behind him in fear: *garayt astakhbîmin qadarî/ laqayt il-makhba'... huwwa qadarî!!*

On page 79 is the following English translation: I ran for shelter from my fate/ Only to find that the shelter....is my fate!!

This is an image of an Egyptian man who tries to run away from his fate in difficult circumstances and finds that there is no escape from it.

On page 128 is an Arabic text with an illustration showing a man with a tail, sitting happily at a table with a drink, and singing: *ayh qîmat abqâ husanan gamîlan/ bassi marbût..../ aw nisr 'azîm mûhannat..mahtût/ lâ ya 'ammi.. khalîni zayy maanâ / qird maghûl.../ bass mabsût !*

On page 129 is the following English translation: What's the use of being a beautiful horse.../ But tied up..../ Or a great eagle, mummified..set aside/ No, sir, leave me as I am/ An unnoticed monkey..../ But happy!

From these examples, one notices a somber attitude. It must be kept in mind that the Arabic book was published in 2008, when Husni Mubarak was president of Egypt, and before the people's uprising of January 25, 2011 which removed him and introduced political changes. The book therefore portrays the general sense of discontent in Egypt; and this was part of its appeal in the country as well as in the rest of the Arab world chafing under mostly undemocratic regimes. But the artistic and literary aspects of the book should not be ignored, for they are also strong elements of the book's popularity and appeal.

Anita Husen is to be congratulated on her beautiful rendering of this book in English, and on bringing Walid Taher's work of dark humor to the attention of the world's audiences, for a better understanding of Egypt and the Arab world before the coming of the hopeful "Arab Spring." **IJB**

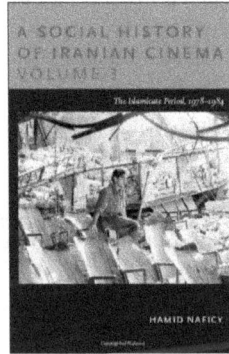

Hamid Naficy. *A Social History of Iranian Cinema Volume 3—The Islamicate Period, 1978–1984.* **Durham, NC: Duke University Press, 2012. 266 pp. Pbk.: $24.95. ISBN: 978-0822348771.**

Professor of Radio, Television, and Film, and Hamad Bin Khalifa Al-Thani Professor in Communication at Northwestern University, Hamid Naficy recently published the third volume of his monumental and unequaled four volume history of Iranian cinema (vol. 1, *The Artisanal Era, 1897–1941*; vol. 2, *The Industrializing Years, 1941–1978*). The third volume covers the period that extends from the early outset of the Iranian revolution movement and the establishment of a republican theocratic state (1978–79) to the period that followed the overhaul of the film industry and the subsequent inauguration of its institutionalization up until 1984. This crucial period initiated the formulation and implementation of what Naficy labels, reviving a Hodgsonian notion, "Islamicate culture," a culture infused with Islamic values and concepts of monotheism, theocracy, anti-idolatry, ethicalism, and moralism, martyrdom, and purification with which this new "imagined community" could be constructed, with assistance of the most efficient tools for Islamic social engineering: media and cinema (pp. 8-10). As Naficy, a social historian, explores and analyzes the dynamics of parallel societal and cinematic developments, he delves into both social history and theory.

The first chapter surveys the "transition period" from the previous culture of "Cinema of Idolatry" (*filmfarsi* cinema), embodied by Western and Pahlavi features, to the new emergent Islamicate culture. This politico-religious "revolution" involved the "purification (*paksazi*)" of all institutions—social, educational, mass media, industrial, bureaucratic, military, and judiciary—including the countless efforts deployed to purify both the film industry and the mass media: policies and initiatives were deployed to destruct and cleanse movie houses (pp. 15-22); curb and realign imported feature films (pp. 22-26); review and censor domestic movies (pp. 26-32); and to muzzle and purge all those associated with the old movie industry (entertainers, performers, and filmmakers) (pp. 32-43). Naficy adroitly sheds light onto the parallel and inseparable developments occurring during this period transition to a new "Islamicate cinema" and the "politics of transition" to an Islamic Republic and its consolidation of Islamicate society, through its emerging and evolving "panoptic control of society and culture" (p. 46).

In the second chapter, Naficy provides comprehensive surveys of the various efforts deployed to document (films and documentaries) the uprising, the revolution, and the emerging opposition. At the outset, he presents films, historical documentaries, and compilations of footage taken by individuals (pp. 48-80) and, then, turns to documentaries produced by opposition groups: the People's Fadaiyan Organization of Iran; the People's Mojahedin Organization of Iran; the Kurdish Resistance groups (*peshmergas*); Jewish and Baha'i films (in exile); and even women's films (pp. 83-109). He ends with the presentation of a number of biographical films about great revolutionaries that were made almost exclusively by the State, through the services of the Voice and Vision of the Islamic Republic and the Ministry of Culture and Islamic guidance: these documentaries recounted the revolutionary deeds of pro-regime and pro-Islam opponents to the Shah, nationalist figures, such as Mosaddeq, Navvab Safavi, Takhti and Bazargan, and leading clerics, such as Moddares, Kashani, and Taleqani (pp. 109-113). With its nationwide distribution, this new "official cinema" ensured that its "official and institutional stamp" would shape a country in need to be "anchored" and "synchronized" ideologically (pp. 112-113).

The third and last chapter covers the period of state consolidation of the new Islamicate Cinema and film culture. Here, Naficy analyzes the emergence and role of new institutions of "development and ideological inculcation and coercion" aimed at "imagining the new Islamicate national identity" (p. 117). This process involved the introduction of "purification measures," and overcoming the financial damages on the industry and institutional rivalries. Naficy analyzes the role of a number of new institutions, such as the Ayat Film Studio and the Islamic Art and Thought Center (pp. 121-127); the Ministry of Culture and Islamic Guidance; the Farabi Cinema Foundation (pp. 127-130); the Foundation of the Dispossessed and the Revolutionary Guard Corps (pp. 131-133); the Ministry of Reconstruction Crusade (pp. 133-136); the Center for the Intellectual Development of Children and Young Adults (136-137); the Iranian Young People's Cinema Society (137-138); the Documentary and Experimental Film Center (p. 138); as well as the professional structures governing the film industry—such as the National Film Archive of Iran, the House of Cinema; the Museum of Cinema; film festivals; periodicals and publications (see Table 4 covering 1979–2003) (pp. 138-150). He also presents the institutional constraints imposed on the film industry and the new censorship laws and regulations that were to govern the film industry (pp. 150-155): the four-phase approval process of the early 1980s; the control of film imports; the "limitations" imposed by the new Islamicate "morality codes"—which expanded or contracted "depending on politics and personalities in charge of the culture industry institutions"—and the policies of support and supervision of the Ministry of Culture and

Islamic Guidance. Naficy also surveys the production of featured movies between 1979 and 2009, discusses taxonomy of film types, genres, and themes of domestic features produced or allowed to be shown in Iran during that period (pp. 166-184).

Naficy thus charts the fascinating emergence of the Islamicate cinema and film industry, while focusing, primarily, although not exclusively, on the first political phase of Islamization and the war years under Ayatollah Khomeini (1980–88). Although some discussions of film productions go beyond the 1978–84 timespan (especially in the latter part of the third chapter), the various periods covered in the available data gathered for the study might help account for discussions that cover three different political periods: the first, and most prominent, political phase under Khomeini, but also, although admittedly to a much lesser extent, the reconstruction era under President Ali Akbar Hashemi Rafsanjani (1989–97), and the reform era under President Mohammad Khatami (1997–2005). Naficy masterfully demonstrates how cinema was quickly adopted as one of the most efficient tools for "edifying" the Islamic Republic's "infrastructure." In fact, very early on, the Islamic Republic began "to internalize cinema by absorbing it into its interstices" (p. 184), the Supreme Guide himself, Khomeini, envisioning how radio and television could become an "educational force" for "shaping public opinion and forming national identity" (p. 159).

No review could do justice to the wealth of information Naficy has gathered and analyzed. Throughout the years, he has had access to original unpublished material—individuals, organizations, and government institutions—flyers and posters; and he has conducted an impressive list of interviews, some going as far back as 1978. He includes over 40 production stills; frame enlargement from films and videos; pictures of posters (his own private collection); cartoons about cinema; flyers announcing film screenings and cultural and political events featuring screenings; and a number of tables: Iranian and international feature movies receiving exhibition permits (1980–82); feature movies produced in the Islamic Republic (1979–2009); and imported theatrical movies that received exhibition permits (1983–84). There are also lists of Iranian feature movies given or denied exhibition permits (1979–82); film periodicals (1979–2003); and themes of features films (1987). More importantly, Naficy appended the oft mentioned, but rarely seen full list of regulations (approved in 1982) that pertains to censorship and the banning of movies, and that regulated exhibition licenses of movies (and videos) submitted by producers (see Appendix, pp. 189-194). Finally, copious notes (pp. 195-216), a bibliography (pp. 217-233), and an index (pp. 235-255) complete the work. Suffice to say that this volume of social history of the Islamicate period of Iranian cinema from 1978 to 1984 will undoubtedly remain, for many years to come, a must for scholars and students of Iranian cinematic culture and all aficionados, young and old, of Iranian cinema. **RDM**

Hamid Naficy. *A Social History of Iranian Cinema Volume 4—The Globalizing Era, 1984-2010*. Durham, NC: Duke University Press, 2012. 631 pp. $99.95. ISBN: 978-0822348788. Pbk: $29.90. ISBN: 978-0822348775.

With the publication of *Volume 4: The Globalizing Era, 1984-2010*, Hamid Naficy, unequaled authority on the history of Iranian cinema, culminates and brings to an end his comprehensive *Social History of Iranian Cinema* (see first three volumes, Vol. 1: *The Artisanal Era, 1897–1941*; Vol. 2: *The Industrializing Years, 1941–1978*; Vol. 3: *The Islamicate Period, 1978–1984*). Once again, Naficy skillfully weaves his analysis of the history of almost 25 years of Iranian cinematographic production together with an analysis of the modern national Iranian identity and the complex sociopolitical developments of post-revolutionary Iran which cover the following periods: (1) the end of the political phase under Khomeini (d. 1989); (2) the reconstruction era under President Ali Akbar Hashemi Rafsanjani (1989–97); (3) the reform era under President Mohammad Khatami (1997–2005); and (4) the "retrenchment era" under President Mahmoud Ahmadinejad (2005–10).

In Chapter 1, Naficy begins with the resurgence of nonfiction cinema bought about by the onset of the bloody Iraq/Iran War (1980–88) and the ensuing post-revolutionary documentaries and fiction war films. He documents the great impact the war had on both national and religious identities, a boon for the consolidation of the nascent Islamic state, with the film industry being mobilized for war: war movies were dubbed "sacred defense war" or "imposed war" cinema. He reviews the evolution of its major forms, both documentaries and feature fiction, including nonfiction films. The first documentary film, a privately funded blockbuster at the time, was produced in 1980 and followed by State sponsored ("official") documentaries by both governmental and para-governmental organizations, from 1982 onward. Naficy then reviews the works of a few war movies directors, also exploring the ethnographic nature of works that focus on social issues of the time.

Naficy then turns, in Chapter 2, to the ways women's representations and women's cinema gradually shifted from the "sexualized" (see Vol. 2 and Vol. 3) to the "segregated." Now, modesty is the lens through which films are surveyed and analyzed, as Iranian cinema's modesty functions as both "social practice" and as "component of gendered subjectivity." Here, Naficy proposes an "Islamicate Gaze Theory" for the ubiquity of veiling (pp. 106-110) and introduces the four phases of Iranian cinema's "modesty:" (1) "women's structured absence" during the early 1980s; (2) "women's background presence" during the mid-1980s; (3) "women's foreground presence" from the late 1980s; and (4) "veiling and modesty as political criticism" from the mid-1990s onward. He then turns to the Persian translation of the Japanese Oshin TV serial (broadcast from 1987 to 1989), analyzes how it was turned into an Islamic role model, and discusses the politics and poetics of love and romance in films. He introduces quite a few women's documentaries (produced in Iran and abroad) that focus on a variety of social issues and ills. Naficy quite astutely shows how a number of women filmmakers became, like many directors, the "social conscience" of Iranian society.

Naficy then focuses on art-house cinema in Chapter 3, with which the West is most acquainted (labelled "postal" cinema). First, he turns to Abbas Kiarostami and his work to explore the idea of the director as an author. He then analyzes the notion of hybridity of art-cinema films, both in production mode (government, private, semi-industrialized, and artisanal), as well as textual production (realist and metarealist narrative strategies), that subvert, according to him, both realism and neorealism. Next, he identifies some characteristics of what he calls Iranian "metarealism" (self-reflexivity, self-referentiality, self-inscription, and intertextuality) and cinema "vérité" esthetics. He proceeds with "research films" (those that fuse fact and fiction), humanist themes and child character films, impressionist esthetics, poetry, and critical synesthesia films. He includes reviews of the "familial mode" of production of art-house cinema, with the likes of Mehrjui, Baizai, Kiarostami, Banietemad, Milani, and Makhmalbaf, as well as "imperial nostalgia and multiplexity" productions. The author not only details international film festivals, film distribution circuits, and the emergence of post-national cinema, he also analyzes post-studio independent films and globalization—criticizing the globalization of art-house cinema, discussing international treatment of art-house filmmakers, and addressing issues of adaptations, copying, copyrighting, and censorship.

In Chapter 4, Naficy explores the new dynamics created by the emergence of "contestatory" films, media culture, and public diplomacy, both in Iran and in the Diaspora. He highlights, first, elements of U.S. "mediawork" treatment of the Islamic Republic as a "treat," discussing the Hostage Crisis, the "Iron Sheik," American films about Iran and Iranians, and video games on war in Iran. Here, mediawork is, in fact, a term he coined "to theorize the 'work' of the totality of the film, media, and consciousness-shaping industries, which operates somewhat like Freud's concept of 'dreamwork'" (p. 273). Then, he turns to the multiple representations of Iran and Iranians produced by exilic Iranian (re)presentations, what he now calls the "exilic mediawork" treatment of Iran and of "exile," both viewed as "oppositional countermedia." mostly televisual, whose three phases he surveys: (1) television (TV) (up to the late 1990s); (2) the 24 h satellite TV (from 2000); and (3) twenty-first century

Internet and satellite-convergent TV. To these two distinct mediaworks, Naficy introduces the Islamic Republic's own brand of "public diplomacy" and mediawork aimed at mobilizing public sentiment to fight against "cultural imperialism" (*estek-bar-e jahani*) or "cultural invasion" (*tahajom-e farhangi*) and prevalent "Iranophobia." Naficy notes that this led to the internal Iranian culture war of the mid-1990s, with the production of "identity" (*hoviyat*) TV shows and its social and political consequences for a number of social actors in the wake of the state's instrumental use of both culture and media. The following decade heralded the cinema of "embodied protest," i.e., the support of the Iranian film industry to the reform movement, inside and outside of Iran, throughout the 2000s (videos, satellite TV, and Internet cinema), developments that are meticulously scrutinized, presented, and analyzed. The cinematic activities and developments presented in these chapters, all serve to "corroborate" what Moaddel's study on the rise of liberal values among Iranians (including filmmakers) has shown: "increasing secularization, individualism, and liberal democratic values" (p. 364) in spite of the ongoing Islamization of the state.

In the last chapter (Chapter 5), Naficy turns to what he has labeled "accented" films—those produced outside of Iran by displaced Iranians—highlighting the therapeutic function of such films and cinema to "process displacement." He surveys what he considers to be both a "cinema of displacement" and a "displaced cinema," which he classifies into "exilic," "diasporic," "émigré," "ethnic," and "cosmopolitan" films and filmmakers (he includes a chronology and the global distribution of those films from 1960 to 2012, the gender of the filmmakers, their types of works, and the countries in which they live). He also surveys the exile and diaspora film festivals, their identity, the cinema and arts documentary productions, as well as the avant-garde, experimental, and animated works, including those of Shirin Neshat, Ghazel Radpay, Marjane Satrapi, with a few pages on "exilic veiling and unveiling," and ending the chapter with examples of "cosmopolitan accented" cinema with works by Sohrab Shahid Saless and Amir Naderi. The work includes 110 illustrations (pp. xi-xiv); three appendices (of Iranian films in distribution in 2005; film house of Iran's film collection; international film and video center Iranian film collection (pp. 513-522); and copious notes, bibliography, and an index (pp. 520-631).

The timespan, the content, and the scope of material included and covered in this fourth volume are just breathtaking. Naficy manages to include detailed and comprehensive micro and macro histories of so many various and interrelated aspects of this social history of Iranian cinema: documentary, feature fiction and nonfiction film, popular genre, art film, and video and Internet productions. Moreover, Naficy's story-telling skills make, at times, for exquisite reading (see, e.g., the few pages on the Ziba Mir-Hussaini's shooting of her *Marriage Iranian Style* and discussion of the Japanese Oshin TV serial). In short, *The Globalizing Era, 1984–2010*, the fourth and last volume of Naficy's magisterial *Social History of Iranian Cinema* spanning from the end of the nineteenth century to the first decade of the twentieth century, brings to a close over three decades of extensive research in archives from around the world. This lifetime project of encyclopedic proportions will remain unquestionably an essential reference for scholars and students of Iranian cinematic culture, as well as for all aficionados, young and old, of Iranian cinema, for years to come. One can only hope that a fifth volume is in the making. **RDM**

Esra Akcan. *Architecture in Translation: Germany, Turkey, and the Modern House.* **Durham, NC: Duke University Press, 2012. 408 pp. $89.95. ISBN: 082235294X. Pbk.: $24.95. ISBN: 0822353083.**

Esra Akcan's excellent book, *Architecture in Translation: Germany, Turkey, and the Modern House* focus on the history of German-Turkish exchanges in residential architecture in the twentieth century. With her analysis of the geographical circulation of major modern housing models and ideas, consecutive chapters trace the translation of the *garden city* model in Germany at the beginning of the twentieth century up to World War I; its transformation into Weimar *Siedlungen* (residential settlements) during the interwar period, and the rise of national architecture under the Nazi regime. In parallel to German architectural discourses and developments, the book describes the translation of the garden city theory and then of the Weimar *Siedlung* theories in Turkey, as well as their hybridization and nationalization with the "Turkish house" discourse. Directing her attention toward questions of urbanity, population, and housing, Akcan successfully situates architecture within the modernization paradigms of the new Turkish republic.

Providing a basic outline of the intellectual debate on modernity and modernization, Akcan distances herself from three influential and competing ideologies of the twentieth century. First, she offers an alternative voice through translation, which does not perpetuate the colonial terms of cultural criticism, such as *civilized* and *backward*, or *international style* and *regionalism*. Second, the book challenges the myth of problem-free modernization, nationalization, and Westernization, which is predicated on the premise of smooth translatability. And third, the author does not support the convictions of untranslatability and refrains from offering a return to a traditional "origin" as a solution. The book leans on the trope of translation, not only to reject the thesis of a clash of civilizations between the West and its other, but also to offer an alternative to passive metaphors such as import, influence, and transfer—all of which deny agency to the receiving location.

Akcan explores the concept of translation to explain interactions between places. The book conceptualizes translation as any cultural flow (traveling of people, ideas, technology, information, and images) from one place to another under any condition. The act of transportation carries with it a process of transformation as well. However, the author challenges the denigration of translation as a second hand and inferior copy of the original. She alternatively argues that it is through translations that a place opens itself to what was hitherto *foreign*, namely a rejuvenating force for changing and developing institutions and cultural forms. Moreover, translation reveals the voice of both sides of a cross-cultural exchange, which differentiates it from narratives that emphasize Western agency alone. The book also challenges the idea of translation as a neutral bridge between cultures, since no translation can be devoid of the geographical distribution of power or capital. Thus, the author analyzes both the liberating and the colonizing forces of translation.

The first architectural translation was that of the garden city model as the basis for urban planning in Turkey's new capital, Ankara. In fact, the advocacy and justification of the ideal was utterly different from the European context, where the garden city concept was put forward as the source of "spiritual regeneration," of not only physical but also mental health, reminding the ideal of "cultivating one's garden" in Voltaire's famous novella *Candide, ou l'Optimisme*. While criticizing the unhealthy, arbitrary and untidy existential conditions of modern chaotic metropolis, proponents of the garden city model assumed that living in gardens and engaging in garden-related activities would cure humanity. Whereas in modern Turkey, the metropolis, in the true sense of the world, has not yet emerged. Therefore, the garden city ideal was translated in a vacuum to the Turkish context without its background on the critique of fast and unorganized urbanism. In fact, this was the case for most of the reform attempts of the new republic. Despite the economic and demographic differences between Europe and Turkey, reformers developed similar concerns insofar as they embraced the broader Western modernizing discourses of the period. Moreover, the Kemalist modernization process relied on the premise that Europeanism was smoothly translatable into Turkey, even if it had to be inserted from above. In this climate, a solution—garden city urban planning—was precociously offered for a problem not yet conceptualized as being that grave. The decision was based on the political will of a new nation-state. For that reason, unlike in England and Germany, where intense professional engagement in the garden city theory took the form of numerous publications and discussions, in Turkey, the garden city theory, like other architectural trends, was brought in from above by forceful state bureaucrats and their chosen architect.

However, the episode of garden city planning was not long-lived. Both the master plans of the Bahçelievler Housing Cooperative in Ankara and later, those of six other cities (İzmit, Adana, Ceyhan, Tarsus, Mersin, and Gaziantep) envisioned (mistakenly) an extremely low density and a sprawling urban development for Turkey. As a result, less than three decades after construction, the houses and gardens of Bahçelievler were torn down to be replaced by taller and larger multifamily apartment blocks, revealing the limits of low-density garden city housing in a rapidly developing and urbanizing country. The second stop on the Germany-inspired architectural transfer was an unlikely successor, the *Siedlung*, which offered metropolitan housing and residential neighborhoods within the city with a small-town image. *Siedlung* architects of the Weimar period defined their task as providing solutions to the problems of the big city, rather than escaping to a new, small town.

Esra Akcan clearly demonstrates the impact of both these trends in Turkey over urban housing projects. However, there is not adequate discussion on the time lag between the German model and the Turkish translation. More specifically, it is not clear why Turkish officials, with the possible guidance of German architects, advocated in the 1930s the garden city model as the basis for master plans for many cities of Turkey, while the same architects had already built the *Siedlung* style housing projects beginning in the 1920s in Berlin. Given the fact that German architects and city planners were already aware of the limits of the garden city model, why not simply bypass this older trend and suggest the most up-to-date solution to urban planning?

The third instance of convergence of architectural trends in Germany and Turkey coincided with the ethnic nationalist climate of Turkey, as well as the fascist context of Europe. Now the emphasis was on the untranslatability of cultural identity and the myth of pure essential culture, which was allegedly radically different and also superior to others. In the 1940s, the rise of fascist architecture in Germany and Italy were praised; and many Turkish architects referred to these examples to justify their demand for state support for the rise of national architecture. Nationalist architects differentiated "technical and material" attributes of architecture from "emotional, creative, and intuitive" ones. The former were translatable as they were parts of a supposedly universal *civilization*, whereas the latter was made up of the untranslatable *culture*. Therefore, they searched for the untranslatable culture, for the so-called Turkish original essence. As the architectural mind behind the Turkish house, Sedad Eldem emphasized the national character of Turkish architecture. The old Turkish house was now regarded as the inspiration for the new architecture of the regime. While in Bahçelievler, government officials asked for a European residential settlement, untouched by the old styles, a decade later the same officials preferred a neighborhood (*Siedlung* Saraçoğlu) that allegedly originated from the old Turkish house. During this period, Eldem even proposed to limit foreign architect's influence on Turkish architecture.

Akcan's book, in that respect, also sheds light upon the denial and exclusionary characteristics of Turkish nationalism. The categorization of anonymous houses under the name of "Turkish house" was a significant distortion of history for nationalist purposes. With this presumption, the house of the Turk was given a higher status than those of the other ethnic and religious groups of the Ottoman Empire. Therefore, hybrid culture that created these houses and terms of coexistence were denied. With the same token, the Turkish government resorted to oppressive practices toward Greek and Armenian architects, who were deprived of equal professional rights with the Turkish architects.

As a minor criticism to an otherwise marvelous book, I think the author's conviction to use melancholy as a metaphor and trope to understand the sentimental and existential mood of some Turkish architects, particularly Sedad Eldem, is a bit exaggerated. Akcan claims that Eldem used his melancholy in a productive way to resolve the dilemma of modernization in Turkey—the simultaneous desire to be a part of the Western civilization and also to establish an identity that would avoid being absorbed by the West—by suggesting the modernism of the Turkish house and the Turkishness of the modern achievements in Europe. However, simultaneous assertion of Europeanism and superiority of the Turks was typical of the entire origin-obsessed nationalist establishment of the new regime—historians, anthropologists, archeologists, all argued within the same lines. In that sense, Eldem's "discovery" of the Turkish house seems to be triggered by the nationalist *Zeitgeist*, rather than his melancholic state of mind. **NM**

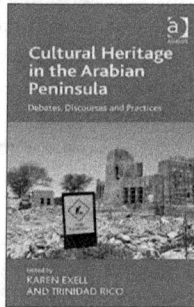

Karen Exell and Trinidad Rico, Eds. *Cultural Heritage in the Arabian Peninsula: Debates, Discourses and Practices.* **Farnham, Surrey, UK: Ashgate, 2014. 226 pp. $103.73. ISBN: 9781409470076; $76.99. Ebk: 224 pp. 1342 KB.**

The focus of this volume is on the multifarious ways that cultural heritage—whether it is found in museums and historical sites or through intangible practices like oral traditions and performances—can be preserved, represented and received within the social frameworks that constitute the Arabian Peninsula. Simply put, in the succinct words of the editors, what emerges from this collection of essays is a relatively straightforward query: "[W]ho do these heritage projects and sites represent, in their production and in their reception?" (p. 7). However, these contests over the management of traditions would be limited to broad thematic concerns without the inclusion of specificities, and fortunately the authors provide the necessary context-rich depth of individual case studies to examine the particularities of heritage schemes in the Arabian Peninsula.

Of course, all of the contributors are acutely aware of the fact that the forms of cultural preservation taking place are almost inevitably fraught with contention between local, state, foreign, and international actors each vying for their own roles in the processes of heritage development. Again, this returns to the central premise set forth by the editors about how cultural properties are identified, packaged and, ultimately, consumed. Currently, the dominant model for the Arabian Peninsula's heritage operations is based on Western notions of marketing cultural properties, a situation that can be attributed to the preeminence of Western-led institutions such as UNESCO as well as the influx of foreign consultants. Therefore, at one end of the heritage spectrum there are the distinctly Eurocentric-aligned examples like Abu Dhabi's Saadiyat Island project which, as discussed by Sarina Wakefield, has sought out globally recognizable franchises for its cultural credentials under the guises of the Louvre Abu Dhabi and the Guggenheim Abu Dhabi. At the other point is the Sheikh Faisal bin Qassim Al Thani Museum in Qatar with its personal, locally constructed sense of purpose that lies way beyond the taxonomic norms of Western-styled exhibitions, and for this very reason, Karen Exell explains, it is disparaged by expatriate experts.

Yet, regardless of the degrees of Western influence that might be present for certain heritage conservation programs across the Arabian Peninsula, what really emerges as a salient objective in every piece is how to ensure that these various cultural ventures will be relevant to the local populations. Clearly, part of the problem is that the proliferation of Eurocentric design strategies, due to their foreignness, are difficult to translate into local values and tastes. Still, instances such as Alaa Alrawaibah's investigation into why Saudi Arabia's Nabatean site of Māda'in Sālih remains suspect in the eyes of the surrounding community demonstrates that often there is a chronic disconnect between the professionals charged with overseeing cultural heritage and the locals who live among it. In Alrawaibah's estimation, it is both the government authorities and the foreign experts who have failed to include the populace in their endeavors, thereby doing little to alleviate their suspicions or mistrust about the project. Similarly, Ali A. Alraouf finds in his study of the revitalization efforts in the historic quarters of Muharraq, Bahrain, that the exclusion of residents from the overall restoration mission has served to foster an atmosphere marred by "the feeling of alienation and separation from the rehabilitation project" (p. 181). Again, this raises the question encountered throughout this book about how to effectively link heritage initiatives to the needs and desires of the region's native inhabitants and, to some extent, its ever-burgeoning influx of expatriate laborers.

Trying to resolve the predicament of fashioning the Arabian Peninsula's local heritage into detached and unfamiliar products is daunting, to say the least, but there are many indications to suggest that it is not an insurmountable obstacle. As most of the researchers in this volume plainly argue, reaching out to and partnering with local communities is a much more valuable approach than trying to work around them. The basis for this precept is evident, since the long-term durability of a cultural project is closely tied to community responsiveness toward it. For the Al-Khamis Museum underway at the site of its namesake mosque in Bahrain's Bilad al-Qadim district, archaeologists Rachel MacLean and Timothy Insoll provide an insightful chronicle of their direct involvement with engaging local sentiments to help shape the project's final rendering. From the outset, MacLean and Insoll document the benefits of incorporating the voices of Bilad al-Qadim into their excavations, analyses and presentations. This was not solely for the sake of authenticity, but also to encourage the area's residents to become active stakeholders with vested interests in the museum's future.

Another possibility for bridging the gap between cultural heritage displays and audience expectations are the methods advocated by Eric Langham and Darren Barker of the UK consulting agency Barker Langham. In their chapter, the consultants are adamant in their views that trying to force Western modes of heritage consumption upon non-Western markets is bound to lead to the latter's indifference, misunderstanding and apathy. Instead, what Langham and Barker propose is that "local context and audience preferences for methods of heritage consumption" (p. 94) must be at the forefront of cultural project design and execution. Drawing from their professional background in the UAE, Langham and Barker contend that its nationals crave cultural activities, interactive exhibits, reenactments, and minimal descriptions, not customary Western-inspired museum standards where object stasis and extensive explanations are fundamental to the whole visitation experience. Hence, the authors conclude with justification that detecting the appropriate cultural materials and pinpointing precisely how locals would prefer to interact with their heritage can skillfully avoid the kinds of dissonance that arise when a single heritage concept is presumed to have universal applications.

Taken in its entirety, this volume offers a well-thought-out thesis about the nature of heritage development on the Arabian Peninsula that seamlessly moves from general topics, like Trinidad Rico's discussion about the position of Islamic values in preservation practices or Ian R. Simpson's overview of the environmental factors behind some of the modern-day nostalgia for Gulf pearling, to more targeted pieces spotlighting the challenges of selecting and promoting certain cultural assets. In addition to the above-mentioned chapters, this second category also contains Victoria Penziner Hightower's contribution on the different ways that the pearl trade is memorialized in the UAE, Mariam Ibrahim Al-Mulla's essay about the sociopolitical aspects of the Qatar National Museum, and Nadine Scharfenort's perspectives on how Qatar's Msheireb Project is blending renovations with locally-infused contemporary architectural ideas in Doha's historic old center. Lastly, there is Stephen J. Steinbeiser's scrutiny of how Yemen's bureaucratic and legal structures have severely under-served one of its UNESCO World Heritage Sites, the city of Zabid. Steinbeiser's work is the obvious outlier here, as it is the lone departure from book's concentration on the oil exporting nations of the GCC, particularly the smaller states along the eastern edge of the Arabian Peninsula. Nonetheless, this observation should not detract from the merits of this volume and its timely exploration of cultural heritage, with all of its meanings and utilizations, in these rapidly changing societies. **JCAR**

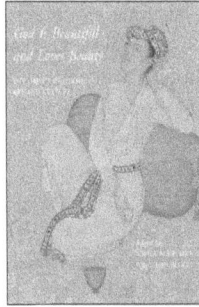

Sheila Blair and Jonathan Bloom, Eds. *God is Beautiful and Loves Beauty: The Object in Islamic Art and Culture.* **New Haven, CT: Yale University Press, 2013. 389 pp. $80.00. ISBN: 978-0300196665.**

Global art aficionados, generally, and the admirers of Islamic art in particular will enjoy how the visual beauty of printed works of art is juxtaposed to scholarly prose in *God is Beautiful and Loves Beauty: The Object in Islamic Art and Culture.* Sheila Blair and Jonathan Bloom, the dynamic-duo authors of works such as *The Art and Architecture of Islam, 1250–1800* (Yale University Press, 1996) and *Islamic Arts (Art and Ideas)* (Phaidon Press, 1997), have once again succeeded in publishing a collection of 15 articles, 12 of which discuss various art objects that collectively provide the reader with a broad understanding of cultural history of the Islamic societies at their zeniths.

The origins of these 12 objects go back to places where Islamic civilization thrived at one point or another. They represent the culture of almost the entire Islamic world, and include the Iberian and Arabian peninsulas, Egypt, Western, Southwestern, Central, and Southern Asia, in addition to the Anatolian and Iranian plateaus. Just as diverse as these objects are in their cultural function, they also relate back to the period between the seventh and the seventeenth century. All the objects discussed in this volume are housed at Qatar's newly constructed (2008) Museum of Islamic Art (MIA) in Doha, and since the contributors were limited to write on the objects displayed at the museum, the book excludes discussion of art objects that originated from Northwest Africa (the Maghrib), Sub-Sahara, Palestine, and Southeast Asia. Hopefully this shortcoming can be addressed in Blair and Bloom's future contributions.

According to Joseph H. Seipel, the Dean of School of Arts at Virginia Commonwealth University who wrote the book's foreword, all the articles published in this volume were initially presented as papers at the fourth biennial Hamad bin Khalifa Symposium on Islamic Art and Culture, in Doha, organized by Blair and Bloom. As co-holders of the Chair in Islamic Art History with the same name endowed within VCU's Department of Art History, the couple had already succeeded in editing *Rivers of Paradise: Water in Islamic Art and Culture* and *And Diverse Are Their Hues: Color in Islamic Art and Culture,* as final words of the proceedings of two previous conferences in 2009 and 2011, which Yale University Press also published.

Refreshingly, the book is as much about the museum as it is about the objects in it. Because I. M. Pei, the much-celebrated Chinese–American architect designed it, the editors chose wisely to include "I. M. Pei and the Challenge of the Modern," written by Paul Goldberger of *The New Yorker* who provides an architecture critique of the building, pointing to the importance of water as an element of serenity in the design of the MIA. Combining traditional with modern concepts in design, Pei closely followed some of Islamic civilization's masterful works of architecture, such as the ninth century Ibn Tulun Mosque in Cairo, to deliver on his philosophy that the old and the new need not be separated and drastically different from each other. Goldberger rightly points to the fact that the design of the MIA closely resembles that of Pei's other works, such as the Suzhou Museum in Jiangsu, where simple geometric shapes figure prominently in his design of that edifice. This is an important point that is made here; and its roots can be explored in the basic Islamic teachings and the concept of beauty in Islam that simplicity is held in highest esteem, as is seen in most works of Islamic art.

Oliver Watson effectively provides a related follow up discussion in the next article. As the first director of the Museum of Islamic Art, he points to a noteworthy fact that not only Pei's design rests on traditional concept of water as the surrounding element of the museum but the layout of the interior essentially benefitted from the fact that the whole project—from the beginning phases of its conception, planning and preparation, to the final stages of building and installation—was envisioned as a museum of a unique civilization. Watson rightly points out that the clarity of this vision was what figured into creating a clear space of the interior of the MIA that was designed by Jean-Michel Wilmotte, who partnered with Pei in the design of the interior of the Louvre pyramid in Paris that has brought the same aspect of clarity to the mission and presentation of the objects to the MIA as well.

The study of the object as a medium of historical and cultural evidence in different civilizations is an emerging genre. This volume emulates other great works such as Arjun Appadurai's *The Social Life of Things: Commodities in Cultural Perspective* (Cambridge University Press, 1986), which Elizabeth Sear and Thelma Thomas emulated in their *Reading Medieval Images: The Art Historian and the Object* (University of Michigan Press, 2002). They focused their scholarship on the idea that objects provide us with a "cultural biography" that fills the void which a narrative may create in text. This book draws its strength from the collection of not only one perspective, but several, as the contributors are archaeologists, art historians, artists, curators, and historians of science.

The articles are appropriately divided into various art media, such as ceramics, metalware, glass, lampas-waves, animal carpets, books and calligraphy, paintings, and architectural/decorative art such as capitals and stucco. As a teacher of the history of the Islamic civilization, one particular point that figures prominently for this reviewer is that what makes the book so much more effective is the fact that some of the articles clearly establish how local pre-Islamic cultures which were exposed to Islam after it expanded out of Arabia in the mid-600s adopted Islam's various cultural tools, such as Arabic as the language of Islam, and adopted it to the traditions that were radically different from that of the Hijaz. For example, in "Murakkaa and the Birth of the International Style," Mohamed Zakariya successfully demonstrates how calligraphy as a form of art that carried the Islamic message through Arabic language adopted non-Islamic calligraphic styles of the Chinese and North Africans by intermixing the pre-Islamic heritage of these regions' past. The creation of various styles of writing is indicative of the claim that generally Islam has never been just a monolithic religious system, but one that should be considered as a civilization that was founded on the ideals of a universal religion that was as diverse as its followers.

Europe's scientific foundation and dependence on Muslim scientific invention and innovation has long been an established fact in a variety of historical analyses but has remained mostly unknown to many Western academic and nonacademics. This point figures prominently in "The Most Authoritative Copy of 'Abd al-Rahman al-Sufi's Tenth-century Guide to the Constellations," by Emilie Savage-Smith. On the same token, the reverse of that direction of emulation from Islamic societies to Europe is vividly discussed in Eleanor Sims's article: "Six Seventeenth-century Oil Paintings from Safavid Persia." It effectively serves as a confirmation of our historical understanding that the Islamic civilization was still a dynamic entity when the West was slowly posing to overwhelm it in the next two centuries. In a somewhat more technical language but still accessible to the uninitiated, Sims demonstrates how the Shi'ite Iranian Safavids (1501–1722) emulated European art, albeit imperfectly, in the case of the six paintings that she discusses in this piece.

All things considered, college and perhaps public libraries should obtain a copy of *God is Beautiful and Loves Beauty*. However, it might be a bit far fetched to assert that all art history courses will greatly benefit from having the book because at times the text becomes technical and one unfamiliar with fields such as astronomy or calligraphy might feel overwhelmed by its specialized verbiage. Specialists and those interested in gazing at medieval or Islamic works of art and science will more than likely enjoy reading the expert opinions of some of the most qualified specialists of Islamic arts. It is difficult to point to one single reason why the book achieves its goal of demonstrating the life of art objects and their cultural importance in the height of the Islamic civilization; however, if we were to consider one reason, it is perhaps the coverage of varied art objects that are not limited to just one medium, place, or era. Just as Qur'anic leaflets of Tashkent can illuminate the devotion and artistic nature of the Turks in Central Asian in "Twenty Leaves from the Tashkent Koran," the design and intense workmanship of stuccos of Samarra in "Three Stucco Panels from Samarra," and the capitals of Cordoba in "Two Capitals from the Umayyad Caliphate of Cordoba" can entice one to ponder upon a civilization that has been mistreated in the current global political climate more than any other. **MMF**

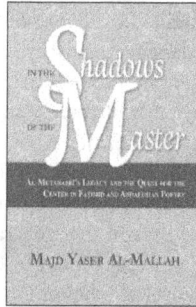

Majd Yaser al-Mallah. *In the Shadows of the Master: al-Mutanabbi's Legacy and the Quest for the Center in the Fatimid and the Andalusian Poetry*. Berkshire, UK: Berkshire Academic Press, 2012. 147 pp. $69.95. ISBN: 1907784071.

Al-Mallah's *In the Shadow of the Master* is an important addition to the study of classical Arabic poetry in a time of political fragmentation, and the creation of new political entities. Specifically, this study investigates the role that poetic discourse played in communicating political and religious legitimacy during the tenth, and the beginning of the eleventh centuries. To this end, al-Mallah takes the reader on a journey to witness the impact of this panegyric poetry in four different Islamic political settings: the Hamadanis in Aleppo under Sayf al-Dawla (d. 967); the Fatimids under the rule of al-Mu'zz (d. 975), and al-'Aziz (d. 996); the 'Amirids under al-Mansur (d. 1002); and the Tujibis under the leadership of al-Mundhir b. Yahya (d. 1022). The book's argumentation is based on the analysis of five odes (with full translations) composed by four poets who were associated with the courts of these rulers.

The starting point of this study is a panegyric written by Abu al-Tayyib al-Mutanabbi (d. 965), who was one of the most acclaimed classical Arab poets. His poetic model was so influential that it served as a paradigm for many poets, especially in the Andalus. Al-Mallah examines al-Mutanabbi's influence on three poets: Ibn Hani' al-Andalusi (d. 973); Tamim b. al-Mu'izz (d. 985); and IbnDarraj al-Qastalani (d. 1030); hence, the book's title *In the Shadow of the Master*. Al-Mallah's central argument is that in composing these odes, the poets emphasize the political or religious legitimacy of the respective patrons seeking to place their leadership at a new "center of history rather than remain on the margins" (p. 2). In so doing, these panegyrics perform important political and ritual functions that demonstrate certain facets of social interaction between the poets, their respective patrons, and the community.

The book consists of five chapters and has a bibliography and an appendix of the Arabic texts. In the first chapter, the author lays down the theoretical framework that explains the book's methodology and objectives. This chapter also offers a historical background of the period in question, where an emphasis is placed on political fragmentation within the Islamic world. Special attention is paid to the "speech act theory" which is used as a framework that "will allow us to explore the formative role that they played in specific political and cultural contexts" (p. 13).

Al-Mallah commences his literary analysis with al-Mutanabbi's panegyric that was composed after his patron, Sayf al-Dawla, suffered disastrous defeat at the hands of the Byzantines in the year 950. The author seeks to show that the classification of this ode as simply a historical document is insufficient to fully understand its real objectives. Placing this ode within the context of court ceremonial, the author argues that al-Mutanabbi applies different rhetorical strategies aiming to legitimize the ruler's position in the community by turning this defeat into military victory. Thus, this defeat serves here as a moral lesson that al-Mutanabbi recast in the form of "a ritual test or contest, a rite of purification through which the weak and the cowardly have been eliminated, the poet declares Sayf al-Dawlah and the Ummah strengthened, renewed, purified, and reinvigorated by experience." (p. 18). Interestingly, al-Mallahdoes not refer to an important book by Margaret Larkin, entitled *Al-Mutanabbi: Voice of the ʿAbbasid Ideal Poetic* (2008) that deals, *inter alia*, with the poet's high status in classical Arabic poetry and his influence on later poets, such as Ibn Haniʾ.

In the next chapter, al-Mallah analyzes Ibn Haniʾ al-Andalusi's ode dedicated to the Fatimid ruler al-Muʿizz after his general, Jawhar al-Siqilli conquered Egypt. The main objective of this ode—according to the author—is to establish, through al-Muʿzz's Imamate the religious and political legitimacy of the Fatimids. At the same time, Ibn Haniʾ ridicules the Abbasid and portrays them as illegitimate rulers. To achieve this goal, Ibn Haniʾ employs motives of noble origin, closeness to the Prophet, restoration and fertility, and generosity.

The scope of the fourth chapter remains within Fatimid politics where the author analyzes an ode by Tamim b. al-Muʿizz, who seeks to strengthen the Fatimids' claim for legitimate imperial power. The author contends that this panegyric should be understood within the Fatimid imperial agenda and not simply as part of their Shiʿa propaganda. He argues that the ode's purpose is "to communicate the Fatimid view (or narrative) to the mostly *Sunni* general public in Egypt and elsewhere, a message that has resonance during the time period of composition (this is the imperial purpose), but that also goes beyond the time period of composition into the realm of poetic immortality for the Fatimids and asserting their claims to legitimacy that are portrayed as not only valid but even more credible than the 'Abbasids" (p. 73). Ibn al-Mu'izz achieves these objectives by employing historical examples borrowed from the *sirah* literature that emphasize the status of 'Ali b. Abi Talib in the critical stages of early Islam.

The fifth chapter visits the Andalus at the beginning of the eleventh century through the analysis of two panegyrics by Ibn Darrajal-Qastalli. While the first ode is dedicated to al-Mansur b. Abi Amir, the second poem is in praise of Mundhir b. Yahia al-Tujibi. Applying the "speech act theory," Ibn Mallah examines the obligatory relationship between the poet and the patron that leads to the fulfillment of the communal duties of the later. These social ties and approvals enhance the patron's legitimacy. Ibn al-Darraj's first poemis modeled on the tripartite structure of the classical Arabic poem (*qasida*) in order to reflect an era of political stability under al-Mansur. By doing so, the poet legitimizes the existing conditions and expects to be rewarded. Composing the panegyric, the poet fulfills his obligation and now "the burden lies on the patron who must reward the poet, symbolically fulfilling his communal responsibilities" (p. 83).

Ibn Darraj's second ode does not follow conventional structure of the *qasida* because it was composed, according to the author, during a civil war. The poet dedicates, therefore, his efforts squarely to praise the patron aiming to gain poem-prize ritual exchange and mutual obligation. No wonder generosity is the central theme of this panegyric. By doing so, "the poet hints at the necessity of re-establishing the role of the community, which has been marginalized in the period of social turmoil" (p. 100).

On the whole, this study adds an important contribution to the study of classical Arabic literature showing the significant role that poetic discourse can play in the ritual communication between poets and patrons. This book will be useful for both scholars and students of classical Arabic. Explaining his theoretical framework, the author uses at times a great number of citations that disturb the flow of his argumentation. It would also be better if the author had eliminated a number of typos found in different places in the book. **AERT**

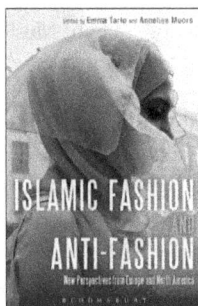

Emma Tarlo and Annelies Moors, Eds. *Islamic Fashion and Anti-Fashion. New Perspectives from Europe and North America.* **New York, NY: Bloomsbury Press, 2013. 294 pp. $88.39. ISBN: 978-0857853349. Pbk.: 320 pp. $29.95. ISBN: 978-0857853356. Ebk.: $15.49. ASIN: B00F943AM2.**

This edited collection of 16 essays brings together fascinating pieces of scholarship on Islamic fashion and its counterpart from Europe, Canada, and the United States. The broadness in geographic range is matched by diversity in approaches, as the contributions hail from experts in religious studies, anthropology, history, cultural, and fashion studies. Highlighting a great variety of different notions of "appropriate" dress, the volume demonstrates how attitudes toward forms of "Islamic dress" are constantly shifting, both among Muslim interpreters, as well as non-Muslims, always depending on a complex mix of contextual factors.

In their introduction, the two editors, Emma Tarlo and Annelies Moors bring together the various themes of the volume, alerting readers to the multiple topics and perspectives to be considered in the volume. Whereas in "the West," Muslim women are often perceived as "dull, downtrodden, oppressed," Muslim women's fashionable styles challenge such notions, as women "distance themselves from the common stereotypes" (p. 20). Yet, instead of positing a Muslim exceptionalism, many of the contributors to the volume discover "overlapping gendered critiques of fashion which draw on both Islamic and secular arguments" (p. 24). Thus, questions related to proper Muslim dress are interwoven with, and influenced by larger issues of the constructedness of gender, perceptions of self and other, fluctuating notions of appropriateness, and shifting understandings of fashion, religion, and modernity.

The first contribution by Pia Karlsson Minganti studies the reception of the burqini in public pools in Italy and Sweden. The author observes that various interlocutors are not in agreement about "Islamic norms" of proper swimwear, as even non-Muslim Europeans themselves have highly variegated attitudes toward covering or uncovering in public baths.

In "Covering up in the Prairies," A. Brenda Anderson and F. Volker Greifenhagen study the perceptions of Muslim identity in Canada, positing that the "covered woman" is simultaneously perceived as both silenced and an "agent of barbarism." Yet, in spite of negative misconceptions about Muslim women, the Canadian "prairie ethos has long been built on an atmosphere of collaborative survival" (p. 67).

The third contribution to the volume "Landscapes of Attraction and Rejection: South Asian Aesthetics in Islamic Fashion in London," by Emma Tarlo, attempts to answer the puzzle that, whereas patterns, textiles, and styles from the Indian subcontinent are ever present in Britain, Muslims from a South Asian background use them sparingly in their own fashion designs. Tarlo interprets this disregard as an expression of intergenerational conflict and an attempt to "cut across regional and ethnic distinctions" (p. 82) to create a cosmopolitan Islamic style that "transcend[s] the limitations of ethnicity and location" (p. 90).

Katarzyna Górak-Sosnowska and Michael Łyszczarz study "Perspectives on Muslim Dress in Poland: A Tatar View," in which they trace the conundrum of Tatar Polish Muslims, whose traditional use and interpretation of the headscarf is challenged by the arrival of new, competing interpretations of Islam. For Tatar women, the headscarf is alternatively associated with rural and peasant folk, or regarded as an "Arab tribal custom" (p. 101); a recent revival of Tatar identity thus constructs "Tatarness and Polishness … as opposites to Arabness and immigrant status" (p. 102).

Rustem Ertug Altinay discusses Şule Yüksel Şenler, creator of the Şulebaş headscarf style that "set standards for urban Turkish Islamic fashion" (p. 107) and paved the way for the later popular tesettür style. The article shows how this Islamic fashion style differentiated itself from "lower-class, rural, elderly, and/or Kurdish women" and instead posited the wearer as an "urban, middle-class, young and modern woman" (p. 113) which found inspiration in Audrey Hepburn's headscarf in the movie *Roman Holiday*.

R. Arzu Ünal studies the "Genealogy of the Turkish Pardösü in the Netherlands," and shows how perception of the overcoat changed from a "modern" piece of clothing to the central piece of an "Islamic" outfit, and how increased mobility between Turkey and Western Europe led to mutual influences, including the introduction of the *Kot* (denim) pardösü.

Maria Curtis' "Closet Tales from a Turkish Cultural Center in the 'Petro Metro', Houston, Texas" combines a series of observations on Turkish American Muslims in Houston.

In their study, "Transnational Networks of Veiling-fashion between Turkey and Western Europe," Banu Gökariksel and Anna Secor suggest that the development of veiling-fashion needs to be seen within the wider context of reorganization of Turkish society, in particular the rise of a middle class: "Veiling-fashion in Turkey is central to the fierce contestation between secular and Islamic versions of cosmopolitanism, modernity, and class distinction" (p. 165), yet both secular and Islamic versions utilize the notion of Europe as a central referent.

Leila Karin Österlind's "Made in France: Islamic Fashion Companies on Display" researches three French Islamic business actors in the French Islamic fashion market, and contends that each company's self-presentation and business narrative answers to an ingrained French valorization of secularism, for which reason the "entrepreneur narrative" of a successful business venture becomes important in these businesses' self-portrayal.

Reina Lewis' "Hijab on the Shop Floor: Muslims in Fashion Retail in Britain" studies hijab wearing retail shop staff in high street fashion shops in Britain. Hijabi store clerks are part of the "fashion spectacle" whose "embodied aesthetic knowledge (of fashion)…could become a form of desirable economic and cultural capital for brands wanting to break into newly discernible markets" (p. 195). Chapter 11 features an interview of Muslim fashion blogger Zinah Nur Sharif, conducted by Emma Tarlo. In the interview, Sharif problematizes the notion of "Islamic fashion" and articulates some of her ambivalence toward fashion.

Degla Salim's "Mediating Islamic Looks" suggests that Orientalist perceptions of the veil as either sexualization of the hijabi, or its portrayal as oppressive can be and are fruitfully exploited by Muslim women themselves to critique one sided stereotypes about Muslim women.

Connie Carøe Christiansen's "Miss Headscarf: Islamic Fashion and the Danish Media" discusses a spring, 2008 headscarf contest launched by the Danish National Broadcasting Company. Christiansen bemoans the fact that media attention focused on controversial aspects of the contest, which was attacked from both non-Muslim and Muslim quarters. Participants in the ensuing public debates largely failed to recognize the "elements of moral and aesthetic self-cultivation found within Islamic fashion" (p. 236).

Annelies Moors' "Fashion and Its Discontents: The Aesthetics of Covering in the Netherlands" raises the question whether young Muslim women in the Netherlands who were not participating in the rise of more fashionable women's dress in the 1990s, and continued to wear more baggy clothes in darker hues should be regarded as taking an anti-fashion stance. Moors posits that these nay-sayers "experienced such an aesthetic as embodying a pure, asexual form of beauty" (p. 253), and a critique of secular notions of women's dress which emphasizes women's sexualized bodies.

Daniela Stoica's "The Clothing Dilemmas of Transylvanian Muslim Converts" studies the dress practices of Romanian women converts to Islam. Utilizing Tarlo's "agency of the hijab," Soica discusses how, while for some of these converts' more conservative choices of dress had to be undertaken within the context of their own family backgrounds, the dress choices themselves impacted their wearers in powerful ways.

Synnøve Bendixen's " 'I Love My Prophet': Religious Taste, Consumption and Distinction in Berlin" studies "how the developing of a specific taste contributes to feelings of belonging within a faith community and mark(s) internal distinctions amongst Muslim communities in Berlin" (p. 274).

The volume has benefited from careful editing, a few minor oversights (such as the occasional grammatical error (p. 274), editorial infelicities (p. 142) or incon-sistencies in spelling (pardesu in the Introduction, pardösü in Chapters 6 and 16, pardesü in Chapter 7) notwithstanding. As is to be expected in an edited volume, the individual chapter's bibliographies exhibit a fair degree of overlap.

The collection of essays is a decidedly successful attempt to demonstrate the com-plexity of notions of gender and Islamic dress, as it highlights the ambivalence of the term "Islamic fashion," thematizes both inner-Muslim debates about appropri-ateness of women's dress and notions of modesty, and provides ample evidence that differences in geographical, socioeconomic, ethnic, religious, and age impact the ways in which conceptualizations and understandings are constructed, and such constructs impact sartorial bodily-physical expressions, which in turn affect the con-ceptualizations. **AHT**

David A. McDonald. *My Voice is My Weapon: Music Nationalism, and the Politics of Palestinian Resistance.* **Durham, NC: Duke University Press, 2013. 338 pp. $25.95. ISBN: 978-0822354796. Pbk.: 360 pp. $23.36. ISBN: 978-0822354796. Ebk.: 360 pp. $16.09. 3954 KB.**

For the general reader, the teacher, and the researcher in Middle East Studies, Da-vid A McDonald's book, *My Voice is My Weapon: Music Nationalism, and the Politics of Palestinian Resistance*, is a contribution of the first order. Two things immediately strike the reader: the superb organization of the material and (for the nonmusicolo-gist in the field) the novel approach. Let's examine the first aspect. The book opens with a "Note on transliteration" which instantly introduces the reader to the com-plexity of the linguistic registers used by Palestinian musicians with vernacular and MSA (Modern Standard Arabic) tightly intertwined together. A "Note on Accessing Performance Videos" follows next. This comes to the readers as a greatly, even if pleasantly shocking surprise because it is here that they realize that what they have in their hands is not just a book, but a "performative" place-event. Here, in fact, the author informs us that because he has deposited examples of his ethnographic field recordings with the EVIA (Ethnographic Video for Instruction and Analysis)

Digital Archive Project at Indiana University, his readers can now access them on-line. To that end, we are given the corresponding audio/video resource locator or PURL for each song discussed in the text. How about the original texts of the songs in Arabic? These are all transliterated in the Appendix at the end of the book while all translations appear in the body of the text. Needless to say, in doing so, McDonald has equipped his readers—whether these are fluent or not in any of the linguistic registers—with the choreographic instrumentation they would virtually require to enjoy the performance. Any reader of the book can now pronounce and understand all the songs in Arabic, hear and see them performed online in a variety of cultural, social, and political contexts by famous Palestinian singers. This helps bring down much of the stockade of impenetrability—the insider and outsider dichotomy—which ethnographers and anthropologists in particular have to contend with in the field. Plenty of photographs help individualize places, ceremonies, and artists. A performative "event" in its own right, McDonald's textual organization succeeds in turning the normally *alienated* reader (in the Brechtian sense, of course) into a fully conscious and knowledgeable participant. By now, readers have acquired their per-formative persona: no longer or simply the detached, objective observers; they have in the course of this multi-media experience become themselves participants. Erwin Piscator's and Bertolt Brecht's theater models may come to mind here. By incorpo-rating the audience into a total performance the resulting *kunstwerk* emerges from the breakdown of emotional and social *entfremdung* as the new locus for the polit-ically conscious and emancipated revolutionary agent. McDonald's polyphony of media has turned the written word into a virtual stage. This is no mean achievement.

Approach-wise too, McDonald delivers much. This ad hoc organization of the texts transforms space and time into a virtual event that invites the reader to con-front and decipher in this new *con*-text writing and orality; phonemes and notes; ethnography and musicology; sociology and history; ideology and art; folklore; cul-ture and politics; a political economy of oppression; and one of resistance. Chapter after chapter, the author beautifully introduces us to some of the greatest hits in the history of modern and contemporary Palestinian music. The core of the book lies in Chapters 2–9. These delineate the history of Palestinian music in the three national loci located in what is now Israel, the West Bank, and Jordan from late-Ottoman times to the Second Intifada. Throughout, narration is grounded in Palestinian folk-lore, ethnography, linguistics, and sociology. In these chapters, the author lays bare the complex web of international, regional, and local references that structure the texts of the songs. With each one carrying its own referents English, Hebrew, MSA, and vernacular resonate in a mutually interlocking game across culture, history, and politics. An instance of this rich repertoire is *Yama mawil al-Hawa* (Oh Song of Longing). A widely known folk song now rearranged to evoke the Palestinian *al-Nakba* (Catastrophe), it is recorded here by the al-'Ashiqin ensemble. The song comes alive before our very eyes as McDonald interviews Adnan Odeh, an *'udist* and a conductor of the famous group. Other songs of equal caliber quickly follow such as

"Muraba' 'Izz al-Din al Qassam" performed by Haifa born Nuh Ibrahim, "Min sijn 'Akka" (From 'Akka prison), "AL-Watan al-Akbar" (The Great Nation) with its stirring melody and black and white visual theatrical orchestration by 'Abd al-Wahab. More recent lyrics include hip-hop performances and the more recent rap tradition that re-appropriated Tupac, now a *shahid*, (martyr) for the Palestinian cause. Page after page deep in the music, glued to the images that roll before our eyes, we realize that McDonald has actually performed many of these songs with Palestinian artists. This book is a *text* literally woven (as the Latin root would have it) in the field with all the cultural threads which McDonald, the scholar, the musician, the folklorist, the ethnographer, and the performer weaves with the choral participation of local people, intellectuals and artists. This seals for us the authority of *My Voice is My Weapon*.

Something, however, perplexes me about the book: its stylistic unevenness. While in Chapters 2–9, writing flows smoothly, channeling a compelling narrative in both the Introduction and Chapter 1, reading is difficult, dragging. Here style rushes down like an impetuous river that at every turn and quite unexpectedly plunges into quick rapids and crushing falls. This is a river that really never seems to reach the plain—not until we turn page to Chapter 2. It is surprising to see, for instance, how often the author feels the need to redefine his goal: is he here simply re-stating the original purpose of the book in an ever-widening context? Is the goal part of his performative strategies and has therefore to remain under construction? If so, is the book perchance conceived as an open work, in which the reader/observer is called upon to add his/her own to the goal? Stylistic incongruity may reveal, after all, a lack of symmetry in his theoretical construction. For instance, it makes sense that the author sees in Palestinian music one powerful way in which "the nation is actively imagined, represented, constructed, and governed under myriad circumstances" (p. 29).

However, in the private and public loci structuring the three Palestinian communities living "in Israel, in exile, and under occupation" music still *re*-presents Palestine as the imagined focus of *national* resistance. Because McDonald rejects the Arab/Jew binary and supports, instead, Perry Anderson's plea for a "relational" history, then I wonder, what happens to Palestinian nationalism? Furthermore, why would someone so wary of essentialism, as the author seems to be, use "exile" so un-dialectically (see Vine Deloria, Jr. *Out of Chaos*, 1985). Again, we find this statement on p. 40: "To perform this music, in many ways, is to perform the nation" that echoes Kamal Khalil's line "If I sing loud enough and strong enough, we can create Palestine in the music" (p. 17). Here, my perplexity deepens more. Is McDonald suggesting that music replaces conscious political action? He goes on saying that, treading in the footsteps of Austin, Searle, Derrida, Faucault, Judith Butler, and Abu Lughod, ethnomusicologists and folklorists, he wants to explore the possibilities for musicians "to fluidly redirect and resignify dominant signs and meanings in accord to their own interests" (p. 25). More particularly, he continues, thanks to folklore studies, sociolinguistics and cognitive psychology, ethnomusicologists have shown music to be a social process and "music performance constitutes a primary process for understanding what it means to be Palestinian and what it means to fight for its self-determination" (p. 33). He is not just saying that music is part of the ideological structures of society, is he? In the end, while McDonald strives to connect in this book his well researched scholarly finds, a deeply felt esthetic experience for the reader/observer/participant with the philosophical and ideological demands of political intervention, one cannot help interrogating the Muses with the question: is the power to re-signify that emerges out of *musico-political processes* under dire conditions of socio-political fragmentation and protracted military attack, capable of subverting the dominant power as only revolutions and mass movements can do?

These critical questions notwithstanding, David A. McDonald has produced a solid, ground-breaking work on Palestine that will guide scholars and public along a more nuanced, humane, and transformative path of discovery for years to come. **FM**

Habeeb Salloum, Muna Salloum, and Leila Salloum Elias. *Scherezade's Feasts: Foods of the Medieval Arab World.* **Philadelphia, PA: University of Pennsylvania Press, 2013. 218 pp. $34.95. ISBN: 978-0812244779.**

Difficult to classify, *Scheherazade's Feasts* is part history, part cookbook, part conveyor of dozens of interesting tidbits of the medieval Arab world. Its focus is on the food of the elite, the ruling Caliphs of various medieval Arab dynasties, emanating from four principal centers: Baghdad and Aleppo under the Abbasids, Cairo under the Fatimids, Cordoba under the Ummayads, and Andalusia. Habeeb Salloum, one of the co-authors, along with Muna Salloum and Leila Salloum Elias, is described in the acknowledgements as being a "beacon of light in a world dim with the knowledge of the Arab past and their achievements" (p. 217).

Throughout the book, the cosmopolitanism of medieval Arab cookery is in evidence: The authors note the breadth of the food trading networks that supplied various foodstuffs to Baghdad's markets from, among other places, Syria, Yemen, Isfahan, Egypt, Oman, and Aleppo. In the *Treasure of the Benefits in Varieties of the*

Dining Table, the unknown author displays a keen interest in the food ways, not only of Syria, Baghdad, Al-Maghrib (North Africa), but also those of Turkey, Nubia, Georgia and Greece, and places beyond (p. 12). The authors highlight the achievements of the medieval Arabs in the realm of agriculture. As they note, the Andalusian Arabs transformed rural Iberia with new irrigation techniques and abundant, diverse crops which eventually shaping the cuisine of the rest of Europe (p. 4). For example, they introduced spinach, *isfanakh*, to Spain, where it became known as *espinaca*, and from there, spinach as a material food item—along with versions of its Arabic name—spread to the rest of Europe. Umayyad caliph Hisham realized that the way in which olives were harvested affected their taste, so he admonished those who shook their trees instead of harvesting olives by hand (p. 15). In this, he anticipated the concerns of modern-day producers of extra-virgin olive oil, who argue that high-quality oil cannot be produced with harsh harvesting methods.

The cosmopolitanism of this time, and the degree to which food items, agricultural practices, and preparation and consumption practices spread and were transformed as they travelled, contrasts with the anti-cosmopolitan and a-historical discourses about food practices in contemporary times. Emphasis on "local" foods erases the history of origins; and diffusions of foodstuffs, and national discourses, as embodied in cookbooks, attempt to "fix" food in time, ignoring the relative recent emergence of the nation state itself. Foods such as hummus, which, as this book indicates, were widely enjoyed throughout the medieval Arab world, get dragged into territorial disputes as Israelis claim hummus as a national dish, a point hotly contested by both the Palestinians and the Lebanese. UNESCO has fanned the flames of long-standing ethnic disputes by naming harissa a Turkish national dish, an act that enraged the Armenians who also claim it as their dish. UNESCO has declared "the Mediterranean Diet" an "intangible cultural relic" in contrast to the openness and fluidity in the medieval period when foodstuffs and practices flowed to and from the "Mediterranean" region.

One of the more interesting aspects of the text is the emphasis on how individuals in the medieval Arab world perceived the healthful qualities or dangers of food. In contemporary North American cuisine, our perceptions of the benefits and dangers of food are influenced by biomedical scientific studies which consider nonvisible elements like calories and vitamins to be the primary factors in determining a healthful diet. Historian Harvey Levenstein calls this ideology "nutritionism," where the consumer is at the mercy of the recommendation of scientific studies interpreted by food corporations. In medieval Arab cuisine, we see a deep concern for the connection between the properties of the food production, the means of its preparation and an individual's health, but in contrast to modern nutritionism, it was couched in terms of the humoral system inherited from the Greeks. Doctors were teamed with cooks: doctors diagnosed, but cooks had the responsibility to fulfil the needs of the humoral system, which included evaluating the properties of food as well as the directive of cleanliness of the food, the cooking vessels, and the cook.

Cleanliness and etiquette were closely intertwined in the medieval Arab courtly society. Cooks and guests were expected to have clipped nails, and clean mouths. In contemporary discourses of hygiene, the emphasis is on the invisible dangers of microbes and germs; in the medieval Arab world, the emphasis is more sensual, depending on the sense of smell to detect odors. In the presence of the caliph, guests were even to wear cotton underwear so as not to perspire (p. 8). Hand washing was enjoined upon them before and after meals, as having food smells on one's hands was considered repugnant. Food esthetics were highlighted in the Abbasid era, as the scholar al-Warraq attests, noting the twinning of the pleasure of the eye with the artful use of garnishes such as pomegranate seeds, celery, cucumber, eggs, and rue, which also produced the pleasure of taste. Abundant spices which ranged from musk, amber, and aloe, to still familiar spices such as saffron, nutmeg, and cloves were thought to still further enhance the sensory experience of food by engaging as many of the senses as possible (p. 12).

Those familiar with the contemporary Arab world will not be surprised at the emphasis on hospitality during the medieval period, its role in diplomacy, and in mediating between rulers and subjects. Rulers encompassed their populations with their generous hospitality, providing the populace with long and lavish multi-course meals, especially at Ramadan. Being a miser, not providing enough food for one's guests was despised. The etiquette extended to the recipients of the hospitality; guests were required to show appropriate restraint. As historians of manners, like Norbert Elias or any ethnographer knows, one becomes aware of etiquette in its breach. One manual decries avaricious guests "who snatch food off a table like a falcon seizing and an eagle swooping, without any friendly familiarity or pleasantries beforehand" (p. 7). The authors include an amusing anecdote about the Umayyad Caliph Sulayman who loved to eat. When his cooks would bring him grilled chicken on spits, the caliph would "pounce" upon them, using the sleeves of his expensive cloaks to dismember the chicken; 70 years later the chicken grease was said to be still evident on his sleeves (p. 101).

The authors argue that the highlighting of gastronomic skills and pleasures underpinned an efflorescence of food writing, poetry, and agricultural tomes. Ibrahim ibn al-Mahdi, the younger half-brother of caliphs Harun al-Rashid and al-Wathiq, is credited with having composed the "first functional and thorough cookbook in the Arabic language" (p. 11). Other food writing included that written by physicians, who presented recipes which combined food products with spices and aromatics that were thought to enhance health. We see that the connection between health and food is not a recent one, as it was commonplace for the medieval caliphs to refuse to eat unless their physicians were by their sides to advise them on the most and least nutritious foods at the table (p. 6).

The bibliography indicates the extent of the careful primary and secondary research that went into this book. A glossary entitled "Tools and Ingredients" notes when modern equipment such as food processors and blenders may be used instead of the medieval kitchen tools. The ingredients list includes translations of the terms from the Arabic and approximations of ingredients like *murri*, a fermented barley salty sauce which is no longer available. The authors recommend using Japanese red miso, since it is also barley based and does not leave the overpowering taste of soya sauce, the usual substitute suggested by specialists of medieval Arabic cooking.

This is a carefully researched book, which is so much more than a mere cookbook. Like some contemporary Middle East cookbooks, like Ottolenghi's and Tamimi's *Jerusalem* (Random House, 2012), it combines the pedagogical and historical context of food with the recipes itself. While it lacks the food photography of the *Jerusalem* cookbook, the page layout is both legible and elegant. The original translated Arabic recipe is presented in italics, with the authors' further "translation" of the recipe following, suggesting alternate ingredients, like filo pastry for the complicated dough recipe suggested by medieval writers, butter or oil for lamb tail fat, which is not widely available. The recipes provide a plausible possibility for nonprofessional cooks to re-create medieval Arab dishes, although many might find "A Dinner Feast Such as that Held in the Caliph's court" which includes 19 courses, a little too ambitious. Perhaps with an eye to undermining the sectarianism which is said by some to define the contemporary Middle East, the menus at the end of the book are ecumenical: a Dinner during Ramadan, a Dinner during Lent, a Dinner during Passover, and a Dinner for Christmas. It is an enjoyable book, adorning inspiring recipes with amusing anecdotes and excerpts from the classic 1001 Nights, drawing our attention to the extent to which food captured the literary as well as the practical imagination of the medieval Arab world. **AM**

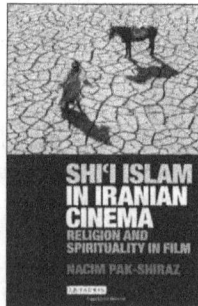

Nacim Pak-Shiraz. *Shi'i Islam in Iranian Cinema.* **Nacim Pak-Shiraz. London, UK: I. B. Tauris, 2011. 239 pp. ISBN: 978-1848855106.**

Lecturer in Film and Persian Studies, Pak-Shiraz wrote a fine study entirely dedicated to religion and cinema in post-revolutionary Iran. The work explores various cinematic representations of religion and spirituality in a number of Iranian films. In addition, fieldwork undertaken at the Fajr International Film Festival (2004–06) afforded her invaluable opportunities to study local Iranian discourses on the relation between religion and cinema.

Since films can be viewed "as a valid and important tool in the understanding of many of the current debates within Iran, rooted as they are in much older historical and traditional discourses on religion, power and politics" (p. 13), the author has chosen socio-historical and cultural approaches for her exploration of how the two interact. Accordingly, long discussions on various aspects of Shi'ism in Iran are included throughout the work, and provide necessary background for those unfamiliar with the religion.

A first introductory historical overview (pp. 1-33) of Shi'ism in Iran (origin, development, role of clergy, and madrasah) presents a number of religious, social, and political elements important for the contextualization of later debates on the role of the clergy. Next, one plunges into a fascinating chapter on how Iranians have attempted to define religion and spirituality in cinema, and the debates that have surrounded discussions on their interrelation (pp. 35-65). For example, the addition of a "Spiritual (*ma'nagara*) Cinema" category during the 2005 Fajr International Film Festival generated further debates the author reviews with a survey of current and previous Iranian post-revolutionary (after 1979) discourses on religion, spirituality, and cinema: Islamic jurisprudential writings, philosophical (mostly Heidegger-inspired) discussions on the "technological art," "official" responses (definitions, critiques), and the approaches of film critics and opponents of this newly coined term of "spiritual" cinema. These discussions remain important contributions to the work, although further analysis of the significance of those debates and of the implications and significance of institutionalized discourses over this contested term, as well as a previous (long before 2005) "official" understanding of the role of religion, and its use (for ideological purposes) could have been further explored.

The following four chapters study the "filmic discourses," or representations and depictions of religion and spirituality. The first chapter looks at the filmic discourse on the role of the clergy (pp. 67-92) deployed by Reza Mirkarimi in his depictions of the clergy in *Under the Moonlight* (2001) and those put forward by Kamal Tabrizi in *The Lizard* (2004). This "formalistic" approach to religion is opposed to the "personal" approach in the chapter that explores the Sufi and mystical filmic discourse that is found in the works of Majid Majidi (pp. 93-121). Concepts such as intuition and inward light, love, the various Sufi states and the spiritual path toward perfection all become vantage points for interpretations of Majidi's *The Colour of Paradise* (1999), *The Willow Tree* (2005), and *Baran* (2001). The third chapter explores the use of elements of the *"ta'zieyh"*—a more popular expression of Shi'i Iranian religiosity in the form of a passion play which eulogizes and commemorates the martyrdom of Imam Husayn—in the "filmic narratives" proposed by Asadi and Beyzaei, offering a preliminary discussion on the origins of this Iranian Shi'i passion play, its historical development, its structure, and social significance (pp. 123-144). Sufficient information is provided to shed light on the *ta'zieh's* dramatic structure and powerful religious symbolism to which Asadi appeals in *The Day of Incident* (1994), based on a screenplay written in 1984 by Bahram Beyzaei; and also Beyzaei in his *The Traveller* (1992) (pp. 123-165). The powerful mediated effects of its cinematic depictions are further explored with Abbas Kiarostami's London Museum installation in 2005, where he projected his experimental film on ta'zieh audiences, providing for insightful discussions on Kiarostami's world. A last chapter (pp. 167-192) proposes a "philosophical" analysis of Abbas Kiarostami's "Koker Trilogy," *Where is the Friend's House* (1987), *And Life Goes On* (1992), *Through the Olive Trees* (1994), and *Taste of Cherry* (1997). An interesting Wittgensteinian (*Tractatus,* 6.44 and 6.45) analysis (furthering a comment by Rapfogel) turns Kiarostami into a "poetic philosopher" who tackled natural disasters and the meaning of life in a "poetic" (mediation of the "feeling" of what "*is*") (pp. 183-184) and "spiritual" manner, in other words, without any attempts at discursive commentaries or explanations.

Here, one needs to bring together this interpretative "spiritual" philosophical filmic discourse with the earlier "mystical" one about Sufism. Both present legitimate vantage points for the study of religion and Iranian cinema. Unclear, however, is why both were selected or, for that matter, applied to those particular filmmakers, since Kiarostami's work is also presented as mystical, defined as beyond the discursive and the dogmatic (formalistic), and Majidi's work as poetic. Could affliction and pain explored by Majidi be analyzed through the proposed Wittgensteinian understanding of the "spiritual" and death and disaster explored by Kiarostami, and be studied with that of Sufism and the "mystical?" A stronger case might have been made had one of these two analytical vantage points been applied throughout the work. It could have provided greater analytical cohesion and perhaps help identify a clearer central thesis to be argued throughout the work.

This issue might be linked with some of the difficulties encountered when defining the parameters of religion and approaches for its study. While some approaches to the study of religion and spirituality in Western cinema are listed (pp. 5-6), some briefly discussed—Jesus/Christ figures; theological approach; mythical; religious function of form and reception; religious interpretation of film with explicit or implicit religious material; film as "hierophany"—(pp. 4-10) and to which, at times, appeal is made in the course of the work, one would have liked better focus and less equivocal discussions of "religion," the "religious," the "spiritual," etc. True, the topic is highly complex, but evaluative statements like, "various subsequent attempts at defining *ma'nagara* cinema by the Farabi Cinema Foundation, academics, journalists, film-makers and others have so widened its scope of interpretation that it is clear there is no one comprehensive definition and no one approach can do justice to the numerous possibilities of studying religion or spirituality in films" (p. 65). This is a view that one encounters a few times, like a persistent reminder of the difficulties at proposing a "definitive explanation" (as if one in fact would ever exist) of "what constitutes religion, who is religious, which members of the social strata endorse a specific religious practice ... or publicly express one's [religious] views in Iran" (pp.

194-195), seem overly reductive. Did the coining of "spiritual" (*ma'nagara*) cinema (and ensuing debates and discussions) occur *only* in 2005? Hence, further elaborations on the significance and implications of the major views and trends uncovered in the study of Iranian understanding of the "religious" and the "spiritual" and cinema, long before 2005 (and after), in the highly ideological and institutional understanding of religion, of post-revolution history of Iranian cinema that one cannot overlook, would have been most welcomed.

Passages that provide insight into the developments of contemporary local Iranian debates and theories not readily available to non-Persian speakers surrounding the nature of what might be spiritual, as opposed to religious cinema remain the most fascinating ones. In short, Pak-Shiraz has written the first exploratory study of religion and Iranian cinema to serve as an introduction to students of film in the significance of religious aspects of Iranian Shi'a society. This is so crucial for the understanding of quite a number of contemporary Iranian films. **RDM**

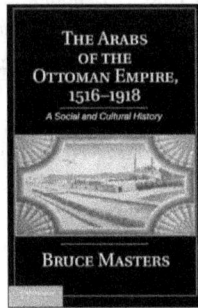

Bruce Masters. *The Arabs of the Ottoman Empire, 1516–1918: A Social and Cultural History.* Cambridge, UK: Cambridge University Press; 2013. 271 pp. Pbk: $26.99. ISBN: 978-1107619036.

Bruce Masters' latest book, The Arabs of the Ottoman Empire, 1516–1918: A Social and Cultural History, is an excellent analysis of the Arabs in the Ottoman Empire dating from Selim I's victory in the Battle of Marj Dabiq and subsequent move into Arab lands to the end of WWI and the division of Ottoman lands. Masters, who is currently the John Andrus Professor of History at Wesleyan University, states that he began his study of Ottoman Arab territories "in earnest" 37 years ago and it shows. In this work, Masters demonstrates a tremendous depth and breadth of knowledge in this field and, as a result, this text is an excellent addition to scholarship.

In the seven chapters that follow the introduction, Masters discusses the establishment and survival of Ottoman rule in the Arab lands; Ottoman institutions; economy and society; scholars and saints; wars against Napoleon; the Wahhabis; and Mehmed Ali's the *Tanzimat*, and the end of "the relationship" as he calls it. In these chapters, Masters deftly explains the nuances of Ottoman rule of the Arab territories.

Masters begins with an analysis of Arab historiography of the period. He affirms that Arab historians in the twentieth century "rarely presented the Ottoman period in a positive light." In fact, until the 1970s, these historians put forth a master–slave narrative through which they explained the period from the Mongols (1258) to Nasser (p. 2). During the 1970s, Masters explains that Arab historians began to develop "a more nuanced understanding" of Ottoman rule over Arab lands (p. 3). Through use of these newer sources, Masters is able to expand academic under-standing of Ottoman occupied Arab lands after Holt (*Egypt and the Fertile Crescent 1616–1922* [1966]) and Holt's student, Rafeq (*al-'Arab wa al-'uthmaniyyun, 1516–1916* [1974]). But, more importantly for Masters is that he addresses the question of whether or not "Arab exceptionalism" existed during the Ottoman period. Finding the view in Istanbul of Arab provinces to be "politically indistinguishable" from oth-er provinces, Masters finds that there was exceptionalism in terms of culture. Being Muslims, Arabs shared certain cultural aspects and were excluded from the Ottoman *devşirme* system—the child levy paid by Balkan and Anatolian Christians.

Another example of a revision to academic understanding is provided by Masters' discussion of the *a'yan*. The category of a'yan has been widely accepted by Ottoman historians since Hourani labeled them "notables" in 1968. Masters, finding this cat-egory to be so broad as to lack meaning, adds nuance and focus to this category by demonstrating that there were, in fact, levels of a'yans. Some a'yans wielded political power, but did not possess the same social status, as evidenced by the fact that other a'yans would not marry off their daughters to them. Following a discussion of nu-merous different levels in the category of a'yan, Masters suggests that perhaps the chroniclers of the time "be considered as voices for the true a'yan" (p. 86).

Throughout this work, Masters does a fine job of explaining the nuances of iden-tity, governors and judges in the Arab provinces, guilds, and other Ottoman institu-tions. At the same time, he attends to his stated theme of Arab exceptionalism. This he sometimes does in very interesting and thought provoking ways. An example of this comes with his discussion of scholars and Sufis. Sufis played a role in Ottoman rule from the beginning. Masters explains that right from the initial battle that led to the conquest of Arab lands, the Battle of Marj Dabiq, Sufis were involved. On one side, Mamluk Sultan al-Ghawri was accompanied by heads of Sufi orders of the Badawiyya, Rifa'iyya, and the Qadiriyya (the most important Sufi orders of Egypt at the time). While on the other side, Sultan Selim I had with him representatives of the Bektaşi order—popular with his janissary forces—and of the Mevlevi order. This appeal to religion was important for Selim as he had negotiated a change in the expansion policy of the Ottomans, who hitherto had expanded largely into Anato-lia and Eastern Europe. But Selim's relations with Sufis did not end here. Masters describes an interesting prophecy concerning famous Sufi mystic, al-'Arabi, who died in Damascus in 1240 and became "a figure with cult status in the Ottoman period" (p. 115). One of Selim's first acts upon entering Damascus was to visit the tomb of al-'Arabi. According to Evliyya Çelebi, writing more than a century and a half after the event, Selim was unsure about whether or not to pursue the Mamluks to Egypt. It is in this moment of indecision that al-'Arabi appeared to Selim in a dream and promised him that he would take Cairo if he restored his grave. Another later story from an apocryphal text of the connection between Selim I and al-'Arabi is that al-'Arabi himself had predicted the restoration of his grave by saying, "When the letter Sin enters the letter Shin ibn al-'Arabi's grave will appear" (p. 117). This was understood to mean that the *Sin* stood for Selim, while the *Shin* meant *Sham* (Damascus in Arabic).

At times entertaining, as evidenced by the example above, at other times revisionist, but always edifying, *The Arabs of the Ottoman Empire, 1516–1918* is an excellent addition to scholarship. This is a text that will be enjoyed and appreciated by scholars of the Middle East and is certainly a text that should be in university libraries and will be on course reading lists—it is definitely one that I will be using in my Ottoman history courses. **DM**

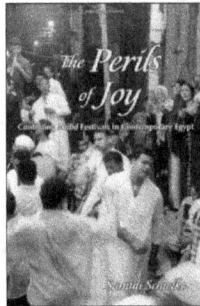

Samuli Schielke. *The Perils of Joy: Contesting Mulid Festivals in Contemporary Egypt*. Syracuse, NY: Syracuse University Press, 2012. 269 pp. $45.00. ISBN: 978-0815633006.

The Perils of Joy is an excellent piece of ethnographical work addressing Mulids in Egypt. The Mulid celebrations are presented as "utopian exceptions to the order of the everyday where everybody is welcome and many things are possible that otherwise would be deemed out of place" (p. 7). Schielke argues that Mulid festivals imply a festive joy for its own sake, and that they also express visions of society, religion, and the self. Mulids are the starting point to address larger issues of contested meanings regarding religion, modernity, class, social order, and moral subjectivity in contemporary Egypt.

The book addresses various views, such as how Mulids are looked upon, where some approve of them; while others argue that it is an innovative practice against true Islam. Yet others argue Mulids are signs of backwardness. The material was gathered in the late years of the Mubarak regime, when Salafi interpretations grew, and neo-liberal politics influenced both the practice and the ideas about Mulids expressed in the book; and it also influences Schielke's analysis. What can the Mulid celebrations tell us about the contested nature of festive joy under conditions of modernist visions of order, progress, and subjectivity? This is the main question that Schielke addresses in *Perils of Joy*.

The book presents the visible aspects of the Mulid: the shape of the celebrations, how they are organized, and where and when. Schielke shows how a Mulid is a festive world with religious meaning for many participants, but not all. The religious aspect to a Mulid is often connected to a saint's shrine, which is visited (*ziyara*), and which bestows blessing (*Baraka*). Each Mulid follows an independent schedule, has a local focus, and is often similar to street festivals. Mulids often appear to be chaotic and manifold, but are embedded in a festive order. Festive lights, music and singers, temporary cafés, amusement areas, colorful tents, and markets all contribute to make Mulids a happening for most people, not just pilgrims.

Considering the function of Mulids, one may ask if a Mulid is subversive and a challenge to dominant norms, or if it is something that distracts people from their real problems. Both are common explanations in Egypt, but, Schielke argues, fail to understand the ambivalent nature of festive time. A Mulid is simultaneously profound and joking, spiritual and commercial, conservative, and subversive. In order to get closer to the function of a Mulid, Schielke argues that we need to consider the meanings given to it by practitioners. The informants' narratives give voice to a view that does not present Mulids as occasions of subversion, but that they may become so when entering the hegemonic discourses and imageries in Egypt. Devout participants rather consider Mulids as occasions of pious devotion and celebration of a saint.

Considering the critical discourses around Mulids, many Egyptians consider them as subversive, as erroneous and backwards, and threatening the order of things. Some may agree to the veneration of saints, but disagree with the festivities surrounding the Mulids; and some people only appreciate the festivities. There are those who consider Mulid celebrations to be innovative, which is not true to Islam, reflecting a struggle of interpretative authority. Islamic reformists and modernists promote a progressive view, where things ought to have a clear and serious purpose, which, in their view, a Mulid fails to provide; a Mulid thus represents a false consciousness and subversion and is considered a threat to modernity. A historical perspective on criticism to Mulids is presented as well where Schielke relates the rejection of Mulids to the Egyptian elite and its engagement with colonial hegemony. The ridicule of festive traditions is seen as a strategy of the modern middle classes who have tried to claim an intellectual and political hegemony over other social groups.

In presenting the various opinions of Mulids, Schielke outlines a contemporary Egypt in transit, with different segments of society relating to religion and modernity in various ways, which is part of the explanation of the contested nature of Mulids. Schielke notes that the problem with Mulids must be related to the modernist view of order and progress, which has dominated Egypt since the twentieth century. He points to the fact that emotions are important to many participants in Mulid-festivities and that the modernist ideals may not always be how things work. Efforts to change the world may often be much more spontaneous and playful than modernist ideals would have it.

However, as Schielke notes, there are not only negative attitudes to Mulids. Many consider them to be authentic and a part of the Egyptian heritage, making them into a folkloristic phenomenon. The image of Mulids transforms into a kind of cultural icon in the popular heritage where it has become turned into folkloric art, and is represented in a way that the middle class can appreciate the esthetic aspects without facing the complex nature of Mulids. However, as Schielke notes, this is not only the case in folklore, but is also found in reformist Sufism, where an attempt can be observed to legitimize Mulids as genuine devotion, against more ecstatic rituals, again reflecting the contestation among religious interpretative stands. The government also initiated a large-scale restructuring of festivals where the government public-planning policies and control of visitors of festivals, made the festive expressions and experiences fragmented. Moreover, even though retaining their character, Mulids move more to the margins. The number of participants seems to decrease, while the number of Mulids seems to be stable. Schielke believes that Mulids will continue, but in a different more marginalized way. In some neighborhoods in Cairo, Sufi celebrations with a more explicitly mystical and ecstatic nature, separated from the amusement and trade prevalent in Mulids, are noticeable. Moreover, the Mulid character as a community festival may attract people who are not there for religious reasons, which Schielke sees as a kind of secularization of Mulids. This leads to a further fragmentation of Mulids and of the festive experience. Schielke notes that such pluralism has been characteristic of Mulids and it remains to be seen if Mulids will make way for new festive traditions or if it will remain one distinct tradition.

The concluding chapter attempts to develop a more general vision of the Mulids as festivals of the extraordinary and the modernist project. Schielke relates a discussion with a friend in Tahrir Square during the 2011 revolution, where the friend said "Isn't this just like a Mulid?" Schielke claims that a Mulid is not a revolutionary event, but that there is a shared tone of extraordinary freedom. The revolutionary space of Tahrir Square can be compared to a Mulid. "Like a Mulid, it was, in itself, freedom" and it is described as a "lived utopian moment of revolutionary freedom" (p. 200). A revolution is exceptional and singular in nature, but something out of the ordinary that makes us see the world differently, like Mulids. From this observation, Schielke goes on to consider festivities in general as inseparable from the social world surrounding them. A Mulid gains its significance based on the relationship it has to participants' general life experiences, their place in society and views of the world. However, they cannot be reduced to the social world outside. And, argues Schielke, here lays the potential for controversy, simultaneously with its attraction and dynamics.

The book is certainly well worth a read. It is informative about Mulids in general in Egypt and anyone interested in religious festivities will enjoy the book. The analysis which attempts to avoid merely putting Mulids in the dichotomous view of "orthodoxy" versus "folk Islam" is a contribution to the analytical perspective and understanding of the situation in Egypt, and elsewhere, where modernist attitudes and liberal politics influence many segments of society. Some religious practices are targeted from such a perspective as being backward, contrary to the more "enlightened" or "rational" forms of Islam promoted by the middle class in Egypt. Schielke manages to discuss this situation without producing yet another account of the meeting between "tradition" and "the modern" as the simple answer to the contestations. In contemporary post-revolutionary Egypt, the religious landscape has changed even more and the Islamist Muslim brotherhood and Salafi groups have gained more influence; one can only hope that Schielke will probe more into the contested nature of Islam and the relation to "the modern" in Egypt in this new historical setting. **SO**

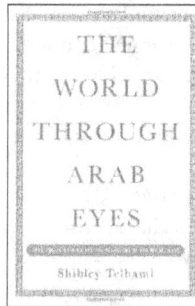

Shibley Telhami. *The World through Arab Eyes: Arab Public Opinion and the Reshaping of the Middle East.* New York, NY: Basic Books, 2013. 228 pp. $27.99. ISBN: 978-0465029839.

Research on Arab public opinion is growing rapidly. Much of it is nationally based and little of that is published in English-language sources. This makes especially welcome a book that reports on a series of surveys encompassing six countries: Egypt, Jordan, Lebanon, Morocco, Saudi Arabia, and the UAE over 10 years, using greatly similar survey instruments. It allows readers to observe trends and also to see the impact of contemporaneous events on Arab attitudes.

Among the extra options offered are comparisons of Arab and Israeli attitudes toward "other" groups, and a chapter on U.S. attitudes toward Arabs, which are notable for their lack of stability over the short period covered. Taken together, the survey outcomes reveal the impact of information especially that which is disseminated by mass media, on ideas and, to a lesser extent, the identities of its consumers. The fact that the author also shares his conclusions about the factors forming these attitudes gives readers a point of departure for engaging both, the results and possible reasons for them.

Identity is a complex set of attitudes that reflect how individuals see themselves in their worlds. Here it is measured as the respondent's first and second choices among four categories: Arab, religion, country, and citizen of the world. With the exception of Lebanon, a state under siege, identification with country has generally declined over the past 10 years, while Arab identity and religion have grown in importance. Differences from country to country are also visible. Saudi respondents consistently claimed their Muslim identity as the most important, but Egyptian identities are more fluid. To Egyptians, the relative importance of country, Arab, and Muslim identity are now about the same, whereas Arab identity had predominated in 2004 and 2005. Telhami thinks that the penetration of new media is a primary reason for the decline of nation as the dominant element of identity but, as the examples of Lebanon and Saudi show, the whole story is likely to be much more complicated.

Empathy is an integral part of identity. What allows individuals to sympathize with the pain of others is carefully probed in questions that are situational rather than global. Here mass media appears to be less important than attitudes shaped over time. Telhami notes that "positive coverage of 'the other side' is often dismissed," while negative coverage may reinforce but does not cause negative perceptions (p. 58). He tests this proposition in questions to Arabs about the Holocaust and to Israelis about the suffering of Palestinian refugees. For example, he asks Arab respondents whether viewing a film or program about the Holocaust makes them feel more empathic toward Jews, produces mixed feelings, or causes them to feel more resentful because such programs build sympathy for Israel. Interestingly, the percentage of those who said they felt empathy for the other was 11% for Arabs and 10% for Israelis responding to a similar question about Palestinians (pp. 60, 64), perhaps a sign of the stability of hardened hearts in both groups. With respect to Arab respondents, even more interesting was that those who identify as citizens of the world (not a large category as can be inferred from the previous) are more empathetic than English speakers. Telhami suggests that this may be because they watch more French TV than English speakers watch U.S. or British TV, an explanation that I find generates more questions than it answers, as well as disagrees with my personal experience in Gulf countries.

The impact of information and events on attitudes is clearer with respect to attitudes toward the United States and Iran, which have changed over the period of the surveys and are especially vulnerable to events whose valences are far from consistent. Telhami's surveys distinguish between "the United States" and "the American people," removing a source of confusion in understanding the question and the answers. Not surprisingly, he finds that Arabs like Americans more than they like the U.S. government, although the distance between these two responses has recently diminished. The impact of economic growth and greater information availability may explain why, from 2005 to 2011, the United States "rank[ed] no better than fourth" among a list of eight countries (including France, the UK, Germany, Japan, Russia, China, and Pakistan) as a place to live (p. 122). In 2005, the United States ranked second as the best place to get an education, but only fourth in subsequent years. Although the difficulties of getting visas to travel to the United States since 9/11 probably contribute to this rating, greater familiarity with Europe thanks to vacations abroad may be a larger factor, along with the migration of foreign universities to the region which both increases familiarity with a variety of education approaches and offers structured opportunities to study abroad for short periods.

Arab attitudes toward Iran reflect what Deborah Amos has called "the eclipse of the Sunnis," particularly the post-invasion rise of Iraqi Shi'a to power (see Deborah Amos, *Eclipse of the Sunnis: Power, Exile, and Upheaval in the Middle East.* New York: Public Affairs, 2010).What Jordan's King Abdullah called "the Shi'ite crescent" has undermined the sense of security among some Sunni leaders of states with significant Shi'a populations, fueling their dread of rising Iranian power and especially the possibility of Iran's developing nuclear weapons. Fleshing out his poll results in an informal content analysis of comments posted on two media websites, Aljazeera.net and Alarabiya.net, both supported by Sunni governing elites, Telhami reports that popular attitudes are more nuanced and varied than the survey data alone can reveal. Looking at the first 36 posts on individual stories, many more of the comments mocked the reactions of Arab governments to Iranian "provocations" such as a story reporting a 2012 "confirmation" by Iran of its claims to the Abu Musa Islands than responded by making hostile comments (some tinged with sectarian slurs). Similar surprises were revealed by reader comments on former Egyptian president Morsi's plans to visit Iran in conjunction with the Non-Aligned Movement summit. Citing a variety of reasons, the majority of the comments were positive—the minority of negative comments was equally varied in their reasoning. The lack of consistent narratives on either side could be a result of the variety of news sources available to respondents, and are evident in different emphases individuals' accord to particular elements of a story—for example, "Egypt," "Iran," "non-aligned."

Of particular interest to Americans is the chapter on trends in Arab attitudes toward the United States and to pressures from the United States for democratization. Although Arab populations favor democracy and see European countries and North American countries as offering more freedom and democracy than their own, they are not convinced that the United States is pursuing democratization in the right way. From 2004 to 2010, nearly half of the respondents chose France as the country with the most freedom and democracy (another reason for investigating Arab attitudes toward France more closely!). The bona fides of President George Bush as an avatar of democracy were erased by the 2003 U.S. invasion of Iraq and the brutal effects of war and occupation on the Iraqi people. Even before, U.S. commitment to democracy in the Middle East was undermined by U.S. support of dictators in return for their support of U.S interests in the region. The notion that Arab populations do not see or understand what is going on between their governments and the United States, or that "the street" displays a mindless anti-Americanism is not supported by the evidence reported in this volume. Observations and aspirations with regard to world order might also be surprising to Americans. Responding to a question asking which country would be the respondent's "preferred superpower," from 2005 to 2011, the United States never got a plurality of the "votes." By now, we should not be surprised that France won a plurality in 2005. But even France came in second in 2009, behind Germany, and fourth in 2011, behind China, Germany, and Russia. The United States did not recover in superpower popularity after the election of President Obama, whose policies toward Israel/Palestine disappointed Arabs more than his policies toward human rights, democratization, and economic assistance. Telhami notes the Arab-centrism of the region, criticized even by Islamists, who resent the priority of Arab over Islamic identity.

This brief and probably idiosyncratic discussion of the 10 years of Arab public opinion reported in this volume is just a sample of what it contains. While I wish Telhami had done more micro-analysis (comparing male and female, urban and rural, Sunna and Shi'a, and other parsing of the combined populations), there is plenty of information in this volume on which to base a more accurate and nuanced picture of contemporary Arab attitudes. Black and white thinking about ourselves and our Arab neighbors is harder to sustain after one has read it. **MAT**

BIOGRAPHY, AUTOBIOGRAPHY

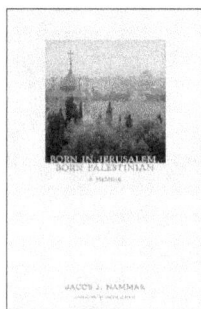

Jacob J. Nammar. *Born in Jerusalem, Born Palestinian: A Memoir*. Northampton, MA: Olive Branch Press, 2012. 152 pp. Pbk.: $15.00. ISBN: 978-1566568869.

Now a retired business executive living in San Antonio, Texas, Jacob Nammar was born in Jerusalem in 1941, lived in it during the remaining years of the British Mandate until 1947, witnessed the Palestinian *Nakba* of 1948, and endured its aftermath as one of the Arabs remaining in (West) Jerusalem under Israel's rule until he immigrated to the United States in 1964. His memoir about this period of his life is a heartfelt account of his experiences, told in an unpretentious language, describing his initial idyllic life before the nakba, and then the hardships he suffered and the discrimination he sustained under Israel, but always remaining free of bitterness, remembering the positive events in his life, and hoping for better days.

His father was a Palestinian Arab, a bus driver and tourist guide; and his mother was an Armenian woman who, before marriage, lived in Beirut to which she had fled as a child from the Armenian massacres of 1915. They had a large family with eight children and lived in the Nammareh neighborhood of Baq'a in (West) Jerusalem, next to other extended family members of Nammar descendants, who owned property and orange groves and who, like other Palestinians, lived amicably with their Jewish neighbors in Palestine during Ottoman times.

Jacob Nammar recalls his happy boyhood in the 1940s until, one day, his school bus was attacked by Zionist terrorists and, in 1946, the south wing of the King David Hotel—where his older brother Mihran worked at the front desk—was blown up by the Zionist Irgun gang and was severely damaged, causing the death of approximately 100 people with many injured. His inner peace was shaken, and it was further disturbed as the British Mandate ended in May 1947, leaving Palestine in chaos, with Israel being created after war with the Arabs.

Nammar personally saw the dispossession and dislocation of the Palestinians, many of whom fled for safety and left their belongings and homes, which were immediately taken over by Israelis. His family decided to stay put and thought they were safe to remain at home. But the Israeli authorities forced them and all other Arabs remaining behind to move to militarily controlled and fenced security zones in (West) Jerusalem. Nammar's lot was to live in Zone A. When the restrictions were removed some years later and they tried to return to their home, they found that it had been occupied by Israelis with the official authorization of the state. Nammar describes the Zionist policy of *nikayon*, the ethnic cleansing he witnessed that Israel was practicing in order to eject the Palestinians forcefully from their country.

Jacob Nammar managed to somehow continue his schooling at the Terra Sancta School from which he graduated in 1958. He gradually began to regain some inner composure, though not without occasional worried disturbance—as when his father and brother were imprisoned by Israel for a period with no explanation, but were later released. What brought him self-assurance and some direction in life was his membership of the Jerusalem YMCA, where he made new friends and became a noted athlete, especially in swimming and basketball.

Finding life in (West) Jerusalem intolerable because of the state's racist and discriminatory practices, five of his mostly older siblings emigrated; and only he, his mother, his sister Wedad, and his youngest brother Zakaria had remained to bury his father when he died in 1961. Six months later, in 1962, his mother and sister decided to leave for the United States to join his other siblings, but his mother was homesick and returned to live in East Jerusalem in 1963, which was then under Jordan's rule. She took Zakaria with her, hoping for a more secure future for him there, and wanting to have contact with her other son Suleiman in Jordan, now married and with children. The close-knit Jerusalem family of Nammar was thus dispersed—replicating the sad reality of most Palestinian families after the nakba.

Now alone in (West) Jerusalem, Jacob Nammar concentrated on his YMCA connection, where he became the assistant director of physical education, taught swimming lessons, and conducted adult fitness classes. He also coached youth basketball and built a good team. He was chosen to play with the Israeli *Hapoel Yerushalayim* team and became a national basketball star, known as Ya'acov Nammar. Yet he noticed he was being increasingly resented as a *goy* (non-Jew), and offensive remarks were made to him such as, "You don't represent Israel! Go home!" and "You don't belong in this country" (p. 117). He was eventually dropped from the team without justification or explanation. That is when he decided to leave his beloved Jerusalem, concluding that learning Hebrew language and culture, having Jewish friends, and trying to fit in Israeli society did not help his integration. On September 1, 1964, he said goodbye to his friends, climbed the YMCA tower for a final panoramic view of the city, went home and packed. The next day he left for the United States.

After a university education, Jacob—earlier Ya'acov, and initially Ya'coub—Nammar had a successful life in the United States, got married, and had children. His mother joined him in 1968 and enjoyed seeing her children and their progeny. She died in 1973 in Toronto, while visiting his brother Suleiman and his family who had emigrated there from Jordan. The Israeli authorities did not permit her burial in Jerusalem as she had wished. She was survived by her eight children, 25 grandchildren, and 30 great-grandchildren as well as her five brothers and three sisters (p. 143).

Intimately personal as this memoir is, it is compelling reading as a description of the quality of family life of Palestinians under Israeli rule and of the effects on them of the *Nakba*. In a compassionately human way, it helps readers understand the reality of the Palestinian tragedy. Its small details bring home the immensity of the injustices Palestinians have suffered, and are still suffering. Yet the author keeps hoping for a rebirth of Palestine where peace and justice will rule, based on mutual understanding and respect among all people living in it. **IJB**

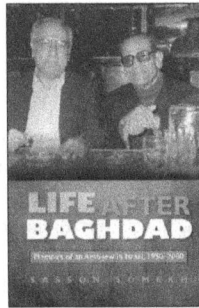

Sasson Somekh. *Life after Baghdad: Memoirs of an Arab-Jew in Israel, 1950–2000.* **East Sussex, UK: Sussex Academic Press, 2012. 168 pp. $22.50. ISBN: 978-1845195021.**

In 1985 Sasson Somekh attended a conference of the Society of Judeo Arabic Studies in Tel Aviv. Somekh, an expert on Arabic and Hebrew language, presented on the subject of the Cairo Geniza, a group of ancient documents relating to the Jewish community of Cairo. The writer of one document "notes the presence of Jews, both Rabbinic and Karaite, as a routine matter at the *majlis*; the anonymous Jewish writer also (subtly) scolds the vizier for making and allowing the attending scholars to make offensive remarks about Jews and the Jewish liturgy" (p. 112). This document presented evidence that Jews had participated, and had their voices heard under the Muslim government of Egypt in the tenth century. However, Somekh's presentation was met with indignation. "Instead of a sympathetic response came shouts of skepticism from two of the most distinguished Geniza scholars, attacking us furiously about the translation and our conclusions" (p. 112). This dispute, about the history of Jews in Islamic countries, symbolized a larger struggle within Somekh's life to bridge the gap between the Arab world and Israel.

Sasson Somekh was born in Baghdad in 1933 to a middle class family. His father was a bank clerk who had spent much of his life trying to learn English in order to accommodate the British. "My father never read an Arabic newspaper" (p. 53). However, the family's life was thrown into turmoil when they decided to immigrate to the newly created state of Israel. Somekh arrived first, in 1951. He was sent to live in a transit camp for immigrants. "I was not familiar with all the social classes comprising the Baghdad Jewish community, not to mention the Jews of northern Iraq-Kurds and those from Mosul" (p. 1). At the camp, he was suddenly thrust into a huge diversity of Jewish immigrants. He was confronted immediately with the problems that immigrants from Arab countries faced in Israel. "The fact that the Jewish Agency clerks spoke Yiddish among themselves (they, too, were new immigrants—Holocaust survivors who had arrived from Eastern Europe not long before), created a feeling, for the first time among many of the Iraqis, that they were second-class citizens, that only a Yiddish speaker could aspire to the status of a full-fledged citizen" (p. 3). The families also found their lives and respect diminished. "Most of these families were used to living in brick buildings, between solid walls. Here they were greeted by rickety canvas huts" (p. 2). Even though the author's father secured decent employment at a bank, many of the people who had been middle class found themselves forced to work construction and manual labor. In addition to the conditions and low wages, the new immigrants were forced to live in a "camp surrounded by barbed wire" where the immigrants "were warned against going outside" (p. 9). Evidently this was not the land of milk and honey that many had imagined Israel to be.

The author decided that in such circumstances he would double his efforts at finding his way into the academy. He had been a budding poet and now he intended to find a way into Israel's intellectual circles. In order to do that he had to master Hebrew. He threw off the Hebrew-Arabic of his birth, with the guttural expressions, and embraced the new European Hebrew that was being used in Israel. As a member of the political left, Somekh began to meet with members of the Israeli Communist party and local Arab intellectuals. He also immersed himself in the Arabic newspapers then published in Israel, such as *al-Jadid*. In one issue of this newspaper, an article appeared arguing for the "mutual translation of the two languages and familiarization of the Jewish readership with Arabic literature, and the Arab public with Hebrew literature" (p. 33). The introduction to this notion of language coexistence was one that would mark the author's long life. However, as Somekh notes, the outcome was not as expected. Not only did some Arabs hesitate to participate with Jews in mutual study groups, in the end "their Jewish counterparts did not acquire a real knowledge of Arabic" (p. 49).

Life after Baghdad is primarily a story about various points in the author's life and people he met. He describes his influences and those professors such as Haim Blanc, whom he deeply respected. In addition, he describes his involvement with such institutions as the Hebrew Language Academy. One of the main themes is his attempt to transcend the conflict in the Middle East in meeting with Arab authors and intellectuals such as Tawfiq al-Hakim, Professor Husayn Fawzi and Nobel Prize Winner Naguib Mahfouz. However, over time he noted that hostility toward Israel was growing in the Arab world. This was particularly the case in Egypt, where high hopes after the peace treaty faded. "The hostility toward Israel would sometime brim over—often because of Israel's actions toward the Palestinians, though sometimes it was very difficult to identify specific actions of our governments as the source of the incitement" (p. 135). Egyptians, such as Hakim, were accused of collaborating with Israelis by hosting cultural meetings. Egyptians spoke out against the "cultural invasion" of Israelis going to Egypt (p. 160).

Somekh's book presents a fascinating life story of a man who attempted to bridge the gaps between Hebrew and Arabic, between Arab and Israeli intellectuals, and between Arabs and Jews within Israel. However, what is most interesting is the degree to which it seems he was able to navigate and familiarize himself with the world of Arab intellectuals and writers in 1950s Israel, in a way that today seems impossible. Another contribution of this book is to present a glimpse into the history of Jewish immigrants to Israel who came from Muslim countries. These immigrants were often shabbily treated in the 1950s, sent by order to far flung development towns where they ended up at low paying jobs and lived out lives of poverty. These social distinctions and the discrimination inherent in the process of immigration in the 1950s are still reflected in Israeli society today. While Somekh found some success in Israel, he was more readily accepted abroad in places such as Oxford. Even today Jewish academics who are descended from Jews that came from Muslim countries are massively under-represented in Israeli higher education. Somekh's story therefore represented a double struggle, against discrimination at home and against discrimination against Arab–Jewish ties in the region. This important book will be a resource to scholars who are interested in the author's work and the relationship between himself and major literary figures such as Mahfouz. **SJF**

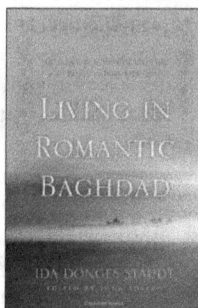

Ida Donges Staudt. *Living in Romantic Baghdad: an American Memoir of Teaching and Travel in Iraq, 1924–1947.* **Syracuse, NY: Syracuse University Press, 2012. 251pp. $29.95. ISBN: 9780815609940.**

Living in Romantic Baghdad: An American Memoir of Teaching and Travel in Iraq, 1924–47 is a timely work which claims a unique place in the literature of travel because of its credible, informative, and eyewitness-inspired style, enhanced by the author's insightful engagement with the subject matter and the insider perspective with which the events are related. The relevance of the book for today's reader, in an admittedly volatile and fractured world, resides in its ability to draw meaningful links, in serving as a reminder of how the past and the present are inextricably tied, and in perhaps lending appropriate context to George Santayana's frequently cited caveat against the suppression of memory and the bracketing of the past: "Those who cannot remember the past are condemned to repeat it." However, as is the case with similar works of art which can be claimed by various fields and genres, *Living in Romantic Baghdad...* appeals to readers of diverse epistemological backgrounds and esthetic orientations. The editor, a graduate of the American School for Boys in Baghdad in 1941, the institution run by the Staudts and where John Joseph taught for four years, emphasizes that the author intended the book to be a description of a journey, an exclusive memoir of teaching and travel, rather than a historical account. The reader, nonetheless, might not see the rationale behind the injunction, for often the line of demarcation between a memoir and a historical account—whether assessed generically or esthetically—is rarely translucent. The way the events are sequenced in Ida Donges' book, and the clear chronological structure of the book, makes the argument against history rather untenable.

The story of *Living in Romantic Baghdad...* is inspired by the innate desire to transgress the territorialized body and the confines of home and domesticity which characterized the period between the Industrial Revolution and World War II, as images of Arabia Deserta and Arabia Felix haunted generations of readers, and as the tradition of travel started moving beyond the luxury-driven Grand Tour to embrace a rugged and risk-laden definition of travel with complex motives and aspirations, but which is consistently marked by compromise, self-denial, roughness, and a relentless bent for endurance and acclimatization. However, as this carefree form of travel, carried out as an essential exploratory act of self-actualization, was steadily gaining ground, it could not be set off from the nascent ideologies of the time which used travel to articulate other types of fulfillment of a fundamentally hegemonic nature. Aware of the contentious political ramifications of the Western presence in the East, the Staudts distanced themselves from ideologues and Orientalists, focusing instead on their philanthropic mission which they adopted as the sole raison d'être of their sojourn in Iraq. Their story, as they would probably wish it narrated, had nothing heroic about it—at least in its inception. Ida Donges Staudt (1875–1952) and her husband, Calvin K. Staudt (1876–1951), an enthusiastic Pennsylvanian couple of German stock, decided in 1919 to embark on an educational journey in the Middle East by first starting a school in Beirut, Lebanon, followed by one in Baghdad, Iraq, where they moved in 1924. Though a success, the Lebanese venture was short-lived. In fact, it was in Iraq that their life and reputation became intimately associated with the American School for Boys, the first of its kind in Mesopotamia, the bastion of human civilization and the land of religious and cultural encounters. The Staudts could boast, a feeling hardly repressed in the book, that the Iraq they made home for more than two decades and to which they contributed in their capacity as educators was a truly romantic and exotic one, but it was also a country on the verge of being tainted by the encroaching global problems which were driving the world toward strife and instability in the 1930s.

To the modern reader who has been following the harrowing political developments in Iraq over the past three decades, the country that Ida Staudt depicts in *Living in Romantic Baghdad...* is undoubtedly idyllic and romantic, but it is not immune to political turmoil and dislocation. In fact, many of the events the Staudts witnessed in their 24 years' stay were premonitory signs that a dramatic transformation was already under way. The 1930s was a turbulent period, as the scramble for Iraq reached an unprecedented level with Great Britain playing a blatant double role of protector and oil scavenger. The Nazis and their agitators and sympathizers were also drawing considerable attention to themselves, thus creating a climate of fear and confusion in the young nation. In addition to the bloody coup d'état and the politically-motivated assassinations, foreign oil companies, aided by their respective countries, took active part in the dramatic change of Iraq; and though, admittedly, the young nation benefitted from the oil boom economically and socially, it sadly lost its political will and hard-earned independence—a déjà-vu scenario for the modern reader. Several of the incidents described in the book assume a prescient nature, thus making the book more relevant and appealing to the modern reader than to the author herself or to her contemporary readers. The belated compilation and publication of the author's diary can, accordingly, be justified.

The Staudts, notwithstanding, considered themselves lucky to have made it before the demise of the romantic narrative, living in an Iraq off the beaten track with modest amenities, but, as inveterate and nostalgic travelers much desire, with abundant opportunities for recklessness, exploration, and heroic aspiration. The author's fascination with Baghdad remains consistent throughout the book, succumbing to nothing but her unconditional loyalty to the "never-changing and ever changeless Baghdad" (p. xxiii), its mythical splendor and glamour. Her story is that of love at first sight, invoking constructive images of The Arabian Nights and particularly the history of Mesopotamia that Ida familiarized herself with before undertaking the journey: "Upon my arrival, I was at once fascinated with Baghdad. Those early days made an indelible impression upon me.... I always felt I was living, not in the present Baghdad but in the Baghdad of the golden age of the caliphs" (p. xxiii). The legendary city is sentimentally associated with the glorious Abbasid dynasty under Harun Al-Rashid, a period, the author makes sure she does not overlook in a book otherwise devoted to modern Iraq, which made significant contributions to human civilization at a time when, oddly enough, ideas, and cultures crossed the globe much faster than human beings. In many parts of the book, the author finds in the past a leitmotif and a panacea for the woos of the present times, insinuating that this very city which has given much to human civilization across the centuries does not deserve the unabated assaults and pains, the "avalanche" of unfortunate circumstances inflicted upon it by human greed and callousness. For the record, Ida traces similar incidents in the past, noting with chagrin the irreparable destruction that Baghdad incurred under Hulagu in 1258 AD. One wonders what Ida would have said about the senseless and large-scale destruction Iraq has witnessed of late. John Joseph, being a graduate of Ida's school and subsequently a teacher there, laments these incidents and particularly the deliberate looting and ransacking of the Museum of Antiquities in Baghdad following the disastrous American invasion of Iraq in 2003.

The Staudts unreservedly embraced the cultural other, and at a time when there was still space for "going native," they reaped the benefits of cultural immersion and interaction. Like the "fearless" Gertrude Bell, a woman of vitality and resilience and one of the last renowned travelers in a fast changing world whom the author met in Baghdad shortly before her death, Ida never shunned people of any creed or social status. Her school, a groundbreaking enterprise of its kind in the region, applied the equity principle and welcomed students from all creeds, ethnicities, and social backgrounds—as long as they could meet the tuition and boarding fees. Well, to be fair to the Staudts, theirs was a self-funded venture, and the school budget was so limited that they had to convert their living rooms into classrooms, the reason why Ida called the project "heroic" and "breathtaking in its audacity" (p. 14). In many respects, the school—a melting pot—was the Staudts' gateway to the Iraqi society using education as a vehicle for cross-cultural interaction. As the size and popularity of the school grew exponentially, the reputation of the Staudts became firmly established among the Iraqis, helping the couple integrate the fabric of society: "We called on kings and queens, on Bedouin sheikhs; attended charming weddings;

breakfasted or drank tea in lovely gardens...." (p. 13). Echoes of their educational project reverberated as far as the royal palace, drawing the attention of King Faisal himself, whom they personally met and whose commendations they were pleased to receive. It is interesting to note that, at a time when foreigners were infiltrating the country for ideological and imperialistic reasons, the Staudts' mission appeared to the locals bona fide, and wherever the Staudts went, they were treated with respect and compassion.

Despite the complexity of the subject matter and the dense historical archives that the author delved into in an attempt to grapple with the story of modern Iraq, *Living in Romantic Baghdad...* is distinguished by its smooth and effective narrative style. To document the genuine romantic aspects of life in Baghdad at the beginning of the twentieth century, the book adopts an essentially fluid, unpretentious, and unadorned style. As opposed to several of the works that Edward Said cites in Orientalism, which are characterized by a clear tendency to distort, "Orientalize," and exoticize, *Living in Romantic Baghdad...* depicts ordinary people with whom the reader can identify in their very human essence and in their quotidian struggles. In fact, Ida Staudt warns against the pitfalls of mythology and Orientalism which permeated Western history textbooks and popular fiction during the author's time. She points out that the stereotypical representations of the other constitute the backbone of a schoolboy's formative years in the West, but she clearly distances herself from them. Without making sound theoretical claims, Ida Staudt strips culture of its abstract matrices and conditioning referentialities. Ida cannot resist being identified with the other and being immersed in his/her cultural sphere, which gains her the trust and respect of her hosts. She would not mind living under a tent, or using a tent in lieu of a classroom out of necessity, eating like the Bedouins, looking favorably on arranged marriages, and welcoming different cultural perceptions. Throughout the book, she shows extreme caution when making observations about religion, culture, and identity. Her perception is not the diametrical or bifurcating one associated with the Orientalist tradition, but rather, a hybridizing one. Even when she does not understand or appreciate a culturally-coded artifact, she does not denigrate it. Arabic music, for instance, does not appeal to her, most likely because she does not understand it, but she derives vicarious pleasure from seeing others enjoy it (p. 236). Quoting her husband who considers himself an "ambassador" of goodwill, Ida writes: "Nations ... must find a means of living together on a friendly basis, for civilization is the result of the common work of all nations" (p. 234). The sense of reciprocity is what eventually makes the self feel incomplete without the other's presence, a condition valorized in Living in Romantic Baghdad... "The East," Ida Staudt writes, "needs the West, and the West needs the East. Each has much to learn from the other. And in that mutual need and mutual richness there will spring a life for mankind richer and better than anything we have known" (p. 234). Ida could already see the effect of the East on her: "I knew the East had done something to me" (p. 90), and this self-confession comes to validate her friend's assertion made earlier in the narrative: "You won't change the East, but the East will change you" (p. 12). It is this awareness of a metamorphosed self which consolidates the author's presence and gains her the trust and compassion of the cultural other; thus helping unleash that "gigantic reservoir of good will" that the editor refers to in the book's Preface (p. xx). In fact, the uniqueness of Ida Staudt's travel experience can be attributed to this unmitigated feeling of complete surrender to the natural state of being, to one's true nature unhindered by hubris or repression, which proves crucial in making of the memoir such a commanding, first-rate travelogue. **JEN**

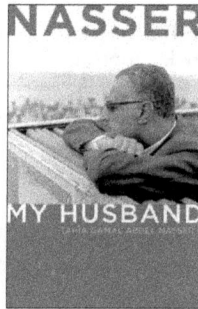

Nasser, My Husband. **Tahia Gamal Abdel Nasser. Translated by Shereen Mosaad. Cairo, EG:** American University of Cairo Press, 2013. 122 pp. $24.95. ISBN: 978-9774166112.

On May 28th, Israeli forces clashed with the Syrian army. President Gamal Abdel Nasser of Egypt turned to his wife "the Israelis will attack Egypt," she recalled several years later. "He indicated the exact day—the following Monday. His prediction came true. Israel attacked on June 5, 1967, in the morning" (p. 96). This is one of several small revelations in Tahia Abdel Nasser's account of her husband's life that has just been published in English. It is an odd revelation, made all the more astounding by the unanswered question: If Nasser knew the Israelis would attack, why was his air force sitting on the ground when the strike came?

Nasser: My Husband was originally compiled by Tahia in 1973, but, as she relates, the idea had come to her in 1959. Starting when Nasser was off in Syria dealing with the United Arab Republic union of Syria and Egypt, she began writing. "I spent nearly three years constantly writing." But then she threw away everything. She attempted again in 1972, but it was not until 1973 that she was able to begin this volume. She claims it was the Egyptian people who encouraged her. "When I go out, I see the looks of the people around me, some wave their hands in greeting, others look at me sadness" (p. 3). But the work that she put into the memoir never saw the light of day in her life. As Hoda Gamal Abdel Nasser explains in a forward, the political climate under Nasser's successor Anwar Sadat, prevented the book from being published. "An organized campaign of character assassination began after 1973" (p. x). According to her, the publication was delayed because the "political mood was hostile to Nasser in Egypt" under Sadat and Mubarak. This is perhaps ironic, since they were continuing the legacy of his revolution. It was not until the upheaval of 2011 that the story came out in Arabic and was then translated to English. The book contains over 40 beautiful pictures, some in color, depicting Nasser's life.

Unfortunately, Tahia's life story is weak on almost every detail that a historian would like to know. It gives us little information about her family history; her father's origin was in Iran. She married Nasser in 1944, but before that, lived a very sheltered life. According to her, her family and the Nassers were friendly before the marriage. Her father died at a young age and her brother, Abdel Hamid Kazem, was her guardian. "He was strict at home and extremely conservative, but outside he had his own private life" (p. 6). Even after they were engaged, she could not see Nasser without a chaperone. Nasser was more liberal it seems, taking her to the theater on a date.

Once they were married, Tahia remained sequestered in the house and although Nasser was not outwardly a conservative or deeply religious man, she lived the life of a conservative Muslim woman. She wore no veil in photographs, an element of the modernizing influence of Nasser, but she rarely met her husband's male friends: "Gamal did not favor mixed social interaction with friends." When a man would visit Nasser, usually one of his military buddies, the wife would be sent to the salon to be entertained by Tahia, while the men sat alone in another room. Tahia seems to have rarely left the house. Nasser had an orderly (*murasil*) as a staff officer, who worked as a sort of butler at the house and seems to have done the shopping. When he came to power, his wife had a driver. When her husband was not at war, and before he became president, "we would go out together once a week, mostly to the cinema" (p. 11).

The conspiracies that Nasser was involved in before the 1952 coup made the house a center of secret meetings. By 1946, guns were being secreted in the cupboards. Banned books appeared as well. Tahia describes various weapons, "the large machine guns were too big to be put in the cupboard, so I kept them in a corner in the dining room" (p. 34). Anti-regime pamphlets also appeared which she secreted away as she could. One day, Nasser appeared with a shoulder holster. His wife thought to herself "he can only be carrying a gun for two reasons: either he believes someone intends to shoot him, or he intends to shoot someone" (p. 44).

Given Nasser's international reputation after the coup, one would think that there might be fascinating insight into the various leaders with whom they spent time. However, her descriptions are bare bones at best. She mentions going to Yugoslavia in 1958, during which time the Iraqi regime was overthrown, and Nasser was whisked away on a secret flight to Moscow. Tahia stayed behind. Later she was seated with Indian leader Nehru, whom she recalls as a lively conversationalist. What they spoke about is not mentioned.

She saw her husband off to numerous wars, beginning in 1948. She describes receiving short letters from him while he was fighting the birth of Israel and also recalls learning of his being under siege at the battle of Faluja. Later, when the British bombed Suez, she describes the events in the simplest of detail. The reality was she just did not talk politics with her husband or others. "I would never broach a political subject with him unless he initiated the conversation, which he rarely did" (p. 102). Nasser does not appear to have been particularly religious, although his wife gave him a *Qur'an* to carry from time to time. She recalls that he "would ask me to pray for victory in my daily prayers and would tell me to 'curse the Israelis'" (p. 102). But for a woman living through momentous events, she does not express much of an opinion on the Israelis, the British, or anyone else.

Tahia can't be blamed for writing an honest memoir, primarily concerned with her children and her life around the house. She was not interested in the public life; yet she remained devoted to her husband and his memory after his death. Most of her children studied, attended university, and became professionals. She was not entirely an uneducated woman—she learned French and English. But if she had strong views on anything in Egypt, it is unfortunately not to be found in this volume. If this was the worldview of the wife of one of the most powerful men in the Middle East for 18 years, what does this say about the views of ordinary Egyptian women, in the narrow world some of them live in due to conservative traditions? She recalls once going through Alexandria and seeing the city's poor. "These are the people I work for" Nasser told her; "they look better than before," she replied. But he was not satisfied: "I want each and every one of those children to have the same education, health benefit and general appearance as Khaled, my son" (p. 112). Those children are now in their 50s. Unfortunately Nasser's dream never came true, as his country remains mired in turmoil, and the level of education does not seem to have improved greatly. **SJF**

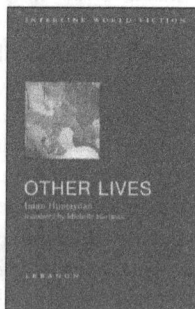

Iman Humaydan. *Translated by* Michelle Hartman. *Other Lives*. Northampton, MA: Interlink Books, 2014. 153 pp. Pbk: $15.00. ISBN: 978-1566569620.

This is Iman Humaydan's third novel after *B as in Beirut* and *Wild Mulberries*, all three novels having been translated from Arabic into English and published by Interlink Books. This is the story of Myriam whose life has become many lives—other lives—as a result of the civil war in Lebanon. From her Lebanese mountain village to Beirut and then to Adelaide in Australia, where she lived with her Druze parents for four years. Then her changing circumstances dictate she move to Mombasa in Kenya where she had a home with her Australian husband Chris for 11 years, and made frequent visits from there to Cape Town in South Africa. The novel, in the beautiful and sensitive translation of Michelle Hartman, captures Myriam's feelings and thoughts, and gives the reader the story of Myriam's return to Beirut where, while waiting to reclaim an ancestral home as it is sole inheritor, she has to confront the ghosts of her past experiences.

The mode of narration of the novel is engaging, as Myriam relates the story of her life in the first person, remembering past events and abiding feelings. The events are not necessarily presented in chronological order, and the feelings are almost invariably unhappy ones; but they all succeed in portraying Myriam's sense of transience, continuous physical dislocation, spiritual restlessness, and unmitigated alienation. This is made vivid by the translator's decision to render much of the narration in the present tense.

From all this we learn that, before ever leaving Lebanon, Myriam was initiated into the sensual pleasures of the body in a lesbian relationship with Olga, who, despite the distances separating them, continued to correspond with her, speak on the phone with her, send her Arabic novels to read, and cassettes of Arabic songs to enjoy. We also learn that Myriam had a happy love relationship with Georges in Beirut, and that he was to follow her to Adelaide but, in the chaos of the civil war, he disappeared and was perhaps kidnapped and killed on the day planned for his departure; hence she subsequently married Chris in Australia. Chris was her father's physician and later a malaria researcher in Mombasa where they both went to live. She did not love him but gave him her body; yet she could not become pregnant because of an abortion she had undergone in Beirut to remove the fetus fathered by Georges.

Now in Beirut again at the age of 40, Myriam began to realize that the Lebanon of her childhood and youth was no longer there. However, the memories of those earlier times continued to haunt her. She went to see the doctor who had performed her abortion, but discovered that he had been killed in the civil war. She found that her friend Olga had cancer, but they, nevertheless, enjoyed sharing intimate moments. She found that her lover Nour, now married, had come back from the United States, and was still endlessly and unsuccessfully looking for his family roots, thinking of them even in intimate moments with her. Memories of her past continued to weigh on her, including the memory of her dead little brother Baha' killed by a bomb, and of her father hit by shrapnel which lodged in his brain and rendered him mentally incapacitated, and of her mother, who, after these events lost her ability and willingness to speak again.

Myriam was a conflicted woman as a result of the civil war and of her continual dislocation, seeking safety where none existed for her. The whole novel is about her restless soul that leads her to refusing to be tied down by men, by places, or by others' expectations. Iman Humaydan's portrayal of her is an excruciatingly painful picture of the evil consequences of the Lebanese civil war that some of its victims endured. And Michelle Hartman's translation is a faithful and perceptive rendering of it for English-speaking readers. **IJB**

Tawfiq al-Suwaydi. Translated by Nancy Roberts. *Tawfiq al-Suwaydi, My Memoirs: Half a Century of the History of Iraq and the Arab Cause.* Boulder, CO: Lynne Rienner, 2013. 570 pp. $39.90. ISBN: 978-1588269034.

Autobiographies are usually suspect because the author has the freedom to tell his story his own way, and exclusively from his own perspective. Originally published in Arabic in Beirut in 1969, this good English translation of the autobiography of Tawfiq al-Suwaydi is welcome, since it provides the Western reader with a firsthand description of part of Iraqi and Arab politics in the first six decades of the twentieth century. The most interesting and informative part of the book is that which deals with Arab–Ottoman relations before WWI and the emergence of pro-Arab nationalism during that period. On the other hand, its shortcomings are pointed out indirectly by professor Antony Sullivan who wrote an introduction to the book. Sullivan and Luay Suwaydi, the son of the author, emphasize that the Iraqi monarchical period between 1920 and 1958 was politically liberal. One may concur with this description in comparison with Iraqi politics since 1958. But at the time, the dominant feature that most Iraqis recognized was direct or indirect British colonialism or dominance. Additionally, the period was far from being democratically stable. Al-Suwaydi himself served as Iraqi prime minister on three occasions, the longest of which did not span more than seven months in 1950. While it is true that Iraq was associated with Arab nationalism in regional politics, its status in that regard was discredited after the nationalist movement of Rashid 'Ali al-Gaylani and four army officers in 1941 during WWII, and received a harsher blow after the ineptness of the Iraqi army in Palestine in 1948. This was followed by the rise of Egypt under Gamal

'Abd al-Nasser as a new type of popular leader of Arab nationalism in the mid-1950s fifties. The inability to understand the impact and magnitude of those two historical turning points, one on the Iraqi national level, and the other on the regional and international levels takes a lot from the book.

Another failure is the omission of about 10 pages of the original Arabic edition of the book due to repetition. These pages appear at the beginning of the original Arabic and speak of, among other things, Ottoman and Arab history, before the collapse of the Ottoman Empire. According to an endnote by Antony T. Sullivan, "[t]he omitted information is presented in a more detailed and comprehensive fashion in [the] English translation ..." (endnote 1, p. 43). Unfortunately for the reader, this did not prove to be the case. The English translation omits two important points made by the author in the Arabic original: His reflection that Iraq was oriented at the time toward not one, but two centers: Ottoman Istanbul and British India. The second is that the Arabs of Iraq did not feel their ethnic identity was threatened after the 1908 coup in Istanbul, but rather in 1909, when Turkish nationalism became more visible. This is important because it could mean that the 1909 March incident, whereby the pro-Sultan Abdul Hamid party staged a failed counter-coup in the Ottoman capital was the actual turning point inside the Arab provinces regarding Arab–Turkish relations after the triumph of the "Young Turks."

Nevertheless, the book is a good read and provides a panoramic picture of Iraqi politics in the period of transition from colonial era to the era of army colonels. **MH**

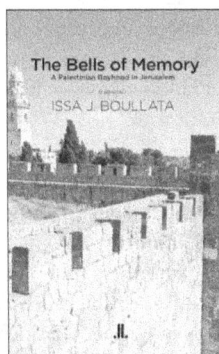

Issa J. Boullata. *The Bells of Memory: A Palestinian Boyhood in Jerusalem.* Westmount, Quebec, Canada: Linda Leith Publishing, 2014. 87 pp. Pbk.: $12.95. ISBN: 978-1927535394.

A pleasant read by a noted Arabic literature scholar, most recently Emeritus Professor of Arabic Literature and Qur'anic Studies at McGill University's Institute of Islamic Studies. What is presented is a picture of a young Orthodox Christian boy, born in Jerusalem in 1929 with strong family ties and support for education.

He presents himself in the cultural and ethnic context of a Palestinian without any further reference to the status of his patrimony, but believes it to be rooted in the Canaanite tribe of Jebusites who inhabited Uru-Salem before the invasion of the Hebrews. Then the author recites his family's long historical connection to the Arab settlement in Jerusalem.

Most important to his rearing is his path in education beginning in the autumn of 1934 at the Thawri Elementary School for Boys and Girls. Here Boullata learned the basic elements of the Arabic language, grammar, and arithmetic. Sprinkled throughout this autobiography are references rich in Arabic literature—many published by Palestinian authors—in addition to standard western and Arab classics. For example, as a part of the author's educational development, the first book he read completely was Al-Dajaja al-Saghira al-Hamra' (The Little Red Hen). The author's education continued in 1938 at College des Freres, where he learned French, and from where he graduated in 1947. Boullata was immediately admitted to the Law School run by the Law Council of Palestine in Jerusalem. His studies there were cut short the following year because the violence in Jerusalem prevented either faculty or students from going to school. Boullata's adolescent years were filled with his initiative in reading—essentially, libraries of books. His father maintained a rather extensive collection of Arabic literature as well as a host of European authors. All of this was further supplemented by gaining access to the library at the YMCA in Jerusalem, even though Catholics were strongly discouraged from reading in a Protestant institution.

Boullata's home life was largely in the Christian Quarter of Jerusalem, but extended to the Muslim Quarter, and it was here that he interacted with the people who would influence his observations and beliefs. This social arena was, therefore, dominated by Arab Muslims and Christians—and notably few Jews, if any. Indeed, he admits that the lack of similar familiarity with the Jewish Quarter was a hole in his social awareness upbringing.

The inter-communal violence that was to threaten the calm of the British created Palestine whose presence was in the form of a mandate to rule, is kept to a minimum in the narrative until the end of the book. While the Palestinian armed leadership, both native and supportive, is mentioned by Boullata, it is only to provide an historical context for his upbringing and orientation. The last chapter of this very brief biography is devoted to al-Nakba, for self-identified Palestinians, the tragedy of losing their homes, livelihood, family and friends as a result of armed conflict with the Zionist–Jewish community and the establishment of the State of Israel is all important. He sets forth here a rather candid and honest historical record, unfortunately without documentary support for what is probably the case but, nevertheless, subject to debate (e.g., the Arab League meeting in Amman in April 1948).

This is but a biography of one Palestinian Arab, but an important member of that community's intelligentsia and literati. One can acquire an important glimpse into the character and quality of life in Palestine in the 1920s, up to the late 1940s; hence an important contribution. **SRS**

Salim Tamari and Issam Nassar, Eds. Translated by Nada Elzeer. *The Storyteller of Jerusalem: The Life and Times of Wasif Jawhariyeh, 1904–1948.* **Northampton, MA: Olive Branch Press, 2014. 304 pp. Pbk: $25.00. ISBN: 978-1566569255.**

Wasif Jawhariyyeh (1897–1972), a noted personality of Arab Jerusalem who was a musician, song-composer, and singer. He is remembered by his handwritten memoirs in three volumes and by a fine collection of Palestinian artifacts and photographs that he left behind. His memoirs are now archived at the Institute of Jerusalem Studies in Ramallah, Palestine. Edited by Tamari and Nassar, the memoirs were published in Arabic in two volumes by the Institute of Palestine Studies in Beirut in 2003 and 2005. This English version, translated by Nada Elzeer is an edited selection of them published in one volume.

The memoirs contain entries about events during Jawhariyyeh's boyhood under the rule of the Ottomans, followed by others on events during his youth and manhood under the rule of the British Mandate. Observant and frank, he writes about life in Jerusalem and its culture as well as about the change he observed over the years in a period of turbulent times, including the Great War of 1914–18, the Balfour Declaration of 1917 and its disastrous effects on Palestinian society, the Arab uprising of 1929 and rebellion of the 1930s, and the *Nakba* of 1948. He also writes about his personal life, his schooling, and the individuals he met and those with whom he dealt during his career as a civil servant.

Since childhood, Wasif Jawhariyyeh loved music and, as a boy, he devised a musical instrument with wires strung across a can; but he eventually acquired a proper *oud* and learned to play it well, and also to sing. He soon became the indispensable musician of celebratory parties in town, many whom he describes in his memoirs, mentioning the names of Christians, Muslims, and Jews present. He himself was a Christian Arab from the Greek Orthodox community, but his friends and acquaintances were from all religions and walks of life. They included notables from the Husseini and Nashashibi families in Jerusalem, and high officials of the British Mandate, such as Ronald Storrs, Keith-Roach, and Humphrey Bowman. When famous singers, such as Badi'a Masabni, Umm Kulthum, and Muhammad 'Abd al-Wahhab visited Jerusalem, he met them in person, along with "the prince of the violin," Sami al-Shawwa. He came to know great Palestinian literary figures, such as Muhammad Is'af al-Nashashibi, Ahmad Sameh al-Khalidi, and Khalil al-Sakakini. All of these events are recorded in his memoirs.

In his lifetime, Jawhariyyeh saw Jerusalem grow beyond the Ottoman city walls; his memoirs chronicle the expansion of the city into its new suburbs, one of which which he moved to when he married in 1924, after having grown up within the city walls in the Sa'diyya neighborhood. Jawhariyyeh witnessed the first airplane to land in Jerusalem, heard the earliest phonograph and radio, saw the establishment of the Palestine Broadcasting Service and the replacement of Egyptian currency by Palestinian currency. In short, although not a professional historian, he wrote memoirs that have been very helpful to any historian.

Jawhariyyeh's writing is witty and sometimes humorous, its editing and translation are good, but the transliteration of names from Arabic into English leaves room for improvement. Furthermore, there are many inconsistencies in them—for example: Dizdar on p. 42 is Duzdar on p. 104; and Iriqat becomes Ereqat on the same page (p. 83), etc. It is not much better with non-Arabic names—for example: Ratzbon on p. 154 becomes Ratisbonne on p. 170. An intimate knowledge of Jerusalem family names is often lacking—for example: Mashhour on p. 136 is meant to be the well-known Mushahwar.

At any rate, as sociologist Professor Salim Tamari says, the memoirs offer readers of history "one of the most valuable records of Palestinian urban life that exists anywhere." **IJB**

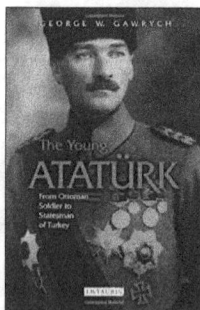

George W. Gawrych. *The Young Atatürk: From Ottoman Soldier to Statesman of Turkey.* London, UK: I. B. Tauris, 2013. 267 pp. $35.00. ISBN: 978-1780763224.

This book focuses primarily on Mustafa Kemal's military career, although it also contains considerable information about his political and diplomatic activities during Turkey's War of Liberation. The main narrative begins with his studies in military high school and ends with the founding of the Turkish Republic in 1923, but Gawrych also includes extremely succinct accounts of Kemal's early life and the reforms he carried out during his 15 years as President of Turkey. The book contains almost no information about Kemal's private life. For example, the important women in his life—his mother, Zübeyde, his mistress, Fikriye, and his wife, Latife—each merit only a single sentence.

Many other biographers, however, have dealt with those matters. The value of this book lies in the fact that it is the first serious, systematic study of the military Atatürk, and the first based on research in Turkey's military archives. Gawrych has pored over Atatürk's own writings, including his personal notebooks and correspondence, and has even examined the books in his personal library, paying close attention to his underlining and marginal notes. Additionally, he personally toured the major battlefields of the War of Independence while writing this book.

Gawrych provides the most detailed, almost minute-by-minute accounts available in English of the battles in which Kemal took part, and reflects critically on the choices he made as a commander and his relationship with the men who served under him. The book includes 13 battle maps drawn by Gawrych's wife, Joan.

This book has benefitted greatly from Gawrych's knowledge of Ottoman Turkish. When translating quotations from Turkish, he often includes the Turkish original of key words, which readers who know Turkish will appreciate. Sometimes this is maddeningly repetitive, however; I think there must be at least 20 instances in which he notes that the Turkish word for "father" is *baba*. The Turkish words are also sometimes misspelled, as in *siysaet* for *siyaset* (p. 63) and *Kauni* for *Kanuni* (p 125). These are no doubt typographical errors, of which there are quite a few in the English text as well, including some howlers, such as the following from p. 118: "Mustafa Kemal trusted [Karabekir] and left him to his own talents and vices." Too often, Gawrych fails to translate Turkish words. Readers who don't know Turkish are sure to be bewildered by the constant uses of *Dağ* and *Tepe* with proper names in the accounts of battles without explaining that they mean "mountain" and "hill." On p. 88, he refers to the "*mutasarrıf* of Malatya," without defining the term. On p. 103, he states that after the *şeyhülislam* issued a "*fatwa*" branding the Nationalists as infidels, 250 other religious officials issued a "counter-*fetva*;" it is confusing to use both the Arabic and Turkish versions of the word in the same sentence.

Gawrych organizes his analysis of Kemal's character around three major concepts that he argues were central to his thought: *his* (feeling, emotion), *dimağ* (intellect), and *vicdan* (conscience or consciousness), the latter referring mainly to "professionalism, patriotism, honor, duty, courage, and sacrifice" (p. 223) rather than to morality in private life. Throughout this book, Gawrych lays great stress on Kemal's intellectualism. He was an avid, lifelong reader, even managing to set aside time for reading during some of the busiest and most stressful times in his life. He read not only military texts, but novels, poetry, history, and philosophy, and he found reading literary works to be a valuable antidote to the dehumanizing effects of the carnage he witnessed on the battlefield. Kemal was above all a student of human nature, and he understood very well the importance of appealing to people's emotions as well as their intellect. He was convinced that the best way to lead others is by personal example.

Although Gawrych clearly admires Atatürk, he does not hesitate to point out occasions when the great man stooped to petty, ruthless, or arrogant behavior. This book is no hagiography but offers a balanced account of the achievements of one of the twentieth century's most brilliant soldier-statesmen.

The book concludes with a useful chronology of the major events in Kemal's life and short biographical sketches of 12 of his closest associates, all of whom figure prominently in the book. **MM**

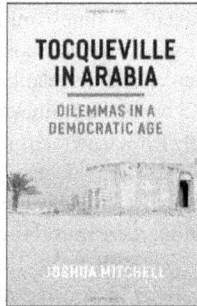

Joshua Mitchell. *Tocqueville in Arabia: Dilemmas in a Democratic Age*. Chicago. IL: University of Chicago Press, 2013. 208 pp. $20.00. ISBN: 978-0226087313.

Joshua Mitchell's *Tocqueville in Arabia* is a memoir on cross-cultural teaching of political thought; a guide for understanding between the West and the Middle East; a Tocqueville-driven critique of current U.S. democracy; and a test of Tocqueville's spiritual sociology on the Middle East's post-Arab Spring prospect for transitioning from aristocracy to democracy. Of particular interest to readers here, is a teacher's commentary on the outlook on democracy by Mitchell's elite university students in Qatar, Iraq, and the United States. More generally, he wants to clarify the contemporary Middle East for the "earnest reader" whom the news media, polemicists, and self-absorbed academicians who prefer arcane language have ill-served. (See his biography at this review's end.)

The subtitle, *Dilemmas in a Democratic Age*, accurately points to Mitchell's questions of the Middle East's prospects for finding a way to merge old and new. In socio-political terms, he compares the declining aristocratic sway in the region to what Tocqueville saw in the United States of 1831. In geopolitical terms, he asks whether the Middle East can move beyond the present constructively. Can it avoid the pitfalls of either trying to recreate a past that never existed (Rousseau), or leaping into a revolution to bring justice and overcome current confusion (Marx, Nietzsche, and Heidegger)? The predictable, inevitable consequence of either would be an injustice and add to further confusion.

In the Middle East, the patronage state assures bounty via family connections, thereby entrenching the extended family. This conflicts with modern individualism of democratic liberty which many Qatari youth find appealing. This disruptive quality became apparent when patronage state failures helped precipitate the Arab Uprising.

Some of Mitchell's Qatari students have a fleeting dream of salvation by the state as a replacement for protection by family and, at the same time, for avoiding the hazards of democracy. Distrust of democracy is in part a bequest of the Middle East's colonial experience; intellectual anti-modernism reinforces their fear of becoming what Tocqueville called a "de-linked" man. Loss of their aristocratic society—each family knowing its place in the hierarchy—would mean the rise of ranking by talent instead of by family, loss of willingness to tolerate humiliation to save the family name, a speeding up and segmenting of time, competition and deadlines and a prospect of public exposure of failure, and the need to find ad hoc ways to collaborate and coordinate across social groups. The authority of persons of recognized name and social standing would have to give way to the authority of public opinion and the right of the individual to dissent. This would be alien and threaten identity.

Mitchell illustrates the present resistance to democracy by pointing out the paucity of civil society in the Middle East: "…it is impossible to form a PTA because certain families will not condescend to talk to or even be seen with other families of lesser stature in the same room" (p. 47).

The culture of family honor and loyalty and obligation opposes Tocqueville's criterion of democratic achievement: a willingness to risk failure. This aversion has two outcomes. First, ineffective enterprises and government agencies do not disappear. Instead, new parallel entities rise; patrons above and dependents below support both the old and the new. Second, the "Arab Street" does not actually exist as a "public space" because each person responds to the family authority, not the larger society. Opinions about others arise from within the family, are primarily about relations with other families, serve to rationalize a family's own virtue in its jockeying for social position, and, thus, tend to explain untoward events as outcomes of conspiracies that other families direct against one's own.

The apprehensions about democracy that Mitchell heard from his students in Iraq and Qatar echo those old nineteenth century fears. Aristocratic man was firmly linked by social codes to "family, to land, to kingdom or empire, and ultimately to the cosmos itself" (p. 34). Social equality in the new world dissolved these links, liberating human beings from past grudges, but also ending the continuity of generations and introducing psychological uneasiness. Tocqueville described the aristocratic dread of uprooting the ancestral order that pervades young and old alike in the Middle East.

If delinked democratic man or the emerging Middle Eastern democrat can "relink" by means consistent with democracy—such as civic associations, an independent but demanding religion, economic discipline, and strong families—he may come to and continue to be able to rule himself. If not, his isolation and anxiety at being alone will cause him to depend on the state to resolve his problems, and define his social roles; to do this will close off his social mobility and exhaust economic resources in attempting to placate voters and interest groups.

Because religion figures large in Tocqueville as a balancing institution in democratic society, Mitchell examines its role in the Middle East. However, he shies sometimes when assessing Islam in relation to democracy. For example, he introduces, but then drops the problem of evil in monotheism and mentions, but does not develop the concept of equality in Islam.

More constructively, Mitchell notes that the *Qur'an* and liturgy are God speaking, a mystique rather like the Incarnation in Christianity. As a "way of life," Islam resists ecumenism or packaging, either as a set of ethical principles compatible with other religion's principles, or as one of several identities one might wear. Islam IS one's identity. Life is a comprehensive whole, not subject to personal view or adaptation or dismissal. This is not fundamentalism in the sense of Biblical literalism. One might say that the *Qur'an* is not lyrics on a page, like a Biblical text that one can interpret; instead it is melody that fills a room and encompasses the believer.

Mitchell observes that "democracy will have to emerge within the context of Islam or not at all." While Islam declares that all individuals are equal and that all Islamic law is "true," these contentions may not stand against the diversity and cultures and expanding global knowledge which are perplexing Mitchell's Middle Eastern students. They wish to avoid the experiments with socialism that produced Iraq's disaster: destruction of family hierarchies and patronage leading to tyranny under a new ruling class less subject to the tribal ethics of accountability and consent. They find disturbing their own inclination to see only two alternative political options: a single "decisive" ruler or chaos; and they tend to equate democracy with chaos. Their perception that separation of individuals from family moorings advances apace today in their own societies disturbs them.

Mitchell's method has limits. Using Qatar and Iraq to stand for all the Middle East shortchanges the likes of Iran, Syria, Egypt, and beyond, and slights older generations anywhere in the Middle East. That his Georgetown students seek "social justice" as equality, and equality as all that justice requires today will not stand as a generalization for campuses whose proportion of Roman Catholics is significantly less than Georgetown's.

This review has concentrated on Mitchell's observations about the Middle East. It leaves aside two thirds of the book: his many trenchant critiques of U.S. politics, both domestic and foreign. Mitchell laments the West's willed ignorance of the economics of debt and growth, the federal government's expanding role in reducing risk and yielding to citizens' impatience, the current equating of justice with equality of outcome, a spiritual attachment to environmental preservation, a growing disinclination to form families, and amnesia regarding religious ideas such as suffering, sin, and redemption.

Mitchell's American students, who have known nothing but democracy, assume that the democratic social order is the inevitable outcome of history. Their assumed duties of citizenship do not include preserving democracy's virtues and fending off its vices. America's challenges, Mitchell thinks, stem from vices such as excessive love of equality, which causes American students and their parents to demand a world in which nobody fails, and excessive impatience with authority and limits, which causes them to adopt an easygoing "spirituality" in place of a demanding religion.

Mitchell closes opining: "the ebullient certainty that brought American troops to the [Middle East] region must never be allowed to guide foreign policy again" and "Tocqueville's claim that the age of democracy is upon us… is not a claim that the political apparatus of democracy is inevitable everywhere (p. 184). The best U.S. policy is to support higher education dedicated to the search for truth.

Joshua Mitchell, Professor of political theory in the Department of Government at Georgetown University, helped establish Georgetown's School of Foreign Service in Qatar, and taught there from 2005 to 2008. From 2008 to 2010, he was acting chancellor of the American University of Iraq, Sulaimani. Cairo-born Mitchell spent part of his childhood in the Middle East and Ann Arbor. He has also authored *The Fragility of Freedom: Tocqueville on Religion, Democracy, and the American Future*. **KLW**

CHRISTIANITY & MISSIONARIES

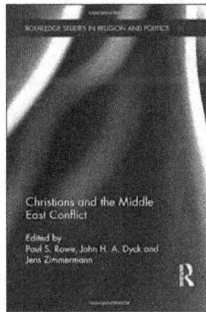

Paul S. Rowe, John H. A. Dyck and Jens Zimmermann, Eds. *Christians and the Middle East Conflict.* New York, NY: Routledge Taylor & Francis Group, 2014. 187 pp. $140.00. ISBN: 978-0415743983.

Christians and the Middle East Conflict brings the thoughts of 10 different authors—all who see the ME conflict through a Christian orientalist perspective. The book is divided into three sections: (1) Theological Perspectives; (2) Historical Perspectives; and (3) Contemporary Perspectives. The first part has three chapters, the second part has three chapters and the third part has four chapters. Paul S. Rowe, one of the three editors of the book is also author of one of the chapters in the book. Rowe says that the purpose of the book is to distinguish the role of Christians in Israel, and to go beyond the theological perspectives of Eschatology and traditional Zionist theologies.

In the first chapter, Salim J. Munayer attempts to provide an alternative theology that could promote reconciliation among the Palestinian Christians and the Messianic Jews of Israel/Palestine. Munayer is the Director of Musalaha Ministry of Reconciliation based out of Jerusalem, Israel. Munayer gives insight on four distinct theologies among Palestinian Christians and Messianic Jews and describes how each of these theologies discriminates against either, or both of the two ethnic groups.

Munayer calls for the reconciliation of Palestinian Arabs and Jews as they continue to live in Israel/Palestine. Munayer says, "I will attempt to articulate a theology of reconciliation for Israel–Palestine in the shadow of the cross that will touch on several key theological issues of some significance in the conflict." (p. 19). Munayer's hope is that through an accepted Theology of Reconciliation not only will the believers of Jesus find reconciliation through the cross, but both ethnic groups would come to accept these terms of reconciliation for an ethnically tolerant Israel.

In the second chapter, "The New Testament and the Land" by Gary M. Burge, the emphasis involves the defense of Israeli claim to the land of Israel/Palestine. In the first chapter, Munayer calls the Israeli claim to the land idolatrous (p. 23). However, Burge argues that the "land is not simply about possessing real estate; land is about security, identity, cultural cohesion and purpose." (p. 27). Although it may seem contradicting, the fact that there are two alternative views of the land of Israel–Palestine, it shows the unbiased nature of the book itself.

The third chapter is an interesting combination of Edward Said's Orientalism and Christian thought. The chapter, "Orientalism in Christian Theology" is written by Magi Abdul-Masih. Abdul-Masih offers Said's analysis and methodology as a way of understanding the scriptures and bettering Christian hermeneutics. He states, "…not only is there Orientalism in various mainline Western theologies and, more specifically, in the representation of Jesus, but also that Orientalism present in theology plays a role in the political arena, especially in the Palestinian–Israeli conflict" (p. 45). He also claims that "for biblical and theological research, the experts are the Orientalists" (p. 48).

The second part, Historical Perspectives, begins with Maher Y. Abu-Munshar's "Christian Reactions to the Muslim Conquest of Jerusalem," where he gives a balanced historiographical description of Christian reactions to the Muslim conquest of the Holy City. He gives two perspectives—those of who have understood the conquest in a negative light due to some contemporary sources, and that of those who have understood the conquest in a positive light as seen in a more abundant view of contemporary sources given by both clerics and common people. This brief synopsis to the conquest ends with a reaffirmation of a positive light to the Muslim conquest of Jerusalem.

The fifth chapter, "Albert Hourani, Arab Christian Minorities and the Spiritual Dimension of Britain's problem in Palestine, 1938–47" by Todd Thomson gives a brief, but well explained synopsis of Albert Hourani, his life and his work. He ends with a brief note, "The concerns of Christians like Hourani remind scholars that the historical actors caught up in the Arab–Israeli conflict have assessed its cost not just in terms of culture, economics and politics, but also in terms of the life of the spirit." (p. 80).

"The Beginnings of a New Coexistence" is the sixth chapter and was written by Akiko Sugase. This chapter deals with the unity of Arabs and Jews through the celebration of the Prophet Elijah (Mar Ilyas) and how the celebration is viewed in the modern day. Sugase states, "I will use the case study of the veneration of Mar Ilyas as a way of refuting the stereotype of Palestine and Israel as the lands of ethno-religious conflict." (p. 84). He gives a response to whether or not a celebration such as this one can truly unite the peoples of Israel–Palestine and ends by saying: "Conflicts always arise from misunderstanding; before thinking about the way to solve conflicts, we should pay more attention to the local cultures, customs and practices of Palestine and Israel." (p. 97).

The seventh chapter is the beginning of the third part, Contemporary Perspectives; it was written by Paul S. Rowe and is titled "In this World You will have Trouble: Christians Living Amid Conflict in the Middle East." This chapter is particularly interesting because it provides a list of various consequences that Christians in various Middle Eastern countries go through as a result of Islamic persecution particularly after any negative interaction with Western countries. Rowe states, "In many cases they have borne the brunt of suspicion that Western foreign policies are deliberately aimed at undermining the faith of Islam and bolstering the Christian and Muslim allies of Western states in the region" (p. 101). The Christian minorities then become a target particularly from radical Islamic groups such as the most recent, ISIS. This chapter provides the response of Christian minorities to political and/or militant attacks in the countries of Lebanon and Syria, Iraq, Egypt, and Israel–Palestine, respectively.

The eighth chapter, "Christians Working for Peace in the Middle East" was written by Peter E. Makari, and gives an analysis of the work being done by Christians in the post-World War era Middle East with more emphasis on the post-Arab Spring situations. He states, "Middle Eastern Christians—be they Egyptian, Palestinian, Iraqi or Syrian—continue to be a resilient and steadfast presence, despite historic challenges. Their authentic witness to their faith in their unique national contexts demonstrates that reliance and steadfastness" (p. 135).

The ninth chapter, "The Crescent and the Cross are the Marks on My Hands" gives a brief insight into the life and work of Father Manuel Musallam. The chapter was written by Alain Epp Weaver who was a co-participant in work produced by Musallam. Weaver gives perspective to Musallam's 1993 speech which was given in Jenin. This speech gives a "…poetic description of the Palestinian nation as a body bearing the marks of the crescent and the cross on his hands…" (p. 141). Musallam's work deals with the reconciliation of Christian and Muslim Palestinians and the desire to have both groups work toward a single Palestinian national identity. Weaver states "National unity is thus narrated through a shared history and a shared geography…" (p. 144) which Musallam uses to bring the Christian and Muslim Palestinians together when he says "As Palestinians, we Christians live with Muslims, and we suffer with Muslims. We did not suffer from them." (p. 146).

This chapter also gives insight into Musallam's work with Fatah and Hamas as a voice for Christian Palestinians. Musallam currently works, not only on the reconciliation of Christian and Muslim Palestinians, but also on the reconciliation of Fatah-Hamas. Musallam states that the Palestinians are "a single civilization with two religions, that of the *Qur'an* and that of Gospel" (p. 146) and as such peace must be found.

The tenth and final chapter, "Palestinian Christian Uses of the Bible," written by Mark Daniel Calder, and, as the title implies, deals with how Palestinians of the Christian faith use the Bible to help in the struggle against their Israeli oppressors. This chapter gives a panoramic view of how the interpretation of scriptures can be, and are used to support various religious or political ideologies. In hermeneutics it is exegesis vs eisegesis. What the text says and means versus what *I* want the text to say and mean.

Interpretation leads to issues depending on who interprets the scriptures and how the scriptures are interpreted. Calder gives insight into ways that the sacred texts are interpreted—both Old Testament and New Testament. And yet various questions remain, "the question of who owns the text, whom it preferences, even what it means…" (p. 169), but that is based on the individual. **MS**

Heather J. Sharkey, Ed. *Cultural Conversions: Unexpected Consequences of Christian Missionary Encounters in the Middle East, Africa, and South Asia.* Syracuse NY: Syracuse University Press, 2013. 328 pp. $39.95. ISBN: 978-0815633150.

Popular perceptions of Christian mission activity in the colonial world are somewhat predictable. The association of missionaries with colonial authorities and Western cultural imperialism is widespread in both popular culture and academia. Take, for example, Barbara Kingsolver's 1998 bestseller, *The Poisonwood Bible* which portrays the destruction of a missionary family amid a disastrous attempt to convert the people of 1960s Congo. In the past decade, revelations such as those about the deprivations that indigenous children suffered at the hands of mission schools in North America, or reports about the efforts of Christian mission activity in Iraq after the United States' invasion of 2003 have done little to improve the reputation of missionaries. The real history of missions is far more nuanced.

The zeal that inspired the development of the modern mission movement in the 1800s was equally propelled by a certain assurance about the predictable outcomes of preaching the Christian gospel abroad. Emulating the ancient mission journeys of the apostle Paul, they sought to globalize the European Christian message that was the product of the Renaissance, the Reformation, and the Enlightenment. Their expectation was that, just as the Pax Romana had facilitated the expansion of Christianity, so would the Pax Britannica. As the world opened up to the European traveler, missionaries would face an open field of harvest similar to the one that greeted the ancient apostles.

This collection of essays seeks to explain the ways in which missions proceeded to have unforeseen, unpredictable, and in many cases, undesired outcomes. It highlights "a history of the unexpected insofar as the changes set rolling often went far beyond, or even astray from, what the missionaries intended" (p. 2). Case studies in the book juxtapose the experiences of people in several countries in the Middle East, Africa, and South Asia, organized thematically. The first section of the book, "Christian Contestations," includes three chapters that deal with situations where Christian religion delivered by missionaries served to divide Christians from Christians and Christians from others. The second section, "Missionaries, Antimissionaries, and Doubters," brings together accounts about colonial societies that resisted or responded to the message of the missionaries. The final selection of essays, under the rubric "Missionaries, Language, and National Expression," provides examples of how Christian missions helped to classify and determine the very understanding of national identity and belonging.

It is difficult to bring together such an eclectic mix of case studies, undertaken by diverse scholars in multiple fields, into a coherent whole. Heather Sharkey has done an excellent job of providing the collection with a united purpose under the theme of the unexpected. She has also managed to balance the three sections of the book by region, including in each section a case study from the Middle East, Africa, and Asia. The unexpected thus emerges wherever missionaries traveled. In Zambia, rival indigenous forms of spirituality rivaled both the Catholic and Protestant missionaries during the early colonial period. Descendants of these indigenous religious entrepreneurs became the leaders of contemporary Zambia. Among Palestinian converts to the Anglican (Episcopal) Church, the politics of the late mandate pitted the Anglican hierarchy against the indigenous church, which pioneered Christian efforts to voice the concerns of an Arab flock. In Sri Lanka, Sinhalese Buddhists embraced the tactics of Protestant Christianity as a means of resisting the missionaries themselves. In India, Christian conversion had an important role in defining legal rights to inheritance; and missionaries contributed to the racialization of Indians in the European mind. In each of these cases, Christian missions expected the spread of the gospel; they did not expect that their own converts would become rivals, or that their efforts would change the regulation of the societies where they ministered.

For scholars of the modern Middle East, the three chapters that deal with mission activity in Arab lands will garner the most interest. First, Laura Robson writes the aforementioned study of Anglican clergy during the period of the Arab revolt of 1936–39, highlighting the Palestine Native Church Council (PNCC) founded in 1905. Fighting suspicions that their association with the Church of England connoted support for the expansion of the Jewish home in Palestine, the PNCC became a vocal opponent of the expansion of Jewish immigration, arguing that it would lead to the expulsion of Christians just as Armenians and Greeks had been expelled from Turkey (p. 56). Their opposition did not persuade then-Archbishop of Canterbury, Cosmo Lang, who instead saw the Palestine question through the lens of Jewish suffering and a theology of Jewish return. The PNCC had little influence on the issuing of the 1939 White Paper that called for limitations on Jewish immigration, which consequently did little to rescue Palestinian Episcopalians from being viewed as traitors to the cause. Robson thus emphasizes the way in which Anglican positions in this period accelerated the emigration of Palestinian Christians.

Emigration is certainly one response that Christians have taken to the Middle East conflict, but one should also note the extent to which the PNCC blazed the trail for Palestinian church leaders to challenge their coreligionists' blindness to the injustices brought by the British mandate.

By the 1980s, Palestinian Anglicans, such as Naim Ateek or Riah Abu al-Assal had become the most vocal Palestinian Christian nationalists, at a time when other Palestinian churches remained in the hands of foreign hierarchs. Their presentation of contextual theology for Palestinian Christians became the pattern that has been followed by the other mainline churches, and today has an impact even upon evangelical Christian leaders, who increasingly present a counterpoint to Western Christian narratives of the Israel–Palestine conflict.

Beth Baron writes the second chapter which deals with mission activity in Arab lands. She focuses her attention on the story of Turkiyya Hasan, an Egyptian student enrolled in a Christian orphanage school in Port Said who was disciplined by caning for refusing to rise for Christian prayers. Turkiyya became a cause célèbrè in Egypt in 1933 when she fled to a local police station and her case was publicized throughout Egypt. It forced the government to respond with a public investigation and the deportation of the school's headmistress who had administered the punishment. This was followed by the announcement that alternative orphanage facilities for Muslims to rival those of the Christian missions would be established. The incident highlighted one of the first instances of a public clash between Christian mission organizations in colonial Egypt, and the rise of the Muslim Brotherhood. Brotherhood activists became increasingly involved in their own mission to protect young Muslims from the influence of the Christian missionaries (p. 136). The outcome, according to Baron, was the acceleration of the spread of Islamic societies, the downfall of the Egyptian government, and the "beginning of the end for American and other missionaries in Egypt" (p. 138). The Islamist movement arose to take their place.

Writing in the same vein, Heather Sharkey provides a concluding chapter that elaborates on the early translation of Christian scriptures into colloquial Arabic in North African countries. Such translations of all or part of the Bible were published in colloquial forms for Moroccan, Tunisian, Algerian, Egyptian, and Sudanese audiences, as well as Judeo-Arabic versions for Arabic-speaking Jews in North Africa. While Arab and foreign scholars derided the use of colloquial Arabic as a vulgar way to communicate eternal truths, missionaries embraced the colloquial form in their work with illiterate rural and urban poor populations, and in particular, women (p. 212). The demise of colloquial translations of the scriptures took place as Western mission activity in North Africa met its demise beginning in the 1930s, as national-ist governments arose and responded to public pressure from Islamists and others to limit foreign mission activity.

The story of mission activity in Egypt in the 1930s is replete with cultural and other offenses that symbolized British imperial overstretch and the deepening an-tagonism of the Islamist trend. The argument that such Christian activity was a device for the expansion of Brotherhood activity is noteworthy, though the Brother-hood would likely have evolved with or without Christian missionaries as its stalking horse. The curtailing of Christian mission activity in Egypt removed the far enemy and revealed the near enemy, *jahili* rulers of the people who became the target of later radicals.

The latter observation begs the question, how crucial was mission activity in caus-ing these unexpected outcomes? Casting one's eye to other chapters in this volume, one sees the centrality of Christian efforts in sparking a resistance movement among Buddhists in Sri Lanka, or the importance of Christian conversion to the reconcep-tualization of identity in India. It is less clear that the Palestinian Christian embrace of nationalism or the rise of Islamism in Egypt were directly related to the mission enterprise.

These histories address the role of foreign Christians and their converts in these societies. They have less to say about indigenous Christian churches. As a next step, the editor and contributors might put their hand to deeper consideration of the relationship between mission societies and indigenous Christians of the historic churches in the Middle East and South Asia. Such stories may reveal even more of the unexpected. **PSR**

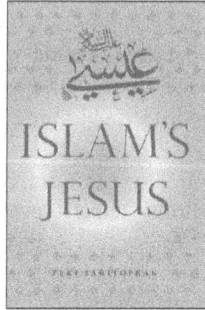

Zeki Saritoprak. *Islam's Jesus.* Gainesville, FL: University Press of Florida, 2014. 223 pp. $74.95. ISBN: 978-0813049403.

Islam's Jesus may first appear as a provocative title because of the diverse understanding of Jesus that Christians and Muslims hold for their religion. Yet, in a day when other books, such as Reza Aslan's *Zealot*, which also attempts to turn a microscope on to Jesus, have stirred such volatile reactions, Saritoprak sets up his book as an academic primer for non-Muslims and Muslims alike to re-discover the revered central figure of the Christian religion as Jesus is understood in Muslim tradition. Saritoprak takes his information from a variety of Islamic intellectual traditions to illuminate why Jesus is not only revered, but important to Muslims, as a way to present Jesus as a figure that should not divide Christians and Muslims, but rather unite them in peace around their shared respect for "God's Messenger" (p. 1). With the insight from *Islam's Jesus*, both Christians and Muslims will have more understanding with which to come together and discuss their traditions with a mutual respect for their differences.

Topics covered in the book include: Jesus as God's Messenger in the *Qur'an*; a Qur'anic Perspective on the Eschatological Role of Jesus; Islamic Eschatology and Jesus as a Sign of the Hour; the Hadith and Jesus's Eschatological Descent; Speculations about Jesus's Return; the Mahdi and Jesus as Allies against al-Dajjal (the Antichrist); Literalist Approaches to Jesus's Eschatological Role in Islamic Theology; Symbolic, Allegorical, and Other Interpretive Approaches to Jesus's Eschatological Role; and Jesus's Descent and Theologies of Muslim–Christian Cooperation.

Saritopriak boldly approaches a controversial but central topic for Christians and Muslims—Jesus—and neither audience can be satisfied fully. While the book does a good job of making the *Qur'an*'s teachings on Jesus accessible to the modern reader, the book would be stronger if the claims of Christian doctrine were also more fully addressed and debated in the book. However, Saritopriak's text is a start from which future scholarly discussions and confrontations may be continued. *Islam's Jesus* is an important academic text to begin true interfaith discussions. Only by understanding Jesus in the context of each tradition will true understanding between his admirers take place. **ALG**

CONFLICTS: POLITICAL, ARMED & CIVIL

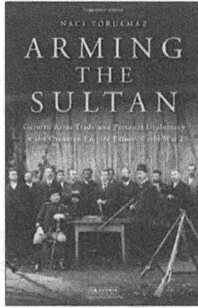

Naci Yorulmaz. *Arming the Sultan: German Arms Trade and Personal Diplomacy in the Ottoman Empire before World War I*. London, UK: I. B. Tauris, 2014. 349 pp. $72.00. *£68.00*. ISBN: 978-1780766331. Ebk: 1877 KB.

The defeat of the Ottoman Empire in the Russo-Ottoman War of 1877–78 not only brought about a financial catastrophe for the Ottomans due to losses of territory and tax base, topped with war indemnities and refugee inflow, but it also meant the end of Ottoman membership in the Concert of Europe. It was, therefore, right after the Treaty of Berlin (1878) when the Ottoman–German rapprochement began to crystallize. The maintenance of good relations with Germany was a cause Abdulhamid II (r. 1876–1909) dearly championed, as the Sultan knew only too well the fatal implications of increased Ottoman isolation in the great age of imperialism. The existing literature has so far addressed certain aspects of this relationship, such as the famous Baghdad Railroad Project, Kaiser Wilhelm II's visits to the Ottoman Empire (in 1889 and 1898), and the ideological impact of Germany on the Ottoman officers. Yorulmaz contributes to this literature by examining Germany's rise as the dominant arms supplier for the Ottoman Empire in the post-Berlin period.

Yorulmaz, an economic historian by training, pays particular attention to the significance of personal diplomacy in the German arms trade with the Orient, examining, not only the roles played by the Sultan and Kaiser, but also the agencies of high- and mid-level German and Ottoman bureaucrats. The first chapter provides a broad view of Germany's entanglement with the Ottoman Empire and analyzes what Yorulmaz calls the period of a first wave of German expansion from the Ottoman request for the dispatch of German military advisers in 1880 to the Kaiser's visit to the Ottoman Empire in 1898. Of particular interest here are the discussions on Bismarck's personal involvement with German war industries—he even leased part of his estate to a powder factory!—and the ways Bismarck promoted the German arms trade abroad. One of those places that witnessed a significant level of economic penetration was the Ottoman Empire where German influence only gained pace after Wilhelm II's coming to power in 1888 and his visit to the Ottoman capital a year later.

The second chapter, aptly titled 'German Military Advisers: Businessmen in Uniform,' is where Yorulmaz highlights the direct correlation between the dispatch of German advisers to the Ottoman Empire in 1882 and the corresponding increase in German arms sales to Constantinople. Here, the author first provides brief profiles of the German military advisers in Constantinople and the posts they had served over the years. One German military adviser who certainly stood out among his peers was Goltz Pasha (1843–1916) who would serve as an adviser to the Ottoman Sultan in multiple capacities from 1883 to 1895—a career crowned by his later round of visits when he was asked to inspect the Ottoman armies in the Young Turk era. Here Yorulmaz provides a number of anecdotes whereby he establishes Goltz Pasha as an important middleman between the palace quarters in Constantinople and the arms firms and political figures back home.

Next, in what appears to be the most engaging chapter of the book, Yorulmaz zooms in on two important contracts the German firms secured: (1) the selection of Krupp guns in 1885–86 for the fortification of the Straits; and (2) the hefty contract awarded to the Mauser Company for the purchase of half a million rifles and 50,000 carbines (topped with 100 million cartridges). The former purchase was done after the suggestion of Goltz Pasha to fortify the Straits in a preventive measure against Russian aggression. The timing of both orders is telling, as they came right in the midst of the crisis over the Bulgarian annexation of East Rumelia (1885) which certainly heightened the security concerns of the Ottomans. The role played by Goltz Pasha in securing the latter contract seems more evident than his role in the first deal. In the end, it was Goltz Pasha who suggested that the German company establish the right contacts among the Ottoman higher-ups in order to ward off competitors in Constantinople. As Yorulmaz notes, "the Mauser rifle may not have been the best rifle but it was certainly the best-marketed" one (p. 115).

Chapter 4 turns attention to the results of the Kaiser's second visit to the Ottoman Empire in 1898. After a fascinating account of the visit which the author aptly situates within the larger German policy of *Drang nach Osten* (Drive to the East), Yorulmaz briefly examines few of the important results borne out of the trip: the concessions secured for the Baghdad Railway Project; the Port of Haydarpasa; the telegraph lines from Istanbul to Berlin; and finally the establishment of a German–Palestine Bank—all illustrating the extent of the penetration of German capital into the Ottoman economy. The chapter ends with a discussion of how Wilhelm II made a number of personal interventions that secured contracts for German arms firms at the expense of their European competitors—a useful thematic section that would have perhaps fitted better to the earlier parts of the study, as it disrupts chronological flow.

Problems of chapter design persist in the next chapter where Yorulmaz provides a portrayal of the Ottoman motivations in aligning with Germany in the aftermath of the Russo-Ottoman War of 1877–78. Here the author skillfully illustrates both Abdulhamid II's personal influence in arms purchases and his unyielding preference for German-made weapons. Yorulmaz observes further that the Ottoman–German rapprochement came to cultivate a cadre of pro-German officers in the Ottoman military ranks who played into the Sultan's personal preference for Germany through providing an endless supply of reports that praised the superiority of German weapons. While this chapter complements the book's overall emphasis on the significance of personal diplomacy, it still reads more like a detailed introductory piece that recaps many of the points already made in the preceding chapters.

The last chapter examines the period of the Young Turk rule from 1908 until 1914, particularly looking at the fate of the German firms after the dethronement of Abdulhamid II in the Counterrevolution of 1909. Here Yorulmaz illustrates how technical superiority as well as competitive prices began to factor in the way in which the Young Turk leadership approached the issue of arms purchases. Yet, the promotion of such objective criteria that initially seem to have worked against the German interests only lasted briefly. The German firms slowly recovered their position, particularly by securing large orders from Constantinople in the months leading up to the outbreak of the First World War. The author ends his discussion by briefly discussing the naval procurements in the post-1908 period in an attempt by the Young Turks to re-invigorate the Ottoman navy long neglected by Abdulhamid II.

Yorulmaz's study is a welcome addition to the literature. With an exemplary use of the Ottoman, German, British, and American records, the author makes a significant contribution to the field through an empirically rich analysis. Yet, the study's conceptual frameworks leave much to be desired. The author puts forth 'German style of war business' and the role of 'personal diplomacy' to explain Germany's domination of the Hamidian arms purchases, but I remain unconvinced to what extent these tactics were at all peculiar to the Germans. In the end, geo-political calculations (e.g., the growing Great Power rivalries and the increasing prestige of German arms following the 1870s) seem to weigh in more heavily in dictating the course of Ottoman purchases. On another note, "three successive waves of German expansion," as suggested by the author, do not seem to yield a useful periodization in analytic terms. Finally, Yorulmaz's work could have benefited from a more careful chapter design. As it stands, the monograph is composed of chronological and thematic chapters, with the end-result of overlapping emphasis and repetitive content.

These minor quibbles aside, Yorulmaz's study is a comprehensive and insightful account of the German–Ottoman rapprochement in general and the German arms trade with the Orient in particular. Its particular value lies in its ability to detail how the German military advisers in Constantinople came to promote the interests of the German military–industrial complex. Moreover, the study is valuable in illustrating how hefty governmental contracts, such as arms purchases, emerged as an important component of the Ottoman diplomatic repertoire of "saving the State." A must-read for the specialists, *Arming the Sultan...* provides much-needed insight into the workings of the global arms trade in the final years of the Ottoman Empire. **RHO**

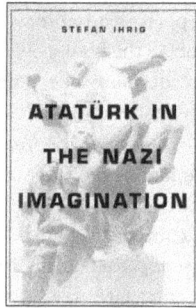

Stefan Ihrig. *Ataturk in the Nazi Imagination.* **Cambridge, MA: Belknap Press, 2014. 305 pp. $29.95. ISBN: 978-0674368378.**

On October 30, 1934, two long rows of Nazi party members marched to the Tiergarten in Berlin. Ernst Rohm, the commander of the Brown Shirts was among them, as was the Berlin police commander. The men stood at attention from 11 am to midnight. At some point during the day, the Nazi dignitaries and police officials paid their respects to the Turkish Ambassador, whose embassy abutted the Tiergarten. It was the tenth anniversary of the Turkish Republic and the Nazi Party wanted to give the country a special honor; just as it was on the verge of taking over Germany.

Why these leading Nazis were present is the subject of a new study by Stefan Ihrig, a Polonsky Fellow at the Van Leer Jerusalem Institute. "For the Nazis, Turkey was not the old East, but a standard bearer for the modern nationalist and totalitarian politics that they wished to bring to Germany," argues Ihrig in his introduction (p. 7). Yet, the author notes, that up until now no study has examined this strange affinity that Hitler had for the Turks. It involved a multiplicity of illusions and false readings of modern Turkey. There were misconceptions about the role of Islam in Turkey and the nature of the founder of modern Turkey, Mustaa Kemal Ataturk, who died in 1938.

The Turkish–German relationship predated Nazism by more than some fifty years.

There was a specific German tradition of caring about the Orient and the Ottoman Empire, an Orientpolitik even, and a deep entanglement with the Ottoman Empire up until 1919. German engineers built a railroad from Berlin to Baghdad through the empire. German military advisors modified the Ottoman army and served in its officer corps. During the First World War the Germans and Ottomans were allies.

But what fascinated the nationalist press in Germany in the 1920s, and thus influenced the nascent Nazi movement, was that Turkey was resisting the allies who had defeated Germany. In the aftermath of the Great War the allies imposed stiff penalties on Germany. For nationalists it was too much to bear—to be a humiliated, defeated nation. The same had been done to the Ottoman Empire, dismembered and carved up into colonies and mandates. The allies occupied Istanbul, and minorities such as Greeks, Armenians, Assyrians, and Kurds dreamed of establishing states on the ruins of the empire.

Then in 1919 and 1920, Turkey underwent a revolution as the young military officer Ataturk emerged to lead a rebellion that swept the "foreigners" out of Turkey and rejuvenated the country. In the German right wing press, from which this book includes many fascinating illustrations, Turkey was shown emerging from the grave to frighten away the British. "The Turks were the only nation that, despite all the weaknesses, despite the decades of warfare, found the strength and the idealism not to bend unconditionally to the destructive will of the Entente," editorialized the *Deutsche Tageszeitung* in 1921 (p. 45). Other articles asked "what do the Turks Teach us?" Papers noted "if Mustafa Kemal and his people sat in berlin right now, they would have a different answer [to the French and British] (p. 81)."

This is all fascinating and the author materials his sources and evidence well. He clearly proves that the German right lionized the Turks. But did the Nazi party? The book notes "it is safe to assume that leading Nazis had read them [leading articles on Turkey]." Later he notes "it is easy to infer" that the Nazis were influenced by calls to establish a "German Kemal Pasha" influenced the Beer Hall Putsch in 1923, when Hitler attempted a coup in Munich. But inferences and assumptions can be dangerous. Where is the evidence in the Nazi party material, diaries or writings of Hitler himself? Yet he notes "the only Turkey mentioned in *Mein Kampf* was the 'Old Turkey,' the Ottoman Empire, which for Hitler was similar to the other 'ancient state,' the Habsburg Empire (p. 110)."

There is no doubt that once the Nazis came to power, they cultivated the Turks as an ally. At a performance of Wagner, the Turkish Ambassador was given a prominent seat. The Nazi party office on "racial policy" claimed that the "Turks are Aryans" in order to differentiate them from "lesser races" in the party policy of hate (p. 128). Later the Nazi press *Volkischer Beobachter* noted the "value the Fuhrer assigns to the continued friendly relations between the young Reich and the young Turkey (p. 145)." Germany and Turkey enjoyed close economic and political relations through the middle of the Second World War.

It is widely thought that one model for the Holocaust was the Armenian Genocide carried out by the Ottomans during the First World War. "Throughout the 1920s, Hitler was to use the Armenians frequently in his speeches as an example of a 'lesser race'" (p. 180). For instance, he compared the Armenian and Greek role in the Ottoman Empire to that of the Jews. "They have become Jews themselves" (p. 180).

This is an important and easily accessible book. It paves new ground and certainly sheds light on an important issue in Germany between the wars. There is no doubt that Turkey was a model for the nationalists in Germany and the Nazis made many efforts to cultivate the Turks as allies. Whether Ataturk necessarily served as a direct model for Nazism is not clear. **SJF**

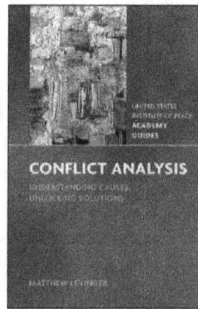

Matthew Levinger. *Conflict Analysis: Understanding Causes, Unlocking Solutions.* Washington, DC: United States Institute of Peace Press, 2013. 268 pp. Pbk: $24.95. ISBN: 978-1601271433.

Conflict Analysis is the second book in a new series of "Academy Guides" being produced by the U.S. Institute for Peace (USIP). These are designed to bridge the gap between academic research and practical applications, and to be accessible to a broad range of practitioners.

This work deals with the emerging field of conflict analysis, and covers a range of methods for anticipating, gaining further insights into, and dealing with social and political conflicts which have the potential for leading to sustained lethal violence. The author has had extensive experience teaching this material in both academic and NGO settings, and presents a balanced compendium of theoretical and applied approaches. The work is generally nontechnical, though some quantitative work such as the political risk metrics of the Political Instability Task Force and the Fund for Peace is discussed.

In addition to covering a number of the common theoretical frameworks for understanding both violent conflicts and organizational responses (or lack of response) to them—for example "groupthink" and conflict phase models—one of the strongest aspects of the book is the extensive use of case studies. These range from short vignettes relating experiences in the field to extended discussions, for example on the reaction of U.S. air traffic controllers to the low probability "black swan" of the 9/11/2001 hijackings. A number of these accounts are centered on elements of several well-studied crises such as 9/11, Rwanda 1994, and the recent wars in Iraq and Afghanistan.

While the book has a well-organized narrative structure, and would be well suited for use as a text, one of the most useful elements of the book may be the series of highlighted checklists, found throughout the volume, which provide a set of "have we considered this?" reminders. (Appendix 6 provides another summary of these suggestions in the USIP "Narrative Analysis Framework.") More generally, the book is clearly designed to be skimmed as well as read, with clear chapter summaries and a number of summary tables.

Consistent with the aim of the series, the book is intended as a reference as well. A series of appendices provide brief references to a wide range of projects and organizations active in the field, as well as a short glossary of some of the technical vocabulary, and an excellent bibliography for further reading. Those appendices may be particularly useful in highlighting the extent of the work being done in this area. For example, the appendices list 19 early warning watch-lists, 13 conflict metrics, 18 conflict assessment frameworks, and 11 sets of conflict mapping tools which have been developed and maintained by a variety of governmental, IGO/NGO, academic, and for-profit groups, largely in North America and Europe. The lists are quite up-to-date, and while some of the links to material on the Web will suffer inevitable and unpredictable changes, sufficient information is provided that it should be easy to locate the projects or their successors through the usual search engines.

This is definitely a book on *assessment*, and to a lesser extent, forecasting and early warning, rather than on mediation or mitigation. These topics are raised tangentially at a number of points but are not the focus, and given that this is only the second book in a series, I would not be surprised if USIP were planning later books specifically addressing these issues. Similarly, while the book deals with a number of issues related to practical considerations for collecting information in conflict-prone regions (this practical advice comes out strongly in some of the stories) it is not by itself a guide to doing such work. Again, this might be addressed in a later volume. **PAS**

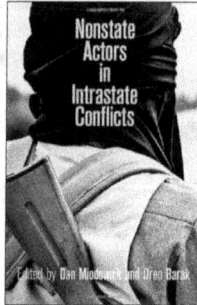

**Dan Miodownik and Oren Barak, Eds. *Nonstate Actors in Intrastate Conflicts.*
Philadelphia, PA: University of Pennsylvania Press, 2014. 243 pp. $ 69.95. ISBN:
978-0812245431.**

The paradigm of political armed conflict has shifted significantly in the post-
WWII era from clearly inter-state to some sort of a transnational character. The
focus of study is now less on the macro universal or state level than on an organizational group, or even individual ones, capable of shifting focus across recognized
geographical borders and often operating within a state. A popular theme taken up
by international relations specialists has been decolonization represented by national
liberation movements, insurgency and its repressive counter which has morphed
into terrorism and in its structured fashion, nonstate actors, who operate beyond the
pale of international rules and regulations. The bounded restraints that Western-initiated international law provided states has somehow unraveled, allowing ancient
ethnic, cultural, sectarian, and national rivalries to emerge again as combatants.

Dan Miodownik and Oren Barak, both political scientists at the Hebrew University of Jerusalem have contributed to our understanding of the complexities of
the relationship between two interrelated concepts, the nonstate actor and intrastate
conflict. The focus of the eight essays is very specific, "the role of external nonstate
actors—particularly foreign volunteers and members of diasporas—in intrastate
conflict" (p. 1). The essays are heavily supported by the theoretical literature, which
can be augmented by the meta-analyses provided by Pearlman and Cunningham
(2012), and Blin (2011). While the geographic concentration is on the Middle East,
examples from elsewhere abound and serve the cause of the regionalist as well as the
Universalist.

Barak and Chanan Cohen investigate violent trans-border nonstate actors to provide a theoretical context as the confluence of statelessness, universal ideologies,
and violent actors. But it is interesting that the authors chose to frame their analysis
within the rubric of Sherwood Forest and the literary figure of Robin Hood. Now,
Robin Hood's goal was wealth redistribution within the confines of a legitimate state,
under the royal crown of King Richard, imprisoned abroad. While the kingdom was

indeed subject to actors' power grab, the perpetrators were native Englishmen and there was no on-going civil conflict. Essentially there were anti-imperial struggles and, the emergence of new states, suggesting a new framework of analysis to explain the interplay of the three factors noted.

Of course, the extent of civic loyalty leads to stability of the respective regime which, in turn, reduces internal threats, but to what extent does it protect the state from external threats? In this case, there are issues of personal identity and the ties they have to their civic identification. What is the foundation for recruitment of foreign fighters to enter a civil conflict not of their own national interest? For Muslims, David Malet found that martyrdom within the context of Islam became an ideal goal. A much more low-grade interest was pure greed, the simple opportunity to loot, which was in evidence in the conflict in Bosnia. A general factor found was identification with the underdog and those who used marginalized groups; case studies here include Texas, Spain, Israel, and Afghanistan. In almost all cases a primary factor revealed was that for political actors, sacrifice was preferable to the consequences of defeat.

Avraham Sela and Robert Fitchette look at the Arab Afghani state–society relationship with the intervening factor of ideology and the role of Islamic *jihad.* They are specifically interested in "explaining the origins and dynamics of transnational networks and their place in a state-society framework" (p. 56). What they found was that Arab Afghans sought benefits by defending fellow Muslims from Soviet infidels.

Gabriel Sheffer, who has been involved with the study of armed conflict for many years now, discusses the notion of a diaspora folk along an ethno-national-religious dimension and their entrance into an intrastate conflict. He notes that any further review takes into account the differences between transnational and a diaspora entity, with the latter becoming an active participant following their expulsion experience.

The sensitive issue of Turkey and its relationship with Armenia and its people is taken up by Nava Löwenheim. This is an elucidating case study because the expatriate Armenian community plays an important role in the operation of the Armenian state, as an extraterritorial political actor, while simultaneously, Armenians are actively involved in anti-Turkish violence from within Turkey and from outside bases of operation in the neighboring states. But Turkey also deals with its ethnic Kurds, who seek sovereignty as a community divided in its state residence between Turkey, Syria, Iraq, and Iran. Kurds are also a multi-sub-group ethnic community, complicating their national identity. The internal and external threat by the Kurds, particularly by those in Northern Iraq has led Turkey to exploit the insurgency in Iraq to conduct military incursions to quell Kurdish militant activity. The Kurdish incursions from Iraq into Turkey have resulted in Turkish military, trans-border reprisals. As an aside, these actions, as pointed out by Gallia Lindenstrauss, have reduced the close relations Turkey has had with the United States. More to the point, Turkey perceives the Kurds and their demand for a greater degree of sovereignty, wherever they may be found, to be a threat either from within the state or external to it.

Lebanon and its Lebanese Maronite Christian community dominated the South Lebanese Army (SLA) with its attachment to Israel covered extensively by Orit Gazit. The author was able to conduct extensive field research in Israel with SLA members resident there. What he found was that nonstate actors' identities can be altered with forces by some level of threat by that native central authority combined with internal chaotic conditions. Sela and Barak conclude this collection with another essay on Lebanon. The case of Lebanon as a multi-confessional state, torn apart from a regional neighbor by a European power, is an ideal case study for this particular study's focus.

While not comprehensive, *Nonstate Actors in Intrastate Conflicts* is a helpful contribution to international relations specialists' understanding of the multiple sides of contemporary political armed conflict. The breakdown of the international system away from the total control of the Western-initiated state system demands a multi-disciplinary approach to match newly emerging understandings of relationships is provided in part here.

Blin, A. 2011. "Armed Groups and Intra-state Conflicts: The Dawn of a New Era?" *International Review of the Red Cross* 93: 287–310.

Pearlman, W., and K. G. Cunningham. 2012. "Nonstate Actors, Fragmentation, and Conflict Processes." *Journal of Conflict Resolution* 56: 3–15. **SRS**

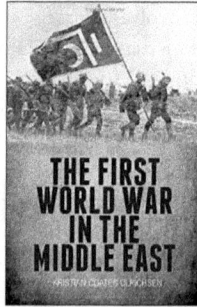

Kristian Coastes Ulrichsen. *The First World War in the Middle East.* **London, UK: Hurst Publishers, 2014. 263 pp. $31.50. ISBN: 978-1849042741.**

In 1915, the British Viceroy of India, Charles Hardinge sent a telegram to London noting the prospects for a successful military campaign in Iraq. "The capture of Baghdad would create an immense impression in the Middle East, especially in Persia, Afghanistan and on our frontier" (p. 133). The expedition, in the spring of 1916, foundered at a little known town called Kut, 100 miles from Baghdad, and resulted in the surrender of 13,000 British and Indian soldiers to the Ottoman army. As they were marched to captivity, a Russian expeditionary force in Persia (now Iran) sat poised to intervene, but choose not to help her ostensible British allies.

These episodes and many others are revealed in Rice University lecturer Kristian Ulrichsen's new book on the *The First World War in the Middle East*. From many perspectives, the war was of great importance because it set in motion the re-alignment of the region that is still being played out today. The breakup of Iraq, for instance, appears to be a direct result of colonial meddling after the war in which Iraq was cobbled together under a British Mandate. Ulrichsen is cognizant of this historical shadow, noting in his introduction that "two of the state[s] that emerged from the legacy of the first large-scale modern Western military intervention in the region lies in ruins" (p. 3).

This book is part military history and part examination of the politics, economics and outcome of the momentous events of 1914–18. It is written in a professional historian's style; those looking for colorful flourishes, descriptions of the agony felt by soldiers in battle, or the *jeux de vie* of Lawrence of Arabia will be disappointed. That being said, there is much to learn in this relatively short but information packed volume.

The author begins with a detailed explanation of the problems militaries faced in the region in the war. He contrasts the "mass industrialized warfare" (p. 37) with the fact that this region had a terrible infrastructure. Logistics for army units was stretched to the breaking point. For instance, when Turkish military leader Enver Pasha launched his third army invasion of the Caucasus in December of 1914, he thought the surprise of a winter campaign would catch the Russians by surprise. Why a Turkish general, leading an army of conscripts used to the warmth of the Mediterranean, thought *the Russians* would succumb to the cold is beyond fathomable; and Enver got what he deserved. His army was trapped on a plateau averaging 2,000 m in the freezing cold around the town of Sarikamis; his army was virtually destroyed.

Similarly, the British at Kut and Gallipoli struggled to gain a foothold against the Ottomans. Even though the Ottoman army, bolstered with German advisors, was corrupt and inadequate, the superior British infantry were stymied. In the desert wastes of Sinai, the Ottomans, led by Freidrich Kress von Kressenstein, a German, sent 25,000 across the Peninsula to raid the Suez Canal. They actually launched inflatable pontoons, something that presaged the Egyptian crossing of 1973 against Israel, but failed to gain much of a foothold on the Egyptian side.

The British, having failed in Iraq and in Gallipoli, realized a long desert campaign to dislodge the Ottomans was their only hope. The author notes the immensity of the task before them. "By December 1916, the British military authorities were responsible for maintaining a force of 200,000 combatants and noncombatants along the border with Palestine" (p. 45). Some 1.2 million gallons of water was needed each day, not just for the men, but also for the horses and camels.

General Sir Archibald Murray led the British invasion of Palestine in early 1917—a campaign best remembered for the fact that he ordered the use of tanks and poison gas to take Gaza in March and April. Despite these new fangled weapons, the

Turkish trenches remained impregnable and he was relieved of command. The rest of the Palestine campaign is perhaps well known, including the famous charge of the Australian Light Horse at Beersheba, which turned the tide and sent the Turks reeling back toward Jerusalem, then Megiddo, and finally, Damascus.

Ulrichsen's book examines, in separate chapters, the military campaigns in Palestine, Iraq, Turkey, Salonika, and the Caucuses. Those unfamiliar with the dates will find it slightly difficult to keep track of due to the fact that it is not organized chronologically. His final chapters examine the post-war period, and the decision to create a Mandate for a Jewish State of Palestine; a nationalist revolt in Egypt; and a tribal rebellion in Iraq. Readers cannot fail to notice too many similarities with today—a breakdown in societies, such as Libya and Syria and the revolt of tribes, combined with religious fervor and nationalism. All of it seems to be playing itself out again, even the poison gas issue in Syria. But the author is not heavy on the politics or blame-game, leaving it up to the reader to decide whether it was colonialism that played a major part in the region's problems today, or the instability created by the decline of the Ottoman Empire and rise of various local Arab elites. **SJS**

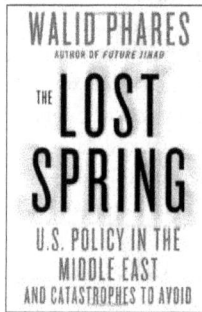

Walid Phares. *The Lost Spring: U.S. Policy in the Middle East and Catastrophes to Avoid.* New York, NY: Palgrave MacMillan, 2014. 258 pp. $19.89. ISBN: 978-1137279033. Ebk: 704 KB. $11.04. ISBN: 1137279036.

It is difficult to determine what type of text Walid Phares has written in *The Lost Spring*. It is not an academic text, as this review will reveal. Neither is it a work of fiction, though the casual reader might mistake it for such. Rather, *The Lost Spring* is little more a political polemic designed to advance the rightwing agenda of its author.

Walid Phares is a former advisor to the Mitt Romney campaign and consultant to various Republican Party politicians, such as Rick Santorum, Herman Cain, Michele Bachmann, and Newt Gingrich. Phares is also advisor to the center-right European People's Party (which he mistakenly calls the European Popular Party), a participant or organizer of various conferences (few of which he bothers to name), and a former associate with the Heritage Foundation.

Phares' thesis is that the Obama Administration is in league with various government funded agencies—(The Endowment for Democracy, the U.S. Institute for Peace, the International Democratic Institute, and the International Republican Institute), liberals, the media (other than Fox News), cultural relativists (the late Edward Said), pro-Islamic and Iranian lobbies, and the academic community—to betray American national interests in the Middle East. The alleged start of this betrayal began with the president's speech at Cairo University in June 2009. At that point, the current administration allegedly turned away from the Bush Administration's "freedom forward" policy and began a long process of accommodation with various Islamists and Salifists groups, the Muslim Brotherhood (*Ikhwan*), and the Islamic Republic of Iran. To use Phares' terminology, "the speech was a version of an undeclared "Yalta agreement" between the administration and the Islamist forces." (p. 170)

The text provides no evidence to substantiate these charges, but is filled with numerous fantastical claims. For example, concerning the overthrow of Hosni Mubarak, and the later election of Mohammed Morsi in Egypt's first democratic election since before 1952, Phares states without evidence "Another factor helped the Muslim Brotherhood in its course, and that was the sympathy of the Obama Administration. With many advisers in its bureaucracy close to the Brotherhood, the administration shepherded the Egyptian revolution in a manner advantageous to the Islamists." (p. 53)

One discovers other claims of conspiracy by Phares. Also without evidence one reads "The Brotherhood's peak [of influence] in the United States came with the victory of candidate Barak Obama in the U.S. Presidential Election of 2008. The network, via its front groups, supported the campaign, not as a formal entity, but as a prelude to receiving influence within America's bureaucracies and the new administration when Obama took office" (p. 138).

Next, according to Phares, the Obama Administration was planning to turn Iraq over to Iran and Afghanistan to the Taliban: "The next goals [after preventing Israel from attacking Iran and reaching out to Hezbollah] were to offer up Iraq, after the U.S. pullout, to Iranian influence as a price for rehabilitation of Iran's regime in the club of nations, and to concede Afghanistan to the Taliban in return for peace with the Jihadists" (p. 183). The sources for these claims are various right wing and conservative publications in the United States. Numerous footnotes reference *American Thinker, National Review, New York Daily News, Cutting Edge News, FrontPage Magazine, American Spectator, National Post*, and *Newsmax Magazine*. Hardly works of scholarly repute. Phares also possesses knowledge of and insights into Middle East politics that border upon the clairvoyant. Apparently he predicted the 2005 Cedar Revolution in Lebanon and the 2009 Green Revolution in Iran (p. 19). Phares also knew the Arab Spring was coming (pp. 38-39), that Iran and Hezbollah would assist the Assad regime in Syria (p. 89), and all but predicted the attack upon the

U.S. Consulate in Benghazi. (p. 101) Of course hindsight always provides one with 20/20 vision.

Finally, throughout the text, Phares refers to himself in the first person. In the first chapter alone this reviewer counted 46 such references. A similar pattern of self-aggrandizement is found throughout the work. Clearly modesty does not become the writer.

Thus, what conclusion does one draw from this text? The main one is that *The Lost Spring* … is not a work of scholarship. Rather as stated in the first paragraph of this review, it is little more than a polemic. One cannot blame or begrudge the author for desiring to ingratiate himself with potential Republican presidential candidates (Romney, Bachmann, Santorum, etc.), for any of these individuals may run in 2016. In fact, Phares' final chapter (excluding the Epilogue) is titled "Romney's Alternative View." Although an analysis of the former governor's 2011–12 positions on the Middle East, the points presented in the chapter might easily be recycled for a 2016 campaign.

Because of the blatant political nature of *The Lost Spring* … and its lack of anything approaching scholarly balance and objectivity, this reviewer cannot in good conscious recommend adoption by individuals or libraries. **WLR**

ECONOMICS, SOCIOECONOMICS, OIL

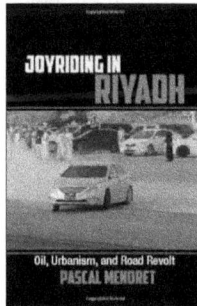

Pascal Menoret. *Joyriding in Riyadh: Oil, Urbanism, and Road Revolt.* Cambridge, UK: Cambridge University Press, 2014. 250pp. $85.00. ISBN: 978-1107035485. Pbk.: $32.99. ISBN: 978-1107641952.

Scholarly works about Saudi Arabia usually focus on issues of regional security, energy policy, Islam, and democratization. *Joyriding in Riyadh*, I am delighted to write, is not one of these types of work. Pascal Menoret's book is an excellent ethnography of youth culture in Saudi Arabia that unpacks the connections between the social practice of joyriding as a form of political dissent with the questions of oil, urbanism, and power. It provides new insight into the categories of masculinity and gender in the Middle Eastern context and the spatial politics of the Saudi state. This work contributes to a growing body of critical scholarship (e.g., Adam Hanieh's *Capitalism and Class in the Gulf Arab States*, Madawi Al-Rasheed's *A Most Masculine State*, and Toby Craig Jones's *Desert Kingdom*) that seeks to reconceptualize the studies of the Arabian Peninsula and situate the region in larger political, economic, social, and cultural contexts and global processes.

In the Introduction, the author lays out the conceptual and methodological framework of the book. Instead of seeing drifting as a criminal youth activity, Menoret re-frames it as an activity that is "embedded in global networks of power and knowledge" (p. 5). It is a product of rapid urbanization and road building, the emergence of a car as the primary mode of transportation anchored in an oil-based economy that fueled rampant land speculation. Menoret then moves to the discussion of politics and sees joyriding as a part of an emerging "plebeian public sphere" which challenges the state through "various genres of opposition (p. 11) and conveys the dissatisfaction of young Saudis with state policies. The final points of this section focus on the author's concern with self-reflexivity during the course of his fieldwork. In the tradition of Pierre Bourdieu, he reflects how his positionality impacts the direction and content of his study and the representation of Saudi youth both at home and abroad.

In Chapter 2, Menoret demonstrates the reality of state surveillance, repression, and violence that Saudi citizens face and how it configures social relations in distinct ways. He remarks that the work of the anthropologist cannot remain unaffected or undistorted in such an environment, and recounts an interesting personal vignette that shows the trajectory of his own research agenda. Chapters 3 and 4 examine how, after the 1972 oil bonanza, Riyadh was transformed into a modern suburban city which has been dominated by the car and underpinned by an oil economy. The process was driven by mass—rural to urban—migration in search of economic opportunities, real estate speculation on a spectacular scale, and the large importation of foreign manufactured cars that reflected material affluence of certain segments of Saudi society. However, in a familiar story around the world, the process of development was contested in different ways. It was accompanied by episodes of violence and expulsion, which contradicted state narratives of harmonious development of the Saudi nation. The following two chapters shift focus from the creation of modern Riyadh to the stories of the young drifters. They are the children of Saudi rural migrants, but unlike the well-connected Saudis, they, by and large, have not benefitted from the new economy. Largely located on the margins of society, they inhabit the new urban landscapes and shape them according to their "use, misuse, and abuse of cars" (p. 20). Indeed, young disaffected, rebellious and marginalized drifters create a new map of the city through driving practices. Menoret conceptualizes these practices as a form of resistance to state policies. The state, in turn, brands the drifters as a deviant element and politicizes their actions.

One of the avenues that could have been explored more explicitly in this book was the multilayered connections between gender, youth culture, urbanism, and political dissent. The brief portion of the text that analyzes the sexuality and masculinity of the drifters was theoretically suggestive.

Joyriding in Riyadh is an excellent and scholarly work that makes a valuable contribution to the field of Middle East Studies. It will appeal to anyone that has an interest in youth culture, urban and gender studies, urban history, and anthropology of the Middle East. Moreover, the book can be assigned to classes on Middle Eastern politics, Arab Uprisings, or any course that deals with the issues of social violence and economic inequality in a comparative or global framework. **FK**

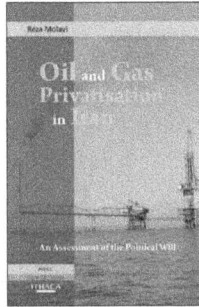

Reza Molavi. *Oil and Gas Privatisation in Iran: An Assessment of the Political Will.* **London, UK: Ithaca Press. 214 pp. $24.95. ISBN: 978-0863724220.**

In an academic environment that is heavily concentrated in Iranian social issues or political matters of state-sponsored terrorism and nuclear capabilities, Reza Molavi's work is a refreshing change of scenery. While scholarship chases social movements and international hostilities, Molavi quietly turns our attention back to the powerful resource that has for decades linked Iranian politics, society, and culture. He does so with an inventive approach centered on assessing the political will to privatize. Examining such a subjective topic takes the discussion far beyond the tired discourse of economy and commodity. It taps into the Iranian social psyche. It engages Iranian political philosophy. The approach transforms oil from a mere domestic resource to a commanding institution that impacts both personal and professional livelihoods. Readers will quickly realize that the ramifications of privatization for Iranian society cannot be underestimated. Whether the wage-earner or the manager, the soldier or the president, the debate over public versus privately held oil has, and will continue to have, enormous domestic and international consequences for Iran.

Thematically, Molavi has chosen a difficult task. Assessing political will requires a broad sweeping analysis incorporating both the technical and abstract. Molavi does just that. With skill and clarity, he interweaves specialized oil economics with the particulars of Iranian culture and society, thereby creating a portrait of political will. For Iran, though, the privatization debate pivots on an "apparent reluctance" rather than a contest between public and private (p. 1). Interestingly, "reluctance" suggests privatization is inevitable, but at what cost? It is from this vantage point that Molavi launches his treatise.

To start, Molavi lays the foundation with four political and economic realities that, he contends, account for Iran's political reluctance to privatize. The first reality is the disjunction between the Iranian state and society, or as scholar Homa Katouzian calls it, the "theory of arbitrary rule" (p. 12). Molavi argues this chasm or disconnect between the state and society severely impacts policy, especially privatization. Molavi identifies the second reality as similar disjunction between economic and socio-political modernization. From the Shah to the Ayatollahs, the history of uneven, government-directed modernization has created a gap between society, politics, and economy. The third reality is Iran's economic dependence on oil. An economy so heavily tied to one product would make it nearly impossible to withstand the market volatility associated with privatization. One temporary economic downturn, Molavi points out, would have devastating consequences. The fourth, and perhaps most influential, is Iran's relationship with the West. Privatization, championed by the West, is suspect in the eyes of Iranian officials. Domestic perspectives in Iran consider the West to be imperialistic, and therefore, taint any substantive dialog over how to privatize. These realities act as philosophies that inform all aspects of the privatization debate.

The body of Molavi's work is segmented into six chapters, frequently transitioning between thematic and chronological. His recursive organization causes redundancy at times, but that redundancy can serve to reinforce technical and abstract ideas that might otherwise be difficult to digest with only one reference. Privatization is such a topic. At first glance the idea seems straightforward, a rather basic economic idea, however, Molavi takes great care in explaining why it is not. Drawing largely on oral interviews with Iranian government officials and authorized publications, Molavi divides privatization between theory and practice arguing that privatization theories arise from interplay between various actors, the international system, and the evolution of ideas. From them emerge practices that are equally varied depending on precedence, experience, and individual circumstances. In short, theories and practices of privatization (even in the West) are projects tailored to the actor and fluid in execution. What makes Iran's situation special, Molavi contends, is the relationship between religion and the state. Privatization would involve the Islamic government, considered to be the ultimate authority over property rights with accountability only to God, to release control over oil. This essential and decisive perspective validates, or at least rationalizes, "reluctance." The reluctance, however, should not hamstring the government, Molavi suggests. Models in Pakistan, Azerbaijan, and India, among others, have implemented varying degrees of privatization based on their economic and geographical circumstances. The result is an assortment of projects in government-owned oil, joint ownership, and private oil holdings.

The next section is a critical juncture in Molavi's monograph, one that readers should review with great care. In Chapters 2–4, Molavi employs a litany of secondary work from credible scholars to painstakingly outline Iran's extensive history of domestic turmoil and foreign manipulation. While interpretations of privatization are important, Iran's recent history is perhaps the greatest contributor to their "reluctance." He first focuses domestically on political fractionalization. This century-old plague on Iranian politics has resulted in political splintering that has given minority groups the potential for absolute rule. Fractionalization, along with the Shah's cozy relationship with the West, he argues, was responsible for the Shah's prolonged centralized and oppressive regime. This is a fundamental reality that spurred anti-U.S.

sentiment and nationalism, which "proved to be critical ingredients in the appeal of the anti-Shah forces in the late 1970s" (p. 52). Molavi also underscores the CIA-led overthrow of Prime Minister Mohammad Mossadegh in 1953 as an event that would later embolden Khomeini's supporters and, for the most part, undo what was left of pro-U.S. sentiment. Referencing Ervand Abrahamian's Khomeninism, Molavi goes on to recount the Ayatollah's convincing populist rhetoric that took sway over the country. Khomeini almost immediately took a position of absolute rule and, as the story goes, Iranian society did not realize the oppressive state that was upon them until too late. In the midst of his historical narrative, Molavi highlights two important factors. First, the Council of Guardians—the supremely appointed committee charged with ensuring all state decisions and political appointees are compatible with Islamic law—and second, the varying interpretations of Shi'ism that fosters further fractionalization. These two characteristics of the Islamic State highlight the difficulty facing the Iranian government in reconciling absolute control with privatization. Molavi's comprehensive retelling does not introduce new information, but instead, summarizes the circumstances leading to the Islamic State's reluctance to privatize.

Molavi begins his descent describing a country in a state of economic turmoil, in desperate need of modernization, and concludes his monograph with a range of his own assessments on Iran's way forward. He first reminds readers there are models to emulate that could lessen the chances of damaging fluctuations associated with privatization. Furthermore, restructuring state-owned companies is a must, even in the face of enormous corruption and efficiencies. The Council of Guardians, in particular, with their rigid control measures remains a serious barrier to essential economic development. Most importantly, Iran is in need of foreign investment, but the only countries able to provide the sizable investments necessary are tied to current sanctions. All this said, Molavi believes Iran "will continue to be sensitive to global issues, since elasticity of its oil revenues is linked to its awareness of, and connection to, the global system" (p. 180). Therefore, he finishes where he started, claiming it is not whether privatization will happen, but more about "a matter of pace and extent" (p. 182).

For his part, Molavi uses incredible detail and clarity in assessing the political will. His conclusions are honest and realistic. The considerable use of oral evidence is particularly interesting. Molavi is sensitive to accuracy, but cognizant of restricted candor among officials. He deserves enormous credit for such balanced interpretations after navigating those waters. His chosen recursive organization, however, may be the only drawback to an otherwise splendid publication. At times, it reads as occasional pieces pulled together to form a book. Redundancies can be helpful, but clearer transitions are absolutely essential with such an approach. All in all, Molavi's broad approach has given scholars the foundation from which to forge specialized studies on oil culture and political will. **DAG**

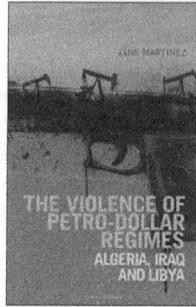

Luis Martinez. *The Violence of Petro-Dollar Regimes: Algeria, Iraq and Libya.* New York, NY: Columbia University Press. 202 pp. $50.00. ISBN: 978-0231703024.

Author Luis Martinez, in his latest work *The Violence of Petro-Dollar Regimes*, poses a simple question: How does tremendous wealth stunt, or even reverse a nation's economic and social development? It seems paradoxical for a nation to simultaneously experience a financial windfall and a domestic decline, but that was the reality for Algeria, Iraq, and Libya. During the early 1970s, each nation experienced eerily similar social and economic decay in the midst of unprecedented oil revenue. To explain the phenomena, the Resource Curse Theory and later "rentier state" theories believe that "the exploitation of bountiful resources in a state with weak democratic institutions is likely to produce irreversible perverse outcomes" (p. 3). Others have drawn direct correlations between the wealth of natural resources and civil war. Martinez considers both explanations to be overly simplistic, and as Martinez's initial question lingers, readers will see that the given theories only momentarily satisfies a serious thinker. We begin to ask ourselves, how truly can being in possession of such a rich resource spell decline for a nation? Martinez unveils a sophisticated, yet lucid argument for the incredible violence and devastation in Algeria, Iraq, and Libya claiming it to be a random intersecting of unique circumstances—a sort of perfect storm—involving revolution, weak democratic mechanisms, and sudden oil prosperity. No stranger to the political dynamics of Middle East petro-regimes, Martinez once again demonstrates his mastery of Arab oil and its socioeconomic nuances by posing the most comprehensive analysis to date on the irony of oil wealth and national decay.

First and foremost, "there is no curse," Martinez proclaims (p. 9). In fact, not only is there no curse, oil was merely a part of larger socioeconomic patterns. To blame oil or even consider the natural resource to be the primary culprit of each nation's economic degradation is far too narrow a position, Martinez suggests. The impact of oil revenue must be understood under the umbrella of nationalism and authoritarianism. Sudden wealth strengthened the nationalist cause and exacerbated oppressive policies, which gradually imbued leaders with a sense of invincibility. Martinez refers to it as "historical meeting" between a sharp rise in oil prices in 1973 and a state takeover by revolutionaries with a penchant for political authoritarianism (p. 8). For the three countries in question, the sudden economic boon helped sustain and then reinforce the power of each regime.

Martinez's work underscores major historical continuities associated with issues of power and leadership. Much like many nationalist and socialist revolutionaries across history, leaders in Algeria, Iraq, and Libya first inspired loyalty and then enforced it. But unlike other movements in history, each took control at a time of untold riches. Tremendous wealth funneled into each nation helping to centralize and consolidate state power. As expected, each regime's authority grew more absolute. Here Martinez distinguishes himself from other scholars by making a subtle, but nonetheless important observation: without the oil rent, they (nationalist leaders in Algeria, Iraq, and Libya) would likely have conducted themselves with "measured authoritarianism restrained by limited resources" like leaders in Morocco, Tunisia, and Egypt (p. 9). However, capturing power around the 1973 oil boon produced "a particularly toxic political alchemy between authoritarian regimes with a destructive potential and financial abundance" (p. 9). Martinez stresses, however, that these revolutionary governments were ill-equipped to handle the abundance—an important nuance in the narrative of oil wealth and national decline.

In the absence of a manager, each state turned to its largest and most organized section to manage the influx, security. Martinez writes that the security apparatus, the regime's enforcement arm, benefited from positions of oversight and a vicious cycle ensued. Financial abundance enlarged the security organizations and expanded the subsequent enforcement of regime standards. Over time, these governments felt increasingly impervious to insurrection, more certain in their power, and further entrenched in their positions.

Martinez's interpretation of power and oil revenue offers new perspectives on the evolution of petro-regimes in the Middle East and, as he states, should force us to ask more thoughtful questions beyond those merely curious about the irony of wealth and domestic decay. What are the political mechanisms that have made oil revenue "the exclusive property of revolutionary regimes" (p. 10)? Moreover, how can we explain the "astonishing similarity" between each country's trajectory (p. 10)? To answer these questions, Martinez segments his work into seven separate chapters to include an introduction and a conclusion. Chapter 1 is purely context, designed to assist readers with a fuller understanding of the Arab perspective immediately before the 1973 oil boon. In it, Martinez makes two important points worth noting: first, the three formerly colonized nations were determined to take control of their natural resources as a means of resisting new forms of imperialism. Martinez argues that controlling oil satisfied each nation's "feelings of revenge" (p. 14). Second, these petro-regimes envisioned oil to be "a weapon of development" (p. 15). Algerian socialists, the Iraqi Baa'th Party, and the Revolutionary Command Council in Libya all championed social change through forms of modernization that were to be compatible with Islam and financed by oil. However, since the project's success hinged on the people's complete loyalty to the revolutionary party, Martinez claims, each state quickly vilified individualism and theories on democratic representation. The party secured "monopoly over people's representation as well as the exclusive control of the state" (p. 34).

With a solid foundation in place, Martinez unpacks his thesis in Chapters 2 and 3 by describing how and why rich petro-regimes turned authoritarian and simply managed their respective state's demise. Martinez posits that newly minted governments used nationalized oil revenue to execute an array of overly ambitious modernization and international projects based on the belief that "oil wealth was unlimited and the rise in oil prices was exponential" (p. 41). Unfortunately, abundant finances exacerbated the worst qualities of leadership in Algeria, Iraq, and Libya. Oil wealth almost immediately made rulers "unreceptive to the demands of societies," even while human development indicators, such as literacy, life expectancy, and morality rate, all saw marked improvement (p. 41). What emerged came to be a fragile combination of social uplift and massive political repression. By 1986, oil crisis and international sanctions caused the fragile balance to shatter and plunged each country into a crisis of political despotism, far worse than before. Martinez claims this began an era of "mafia regimes" (p. 86). To summarize, from 1986 to 2003 economic instability and social upheaval threatened each regime's authority, and they (the mafia state) reacted swiftly by consolidating power along tribal lines and siphoning off billions in capital from within their otherwise bankrupt countries. Martinez notes that Iraq, in particular, experienced the deepest devastation due to the Baath party's "destructive potential to perfection" (p. 100).

Then the unexpected happened; oil revenue once again skyrocketed in 2004. After leading readers through the details of mafia politics, Martinez concludes on a contemporary note arguing that past failures did little to change authoritarian practices. Forward looking in Chapters 4 and 5, Martinez observes that Europe's twenty-first century energy investment has once again increased revenue for Algeria and Libya, but does not appear to be altering, into democratic forms, ever-present institutional inefficiencies, and government patronage. On the other hand, the United States' invasion of Iraq has at least equipped the country for managing wealth and promoted the transition to representative government.

Readers are left to wonder whether each country will be able to handle the new "financial bonanza" (p. 135). However, one thing is certain. Martinez's superb and succinct explanation clarifies the otherwise puzzling questions surrounding the durability of each regime and erases any notion of a mysterious force, both unexplainable and unstoppable, that causes oil-laden nations to resort to authoritarian practices. Typically perplexing topics such as this are susceptible to critique, but Martinez's argument is sound and his evidence is solid. Therefore, Martinez has given scholars a tremendous gift. He has offered a new perspective on Arab petro-regimes that provides scholars a new lens through which to examine concepts of political power in the Middle East. Broader still, his work should also be considered applicable to other places where oil reigns supreme outside the Arab World. In sum, the potential is enormous. **DAG**

EGYPT

❁

Jessica Barnes. *Cultivating the Nile: The Everyday Politics of Water in Egypt.*
Durham, NC: Duke University Press, 2014. 230 pp. $70.92. ISBN: 9780822-
357414. Pbk: $19.80. ISBN: 978-0822357568. Ebk: 4364 KB. $15.87.

In June 1990, Egyptian Minister of State for Foreign Affairs and soon-to-be U.N.
Secretary General Boutros Boutros Ghali inaugurated a Global Water Summit Initiative at the Intercontinental Hotel Semiramis, Tahrir Square, Cairo—just meters
from the banks of the Nile. In attendance were representatives from every country
in Africa except the two pariahs of the day: Libya and South Africa. Speaking before this group he and Dr. Joyce R. Starr (who was my boss at the time), outlined
a future for both Sub-Saharan Africa as well as North Africa that emphasized one
basic theme—unless the riparians of rivers such as the Congo, the Niger, the Zam-
bezi—and most especially—the Nile worked cooperatively in the coming days to
manage, share, and allocate their resources more efficiently and effectively, a rising
population and increased demand would surely lead to fierce competition—if not
outright conflict—over clean and plentiful water.

A quarter of a century later, Jessica Barnes has written a monograph which, for all
intents and purposes, echoes this theme. Her perspective, however, is less grandiose
in scope; while our work in the 1990s was oriented toward a more regional if not
global outlook, Barnes's work is concentrated more on the political aspects of water
resource management at the national and indeed, local levels.

The book's main arguments then are relatively straightforward. Barnes contends
that water (in this case, Egypt's Nile) is *made* by a number of human actors who

are interacting at a number of levels and in a number of ways which, at times compliment, and at other times contradict each other's goals and interests. Water is not—she wishes to emphasize—a natural and existing entity but rather, ebbs, flows, deluges, and retreats, all due to the actions and behaviors of human intercession. As such, water is not merely a resource, but a constructed entity which—depending upon who has it, who does not, who wants it, who needs it, and above all, who controls it—wields significant power. From Barnes's perspective, there is nothing "natural" about this natural resource.

The book takes the reader through the various steps and stages of resource management, distribution, and allocation. While local agricultural users are the primary subjects of the study, it is clear too that as Egypt's only lifeline, the Nile is essential to cash-crop production (most especially cotton), industry, the raising of livestock, sewerage, and a host of other competing uses (p. 49).

Indeed, this is where Barnes's argument is particularly strong, with relevance which surpasses the issue of water resource management alone. Through her analysis of this complex system of local, national, and global users, as well as funders and managers, Barnes is able to document the degree to which system breakdown is endemic when competing interests, communication gaps, inefficiencies, and cultural clashes all conflate.

Similarly, her discussion of the politics of dams (pp. 156-158) is particularly compelling. Like similar cases on the Ganges and elsewhere, the building of the Aswan High Dam offers the reader a well-developed case for how damming as a primary water-resource management tool and its related objectives of electrification, resettlement, and nation-building converge, often have deleterious results.

In short, Barnes offers some interesting insights complete with numerous attending charts filled with statistics which further solidify her arguments. And yet, there are a few concerns here which I wish to note. First, some mention of population growth, not to mention water-borne disease—a scourge throughout Upper Egyptian society—surely would have been in order as a part of the story here, but these areas are not covered to any degree.

Second and perhaps more confounding is the *way* that Barnes tells her story. The writing of this monograph is often informal, anecdotal, and presented in a style which I found rather distracting. I am not at all opposed to the occasional use of first person and yet, much of the text is written in a personal narrative form which, from my perspective at least, contributed little to my knowledge of the specific subject at hand.

More to the point, Barnes uses a writing style through which she repeatedly informs the reader of what she is "going to do," much like the style of a proposal. Initially I took no issue, as this is a useful technique early on, laying out a roadmap for the reader to help guide him or her through the text. But after a while I felt as if I were watching a local news cast where a refrain of "Coming up next!" seemed to infiltrate the text. Indeed, had there been less of this, I cannot help but feel that, in truth, the book would have been considerably shorter.

That being said, Barnes has written an interesting text worthy of consideration for any scholar presently thinking about the relationship between population, resource scarcity, and future global conflict, especially in an era of changing climactic conditions. While this text does not directly address these relationships, it does provide one piece—and a significant one at that—of this increasingly significant (and dare I say fluid?) dynamic. **SD**

Karin van Nieuwkerk. *Performing Piety: Singers and Actors in Egypt's Islamic Revival.* Austin, TX: University of Texas Press, 2013. 320 pp. $60.00. ISBN: 978-0292745865. Ebk: $48.00. 4061 KB.

This book addresses the impassioned religious debate and cultural politics in contemporary Egypt, particularly during the era of Hosni Mubarak. Through focusing on retired and repentant celebrities, the book provides a general description of the development of Islamic movements in Egypt showing not only the influence of Islamic activism that developed in the 1980s, but also the impact of pious stars on the everyday practices of large Egyptian audiences.

The literature of the Muslim piety movement in Egypt is rich. However, the unique feature of van Nieuwkerk's work is that it assesses the transformation of Islamist movements through the lens of performing arts. Performing art is portrayed here as a form of religious and political activism. Further, the book proposes that the pious lifestyles of repentant celebrities in Egypt have become an accepted alternative to Western and secular styles of living.

The study is contingent on rich and diverse sources including, for example, ethnography, media, literature reviews, autobiographies of stars, and local print material, published mostly in Arabic. The author conducts interviews with mostly female performers, intellectuals, and critics. The interviews with artists make the book enjoyable and accessible to nonspecialist readers. Despite the rich and fresh material, however, the book is basically a historical and descriptive account that does not offer new theoretical insights to help understand the complicated phenomenon being addressed.

The author divides the book into three parts and tackles three chronological decades in the development of the phenomenon of performing piety—the 1980s, 1990s, and 2000s. To begin, the author discusses the narratives of the celebrities who retired in the 1980s with special focus on the connection of the stars with the piety movement that resulted in the spread of "pietization" among Egyptian audiences. Repentant stars publicly rejected and denounced disgraceful behaviors such as dancing, unveiling or immorally exposed acting, and inappropriate singing. The book highlights the idea that women and minorities became involved in the fields of political and religious discourse. Through the venue of Islamic salons within which religious learning, *da'wah* and charitable deeds were facilitated, veiled and repentant celebrities had the opportunity to Islamize their lifestyles.

The book also shows how, in the 1990s, Islamists and secularists in the politically divided country were engaged in the public sphere debating Islam, art, and gender. Islamist authors challenged and opposed the secular nationalist discourse by formulating their own conservative Islamist ideology. The retired and veiled artists became involved in the public zone disturbing the ruling regime and the secular field of art. Due to the rising power of various forms of Islamic movements, the state launched a heavy assault on all forms of Islamists without differentiating between militants, extremists or terrorists, and moderate reformists. Further, the state attempted to generate its own form of Islam by allowing secular players in the cultural domain to act against Islamism as well as by encouraging conservative shaikhs of al-Azhar to attack the secular cultural players.

Van Nieuwkerk observed that the debates of the repentant celebrities highlighted the intense use of media. And because of the spread of new communication technologies such as cassettes, video, satellite TV, and the Internet, the public sphere developed beyond the control of the central government. For example, while the Islamist version of Islam was countered and challenged by official or government media, it received tremendous supported from other media.

The book further discusses the emergence of Islamic esthetics in the 2000s as represented in the production of pious performances known as the Islamist project of *art with a mission*. The author points out that the gendered character of performing piety and the critical role of the body were central issues in the development of Islamic esthetics. In addition to religious soaps, talk shows and historical plays about the glorious period of Islam, this period also witnessed the emergence of religious entertainment and leisure in various forms, including religious songs, and Islamic weddings performed by religious wedding bands. These new forms of Islamic art performance developed particular ethics and esthetics that depicted such activities as purposeful art. Likewise, the soaps presented a constructive discourse of Islamic values promoting religious ethics and appropriate family virtues. Many veiled stars produced and participated in religious soaps during Islamic occasions, such as the holy month of Ramadan disseminating social and religious values. The author maintains that mainstream Islamist actors aim at Islamizing art, popular culture, and the public zone.

The author makes a useful distinction between conventional or classical and new forms of religious media. For example, the new religious media focuses on participation and personal piety through the context of mixed-gender audiences in the studio setting instead of discussing Islamic law and jurisprudence in a formal gender-segregated environment of the mosque.

The book does not provide a list of figures and pictures at the beginning of the manuscript that would make it easy for the reader to locate particular images within the text. The author also fails to mention her article entitled, "From Repentance to Pious Performance" (2007 in *ISIM Review*, *20*, 54-55. See also, https://openaccess.leidenuniv.nl/bitstream/handle/1887/17188/ISIM_20_From_Repentance_to_Pious_Performance.pdf?sequence=1). This particular article has two pictures that are included in the book (6.1, p. 161 and 6.2, p. 171) without reference to the original work.

Toward the end of the study, the author mentions that she visited Egypt in December 2011 (10 months after the revolution of January 25, 2011). She interviewed a media specialist focusing on his career as reflecting his artistic development through the three periods of political development discussed in the book. It would have been fruitful if the book had examined more clearly the impact of the phenomenon of performing piety on the 2011 revolution and the rise of the Islamists, particularly the Muslim Brotherhood when one of its members was elected president in the country's first democratic election. Nevertheless, this does not negate the value of the book as an invaluable contribution to the anthropology of performing piety, in general, and the study of Islamic revival and Muslim piety movement in Egypt, in particular. **ESEA**

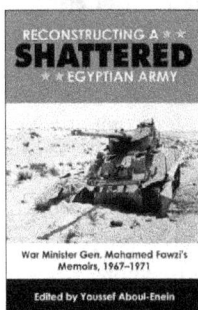

Youssef H. Aboul-Enein, Ed. *Reconstructing a Shattered Egyptian Army: War Minister Gen. Mohamed Fawzi's Memoirs, 1967–1971.* Annapolis, MD: Naval Institute Press, 2014. 320 pp. $64.95. ISBN 978-1612514604. Ebk: $43.00. 1975 KB.

On June 6, 1967, Egyptian forces received orders from Abdel Hakim Amer to withdraw from Sinai. Amer was the head of the armed forces and a close colleague of Egypt's President Gamal Abdel Nasser. The day before, Israel had launched a surprise attack on Egypt and Syria, with the intention of using surprise to overturn the Arab countries' military might. But the Israelis never counted on the delusion, corruption, and incompetence that shot through the Egyptian ranks as the battle unfolded.

In *Reconstructing a Shattered Egyptian Army ...*, U.S. Navy Medical Corps commander Youssef H. Aboul-Enein tries to examine the memoirs of the key Egyptian figure tasked with picking up the pieces of 1967. General Mohamed Fawzi's memoirs are a rare insight into the functioning of an Arab military regime. After the end of the colonial period in the Middle East, almost all of the Arab regimes in the region became dictatorships; and some were racked by coups. In the 1950s, a series of military officer regimes—inspired by Arab nationalism—came to power. The most prominent of these was Nasser's. Often these regimes have remained opaque; and even the memoirs that are translated into English or do exist, are full of boasting that have little connection to reality.

By contrast, Fawzi's memoirs are candid and critical. A former commander of the war college in Egypt, he became disillusioned with Egyptian military failures in places such as Yemen, where Nasser had sent the army in the 1960s to prop up a fellow Arab nationalist regime. "Unified plans against Israel were on paper only," he writes (p. 24). More troubling: "... only 9 percent of personnel within the army had high school diplomas" (p. 30). Illiteracy was rampant in the army, which was drawn from conscripts in a country that was still largely rural. In cases where reserve units were called up, sometimes only 70% would report for duty.

This book is an interesting combination of edited volume, memoirs and analysis. Ostensibly it is an edited volume because each chapter includes an introduction by experts such as George Mitroka, director of the Denial and Deception Studies Program at the National Intelligence University. But it isn't clear why these short introductions to each chapter are necessary, or what they add to the text. Most of them include a sentence like "I look forward to the discussion this series will generate... [and hope] America's military classrooms will choose to use this series" (p. 47). Aboul-Enein writes most of the text himself with some block quotes from Fawzi. For instance, he allows Fawzi himself to tell the story of the incompetence involved in moving military units before the 1967 war. "The 14th infantry Division moved from Cairo to Jebel Libni on May 18, and when they began to set up the perimeter, the entire division was moved again" (p. 31). This constant movement led to equipment delays and many units not being prepared to fight Israel.

The disaster of 1967 was clear in the amount of equipment abandoned in Sinai. Hundreds of tanks were simply left in the desert. Some 85% of the Air Force's planes were lost, and 85% of the armored equipment. More than 9,000 men were reported missing. After the disaster there was a challenge to Nasser's authority, which ended with the suicide of Amer. By June 9th, Fawzi realized that the army would have to be reconstructed "starting from zero" (p. 66).

The reader is left with an assumption that Fawzi was a key player in most of the reconstruction of the Egyptian army, without the author's making clear in which efforts he was specifically involved. As Egyptian war minister from 1967 to 1971, it is assumed he played a major role, alongside Soviet military advisors, in rebuilding the forces. Several key elements of this reconstruction are highlighted. For instance, 1.5 million people had to be evacuated from the Suez Canal Zone, and bases made ready for the "war of attrition" against Israel (p. 89).

The concept of attrition was to use Egypt's large resources and Soviet support to slowly bleed the Israelis. Israel was good at lightning warfare, but unprepared for sustaining losses. Fawzi and his commanders began to probe the Israeli defenses along the Canal. They sunk an Israeli ship, the *Eilat* with an anti-ship missile. "Egypt was provided the latest weaponry even before many of the Warsaw Pact nations" (p. 98). The U.S.S.R., with its Soviet arms, saw the war with Israel as one of pride, since the Israelis were using the latest American equipment. They wanted to test their SAM anti-aircraft systems and other weapons. Hundreds of Egyptian pilots were trained; and Ilyushin-28 bombers were introduced. Compared with the humiliating destruction of the Egyptian Air Force in 1967, by September of 1969 the Egyptians were able to launch massive 100 jet sorties into Sinai to take on the Israelis. Fawzi played a personal role; he "took great interest in Israeli radar and air defense systems that provided early warning of mass Egyptian MiG formations" (p. 126).

The author concludes that the efforts of Fawzi were part of a major reordering after 1967. The war drove many to reconsider Arab nationalism and embrace Islamism as an answer. He notes that this book can help American policymakers understand the region "and ourselves" (p. 171). He remarks that the United States must confront a balkanized region that is becoming more chaotic. But what lessons does Fawzi give? He was an Egyptian general who tried to apply modern military science and logic, including civilian control of the military. He tried to reduce corruption and introduce discipline. But are there modern-day examples of Fawzis in the Middle East? The problem is that this book takes an exceptional military figure without posing the question of whether reformers like this have prominence today. Fawzi was self-critical and honest about his country's weaknesses and sought to remedy them. Are there memoirs being published like this today in the Middle East, which call for major reforms along modern scientific lines? That is a question left unanswered in this slim and well-written volume that sheds light on an important topic. **SJF**

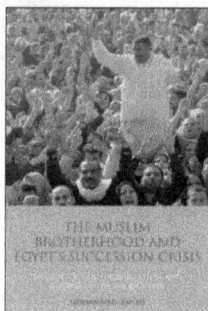

Mohammad Zahid. *The Muslim Brotherhood and Egypt's Succession Crisis: The Politics of Liberalisation and Reform in the Middle East.* New York NY: I. B. Tauris, 2010. 224 pp. $85.00. ISBN: 1845119797. Pbk: $28.00. ISBN: 978-178076217.

Mohammed Zahid's *The Muslim Brotherhood and Egypt's Succession Crisis* focuses on the economic and political reform process in Egypt in the last few decades and examines the impact of this reform process on power dynamics. Although the book has three major themes—the economic and political reform process based on neo-liberalization in Egypt, the increasing power of the Muslim Brotherhood (MB), and the rise of Gamal Mubarak in the political life of Egypt—Zahid briefly deals with a large number of theoretical and popular issues, such as the lack of democracy in the Middle East, the relationship between economic and political liberalization, civil society in the Middle East, Western intervention, "9/11," etc., in order to support his ideas in this short book.

Zahid firstly examines the neo-liberalization process of Egypt and its usual results, such as the increase in unemployment rates, the decrease in social policies and state subsidies, and the extent of poverty. Zahid then argues that these developments lead to the emergence of NGOs providing some basic services due the decline of the state's social policies. At this point, Zahid takes into account the MB and shows how the MB uses the opportunities created by the economic and political reform process in order to challenge the Mubarak regime within civil society and to delegitimize it in the eyes of people. Therefore, Zahid focuses on the MB's syndical activities as an "art of politics" and the mobilization of the middle class through the politicization of syndicates.

Zahid believes that the adaptation of the MB into new developments, such as participation in syndicates and parliamentary elections, is the result of the emergence of a new pragmatic generation within the MB in the late 1970s and early 1980s. He examines the transformation of the MB from its beginning to recent times, and tries to show how the MB became a political movement at the hands of a new pragmatic generation, although initially, it was a religious movement aiming to increase spiritual piety.

Zahid's book can be useful in order to construct background knowledge about the emergence of Egypt's Arab Spring, the collapse of the Mubarek regime, and the rise of the MB; however, it is going to be disappointing to expect rigorous and advanced research because of the book's rudimentary approach to a large number of important issues. **FV**

GULF STATES

✿

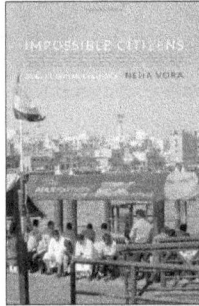

Neha Vora. *Impossible Citizens: Dubai's Indian Diaspora*. Durham, NC: Duke University Press, 2013. 245 pp. $24.95. ISBN: 978-0822353935.

Impossible Citizens is a very welcome addition to the growing body of anthropological literature on the Arabian Gulf and, particularly, the millions of foreign migrants who work there. Vora's ethnography of Indians in Dubai is detailed and quite intimate, for, as she notes, Dubai is her second home. Her access to businesses, families and, indeed, the areas of "old Dubai" was aided by the fact that she speaks Hindi. Vora carefully examines several pertinent questions throughout the book such as diaspora, democracy—and, to me, the most fascinating—citizenship. What does citizenship mean in Dubai? As she points out, following Longva, to be a citizen of a Gulf country usually means that one is a part of the "ethnocracy" that is made of tribally connected (if only on paper), Arabian Gulf Muslims with a few, very few, notable exceptions. Then, since the Indians of Dubai, the NRI (nonresident Indian population) recognize that they can never be a part of that class of people, "impossible citizens" takes on a poignant trope. Citizens they may never be, but economic actors they are and *sine qua non* in the story of Dubai's success. *Impossible Citizens* also underscores the disjunction between the official stance on "temporary foreign workers" and the reality of long-term foreign residents who have worked for multiple contracts, often various sponsors, and have in many cases, invested time, creativity, entrepreneurial energy, and money in ventures and businesses. This is a refreshing perspective into the "other" migrants who populate the Gulf, as it has commonly been the unskilled, lower class laborers who are confined to labor camps on the outskirts of the city, and whose conditions have drawn attention and outrage.

Dubai is a bit of a lightning rod, and is often mistakenly portrayed as the UAE *in minima forma*. Vora leans dangerously toward that with shifting levels of analysis that imply that what happens in Dubai happens everywhere; and that is decidedly not the case. Each of the seven emirates is a sovereign state whose rulers can—and do—make *Amiri Decrees* that have jurisdiction only within that particular emirate. Federal laws theoretically outweigh such local rules, but in practice that is not always the case and hence, the "climate" of doing business in Dubai is very different from that of Abu Dhabi, Ras al Khaimah, Ajman, Fujairah, and Um al Quwain. The populations—both of citizen and migrant—are very different in each emirate as well and the economic integration of the Indian population in Dubai is seen by most Emiratis as a "uniquely Dubai" circumstance not dissimilar from the Ajami, originally Persian population there. In fact, Emiratis in Abu Dhabi jokingly claim that to "find out what is going on in Dubai you have to ask an Indian or an Iranian—just not an Emirati." The socioeconomic histories of each of the emirates is quite distinct, especially those of Abu Dhabi and Dubai, and so it is necessary—and much safer—to consider them separately and not extrapolate one from the other.

Vora's examination of Dubai and her theoretical perspective, neo liberalism, extends far beyond the earlier work by Kanna (2011) and Ali (2010). However, to what extent Vora's Indian migrants consider themselves to be economic actors in a neo-liberal paradise is questionable and, like many anthropologists, I rebel against the heavy application of theoretical perspective, especially when it is used to reframe an interlocutor's comments. The strategies and skills required to negotiate the shifting alliances, changing priorities, vacillating sponsors, and Dubai's lately turbulent economy probably have much more to do with the indispensability of a merchant under-class than neo-liberal greed and its supporting ideology. When Vora describes the situation for Indians in Dubai as "an inconvenience to be tolerated for the moment," she has touched upon a very raw nerve because it is becoming increasingly evident that "the moment" now stretches far into the future as Dubai cannot be maintained—much less enlarged for Expo 2020—without the Indian and other foreign populations.

See also Ali, S. 2010. *Dubai: Gilded Cage*. First Edition. New Haven, CT: Yale University Press, and Kanna, A. (2011). *Dubai: The City as Corporation*. Minneapolis, MN: University of Minnesota Press. **JBR**

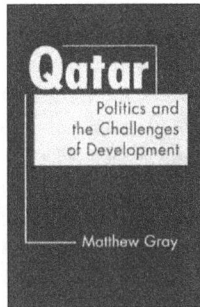

Matthew Gray. *Qatar Politics and the Challenges of Development.* **Boulder, CO: Lynne Rienner, 2013. 271 pp. $65.95. ISBN: 978-1588269287.**

The growing interest in writing about Qatar has increased in the last decade. This interest has come after the emerging role of Qatar as a serious mediator in many conflicts all over the globe. *Qatar Politics and the Challenges of Development* focuses on the developments that took place after 1995, when Shiekh Hamad bin Khalifa Al Thani seized power from his father. This book is one of the latest publications which analyzes the challenges of development in Qatar from the political economy perspective, and addresses the questions of "where Qatar came from and what has changed, or not, and why; [and] the centrality of oil and gas to the political economy" (p. 3).

The book comprises eight chapters. Chapter 1, "The Transformation of Qatar" sets the tone of the topic under investigation. This chapter also presents the theoretical framework and the argument of the book. The author describes Qatar as not being a typical "rentier State" and suggests that Qatar's economy, the state-society relations, and the international political role have shifted Qatar to be a "late rentier state." Gray has presented detailed assessments of the publications which have reported on Qatar in recent years, which offer insight into the different observations and opinions concerning Qatar's developments. Chapters 2–4 following the introduction are more concerned with the economic history of Qatar. The author acknowledges that "History is ... prologue to the present," and without understanding the dynamics that shaped the Qatari economy in the past, it is hard to identify the changes, if any, of the new dynamics.

Chapter 2, "The Historical Context" focuses on the rise of the al-Thani Family, the political economy after discovering oil in 1938, Qatar under Khalifa, 1972–95, and the developments which occurred after Hamad Bin Khalif seized power from his father in 1995. The chapter offers the reader a comprehensive background about the history of Qatar since 1766, with the focus on the developments that took place prior to 1995.

Chapter 3, "The Political Order" presents a detailed analysis of Qatar's energy-driven economy, the Royal Family, state mechanism and state-owned firms, the business families, tribes, social changes, and the international business actors. This chapter continues what was begun in the previous chapter, but with more focus on the economy, and the role of the state in the economic sector. It also focuses on the role of the energy sector in the Qatari economy.

Chapter 4, "Oil, Gas and Rent" covers Qatar's energy resources and political economy, the scope and the future of the oil sector, the centrality of gas, the role of other sectors, and the place of energy. The author carries on the discussion which began in the second and third chapters; however, in this chapter there is more focus on the oil and gas sectors, with more analysis concerning the contribution of those two sectors in Qatar economy.

Chapters 5–8 cover the period after 1995, and present a comprehensive analytical view of the ideas and initiatives which have appeared within the last 18 years. Chapter 5, "Energy-Driven Economic Diversification" includes the 2013 Qatar National Vision, the liberalization of economic and business reform, the direct beneficiaries of the rent, the education developments, Qatar Airways and the promotion of Islamic finance. The author assesses Qatar's economic steps to diversify its economy.

In Chapter 6, "The Strategy of National Branding," the author discusses the elements that contribute to the "Planned Branding Process." Those elements include establishing the Al Jazeera Media network, hosting major sport events, organizing major cultural events, and promoting tourism and museum industry. The author indicates that the branding strategy has economic aims, which supports his earlier argument that Qatar has moved from being a "rentier state" toward a "late rentier."

Chapter 7, "Qatar in the International Arena" covers Qatar's political role by focusing on the country's relations network, especially the relations of Qatar with countries such as the United States, Iran, Israel, China, and emerging Asian states. This chapter also discusses Qatar's regional security issues and the position of Doha toward Arab Spring. Gray argues that Qatar, by building its own network of foreign relations and playing a controversial role, is seeking image building globally, and gaining economic security and business opportunities.

Chapter 8, "Challenges for the Future" aims to identify the challenges that face Qatar's economic developments and the challenges ahead. Those challenges can be categorized into the following: first, economic challenges such as the global economic crisis; second, socioeconomic challenges such as the problem with labor market and promoting "Qatarization," the question of Qatari culture and identity and the future role for women and youth; and third, the political challenges where the author discusses the political situation after the Arab Spring, and asks the question of whether democratization is inevitable. The question of whether Qatar can be considered as a model of development is in the last chapter of the book; yet, it invites more discussion concerning the question: is Qatar a model of development?

The book is well written and well organized. The structure of the book reflects the serious and comprehensive research done by the author. It has presented new views on Qatar's development and challenges. However, the book opens the door for more research and views on how contemporary Qatar, "as one of the vibrant states in Middle East" will handle the ongoing challenges. **MZ**

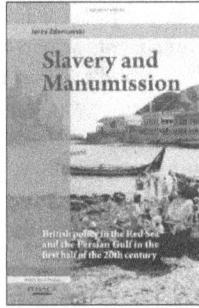

Jerzy Zdanowski. *Slavery and Manumission: British Policy in the Red Sea and Persian Gulf in the First Half of the Twentieth Century.* **Reading, UK: Ithaca Press, 2013. $74.95. ISBN: 978-0863724381. Ebk: $8.99. 1318 KB.**

Jerzy Zdanowski's *Slavery and Manumission: British Policy in the Red Sea and the Persian Gulf in the First Half of the Twentieth Century* contributes to the growing body of literature published since 2000 concerning the nature of slavery in the Middle East and Africa. This literature includes Kevin Grant's *A Civilized Slavery: Britain and the New Slaveries in Africa, 1884–1926* (Rutledge, 2004), Kenneth Morgan's *Slavery and the British Empire: From Africa to America* (Oxford, 2008) and *The Slave Trade and the Origins of International Human Rights* (Oxford, 2012) by Jenny S. Martinez. The above titles, though, are fairly broad in their focus, choosing to examine slavery from a macro-level. In contrast, Zdanowski's examination of British policy toward slavery around the Arabian Peninsula is very much one of a micro-level analysis.

Zdanowski presents the reader with a work that is thoroughly researched. An analysis of his bibliography indicates his mastery of both primary and secondary material. This detailed analysis allows Zdanowski to present the individual stories of both the British civil servants involved in the policy of manumission and the various slaves that the policy was attempting to benefit. As he states in the preface: "The book is on slavery, manumission and British politics in the Red Sea and Persian Gulf in the first half of the twentieth century. It presents these problems at the level of regional and international politics but also at the level of the everyday life of the slaves and the everyday work of British officials involved in the affairs of the region" (p. xxix).

This is Zdanowski's thesis and main strength. His work examines the role of various British agents, their relationships with various slave dealers and the efforts undertaken by specific representatives of the Crown to grant manumission. Zdanowski paints the canvas of his story with a fine brush. The struggle against slavery is examined is as government policy, along the Persian Gulf and in the Red Sea region. The reader is also provided with an overview of the status of slavery within the Arabian Peninsula at the dawn of the twentieth century.

British policy was to oppose slavery in all of its manifestations. The manumission of all slaves was the long term goal of the Crown. Unfortunately, slavery had a long history within Islam. The *Qur'an* and reliable Hadith attributed to the Prophet Muhammad both permit slavery but also give honor to the owners that freed their slaves. Unlike the *Uncle Tom's Cabin* image of slavery in the West, the institution was very complicated in the Muslim world. Yes, some slaves were little more than chattel, but many occupied trusted positions within the household of their owner. Thus, the British rarely interfered with domestic slavery. Instead, they focused upon the slave trade and freeing those slaves that were subject to verifiable mistreatment and deprivation.

Along the Persian Gulf, slavery was a fundamental component of the pearl diving business. Slaves caught up in the pearl business might come from Africa, Persia, or British India. In the case of the latter, manumission was easily obtained, but for others the situation proved more complicated.

Although most pearl divers were slaves in the Western since of the term, many were also what one might think of as indebted or indentured servants. Their status as a slave came, not from being born into the institution of slavery, but rather being deeply in debt. As noted:

> The African population, mainly slaves, was engaged chiefly in the pearl diving industry and was indebted. An agreement had been in force since 1879, concluded by the sheikhs of the Trucial Oman, regarding the treatment of indebted divers absconding from one principality to another to evade debt. (p. 259)

Followed by:

> The main point was to determine whether a refugee Negro [Zdanowski's term] was really a slave or just a fugitive from justice or debt. This had to be established properly *before* a certificate was granted (and not afterwards). (p. 260)

Thus, slaves that were simply indebted were not granted a manumission certificate. In contrast, maltreatment, when proven, resulted in freedom for the slaves in the Persian Gulf.

Slavery was commonplace within the Red Sea region. Its existence was complicated due to several factors. First, many slaves were brought from the Sudan into the Arabian Peninsula through Jeddah. As the Sudan had been a British protectorate since the 1880s, individuals taken from that country could obtain a certificate of manumission from the British agent in Jeddah. This rapid action by the British contrasted with the generally slow response of the Sudanese government and the latter's policy that "all slavery in the Sudan was to end in due course" (p. 172).

A second source of slaves in the Red Sea environ was Ethiopia (referred to as

Abyssinia by Zdanowski). Raiding parties would capture people from Abyssinia, Eritrea, and Somalia and bring them either to Yemen or Jeddah for sale. Once they were landed in Arabia, the captives were then mixed with those from the Sudan to be sold in the interior of Arabia, especially in the Najd. Adding to this illegal trade were individuals kidnapped during the Hajj, which was the third source of slaves. The large influx in individuals into Jeddah during the Holy Pilgrimage was simply too tempting for slave dealers to ignore. Zdanowski notes:

The role of the pilgrimage in buying and selling slaves, especially children, was stressed many times in reports of the British Consuls at Jeddah. In 1925, a report was prepared by Consul Bullard, who explained that the stock of slaves in the Hijaz was very large... mainly from Abyssinia, but partly by the enslavement of Africans who came or where brought to the Hijaz on pilgrimage. It was not uncommon for a caravan of Nigerians or Sudanese travelling to or from Medina on foot to be raided by Bedouin...." (pp. 205-206)

Following his successful conquest of the Hejaz, Ibn Saud did sign the Treaty of Jeddah in 1927 with Great Britain. In Article 7, the king (Ibn Saud) "undertook to cooperate by all the means at his disposal with the British Government in suppression of the slave trade" (p. 217). This eventually made slavery and the slave trade unappealing in Jeddah, but the slavers simply moved their illegal activity to more remote areas of the coast. In the interior of Arabia, especially in the Najd among Ibn Saud's most fanatical Wahhabi followers, the suppression the slave trade and manumission of slaves was little more than an illusion.

One leaves Zdanowski's work informed, but also deeply disappointed, not in the level of research and presentation, but the fact that by 1950, even though the slave trade had all but vanished, slavery still was commonplace in the Arabian Peninsula. For, as Zdanowski notes, [the] "extinction of slavery as such was the secondary goal of British engagement in the region, although this goal was not achieved in the time under discussion" (pp. 321-322).

The conclusion that Zdanowski presents will provide the reader with an important body of information about both British policy and domestic politics in the Arabian Peninsula concerning slavery and the slave trade. This reviewer recommends the work for library adoption. **LR**

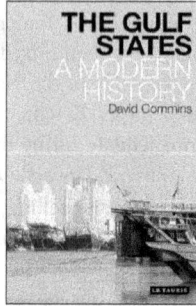

David Commins. *The Gulf States: A Modern History.* **London, UK: I. B. Tauris, 2012. 318 pp. $69.50. ISBN: 978-1848852785.**

The first image of the Gulf that flashes into the minds of nonspecialists is one of conflict. From the unanticipated (by the West) assertion of sovereignty by members of OPEC to the equally unanticipated Iranian revolution, and then the bloody destruction wreaked by three Gulf wars, conflict is an important dimension of the story of this region. Even so, it is far from the only one. Absent from the mental maps of most scholars of the "third wave" of democratization, liberalization of the economies and societies of the Gulf monarchies is still a virtually untold story (Tétreault 2006). This is too bad, too, because the lack of interest in and appreciation of the distance traveled along that dimension is a key factor in the ease with which Gulf monarchs have been able for the past several years to reverse significant elements of the progress made since the early 1990s. We are by no means back to the future yet but, as the harrowing situation in Bahrain reflects, such an eventuality is far from imaginary.

Ignorance of the Gulf is surprising in light of the region's critical importance as a nexus of trade, investment, and involvement in global policy. Indeed, when we think "globalization," the Gulf should be at or near the top of the list of actors. From the hydrocarbon exporters that fuel the economies of much of the developed world, to the owners of huge piles of ready cash, much of which has flowed into a wide range of investment vehicles across the world, to their expanding activity in foreign policy, Gulf governments are major global players. Gulf citizens loom large as participants in the globalization of entrepreneurial violence, both as actors and, along with their governments, as financiers. While that aspect of the Gulf is more widely known, how it fits into globalization writ large is rarely asked.

This is why the current upsurge in publications on the Gulf is so welcome. As one of several general histories of the region, David Commins's book on the Gulf States has much to recommend it. It is wonderfully written, able to engage the reader from its first pages. It is broad in scope, beginning with a short summary of "ancient" history that touches on such fabled places as Dilmun and exotic peoples like the

Carpathians. Despite its brevity, this quick overview manages to site the inhabitants of the region as agents firmly anchored in world historical time. They are by no means pictured as what anthropologist Eric Wolf has called "people without history," peoples and cultures envisioned as primitives suspended in timelessness until the Europeans came along (Wolf 1982).

Among the substantive virtues of Commins's book is its detailed picture of the Gulf as a "globalized" region as far back as history goes. This approach foreshadows the emphasis on migration in the chapters devoted to the post-1500 Gulf. Consequently, it projects what I believe is a more accurate and useful picture of the movement of money, people, ideas, and goods than we generally find in the literature on globalization, and locates it appropriately in a cross-roads of sea and land migration.

The bulk of the volume concentrates on describing how the Gulf fitted into succeeding global and regional regimes. The early chapters focus on "eras" defined by local and extra-regional empires whose influence penetrated its political and social formations. Both God and Mammon are represented as engines of empire. Competition among imperial powers such as the Portuguese, the Dutch—and the Safavids—is integrated into discussions of the fortunes of local rulers. Even pirates get their due, their status and character reflected in a quote from Augustine's *City of God* that has a pirate challenging Alexander the Great's castigation of him for taking hostile possession of the sea. To this the pirate retorted, "What thou meanest by seizing the whole earth; but because I do it with a petty ship, I am called a robber, whilst thou who dost it with a great fleet art styled emperor" (Commins, p. 71). Similar mental images of the Gulf shaped the attitudes of Europeans, who saw exploitation of the region's trade and then its hydrocarbon resources by their powerful navies as in the natural order of things while local resistance by sea was called piracy and condemned (al-Qasimi 1986).

In partial contrast, relationships on land in the smaller Gulf settlements were mediated by what I think of as the romance of tribalism, which charmed British agents such as Gertrude Bell and Percy Cox who allowed local rulers more leeway than was enjoyed by British dependencies in south Asia or Africa (Dickson 1956; Wallach 2005). It never went far enough to concede real autonomy, but it did soften destructiveness so evident in places such as Palestine, Lebanon, and post-1857 India, where European imperialism left a huge legacy of inter-group hostility.

State-formation and state-building are primary concerns as Commins moves into more recent times. Many Western observers (e.g., Draper 1992; Fromkin 1989) tell this story as a saga of misguided European politics. Commins joins other historians (e.g., Anscombe 1997) to view nineteenth and twentieth century Europe as components of an extensive *dramatis personae* and not as the sole stars of the Gulf-politics show, even in the era of U.S. dominance. Ruling families, intra-regional struggles for power and authority, and the growing impact of the oil industry, including revenues and how rulers chose to use them, are examined as well. How local forces used Europeans, including the ambidextrous Ottomans, to beef up their competitive advantage in domestic quarrels, adds to the argument that agency was not one-sided.

Commins's efforts to address the region as a whole carries through even in these later chapters which trace twentieth century state-building in a time of profound changes in world order. Although there is a strong regional and global focus in these chapters, they are organized using a nation-by-nation framework that includes Iraq and Iran in addition to Bahrain, Kuwait, Oman, Qatar, Saudi Arabia, and the United Arab Emirates, the six members of the Gulf Cooperation Council (GCC). Commins is particularly interested in struggles within ruling families and, in the case of the two "republics," struggles among elites, as important contributors to the development of today's modern states. Although this volume, like others (e.g., Foley 2010), emphasizes Saudi Arabia, the state-by-state organization ensures that all the Gulf countries are covered under each of the chapter topic frames.

The volume, however, is not without flaws. It takes a top-down approach. Consequently, in spite of the attention paid to state-building, it reflects little of the flavor of local activism which, in the twentieth century if not before, exercised significant influence on the decisions of leaders. The texture of individual societies is missing, not only as a contrast between Iran and the Arab states or between the two "republics" and the monarchies, but also among the monarchies themselves. Religion is portrayed as an important structural element of politics, but its affective power is not explored and neither is the way it is embedded in the conduct of politics and the rhythms of everyday life.

These omissions, along with a few minor factual errors do not detract from the overall value of this volume, however. It would be a good introduction to the region for general readers and lower-level undergraduates in Middle East studies; inadequate sourcing makes it less useful for advanced students. It is most attractive as a survey of globalization, its long history, and its operation in a key cross-roads of migration and trade.

References:

al-Qasimi, Sultan M. (1986). *The Myth of Arab Piracy in the Gulf*. Dover, NH: Croom Helm.

Anscombe, F. F. (1997). *The Ottoman Gulf: The Creation of Kuwait, Saudi Arabia, and Qatar*. New York, NY: Columbia University Press.

Dickson, H. R. P. (1956). *Kuwait and Her Neighbours*. London, UK: Allen and Unwin.

Draper, T. H. (1992). "The Gulf War Reconsidered." New York Review, retrieved from http://www.nybooks.com/articles/archives/1992/jan/16/the-gulf-war-reconsidered-2/

Foley, S. (2010). *The Arab Gulf States: Beyond Oil and Islam*. Boulder, CO: Lynne Rienner.

Fromkin, D. (1989). *A Peace to End All Peace: The Fall of the Ottoman Empire and the Creation of the Modern Middle East*. New York, NY: Avon.

Tétreault, M. A. (2006). "Kuwait's Annus Mirabilis." Middle East Reports Online, retrieved from http://www.merip.org/mero/mero090706.html

Wallach, J. (2005). *Desert Queen: The Extraordinary Life of Gertrude Bell: Adventurer, Adviser to Kings, Ally of Lawrence of Arabia.* New York, NY: Anchor.

Wolf, E. 1982. *Europe and the People without History.* Berkeley, CA: University of California Press. **MAT**

Iran: Politics & History

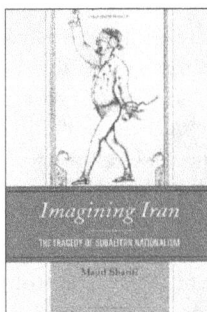

Majid Sharifi. *Imagining Iran: The Tragedy of Subaltern Nationalism.* **Lanham, MD: Lexington Books, 2013. 357 pp. $99.00. ISBN: 0739179446. Ebk: $65.99. 832 KB. 374 pp.**

Sharifi takes a "critical theory" path to illustrating the decades-old discussion of whether "modernization" is "westernization." He labels "westernization" as "imperiality" that causes "subalternity." This condition of "subalternity," he argues, prevents Iran from "modernization"—which he paints as the focal point of an unending, multi-sided debate in Iran. This debate keeps the country from being able to find effective unifying images and condemns it to cycles of revolutionary violence and subsequent coercive violence by each new regime.

If one pares away the coded vocabulary of critical theory, one may find an easier to understand image: Iran suffers from the wound of colonialism. Sharifi's thesis does add valuable components, however. He has patiently examined scholarly, media, and historical sources to illustrate that Iran's wound is similar to that of other former colonies in some respects, but unique in others. It is similar in the subaltern character of Persia's response to being subject to imperial conquest. Iranians shared with many others the impulse to blame themselves for becoming others' subjects and tried first, to accommodate the economic and political challenges by becoming as much like their metropole masters as they could.

What Sharifi parses as different or especially notable in Iran's last 12 decades is how groups in Iran competing to become the recognized, legitimate rulers have used contrasting versions of the country's history, purpose, and basis of authority—but in service of goals that sound much alike. Each of several narratives combine these elements to appeal to the country as a nation that is (or should be) sovereign, developing in its economy, education, and social stature; democratizing, and politically constitutional. But because of how each opposition group pitched its campaign to justify throwing out its predecessor regime, no new regime won over those it replaced. Each resorted to the same destructive tactics which, instead of unifying the country, kept it divided. It came to power in the name of the rule of law, upholding the constitution, superseding the violent maneuvers and authoritarianism to bring together all of Iran.

But no new regime—of the five since 1905 that Sharifi analyzes—has convinced enough of its elite and subordinate groups that its version of "Iran" qualifies as "true Iran;" thus, the nation of Iran does not yet exist. And the seeds of ideological difference (Islam, secularism, uniqueness, absolutism) and the violence each regime wields in searching for compliance and legitimacy only worsens the divisiveness that neither "new narratives" nor intimidation have overcome. The new government's "official identity"—whether secular, Islamic, expansive, or anti-imperial—has never equated to "Iran, our nation."

Sharifi's book is a case study of the dynamics of regime change in Iran: erosion through media and political dissent of even partial consensus on a narrative, bloody contention and takeover, return to oppression—all wrapped in a promise of unity and the future glory of Iran and all for which it stands.

In contrast to typical political science approaches to regime weakness and disruptive change (think Arab Spring), Sharifi does not assume autonomy of, or a disconnect between nation (the people) and state (constitutional authority). Rather, he seeks to understand how a people's perception blends these concepts. The people's interaction with their leaders and with outside influences affect their ability to share a common identity, respect a common government, or find common cause that could subordinate attachments to local authority or personal interests. Sharifi examines how each regime came to understand itself through its relations with major powers outside. For example, Iran between the World Wars in its first efforts to institutionalize not only ran head-on into clergy and local elites whose privileges the new "modernists" (imitators of the west) tried to confiscate—an act guaranteeing opposition to the center. As a regime, it also found itself torn among various models: German, Turkish, British, and Russian. So when it tried to link "the people" with efficient, effective management styles, it failed because, as a government, it lacked the cooperation it needed from sub-groups and local controllers of industry, religion, and schools.

More tendentious is Sharifi's treatment of "the wound." He blames Iran's inability to develop its own institutions of conflict resolution and effective administrative management not only on the first wounds inflicted by the imperial masters, but also on the contemporary "world system." The liberal order of globalization (dominated by "the center" that is primed to intervene to exacerbate internal dissentions) keeps the Iranian body too weak for the major surgery of thoroughgoing political reform; the first aid each new regime has applied has not brought the political health that Iran will need to find its own modernity, one that is positive, inclusive, and respected inside and out.

Sharafi summarizes his own work as applying not only to Iran but to others in the Middle East, "weak states, fragmented societies, contending and confrontational visions of secular and Islamic nationalisms, and in many cases, the political disengagement of a large body of the masses who form into small social/private spaces where rumors and conspiracy theories replace political debates with fictional stories, dramas, and theatrical tragedies." In language more clear than much in this book he continues, illustrating part of his thesis about the damage imperial binary thinking imposes: "people of these states have no voice, their states have no power, their societies are hopelessly fragmented, and their mainstream scholars continue to live on borrowed knowledge produced by imperial states. This borrowed body of knowledge continues to shape the meaning of security/insecurity, development/ underdevelopment, democracy/authoritarianism, and the rationality/irrationality of human rights."

http://tirnscholars.org/2013/09/08/new-book-majid-sharifi-on-imagin-ing-iran-the-tragedy-of-subaltern-nationalism/#sthash.kHb02bRU.dpuf

In support of his model of the self-image outcomes of interaction of contentious relations within Iran and impositions of imperial or modern state-system actors from outside, Sharafi examines five regime changes in Iran since the constitutional revolution of 1905–06. Each regime wished to impose its version of "Iranianness" as the official, accepted narrative, but all five failed: from monarchic absolutism to constitutionalism; to Reza Shah centralization; to tentative democratic nationalism disrupted by imperial intervention (1941 and 1953); to return of "the shah" (Pahlavi) and imitating the imperial; to Islamic Nationalism to Khatami's failure; to state power—a military–industrial complex—but still no nation.

In his final turn of this model, Sharafi says of the present Islamic Republic of Iran (IRI): "It came to power, not by negating the embodied knowledge of imperiality, but by criticizing the Pahlavi regime for not being sovereign, having a dependent economy, governing without the democratic consent of the people, and violating its own rule. Not surprisingly, the opposition to the IRI has accused it of failing to become a sovereign, developed, democratic, constitutional state" (p. 321). The conundrum for the IRI is that it "lacks the political capacity to change without collapsing, so it prefers going to war than imploding" (p. 325). Alternately, says Sarafi, normalization of U.S.–Iraq relations might free "romantic nationalism" from its imperial bonds—being the "other." This transformation of thought will occur only if global discourse fully embraces "positive politics" by becoming "human-centric, sustainable, and environmentally friendly" (p. 330).

The contents of this book, both in history and in theories of political communication, deserve a wider audience than they will receive. The author's use of post-modern deconstructionist terminology and his philosophical weakness of treating ideas (instead of persons) as actors detract from, rather than adding meaning; ideas do not act; persons do. How can "constitutionalism" "overthrow authoritarianism" (p. 44)? A reader from outside the critical theory fraternity has to translate to get past the unnecessary erudition demonstration effect; for example, "analysis of hegemonic and counter-hegemonic discourses" (p. 315).

Also disconcerting are the too frequent proofreading and editing errors. For example, bibliographic entries for Foucault include one that the author probably found in an early search (the wrong Foucault) that sneaked through into the published work (p. 335).

Majid Sharifi is an Assistant Professor in the Department of Government & International Affairs at Eastern Washington University. **KLW**

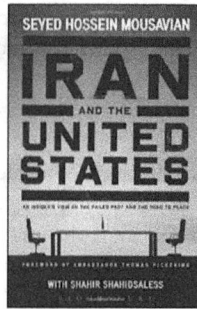

Seyed Hossein Mousavian and Shair ShahidSaless. *Iran and the United States: An Insider's View on the Failed Past and the Road to Peace.* New York, NY: Bloomsbury Academic, 2014. 368 pp. $23.54. ISBN: 978-1628920079. Ebk: 748KB. $17.04.

As dark clouds of hostility and conflict continue to overshadow U.S.–Iran relations, a global public, including many in the United States, continues to look for a silver lining in this foreboding atmosphere. Unfortunately, Hossein Mousavian and Shair ShahidSaless appear in this storm as a bolt of lightning and thunder rather than a silver lining, offering little light and a lot of noise. *Iran and the United States: An Insider's View on the Failed Past and the Road to Peace*, Mousavian's latest work—assisted by Shair ShahidSaless—is propagandistic, tedious, defensive, and superficial; and thus fails to address the crux issues that created the four decades of enmity between Iran and the United States.

Mousavian's lengthy and impressive credentials as an Iranian diplomat, security professional, scholar, and member of Iran's formal and informal executive decision-making circles is compromised by his nearness to the subject—and some of his critics would add outright complicity in Iran's subversive and aggressive activities. For the sake of this review, the focus of commentary will remain on the actual arguments posited by the authors. Nevertheless, simply ignoring the fact that Mousavian's insider perspective involved leadership in one of Iran's chief propaganda organs—the *Tehran Times*—would create an artificial background that obscures the main points of the book.

The author's intentions for writing the book are explicitly admirable. He states directly: "As a proponent of the maximum engagement school of thought between Iran and the West/United States, based on 35 years of experiences and diplomacy, in order to address mistrust and promote better and enduring friendly relations between Iran and the West/United States, my aim is to formulate a workable, realistic, win–win roadmap to resolve the protracted standoff in Iran–U.S. relations. I wish to substitute friendship and peace for hatred and hostilities between the two great countries of Iran and America" (p. 14). Yet, this diplomatic tone which pervades the book is punctuated by outright denials of Iranian aggression at home and abroad, and is diluted by bold statements by Mousavian in the text and elsewhere claiming the United is completely to blame for the "impasse" in U.S.–Iran relations—a position that undermines the author's quest for "mutual forgiveness."

Mousavian's thesis is that Iran is misunderstood by the United States because of its lack of cultural insights and its inept policymakers, and subsequently applies an aggressive and provocative policy, including regime change, support of terrorist organizations such as the MEK (*Mujahedeen-e-Khalq*), interference in Iran's domestic life, aid to Iran's archenemies Israel and Iraq (under Saddam Hussein), and economic sanctions aimed at crippling the regime. Furthermore, he laces his thesis with warnings of potential conflict, missed opportunities for peace, and dangers of escalation that could have dire regional and global consequences.

What follows next in the authors' discourse is a tedious, shallow, and grossly biased explanation of the key events in U.S.–Iran relations. Subsequently, Ayatollah Khomeini emerges in the narrative as a victim, not an agitator in the Iran Hostage Crisis; the overthrow of Mohammad Mosaddegh in the 1953 Iranian coup as a subversive act of the United States with no mention that the Iranian clerical class also opposed him; and Mahmoud Ahmadinejad's statement that Israel should be "wiped off the map" as a misunderstanding rather than common discourse in Iran deeply embedded in its social fabric.

The most disturbing aspect of Mousavian's assertions is more than blatant denials of Iranian aggression in Lebanon, acts of terrorism in Europe, interference in Iraq and Afghanistan, and gross human rights violations including the systematic persecution and execution of organized dissenters (religious and political). *Iran and the United States* ... asserts "rogue cells" within the Iranian government or "false flag" operations account for the terrorist acts of which Tehran has been accused (pp. 140-141; 160; 174). The danger in such assertions by the author who is seeking deniability is that it removes accountability for terrorist acts and emboldens further state aggression, which risks escalation of an already volatile situation. Furthermore, for those of us who served in Southern Iraq in Operation Iraqi Freedom, and have witnessed or analyzed up-close Iranian training of Iraqi insurgents, agitation, explosively formed penetrators (EFPs) and other forms of lethal aid, and direct action (Quds Force operations in Iraq), the statements appear to be the same denial and deception tactics Tehran used in the past rather than conciliatory efforts to resolve this major impasse.

Mousavian's experience as a member of Iran's nuclear negotiation team for the European Union, and for engagement of the International Atomic Energy Agency (IAEA), coupled with his scholarship on the subject—he authored *Iranian Nuclear Crisis: A Memoir* (2012)—should have generated some of the more insightful analysis of this subject in his current work. Instead, the author continues his dismissive attitude toward the IAEA while asserting Iran's benign and peaceful intentions for developing nuclear power. When addressing the issue of Iranian concealment of its nuclear activities, a finding by the IAEA, the Iranian diplomat softens the cover-up by stating: "no gas was introduced to the centrifuges and no enrichment was carried out at Natanz" (p. 183).

Iran and the United States ... makes the case for deeper cultural understanding including an accounting of Iranian "national pride," "anti-foreign domination sentiments," and desire for reciprocity. Yet the author overlooks major American sentiments, including the United States' deep revulsion of state violence, typified in cases like the Satanic Verses controversy and fatwa by Khomeini ordering the execution of Salman Rushdie—a fatwa affirmed by the current Supreme Leader and his Iranian Revolutionary Guard Corps—and supported by public monuments honoring an assassination attempt on Rushdie.

However, Hossein Mousavian and Shair ShahidSaless do offer some hard truths for an American audience seeking a better understanding of Iran. The Iranian Green Movement that brought hope of reform in the aftermath of the disputed Iran presidential elections of 2009 did not represent the majority of Iranians, but an urban, intellectual, and professional sentiment hotly contested at the grassroots level, the authors note. [The Green Movement was crushed by the powerful state security forces that had significant local support, including the well-organized Basij.] Even Mousavian's brief imprisonment on espionage charges by President Ahmadinejad in 2007, a major episode discussed in the book, demonstrates not only the fierce factional conflicts among Iranian leadership, but also the ability of the state to maintain control amid such convulsive domestic forces. Therefore those optimistic reformists hoping for domestic organized political change in Iran should understand clearly the potent reactionary forces dampening such prospects.

Mousavian concludes his current work with a Road Map for Peace, an anti-climactic appeal to the United States to acknowledge that Iranian policy is defensive and thus amenable to a "comprehensive agreement" that would allow communication, peace, and economic benefits for all parties. But here is the problem with his work, the very arguments he presents in the book generate further mistrust, suspicion, and alienation, the very "impasse" he laments. **MSC**

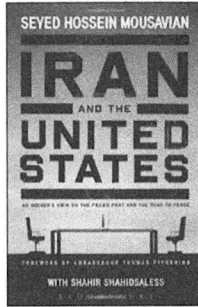

Seyed Hossein Mousavian and Shair ShahidSaless. *Iran and the United States: An Insider's View on the Failed Past and the Road to Peace (This is a second review of this title).* **New York, NY: Bloomsbury Academic, 2014. 368 pp. $35.00.ISBN: 978-1628920079. Ebk: 748KB. $17.04.**

Covering more than 150 years of bilateral U.S.–Iran relations which have oscillated between the cordial and the frozen, the pragmatic and ideological, the engaged and contained, this book is a useful summary of all that has gone right—but more often wrong—in the relationship. It is written by a former Iranian diplomat, Seyed Hossein Mousavian who was formerly Iran's Ambassador to Germany (1990–97) during the period when four Iranian Kurdish dissidents were killed in Berlin. This was later found to have been officially sanctioned by the Iranian government and effectively halted Iran–West diplomatic relations, as the EU states recalled their ambassadors from Tehran. Mousavian was then made head of the Foreign Relations Committee of Iran's National Security Council (NSC) (1997–2005), when President Khatami attempted to engage the United States through a bold attempt at public diplomacy amid opposition from hardliners in Iran, including Ayatollah Khamenei (p. 149), and from the U.S. Congress as reported by the *New York Times* in 1999 (p. 155).

In 1996, the Khobar bombing in Saudi Arabia which the Clinton Administration originally blamed Iran was later found to be more likely commissioned by al-Qaeda. If not for the distrust—of which the bombing episode was a part—Mousavian argues that this period could have been a golden opportunity for the reformist Khatami government to engage with the Clinton Administration. In 2001, 9/11 undermined another potential renaissance in relations through G. W. Bush's conflation of U.S. grievances against various states by labeling Iran, Iraq and North Korea as an "axis of evil."

Mousavian's post at the NSC overlapped with his becoming spokesman for Iran in its nuclear negotiations with the European Union from 2003 until 2005—the basis on which a broader engagement might have been made with the European states (and by extension the United States) after the particularly negative period which preceded it. However, it was impossible to make headway with the G. W.

Bush Administration at this time since it was clear that Vice President Dick Cheney and Secretary of Defense Donald Rumsfeld sought to extend the Iraq War in 2003 into regime change in Iran (p. 202). Even though President Bush may have been open to discussing all the bilateral grievances with Iran, his axis of evil speech, like Ahmadinejad's controversial "wiping Israel off the face of the earth" speech in 2005, negated that possibility. However, Mousavian denies that the phrase attributed to Ahmadinejad was ever made, giving the Persian translation on pp. 184-185. The more deliberate Holocaust denial (p. 213) would be harder to retract, but is inherently linked to Iran's identification with the Palestinian occupation which forms another unresolved piece in the U.S.–Iran relations puzzle.

As Foreign Policy Advisor to Saeed Jalili, the Secretary of the Supreme National Security Council and Iran's nuclear negotiator (2005–07) and Vice President of the Center for Strategic Research for International Affairs (2005–09), Mousavian, by choice, had a less high-profile input into Iranian foreign policy. This was wise since it is made clear from Mousavian's first meeting with Ahmadinejad, when he was being considered as a potential Foreign Minister, that he would not be able to work with Ahmadinejad effectively. Conservatives had control of all the levers of power, and mistrust once again dominated official decision making. Ahmadinejad was clear in his criticism of America and its inability to impede Iran's freedom of movement in developing the nuclear program. This was despite facing possible referral by the Western dominated IAEA to the UN Security Council (p. 209). Iran was duly referred to the UN Security Council in 2006 at a time when the United States viewed Iran as a pre-eminent threat in its second National Security Strategy document (p. 219).

The most interesting part of the book is not the inclusion of all the stages in the evolution of the U.S.–Iran relationship. These have been covered by various volumes looking at the Islamic Revolution, U.S. hostage crisis, the Iran–Iraq War, and Iranian foreign policy in general. It is in the personal encounters with leading figures of Iranian politics and in the West which brings Middle Eastern politics and IR theory to life. With years spent working at the forefront of the major issues which continue to govern Iranian foreign policy and Western policies toward Iran, his conclusions are invaluable.

There are some pertinent points made by the author throughout the work which should be the basis for further reflection on both sides. First, the superior attitude of the West felt by Iranian politicians and diplomats, when a more open and balanced exchange may have received a much more positive reaction from Tehran. Second, the motivation of Iran in its foreign policy: independence, dignity and freedom, as espoused during the 1979 Islamic Revolution, which has often been ignored in Western policy circles. For example, Mousavian states that Mossadegh may have been a modernist, but he also rebelled against foreign domination, and the West punished him with a coup in 1953 (p. 149). The result is a struggle rather than an accommodation of wills within international affairs which has persisted throughout the past three decades.

Third, the defensive nature of Iranian attempts to block U.S. domination or hegemony in the Middle East and tip the balance of power back in its favor (p. 261). Fourth, the unusual situation in which Iran has been denied its right to enrich under the Non-Proliferation Treaty (NPT) and yet has not been able, until recently, to conduct an effective dialog with its main adversary on the matter. Rightly, the book dismisses any "Clash of Civilizations" as being redundant in explaining the U.S. (liberal) versus Iran (Islamic) dynamic (p. 262) since values are only a part of the foreign policy decision-making process. After all, Saudi Arabia is another Islamic state with which the United States has enjoyed cordial relations for many years. Certainly, Israel is identified as a major irritant in the relationship, but again Mousavian states that only 11 of the other 57 members of the Organization of the Islamic Conference have recognized Israel (p. 264). Fifth, there needs to be consistency in the foreign policy approach employed by both sides in order to sustain a peaceful solution and better social ties to support dialog, understanding and tolerance.

There are vital and common interests upon which both states could cooperate, including: Syria, Iraq, Afghanistan, and al-Qaeda. United States support for a regional security organization would also boost regional cooperation (p. 289). Progress on any of these would elevate and enhance international stability and security and should therefore be a policy priority in Iran, the West, and among Arab states once a nuclear deal has been reached. Mousavian rightly prizes détente over the Middle East Cold War struggles and proxy conflicts which are apparent today. It is in that spirit that the Comprehensive Joint Plan of Action should be taken forward. **RM**

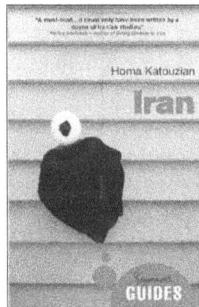

Homa Katouzian. *Iran: Beginners Guides.* **London, UK: One World Publications, 2013. 248 pp. $14.95. ISBN: 978-1780742724.**

Iran politics and history have been considered one of the most important topics in Middle Eastern studies in the past 30 years. This comes as a result of the changes that have taken place in the Islamic Republic of Iran and abroad. Iran has been witness to the last revolution in the twentieth century that produced the first

Twelfth Imam Shi'a state in the same century. The ramifications of such fundamental changes have opened the door for more publications in order to offer a better understanding of Iran.

The primary target of this book is the general public. These kinds of books normally present more information/facts rather than analyses. Therefore, the author, Homa Katouzian, who is a leading figure in the area of Iranian studies takes the reader on a tour to explore Iran's history prior to, and after the introduction of Islam. He follows a periodical method as a tool to structure his book, beginning with ancient Persia, and progressing to the medieval period. The modern period, beginning with the sixteenth century has received more attention, so that the author has allocated four chapters to discuss nearly 400 years of modern Iran.

The author admits that Iranian history is marked by dramas of various dimensions: the first was the conquest of the Achaemenid Empire by Alexandria the Great; the second, the conquest of the Sasanian Empire; the the third, the Mongol invasion; and the last, the invasion of the Afghans in the late eighteenth century which ended the Safavid empire.

There are six chapters, Introduction, timeline, index, and bibliography. In the Introduction, the author explains the elements that contributed to shaping the Iranian personality, followed by a discussion of the geographical location of Iran and its people. In this context, he presents information about the social structure that includes nomadic, rural, and urban structures. Furthermore, issues such as state–society conflict, nomads and ethnicity, "Iranianism," and conspiracy theories in the Iranian culture are discussed.

The first chapter of the book focuses on Ancient Persia. The author suggests that the Persian Empire is the first world empire which was founded more than 2,500 years ago by Cyrus the Great. The chapter covers the four periods of ancient Persia: the Achaemenid Persia; the Hellenistic interlude; Arsacid Parthians; and the Sasanian Persia.

Chapter 2 offers a detailed discussion of issues related to medieval Persia. The chapter starts with an overview of the emergence of Islam in the Arabian Peninsula. This is followed by the following: the Muslim belief, Shi'ism, Arab Caliphates, the role of Persians under Abbasids, the rule of Turks, the Ismailis, the Mongols, Timur and his descendants, and the Safavids Empire which could be considered the starting point of modern history of Iran. This chapter covers nearly tenth centuries of Iran's history.

Chapter 3 focuses on the dilemma of modernization and the revolution of law. This period started around the end of the eighteenth century. However, serious efforts at modernization can be seen in the middle of the nineteenth century. The chapter also discusses the Russo-Persian Wars, the rise of u'lama, Amir Kabir's reform, Anglo-Russian rivalry, the discovery of law, the Tobacco Revolt, and the Iranian economic situation in the nineteenth century. This chapter includes interesting information about literature and the arts, the revolution of law (Constitutional

Revolution, 1905–06) and its ramifications for Iran and the 1921 coup which brought the Pahlavis to power in Iran.

Chapter 4, which focuses on Iran under the Pahlavi, offers a discussion of modernization and dictatorship in Modern Iran. It also covers the policies of Reza Khan and the Iranian Mustafa Kemal Ataturk. Those policies focused on what has been considered an important milestone in building modern Iran. This included reform of the army, in addition to judicial and educational reforms. The chapter also covers oil and the economy; dress code and forced unveiling; foreign policy and the allied invasion, 1926–40; the constitutional chaos, 1941–51; political movements in the 1940s; the Azerbaijan revolt; oil nationalization, 1951–53; and the 1953 coup. This chapter presents brief information on land reform and the revolt of June 1963, the return to arbitrary government, one-party state, and the impact of the white Revolution.

In the fifth chapter, the focus is on the 1979 revolution and the Islamic Republic. In this context, the author discusses the rise of anti-Westernism in modern Iran; the opposition to the Pahlavi regime in Iran and abroad; the origins of the 1979 revolution, the impact of the oil price increase; the protest movement of 1977; and the nature of the Islamic revolution. This chapter also deals with the developments concerning Iran's relations with the United States. This includes the hostage-taking, and the Iran–Iraq War of 1980–88.

In the last chapter, the focus is on the Post-Khomeini Iran. The author discusses the transition from pragmatism to reformism, the rise and decline of Islamic reformism, and the return of fundamentalism. As mentioned earlier, this book is aimed toward public readers. Accordingly, it does not offer a deep analysis of the issues it covers. However, it provides readers a basic overview of issues related to Iran's history and politics. **MZ**

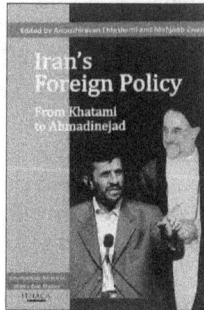

Anoushiravan Ehteshami and Mahjoob Zweiri, Eds. *Iran's Foreign Policy From Khatami to Ahmadinejad.* **Reading, UK: Ithaca Press, 2011. 2nd Ed. 165 pp. $69.95. ISBN: 0863723241. Pbk: $19.95. ISBN: 978-0863724152.**

Revising an edited book is a challenging task. The editors have basically two choices. First they could ask their contributors to update their chapters, as David Lesch and Mark Haas have done in producing five editions of *The Middle East And The United States* (Boulder, CO: Westview Press, 2012). The other alternative is to keep the original chapters as they are, and include a final, updated chapter. The latter choice was made by Ehteshami and Zweiri, with mixed results. While the final chapter, by the editors, is very solid, and captures the essence of Ahmadinejad's policies, the book would have been improved had a number of chapters, especially the ones on the relations between the European states and Iran, been updated.

That having been said, several of the chapters stand the test of time. R.K. Ramazani, perhaps the Dean of Iranian scholars living in the United States, has produced an excellent introductory chapter, comparing pre-Islamic, Islamic, and Revolutionary Iran and noting some major communalities. Another very solid contribution is Judith Yaphe's chapter, "The United States and Iran in Iraq: Risks and Opportunities" which outlines the key issues, especially since the U.S. invasion of Iraq in 2003. This is a chapter that should have been updated, given the U.S.–Iran struggle over influence in Iraq in the Maliki era. The same could be said for Zweiri's chapter on Arab-Iranian relations which also goes into depth on Iranian-Iraqi relations. In addition, Zweiri goes into great detail on the Sunni–Shia conflict as well as on the impact of Iran's nuclear program on the Arab World; additionally, the book would have been improved had this chapter been updated to cover the critical years 2006–10. Two chapters are devoted to relations between Iran and the United Kingdom. Both are written by diplomatic practitioners with experience in Iran—Christopher Rundle and Michael Axworthy—and both give the reader a good feel for the dynamics as well as the frustrations of Western diplomats who deal with Iran.

The two chapters on European-Iranian relations are the weakest in the volume, as they simply do not stand the test of time. Thus in his chapter, "Iranian-European

Relations: A strategic Partnership?" Shahriar SabetSaeidi, asserts "Even with a conservative president in Iran (Ahmadinejad) and closer ties between the United States and European countries, especially Germany and France, Europeans are still trying to avoid imposing unilateral sanctions against Iran..." (p. 68). Clearly this situation has changed as the EU is now taking a very aggressive position on anti-Iran sanctions. Similarly, in her chapter "Iran: Caught between EU-US Rivalry?" Anastasia Drenou, writing from a perspective unsympathetic to the United States, sees Iranian issues "as safe ground for Europe to contest American hegemony" (p. 78), and "the European Union has chosen Iran as its 'test subject' to stand up to U.S. interventionism" (p. 84). Here too, the chapter needs, if not a change in perspective, then an unbiased update detailing how U.S.–EU cooperation on Iran has greatly improved.

In sum, while the book has some useful material, it would definitely have been strengthened by the contributors updating their chapters. Hopefully, the editors will consider a third edition of the book, this time updating all the chapters to include the entire period of the Amhadinejad presidency. **ROF**

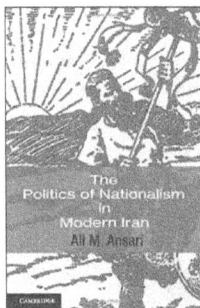

Ali M. Ansari. *The Politics of Nationalism in Modern Iran.* New York, NY: Cambridge University Press, 2012. 327 pp. $30.99. ISBN: 978-0521687171.

There have been a number of academic writings by Iranian intellectuals recently—especially those of liberal or secular sentiment, dealing with what the Islamic revolution of 1979 was actually about—and how to understand it in the larger context of Iranian history. *The Politics of Nationalism in Modern Iran* is written along these lines. The author, a Professor of History at the University of St. Andrews, traces the development of Iranian nationalism from the Constitutional Revolution in 1905 to the presidency of Mahmoud Ahmadinejad. This excellent work asks these basic questions: What is an Iranian; and how has Iranian identity been shaped over the past 100 years? The book is particularly focused on the role of the Iranian political elite and intelligentsia in attempting to define Iranian identity by using Iranian history, Iranian myth, Shi'a Islam, and the racial concept of Aryanism.

The author maintains that, although the book traces the beginning of Iranian nationalism back to the French Revolution in the late eighteenth century, and to the influence of nineteenth century philosophers such as Jamal al Din Afghani, the evolution of modern Iranian nationalism began with the Constitutional Revolution of 1905. This revolution occurred toward the end of the rule of a corrupt and incompetent Qajar monarchy. It brought together nationalists, local dignitaries, and Shi'a clergy to force a constitution on a reluctant monarch. This constitution outlined a new form of representative government, the author suggests, with a parliament and human rights. Never mind that the constitution was, in fact, never fully implemented, and the early convening of the parliament was only a partial success. Nonetheless, the author argues, the Constitutional Revolution brought an expectation of representative republicanism to Iran—a concept that the author believes lasted until the 1960s.

The constitutionalists soon realized, the book argues, that a representative form of government also needed a strong leader; and the constitutionalists eventually found this in Reza Shah. This combination of constitutionalism with a strong monarch lasted several decades, but was eventually abandoned by Reza Shah's son, Mohammed Reza Shah, who abolished any traces of a constitutional government, becoming a monarch with absolute power.

The book describes how the various Iranian leaders developed their own concept of Iranian nationalism. In the early twentieth century, Iranian identity had not coalesced, and it was not obvious what Iranian nationalism meant, or how it was to be defined. After all, at the time of the Constitutional Revolution in 1905, only about one half of the population of the country spoke Persian; the Qajar dynasty in power at the time were originally Turks, and Iran was referred to as Persia—the Greek name for the country—in the larger world. So what was an Iranian? There was, however, incipient Iranian nationalism present even at this early time. In part, Iranian identity at that time was found in the ancient myths of Iran, primarily in the stories of the *Shah Nameh*, or Book of Kings, by Ferdousi. This epic poem of over 50,000 couplets was written over 1,000 years ago and tells the largely mythical story of the kings and heroes of ancient Iran until the time of the Islamic conquest of Iran in the seventh century. Many of the stories of the *Shah Nameh* are known to average Iranians, even those who cannot read, as these stories are told and retold by storytellers across all sections of Iran, even to this day.

As important as the *Shah Nameh* is to Iranian nationalism, the tales are largely mythical and are not an accurate history of Iran. In fact, Iran has a rich history which goes back over 2,500 years to the Achaemenids civilization of Cyrus the Great. Cyrus and other Achaemenid kings were heroic figures who fought the Greeks and built the magnificent capital of Persepolis in Southern Iran. The author chronicles how this history has provided a rich fodder of heroic stories on which are built Iranian identity and national pride. Leaders of Iran have used the history of Cyrus the Great, and in general the history of the Achaemenids, to great effect. For instance, the author points out that Mohammed Reza Shah compared himself to

Cyrus the Great and even changed the Iranian calendar to make it coincide with the reign of Cyrus the Great 2,500 years ago.

The author also describes how, in the early twentieth century, Iranians became aware of the concept of Aryanism that had developed in Europe, particularly Germany. Since the Iranians believed that they were the original Aryans, ("Iran" and "Aryan" are cognates), this view, for a short time, led to a new kind of nationalism based on race, in which Iranians and Europeans were seen as brothers. The Iranian intelligentsia largely abandoned this argument, the author points out, particularly after the Second World War, in part because of the association of Aryanism with Nazism. However, one still finds the claim that Iranians are the original Aryans in some Iranian publications.

Although as much as Iranian nationalism is focused on ancient Iran before the Islamic conquest, the author also describes the importance of Islamic symbolism in defining Iranian nationalism. Although Islam originated in Arabia, Iranians particularly dislike being associated with Arabs and blame the Arabs for many of their problems; nonetheless, a unique version of Islam was developed in Iran, namely Shi'a Islam. In fact, the author points out that some Iranians, especially Shi'a clergy, argue that Iranians are special or enlightened Muslims. While Shi'a Muslims are found in other areas of the Islamic world, Shi'ism remains particularly Iranian. In addition, Iranians take pride in their contribution to Islamic history, as many of the early Islamic philosophers and scientists were Iranians.

How did the Islamic Revolution in 1979 change the concept of nationalism in Iran? Not much, the author argues. In fact, he sees the government of Ayatollah Khomeini as largely a continuation of the government of Mohammed Reza Shah. There was not great change in the governing machinery if one looks closely. The concept of Iranian nationalism under Ayatollah Khomeini changed little from Mohammed Reza Shah's. In fact, the author suggests, the major changes in Iran did not take place until the rule of Ali Akbar Hashemi Rafsanjani after the end of the Iran–Iraq War.

Although the book flatters some Iranian leaders—Reza Shah and Ayatollah Khomeini for instance—the author has particularly harsh words for Mohammed Reza Shah and President Ahmadinejad. (The book was published in 2012, when Ahmadinejad was still president of Iran.) The author argues that while the beginning of Mohammed Reza Shah's reign was relatively benign, after returning from a brief exile in 1953, Mohammed Reza began to consolidate his power and abandoned any pretext of constitutionalism. By the late 1960s and especially with the promulgation of the White Revolution, Mohammed Reza Shah had developed a national ideology based on two principles: that he was the new incarnation of Cyrus the Great; and that he governed with "divine right" and was therefore beyond any legal or governmental framework. The author describes how this special status was further inflated when the Shah had himself referred to as *Shahanshah Aryamehr*, king of kings and light of the Aryans.

Professor Ansari is particularly contemptuous of President Mahmoud Ahmadinejad, largely for creating a self-aggrandizing myth of manifest destiny. (The author has written a separate book about Ahmadinejad, *Iran Under Ahmadinejad*, 2008) Ahmadinejad invoked both a connection to ancient Iran and to Islam. The author describes an event in 2005 in which Ahmadinejad claimed that documentary footage showed a green halo appearing over him while he was speaking at the UN, indicating his holiness. This claim caused a great controversy among the Islamic clergy in Iran, most of whom found it untrue and embarrassing. Also, like Mohammed Reza Shah, Mahmoud Ahmadinejad also referred to himself using a reference to Cyrus the Great. The book reports "Ahmadinejad was the first post-revolutionary leader to fully exploit the Achaemenid heritage and to praise [it] in terms that may have made Mohammed Reza Shah blush..." (p. 278).

This rewarding book is not an easy read, but it is an insightful discussion of issues of nationalism in modern Iran. The book is not a history as such, and readers looking for a chronological description of modern Iranian history will not find it here. While the author discusses most of the major historical events in the last 100 years of Iranian history, the reader must know the actual histories of these events in order to make sense of the author's arguments. In addition, some scholars of Iran will not agree with everything that is in this work. Although he is not the first to suggest that there was little difference between the government of Mohammed Reza Shah and that of Ayatollah Khomeini, this argument may surprise some. **GF**

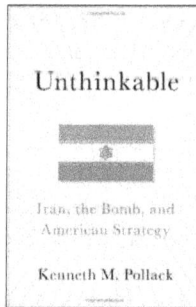

Unthinkable

Iran, the Bomb, and
American Strategy

Kenneth M. Pollack

Kenneth M. Pollack. *Unthinkable: Iran, the Bomb, and American Strategy.* New York, NY: Simon & Schuster, 2013. 560 pp. $20. 57. ISBN: 978-1476733920.

Kenneth Pollack is a former CIA agent and a Middle East expert at the Brookings Institution. Pollack is well known for devotedly justifying the Iraq War (2003), which turned out to be disastrous and humiliating. Today, he asks his readers to listen to what he says about the Iranian nuclear dilemma and the strategy from which America benefits. Let us, once again, listen to Pollack—yet this time more carefully.

The thesis of *Unthinkable* is simple: the United States must make a deal with the

Islamic Republic of Iran. In this regard, at one end of a spectrum, since the Right Wing advocates going to war against Iran, they feel no pressure to make a deal. At the other end, the Left Wing believes that they can live with a nuclear Iran, and therefore, any deal seems good enough to them. This is problematic because as long as the Islamic state prevails, it may evolve into a nuclear regime that pursues its anti-American policies more confidently. Thus, one should hit the nail on the head by removing the Islamic state. This end, Pollack suggests, cannot be easily achieved by going to war because of many reasons, such as unpredictable outcomes of any war; lack of America's public support for another war in the Middle East; and Iran's retaliation—particularly through international terrorism. Pollack argues that limited airstrike (as against a full-scale war) is even more objectionable. His argument is straightforward: Israel does not have the military power to demolish Iranian underground nuclear sites. This job, nevertheless, can be accomplished by U.S. forces. But, even if the United States does so, it only worsens the situation because it gives more incentive to Iranians to ignore the Non-Proliferation Treaty, re-establish their nuclear sites, and reach a break-out capability, or perhaps develop a nuclear arsenal. In addition, one must take into account the fact that Iranians may have hidden sites, which are therefore invulnerable to American airstrikes. Having various scenarios crossed out, the most effective policy remains containment, that is, to prevent the Islamic Republic from hurting the U.S. interests until the regime dies out.

What happens when the Islamic Republic does fall? Fall it will, someday, and hopefully soon. We may desire it to happen, but we may not be ready for it when it does. The structural flaws of the Islamic republic are deep and pronounced, and while the regime could continue to creak along for several more decades like Cuba and North Korea, it could also collapse within the next few years (p. 367).

Elsewhere, Pollack reveals another shocking lesson. Clearly it is not American behavior that generates Iran's objectionable actions. It is either the Iranian leadership's pathological perceptions of the United States or its own aggressive ambitions, neither of which appears to be affected by less threatening American behavior (p. 115).

Pollack does not stop short in surprising his readers. On another occasion, he sadly sounds like a youngster rather than a serious scholar or a pragmatic politician.

Many Iranians bristle at the cliché 'carrot-and-stick' because they say it is derived from the metaphor of how one leads a mule. They say that they find this humiliating and offensive. [...] And as for Iranian sensibilities ... well, what I find objectionable is 30 years of Iran killing Americans in Lebanon, Saudi Arabia, Iraq, Afghanistan, and elsewhere. When the Iranian regime stops doing that, I would not only be willing to change how we describe our policy, I would be willing to change the policy itself (p. 157).

Pollack's artless wording is a good indicator of his way of thinking, which shows how serious a scholar he is. The abovementioned (and his other) statements should be sufficient for a reader to quickly question whether Pollack understands his case study, particularly the Iranian side of the equation. (It is worth mentioning that there is not even a single source in Persian in the bibliography.) Nevertheless, for some reasons unknown to this reviewer, Pollack is taken too seriously and with far too little criticism.

For instance, Shahram Chubin, a nonresident senior scholar at Carnegie Endowment for International Peace, recently wrote a review of the *Unthinkable* in *Middle East Policy Council* (Spring 2014, *XXI*, (1)). Chubin ends his review by suggesting that when diplomacy fails, and the Iranian nuclear dilemma reemerges, "then we will need the wise counsel offered in this excellent book" (p. 2). In what sense is Pollack's *Unthinkable* an "excellent" book; how does consulting it provide us with an answer to Iran's nuclear dilemma? Unfortunately, Chubin does not elaborate on this point. Chubin's review is, in effect, friendly praise rather than a critical review from which Pollack and his audience could benefit. The feeling is mutual: to Pollack, Chubin is "one of the wisest scholars of Iranian politics and strategy" (*Unthinkable*, p. 5). This may or may not be true—regardless, one should ask why this book is recommended as an excellent source by a senior scholar? In the same review, Chubin states that Pollack's "study of the Iranian side of the picture is sensitive and nuanced" (*Review*, p. 2). It is curious to know where Chubin found "nuanced" analyses of the "Iranian side of the picture" in *Unthinkable*. What are some examples of a nuanced analysis of the Iranian side that Chubin claims the *Unthinkable* offers? Moreover, what is original in Pollack's thesis? What is Pollack's contribution to the literature? What did he reveal that scholars of Iran did not already know?

The fundamental weakness of the book is Pollack's lack of knowledge of the Iranian side of the picture, which he wittily admits. "It's actually not hard to be an expert on Iran," Pollack acknowledged, "You only need to know two phrases: 'I don't know' and 'it depends'" (p. 4). On a number of occasions, when Pollack does not know about a topic, he frankly confesses the fact. This confession, however, does not mean to suggest that Pollack does not know anything about Iran. He is an accomplished author and has worked on Iran for quite a long time. Pollack's *Unthinkable* is a comprehensive book, in which a handful of conventional scenarios (e.g., carrot-and-stick, airstrike, invasion, and containment) are analytically examined. To non-academicians, Pollack's writing style may be engaging but unbearably wordy. The historical references and parallels that he makes between different nuclear regimes are insightful. His logic is sound, and his arguments are easy to follow. However, sound logic and some historical knowledge do not a substitute for a through understanding of the Iranian side of the picture; and when such an understanding is missing; one ought to doubt excellence, sensitivity, and nuance of any work on the Iranian nuclear dilemma, including *Unthinkable*. **MMM**

Iraq: Politics & History

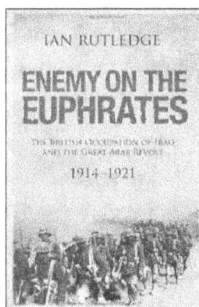

Ian Rutledge. *Enemy on the Euphrates: The British Occupation of Iraq and the Great Arab Revolt, 1914-1921*. London, UK: Saqi Books, 2014. 471 pp. $23.52. ISBN: 978-0863567629.

The American invasion of Iraq in March 2003, "Operation Iraqi Freedom," with the stated aim of toppling the tyrannical regime of Saddam Hussein can be inducted into the Hall of Fame of great events leading to unintended consequences. Iraq has been ruled for the last seven years by a Shi'a government, heavily supported by the Islamic Republic of Iran, and heavily supportive of the Alawite regime of Bashar al-Assad in Syria. Iraq has thus become a central link in the new emerging Shi'a crescent, stretching from Iran to South Beirut, and this clearly is not what President George W. Bush and the Neo-Cons around him wanted to achieve.

It is the case with Iraq, as with other states established in the post-Ottoman era Middle East, that the questions of political legitimacy and historic narrative are the ones which give the key to understanding their current history. The history of Iraq did not start with the American invasion; in fact, most of what has happened since then can be related to the very circumstances of the creation of Iraq, what Christopher Catherwood called *Churchill's Folly: How Winston Churchill Created Modern Iraq* (Constable, 2004). Hindsight is one thing and reading correctly complicated socio-cultural-political situations in real time is quite another, so when Iraq sunk into the undeclared but cruel ongoing civil war of the post-Saddam days, it became the order the day to refer to the "folly" of establishing modern-day, multi-sectarian, fragmented Iraq.

Rutledge's book may be conceived as one of these books, but it really goes beyond that, and provides the reader with a good, balanced and nuanced picture of the background of the establishment of Iraq. Rutledge is a relatively newcomer to the field of Middle East Studies, and in his case, it is relevant to invoke the old adage, about better late than never. He is quite right when he says that the answer to the question "on what side did the Arabs fight in WW1?" is "not Britain," which is the accepted account. Such an account, he pointedly wrote is "emanating from the glorification of 'Lawrence of Arabia' and the 'Arab Revolt' of Sharif Hussein and his sons. True enough in this case, and to follow Rutledge's own logic, there is the question to ask as to why the writer refers to the "Great Arab Revolt"? (p. 395), if he talks about the revolt in the desert? The answer is clearly that the revolt had no military value, rather a huge political value, as it put the nascent Arab National Movement, hardly in existence prior to 1914, firmly in the world affairs arena with the Paris Peace Conference of 1919 and afterwards. If the "Great Arab Revolt" refers to the Iraqi rebellion of 1920, then it should be coined the "great Iraqi Revolt," a point which is one of the main topics of this book.

I am impressed with how Rutledge dealt with the question of whether the rebellion in Iraq in 1920, was an Iraqi nationalist insurrection against British colonial designs, or a mostly Shi'a outburst. Rutledge opines, rightly so, that it was the latter; though admitting that it was not only the Shi'a, and is debating with those historians who referred to the rebellion as the founding stone of the modern Iraqi state. He refers to the rewriting of history under Saddam, when "marginal" Sunni figures became elevated to the status of great heroes of the rebellion, which they were not. Rutledge touches here upon the question of historic narrative and its usage by different regimes in order to serve their political purposes.

In February 2014, the Iraqi government officially opened a museum in the Shi'a holy city of Najaf, commemorating the rebellion. The fact that the museum was opened in Najaf served notice as to how the current rulers of Iraq view the rebellion which ended when Iraq was handed over by the British to a non-Iraqi, but prominent Sunni leader, Faysal al-Hashimite, who became the first King of the newly established state.

Where Rutledge is wrong, is when he writes (p. 395), that the orthodox, romantic myth about the "Great Arab Revolt" was questioned only in the last two decades. Elie Kedourie did it much earlier (*The Chatham Version and other Middle Eastern Studies*, Praeger, 1970).

Rutledge gives us a well-researched and well-written account of the rebellion and the consequent establishment of Iraq. He clearly describes British policy, gives a realistic picture of the local Iraqi scene, and altogether produces a readable, interesting and very useful contribution to the understanding of modern Iraq. **JO**

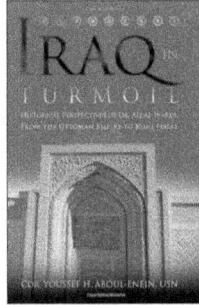

Youssef H. Aboul-Enein, Ed. *Iraq in Turmoil: Historical perspectives of Dr. Ali al-Wardi, from the Ottoman Empire to King Feisal.* **Annapolis, MD: Naval Institute Press, 2012. 189 pp. $26.95. ISBN: 1612510779.**

Between 1969 and 1976 Ali al-Wardi, an Iraqi born sociologist published an eight volume Arabic history of Iraq. His massive tome was an epic achievement and he himself was a product of interesting times. Born in Iraq in 1913, he was just a boy when the revolt against the British broke out. He traveled to Beirut in 1943 and, like so many influential men of his generation, attended the American University of Beirut. It was in the United States that he received his Ph.D.; yet he chose to write his epic in Arabic, his mother tongue. *Iraq in Turmoil* is an attempt to provide a much abridged analysis of this important work and draw conclusions about modern-day Iraq from it. As the editor notes "[this] volume provides an abridged translation with commentary of the most significant aspects of the work for an American military audience, coupled with analysis of all eight books" (p. xii).

Commander Youssef Aboul-Enein is chair of Islamic studies at the Industrial College of the Armed Forces and is a U.S. Navy Medical Service Corps officer. As he notes "apparently, al-Wardi's volumes are among the reading selections offered to Iraqi prisoners…[they] exploit the image of Iraq's history with the Shi'a, Sunnis, Kurds, Wahhabis and Persians to their advantage…I uncovered a treasure trove of historical information ital. to the understanding of Iraq" (p. xii). The author and subsequent chapter editors don't attempt to hide the intentions behind this volume, which was produced primarily for the American military. As General H. R. Mc-Master, who writes the forward to Chapter 1, states "soldiers who have conducted counterinsurgency operations in Iraq and Afghanistan understand the importance of developing and understanding the culture and history of the regions in which they are fighting" (p. 1). That being noted, this volume nevertheless offers much to scholars outside of the military academy. Portions of Ali al-Wardi's work have been translated into English before, but those books are not widely available and knowledge about them is lacking. Therefore another refresher on this important piece of history is of great worth for which scholars on modern Iraq to take note. For those studying the history of the United States in Iraq, the comments in the text are also of interest. For instance, McMaster writes "the heroic narrative related by al-Wardi is significant to American Soldiers [sic]. In this popular portrayal of the Revolt, tribal leaders rebel against the arrogant and insulting British occupation, asserting their sovereignty through a tribal call to arms strengthened by Jihad" (p. 5).

Wardi's narrative is not strictly about Iraq. In fact he wrote a history of Safavid Persia, the Ottoman Empire, the Wahhabis of Saudi Arabia and modern Egypt. Of course this made sense because Wardi Iraq was not living in a vacuum; it was deeply impacted by the major currents in the Arab world. Napoleon's invasion of Egypt had an impact because it set in motion trends that would change Iraq, for instance. Wardi was unsparing in his critique and harsh analysis. For instance, in describing Shah Abbas' raids on the Ottoman Empire in the seventeenth century he notes "Abbas inaugurated his arrival in Baghdad with a Sunni genocide. Rolls were distributed with the names of Sunni families to be killed" (p. 13). The use of the term "genocide" here is one used by the editor in his abridgement of the al-Wardi text and this presents a partial failing. Since al-Wardi's eight volumes cannot be condensed into 200 pages, the authors felt it better to describe or redact the al-Wardi original. Thus excerpts are not provided, but rather a dumbed down version of the text. The reader is left to trust the redactor.

In his description of Ottoman Iraq, al-Wardi presents a state always seemingly at conflict with the Shi'a empire in Persia, and also with various tribal rebellions. Minority populations were sometimes persecuted. For instance, in modern-day Iran, Sheikh Mohammad Baqir al-Majlisi "led a zealous inquisition in 1699 and forced conversions of Sunnis, Zoroastrians, Sufi Muslims, Christians and those 'Hellenized' Muslims that had been influenced by Greek classical philosophy" (p. 16). Subjugating and defeating Bedouin tribal rebellion seems to have taken up a great deal of the time of Ottoman governors. In 1708, for instance, "one of the largest confederations [of tribes} in Iraq's history (p. 17)" set upon the outskirts of Basra in southern Iraq. With supposedly 100,000 fighters they were met on an open plain by the Ottoman army which brought along "cannons, muskets and grenades" (p. 17). Some 10,000 Bedouin were killed. Some 10 years later Ahmed Pasha was again at war with tribes that he accused of aiding Persia.

Another interesting historical issue that is raised is the accusation that many tribal rebellions sprang from seeming insignificant incidents that could be describes as insults to one's honor. In one instance in 1836, Sherief Pasha in Damascus ordered the conscription of 170 Druze men to the Ottoman army. The Druze leader refused, claiming he needed the men to fight the Bedouin who were threatening his villages. "In response the Ottoman *vali* slapped him, thereby initiating a revolution by this assault on the dignity of Sheikh Yahya" (p. 31). The 1920 revolt, which is the center of al-Wardi's narrative, was also engendered by an insult. "The instigating event involved the British Army captain Lyle and his insult of Sayyid Alwan al-Yasri by throwing Alwan out of his office one day in late 1919" (p. 89). In another instance it was claimed that "British officers allowed their dogs into the tent of Bedouins" (p. 82), the dog being considered unclean and not permitted into the homes of a pious Muslim. During the Egyptian campaign in what is now Saudi Arabia in 1816, the Egyptian soldiers believed that their officers routinely drank alcohol, which caused them to sympathize with the Wahhabis they had been sent to subdue.

All these stories have a similar thread, of dishonor and non-Islamic behavior justifying rebellion. The question is not raised to what extent the story may have been embellished after the fact to justify the rebellion or whether it actually took place. For instance the British colonial officers and their advisors in Iraq consisted of men like T. E. Lawrence and women like Gertrude Bell, who even if they are today considered arch-colonialists, were particularly knowledgeable and respectful of the customs of the people they dealt with. Is it reasonable to assume that British officers routinely brought their dogs into the tents of Bedouin leaders they met? The authors of this volume don't examine the degree of accuracy in al-Wardi's text, allowing it to speak for itself. This is commendable, but it leaves it for other scholars to inquire about.

The central portion of this book, as with Wardi's original text, is the 1920 Arab revolt. Likely the editor felt that the 1920 rebellion has parallels with today's Iraq and that much could be learned from it. "The 1920 Revolt began in Ramadi and spread throughout Iraq in opposition to the British mandate system imposed on Iraq" (p. 80). The editor notes that "starting in 2003 insurgents used Tel Afar as staging points for attacks against US forces that led to Operation Black Typhoon (p. 95)." Likewise Tel Afar had been a center of the 1920 revolt. The problem is that the 1920 has always been confusing to understand in almost every narrative of it. Perhaps this is because no full length modern text has struggled to provide a good account of it either for an academic or a popular audience. Unfortunately *Iraq in Turmoil* also does not provide a clear account that keeps tracks of the various interests and groups. Nevertheless *Iraq in Turmoil* is an important contribution and one that sheds light on a very important scholarly work by an Iraqi who was intimate with the events that he mentioned. **SJF**

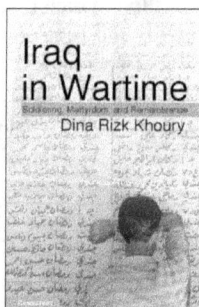

Dina Rizk Khoury. *Iraq in Wartime: Soldiering, Martyrdom, and Remembrance*. New York, NY: Cambridge University Press, 2013. 281 pp. $76.50. ISBN: 978-0521884617. Pbk: $26.99. ISBN: 978-0521711531. Ebk: $18.69. 3265 KB.

In honor of the centennial of WWI, I've been re-reading Paul Fussell's classic, *The Great War and Modern Memory*. Dina Rizk Khoury's book on Iraqis and how they experienced the three Gulf wars: Iran–Iraq, Kuwait, and the end of Saddam, is equally evocative and surprising. The experiences of the soldiers was very similar, but the home front of each was a different story, with British women publicly shaming young men avoiding service by handing out white feathers, and organizations like the Baaʻth Party and the Women's Federation identifying them and turning them in to the authorities. Both London and Baghdad executed deserters, but only the latter punished their families as well. Punishing families whose members did not conform to Saddam's patriotism model du jour is appalling, but so is the way widows and their children were victimized by male relations eager to claim inheritances from the fallen. The instrumental value of women to the state and their families during this period is well set out in Khoury's book, and contrasts strongly with the pre-war pictures of Iraqi women as the most modern and autonomous in the Middle East. But much in this volume contrasts with what we used to know.

Like WWI, the Iran–Iraq war was depicted as defensive by both sides. At the start, young Iraqis, like young Britons, were eager to fight. As the wars continued under the execrable quality of leadership in the capitals and on the battlefront, they lost their glamor and the fighters their idealism. For Saddam in Iraq, the adversaries were not only Iranians, but also other Iraqis—Kurds in the north and a range of unsatisfactory Iraqis in the south, such as deserters, villagers who sheltered them, Communists, and Shiʻa activists (many of whom fled the country). To Baghdad, they were indistinguishable, but soldiers in the field saw distinctions, not only among other Iraqis but even among Iranians. Soldiers were taught to ridicule the young Iranians who were sent into battle with wooden keys to paradise around their necks, but some saw themselves as serving their secularist ruler in much the same way.

The wars instantiated new powers and techniques of population control. The

Ba'ath Party assumed the bureaucratic functions of a mukhabārāt. It formed and trained two major militias whose main function was to capture deserters and provide intelligence for the army. The party kept track of Kurds and other anti-regime insurgents. They mapped Iraqis into categories of people, many created as byproducts of war. Bad categories were filled by enemies and good ones its bulwarks. Soldiers distinguished by exemplary action on the battlefield were designated "Friends of Saddam," but the label soon was applied to civilian bureaucrats, clan leaders, and others whose service to the regime was repaid by preferential increases in entitlements. As corruption and financial shortages squeezed resources, entitlements were transformed into "acts of mercy," gifts from the leader. Iraqis often found themselves unable to navigate obstacles generated by their increasingly "improvisational" nature. The expansion of entitlements was seen as insulting: soldiers, families of "martyrs" (persons killed as the result of war), and disabled veterans resented putting what they saw as earned entitlements on the same level as rewards for reconstruction, intelligence work, and even coming to work during bombardments. Entitlements grew more erratic as additional recipients were added, claims to benefits were negotiated, and corruption continued. Notices of rewards to poorer Iraqis and those without intermediaries to speak for them were often as much as "recipients" got.

Punishment of those who betrayed the regime or engaged in behavior that threatened the established order, such as harboring deserters or having a bad attitude toward the Kuwait war and the subsequent popular uprising was also improvisational. Dissent was concentrated in the Kurdish north and the Shi'a south. The Intifada following the Kuwait war was concentrated in these regions. The Kurdish north was protected as the result of individual actions by a handful of reporters and U.S. officials. Its most effective aspect was a no-fly zone that kept the regime from bombing the area or using helicopter gunships to attack particular individuals or groups. The south, where insurgents thought that George Bush's exhortations to rise up against Saddam implied that some assistance would come from the coalition if they did so, were neither aided nor protected. Coalition commander Norman Schwarzkopf allowed the Iraqi military to retain the use of its helicopters which were deployed against insurgencies in both the south and the north. Air interdiction of the insurgency in the north ended with the implementation of the no-fly zone, but in the south, helicopter gunships destroyed it, aided by bickering among former Shi'a exiles, most of whom had taken refuge in Iran, unable to agree sufficiently to test Saddam's offer to include them in post-war governance.

Successful tactics for suppressing insurgency in one region were applied in the other and, as they became more brutal, further reduced the likelihood of post-conflict reconciliation. In the south, the razing of villages, public executions of deserters, and the relocation of survivors to block housing along major highways where they could be kept under surveillance more easily, embittered the population against the regime. The use of chemical weapons against the Kurds in the north alienated the population completely. The regime had not foreseen the impact of this action; as

Khoury notes, using chemical weapons against Kurds was seen as no different from using them against Iranians, a move that had elicited little notice from the "international community." Other atrocities included draining the marshes in southern Iraq, initiated on a small scale toward the end of the Iran–Iraq war with the uprooting of vegetation in which school children were enlisted to help. It culminated in a full-scale obliteration of this ecologically rich habitat, leaving dissenter/insurgents no place to hide, and eliminating plants, animals, and recharge zones for ground water. Poison was used in the southern marshes, too. In both regions, poison was intended to make it impossible for residents to move back and support themselves on the land.

The post-Kuwait war period inflicted more suffering on the Iraqis, hounded by the regime for their actions and attitudes, and the sanctions and occasional bombing inflicted by the United States. Deteriorating public health, increased infant mortality and higher death rates overall from a lack of medication and adequate food resulted from the sanctions and how they were managed by the regime. Even after the "Oil for Food Program" went into effect, the impact of shortages continued to be severe and was unevenly distributed. The dual culpability of foreign antagonists and the leader of Iraq was no mystery to the Iraqis, and although many were relieved by Saddam's ouster in the third Gulf war, there were no roses and chocolates for the "liberators."

WWI shaped modern memory, but Khoury shows that Iraqi memories of the three Gulf wars were post-modern. Saddam feared the development of solidarity among men from different regions and backgrounds. Propaganda designed to depict a unified Iraq shifted narrative toward historical images, like Qadisiyya, and projected the unity arising from the current wars as the result of the successes of Baa'thist-led modernization. For individual stories, they substituted tales of boys achieving manhood in the heat of battle, defending against an unworthy enemy. Photographs projected soldiers and their weapons in heroic poses (pp.190-194), and were accompanied by stories of victories to keep up the morale of those at home. Women had no place in these narratives which explains why Khoury's attention to women and families throughout her volume is especially revealing, in much the same way as posts appearing on Riverbend's blog. Historical memory of the Gulf wars, especially the first one, remains fragmented, appearing now and again in short stories and personal accounts amid officially sanctioned memoirs.

Official memorials also have a prominent place in this account, such as the Martyrs' Monument and museum erected in memory of those killed in the Iran–Iraq War (p. 226). The Martyrs' Monument was the site of highly choreographed ceremonies on Martyrs' Day, whose trajectory followed the ups and downs of the war itself in differently inflected stories of sacrifice, the evil of the enemy, and loyalty to the leader. Visual imagery included Iraqi families in their homes, proud of the sacrifices of the men in their families. Khoury notes how the insistent repetition of images in these photographs also homogenized the war experience.

The Kuwait war and the Intifada presented problems for those in charge of war rituals. Who were the martyrs? Why had they died? Unable to confront these questions, the structure chosen as a symbol of Iraqi unity in war was really a mausoleum, the al-'Amariyya shelter. Public shelter 2.5 was built in a suburb of Baghdad to protect civilians from bombing during the Iran–Iraq War. It became a casualty of shock and awe as the result of two "smart bombs" fired on February 13, 1991 that killed the occupants, some 400 women and children, in particularly gruesome ways. Rituals at the site were spontaneously organized once it could be approached. The regime took over annual rituals at the shelter in its ceaseless efforts to muffle stories of individual suffering that ended up as events protesting the victimization of the Iraqi people by the embargo. By usurping the role of locally expressed grief and memory, the Iraqi state reinforced the fragmented quality of historical memory of these three horrible conflicts. Khoury notes especially the impact on those who had fought and died in the Iran–Iraq War. After the collapse of Saddam's Ba'athist regime, how should Iraqis remember them, and how should we? **MAT**

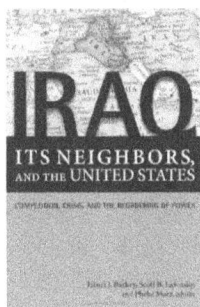

Henri J. Barkey, Scott B. Lasensky, and Phebe Marr, Eds. *Iraq, its Neighbors, and the United States: Competition, Crises and the Reordering of Power.* **Washington D.C.: United States Institute of Peace: 250 pp. $19.95. ISBN: 1601270771.**

The American-led invasion of Iraq in 2003 was a momentous game-changing event in the region. The importance of it may not be apparent for years to come. In *Iraq and its Neighbors*, the authors set out to compile numerous important essays examining the regional strategic issues that Iraq confronts. In the Introduction, the editor's note that the invasion "upended Iraq's relations with its neighbors, profoundly altered both the regional balance of power and America's role in the region, and fundamentally changed the assumptions about Iraq's future" (p. 1).

The book generally presents a series of case studies of individual countries and how they have related to Iraq before and after 2003. As the editors claim, "Iraq's strength, ambition and aggressiveness were the source of instability in the region" (p. 3). Iraq is accused of being this source of instability because it had fought an almost decade long war with Iran in the 1980s and then launched an invasion of Kuwait which resulted in it becoming a pariah state in the 1990s. The notion is that after 2003, the state became a source of instability, not because it projected its power, but because it became a power vacuum into which Iranian, Saudi, and other interests were poured. Nevertheless "the traditional cross-border tensions Saddam so eagerly exploited have not disappeared and are likely to plague regional relations for years to come" (p. 5).

The editors, a professor of international relations at Lehigh, and two scholars working with the U.S. Institute of Peace bring expertise and experience to this volume. They have combined an excellent assortment of articles and secured a forward by James Baker and Lee Hamilton, who worked with the Iraq Study Group and, in Baker's case, played an important role in shaping the U.S. role in the region.

In 'the new Iraq', Phebe Marr and Sam Parker argue that the "Iraqi state is slowly reemerging and, with it, so too are its long-established traditions of statecraft and power maintenance" (p. 14). However, they correctly note that Iraq is, in some ways, a threat to its neighbors through having become a weak state. This problem is ever-present, as illustrated by the continuing low-level terrorist insurgency in Iraq that has taken place in 2012, after the book was published. What role Iraqi instability played in encouraging the Arab Spring or the rebellion against Bashar al-Assad in Syria is not clear. Henri Barkey, a professor at Lehigh University, writes in "a transformed relationship" that Iraqi relationship has changed in recent years. "During much of the Cold War the two countries were on opposite sides of the global divide" (p. 46). Barkey notes that, beginning in 2009, the Turkish government began a new policy of dialog with the Kurds and thus, was seeking to transform what had been a conflictual relationship with the Kurdish proto-state in northern Iraq. The author argues that Turkey's AKP party's Islamic outlook allowed it to renew relations with the Kurds more easily than past Turkish nationalist parties. However, the article notes that there is a "time bomb" in relations with the two countries. The Tigris and Euphrates rivers originate in Turkey; this could become a bone of contention in relations between the two countries. In the final analysis, however, this article does not seem to offer a clear view of what Turkey's ongoing policy of incursions into the Kurdish areas of northern Iraq mean for long-term relations.

Mohsen Milani argues that, regarding the Iranian relationship with Iraq, "the first one began when the war started in March 2003 and ended with the victory of the Tehran-supported, Shi'a-dominated United Iraqi Alliance in the elections for the Transitional National Assembly in January 2005" (p. 81). Milani sees a cautious Iranian policy where Iran fears the loyalty of the Shi'a Arab parties it has supported, and also fears a powerful Iraq. "This strategy is designed to decrease Iran's chances of being unpleasantly surprised in Iraq" (p. 85). Iran has also used its policy to pressure the Iraqi government against the Muhadin el-Khalq, the Iraqi-based Iranian dissident group. Like many of the authors, Milani concludes that the Arab Spring may change Iranian policy in Iraq in the future. As with other articles, it means that the reader is left without a clear conclusion, which weakens both this article and the volume as a whole.

The entry on Iraqi–Saudi relations is of great interest because of the role the Saudis have played in Iraq over the last two decades. Saudi Arabia helped encourage Saddam's invasion of Iran in the 1980s and bankrolled Saddam's armies. At the same time, the Saudis became afraid of the increasing power of Saddam, especially after the invasion of Kuwait. However, since 2003, the Saudis have faced the nightmare of Iranian influence pouring over the border into Baghdad. Losing the Saddam bulwark against Shi'a Islam means that the Saudis see a destabilizing influence in their own Qatif region, as well as with Shi'a adherents in the Gulf. Toby Jones writes that "Saudi Arabia has also openly expressed dismay over the dismal state of sectarian relations in Iraq and particularly the continued marginalization of its Sunni minority" (p. 108). Yet, at the same time, Iraqi leaders "have been even more critical of Saudi Arabia's reported financial complicity in the violence in their country" (p. 113).

Judith Yaphe provides an interesting analysis of Iraq's relationship with its Gulf Arab neighbors. Most recall that it was rancor that led to Iraq's invasion of Kuwait, and threatening the Gulf Arab States. The Gulf States also played host to the American military bases that made the 2003 invasion possible. The author concludes that the Gulf States will always remain weaker than a reconstituted Iraq, and they will rely on an American military presence for years. Like many of the conclusions in this book, this is an obvious fact; the questions remains what other insights can be gleaned.

The article by Mona Yacoubian is no longer relevant in light of current events in Syria. It isn't clear what will become of Syria, so it is hard to know what will be the policy relationship between Syria and Iraq in the coming decade. However, Scott Lasensky's article on Iraq's renewed relationship with Jordan is of interest. Jordan was one of the few states that stood by Saddam Hussein and also hosted several defectors from the regime in the 1990s. Jordan suffered "spillover" from Iraq after 2003, with hundreds of thousands of refugees coming and going from Amman (p. 168). Yet "Jordan can claim little if any influence on developments in Iraq" (p. 175). Jordan's policy has been to work closely with the Americans on the continued development of a secure Iraq.

In a 'lessons learned' chapter, Hesham Sallam notes that "the national building experiment in Iraq may have fallen short of delivering the promise of democratic change to the rest of the Middle East that supporters of the U.S. invasion had anticipated" (p. 205). This is the central issue with Iraq: it is not entirely clear what will become of the country. Following a period of chaos in 2004–06, the country seemed to be getting back on its feet with the outbreak of the Arab Spring. The 'Spring' has taken focus off the continued intractable problems in the country. What will become of Iraqi Kurdistan, the Iranian role in the country or the Sunni insurgency? What is clear from this book is how decisive 2003 was in terms of a turning point in the history of the country. It is well worth a read by scholars and policy analysts alike. **SJF**

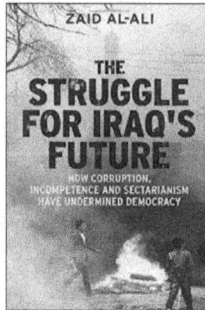

Zaid al-Ali. *The Struggle for Iraq's Future: How Corruption, Incompetence and Sectarianism have Undermined Democracy.* **New Haven, CT: Yale University Press, 2014. 295 pp. $21.47. ISBN: 978-0300187267. Ebk: $13.99. 304 pp. 649 KB.**

The trouble with writing on a current event or ongoing crises is that the publication is sure to be outdated by the time it goes to press. This is particularly evident when writing about Iraq. This book ends around late 2012–early 2013. The rise of ISIS, the ethnic-cleansing of the Yezidis, and the forced relocation of many Christians, Shi'a, and Kurds, were all incidents which followed publication of this book. Of course these issues had roots in the period before. Because of that, this text remains relevant for analyzing, and in some ways predicting the future failure of an already failed state. Any review of *The Struggle for Iraq's Future…* must keep in mind these ongoing events.

Ziad al-Ali is a lawyer specializing in comparative constitutional law and was a legal adviser to the United Nations in Iraq from 2005 to 2010. As such, he is excellently placed to provide a diagnosis of what happened to the state after the U.S.-led invasion of 2003. The author is also an Iraqi who was exiled as a child. "I was involved in the effort to rebuild the state—not for professional or financial reasons, academic interest or curiosity, not as a stepping stone to other opportunities, nor to kill time while I waited for something else to do" (p. 5), he writes. In that sense this is an intense "rediscovery"—in his words—of the country he had been deprived of as a child. But his interest and view also betrays a more prosaic view: Iraq has been feasted on by outside vultures, particularly that laundry list of groups who used the country precisely as a stepping stone to better careers and jobs, and by outside powers.

The author is cynical in painting a trajectory of Iraq falling into the grip of sectarian violence and corruption. "In the 1970s Iraqis generally eschewed corruption and theft… by the time Nouri al-Maliki's second government was formed in November 2010, moral standards had plummeted, in large part because of an understanding that anything that was not stolen would just be wasted or gobbled up by the political parties anyway" (p. 9). This is a romantic picture perhaps of the past. We know today that the regime of Saddam, despite mass human rights violations, did invest in infrastructure and also healthcare reform. It is a double edged sword one finds in histories of the Soviet Union. Crime, corruption and other issues may have been kept under control by the Soviet system, but the dark side is that they came exploding to the surface after. Ali's assessment doesn't necessarily take this issue into account.

Ali paints a dismal picture of modern Iraq. Born under the British and their support for King Faisal, who was from the Hijaz in what is now Saudi Arabia, the state was cobbled together and dragged into the modern era after a brief rebellion in the early 1920s. When the monarchy was overthrown in a brutal military coup in 1958, Iraq was restructured as a republic. But hopes for a more open system faltered. The Communist party was suppressed. "An election law was promised but never delivered, and in time all ministers who were affiliated to political parties or ideologies were dismissed from government" (p. 27). Then came Saddam Hussein, the Gulf War, and finally the 2003 invasion. Iraq already had a bloody and chaotic past; the question was whether it could be reconstructed.

In analyzing the post-2003 period, the author first concentrates on the ruling elites that emerged under U.S. auspices. "For decades the U.S. and the UK had been cultivating allies among the Iraqi exile and opposition groups" (p. 39), notes the author. He paints a picture of an immature class of people, such as Ayad Allawi, who grabbed onto power despite having little support in Iraq. In his analysis tribalism and corruption had emerged in the 1990s as the state turned inward during its isolation. "Many exiles did not have any valuable work experience… many of those who expected to occupy senior positions had never worked for the state at all" (p. 53). This was one of the other results of Baa'thism and the attempt to remove all the Baa'thists after the invasion. Unlike rebuilding, say Germany, after the Second World War, or the U.S. south after the Civil War, there was no large professional class to rely upon. The middle classes had been eviscerated during the period of sanctions. Except for Iraqi Kurdistan where "Kurdish officials worked against the odds and made incredible strides in developing their region," the country was falling apart.

From the start, the new Iraq was plagued by sectarianism. This was, according to the author, particularly true in the new parliament. It was "the most sectarian institution in the country. Posts in parliament were distributed on the basis of what was described as 'balance'—each of the country's three main ethno-sectarian groupings was given adequate representation, based on their respective demographic weight" (p. 59). This was a recipe for worse to come.

The initial political developments were hampered by U.S. occupation and a violent insurgency that tore the country apart and caused thousands of deaths, primarily of civilians targeted because of their religious background. But security began to improve in 2007. The author describes how it once looked to drive north of Baghdad. "What should have been a two-hour drive could often take half a day or longer… by 2009 over sixty Iraqi army checkpoints dotted the highway"(p. 119). Driving to the Shi'a holy city of Najaf required driving on "one of the most dangerous stretches of road in the world" (p. 119). Burnt out cars and corpses were common sights along the road.

The rise of Nouri al-Maliki was the last nail in the coffin of what seemed like an improving state in 2009, but one built on faulty foundations. Maliki sought to aggrandize power in the hands of the Shi'a. "Service delivery and standard of living" did not improve (p. 148). The author concludes that this "will spell disaster for the state's survival in the mid to long term" (p. 148). This is a prescient analysis. We know now that it did spell disaster. It is ironic to think of now, but one of the disputes in 2012 was the attempt of the telecommunications minister Mohammed Allawi to construct a fiber-optic cable to link Iraq to Turkey and the rest of the world. Maliki blocked it because of his dislike of Turkey.

The author describes the country as lurching from one failure to the next. Minority Christians were attacked and bombed and kept fleeing the country. Yet even as violence increased in 2012, the government ministers continued to praise themselves. Ali describes a meeting in Amman where Iraqi government officials "showered themselves with praise, describing success after success" (p. 187). It was all a charade. He also describes conferences about Iraq attended by Europeans "who had nothing to do with Iraq" (p. 210). This was part of the parade of internationals, bureaucrats and others, punching their tickets on the way to better jobs at the EU or better academic appointments.

One of Ali's pet interests is the decline of the Iraqi environment and the increasing deterioration of farmland due to dust storms. Villages were buried and farmers driven from their land. Unemployment rose. He describes this environmental destruction as "the third insurgency," comparing it to a terrorist war (p. 219). That is an interesting point. It is perhaps symbolic of the rest of the tragedy of Iraq, decimated by dust storms and real storms sweeping over the Middle East. **SJF**

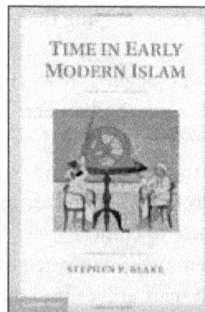

Stephen P. Blake. *Time in Early Modern Islam*. Cambridge, UK: Cambridge University Press, 2012. 209 pp. $90.00. ISBN: 978-1107030237.

This book represents the latest in a series of works that have sought to compare the differing historical trajectories of the Gunpowder Empires of the Ottomans, Safavids, and Mughals in the early modern era. It is also indicative of a growing interest among researchers about what role cultural conceptions of time played in various historical contexts. While most researchers working with pre-modern sources in Islamic history are always aware of the need for multiple conversions between Muslim and non-Muslim chronologies, the simplification of this process in the digital age can obscure the decisive impact that Muslim conceptions of time have had on history. Stephen Blake's comparative study aims to demonstrate that the ways in which different groups of Muslims marked time cannot be reduced to simple *hijri-miladi* conversions. Furthermore, the peculiarities of the relationship between Muslim cultures and their marking of time contributed to major advances in astronomy and mathematics that made Muslim societies among the most advanced of their time.

For starters, the adoption of a lunar calendar by Qur'anic fiat (9:36-37), coupled with a strict prohibition of the practice of intercalation (i.e., the periodic insertion of an extra month into the calendar to keep it in line with the seasons), meant that the names of the original Arabic months, which were tied to seasonal characteristics or activities, soon lost their original meaning (pp. 7-8). More importantly, the adoption of a strict lunar calendar meant that the most basic rhythms of pre-modern agrarian societies were gradually decoupled from the march of chronological time. As Blake points out, as early as the Umayyad period, Muslim rulers and their nascent bureaucracies realized that to rely solely on the Muslim lunar calendar would lead to problems with taxation. Since the lunar year is roughly 11 days shorter than the solar one, this meant that lacking some kind of adjustment, the harvest season would eventually suffer from double-taxation, which could lead to trouble for both rulers and subjects alike. To meet this challenge, both the Umayyad and 'Abbasid caliphate resorted to strategies like *izdilaq* ("sliding") or a "Kharaji Fiscal Era," tied to alternative non-Muslim calendrical models that underwent consistent modification in later eras (p. 108).

In the introduction to the work, Blake defines three key categories by which pre-modern Muslim societies marked time: calendrical, ceremonial, and chronological. This is followed by five chapters and a conclusion. The first provides a basic overview of the Ottoman, Safavid, and Mughal empires for the uninitiated reader. The second takes a comparative look at the various calendar systems employed by these empires. The third chapter examines how the different empires honored various forms of ceremonial observance over the course of a year. The fourth chapter examines the empires' use of chronological time in regard to both fiscal matters and historical dating, whereas a separate fifth chapter focuses specifically on how these polities dealt with the issues surrounding the Muslim millennium at the end of the tenth/sixteenth century. The conclusion focuses specifically on comparison of the issues raised in the book with Christian and Jewish chronological systems.

Although the author does not include much in the way of extensive primary source research as part of the study, the comparison does prove illuminating, and is well worth the effort. We learn, for instance, that Persian attempts to harmonize the Muslim lunar calendar with various solar calendars inherited from the Zoroastrian era or imported by Turkic migrations played an important role in the founding of observatories in the Saljuq, Mongol, and Timurid eras. The work done by thinkers in these institutions, along with many of their millenarian ideas, was inherited not only by the Safavid Dynasty, but also by scholars in the Ottoman and Mughal realms (p. 171).

But from this common core of medieval knowledge production, divergences were plentiful. The Ottomans included Christian solar calendars, but largely stuck closely to the *hijri* calendar in a way that the Persians and Mughals did not. The Mughals drew on Indic calendars, and during the rule of Akbar (1556–1605), even designed an entirely new calendar known as the *tarikh-i ilahi* in conjunction with his novel religious ideas, which intersected with the Indic, Persian, Turkic, and Muslim calendars already in existence (pp. 118-119). The result was often confusion in the process of dating the course of events in various histories following Akbar's reign; a problem not shared by Ottoman historians, who usually stuck pretty closely to the hijri calendar in their works. On the other hand, the Ottoman predilection for strict adherence to the Muslim lunar calendar meant that the empire struggled with the aforementioned problem of over-taxation as the lunar calendar lapped the march of the seasons; however, this problem was not as marked among the Safavids and Mughals (pp. 133-134). And finally, the combination of a grand conjunction of the planets Jupiter and Saturn in 1583 (which had last occurred at about the time of the Prophet Muhammad's emigration to Medina) and the advent of the Muslim millennium in 1591 led to the appearance of various millenarian movements in all three empires, followed by a backlash against their excesses once the events had come and gone (p. 173).

The chapter on ceremony is somewhat less enlightening. It is not surprising that the Safavids would emphasize and develop Shi in 1591 led to the appearance of various millenarian movements in all three empires, followed by a backlNor is it surprising, given Mughal India's substantial non-Muslim elite and populations, that non-Islamic holidays and ceremonies would play a heightened role there. And the Ottomans, given their control of the Holy Cities, would certainly highlight the equipping and departure of pilgrimage caravans to mark each year. Moreover, Ottoman ceremonies highlighting rites of passage for members of the dynasty seem more political than chronological in nature, although Murad III's massive circumcision ceremony for his son did seem to be connected to the grand conjunction of 1583 (p. 170).

This does not detract from the contribution of the work as a whole, however. It is a well-written and well-organized summation of the complexities of time management in Muslim societies, not only in the early modern period, but throughout Islamic history. The book will prove useful as an introduction to these issues for both advanced undergraduate and graduate students. Two quibbles, however: first, the extensive writings of George Saliba on Islamic astronomy were insufficiently consulted for this study, with the result being that the work of Ibn al-Shatir of Damascus (d. 1375) was ignored. Given that Ibn al-Shatir's work has many novel aspects, and the bulk of his work was tied to timekeeping practices, this omission should be noted as an important adjunct to the material covered in this study. Second, although the author alludes to how European scientific achievements began to surpass those of the early modern Muslim empires by the eleventh/seventeenth century (pp. 74-75), the conclusion of the work does not directly address why that might have been so. Given the centrality of this type of question to world historical debates, a brief discussion of that issue might have helped to conclude the study more effectively. See, for example, On Barak. *On Time: Technology and Temporality in Modern Egypt* (Berkeley, CA: University of California Press, 2013). For Ibn al-Shatir, see George Saliba. *A History of Arabic Astronomy: Planetary Theories during the Golden Age of Islam* (New York: New York University Press, 1994), 233–241. **JJC**

Islam & Muslims

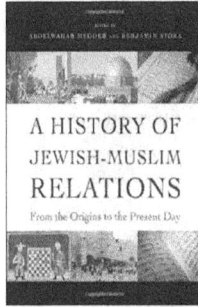

Abdelwahab Meddeb and Benjamin Stora, Eds. *A History of Jewish-Muslim Relations from the Origins to the Present Day.* **Princeton, NJ: Princeton University Press, 2013. 1146 pp. $75.00. ISBN: 978-0691151274.**

I have to say, first of all, that this is a very beautiful book. It is also a very important and timely one. The general editors, Abdelwahab Meddeb and Benjamin Stora (a Muslim from Tunisia, and a Jew from Algeria) state in the Introduction that their intention in compiling the book was to "prompt exchanges and dialogue" so that "each side will be in a position to make a final assessment of the contentious issues, reaching a compromise that will allow them to work toward a reconciliation (without necessarily obscuring what is irreconcilable)" (p. 16).

The book is divided into four parts: the Middle Ages, the Modern World, the Present, and "Transversalities" (the rather peculiar term by which the editors designate areas in which the two religions overlap or converge). Each of these sections is introduced by a separate prologue, followed by numerous essays on different sub-periods or aspects of the subject under consideration. Additionally, each section contains short asides designated as "Nota bene," featuring biographies of important figures of the period or more detailed information about a particular subject; and others entitled "Counterpoint," which are significant excerpts from primary sources. Marginal notations usefully connect each of the essays with other references to a particular subject elsewhere in the book. The book contains more than 250 well-chosen illustrations, many of them in color. There is also a very extensive bibliography and separate indexes of names and places.

The authors of the essays are among the world's leading experts on the subjects they address. The essays average about 10–15 pages in length. This format works well when addressing very specific, well-defined issues, such as "The Jews in Jerusalem and Hebron during the Ottoman Era," but is simply incapable of dealing adequately with such vast and complex topics as "Sufi and Kabbalistic Hermeneutics." With very few exceptions, the authors have managed to write serious, scholarly essays in language that is accessible to the nonspecialized reader. The fact that many different authors have contributed articles on closely related topics leads at times to annoying repetition and overlapping. This is particularly true of the essays in Part IV, Chapter IV: "Philosophy, Science, and Intellectual Movements."

The section on "The Present" must necessarily confront some of the most controversial issues in the book, yet it manages to be the most satisfying. I would particularly single out Denis Charbit's articles on "The Balfour Declaration and its Implications," "Zionism and the Arab Question," "From the Judeo-Palestinian Conflict to the Arab–Israeli Wars," and "Israel in the Face of Its Victories," as exemplary in their honesty and fairness to both sides. By contrast, the section on "Transversalities," in my opinion, does a rather poor job of examining the many points of convergence between the two religions.

Many of the book's articles have been translated from other languages (mainly French) and some of the translations are awkward or inaccurate. Take, for example, the reference to "the amorous Jewess of an Arab" (p. 568), where what is meant is "the Jewish woman enamored of an Arab;" or the reference to "Pierre de Castille" (p. 957) for Pedro I of Castile. As one would expect in a book of this size and complexity, there are also numerous typographical errors and misprints. On p. 483, for example, one reads that "five to eight *million*" settlers withdrew from the Gaza Strip in 2005." Oddly, Hebrew words on pages 655 and 1016 are printed backwards (i.e., from left to right).

In spite of these minor quibbles, however, I highly recommend this book to everyone who is interested in Jewish–Muslim relations. I can easily imagine using it as the principal textbook for a college course on the subject, and I am sure that others will do just that. **MM**

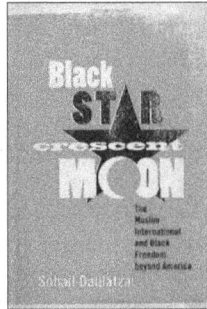

Sohail Daulatzai. *Black Star, Crescent Moon: The Muslim International and Black Freedom beyond Americca.* Minneapolis, MN: University of Minnesota Press, 2012. 257 pp. $22.50. ISBN: 0816675864.

Black Star, Crescent Moon by Sohail Daulatzai identifies the history and contours of the 'Muslim International', "a dissident and exilic space that encourages transgression, applauds border crossing, and foments forms of sabotage and resistance not possible within European and U.S. discourses about individualism, the nation-state, "democracy," and the broader philosophical and juridical frameworks of the Enlightenment, modernity and Western liberalism" (p. xxiv). If this explanation sounds broad or enigmatic, the following chapters clearly demonstrate that the Muslim International is an intellectual tradition and cultural space, if not network, within which American Black Muslim intellectuals, activists, writers, and artists have located themselves politically since World War Two. Within the global context of the Cold War, globalization, the "war on terror," the American Empire, European colonialism and neo-liberalism, the chapters "explore popular culture as a powerful site for revealing the struggles over ideology and power, race and nationhood, and the politics of identity" (p. xxvi).

To put it simply, Daulatzai's Muslim international is a conceptualization of a pronounced Muslim (not Islamic) sub-trend, or perhaps better, intellectual, cultural, and political tradition within Third World anti-colonialist and anti-racist struggles since the end of World War II. The idea is not a mapping of a pan-Muslim network, but an excavation of how American Black Muslims, and indeed radical American blacks, foregrounded their own ant-racist, anti-capitalist, and civil rights (read: human rights) struggle within the larger anti-colonial, independence, and revolutionary struggles of the "Muslim Third World."

The book's first chapter posits the life, thought and activism of Malcolm X as a foundational radical thinker, who used "the national liberation movements in the Muslim Third World as a critical lens that served to define the contours of Black identities, liberation struggles, and their solidarities with the broader Third World" (p. 3). Even those who are familiar with the life of Malcolm X will find Daulatzai's anatomy of his "shifting Muslim identities" riveting (p. 2). The author maps the shifts within the leader's political identification with African and Arab (read: Muslim) anti-colonial liberation struggles, posing the 1955 Bandung Conference as a central event and reference point that set up for Malcolm X "an analogy between black people in the United States and people in the Third World" (p. 29).

Yet, if "Islam came to be seen as an alternative form of radical Black consciousness," Malcolm X, along with the Nation of Islam pioneered it as "quite distinct from what was perceived to be the integrationist goals of Black Christianity" (p. 18) and a rejection of the cooptation of the white liberal and Civil Rights establishments into the anti-communist, jingoistic patriotism of the day by the U.S. government. To this end, the author forcefully communicates how Franz Fanon, Bandung, the Third World, the Muslim International, and Islam gave Malcolm X a "grammar of resistance" (p. 21) that conceptually helped internationalize his thought and, in turn, the Black liberation struggle. Daulatzai sensitively gives credit to the relevance of the Nation of Islam in forging Malcolm X's Third World perspective while fairly noting his growth into a full-fledged internationalist thinker, whose Organization for Afro-American Unity emulated Kwame Nkrumah's revolutionary Organization of African Unity (p. 36).

While each clearly express its own integrity and separate argument, the remaining chapters of the book demonstrate the legacy, force, contribution and, indeed, haunting of Malcolm X's life and works, showing how he was the central figure in converting the mainstream "Negro Revolution" of Civil Rights into a "Black Revolution," the former being "domestic and national" if not domesticated and co-opted, while the latter being "global and international," influencing, along with Fanon, the next generation of Black revolutionaries, including the Black Panther Party (p. 32).

In demonstrating how "the Muslim Third World became a literal and ideological backdrop to the narrative of resistance" of the Muslim International, Daulatzai moves in Chapter 2 to explore how the Muslim Third World influenced Black radical politics, Black resistance literature, and radical cinema in the United States. The author charts a constellation of voices from James Baldwin to Black Panther leaders that located the Black struggle in America within a universe of anti-colonial politics and cultural productions, including the Third Cinema. In doing so, he considers Fanon's *Wretched of the Earth* and its cinematic analog *The Battle of Algiers* as master texts that informed black cultural production in the United States. The chapter then discusses Sam Greenlee's *The Spook Who Sat by the Door* (1969) and *Baghdad Blues* (1976) posing them, and other films such as *Sweet Sweetback's Baadasssss Song*, as domestic analogs to Fanon and Pontecorvo and Hadjaj's work, as well as a critical counter-point to the nonthreatening, domesticated representations of black characters played by Sidney Poitier.

Highlighting the legacy of Malcolm X to the Black Power movement and rigorously historicizing the context of the Muslim International, the author shows that activists, film-makers, poets, writers, and artists within the Black Power movement "positioned themselves, their art, and their politics in relation to the anticolonial and anti-imperialist movements" of the Cold War (p. 69). These acts of cultural positioning intended to disentangle black identity from white majoritarian American culture and nationalism, realigning those "Black identities Diasporically and internationally" more accurately in "relation to the popular struggles taking place in the Muslim Third World" (p. 69).

Chapter 3 provides an impressive mapping of the cultural dimensions of the Muslim International as it intersected with the hyper-nationalist post-Vietnam age when the figure of the "black criminal" synchronically arose with the figure of the "Muslim terrorist." After the destruction of the Black Power movement by the U.S. government and the subsequent post-Civil Rights era demonization of poor urban, Black communities, "Black Islam in hip-hop culture reclaimed the interpretative authority over Black destiny…and imagined a different community of belonging with very different possibilities for freedom, in which Black people would be seen not as national minorities but as global majorities" (p. 97). Undergirding hip-hop, the legacy of Malcolm X "deeply influenced a younger generation of activists" (p. 101) including the Black Arts Movement, which "was inflected by ideas and symbols of Islam and the Muslim Third World, for the artistic and esthetic tradition that it forged was a part and parcel of the Muslim International" (p. 107).

If Malcolm X and the Black Arts Movement mobilized Islam, Third World, and international themes and motifs to forge narratives of liberation and struggle, the "golden age" of hip-hop artists "sought to reclaim a history of Black radicalism and internationalism in the context of criminalization of Blackness, mass incarceration" and the "rise of the carceral imagination of the United States" (p. 109). Daulatzai thoroughly documents the Black Muslim and Pan-Africanist voices, nomenclature, themes, and narratives of Black liberation, including those generated by the Nation of Islam—and particularly Malcolm X—in artists ranging from Gang Starr and the Wu Tang Clan to Ice Cube, Rakim and Mos Def (Yaslin Bey). Daultatzai's assertions regarding the redemptive potentiality of political rap finds itself in, and adeptly draws from, an established scholarship on hip-hop. However, he contributes to that canon by carefully historicizing a nuanced and intertwined trajectory of radical Black liberationist narratives from Malcolm X, Fanon, Amiri Baraka, and Patrice Lumumba to Afrika Bambaata to Public Enemy, "the benchmark of hip-hop's political radicalism" (p. 120).

Chapter 4 is a critical examination of the rise and transformation of Muhammad Ali as a radical political figure to a co-opted icon of liberalism in post-Civil Rights America. Muhammad Ali's "legacy is a lens through which to view the shifting ideological currents of American national identity from the Black Power era and Vietnam through the post-Cold War 1990s and into the post-911 moment." Again in the political context of "culture wars" and the "clash of civilizations," Ali was "transformed into an American hero" that assuaged the "bitterness of Black Power" and" the fears of Black Internationalism" so that "the wounds of the past can be healed and American redemption can be the moral imperative for global dominance in the new American century as Islam became the preeminent threat to U.S. national security" (p. 139).

As elsewhere in *Black Star...*, Daulatzai seamlessly weaves primary and secondary sources into an analytic prism showing "Ali was an extension" of "a tradition in which Black Islam saw the Muslim Third World...as deeply informing black liberation struggles," which offered "a trenchant critique of U.S. domestic racism and its imperial foreign policy..." (p. 166). However, the re-imagining of Muhammad Ali by mainstream American media, sports, and Hollywood coincided with "the sense of collective triumphalism that gripped the nation" in the unipolar era (p. 149). This re-written narrative erases the memory of America's intervention in Zaire, Indonesia, and the Philippines as well as Ali's complicity with Mobutu, Suharto, and Marcos. The "recuperation of Ali as a national hero," therefore, "sought to domesticate and contain Black Islam" and "fracture Black Islam from the larger Muslim Third World" in order to undermine the possibilities of resistance that the Muslim International might offer (p. 167).

Chapter 5 is a powerful exploration of the historic and racial basis for "carceral logic" of America's war on drugs and urban poor, demonstrating the dialectic between the United States' domestic carceral regime since the Civil Rights movement and the domestication of the United States' war on terror.

In *Black Star, Crescent Moon*, Daulatzai shows how this logic has been folded neatly into "homeland security" and the war on terror by federal, state, and municipal authorities, showing that the United States' "global archipelago of prisons is really the logical extension of the dirty war that has been fought in the United States through the containment, incarceration, and torture" of black Americans in the government's "war on drugs" and criminalization of black men (p. 171). Daulatzia uses the conviction and incarceration of black activist and thinker Jamil al-Amin (formerly H. Rap Brown), and his subsequent remanding to a Supermax prison (America's "domestic Guantanamo"), as a backdrop to how the "fears of the Muslim terrorists are being conflated with Black criminality. The author maps out the cultural and juridical processes by which Black Muslims are configured as the "enemy within" and "homegrown terrorism." These processes contain "a deeper anxiety" with how Black Islam has "continually challenged domestic racial control and imagined black freedom beyond the United States' Muslim Third World.

The author successfully shows "the relatively recent histories linking blackness, Islam and the Muslim Third World through politics and art" (p. 190). In doing so, the author powerfully "de-parochializes" a tradition of cultural, literary, cinematic, and musical productions and producers form a bedrock of Black Muslim activism and radicalism that internationalized the larger American Black struggle for freedom within the contexts of racism, white supremacy, capitalism, colonialism, and imperialism. As a result, he provides an invaluable contribution—indeed intervention—into the critical study of the ways in which Islamophobia is intertwined with America's tradition of controlling dissent. But more so, he provides a historical cartography of how the struggle for Black liberation has been itself interwoven with the political struggles of the Muslim Third World. **SS**

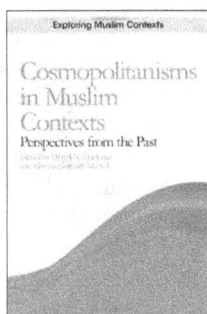

Derryl N. MacLean and Sikeena Karmali Ahmed, Eds. *Cosmopolitanisms in Muslim Contexts: Perspectives from the Past.* Edinburgh, UK: Edinburgh University Press, in association with the Aga Khan University, 2012. 208 pp. $90.54. ISBN: 978-0748644568. Pbk: 2013. 190 pp. $36.98. ISBN: 978-0748689859. Ebk: 208 pp. $22.9

This volume is a collection of essays loosely centered on the notion of cosmopolitanism, the editors' choice of the plural *cosmopolitanisms* was wise, as the individual essays have rather different perspectives on what constitutes "cosmopolitanism." This is not to say that these perspectives are mutually contradictory so much as address fields so disparate as to have comparatively little in common. While many of the essays are quite interesting and thought-provoking, and all are thoroughly researched and documented as well as being carefully written, this volume suffers greatly from a lack of interconnectedness, a quality often characteristic of thematically-oriented collections. Many scholars will find at least one of the essays very relevant and useful; few will view the entire collection in the same way.

Most significant about this collection is its orientation toward cosmopolitanism within Muslim contexts during the last two centuries rather than during the classical or medieval periods, and toward comparatively mundane rather than official or high-culture cosmopolitanisms. MacLean argues in the first chapter that he and Ahmed expect that these essays will encourage larger reflections on commonalities and differences: "In particular, this book seeks to ask the question, is the concept of cosmopolitanism useful for the study of Muslim societies and cultures of the past?" (p. 1) MacLean continues by giving a clear definition of cosmopolitanism, and states that contributors were asked to explore the relationship between "the high pan-Islamic and the grassroots vernacular form of cosmopolitanism within Muslim contexts." (p. 2) The contributors undeniably explore the vernacular, but the degree of engagement with the high pan-Islamic varies greatly from one essay to the next.

The most compelling essay in the collection is the fifth chapter: Ariel Salzmann's "Islampolis, Cosmopolis: Ottoman Urbanity Between Myth, Memory and Post-modernity," which addresses the status of various non-Muslim communities in Ottoman cities before the establishment of the modern Turkish state. Salzmann's text repositions this issue from previous studies by conceptualizing urban space as not "the experience of subordinated groups in terms of binary relationships between *a* subordinated group… and *the* Muslim political authority," (p. 71), but rather as the interplay *among* the subordinated groups, as well as with the dominant authority. The contrast between medieval Istanbul, where members of different faith communities often lived in mixed neighborhoods, and Venice of the same period, where Jews and Muslims were confined to literal ghettos, is illustrative. Salzmann documents how disasters such as plagues, floods and fires brought members of different communities together in mutual support, especially given the Ottoman state's general inability or refusal to provide much in the way of social services for these largely impoverished groups. Salzmann's most compelling example is of a lottery sponsored by a Jewish group to raise funds for the marriages of orphans; the ticket is printed in multiple languages, demonstrating that members of other faith communities, including Muslims, found the cause worthwhile. Such solidarity appears to be the exception rather than the rule in twenty-first century Istanbul; Salzmann begins the essay with the extraordinary event of the murder of a Turkish-Armenian journalist in 2007, which brought the city together.

Also of note is Thomas Kuehn's "Translators of Empire: Colonial Cosmopolitanism, Ottoman Bureaucrats and the Struggle over the Governance of Yemen, 1898–1914," which describes how Ottoman leaders learned from the British experience of managing subjects of different civilizational levels. Kuehn argues that to the Ottomans, "the principal reason for the success of British colonial rule seemed to be the native chief or local ruler under British sovereignty who governed on behalf of the crown and ensured British domination in a cost-effective way, not the Oxbridge-educated district officer of the Indian Civil Service who managed the locals under his charge" (p. 64). But actually, using British principles of indirect rule were problematic, especially given the perceived threat of British intervention in a Yemen not fully under Ottoman control. This issue led to a complex understanding both of principles of governance and of the (declining) Ottoman state's place in a world being divided up among more vigorous imperial states.

Other essays in the volume range farther (and further) afield, taking as their subjects the adoption of Islam among Tanzanian hinterland villagers in the interwar period; the means by which different groups of Muslims were (largely) integrated into a cosmopolitan whole in Mombasa; the use of curse words in colonial Alexandria and their problematic status with regard to laws intended to enforce respect for the dignity of officials; British and Persian perceptions of each other's cuisine during the early nineteenth century; a look at the work of the Muslim Indian artist

Abdur Rahman Chughtai and the tension between its comparative timelessness and cosmopolitanism and the poetry Chughtai's paintings accompanied in a published volume; and various understandings of the doctrine of *al-tashabbuh bi-l-kuffar* or "imitating the infidel." This last essay suffers from too broad a perspective, while the first essay, on the Tanzanian villagers, presumes a bit too much background knowledge on the part of the reader: while the endnotes provide ample references, a few paragraphs of explanatory background information would have greatly improved the otherwise informative essay.

Again, the plural "cosmopolitanisms" is perhaps the best indicator of this volume's content. MacLean and Ahmed are to be commended for bringing together such a wide range of scholarship under the same theoretical umbrella. The book undeniably manages to ask the question posed by its editors; however, given the plurality of cosmopolitanisms within the volume, whether that question has been fully answered has yet to be seen. **IC**

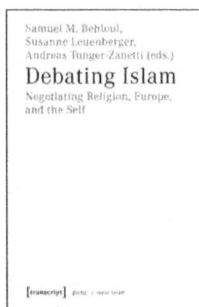

Samuel M. Behloul, Susanne Leuenberger and Andreas Tunger-Zanetti, Eds. *Debating Islam: Negotiating Religion, Europe, and the Self.* **Bielefeld, DE: Transcript Verlag, 2013. 372 pp. $45.00. ISBN: 978-3837622492.**

Since 9/11, much academic literature has discussed the integration/assimilation of Muslims in the West, and the need—or lack thereof—for socio-political accommodations. The current book under review, *Debating Islam: Negotiating Religion, Europe, and the Self* contributes to this discourse by offering new insight into the experiences of European Muslims. Developed during and after an international conference at the University of Berne, "Debating Islam: Switzerland-Europe," the text's primary aim is "to bring together case studies on various national Muslim debates and apply a comparative perspective on Europe and its specific perception of Islam" (p. 9). Strategically divided into three sections, each of which contains a brief introduction regarding its chapters' main themes, the text offers an array of in-depth analyses employing various theoretical frameworks to articulate its points. In doing so, it addresses many of the misconceptions percolating in European discourses about Muslims, and its findings ultimately dispel many of these misconstructions.

In his introduction, Samuel M. Belhoul explains that the chapters' objectives "exemplify what power relations dominate the current Western-European Islam debates and how these debates influenced individual and collective self-images and images of others" (p. 13). Belhoul asserts that, unlike former research on Muslims in Europe, this text brings to the foreground research on Switzerland, currently under-developed in the field, and more broadly highlights the "epistemic conditions" that facilitate how debates about Islam are constructed and perceived (p. 14). In order to address the aforementioned objectives, the author explains that the chapters address how Islam becomes a topic in socio-political debates, the conditions under which such debates take place, and the actors implicated in these debates. More importantly, the chapters also explain the ways in which these debates are "ultimately incorporated into an individual and a collective 'self-image' and 'image of others' by Muslims and non-Muslims respectively" (p. 17). Ultimately, Belhoul concludes that the chapters' empirical examples demonstrate how various European countries are currently dealing with religious and cultural diversity (p. 31).

Part I, entitled "Rules and roles" is comprised of five short chapters that address the varied and contradictory socio-political and normative-juridical conditions giving rise to Western–European debates on Islam, as well as how the actors involved are situated in, and respond to these debates. The first chapter by David Tyrer analytically discusses the racialization of Muslims in order to "shed light on the epistemic conditions surrounding Islamophobia and historicize its emergence" (p. 44). Frank Peter's contribution introduces a new way to approach the discourses surrounding Muslim religiosity in France. By looking at members of the Union of Islamic Organizations of France, Peter illustrates how the structural ambiguity of the law provokes the espousal of variant views concerning its nature and force, as well as issues pertaining to citizenship. Amélie Barras's chapter speaks to a growing body of literature that critically assesses the national and political discourses fixated on Muslim women's self-hood, autonomy, and their bodies, which often posit a monolithic presentation of the "Muslim woman." Mallory Schneuwly Purdie offers a compelling and insightful case study of the experiences of Muslim inmates in Swiss prisons. Incorporating collected data from interviews with Muslim inmates and wardens, this chapter demonstrates how many of the stereotypes surrounding Islam and Muslims infiltrate the prison system, and how these negative images affect the ways in which Muslim inmates turn to religion. The last chapter in this section by Katy P. Sian traces the history of Sikh Islamophobia in Britain to the Indian subcontinent, and explains how the complex relationship between Sikhs and Muslims acquires new meaning in the diasporic context.

Part II, entitled "The one facing the many" contains four short chapters that "work out the constitutive effects of public framings and imaginaries on current processes of Muslim self-formation" (p. 137). Petra Bleisch Bouzar employs the concept of "small stories" found within narrative theory to describe the religious self-formation of a female convert in Switzerland as she maneuvers through variant discourses about Islam and Muslims. Leon Moosavi, through in-depth interviews, reveals how the self-perception of British Muslim converts is radically different from how they are imagined by their non-Muslim peers. By incorporating the concept of "hybridity," Moosavi imparts the views of British Muslim converts who identify as both British and Muslim despite public skepticism concerning their loyalty to British society. Susanne Leuenberger's chapter employs participant observation methodology, and Butler's concept of "subjectivation" to analyze the speech of Gibril, a Swiss convert who reflects upon the public perception of his religiosity. Jörn Thielmann's contribution links Bourdieu's discussion of "fields" and Foucault's discussion of "techniques of the self" to address how German Salafi converts and reverts navigate Islamic "fields" and compete with their religious peers over who can be considered a "true" Muslim.

Part III, "The many facing the 'other' (within)" contains six chapters that account for the ways in which various actors position themselves in different debates about Islam in Austria, Denmark, and Switzerland. Farid Hafez describes how localized Austrian Muslim groups have struggled with and put pressure on the Islamische Glaubensgemeinschaft in Österreich to more effectively represent the community. Lene Kühle explains how the Danish Cartoon controversy of 2005–06 was a catalyst for positive socio-religious changes including, but not limited to, changed perceptions of Muslims and their requests, and the establishment of Muslim organizations. Marius Rohrer relies on newspaper analysis, interviews, and other documents, and employs Distinction Theory Text Analysis to discuss the case of Muslim parents in Basel, Switzerland who refused to have their children participate in coeducational swimming lessons in state primary schools. His findings contribute to debates regarding social structural change and diversity management practices. Andreas Tunger-Zanetti sheds light on how religious illiteracy and the "second public sphere" affected how Swiss citizens cast their votes during the federal referendum regarding the building of minarets. The last chapter in this section written by Matteo Gianni discusses how the renewal of assimilationist discourses in Switzerland "follows a conception of integration which is seen as entailing the mere adjustment (or normalization) of the 'Other' to (supposedly) 'common' democratic and liberal norms" (p. 314). In the last portion of his chapter, Gianni proposes an alternative conception of integration.

In the text's epilogue, Reinhard Schulze claims "debating Islam does not mean to debate Islam, but to use Islam as a self-referential tool with which to debate society" (p. 349). Each chapter in this text takes up this call successfully and the chapters' various theoretical approaches can be fruitfully employed in addressing future case studies in Europe. The text does not slip into polemical debates and its case studies expose readers to the myriad of opinions, experiences, and concerns shared by European Muslims and non-Muslims. At the same time, given the limited space allotted to each chapter, readers may want more examples and details regarding some of the respective cases to verify whether they are "exceptional" or can be qualified as a more normative reflection of the experiences of European Muslims. This might be particularly true for readers who are skeptical of Muslim integration in Europe and those already swayed by Islamophobic rhetoric. However, these chapters do offer a vital contribution toward the fostering of dialog and they propose examples that counter the aforementioned doubt. This text appeals to both academics and nonacademics alike, as it provides quality work treating the varied landscape of European countries' Muslim communities. Ultimately, the chapters seamlessly interweave empirical data with theoretical frameworks, all the while enabling larger thought-provoking questions regarding the religious and cultural diversity of Europe to loom large. **SF**

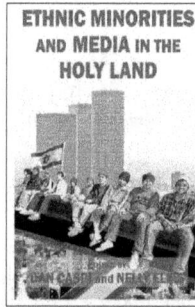

Dan Kasp and Nelly Elias, Eds. *Ethnic Minorities and Media in the Holy Land.* Portland, OR: Vallentine Mitchell, 2014. 252 pp. $89.95. ISBN: 978-0853038979.

Any discussion of ethnic issues in the Middle East is relevant in these times when, like now, when sectarian and ethnic issues seem to tear apart the fragile fabric of Middle East societies, the region seems to be in a relatively quiet and stable situation, and surely much more so in these times

Israel is in the eye of at least one of the storms happening just now, the current round of hostilities with Hamas in Gaza, but usually any discussion regarding ethnic issues in the Middle East deals with the state commonly referred to as the "Jewish state." So, to publish a book about exactly that issue amid the overall regional turmoil is important, timely and intriguing.

With Arabs in Israel (20% of the population) mostly regarding themselves as Palestinian citizens of Israel, not Israeli Arabs, it is relevant to discuss their situation, and while reading the book, I watched the media reports from there, describing the restiveness, if not outright hostility of many Palestinians in Israel toward "their" state, a clear indication of the relevance of the book on hand.

It was with great expectation that I read this compilation of articles, but I was disappointed. First, I cannot understand the name of the book. Since it is about Israel, why does the title refer to the Holy Land? This is a Christian term, and those who use it—particularly the Catholic Church—do it as part of their on-going theological debate with the Jewish claim to the land. Evangelical Christians, mostly supporters of Israel, tend to also use this term, but do it from a theological standpoint of support for the Jewish claim to the land. Be that as it may, the choice of the title stimulates questions; and as I usually do not subscribe to conspiracy theories, I will not raise some of these here.

Then there is the question of ethnicity. The editors are both noted experts in mass communication and the media in Israel, but if they edit a volume on issues concerning ethnicity, they owe the reader a thorough explanation as to their decisions to refer to Jews from the former Soviet Union and Mizrahi Jews (Jews from Muslim and Arab countries) as being an ethnic minority. Well, they can be defined as a cultural sub-group within the overall Jewish population, but they cannot be defined as ethnic minorities. If the editors believe it to be the case, they need to amplify on it.

The writers made an easy job of using definitions which may make sense in the Western world, but much less so in Israel itself. Does the reference to the Holy Land also fall within this category? But if they stand behind their classifications of Jews from the former Soviet Union and Muslim countries as ethnic minorities, it makes no sense at all not to try and classify and categorize the various sub-groups among Palestinians in Israel. There are Druze who are different from the Muslims, Christians and other sub-groups, but in the book they are all lumped together. Consistency is something to be expected from a book like this, but clearly, it is missing here. However, it is appropriate to include a chapter on the community of migrant workers in Israel, although I expected it to be about the growing community of Sudanese and Darfuris who make up a larger part of the population than the Filipinos in Israel.

Another miss in this book is a chapter—really an introduction to the book—in which the editors refer to the role, impact, and image of Israel's media in society at large, and body politic, in particular. Were a chapter like this to be correctly representative, the questions relating to Jews from the former Soviet Union and Muslim countries would have to be described in a way that would annul any reference to them as ethnic minorities. Many Israelis, particularly from the Right Wing feel alienated by what they consider to be the elitist, Left Wing oriented Israeli media. Most of the voters of the Right Wing in Israel are Jews from the former Soviet Union and Muslim countries. A coincidence?

In spite of all the above criticisms, I still recommend this book, if not for any other reason than for the three particular chapters—Anat First on Arabs in Israel; Amit Kama on Manila in Tel Aviv; and Amit Schejter, on the Palestinian—Israeli minority and the complexities of their broadcasting in Israel. **JO**

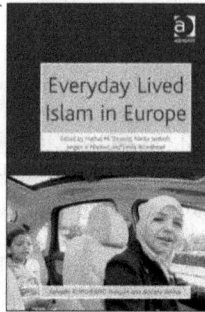

Nathal M. Dessing, Nadia Jeldtoft and Jørgen S. Nielsen, Eds. *Everyday Lived Islam in Europe.* **Surrey, UK: Ashgate Publishing Ltd., 2013. 183 pp. $99.70. ISBN: 978-1472417534. Ebk: $83.86. 986 KB.**

Everyday Lived Islam in Europe is part of a series on Religion and Society by Ashgate AHRC/ESRC publishers, along with other titles including: Social Identities Between the Sacred and Secular; Religion in Consumer Society Brands; Consumers and Markets; Discourses on Religious Diversity Explorations in an Urban Ecology; Understanding Muslim Chaplaincy; Ageing, Ritual and Social Change Comparing the Secular and Religious in Eastern and Western Europe; Varieties of Religious Establishment; and Media Portrayals of Religion and the Secular Sacred Representation and Change.

Everyday Lived Islam in Europe stands out in the series for both its breadth and attention to the particularities of localized practices of Muslims in Europe. The theoretical and methodological contribution of the book situates itself in a long tradition of ethnographic fieldwork and embedded observation, but nicely packaged as a theoretical whole. The authors' aim to "shift the gaze from 'hypervisible' forms of institutional religion" to the ways Muslims "live" their religion everyday in "shops, schools, workplaces, health centres" over the lifecourse (p. 2).

Topics covered in the book include: theoretical and practical methods for studying "everyday lived Islam;" case studies so diverse that Muslims included Gujarati Women in Leicester, England, young Bengali Muslims in the East End of London, minority Muslims across Germany, Denmark, Spain, and even Somali Muslim women in Finland. The theoretical approaches to illustrating "everyday lived Islam" included such diverse perspectives as incorporating individual spirituality and emotions, healing practices, understanding identity through labels, and "otherness" in the context of both current and historical conflicts. The methods used to understand less visible religions included placing identity cards on a table in order, many in-depth interviews, and years of embedded ethnographic field research.

The project is ambitious, and the authors naturally can only contain slices of life to illustrate, but cannot fully convey, their theoretical aims in 183 pages. However, the attention to the little "traditions" of "less-visibly institutional" forms of religiosity among Muslims in Europe is—and I agree with the authors here—of utmost importance in understanding how Islam in Europe both conforms and responds to the larger de-institutionalization of religion in Europe over the last century. Scholars of religion can look to this work, comprised of both senior scholars of religion and Islam in Europe, as well as up and coming stars, as a good example of the kind of inter-generational insight and innovative theoretical framing that is necessary to contribute to the larger discussion of religion's meeting places among a variety of metamorphosing cultural traditions. **ALG**

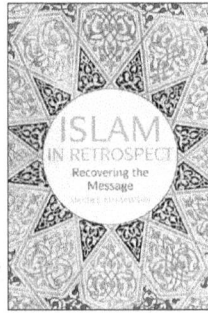

Maher S. Mahmassani *Islam in Retrospect: Recovering the Message.* **Northampton, MA: Olive Branch Press, 2014. 800 pp. $35.00. ISBN: 978-1566569224.**

For the innumerable Westerners who believe that Islam mandates wife beating, suicide bombings, honor killings, and any number of other heinous acts, *Islam in Retrospect: Recovering the Message* would come as quite a surprise. Mahmassani writes of an Islam that is pacifist, humanist, secular—something rather alien to the Islam found in the mainstream Western media. For many with limited knowledge of Islam, this book will be welcomed and celebrated. However, academically speaking, Mahmassani's methodology presents challenges. Likewise, although a good deal of the author's points are valid, *Islam in Retrospect* should be read with a grain of salt, as not all aspects of the book may be practical or desirable. Mahmassani's work could be considered, perhaps, similar to Abou El Fadl's *The Great Theft* (HarperCollins, 2007), yet a less concise and less meticulously researched version of it.

Mahmassani introduces his work by stating a number of prevailing "myths" about Islam, including that it is "incompatible with reason" and modernity and that it is a fascist, all-encompassing political and economic system. Each is followed by brief challenges of these myths, which he expounds later. The book is then divided into three parts. Part One discusses the universality of Islam, while Part Two covers the issues of secularism, Islamic state, and Shariʻa. Finally, Part Three considers "progressivism" and human rights concerns. The crux of Mahmassani's argument is that the *Qurʾan* is the only "universal" part of Islam, and as such, *Islam in Retrospect...*

seeks to unread centuries of character and practice to make Islam more applicable to today. Asma Barlas engages in a similar exercise in her book, *Believing Women in Islam* (University of Texas Press, 2002).

This "recovered" form of Islam, as proposed by Mahmassani, is decidedly familiar, reminiscent of Protestant Christianity—anyone, regardless of educational level, has the right to approach the text and interpret it in anyway he so chooses. However, one must not forget the flipside of this coin; Salafism, the phenomenon Mahmassani implicitly desires to undermine, is also regarded by some scholars, like John Esposito, as "Protestant Islam." Furthermore, when anyone is able to offer his own textual exegesis, extremisms and puritanical interpretations of the *Qur'an* and Hadith can be read into these texts, albeit falsely, as a result of a lack of religious education. Hence, this is why a majority of Muslims practice *taqlid* that is, following or imitating the interpretations and rulings of those who have expertise in Islamic jurisprudence. Yet, taqlid is not "elitist," as Mahmassani believes; no Muslim is *mandated* to follow someone else's interpretations. Rather, there is the implicit recognition that correctly interpreting and understanding religious texts is arduous. Therefore, in the absence of formal religious jurisprudential education, if a Muslim chooses to engage in one's own exegesis, it is only binding on oneself. Otherwise, as some suggest, this can give rise to harmful and incorrect renditions of the religion, as in the case of Salafism.

The topics covered by Mahmassani, including Shari'a, the Islamic state, governance, and the role of textual sources, are certainly of interest to both Sunnis and Shi'a, yet it is unclear in *Islam in Retrospect* ... whether Mahmassani intends to write about Sunni Islam, Shi'a Islam, conflates the two, or imagines a future in which these sectarian divisions do not exist, as his intention in this regard is never discussed. In fact, he rarely, if ever, mentions the terms "Sunni" or "Shi'a." Rather, the clearest evidence of such division comes in the form of his chapter on "Islam and the Mind," in which he argues for a sort of neo-Mutazili conception of free will. In this, the author implies that God does not yet know the future and that this is the mindset most compatible with modern, revisited Islam. This assertion arises from a notion that predestination is inherently fatalist and that it somehow removes the justness intrinsic to God's being. However, there seems to be a lack of comprehension of the Ashari concept of *kasb*, or acquisition, on the part of the author, a particularly troubling issue considering that Sunnis today most often align themselves with this doctrine. Kasb is not fatalistic, nor does it make God unjust or unknowing. This argument conflicts with majority Muslim opinion. Hence, as this book is a sort of prescription for the future of Islam, it is relatively implausible to think that such an idea would be welcomed by the majority of Muslims.

A final issue concerns Mahmassani's position toward secondary sources, i.e., Hadith (prophetic tradition). Methodologically, he adheres solely to the *Qur'an*, questioning the authenticity and applicability of Hadith, arguing that they, largely, are context-specific and thus irrelevant and potentially detrimental to modern times. However, when a Hadith is "meaningfully relevant," the author may use it to aid in his interpretation of the *Qur'an*. While it is true that Hadith have been used and abused to "sacralize" harmful cultural or societal practices, dismissing a large segment of the Hadith collection on the grounds of lacking authenticity indicates poor understanding of how prophetic traditions have been used in the traditional Islamic scholarship, i.e., level of authenticity, context-specificity, and generalizability. Rather than rejecting negative Hadith and accepting positive ones, there has been a tendency in traditional Islamic scholarship to reject the weak and trust the strong. Mahmassani fails to offer a convincing argument as to why Islamic scholarship should depart from this approach. Likewise, the author suggests that the fact that Hadith are not "divine"—in contrast to the *Qur'an*—is grounds to reject them.

In light of these considerations, *Islam in Retrospect...* does serve to remind us of some very important realities, including the ontological sameness of men and women, of the applicability of Islam to all times and places, the ease of practice of the religion, and the fact that Islam absolutely can peaceably live beside other religions and within secular political systems. Indeed, much of this has been lost over the years, and as such, Mahmassani's goals are noble. Yet, we must remember, religion is not a competition. As such, apologia and reformation is not the way to proceed in order to appease others. **CL**

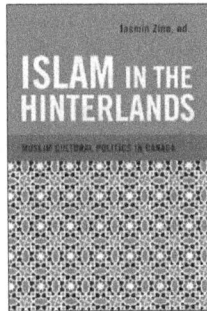

Jasmin Zine. *Islam in the Hinterlands: Muslim Cultural Politics in Canada.* Vancouver, BC, Canada: UBC Press, 2012. 340 pp. $90.00. ISBN: 978-0774822732.

Since the events of September 11, 2001, Muslims across the Western world have endured challenges to their citizenship and sense of belonging. The security concerns that arose in the wake of that day have had a deep impact on Muslims, as their loyalties have been questioned, their lives marked for surveillance and criminal profiling, and their status as residents called into doubt. The concern that Muslims might constitute a sort of fifth column of radical Islamism has become a common theme of numerous speaking tours, books, and websites. Many Muslims and others have raised concern over the spread of "Islamophobia" as a result of the fear generated throughout these media.

The impact of these influences on the cultural politics of Canada sets the backdrop for this collection of essays. While cultural pluralism is a source of pride for most Canadians, several developments over the past decade have drawn attention to the ways in which Canadian cultural politics have proved punitive toward Muslims. One was the 2004 refusal of the Ontario government to contemplate adding Shari'a courts to approved forms of personal arbitration amid widespread suspicion of Muslim social mores. Another was the ongoing use of "security certificates" by the Canadian government to detain a number of Muslims suspected of ties to international terrorism without publicly revealing any evidence. Yet, another was the passage of an infamous 2007 Citizen's Code in the town of Herouxville, Quebec, which pointedly sought to "inform new arrivals" to the way of life in Quebec where women could drive, hold a job, and be certain that they would not be killed or publicly beaten, the assumption being that immigrant cultures did not share similar values. That same year saw the death of Aqsa Parvez, a Pakistani teenager killed as the subject of a so-called "honor killing," The scholars contributing to this book hold that these developments and others provide normative ways in which Canadian society forms boundaries to marginalize and exclude immigrant communities.

The collection holds together well as a set of critical reflections. The contributors are almost all Muslim scholars based in Canadian universities, working in the fields of communication, sociology, political science, religion, and education. Most of the authors view the issue of Muslim absorption into Canadian culture through the lens of critical theories of race, culture, and gender. In this sense, the editor understands the effort made by these scholars as a sort of authentic jihad for understanding, awareness, and social justice (p. 34). The contributors use several different methods, including content analysis of prominent local newspapers, interviews with young Muslim women, and historical and documentary analysis of relevant texts. Their focus is on the use of media and public policy as a means of reinforcing how the essentialized Muslim "Other" differs from the equally essentialized Canadian identity. The collection is well written and the difficult editorial task of bringing together a diverse set of scholars on a topic such as this has been ably performed by Dr. Zine.

Throughout the text, the contributors marshal evidence well to make the point. They use a widely varying analysis to point to ways that Muslims are classified as outsiders to an essentialized Canadian identity. The two content analyses of Canadian news media demonstrate how they "have reproduced Orientalist thought and frameworks of meaning" (p. 132) according to analyst Yasmin Jiwani, as well as how they have manipulated the idea of "threat" implicit in the presence of immigrant communities, according to Jacqueline Flatt (p. 252). Shaista Patel conducts a critical analysis of Canada's anti-terrorism act, voicing the concerns of Muslims that the act veers toward criminalizing motivations rather than acts, since "if there were two equally heinous acts of terror, one committed for an ostensible religious purpose and the other for the sake of creating fear itself, the former would be designated a 'terrorist' act, whereas the latter would be labeled merely a criminal act" (p. 286). Several contributors are able to contribute their own experiences, and their knowledge of Islamic schools, students, or activists to help demonstrate their points.

They also admit ways in which Muslims themselves contribute to the marginalization of their community. Jasmin Zine's fascinating account of her conversations with veiled Islamic school students reveals the ways in which they deal with "racism and Islamophobia in society at large… at the same time contending with patriarchal forms of religious oppression in their communities" (p. 208). Reflecting on the furor over the approval of Shari'a arbitration in Ontario, Itrath Syed points out that "[t]he irony is that much of this construction of Muslim women as universally oppressed originated with Muslim women and their representatives, who themselves were not without power" (p. 73). In an assessment of literature by prominent Canadian Muslim dissidents Raheel Raza and Irshad Manji, contributor Meena Sharify-Funk points out that Manji's "reluctance to articulate what it is that genuinely *inspires* her about Islam renders her critique unpersuasive and unmoving even to worldly and self-critical Muslims" (p. 156). Ironically, though Muslims are said to be marginalized by Orientalist and racist tropes in Canadian society, they do possess enough agency to become a part of the story of their own marginalization.

But this complexity points to some of the limitations of race theory, Orientalism, and Islamophobia as theoretical tools. Critical race theory often seems a little over determined and occasionally petulant in the Canadian context. First, Canada has not (yet?) seen the most egregious forms of Islamophobia, like arguments over mosque construction, or wide-ranging headscarf bans. Muslims are well-connected in Canadian society, boasting a higher-than-average level of education and participating in both formal electoral politics (indicated by the number of Muslims voted into electoral office) and in informal politics of community organization (as indicated by Katherine Bullock in her contribution to this volume). Canada has also provided the context in which the reconstruction of the social imaginary of the Muslim in the form of the unique sitcom "Little Mosque on the Prairie" has taken place, as is explored by Aliaa Dakroury in her chapter.

There are other problems and limitations that arise out of the use of critical and race theory. The first is that Muslims are not all immigrants and the category of Muslim, though most often tied to immigrant communities, is also a religious category that can be divorced from race. Religion as a category can be understood as a concept that is different from race in the sense that it is cognitive: it is subject to defense and debate, and its very nature is heterogeneous and malleable over time, making it a unique social category. Many of the problems that are identified with race in this volume could also be said of other religious communities who do not suffer the same racial stigmas as Muslims. For example, the assertions about gendering in certain cultures are frequently made about fundamentalist, evangelical, and Mormon communities. Equally, the refusal of the government of Ontario to countenance Shari'a law courts also led to the elimination of all forms of religious arbitration in that province, granted as a means of seeking to overshadow what might otherwise have been a basic form of racial prejudice. What is more, the problems faced by Muslims in achieving their rights amid the educational system in Ontario are shared by many religious communities. Nadeem Memon's observation in his chapter that Islamic schools are a creation of "parents who espouse a sentiment of selective engagement with public institutions in Canada" (p. 200) could just as easily describe the motivations of Christian school parents. One wonders how the constructivist use of religion as a social category might be helpful to put in dialog with these critical assessments.

Occasional logical jumps and editorial problems mar the text. For example, Flatt's content analysis judges perceptions of Muslims in sample that is already selected based on references to security certificates. The application of this sample to coverage of Muslims as a whole suffers from an ecological fallacy. She also immediately associates these articles' depiction of immigrant men as "Muslim males," even if those descriptors are not evidenced in the manifest content. Finally, there are occasional editorial problems that are relatively minor but nonetheless irritating. Strangely, the editors seem to have used an odd variant spelling, ignoring the usual standard transliteration of the term "Shari'a."

Nevertheless, *Islam in the Hinterlands* stands as a fascinating contribution to scholarship of critical race studies, Muslim status in Western societies, and the politics of Islam and politics in the Canadian context. **PSR**

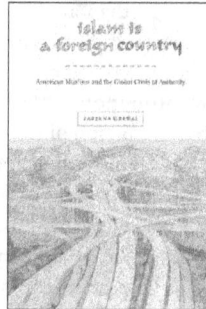

Zareena Grewal. *Islam is a Foreign Country: American Muslims and the Global Crisis of Authority.* New York: New York University Press, 2014. 409 pp. $71.10. ISBN: 978-1479800889. Pbk: 393 pp. $25.00. ISBN: 978:1479800568. Ebk: $11.99. 1720 KB.

In the aftermath of the 9/11 attacks there was an intense interest in learning about Islam and American Muslims. A number of books on Islam and Muslims came out with varying degrees of usefulness. Some of these books were written by American Muslims. One of these books is Zareena Grewal's *Islam is a Foreign Country*. In this book, Grewal weaves the stories of "Muslim student travelers"—American Muslims who travel to Muslim majority countries to advance their religious knowledge—into the controversies and issues surrounding Islam and American Muslims.

In the Introduction, Grewal writes that her book "does not offer a definitive re-form program in order to resolve Islam's presumed crisis; rather it offers a far more complex and revealing picture of global debates, both about and among [Sunni] Muslims that get at the heart of anxieties (both most Americans and Muslims' own) about Islam's place in the world" (p. 22). Grewal does not clearly state the two key reasons that there is a "global crisis of authority" in Sunni Islam: the abolition of the Caliphate in 1920, and the al-Azhar's loss of its legitimacy and moral authority due to Nasser's transforming the office of the Sheikh al-Azhar into that of a political appointee who is globally perceived as issuing fatwas on demand from the head of the Egyptian state. These two factors, more than anything else, helped create the "global crisis of authority" in the world of Sunni Islam. But, in Sunni Islam, neither the Caliph nor the pre-Nasser Sheikh al-Azhar had the position that the Pope has, or the Imams have in Shi'a Islam. Hasn't Sunni Islam survived with four schools of thought and a multitude of religious opinions on the same issue? Grewal herself recognizes this characteristic of Sunni Islam: "[H]istorians emphasize the enormous importance of this failed inquisition to the development of the highly decentralized structure of Sunni Islam in particular, noting that had the inquisition succeeded, it may have formed a hierarchy similar to those in other religious traditions" (p. 40). Given the history and the diversity of the tradition of Sunni Islam, why is having disputes as to religious authority a problem? Grewal identifies "incoherence" of the religious debates as the problem: "[D]isagreement over the criteria that make one a religious authority do not in and of themselves constitute a crisis, because crisis is more than mere confusion, even communal confusion, as a result of an unresolved religious debate. The sense of crisis derives from the sense that religious debates are "becoming incoherent" (p. 41). Grewal does not explicate fully what is this "incoherence."

Grewal's book is very useful in its study of American Muslims. One of the major contributions of her book sheds light on the phenomenon of the "Western stu-dent-traveler," men as well as women, a type of traveler that became an object of suspicion in the post-9/11 United States (p. 31). What makes the book readable and her ideas accessible to the reader is her opening each chapter with personal stories of the student traveler. She brings to life the abstract and theoretical discussions by weaving these stories into the narrative of Islam, and particularly American Islam.

Grewal's book comes up short when she describes and analyzes the activities of American Muslim activists and the government authorities in reacting to the 9/11 attacks. In Chapter 7, for example, she discusses the two "transformations" of Hamza Yusuf, giving the impression that the sincerity of the man is to be ques-tioned. Is it possible that the magnitude of the shock and the absence of readiness to deal with it, along with a changing perception of reality, have caused a genuine and sincere struggle to cope with the aftermath of the 9/11 attacks and caused a change of heart? Is the U.S. government only concerned about suppressing dissent and shaping Islam? Where is the recognition of the real issue of national security threats and the real concerns about radicalization and violence in the name of religion? Even paranoid people have real enemies.

Grewal begins the book with a reference to Dearborn and ends the book with a reference to Detroit. As a former Detroit resident, that hit home. A few days after the 9/11 attacks, while living and practicing law in Detroit, this reviewer heard the Detroit FBI special agent John Bell say: "We are in your community because the attackers were Arabs and Muslims." I doubt that he, or the FBI "higher ups" in Washington, DC thought of or cared about the nuances of Islam and its crisis of authority. There was a bona fide fear that more attacks were in the works and the mandate of the FBI, as revealed in the then Attorney General John Ashcroft's book *Never Again*, was not only to catch the perpetrators of terrorist attacks but to prevent future attacks as well (2006).

This surveillance and scrutiny, Grewal believes, hurt the ability of Muslim Americans to effectively deal with and resolve the crisis of authority: "As we will see, the presence of external scrutiny, both the presumed presence of governmental surveillance and the mainstream media spotlight, actually transforms the ways Muslim American intellectuals and religious leaders speak to one another, profoundly shaping their debates about the crisis of authority" (p. 296). It is not clear if there is self-censorship on matters of foreign policy or a generalized self-censorship that includes debates and discussions on the crisis of authority in Sunni Islam in America and elsewhere. It is more likely that it is the former.

The Epilogue closes on an unduly pessimistic note about the future of Islam and Muslims in the United States. Grewal ends the book with the tragic death of Imam Luqman Abdullah. But the Imam Luqman tragedy is hardly representative of the challenges of American Muslims, and it is not a fair representation of the past or present relationship between American Muslims and the government. It is a stretch to move from the Imam Luqman tragedy to draw this conclusion: "The shrinking place of dissent in U.S. mosques brings together many of the threads of this book: the competing constructions of Sunni religious authority, the significance of religious knowledge, the relationship of devout Muslims to the state, the diversity of the Umma, and the place of Islam in the U.S. and in the world" (p. 354). The challenges facing American Muslims include the thinking behind the case for a guilt-by-association policing as argued for by Marc Sageman in *Understanding Terror Networks* (2004). A more pressing concern is the fear that the FBI is manufacturing terrorism threats in the community. In *The Terror Factory: Inside the FBI's Manufactured War on Terrorism*, Trevor Aronson examines a number of FBI investigations where, he argues, the government pushed unstable American Muslims down the radicalization path, and in sting operations, provided these individuals with the means to act on violent inclinations. The American Muslim interest is pulling their young and unstable from the radicalization path and rehabilitating them. There is also Grewal's calling Dearborn "little Beirut." Beirut is a cosmopolitan city, Dearborn a village in comparison. Very few Beirutis live in Dearborn. Those who know Dearborn and Dearborn Heights know that the joke is that these two cities are Bint Jbail and Bint Jbail Heights, referring to the strong demographic presence in Dearborn and Dearborn Heights of Americans who hail from the Lebanese Shi'a southern village of Bint Jbail. As to the endangered species of American Muslim charities, Grewal briefly mentions American Muslim charities and the challenges they faced in the post 9/11 world (p. 313). These American Muslim institutions deserved more attention from Grewal due to the role they play, along with Islamic centers and Islamic schools, in the life of American Muslims.

Despite the concerns outlined above, I recommend this book. Anyone interested in Islam in general and American Islam in particular would find the book readable and highly informative. This book is useful for classes on Islam, American Muslims, or Terrorism and, because it is inexpensive, it is an ideal supplementary book to go along with a course textbook. **IAA**

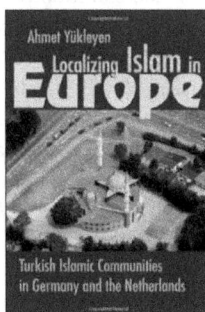

Ahmet Yükleyen

Localizing Islam in
Europe

Turkish Islamic Communities
in Germany and the Netherlands

Ahmet Yukleyen. *Localizing Islam in Europe: Turkish Islamic Communities in Germany and the Netherlands.* **New York NY: Syracuse University Press, 2012. 304 pp. $39.95. ISBN: 0815632622.**

Throughout the past decade, the topic of Muslims living in the West has remained one that is simultaneously controversial, confounding, and heavily discussed within the social sciences. Despite this extended and continued period of discussion, there are few texts within the genre that are based on extensive fieldwork, or provide the detailed and concise descriptions that are often necessary in understanding a particular social occurrence. Political scientists and policy analysts alike may look to *Localizing Islam in Europe: Turkish Islamic Communities in Germany and the Netherlands* to present the necessary components that are to be considered and utilized when drafting policies to better the lives of this particular demographic. The ethno-national identity of Muslims and the European country they live in is significant in understanding the development of Islam in Europe. Yukleyen illustrates this, examining Islam and Turkish Muslim immigrants within the context of their countries of origin, as well as current countries of residence within Western–European nations.

Yukleyen addresses many aspects that characterize Muslims in the West, drawing from research and fieldwork which examine Turkish Muslim immigrants living in Germany and the Netherlands, as well as the complex individual traits present within five different functioning Islamic communities. Making use of case studies canvassing the Gulen, Süleymanli, Northern and Southern Milli Görüş, and Kaplan communities, he aptly shows the different possible outcomes that arise as a result of Islamic communities responding to the conditions and stresses of their environment.

There are several facets to his research, each sufficiently explained through detailed descriptions of the methodological framework used in order to survey and interpret each of the communities. Stating that "Islamic communities have the strongest influence on Muslims in Europe in shaping their religiosity" (p. 3), Yukleyen illustrates how Islam and Europe influence each other through the development of varying Islamic interpretations. Throughout each chapter, he presents the different components active within each of the communities and describes how social and contextual interactions bring about specific differences in Islamic interpretations.

His approach to this topic has various related focuses, such as "who has the authority to speak in the name of Islam" (p. 303), which influences how the communities adapt within the European setting. The mechanics of this relationship work toward establishing that Islam and European ideals are not necessarily two contradictory ways of life. In doing so, the author analyzes how religious authority (the proper practices of a 'true Islam') is established based on differences in religious Islamic community, relations between the community and the state's legal framework regarding state policy, and the integrative measures that Islamic communities provide for Muslim immigrants. The components operate simultaneously resulting in "an internal authority formation and interpretation unique to each Islamic community, which creates internal checks and balances" (p. 109).

With each chapter, Yukleyen presents each of the components for analysis and discussion. Policymakers and analysts would take particular interest in the chapters devoted to the integrative measures taken by the European countries as well as the integrative opportunities Islamic communities provide. For example, in comparing the Milli Görüş communities of Germany and the Netherlands, he finds that the multicultural policies characteristic of the Netherlands result in greater social acceptance of Muslims; conversely, Germany's Milli Görüş ranks among the highest threats to German society due to the nation's 'partially-exclusionist' policies. Yukleyen uses the disparity between two branches of the same community to show that "multicultural policies help Islamic organizations to integrate and adapt their interpretation of Islam to their European setting" (p. 220).

With *Localizing Islam in Europe*, Yukleyen expertly adds to the discussion of Muslims living in the West. Perhaps the most pertinent of his additions is his description making up the levels of the Islamic field in Europe. The first level relates to Muslims' production of religious authority within any given community; the second level describes the competitive relations that Islamic communities have with one another; the third level of the Islamic field refers to the relationship established between the community and the state in which they exist. Throughout the book, the depth of his research and analysis work to present his overarching argument that "one can be equally European and Muslim (p. 221). In the continuing discussion of Muslims in the West, Yukleyen's publication provides a thorough reserve of knowledge of the symbiotic relationship between Western Muslims and the nations in which they reside. **ET**

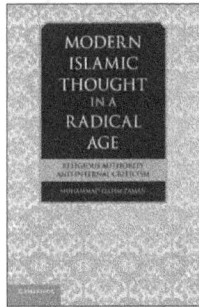

Muhammad Qasim Zaman. *Modern Islamic Thought in a Radical Age: Religious Authority and Internal Criticism*. Cambridge, UK: Cambridge University Press, 2012. 363 pp. $94.00. ISBN: 978-1107422254.

Modern Islamic Thought in a Radical Age: Religious Authority and Internal Criticism, authored by Muhammad Qasim Zaman, provides a scholarly synopsis on internal debate between traditional and contemporary religious authority in Islam. Zaman focuses his analysis on the works and deliberations of scholars of the Middle East and South Asia. The book offers a comparative perspective in the evaluation of the works and debates of Muhammad Rashid Rida and Yusuf al-Qaradawi from the Middle East, and Ubayd Allah Sindhi, among other Deobandi scholars from South Asia. Over nine chapters, Zaman overviews a broad-ranging discourse on consensus, *ijtihad*, contestations of the common good, deliberations on religious education, the legal rights of women, social and economic justice, and denouncing violence.

The book provides an intellectual assessment of debates amongst scholars on issues where the foundational texts of the *Qur'an* and Shari'a do not provide a direct provision. Zaman not only highlights commonly recognized disagreements amongst modern and traditional scholars over matters such as identifying *maslaha* or the common good, but he brings forth the ambiguity of internal criticisms.

Such matters as the traditional scholarly background of the ulama roster were contested by the Ulama Union, founded by Qaradawi in 2004. Zaman further portrays the debates of contemporary ulama concerned with the image of Islam, particularly with disputes relating to women, and how such issues led the Deobandi Fiqh Academy to revisit some of the long-standing norms of the Hanafi School.

Throughout the book, Zaman portrays the debates and critiques of contemporary scholars, or ulama with a special focus on Qaradawi, Rida, and Sindhi. Yet he was careful to indicate the tenuousness of their work, as they all lacked a broad social base and portrayed a pragmatic leaning. None of the three scholars, though prominent, had any formal students; and all three at some point in their lives, had received some form of patronage from various authorities.

Zaman is the Robert H. Niehaus 1977 Professor of Near Eastern Studies and Religion at Princeton University and has extensive works on religious and political thought in traditional and contemporary Islam in both the Middle East and South Asia. Furthermore, Zaman relies on a rich bibliography of 31 pages with references dating from 1883 until 2011, and a nine page index. The 363 page book is divided into sections: the first one focuses on the debates on consensus, ijtihad, and on the common good, or maslaha; the second section provides case studies on religious education, the legal rights of women, social and economic justice, and denouncing violence. A recommended scholarly work. **DW**

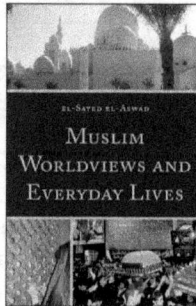

El-Sayed el-Aswad. *Muslim Worldviews and Everyday Lives.* Lanham, MD: Altamira Press, 2012. 248 pp. $85.00. ISBN: 978-0759121195.

Muslim Worldviews and Everyday Lives examines how religiously constructed images of the world influence "ordinary" people's everyday lives. The book is divided into six main chapters with case-studies from Egypt, the UAE, Bahrain, and the United States, including informants from the Sunni, Shi'a, and Sufi sects. The material is mainly gathered ethnographically and the approach is a welcome contribution to contemporary studies on Islam. As el-Aswad observes, many studies on Islam and Muslims are politically oriented and focus on ideology, while he makes a conscious choice of separating "worldview" from "ideology," focusing on ordinary Muslims and their everyday lives. Worldview relates to belief systems and symbolic actions, while ideology is defined as related to more worldly orientated power. A world-view includes assumptions concerning how the universe is structured, which may go largely unquestioned, and are often unsystematized. For example, it is manifested in images and stories as well as beliefs, shared meanings and practices that render social life possible and plausible. The separation between ideology and worldview does not mean that worldviews are apolitical since they may be of importance to grass-root activity. As a part of a larger trend among scholars of religion, this approach to lived religion is an important contribution to the scholarship of religion in general, and illustrates how religion is apprehended and practiced among ordinary people.

An overarching aim with *Muslim Worldviews and Everyday Lives* is to present in-sights to scholarship about Islam and Muslim societies and to question the often derogatory misconceptions found in the global media discourse. El-Aswad is also critical of "New Orientalism" which he regards as an ignorant approach to Islam, focusing violence; and he holds it responsible for what he perceives as the emerging conflict between the West and Muslims, as it is seen as not only a fight against vio-lent interpretations of Islam, but against Islam as a whole. El-Aswad, on the other hand holds a view of Islam that appears as idealized when he argues that Islam never advocated terrorism. Islam is presented, as if it had agency, as having asserted its encompassing worldview, without completely rejecting secular modernity, accepting it in its moderate form. El-Aswad can be considered to perform "engaged research" in this book which is expressed in his hope that the approach used may increase cultural understanding and dialog between Muslims and non-Muslims, leading to more effective and peaceful policies. El-Aswad also holds that religious cosmology is re-emerging as an important player in the public arena; and he argues in the conclusion of the book that Muslim worldviews provide with a unified spiritual–social-meaning system, which could be mobilized for building a unified Muslim power structure.

The main thesis is that Muslims are influenced by an overarching Muslim worl-dview, based on the *Qur'an* and Sunnah, but that local and sectarian differences are important to consider when studying the variety of Muslim worldviews that can be observed. El-Aswad notes that worldviews are characterized by a diversity pertaining to ethnicity, culture, region, and religious orientation, which in his view strengthens and enriches the underlying shared unity. He emphasizes that there are no emic categories found in his material such as the outsider concepts of "Islams" or "local Is-lams" since his informants rather lay weight on the view that Islam is one and unified, encompassing various traditions and worldviews. The underlying worldview, which, to a large extent is captured in the declaration of faith in one God and Muhammad as his prophet, is the foundation for his informants' worldviews; but depending on region and sectarian belonging, their worldviews in more detailed form differ, and cause them to apprehend the world differently which informs how they act in this world, and relate to the unseen. The analysis shows that the worldviews can function as sanctifying mundane areas, such as connecting religious perspectives to economy and ecology, which may help people cope with various problems, find explanations and solutions, and make life comprehensible from within religious worldviews. In the opinion of el-Aswad, belief in sacred "invisibility" (*al-ghaib*) strengthens the Muslim worldview and identity, and has the power to influence ordinary people and their everyday actions, which is illustrated in the various case-studies.

El-Aswad argues that Western worldviews and ideologies impose an essentially secular perspective, and that global flows and cyberspace have opened new venues for Muslims to rethink their worldviews and social lives. Informants adapt their worldview to circumstances at the same time as they remain Muslim in their orientation to the world. One case-study illustrates how hybrid identities appear among Muslims in Detroit, who make use of the material and technological advancement in the U.S. El-Aswad notes that this does not mean that Muslims who are not in a diasporic situation are not making use of new technologies. Among informants in the Middle East, globalization and secularism are met with a Muslim worldview as a shield, without implicating a complete rejection. It appears to be a strategy of approaching changes through a religious worldview. The analysis shows that geographical borders are not the only important factor to identity construction. Rather, a dual consciousness develops which bridges real and imagined spaces. The hybrid American Muslim identities, for example, appear as plastic and flexible, and are colored by informants' ethnic and national origin as well as sectarian differences. El-Aswad explains that his American Muslim informants consider their Islamic worldview to be a balancing factor to materialism and secularism, not an alternative. The analysis illustrates that transnational and hybrid identities change and reconstruct in unpredicted ways; el-Aswad holds that Muslim Americans can be viewed as cultural mediators able to bridge dichotomies such as East and West.

The esoteric worldview of Shi'a in Bahrain constitutes another case-study, where the social side of the worldview is addressed in order to examine how religious practices impact the sociopolitical life of informants. The notion of revealing hidden truth and justice appears as the informants highlight how the unseen cosmology, reproduced through art and ashura-rituals, for example, are relevant and present in everyday life and is believed to have implications for the future of the informants. In placing the past in the present, the informants focus on a vision of the future which includes a belief that the hidden Imam will return and bring justice. Another case-study is the relationship between Sufi beliefs and practices in Egypt. Sufis are presented as living in an enchanted world, which is described as "embodied spirituality" requiring ethical and esthetic attitudes to the seen world. For example, saint's shrines are places of ritual activities linking the sacred and the everyday life. Those participating attempt to maintain good relationships with their saints and visitations (*ziyāra*) to a shrine establishes spiritual networks, not only with the saint, but also with other visitors. Another interesting case-study concerns the place of dreams and imagination which is related to the seen and unseen dimensions of worldviews. The author demonstrates the socio-cultural conditions that bring about support to certain dreams for constructing and understanding reality. Certain dreams are sanctified by religious worldviews and some aspects of worldviews are validated by dreams. A conclusion is that dreams are an integral part of his informants' world-view, and are regarded as giving clues for understanding spiritual reality and antic-ipate future events, and to glimpse the unseen, hidden reality, that is believed to influence people's lives in everyday reality, and also to give it meaning.

This is a rich and comprehensive book that poses questions to contemporary studies on religion in general and Islam in particular. The ethnographic approach and focus on ordinary Muslims illustrated through informants' practice and percep-tions of the world presents Islam as a lived religion that must be understood in local contexts informed by global processes. The book shows how worldviews inform and are informed by practice, and is a valuable comment on how Islam and Muslims are being studied and perceived today; and it highlights the need to rethink methods and understandings found among some scholars as well as journalists. It further illustrates the need to study religion as, to a large extent, being created, understood, reformulated, and practiced by ordinary people in connection to their daily life, dis-regarding what established religious scholars or acknowledged ideologues consider as being true religious belief or practice. **SO**

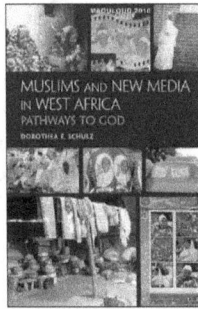

Dorothea Elisabeth Schulz. *Muslims and New Media in West Africa: Pathways to God.* **Bloomington, Indiana: Indiana University Press, 2012. Index. 306 pp. Pbk.: $27.95. ISBN: 978-0253223623.**

Dorothea Schulz's *Muslims and New Media in West Africa: Pathways to God* is a thoughtful project that aims at investigating the mass-mediated religious discourses and practices creating new, publicly engaged Muslim communities in West Africa. The book consists of seven chapters, of which parts of three chapters have been pre-viously published in scholarly journals. The book addresses Islamic renewal in West Africa, particularly in the urban areas of southern Mali where the author conducted ethnographic studies, especially in the town of San, and among other neighbor-hoods around the capital city of Bamako. Through utilizing comparative data, the author attempts to locate ethnographic findings within a broader politico-economic framework.

One of the book's objectives is to trace the recent movement of Islamic renewal in Mali from domestic realms to domains of public debate and interaction. Schulz's central point is that the integration of media into religion and politics has transformed the public sphere of the Islamic renewal movement more than other traditional Islamic groups. She examines the role played by new media technologies in sustaining and developing religious beliefs and practices of Malian people. The key concept on which the study is based is "pathways," included in the subtitle of the book. The author successfully uses this concept to expound the effort of Muslim revivalists in Mali to promote their religious tradition through using mass-media technology as one of the numerous pathways to God.

The author views the new political movement of Islam in Mali as the paradoxical outcome of the interaction between transnational networks, implying dependence, and national efforts to manage the economic and symbolic resources of the state. For instance, the family law reform, announced in March 2000 by Malian national radio encouraging democracy and public discussion, was critically reviewed and opposed by Muslim religious activists who thought that the law reflected Western influence, threatening women's traditional role, and Mali's authentic culture. By articulating their struggle with the states' official and political constructions in the language of religious rights, Muslim leaders accentuate Islam as central in a politics of religious and moral difference.

The book tackles the changes in the economic and social domains in Mali since the late 1980s with special focus on gender and intergenerational relations in middle and lower-middle-class households. The new economic conditions have resulted in a yearning for moral, rather than structural, reform. Schulz argues that economic liberalization of the mid-1980s, which shifted financial obligations between men and women or husbands and wives as well as between generations, has compelled women to engage in new domains of responsibility and self-reliance. With such new changes, many women from low-income households do not view themselves as marginalized or excluded. Rather, they show a distinct sense of dignity and self-containment.

One significant contribution of the book is that it addresses media engagements by Malian television viewers as a way to comprehend how people make sense of the changing moral domain of family life. Shulz points out that television audiences of urban Mali tend to apply a double process of media involvement by viewing different aspects of televised serials or soap operas as well as through engaging in debates about the moral issues generated by these serials regardless to their Western or American origin. Such serials encourage debate concerning gender and generational relations within broader religious and social contexts.

The author discusses the institutional foundations of Islamic renewal with special attention to Muslim women and their leaders, showing their initiatives related to the reassessments of gender relations. Most Muslim women's groups, formally recognized as part of civil society, are registered as an association under the auspices of the National Union of Muslim Women of Mali. Muslim women's groups integrate ideas from transnational Islamic revivalist trends, especially concerning women's leading role in societal renewal. Muslim women's groups, coming from the lower strata of urban populations, draw women who seek Arabic literacy and knowledge of ritual precepts. The social institutions of Muslim activism, visible in Mali's public arenas since the mid-1980s, at once challenge and reinstate the central importance of the state.

The author expounds the understandings of religiosity guiding Muslim Malian women in their search for piety. She argues that Malian women's personal efforts to cultivate a pious disposition intersect with broader social transformations that emerge at the interface of the institutions of state power and transnational intellectual trends and communication flows. Younger and unmarried women adopt a reformist identity stressing their effort to formulate a modern and cosmopolitan Muslim orientation distinct from a traditional Muslim identity through advocating for a stricter adherence to the rules of Islam and rejecting Western consumerism.

Schulz elaborates on the Muslim movements giving special attention to the popular movement of the Ansar Dine and its leader Sharif Haidara as an example of the increase in public and mass-mediated religious discourses. Both the diversification of a media market that, until 1991, had been under close state control, and the privatization of economic and religious activities encourage new forms of publicizing Islam. These forms include various Muslim orientations such as those associated with reformist trends in Saudi Arabia and Egypt, or those associated with the moral reform movement developed by "authentic" African Muslims. The latter movement is represented by the Ansar Dine whose leader depends on media technologies such as audio tapes, cassette sermons and radio broadcasts for delivering religious messages and creating a new sense of community—not through shared locality, but through circulation of tapes.

Schulz extends the discussion of the relationship between new media technology, personal spiritual experience, and religious discourses in Mali's public life. Media technologies such as audio-recording and visual representations are viewed as effective means that carry an ideology of enlightenment and progress. Similarly, the newly adopted media technologies have enabled the Islamic renewal movement in Mali to spread its moral and religious practices. However, these practices do not replace conventional forms of religious expression. The supporters of Islamic renewal in Mali, including members of the Ansar Dine do not view new media technology as connected with a Western ideological project of modernity threatening their local culture. Rather, they use these technologies to disseminate their religious and moralizing messages beyond the reach of the state. Within this context, the author argues that the prominence of an Islamic symbolic repertoire in broadcast genres refutes Habermas's view of the diminishing significance of religion and religious communication to the rise of the modern public sphere.

Although it is acceptable to state that new media technologies facilitate the publicity of a Muslim movement like that of the Ansar Dine, it is hard to apply such a statement to all popular Muslim movements. For instance, the Muslim Brotherhood, established in Egypt in the1920s and suppressed for decades by the state, has not entirely relied on media technologies for its continuation in popularity. Even before the establishment of new media, the Muslim Brotherhood had been publicly, nationally, and globally recognized, and has become, not only one of the predominant Muslim movements, but also the largest political opposition organization in many Muslim countries. The first democratically elected president of Egypt, Mohammed Mursi, is a member of the Muslim Brotherhood.

This book, had it been written in simpler or less wordy language would have been more readily comprehensible. For this reason, it is not recommended for undergraduate students. Overall, however, the book is a welcomed contribution to the scholarship of Islam, West Africa, and New Media studies. **ESA**

Katarzyna Górak-Sosnowska, Ed. *Muslims in Poland and Eastern Europe. Widening the European Discourse on Islam.* Warsaw, Poland: University of Warsaw, Faculty of Oriental Studies, 2011. 343 pp. ISBN: 9788390322957.

Various aspects pertaining to Islam have currently gained a prominent place in global academic and public discourse. However, in many, if not most instances the debates on Islam tend to focus on those geographic areas where Muslims constitute majorities, as in the Middle East, North Africa, and Southeast Asia; or where they are perceived by many as suspect minorities with implications for national and personal security, as in parts of North America and Western Europe. Until very recently, Eastern Europe and, indeed much of the post-Communist world, has been overlooked by the global English-language mainstream and more local (West) European discourses on Islam. In a few instances, when attention is focused on East European Islam, it is viewed through the prism of national and regional security and stability. This volume edited by Górak-Sosnowska enriches this debate by adding an array of important experiences, observations, and analyses from Central and Eastern Europe, which in some cases affirm the global trends, but in many others challenge or moderate them.

The book features 20 distinct chapters by some of the most prominent country and area experts, which are preceded by a forward and introductory chapter by the editor. The volume examines Islamic encounters in a total of nine countries through a multitude of theoretical and methodological lenses. Specifically, among the topics included in the analyses are cultural and literary studies, issues in migration, linguistic behavior, gender relations, relations between various groups within the Muslim communities, conversion, interfaith dialog, revival and survival of autochthonous Muslim groups, social justice, and intersections between religious and ethnic identities of minority groups. These issues are examined using predominantly qualitative methods, including interviews, participant observation, mass media analysis, examination of online forums, and Internet surveys. The book is divided in two major parts. A larger part (12 chapters) is devoted to examining Islam and Muslims specifically in Poland. In the second part of the book, eight chapters look into the questions pertaining to Islam in other parts of Eastern Europe.

It is difficult to do justice to all of the chapters examined in *Muslims in Poland and Eastern Europe* in a short book review; however, I see at least two major contributions that the authors of this volume have made. First, and foremost, I agree with the editor that this volume importantly qualifies "the deterministic approach," which predominates (West) European, and, generally, "Western discourse on Islam" which sees Islam as a force that "hinders integration of Muslims in the mainstream society of the West" (p. 24). In contrast, this volume shows that Islam has been a fact of life for hundreds of years in the central and eastern parts of the continent. Consequently, transferring unquestionably West European intellectual and policy-oriented approaches for understanding or dealing with East European Muslim populations is inappropriate. After all, an average Muslim of the West is fundamentally different from an average Muslim of the East. While low levels of integration and socioeconomic conditions are among the key problems pertaining to West European Muslims, autochthonous East European Muslims have shaped the cultures and societies of their homelands, often at the risk of assimilation or losing a distinct cultural identity, which are among the challenges currently faced by these collectivities.

Despite the caution that East European governments and societies should exercise in adopting West European approaches while dealing with their Muslim populations, this volume implies that the positive developments of West European nations in integrating immigrant Muslim populations constitute an important lesson for Eastern Europe as the region is swiftly changing its status from a place of net outmigration to that of a final destination for Muslim immigrants.

Second, this volume brings together and succinctly provides up-to-date information on the status, number, inner politics, and functioning of Islamic institutions and groups, and on biographical information concerning Islamic leaders in these countries. This alone is a major contribution to the English-language scholarship on Islam in the region. Consequently, this volume is likely to become an important guide for scholars and the general public interested in the issues of Islam in post-communist Europe. It is equally noteworthy that each individual chapter also contributes to the literature on the specific theoretical issue of interest, which renders this book relevant to numerous intellectual audiences.

Among other laudable points is the fact that the book covers some of the most interesting and under-researched cases, such as Hungary and Slovakia, where Islamic presence is not large. Since the countries with relatively large Muslim populations, such as Albania, Bosnia and Herzegovina, Kosovo, and Macedonia draw more attention in the general literature, it is understandable that they are not included in this volume. Yet, it would be intriguing to read about Islam in the Czech Republic, Croatia, Estonia, Latvia, Moldova, and Belarus in a subsequent work, when resources permit doing work on these cases.

In a similar vein, the book made me think about the way, in which its line of research might develop to consider transnational relations between autochthonous Muslim groups in the region. The volume makes it clear that cross-border relations with the Middle East are especially strong among the migrant Muslim communities. Moreover, it is understandable that some autochthonous Tatar communities may feel uncomfortable interacting with those across the border, possibly due to uneasy relations between the "parent" states. For example, as this volume points out, a leading Lithuanian Tatar imam would emphasize the distinct Lithuanian Tatar identity over a common identity with Polish Tatars. Still, one might expect that the process of democratization in Eastern Europe and its ongoing integration in the European Union and Schengen would make it easier for at least the Tatar communities in Poland, Lithuania, and Romania to communicate with stronger and well-established Finnish Tatars, and with those who arrived more recently to Central Europe, such as the Tatars of Germany. The First European Tatar Youth Forum held in Riga, Latvia, in April of 2012, shows that such trans-border relations are possible.

Similarly, it is interesting to note whether an active participation of Poland in NATO operations in areas populated by Muslims, such as Kosovo, Bosnia, Macedonia, Iraq, Afghanistan, Lebanon, and the Golan Heights, was facilitated by the presence of indigenous Muslim populations within Polish borders.

The book is well composed and the production errors are minor. Even when they are present, it is possible to discern the intended meaning from the context. For example, in a chapter on Polish Tatars, the author selected for research those Polish Tatars who identify with the Tatar ethnic group, as opposed to those who would think of themselves as Poles of Tatar descent, and are "practicing Islamists" (p. 54). From the rest of the chapter it appears that the author probably meant "practicing *Muslims*," not politically minded Islamists. However, language-related issues are insignificant and the substantive contribution of the book by far overshadows any formatting and stylistic deficiencies, which are minor.

In conclusion, this volume represents an important contribution to Islamic, East European, and Slavic studies. It, therefore, is a must-have book for anyone interested in the cross-section of these areas of study. The book should also be of importance to audiences interested in theoretical issues elaborated in the volume, which go beyond Islamic and Post-Communist studies. **RS**

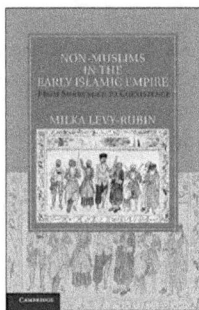

Milka Levy-Rubin. *Non-Muslims in the Early Islamic Empire: From Surrender to Coexistence.* Cambridge UK: Cambridge University Press, 2011. 267 pp., $90.00 (£55.00). ISBN 978-1107004337.

In *Non-Muslims in the Early Islamic Empire: From Surrender to Coexistence*, Milka Levy-Rubin brings a new approach to the study of the *Shurūt Umar* (Conditions of Umar) and the status of the *dhimmīs* under the early caliphate. She does this by focusing on questions of their *Sitz im Leben* and their sources of inspiration, looking for "the *longue durée* process that stood behind the formation of the status of non-Muslims under Muslim rule" (p. 2). By focusing on both "the *origins* and on the *process* of the formation of the status" (p. 2) rather than on the final product of the Shurūt Umar, Levy-Rubin is able to look beyond the Islamic milieu of the Shurūt Umar and focus instead on the precedents set by both the Byzantine and Sasanian Empires and the paths these traditions may have taken into Muslim law and society. Levy-Rubin organized the book in a way that breaks down the development of the Shurūt Umar and other regulations related to non-Muslims, and then demonstrates that the component parts of these regulations were present in the pre-Islamic worlds of the Byzantines and Sasanians.

Chapter 1 focuses on the authenticity of the surrender agreements between Muslims and non-Muslims as presented in early Muslim historiographical and legal literature. While many historians have looked at the surrender agreements recorded in texts such as the histories of al-Balādhurī or al-Tabarī with a suspicious eye as attempts to retroject later conventions into the past (a whole field of source critical approaches to these documents has developed over the past decades), Levy-Rubin places these treaties within a context of international treaties common across the Near East before the rise of Islam. Here she provides a summary of Greco-Roman, Byzantine, and Sasanian practices regarding international treaties, including treaties of surrender, and demonstrates that such treaties would have been familiar not only in the lands the Muslims conquered, but also in the Arabian Peninsula itself. When compared with such pre-Islamic treaties, Levy-Rubin argues that the treaties associated with the Muslim conquests appear to be outgrowths of pre-Islamic practices and, therefore, are more likely authentic, or at least closer in content to the original documents than suspected. This chapter perhaps best demonstrates Levy-Rubin's context-focused methodology and best makes the argument for the value in situating early Islamic history into a much broader Near Eastern context while also making a strong argument for the agency of the conquered peoples in determining the immediate outcomes of conquest.

Chapters 2–4 trace the evolution of the Shurūt Umar, *ghiyār* codes (codes of differentiation), and their enforcement over the seventh through ninth centuries. At the heart of Levy-Rubin's argument is the assessment that as the Muslim community grew and, most importantly, became increasingly urban, there occurred greater interaction between Muslims and non-Muslims. Therefore, she argues, the conditions outlined in individual treaties written at the time of conquest became increasingly unsuitable, making it necessary to redefine the status of non-Muslims in a unified manner. In Chapter 2, Levy-Rubin examines the development of such a canonical definition into the form of the Shurūt Umar in early ninth century juristic sources (particularly Abū Yūsuf's *Kitāb al-Kharā* and al-Shāfi'ī's *Kitāb al-Umm*) tracking a development in which restrictions on non-Muslims became increasingly tight, while the size and stability of the Muslim community increased, hitting a peak in the ninth century during the reign of the Abbāsid caliph al-Mutawakkil, when the *Shurūt Umar* achieved priority over other competing approaches. Chapter 3 focuses on the *ghiyār* codes, attempting to date a "*structured code or set of rules* rather than this or that particular regulation" (p. 88). Here, Levy-Rubin notes that, while many of the clauses found in the Shurūt Umar have origins in Byzantine legal codes, those "pertaining to the presence, dress, appearance, and behavior of dhimmīs in the Muslim public sphere" do not share similar origins (p. 167). Instead, Levy-Rubin argues that the ghiyār codes originate in Sasanian practices in which such distinguishing marks were an established principle of social hierarchy. By arguing such, she has moved beyond an understanding that places the codes of ghiyār not only in a Muslim context, even beyond an Abrahamic context entirely, placing it instead in the adoption of (what Levy-Rubin calls) the Sasanian aristocratic ethos. Chapter 4 examines the enforcement of these codes, finding early adoption of these restrictions on non-Muslims under the Umayyad Caliph Umar b. Abd al-Azīz, but little formal (or at least standardized) enforcement until the reign of al-Mutawakkil. Even in the ninth century, Levy-Rubin shows that enforcement of restrictions on non-Muslims was difficult and uneven, demonstrating a tension between the desires to elevate Muslim social standing with the realities of a diverse empire.

Chapter 5 explores the provenance of different statutes within the Shurūt Umar. Levy-Rubin admits that the Shurūt Umar is a unique legal document with no analogous documents found in the contemporaneous Mediterranean or Near East, but she finds companions for many of the individual rules found in the Shurūt Umar in legal treaties related to the treatment of the *metoikoi* in Athens, the *gerim* in Israel, as well as Jews and Samaritans under Byzantine rule. Uncovering a similar pattern in the Sasanian world for the treatment of non-Zoroastrians is more difficult due to the lack of a well-documented legal system, but, instead, Levy-Rubin can here focus on the better understood rules of Sasanian social hierarchy and associated laws of distinction, including sumptuary laws, which she argues is a model for the later Muslim ghiyār codes.

In the end, Levy-Rubin argues that the Shurūt Umar "thus reflects the completion of a process in which Muslim society was redefining itself versus the conquered societies" (p. 167). While the conclusions, both that the Shurūt Umar developed over time as the Muslim community evolved, and that these laws were largely inspired by Byzantine and Sasanian predecessors, are not that surprising, the detail with which she builds her argument solidifies our understanding of this transformation. The manner in which Levy-Rubin brings together Greco-Roman, Byzantine, Sasanian, and early Islamic sources provides a great resource for scholars interested in the development of early Islamic society. Levy-Rubin's work here is an important contribution to a growing body of research that is seeking to understand the development of the early Muslim community in its broader historical context. **RJH**

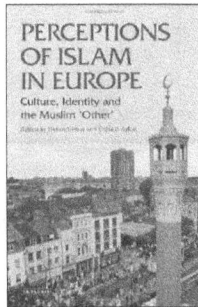

Hakan Yilmaz and Cagla E. Aykac, Eds. *Perceptions of Islam in Europe: Culture, Identity and the Muslim 'Other'.* **New York, NY: I. B. Tauris, 2012. 214 pp. £56.50. ISBN: 978-1848851641.**

According to the editors, there exist today four types of books that treat Islam and Muslims in Europe. There are the "Islamic threat" or the so-called "Eurabia" books, popular writings that warn of the immediate threat of Islam in its purported effort to subvert the European way of life and its civilization from the continent and replace it with Islam. Then there are the histories that provide analyses of the interaction between Europe and Islam in the *longue durée*, written by historians, such as Bernard Lewis. The third category in what is referred to as "free essays on Islamic movements and communities in Europe." These are monographs that treat the problems of integration faced by Muslim communities in Europe today, emphasizing conflicts between Islamic beliefs and Western institutions, and between Islamic political movements and Western democratic systems. Finally, there are the social scientific studies of Islam in Europe, which focus on various difficulties faced by European Muslim communities from the perspectives of sociology, politics, and cultural studies.

This book lies in the fourth category, but with a different and innovative perspective. Rather than focusing on ways in which European Islam is changing by virtue of its contact with Western notions and norms that it encounters in its new home, the goal of this book is to consider the cultural and institutional changes in Europe that have evolved through its present-day engagement with Islam. Europe is currently struggling as theological, political, social, and cultural questions bump into human rights issues, gender concerns, integration schemes, and security interests. "The debate about Islam in Europe is in reality part of a wider questioning of the new meanings of citizenship, pluralism, the evolving form of the European project, the nature of 'European values' and the relation between the state and religion" (p. 2).

The book is composed of 11 essays in two parts: "Theoretical Studies" and "Case Studies." They hold together well and are solid overall. The first, by Gerard Delanty, argues in his "Islam and European Modernity in Historical Perspective" that Europe and Islam are idealized notions. Although this notion is not new, Delanty develops it well in the context of the present discussion. Europe has always been a constellation of traditions, since its borders within and without were always fluid and it was always composed of a mosaic of civilizations. It was neither purely isolated nor purely Christian; and during much of the history of relationship with the Muslim world, it admired as much as feared its Muslim neighbors. Islam was considerably more tolerant in the Middle Ages and allowed for greater cultural and religious variety than has generally been recognized, in part because it never had a hierarchical and ecclesiastical structure. While the relationship between Europe and Islam has often been defined as contrary or conflictual by modern observers, and used as a means of defining a "European" identity by seeing Islam as the ""Other," that perspective does not adequately describe the actual history of Europe's relationship with Islam.

Deniz Kandiyoti's essay on Europeans' perspective on gender and citizenship in relation to Islam treats the problematic of how issues and boundaries are currently defined. The natural assumption of European superiority within the trope of "the West versus the East" tends to objectify and essentialize the true complexity of Islam, including Islam as practiced in Europe. Stephanos Pesmazoglou also treats European views of Islam. Jeffrey Haynes treats the effect of globalization on Islam and on politics and pluralism in the Muslim world, while Sia Anagnostopoulou examines the effect of European colonialism and colonial mentality, not only on European attitudes toward Islam, but also on their impact on Islam itself under the influence of colonialism. She cautions the tendency toward essentializing and aptly cites the Patriarchate of Constantinople in response to the rise of Western dominance in the early modern era: "In our times the devil has come up with another deception, the concept of Freedom, which is an alluring plan of the devil, so that nations are led to destruction and disorder" (p. 73).

Cagla E. Aykac treats the many and complex challenges that the European Union faces as it expands and incorporates more national communities and cultures while trying to maintain a sense of unity. Her essay treats the otherness of Muslims within the historical context of the otherness of various Europeans within the EU realm. The current tendency to associate racism with migration and security "gives a sense that racism in Europe is motivated by the growing presence of 'others' in Europe and thus fails...to recognize the very internal and historical precedents of racism in construction of European nation states" (p. 103).

A series of articles follow that concentrates on particular European countries. Katarzyna Gorak-Sosnowska treats the integration of the indigenous population of Polish Muslims who originated from Tatar migrations and invasions. Gerdien Jonk-er examines the portrayal of Muslims in German language text books from the early nineteenth century to the present, showing how the images conform with German views of self and other from the rise of modern nationalism through national so-cialism; and then a Germany divided all the way to newly developing post 9/11 narrative that is profoundly influenced by media fascination with whipping and stoning, the oppression of women and arbitrary rule. She cites an 1803 geography textbook in which was written, "Mohammad wrote a book of law full of ridiculous insinuations...There will be a day of atonement when Mohammad is transformed into a large ram and the Turks into fleas who hide in his fleece and he will swim over the ocean to Paradise where there exists a spring 70,000 miles in length, filled with honey-sweet wine. Otherwise he has forbidden his followers from drinking so that they may battle without drunkenness. The book of law is called Al-Quran" (p. 132).

Welmoet Boender examines the teaching of integration in the Netherlands, and notes, among other things, how the secular government overestimates the influence of imams on local communities. Sarah Silvestri compares the quite different struc-tures of the Muslim communities in the UK and Italy and the attitudes and policies directed toward them. Kenan Cayir studies changing perceptions of Europe among religious Muslims in Turkey, with its radical westernization history and current movement toward a less secular and more obviously Islamic nation-state. Islamist perspectives vary, and the conventional anti-European stance of Islamism has been in retreat since the late 1990s "due to the Kemalist circles' continuing pressures on Islamic groups in internal politics, the Islamic actors' upward social mobility and their re-conceptualization of Europe as a site where they can further their economic and political interests while enjoying the freedom of belief" (p. 198).

The editors manage to pack a lot of useful information and productive analysis in this slightly more than 200 page collection. It represents an important contribution toward current efforts to make sense of the often confusing disconnect that many observers note between the liberalization of Europe and the difficulty of encounter between Europe's old and new citizens. **RF**

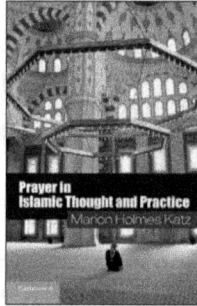

Marion Holmes Katz. *Prayer in Islamic Thought and Practice.* **New York, NY: Cambridge University Press, 2013. 243 pp. Pbk: $29.99. ISBN: 978-0521716291. Ebk: $16.00. 1003 KB.**

From the beginning of Islam, prayer has punctuated the life of Muslims; and the presence of mosques and the activities within have been a distinguishing feature of Islamic societies. The call to prayer is heard five times a day in most Muslim countries and has been unfailingly noted by observers traveling through Islamic lands. Yet, until recently, there had not been a general study surveying the phenomenon of prayer in Islamic societies, both with respect to the way it has been interpreted by Muslims (whether they are theologians, legal scholars, mystics, or philosophers), and the way it has been practiced by a variety of groups and societies from the early days of Islam until the twenty-first century. Marion Holmes Katz has written a wonderfully clear and comprehensive study to address this deficiency. Her book, as its title suggests, addresses the centrality of prayer in Islamic thought and practice. In it she asserts that prayer— the second pillar of Islam—is not only a ubiquitous phenomenon in Islamic societies, but is first and foremost a ritual, and as such, is governed in legal manuals by concepts of obligation and validity. She expresses the hope that her study will to some extent "help in restoring ritual to its proper place in the study of Shari'a, and legal analysis to its proper place in our understanding of this category of ritual" (p. 8).

Prayer in Islamic Thought and Practice is divided into an introduction, five chapters, and a short conclusion. Each of the chapters focuses on one thematic concern relating to prayer. Within each chapter, the treatment is thorough, historical and nuanced and backed by extensive research, as evident from the wide range of sources cited. In her analysis, the author relies primarily (but not exclusively) on Arabic-language sources produced in the Middle East and North Africa between the ninth and sixteenth centuries, though she also briefly addresses for each theme "cases where modern developments have introduced major changes in practice or interpretation" (p. 2). Holmes Katz does a fair job of addressing the diversity of thought and practice among various Muslim sectarian groups, reporting on Twelver Shi'a and Isma'ili interpretations and practices, though the overwhelming focus in the book remains on Sunni theological and legal understandings of the phenomenon of prayer and on practices in predominantly Sunni milieus. In many of the chapters, she also analyzes and dwells on the influence of the Sufi tradition on scholarly attitudes and interpretations, as well as on popular manifestations relating to prayer.

The themes dealt with in each of the chapters are varied but essential to a well-rounded interpretation of the ritual of prayer. Chapter 1 addresses the development and rules relating to both canonical prayer and supplication. After tracing the origin of the term *salat* and its pedigree, the author moves on to address the historical institution and the development of the practice of canonical prayer, dwelling on the conditions and components of the practice and contrasting it with the more free-form and less regulated practice of supplication (*du'a*). Although salat was obligatory and du'a was encouraged in many instances, Holmes Katz points out as well to tensions raised by the latter practice, certainly to debates regarding the petitioner and his acceptance of God's decree and as to whether God's decree could be altered by human supplication and intervention.

In Chapter 2, the author addresses the rules of validity for prayer set by legal thinkers. Discussing issues of intent, reverence and concentration, emotional involvement, and ethical transformation, she analyzes how Muslim authors "pondered the relationship between legally adequate and spiritually ideal prayer" (p. 44).

Then, in Chapter 3—the most complex of the chapters—Holmes Katz considers the meaning of prayer as understood by various Muslim authors, offering a very wide spectrum of interpretations. Here, the interpretations of the ritual by the main schools of law as a pure act of servanthood lacking an identifiable rationale that would be comprehensible to humans is contrasted with Sufi, Isma'ili, Mu'tazili, and philosophical interpretations of the subject. In this chapter, Holmes Katz offers a thorough analysis of the various interpretative frameworks used by Muslim thinkers from all walks for the understanding of salat—ranging from the interpretive model of prayer as akin to a royal audience, or as a form of intimate conversation/communication with the divine, to that of prayer as an exercise in self-discipline and as reflection on the cosmos.

Chapters 4 and 5, although grounded in legal and theological debates among Muslims, deal with practice somewhat more elaborately than previous chapters, and will be of great interest to social and gender historians. Chapter 4—dealing with communal prayer—begins with a definition of what constitutes congregational prayer, and the conditions and qualifications necessary to fulfill Friday prayers. It moves on to discuss many issues such as leadership in prayer—expounding on opinions as to who should or could fulfill that role, whether it is appropriate or even allowed to pray behind a leader from another school, whether or how much compulsion is allowed in enforcing matters of ritual performance, and whose responsibility it was to exhort Muslims to good practice and who, in reality, was most effective at it. The chapter deals as well with matters of nonperformance and how these were dealt with, justified and, to a great degree, accommodated in many circumstances, both in theory and practice.

Chapter 5—dealing more specifically with women and prayer—is perhaps the most relevant to a modern audience where debates about the participation of women in Islamic societies have been raging. Like the previous chapter, Chapter 5 surveys a multitude of medieval and modern opinions on a number of wide-ranging issues with relation to women's ritual participation in prayer. These include whether "the enhanced merit of congregational prayer applied to both sexes" (p. 180), where women should position themselves if they did partake in such prayers, the limits of their participation, and whether it was permissible for them to lead a male audience or a mixed audience in prayer. The chapter also deals with the fluctuation over time that the sources reveal with regards to women's access to mosques, as well as with the various limitations that circumstances imposed on women's ability to perform their prayers correctly, be they lack of proper education in matters of performance or lack of access to the requisite instruction.

A review such as this can only whet readers' appetites and encourage them to read this richly erudite and enjoyable book. It is truly a feat of scholarship, not only thoroughly researched, but also written in a clear style that makes it accessible to relative beginners and more advanced scholars alike. Marion Holmes Katz is to be commended for taking on this difficult task and executing it almost perfectly. **MY**

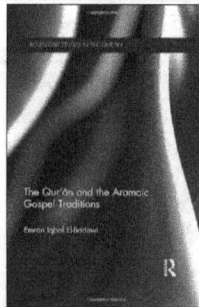

Emran El-Badawi. *The Qur'an and the Aramaic Gospel Traditions*. New York, NY: Routledge, 2014. 280 pp. $160.00. ISBN: 978-0415821230.

In this work, El-Badawi has made a detailed comparison between the text of passages of the Qur'an and the corresponding passages of the Aramaic Gospels. He does this in order to prove his assertion that the Qur'an as a text was produced within a milieu that was dominated by what he terms the Aramaic Gospel Tradition.

El-Badawi is careful to avoid the use of the term "influence," due to its negative connotation in light of previous theories regarding the origins of Islam. He states, "This study will demonstrate how the Qur'an ..., selectively challenged or re-appropriated, and therefore took up the 'dogmatic re-articulation' of language and imagery coming from the Aramaic Gospel Traditions, in order to fit the idiom and the religious temperament of a heterogeneous, sectarian Arabian audience" (p. 5). By dogmatic, he means here a more indefinite sense of belief rather than a definition of the word connected to any particular religious institution. The system of belief studied in this work is that which will eventually become Islam, but that is described by El-Badawi as originally "anti-Trinitarian, post-Rabbinic and apocalyptic," what he terms "strict monotheism" (p. 5).

In El-Badawi's opening chapter, "Sources and Method," he discusses the historical context of the Qur'an and the Aramaic Gospel Tradition, his thesis and definition of terminology, an extended section on secondary studies of the Qur'an, his methodology, and the organization of the book. It is in this chapter that he discusses certain aspects of the work that might be questionable for some scholars. He recognizes that the sources that relate the historical context of the origins and compilation of the Qur'an, most notably the sira works, are problematic, and yet notes that he accepts them for the purposes of this study. He follows Fred Donner's notion of the "historical kernel" in the Islamic source material, but does not really indicate how he determines which aspects of Muhammad's life story he accepts and which aspects he rejects. In addition, he utilizes the canonical versions of both the Qur'an and the Aramaic Gospels, but does discuss the noncanonical sources that could impact his analysis of these texts.

El-Badawi's methodology is clearly laid out, detailed, and extremely well organized. He states that he chooses texts within both the Qur'an and the Aramaic Gospels "if general linguistic relationships are outwardly apparent" (p. 49). The text of the Qur'an is then read within the context of the surrounding verses. Then, it is compared to earlier works ("Biblical, Rabbinic, Apocryphal, Pseudepigraphal, homiletic, historical, and epigraphic literature") to ensure that the text is not connected to a source other than the Aramaic Gospel Traditions. Once a firm connection between the Qur'an and the Aramaic Gospels is established, he states that he will then consult the Islamic literary works and secondary sources. Only after all of these steps have been completed will he "formulate a hypothesis" about the relationship between the scriptural passages in question.

El-Badawi's second chapter, "Prophetic Tradition in the Late Antique Near East," spells out the context within which the works studied, especially theQur'an, were developed. He terms this historical context "prophetic tradition," and defines it as follows: "Prophetic tradition may designate a religion, faith, denomination, sect, school, or group of adherents which tends to be monotheistic in a general sense. More explicitly, it is the social lifestyle of abiding by the teachings, ethics and law of a divinely inspired or sanctioned leader.... Their teachings are: (1) dogmatic in nature…, and (2) passed down from one generation to the next" (p. 51). He describes the Judaeo-Christian and Zoroastrian background for the Aramaic Gospels—the product of a Syriac church desperate to survive in the face of religious sectarianism—and the Arabian background, both of which will serve as source material for the text of the Qur'an and the religion of Islam. It is here that El-Badawi engages in his first comparison of the two languages involved. He states that the "Syriac speaking Christian groups and the tribal and urban centers of Arabia… submitted to the ethics, laws, and teachings of Syriac Christian literature…. This act of submission was called in Syriac ašlem" (p. 59). This term is then connected to the Arabic islām with a similar correspondent meaning. However, El-Badawi is careful to point out that the Islam of Muhammad was only one of many such movements (what he terms islāms) in Arabia during the sixth and seventh centuries, all of whom were informed by the continued presence of the Aramaic Gospel Traditions due to the continued presence of Christian communities and individuals with whom the Arabians would have been familiar.

The work is then organized into four chapters that each dwells on a specific theme. There are far too many sub themes in each chapter to discuss in detail here, and so I have limited my discussion to those that I find most intriguing. The first of these, "Prophets and their Righteous Entourage," discusses Jesus' place among the Hebrew prophets in the Aramaic Gospel Tradition and then the place of these same prophets in the Qur'an. The chapter then goes on to discuss the "alienated, oppressed and disenfranchised members of society" (p. 78) who would become members of a prophet's entourage. The following chapter, "The Evils of the Clergy," compares the negative dictates by both Jesus and Muhammad about the clergy of their day, and includes themes of persecution by and the materialism of the clergy, as well as discussing the issue of hypocrisy, themes prevalent in both the Aramaic Gospel Tradition and the Qur'an. The next chapter, "The Divine Realm," includes discussions of the themes of God's majesty, light, the Word, and God's mercy. El-Badawi points out in this chapter that the Qur'an replaces Jesus with God in many passages in order to maintain the "strict monotheism" necessary in Islam (pp. 160, 162). The final thematic chapter, "Divine Judgment and the Apocalypse," reveals important differences between the Aramaic Gospel Tradition and the Qur'an, including an especially fascinating section that covers the idea of death and judgment. In the former, followers are promised that they "will never see death" (p. 168), while in the latter, followers are told in no uncertain terms that "every soul will taste death" (p. 169). Again, Jesus' role in the Biblical texts is removed when re-articulated in the Qur'an's depiction of the Final Judgment, as El-Badawi points out the use of passive verbs in Qur'an39 to replace any possible Trinitarian interpretation. In the sections in this chapter on Hell and Paradise, El-Badawi deftly brings the depiction of both the "Righteous Entourage" and the evil clergy full circle, as these groups switch places—with the clergy in Hell and the faithful followers of Muhammad and Jesus in Paradise, enjoying the material benefits denied them in life.

The final chapter of the work serves as El-Badawi's conclusion. He includes a discussion of typology, and explains that he has limited his study to those passages that lend themselves most obviously to comparison, but then points out that the number of passages that could be compared on, for example, a rhetorical basis, are statistically small enough to warrant their exclusion. He notes that the Qur'an was very much aware of Gospel texts, but that it did not, as some scholars have claimed, have origins "as a purely Syriac lectionary…, or, alternately, as a Christian scripture for the Arabs" (pp. 213-214). He notes that the Qur'an "may be appreciated as both a collection of divine revelations as well as a product of religious cross-pollination. Therefore, it is not the finality of an individual prophetic tradition nor its written legacy—scripture—but rather the continuity of prophetic tradition and scripture that bestows upon us the broadest perspective from which to appreciate them both" (p. 219).

Overall, El-Badawi's work is an important addition to our understanding of the Qur'an within its historical and religious milieu. His detailed analysis is supported by a number of appendices that reflect the passages of the various Gospel texts and their corresponding passages in the Qur'an, as well as the typology involved in their comparison. He also provides a number of tables throughout the text that are fairly useful. El-Badawi's acceptance of the story of theQur'an's origins and composition is problematic, despite his nod to the issues with the source material, because so much of his analysis rests upon the story they tell, especially in those sections dealing with Muhammad and his historical milieu. The work is unfortunately marred by a number of typographical errors that are quite distracting, especially in the beginning sections of the book. That being said, this remains a very important work that will hopefully serve to further our understanding of the Qur'an and its relationship to the belief systems and scriptures among which it originated and with whom it continues to interact. **RRW**

ISLAMIC LAW & POLITICS

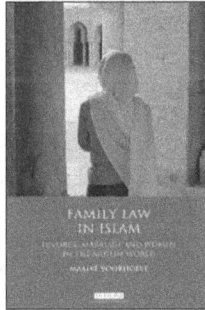

Maaike Voorhoeve, Ed. *Family Law in Islam: Divorce, Marriage and Women in the Muslim World.* London: I. B. Tauris, 2012. 240 pp. $99.00. ISBN: 978-1848857421.

This collection presents recent and ongoing research by several scholars in law, anthropology, and sociology. As such, some of the chapters have the feel of preliminary reports, but they are, nevertheless valuable for their insight and contemporaneity. In modern times, "family law in Islam" really means the plethora of codes based on Muslim jurisprudence that govern family life. The differences from one personal status law (PSL) to another—not a theme emphasized in this volume, but something apparent in the reading—indicate that Muslim jurisprudence becomes nationalized when codified. One wonders whether we can speak of family law in Islam as opposed to law and the family in different Muslim countries. In spite of the subtitle invoking the Muslim world, the legal systems actually discussed are those of Iran, Yemen, Lebanon, Egypt, Syria, and Tunisia.

The chapters are organized in two sections under the rubrics "discourses on the law" and "discourses of the law." The former refers to the law as a subject of public discussion and debate, and the latter to the law as it is practiced, including what legal practitioners have to say about it. In the first section, Susanne Dahlgren's informative chapter on Yemeni PSL shows how the gains achieved for women in the Arab world's only Marxist state, the People's Democratic Republic of Yemen (PDRY), 1967–90, were rolled back after unification with the more conservative Yemen Arab Republic. The 1974 PSL of the PDRY incorporated reforms adopted elsewhere in the Muslim world in the twentieth century. It ended forced marriage, reined in excessive dowers (*mahr*), restricted polygyny, and limited men's right to unilateral divorce. More unusual was a provision making both spouses financially responsible for the household. These reforms were embedded in a modernist rhetoric proclaiming women's vital role as mothers and participants in state building. Post-unification, the rhetoric shifted from modernity to the prescriptions of Islam for family life. A more conservative PSL was adopted in 1992, promoted by the Islamist Islah Party. Women's rights activists have also shifted their rhetorical appeals from modernism to Islamic correctness. This strategy has met with some success: the re-introduction of *bayt al-ta'a* (house of obedience) was blocked, as was a proposed Saudi-style committee for promoting virtue and combating vice.

A similar dynamic driven by contestation between religious conservatives and women's rights advocates is apparent in Arzoo Oslanloo's discussion of how women and family issues have been framed in post-revolutionary Iran. A pre-revolutionary discourse of women's rights was discredited by its association with Western-style individualism, denigrated as "entitlement without responsibility." Revolutionary discourse replaced "rights talk" with an emphasis on women's status as "the crowning jewels of the family," the family being understood to be "the foundation of society." As in Yemen, the socially important role of women as wives and mothers was embraced in Islamist thought and rhetoric. President Muhammad Khatami (1997–2005) sought to enhance the status of women through a state-sponsored Center for Women's Participation (CWP), which, among other things was charged with studying how Iranian law could be reconciled with the UN Convention on the Elimination of All Forms of Discrimination against Women. Had that move been successful it would have re-instated an agenda of women's rights. But his successor, President Mahmud Ahmadinejad, renamed the CWP the Center for Women and Family Affairs, signaling a shift in focus, again, from rights to status. However, in another parallel with Dahlgren's narrative, Iranian legislators recently shelved a proposal to make it easier for married men to contract temporary marriages on the ground that permanent marriage is foundational to society (and viewed as more religiously correct). The point that emerges in both chapters is that Islamist thought has embraced the modernist ideal of the conjugal family to a large extent, and that, within that discursive frame, women's status can be enhanced by appeals to religious principles.

A similar point is made in Massimo di Ricco's study of Druze female activists in Lebanon. In Lebanon's confessional system of government, 19 different religious communities have official recognition, and there are 16 different PSLs. The officially recognized sects are more independent of the state than in any other Arab country, their autonomy extending, for example, to educational affairs. All Lebanese citizens are required to belong to one of those recognized sects. This, in effect obliges women's rights activists to operate within their "community public sphere" rather than the national sphere. In site of that difference, di Ricco shows how Druze activists have promoted reforms by appealing to Druze religious doctrines, which are constructed as more gender-egalitarian than Muslim family law. Developments in the Druze PSL will bear watching since the suggestion here is that they may run counter to the more common pattern of entrenched conservatism in the family law of religious minorities (Copts in Egypt and Muslims in India, for example) in plural legal systems.

Nadia Sonneveld's rich study shows how the lines drawn clearly between formal and informal marriage in Egyptian public discourse become less clear upon close examination. Informal marriage includes so-called *'urfi* or "customary" marriage and *misyar* or "ambulant" marriage, neither of which is consistent with the Egyptian PSL. Both forms of marriage are usually clandestine or semi-clandestine, hence often not registered with the civil authorities. Also, in a *misyar* marriage, the couple agrees to forgo a dower and cohabitation. Whereas public discourse construes these forms of marriage as engaged in primarily by youth, and hence as a threat to the familial and social order, it is often married men who resort to *'urfi* and *misyar* marriage as a means of concealing their polygyny from their first wives, who could sue for divorce if informed of it. The women who become second wives benefit socially from their married status. Older, independent women resort to *misyar* contracts of marriage with younger men, also for the social benefit of marriage, while keeping their autonomy. The phenomenon of informal marriage mirrors social changes occurring in family life. Although public opinion maintains that it is the husband's duty to provide financially and his wife's duty to obey him in return, the "maintenance-obedience relationship" is inverted in many informal marriages, which allow self-supporting women to live independently. Moreover, women often contract informal marriages with no intention of forming a conventional household or raising children. Thus two assumed aspects of marriage are called into question by informal marriage, as is men's masculinity.

The four chapters in the second section focus on what happens within the family law courts, or in other words the law in application. Each is based upon fieldwork and aims to go beyond consideration of the formal law by looking at the way that legal processes influence outcomes. The chapters by Christine Hegel Cantarella, Sarah Vincent Grosso, and Maaike Voorhoeve discuss tactics of delay, the production and crediting of evidence, and judicial discretion, respectively, in divorce proceedings. These foci result in nuanced accounts of how the law can work for, as well as against the interests of women litigants. Delayed decisions are universally portrayed by reformers as detrimental to women, but some Egyptian women used delaying tactics successfully to enhance their opportunity for a favorable out of court settlement. Similarly, while Tunisian women seeking a divorce find it difficult to produce credible evidence of "harm" at the hands of their husbands, it is equally difficult for the latter to prove their wives "disobedient." Here, gendered expectations play a role, and the challenge is to prove one's spouse to be a "bad" husband or wife. And as Voorhoeve points out, judges are left with plenty of room for discretion by the wording of the law.

Esther van Eijk's chapter offers an interesting comparison between the efforts of Syrian Muslim and Catholic courts in attempting to mediate between couples requesting a divorce. Catholic judges put more effort into reconciling couples before granting annulments than Shari'a court judges do when granting divorces, which may reflect the differences in doctrine on the sanctity of marriage. But it is also probably due to the much lower case load in the Catholic courts.

These chapters are informative and sophisticated studies, and they advance our knowledge of how family law in several Muslim countries is debated as well as how it actually works. **KMC**

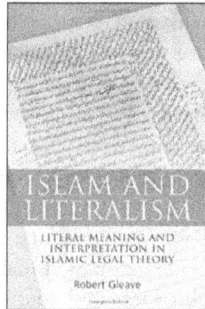

Robert Gleave. *Islam and Literalism: Literal Meaning and Interpretation in Islamic Legal Theory*. **Edinburgh, UK: Edinburgh University Press, 2013 [2012]. 224 pp. $112.00. ISBN: 978-0748625703. $39.95. Pbk.: ISBN: 978-0748689866.**

Is reading to be equated with comprehension? While that is the expectation and hope, the former does not ensure the latter. Comprehension has embedded in it the issue of interpretation, and different readers may process the same information differently. This becomes all the more important for rule-making in understanding the messages—as part of the Message—in the scripture. Is the statement a command (obligatory), recommendation (preferred), or merely permissible (acceptable)? The issue here is not who has the interpretive authority, but what is the message? How is the meaning to be understood? For Muslims, the question is how to be sure about understanding the meaning of the *Qur'an*—the text (*kitab*) that is the compilation of messages from God (Allah). In particular, how to glean the law (*shar'*)—the system of laws (*shar'iyya*)—through the correct understanding of the meaning (*ma'na*). In other words, what is the mechanism—the systematic procedure—for understanding? Thus emerged a methodology *usul*) for a specific ruling (*fiqh*) based on that understanding, which resulted in the corpus of Muslim legal theory (*usul al-fiqh*). Schools of thought (*madhahib*) developed around these activities.

Whereas the objective had always been to fathom the *intended* (actual) meaning of Allah, the Judge on the Day of Judgment, a perceived intermediate proximate step was to focus on the *literal* (given) meaning of a word and assign it a privileged status. Given that Muslim legal scholars studying the methodological principles of interpretation (hermeneutics) have been mostly "literalist" (p. 26), in *Islam and Literalism,* Robert Gleave traces the evolution of "literalism" in *usul al-fiqh.* Divided into seven chapters, the first two lay the conceptual, theoretical, and methodological foundations for the work in borrowing from communications theory. Chapters 3 and 4 are the heart of the book, where the author examines the formative and developed phases, respectively, during the early period of Sunni usul al-fiqh. The next chapter provides the Shi'a perspective from the early Imami era through the hadith and fiqh literature. The remaining two chapters are case studies of Zahirism, Salafism, and the [Shi'a] Tafkiki school.

For Gleave, literal meaning is what the text "in itself" imparts on account of the words and grammatical rules of the language. It is characterized by singularity, certainty, and accessibility. Akin to the "conventional meaning" of linguist Paul Grice, literal meaning is conceptually distinct from both the writer's intent and the reader's understanding of the text. Antithetical to the postmodern counterpart of constructivism (including feminism and critical theory), the "authorian" link to Allah is definitely not questioned for its literal meaning. When this textual meaning is privileged in being given priority over other interpretations, that approach is literalism. Cognizant of ambiguity in the text, Grice separated "Sentence Meaning" from "What Is Said." As the sentence meaning can be ambiguous, there is a distinction between literal and nonliteral meanings. With vocable (*lafz*) as the linguistic unit of analysis, correspondence between intended meaning and the utterance is true (*haqiqa*) usage, which is identified with literal meaning. Otherwise, it is diverted (*majaz*) usage, which is associated with nonliteral meaning. Furthermore, establishment of the sound-meaning relationship with the act of "placing" (*wad'*) is considered the benchmark in the time-line. This haqiqa/*majaz* pairing is the important broad distinction that is pervasive throughout the book. The rest of the analyses—critical textual interpretations (exegeses, *tafsir*)—entail examining the various subcategories of haqiqa and majaz uses. Borrowed from linguist Francois Recanati, the usefulness of the three types of literal meanings (t-, m-, and p-) becomes evident much later in the chapter on Zahirism.

As a way of delineating the nascent and subsequent early Sunni exegeses, Gleave refers to them as "thought" and "theory," respectively. One tool employed for distinction in the nascent phase was the obvious (*zahir*) implied (*batin*) pair. Other words used for unclear meaning were ambiguous (*mutashabih*), corrupted (*harrafa*), and interrupted (*ta'wil,* but referring to an event). Attributed to 'Abd Allah ibn 'Abbas, a companion and relative of Prophet Muhammad, a well-known interpretive rule was *kull shay' fi al-Qur'an,* abbreviated as the *kull shay'* rule. For grasping the simile or metaphor in a gloss (linguistic ambiguity), the exercise involved "X" text in the *Qur'an* interpreted to mean "Y" with reference to the Arabic of the Bedouin (*kalam al-'Arab*) in which the *Qur'an* was revealed. Thus, "to fight" (*qatala*) in Surah al-Tawba (9:30) was interpreted to mean "to curse" (*la'ana*).

Muhammad bin Idris al-Shafi'i, who elevated the Sunna of the Prophet (recorded in the *Hadith*) to another primary source, along with the *Qur'an* for developing interpretive rules, was credited with launching the subsequent theoretical phase. However, the word used in his treatise was *zahir* (and not haqiqa), noted Gleave. The key contribution of Al Shafi'i was a fivefold typology of elucidation (*bayan*): (1) the *Qur'an* clarifying itself; (2) Sunna clarifying the *Qur'an*; 3) Sunna clarifying in details and duties mentioned in the *Qur'an*; (4) Sunna clarifying details not mentioned in the *Qur'an*; and (5) external sources—other revelatory texts or ordinary language use—clarifying ambiguity in both the *Qur'an* and the Sunna. In regard to the scope of the meaning of zahir, al-Shafi'i identified a fourfold typology of use: general; general with inclusion of particular; particular; and nonzahir warranted by context (*siyaqihi*). Al- Shafi'i connected the obvious (zahir) implied (*batin*) dichotomy and the general (*'amm*) particular (*khass*) pair. Thus, in view of Prophetic Sunna, cutting off the hands of a thief in Surah al-Ma'ida (5:38) would hold if the amount was a minimum quarter of a dinar. By the same token, "100 lashes" for fornication in Surah al-Nur (24:2) would apply only for free virgins (and not for nonvirgins or slaves).

Three other theoretical rules of interpretation by three different scholars were explored for the theoretical phase. Abu Bakr al-Jassas, a Hanafi Mu'tazili scholar, placed the capacity for understanding the literal meaning on everyday people who spoke the language of the Arabs (*lughat al-'Arab*). Reverting to ancient Arabia during the time of the Prophet and his companions, Ali bin 'Amr ibn al-Qassar, a Maliki jurist, directed attention to the ancient Arabic language. Thus, the emphasis shifted from ordinary people to experts in language (*ahl al-lisan*). For Abu Bakr al-Baqillani, another Maliki scholar, the focus changed from expertise in ancient Arabic vernaculars to expertise in linguistic and grammatical rules. The statement "Do not go near to zina' (17:32) is unambiguous. Not to say "uff" to parents in Surah al-Isra' (17:23) has the implication (*mafhum*) of not hitting one's parents and does not require reasoning. The literal meaning is obvious in both cases from the text itself, but in the second example, it is not coming from utterance of the vocable. Consequently, al-Baqillani proposed a fourfold typology for identifying haqiqa usage: assigned in a general manner, from the roots of the word, plural of the word, and applying to all cases within a category.

Zahiri hermeneutics is adamant about the general meaning (disregarding a search for the particular); Salafi approach is emphatic about context. Both positions are relevant for grasping violence in Islam. The discussion on *haqiq[a] shar'iyya* was detailed and interesting; however, Chapter 5 on early Shi'a exegeses was vague.

Even though Gleave noted that al-Baqillani moved away from the notion of an immediate understanding of the literal meaning, the explanation of that understanding not coming from the utterance was not articulated (p. 118). It was not the selection of al-Jassas, al-Qassar, and al-Baqillani as case studies, but the rationale for their placement sequence in Chapter 4 which was confusing; al-Jassas, al-Qassar, and al-Baqillani stressed the capacity of the ordinary Arabic speakers, experts knowledgeable in Ancient Arabic language, and experts in Arabic linguistic and grammatical rules, respectively. Aside from their life-parameter dates, one would expect from this learning curve of interpretive analyses to read about al-Qassar before al-Baqillani, but it was the other way around (pp. 96-97). Gleave rightly observed that al-Jassas exemplified a continuation between initial and later methodologies in early Sunni hermeneutics, but the differences from the various chapters were not explicitly compared along a development trajectory. With attention to Arabic language, the kull shay' rule in the nascent phase placed emphasis on Bedouin Arabic (kalam al-'Arab) and that reference point changed during the second phase from everyday Arabic (lughat al-'Arab) for al-Jassas to Sahaba Arabic for al-Qassar to Arabic grammar for al-Baqillani. There is an urban–rural dimension to cosmopolitan and desert Arabic. Sahaba Arabic stressed by al-Qassar took the reference point back to Bedouin Arabic at the time of the Prophet. Thus, there was a nonlinear trajectory regarding language usage, but an overall linear trajectory for the development curve of Qur'anic tafsir within the mainstream Sunni tradition.

Listing hermeneutic nuances was helpful; specific Qur'anic examples were insightful. The bibliographic technique of key reference followed by full citation was innovative and useful. Lucidly written and well-researched, *Islam and Literalism* is an invaluable contribution. It is a must read for graduate students and scholars interested in usul al-fiqh. Those in security studies with an interest in terrorism would also benefit from the book. **RM**[1]

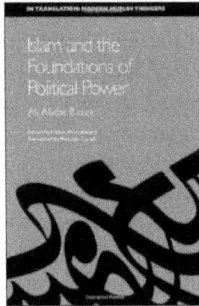

Ali Abdel Razek and Abdou Filali-Ansary, Eds. Translated by Maryam Loutfi. *Islam and the Foundations of Political Power*. Edinburgh, UK: Edinburgh University Press, 2013 [1925]. 144 pp. $89.95. ISBN: 0748639780.

One of the most contentious debates within the Islamic world over the last century centers on the degree to which religion should shape and influence politics and governance. This debate helped spur and sustain many of the great political reform movements—progressive, conservative, and radical—of the twentieth and twenty-first centuries. From the struggle to open Turkey's political system to the Islamic Revolution in Iran, and from the rise of transnational jihadi networks to the constitutional debates of budding post-Arab Spring democracies, the question of Islam's role in politics shaped and continues to shape public discourse on legitimate political power throughout the Islamic world.

Given the resonance of this issue throughout the Islamic world today it is refreshing, if unsurprising, that a newly translated edition of Ali Abdel Razek's seminal work, *Islam and the Foundations of Political Power*, should appear. Part of Edinburgh University's Modern Muslim Thinkers in Translation series and edited by Abdou Filali-Ansary, founding director of the Aga Khan University Institute for the Study of Muslim Civilization in London (2002–09) and of the King Abdul-Aziz Foundation for Islamic Studies and Human Sciences in Casablanca (1984–2001), this new edition highlights the lasting impact and contribution Abdel Razek made to debate on Islam and politics, despite having been originally published in 1925.

Ali Abdel Razek's essay was published in a mature political and intellectual milieu already steeped in the religion-state debate. He was born (1888) just as leading Islamic thinkers in Egypt, like Muhammad 'Abduh and Jamal al-Din al-Afghani, began publishing their ideas on Islamic revivalism, modernization, and anti-colonialism. Journals like 'Abduh's *al-'Urwa al-Wuthqa* (The Indissoluble Bond) and that of his disciple Muhammad Rashid Rida, *Al-Manar* (The Beacon), were widely circulated and generated considerable debate as political activism against British occupation intensified during the first decades of the twentieth century. Following the 1919 uprising against the British and the subsequent political battles between the nationalist Wafd party and the British-backed monarchy, politics and the question of legitimate political authority took center stage in the Egyptian public sphere. It was against this backdrop—and that of Mustafa Kemal Atatürk's abolition of the Ottoman Caliphate in 1924—that Abdel-Razek's controversial work appeared.

As Filali-Ansary notes in his introduction, Islam and the Foundations of Political Power caused an uproar in Egypt among members of the Sunni religious establishment and intellectuals alike. Abdel Razek's essay, only 118 pages in its current edition, challenged not only the foundational political assumptions of the conservative religious and monarchist classes, but also those of the "modernizing" constitutionalists in the Wafd movement. On one hand, Abdel Razek refuted traditional/monarchist authority claims by disentangling, deconstructing, and systematically challenging the core tenets of the millennia-old scholarly political consensus developed after the time of the Prophet Muhammad. On the other, he upset the secular-nationalist Wafdists by legitimizing the use of scientific rationality and historical criticism in "religio-political matters," tools they had sought to use as a means of public differentiation from the "backwards" *ulama* and monarchy (p. 5).

The backlash against the essay was immediate and overwhelming. Abdel Razek

was put on trial by the faculty disciplinary committee of al-Azhar, stripped of his title as an *'alim*, and banned from teaching. But what made his essay so inflammatory?
The obvious answer is the essay's subject and the manner in which it is addressed;
however, perhaps more pointedly, Abdel Razek's position as an *'alim* and faculty
member at al-Azhar—the bastion of Sunni Islamic orthodoxy—made his essay all
the more shocking and discomforting for the ulama.

Ali Abdel Razek begins his investigation with a simple premise: "None of the
scholars who attested that the appointment of an imam [caliph] was a religious duty
could substantiate this thesis with a verse from the *Qur'an*" (p. 36). From here, he
proceeds to steadily unravel the traditionalist argument by poring over the chief
source materials of Islamic scholarship, the *Qur'an* and Sunna of the Prophet. Abdel
Razek supports his arguments by elaborating on Muhammad's prophetic mission
and distinguishing it from its oft attributed political dimensions. After close examination of some 53 Qur'anic verses, he concludes, "Muhammad was strictly a Messenger, entrusted with a purely religious mission, uncompromised by any desire for
kingship or temporal power...According to this view, Muhammad was no more and
no less than an envoy sent by God, in no way different from his brethren-prophets
who preceded him. He was not a king, nor the founder of an empire, nor someone
preaching in favour of a kingdom" (p. 81). Thus, Abdel Razek stipulates that justifications for the caliphate cannot be based on the "traditional" claim that Muhammad's mission combined elements of political stewardship with religious prophecy.

From a historical perspective, Abdel Razek goes much further in his refutation
of Islamic political authority, arguing that Islam provides no basis for sovereignty,
and the historical sovereignty imposed upon Muslims in the form of the caliphate
has been overwhelming un-Islamic: "History does not offer us a single example of a
caliph whose image is not associated with the fear inspired by the brutal force surrounding him, with the armed force surrounding him, and the unsheathed sword
that lent him protection" (p. 47). And, additionally, "The caliphate has always been,
and still remains, a disaster for Islam and for Muslims. It has been a constant source
of evil and corruption" (p. 54). With arguments such as these, it is little wonder
Abdel Razek won few friends among Egypt's aristocracy and ulama.

At the end of his essay Abdel Razek concludes, "One looks in vain to either the
Qur'an or the hadith for a simple allusion, whether explicit or implicit, which might
give succor to the proponents of a political interpretation of the Islamic faith" (p.
92). Political organization and governance are therefore matters "religion has left to
humankind, for people to organise in accordance with the principles of reason, the
experience of nations and the rules of politics" (p. 117).

Abdel Razek's brief but powerful and thoroughly reasoned essay shocked, offend-
ed, and inspired. Filaly-Ansari even goes so far as to suggest that scholarly backlash
against the book from figures such as Muhammad Rashid Rida spurred the development of modern Islamism and Islamic political thought. Although perhaps
a stretch, there is no doubt that Abdel Razek provoked the Sunni establishment

into defending positions on Islam and political sovereignty it had long thought canonized. By invoking Ibn Khaldun's admonishment for critical historiography and Muhammad Abduh's call for a return to the fundament of the *Qur'an* in legal exegesis, Abdel Razek also reopened the debate among Muslim scholars on the role "reason" could and should play in the interpretation and application of scripture and tradition. These issues remain hotly contested to this day.

In light of the reinvigorated global debates among Muslim scholars, intellectuals, and the public on the role of Islam in politics, Ali Abdel Razek's essay is perhaps more relevant than ever. His provocative insight and methodically reasoned arguments provide readers—scholars and laypeople, Muslims and non-Muslims alike— an excellent springboard from which to begin their investigations of a deeply divisive but nevertheless intriguing subject. Filali-Ansari has rendered the public a great service in editing and publishing a new version of *Islam and the Foundations of Political Power*. As a foundational text in the scholarly study of Islamic political thought and a fascinating treatise on the relationships between religion and sovereignty more broadly, this new edition of Abdel-Razek's timeless essay is a must-read. **DHG**

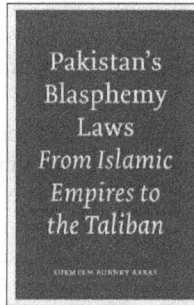

Shemeem Burney Abbas. *Pakistan's Blasphemy Laws from Islamic Empires to the Taliban*. Austin, TX: University of Texas Press, 2013. 204 pp. $55.00. ISBN: 978-0292745308.

This book addresses a pressing issue that agitates interfaith relations and theological politics in many Muslim countries, particularly Pakistan, Iran, Egypt, Malaysia and Bangladesh. The criminalization of blasphemy, simply understood as insulting Islamic religious symbols, has become an instrument by which religious minorities and social critics, scholars and intellectuals are harassed and silenced by clerical orthodoxy. These laws are also used as impediments to social reform, especially with regard to minority and women's rights. In Pakistan, the assassination of Salman Taseer in 2011, then governor of Punjab, by his own security detail, brought global attention to the problem of blasphemy laws and their abuse in Pakistani politics.

Professor Abbas, herself a victim of false persecution under the blasphemy law of Pakistan, tries to argue that the culture of intolerance and persecution of alleged blasphemers is a historical consequence of Muslim empires using religion to discredit and delegitimize dissent. She claims that the criminalization of blasphemy—she understands it as *kufr* (also understood as disbelief)—cannot be supported from the *Qur'an* and is essentially an un-Islamic law exploited as Islamic by the continuing collusion of state and the clerical establishment in the Abbasid and the Umayyad empires, as well as in Pakistan under President Zia-ul-Haq.

I am sympathetic to her claims and also applaud her personal courage in dealing with the horrors of persecution, but I do have a few reservations. Throughout the book, Professor Abbas makes categorical claims that are not factually true. Such claims weaken her case and make the reader less inclined toward the normative goal of her book, which ostensibly is a call for more intellectual freedom, religious tolerance, and gender equality in Pakistan.

Abbas claims that the *Qur'an* does not explicitly acknowledge Prophet Muhammad (pbuh) as the last prophet (p. 44). Most English translators translate verse 33:40 as follows: *Muhammad is not the father of [any] one of your men, but [he is] the Messenger of Allah and last of the prophets. And ever is Allah, of all things, Knowing.* The Arabic term in the verse *Khatima al-Nabi* is translated either as the last Prophet or the seal of Prophets. I found it a bit surprising that Abbas would make the said claim without any discussion of how it is understood by a vast majority of Muslims, and not just the state or clerical orthodoxy. Nearly all Sufi traditions—and Professor Abbas claims that she is a scholar of Sufi Islam—also believe that Muhammad was the last Prophet of God. Additionally, there are many authentic traditions (*ahadith*) which assert the Prophet Muhammad was the last Prophet of God. Abbas does not engage with this. She does make a general point that not all Hadith are authentic, but that is not enough. She must show the inauthenticity of specific traditions in order to strengthen her case.

On p. 133, Abbas argues that the Pakistan's blasphemy laws are a product of three empires, and one of them is the "CIA-led Empire in Afghanistan (1978–89)." Frankly, I don't understand what that means. Afghanistan was under Soviet occupation from 1979 to 1989. The CIA did not have an empire in Afghanistan, like the British or the Islamic empires, the two other empires that the author mentions. While it is well know that the British introduced modern blasphemy laws in the subcontinent, Abbas' attempts to implicate the CIA, and by extension, the United States, are tenuous and undocumented. She makes similar claims elsewhere in the book (p. 6) that *hudood* and blasphemy laws in Pakistan under President Zia were "underwritten by the CIA." This line of "sidebars" actually undermines her main argument that the practice of oppression using blasphemy is a historical practice developed by clerics and emperors to consolidate power and delegitimize dissent.

The broad idea or strategy of the book is to show how the mixing of religion and politics has engendered a culture of intolerance that often backfires, and rather than fostering homogeneity and solidarity, leads to fragmentation and oppression. I agree and find that argument compelling. The book provides useful historical details about blasphemy laws in the subcontinent and provides a context to understanding current challenges.

The best chapter of the book is Chapter 5, which deals with the case of the Sufi Al-Hallaj who was brutally executed for blasphemy. In this chapter, which is both rich in historical details and discussion of the various elements of the Al-Hallaj episode, Abbas successfully shows how politics have abused Islamic law, and especially how blasphemy laws are used as the stick of the orthodoxy in collusion with state apparatus to punish the dissenting or subaltern voice which may speak up for justice. I wish she had examined more cases as thoroughly and with as much richness of detail and nuance as she did this case. It would certainly have made the book stronger and more interesting.

This book is for experts, for those who are interested in Shari'a politics in the Muslim world, in historical aspects of Islamic law, and in challenges for human rights in the Muslim world. It is not a good fit as a textbook for undergraduate or graduate classes, but can be used as supplementary readings in graduate seminars. **MK**

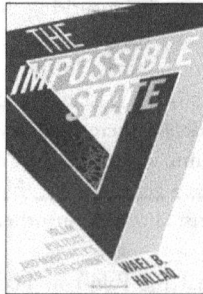

Warl B. Hallaq. *The Impossible State: Islam, Politics, and Modernity's Moral Predicament.* **New York, NY: Columbia University Press, 2013. 256 pp. $33.75. ISBN: 978-0231162562.**

Wael B. Hallaq, the leading scholar of Islamic law, in his recent book, *The Impossible State: Islam, Politics, and Modernity's Moral Predicament* makes a powerful argument for the relevance of Shari'a as a moral discourse while staying critical of its compatibility with the modern state. It can hardly be placed in a single discipline as it touches and transcends a number of debates within social sciences, legal studies, and philosophy. The book has been divided into seven chapters that lay the foundation and build arguments the author presents in the Introduction. By the final chapter, all of the arguments have been resolved.

Hallaq's main argument is a refreshing take on the modern state and Islamic governance; he states that Islamic governance—as understood by any minimal standard of what Islam is—through the embedded position of Shari'a is incompatible with the modern state. But unlike the clichéd arguments, coming primarily from the liberals, about the primitiveness of Islamic law and rules of conduct, the incompatibility stems from the different positions or "paradigms" that are at play. For Hallaq, the very notion of an Islamic state is ridiculous because the state is a creation of modernity, and modernity is never ahistorical or neutral. The morality that the modern state espouses is incommensurable with those of Islam. And herein lies the challenge for modern Muslims "Modern Muslims are therefore faced with the challenge to reconciling two facts: ontological fact of the state; deontological fact of the inevitability to bring about Shari'a governance" (p. x). Therefore, he makes the case that pre-modern governance that was based on Shari'a was a result of Islamic control, and not the state.

The author starts with a number of assumptions. He states that modern Islamist thinkers and scholars accept the modern state as a given; and that the state remains the "favored template of the Islamist and the Ulama" (p. xi). And it is this assumption and practice of the *ulama* that the book questions; there is stark a contradiction between Nation-state and Islamic Shari'a which cannot be reconciled.

The conception of a modern Islamic state is inherently self-contradictory, which is primarily grounded in modernity's moral predicament. This moral predicament can be filled by Shari'a. Hallaq predicts and answers an obvious question at this point: What kind of Shari'a? And has Shari'a not been tried and rejected already? He answers that Shari'a in the modern state is a failure, and thus can be left out. The morality that needed to be derived from Shari'a was not present in the modern state. Thus, pre-modern Shari'a, as the central domain, or paradigm through and by which all other peripheral domains can be understood is taken into consideration. Here the central domain in Shari'a is morality; economic and politics are periphery domains.

But Hallaq's is not a nostalgic exercise. His investigation of the pre-modern morality located in the Shari'a is based on his deconstruction of the modern state using morality as a measuring gauge. Morality is important because there is a need to bring back moral accountability into modernity. In this way he charts the paradigmatic Islamic governance, while accusing the state of being at the center of the "Project of Destruction" (p. 4).

For Wael Hallaq, Islam's interface with modernity is a process and not an event in the past. Unlike the first band of Arab and Muslim intellectuals like Muhammad Abduh and Jamal Uddin al-Afghani, who were trying to reconcile Islam and modernity, Hallaq has called into question the ability to reconcile the two. According to Hallaq, al-nahda is a failure. Modernity has failed the Islamic state and there is a need to go back into history and find the source of morality—Shari'a—to save community and individuals from the sense of narcissism, and moral unaccountability that society and individuals have developed as a result of the project of modernity.

The author sets out to define the paradigmatic modern state. Modern state is a bit amorphous, yet he equivocally argues that modern nation-state can be thought of—for the purposes of this argument—in terms of content and forms. Content he argues is a set of variables that are changeable, or possibly changeable. Form, on the other hand, consists of "fundamental structures or properties that the state has in reality possessed for at least a century and without which it could never be conceived as a state, being that essential" (p. 21). He gives the following attributes to the state: (1) its constitution as a historical experience that is fairly specific and local; (2) its sovereignty and the metaphysics to which it has given rise; (3) its legislative monopoly and the related feature of monopoly over so called legitimate violence; (4) its bureaucratic order; and (5) its cultural hegemony engagement in the social order, including its production of the national subject.

Halleq introduces the concept of the sovereign will through his diagnosis of separation of powers. The sovereign will of the modern is represented in its law which is complete in itself. Max Schelerhe argues that Western thought has been one in which there exists a systematic justification for domination. This urge for domination finds roots in the separation between value and matter. This separation gets translated, though legal positivism, in which the mechanical view of the world, separates nature with value. This separation between "is" and "ought" was made most prominent through the works of John Austin. This is/ought dichotomy in moral reasoning is where the moral unaccountability of the modern state stems from. And since moral reasoning is not ahistorical, other forms of moral reasoning are possible, if not wanted.

The legality of the modern state functions through this dichotomy. But this dichotomy becomes problematic to a Muslim. In pre-modern concept, the difference between the moral and the legal didn't exist. The *Qur'an* presents a cosmological morality that grounds Muslim subjectivity through moral accountability. To accept the positive law of the modern state sets aside Shari'a and draws its inspiration from the *Qur'an* which sees no difference between "Is" and "Ought." The modern state, even though it may be Islamic, sets aside the universality of the *Qur'an* in favor of the context-based man-made laws. The modern state is deemed amoral, yet it asks for sacrifices for its own sake. How can this be reconciled with Islam?

Hallaq favors Shari'a because the concept of *ijtihad* allows a flexible interpretation without losing the divine and moral compass set by the *Qur'an*. According to the author, the pre-modern forms of self, state, and community are stronger and can teach an important lesson for modern morality.

Halleq's work transcends the work of a social theorist, as he moves beyond a particular framework of thinking, and uses the best of everything. Some might find this academic "ship-jumping" problematic, but it is highly useful in criticism of modernity and the enlightenment project. Yet, the book fails to account for the various ways in which Islamic society has appropriated both Islam and modernity. While Halleq tries to justify Islam through ijtihad, no such emphasis is given modernity; nor does he explain how we would negotiate some of the blunt inequalities within the *Qur'an* and Shari'a. Although the author assumes an unquestioned acceptance of Shari'a by Muslim society, surely such acceptance is not universal.

Overall, the book is an excellent attempt at productive engagement between two different modes of thinking, except the less privileged and much marginalized paradigm wins this round. It should form part of recommended reading for scholars and lay readers with a special interest in topics related to modernity, Islam and politics. **MMR**

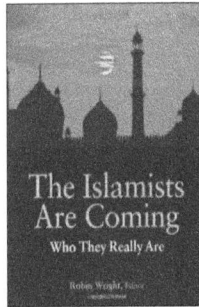

Robin Wright. *The Islamists Are Coming: Who They Really Are.* Washington, DC: Woodrow Wilson Center Press and United States Institute of Peace Press, 2012. 169 pp. $16.65. ISBN: 978-1601271341.

By all rights, this book should be excellent. It addresses a topic that policymakers and analysts urgently need to understand: the Middle East's Islamist parties, their origins, policy positions, and likely future directions. The book is a collaborative effort uniting two prestigious think tanks. The editor and contributing authors are highly recognized experts in Middle Eastern studies based in leading research centers. In short, all the ingredients have been assembled to produce an excellent analysis of an important topic.

The recipe for combining these ingredients has also received professional consideration. The book begins with an excellent introductory chapter by the editor, followed by a regional overview and 12 country profiles covering 11 countries from Morocco to Yemen (Egypt gets two, one to introduce the Muslim Brotherhood and another for the Salafis). A final chapter offers capsule profiles of 50 Islamist parties across 14 countries. To make the material accessible and to facilitate comparison, authors have been enjoined to follow a standard outline, beginning with the origins of the movement in their assigned geography, tracing its progression institutionally and ideologically to the present time, looking ahead to likely developments in the near term, and reviewing positions on selected key issues.

Despite these assets, the whole falls short of the sum of its very promising parts. Before considering why this is so, the book's strong points deserve recognition. Three stand out. First, this work offers a comprehensive, if abbreviated overview of the Islamist parties that are now the largest parties in many countries. One can imagine a harried Congressional aide turning to this book repeatedly to make some sense of Islamist movements in countries her boss is about to visit.

Second, the treatment is uniformly fair, even-handed, and thoughtful. Within the strictures of the format, the authors have striven not only to distinguish radicals from reformers and to do so over time, among countries, and across the current political spectrum, but to provide some explanation for this diversity and how it has evolved. Facile, broad-brush generalizations have been avoided, although at times, this results in the opposite effect, an analytic pointillism that resists resolution into a coherent picture.

Third, the book is well-written in clear prose that is accessible if rarely compelling, sharply focused on the main storyline, and devoid of jargon. The authors' evident expertise enables them to assemble the key events and their leaders into a straight-forward narrative covering the past eight decades.

What, then, are the shortcomings causing the work's reach to exceed its grasp? They fall into two categories: the analysis itself and how it is presented. While the first category holds much more significance in the broader scheme of things, some quick fixes to the latter would have made the book more useful to the reader. First, and most important, the analysis does not put the emergence of the Islamist political movement into its socioeconomic or religious context. The narrative tells us that the Islamists are coming, how many groups there are, and how fast they are moving, but it does not make clear why they are coming. What are the social and economic forces that have attracted people to these movements? What types of people have supported them? We are given a sense of the movement's leaders but much less of their followers, rich or poor, urban or rural, young or old, educated or otherwise. What are they looking for and why do they believe that the Islamist parties offer the best chance of finding it?

The defining feature of Islamism is the leading role it assigns to Islamic doctrine in the political sphere. By choosing to leave this central and essential aspect of Islamism largely off the table, the authors have undercut their ability to explain who the Islamists are and what they hope to achieve. The religious and doctrinal issues uniting or separating Islamists are admittedly very difficult to summarize, particularly for readers lacking much if any familiarity with Islam—precisely those readers presumably targeted by this work. Nonetheless, the result is a denatured discussion that is oddly distant from its topic. As it describes the long struggles between the old regimes and the Islamists, no real sense emerges of what the latter are fighting for or how they will govern now that power is within their grasp. Where they have come from is important, but it tells us only so much about where they are headed.

Second, the text barely addresses the place of the Islamists within the current political spectrum. The decades-long battle between the Islamists and the previous regimes, which many of the authors have focused on for much of their careers, gets most of the attention. These events are still relevant—they shaped the older generation of Islamist leaders and many of their old regime opponents are still on the scene—but this history does not tell the whole story. The Manichean struggle of Islamists versus authoritarians does not tell us enough about the current political dynamic without a parallel examination of relations between the Islamists, on the one hand, and the secularists, liberals, socialists, religious and ethnic minority groups, and the all-important military, on the other. Third, the analysis barely scratches the surface of what could be called the Islamists' secular agenda. What are their policies toward business and economic reforms? How will they try to reshape the horrific education and health systems, address youth unemployment, or fix the social safety net? Are they pro-labor, pro-trade, interventionist, or laissez-faire? Will they work to end corruption or belly up to the trough themselves? Their ability to manage sky-high popular expectations for social justice and economic opportunity will arguably have more impact on the Islamists' political trajectory than their history of oppression and secretiveness, but, again, these are hardly addressed.

A final shortcoming, and one the authors could do very little about, is the detrimental impact that the speed of events in the region will inevitably have on the book's value. While the historical context is certainly not going to change, everything else is a moving target. The descriptions of the parties and their positions in Egypt are already out of date, given reconfigurations in the run-up to the 2013 parliamentary elections. None of the political forces have ever faced the open political scene that they find themselves in, leading to continual redefinition and evolution in Islamist and non-Islamist positions and political structures.

Naturally, no work of this kind could cover all of the above, certainly not on a country-by-country basis. Within the confines of a book-length treatment, however, the choice to use a uniform country case format with a heavy historical emphasis, in effect, limits the book's ability to do its job of introducing the Islamists. The presentational issues, to which we now turn briefly, exacerbate this problem.

The evident effort to make each chapter self-standing has necessitated covering the early history of the movement over and over, even though most groups share a common origin in Egypt's Muslim Brotherhood and have followed quite similar trajectories of state repression and back-and-forth struggles against authoritarian regimes. This eats up a lot of space without adding much value, forcing several authors to compress events since 2000 into a page or less. Good writing cannot entirely overcome the resulting space constraints, leading to very condensed treatment, at times verging on the cryptic, as each author attempts to cover the eight decades from the Brotherhood's 1928 founding to the post-Arab Spring elections.

The parallel case-study approach makes it quite difficult to read the book cover to cover, given inevitable repetition. The brief issue descriptions also become repetitive, particularly where very similar positions on such questions as Israel and democracy have been adopted across countries. Although each chapter can be read on its own, this comes at the cost of using up space that might better have been devoted to analysis of economic issues, the Islamists' socioeconomic support base, or relations with non-Islamist political forces. Treatment of this broader set of issues could have given readers better insight into what will drive the Islamists' decision making in the future rather than focusing so much on recounting their past. **JB**

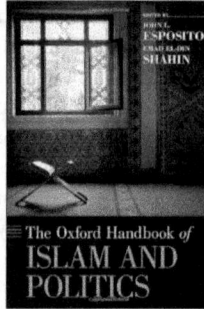

The Oxford Handbook of
ISLAM AND
POLITICS

John L. Esposito and Emad El-Din Shahin, Eds. *The Oxford Handbook of Islam and Politics.* Oxford, UK: Oxford University Press, 2013. 684 pp. $150.00. ISBN: 978-0195395891.

This book was published one year before ISIS (or ISIL) appeared on the international scene and involved Syria and Iraq and a coalition of Western and other nations in fighting it as it attempted to establish, by violence, an "Islamic state" or a "caliphate" in the Levant, meanwhile causing loss of life and destruction, and committing barbarities of untold proportions. The book, therefore, does not deal with ISIS, but with previous movements, some more radical and militant than others, that called for the Islamization of society and the state; and it offers encyclopedic knowledge about their ideologues, activists, intellectuals, and the dynamics of Islam in the politics of different regions of the modern world.

The two editors have assembled contributions to the book from forty-two prominent scholars to cover this vast subject crucial to modern-day life, and they have planned their book diligently in order to give readers comprehensive information about Islam and politics around the world. In their introduction, they explain that "political Islam" has recently manifested itself in two opposed orientations: (1) an increasing involvement by mainstream movements in the democratization process after successfully toppling autocratic regimes in many cases, and (2) an inclination toward violence by fringe groups. The two orientations have different views of the place of Shari'a (Islamic law) in society and of the process of change they advocate; hence their different political actions.

Part One of the book has seven chapters and deals with major themes related to the problem of Islam facing modernity; it has discussions of basic issues of revival and reform regarding Shari'a, the nation-state, democracy, political economy, and gender. Part Two, with 10 chapters, offers studies of the major Islamic thinkers and activists: founders like Hasan al-Banna and Abu al-A'la Mawdudi; revolutionary ideologues such as Sayyid Qutb, 'Ali Shari'ati, and Ayatollah Khomeini; and intellectuals like Hasan Turabi, Rashid al-Ghannushi, Yusuf al-Qaradawi, Mohammad Khatami, and Abdolkarim Soroush.

Part Three has eight chapters about Islam and politics in specific regions of the world: North America, Europe, the Middle East, Central Asia, South Asia, Southeast Asia, North Africa, and Sub-Saharan Africa. Part Four concentrates on the dynamics of Islam in politics and has three sections: one with six chapters on political Islam when in possession of state power as in Iran, Saudi Arabia, Turkey, Sudan, Afghanistan, and Egypt with the Muslim Brotherhood; another section with seven chapters on Islamic movements in the political process such as Hamas in Palestine, Hizbullah in Lebanon, the Islamic Action Front in Jordan, Nahdatul Ulama in Indonesia, and Jama'at-i Islami in Pakistan, as well as the Islamic movements in North Africa and in Malaysia; and a third section on Jihadi political Islam with three chapters: one chapter on Egypt's al-Jama'a al-Islamiyya and the al-Jihad Group; another on Jihadists in Iraq; and a third on al-Qa'ida and its affiliates.

From this quick conspectus, it is clear how comprehensive the contents of this large book are and how important it is to the understanding of the relation of Islam and politics in contemporary times. Each of the chapters is written by a specialist and has up-to-date information on its topic. Some chapters offer a useful preliminary history of their topic before their analytic account of it, like the one on Islam and politics in North America; but it is unfortunately limited to the United States. Several of chapters, like the one on Islam and politics in Sub-Saharan Africa, whet the reader's appetite for more information, but unfortunately, it is not provided, such as when the Boko Haram movement of Nigeria is mentioned in only one line (p. 388). But on the whole, all chapters are elaborate, precise, erudite, and well-documented. The treatment of non-Muslims as manifested in the politics of Muslim countries is dealt with in several chapters and in some of the chapters containing the principles advanced by ideologues and activists; a special chapter on this topic might have been relevant in Part One as one of the major themes, but this and other desiderata would have lengthened this already full book even further.

When all is said and done, this book is a welcome addition to the writings on Islam and politics, which is a subject of great consequence and urgency in the modern world's scholarship. Islam is shown to be a living religion and way of life, and a significant factor in the politics and the social fabric of contemporary human existence. The diversity of the political manifestations of Islam in various regions as it faces modernity does not negate the unity of Islam as a belief system. The book demonstrates how a Muslim people's culture is still accommodated within their modern vision of their religious beliefs—a good example being the contemporary political structures of Saudi Arabia under the rule of its Wahhabi dynasty (pp. 411-422) and Turkey under the leadership of Recep Tayyip Erdogan and his Justice and Development Party (pp. 423-439). The former country has an established tribal culture with time-honored traditions and the latter has a secular twentieth century experience with a robust democracy, but both identify themselves as Muslims in their devised contemporary political structures.

This book is highly recommended as a reference book and also as a textbook for advanced students of Islam and political science. **IJB**

ISRAEL

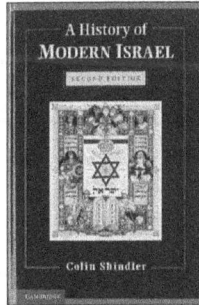

Colin Shindler. *A History of Modern Israel.* New York, NY: Cambridge University Press, 2013. 2ed. 496 pp. $80.75. ISBN: 978-1107028623. Pbk.: 352 pp. $27.09. ISBN: 978-1107671775. Ebk.: 3919 KB. 497 pp. $15.19. ISBN: 1107028620.

In January of 1989, Israeli Prime Minister Yitzhak Shamir and Foreign Minister Moshe Arens came up with a novel idea. "Shamir said that Israel would accept a Jordanian-Palestinian confederation and a common market of Israel, the Palestinian territories and Jordan, with open access to Israeli ports" (p. 214). Shamir proposed that a token 40,000 houses be built for Palestinians living in refugee camps, as a nod toward the demand for a "right of return." Rabin, the Labor party leader, concurred and considered joining a national unity government. In the end, the plan never got further, as Likud rebels led by Benjamin Netanyahu bucked the consensus.

This is one of many fascinating historical episodes to be revealed in the second edition of Colin Shindler's *A History of Modern Israel.* Shindler is an Emeritus Professor at the School of Oriental and African Studies, at the University of London. He is a founding chairman of the European Association of Israel Studies. As such, he is well placed to provide a narrative history of Israel in one volume. The first edition of this book was published in 2008. The author notes that new social and international concerns necessitate a second volume. For instance, Israel has continued to develop economically, and its scientists have continued to receive international acclaim. This is overshadowed by other problems—for example, the Iranian nuclear threat. "Given that Iran possessed a land mass eighty times that of Israel and nine times the population, it seemed unlikely that Israel would actually unleash a military attack on Iran despite a cacophony of bellicose noises emitted from Netanyahu and

[Ehud] Barak" (p. xliii).

Shindler begins his account by discussing the origins of Zionism. He notes that Theodore "Herzl changed the course of Jewish history" (p. 14). This "pragmatist" and "utopianist" (p. 14) who was born in Hungary but lived in Vienna, wrote *Der Judenstadt* in 1895. At the time, the "founder" of Zionism had never heard the term "Zionism," even though it had been coined by Nathan Birnbaum in 1890. He spoke no Hebrew and, as Shindler points out, "there was no mention of Palestine" (p. 14).

Shindler hoes a well-manicured narrative that positions Zionism as a European ideology, which it was, and moves forward linearly without questioning other aspects of this movement. Gone from the analysis are some of the ideological questions that require exploring. For instance, to what degree was racism and supremacism at the heart of this movement and its competing ideology, and how would those differences play a role later in the state? The author provides no background to the founding, for example, of the ethnically pure kibbutzim, a Labor Zionism innovation, that creates Ashkenazi (European) Jewish communities, where, in practice, non-European Jews and local Arabs were prohibited from living. This has immense importance for the future state of Israel and its internal conflicts; where each community lives separately—Arabs and Jews in different schools; Jews from Ethiopia, Russia and Morocco in "development towns;" and Haredim in other areas—the opposite of a modern notion of a state—and an issue intimately related to the "conquest of labor" that Labor Zionism innovated after 1908. It would be like writing a history of the United States without discussing 'Manifest Destiny' or the racial arguments of the nineteenth and early twentieth centuries.

Shindler compounds the text's blindness by stigmatizing all the Jews who emigrated from the Arab world as lacking skills. "Only a small fraction of the immigrants possessed any kind of training or marketable skills" (p. 97). In fact, many Jews from Yemen, Iraq, Morocco, Iran and Turkey had skills; some had been incredibly wealthy, and many left behind accounts of meeting with extreme racism in Israel. Schindler interprets this as "the Sephardim felt undervalued and suffered from Ashkenazi disdain for their way of life" (p. 97). Today the descendants of these Jews make up half the Jewish population of Israel. What was their "way of life"—as diverse as the "way of life" of European Jews, from the wealthiest people in Baghdad to cave-dwellers from Fezzan in Libya.

This book's bias, and where it is strongest, is in describing political infighting, rather than social issues. However, it does contain some nuggets that address the social problems plaguing Israel. The early chapters discuss the first politicians to address Arab minority rights in Israel. The fascinating chapter four deals with the "politics of piety" (p. 78) and how Israel's early leaders dealt with the ultra-Orthodox population. An early case dealt with "who is a Jew." Interestingly, the author quotes Vladimir Jabotinsky, the Revisionist Zionist, who had once noted "if a people voluntarily encased their religious consciousness within an iron frame, dried it out to the point of fossilization, and turned a living religion into something like a mummified corpse of religion, it is clear that the holy treasure is not the religion, but something else… for which this mummified corpse was supposed to serve as shell and protection" (p. 88). This is a fascinating quote; unpacked it makes us recall his phrase "an Iron Wall" and also British historian Arnold Toynbee's claim that Judaism was a "fossil" religion. Unfortunately the text does not make this connection.

This volume gives a healthy and interesting examination of the worldwide criticism of Israel since the 1960s, as well as an internal critique of the country's policies. For instance, in July 1970, the World Union of Jewish Students at a meeting in Arad noted that Zionism's goal "can only be realized if the national rights of the Palestinian Arabs are considered" (p. 183). The students called the Palestinian aspirations a "consequence of Zionist ideology." This is critical and strong language, so soon after 1967, very clearly supporting Palestinians in a way most Jewish youth movements do not do today. Yet, again, there is little analysis of this trend by the author. However Shindler does note that "what was used for propaganda [by Israel] for non-Jews was simultaneously being distributed to Jews as information. For example, British Jews were repeatedly told that the Israeli Ambassador [Shlomo Argov] had been shot by the PLO and not by members of the anti-PLO Abu Nidal group" (p. 195). The author notes that the blanket "blind support" for Israel by Diaspora Jewish organizations worked well under Mapai-led governments, when Israel was effectively a one-party government state from 1948 to 1977; but became "political schizophrenia" after 1977 because of the alternating policies of "left" and "right" (p. 195). He notes that the ascent of Menachem Begin to power in 1977 alienated some Jews, and left pro-Israel Jews associated with the right in Israeli politics. This was problematic when Yitzhak Rabin explored peace opportunities in the 1990s. But what Shindler doesn't examine is whether there was really any difference politically between the left and right in Israel, with regards to issues such as settlements and the Arab states. In fact, there was little. The left inaugurated the settlements, including in the Sinai, and Shimon Peres, a "dove" in this book, supported or approved a fair share of them. The right sided the peace with Egypt and the left with the Palestinians. Some of the differences are more semantics than reality; one politician may be a dove, even though he ordered the blanket bombing of Lebanon in 1996 called "Grapes of Wrath." Whether this is schizophrenia or basically one policy over time—and thus any foreign support for it is consistent—is worth examining further.

The last chapters of the book examine events since 2008, including the raid on the Mavi Marmara flotilla that was trying to reach Gaza in 2010; the Goldstone Report on Operation Cast-Lead; and the Arab Spring. It looks at the decline in Israel–Turkish relations and Israel's continuing "sense of isolation" (p. 410). This is an immensely readable and accessible book and a good primer for students. The main problem is the lack of analysis and critical examination of some of the accepted narratives regarding Zionism and Israel. However, a helpful glossary, and a fast-paced and interesting narrative make this one of the few good and balanced one-volume histories available. **SJF**

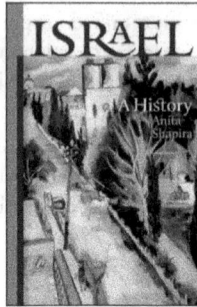

Anita Shapira. *Israel: A History.* **Waltham, MA: Brandeis University Press, 2012. 502 pp. $35.00. ISBN: 978-1611683523.**

Soon after the creation of the State of Israel, large numbers of Jewish immigrants began arriving from Arab countries such as Iraq and Yemen. Many of these Jews came from relatively traditional religious families. The Israeli government's bureaucrats however were mostly European-born secular Jews who sought to mold these immigrants into a new image. "The teachers did not hesitate to tell students to cut off their [traditional] sidelocks, throw away their hats, and turn their backs on religious tradition. Boys and girls sat together in the same classroom and learned not to respect the traditions of their forbears" (p. 241). Yemenite Jews took this especially harshly. This controversy, over whether Jews from Arab countries should be "modernized" or educated in a system more closely resembling the one they were used to was at the heart of a *Kulterkampf* in Israel's early years.

Anita Shapira, a Professor Emeritus at Tel Aviv University, has set out in *Israel: A History* to present an accessible, one volume account of the country that can be accessible, both to a popular audience, and students of Israeli history. In the opening sections she notes "most histories of Israel focus on the Arab–Jewish conflict… without shying away from examining the conflict, the history should encompass internal Jewish politics, immigration and nation building" (p. xi). This history book therefore sets out to provide a more social history of a country whose history has been told previously in one volume accounts by Martin Gilbert and Howard Sachar.

From the first chapter it is obvious that a history of Israel in Shapira's conception is in fact a history of Zionism. This sets up a paradigmatic problem. If Israel's history is primarily tied into Zionism, then what should be made of the people who were already in Israel before the advent of Zionism, namely the Arab population and the religious Jewish groups? Any new country faces this issue. Does a history of Turkey involve the story of Troy, the Armenians and Byzantine Christianity, or is it just a history of the Turkish people and the country they built up? Shapira's narrative follows the traditional Zionist history of Jewish emancipation in Europe in the nineteenth century and the writings of Theodore Herzl, the father of the Zionist movement. Although the Zionist movement, which sought a national home for the Jewish people, considered offers to immigrate to Africa and elsewhere, their hearts were set on Ottoman Palestine, where Judaism had been born. "At the beginning of the nineteenth century, Palestine was a remote, backward province of the Ottoman Empire...the country was almost empty, with some 250,000 inhabitants" (p. 27).

As Shapira narrates it, the first Zionists from Europe who arrived in Palestine were confronted with a foreign landscape. "Members of Yesod Hama'ala Committee, who came to purchase land for the first moshav, established by Hovevei Zion... were warmly welcomed at the Chelouche [Jewish] family home, though with some puzzlement...there remained a gnawing doubt whether they were really Jews" (p. 29). Given the fact that Israel's government would later wrestle with the question "who is a Jew," this was an interesting irony; the local Jews wondered whether the early Zionists were in fact Jewish. Here Shapira has a chance to pause and consider that the story of Israel's history involved the Chelouche family of Sephardic Jews, who were in the land that became Israel *before* the arrival of European Zionists. And yet her narrative quickly moves on to focus on the work of Jews at places like Yesod Hama'ala, ignoring the activities of people like the Chelouche family.

This "new Yishuv" of Jewish settlements that grew up was riven by its own internal controversies. One issue was whether the labor on the Zionist villages should be done by Arabs and Jews or just by Jews. Shapira rejects the interpretation that there was a European colonialist element to the Zionist enterprise. "The new Jewish Yishuv was not established so that the motherland could send its sons and daughters to settle in a country it ruled and exploit the colony's resources" (p. 47). However, Palestine did come under the control of a colonial power, England, beginning in 1917. Britain was dedicated to creating a Jewish national home in the country through the Balfour Declaration, but it quickly saw that this would be no easy task. "The story of the thirty-year long British rule in Palestine is a tale of Britain's slow withdrawal from its pro-Zionist commitments, the Zionist leadership's efforts to exert pressure on the British to meet those commitments, and the Arab pressure in the opposite direction" (p. 75). The book's discussion of the British Mandate is cursory and seems to miss some of the more important issues, such as the development of the Jewish underground groups (Haganah, Irgun, and Lehi), their decision to engage in a campaign of bombing and assassinations against the British, and the short civil struggle between them known as the *saison*. This is part of the overall pattern to stay away from politics and conflict, but by skipping some of these formative issues, the book seems to ignore basic events that would haunt Israel in its post-independence years. This was particularly true of the Palestinian refugees who were not allowed to return to the nascent and fragile state of Israel. Shapira argues that "in the context of the time, Israeli policy on the refugee issue was not considered out of the ordinary" (p. 175).

Some of the book's most interesting, and problematic content is focused around the first decade of the state and the issue of immigration. The first Knesset, Israel's parliament was elected in January of 1949. It was supposed to create a constitution, "instead the Knesset would enact a series of Basic Laws" (p. 182). In lieu of a constitution, Israel has been governed based on these laws ever since. Shapira argues that this was a major mistake. "A constitution's importance goes beyond its purely legal aspect. Such a document is a tool for creating civic ethos as a significant component of the state's identity" (p. 183). This was "one of [Prime Minister David] Ben-Gurion's greatest mistakes, largely because he never imagined that the influence of religion and the power of the religious parties would grow" (p. 183). In Shapira's analysis, the lack of a constitution opened up a can of worms that allowed the power of the religious to grow over the state's institutions and early exemptions made for the religious Orthodox Jews came back to haunt the state later as more and more of them opted out of things such as army service. Once again, the book clearly sides with the secular European Jewish section of Israeli society in arguing that a history of Israel is necessarily a history of this group, while other groups in society, such as the religious, are painted as posing a threat to this group or undermining the state by making demands of it. The author posits that Israel's transition to democracy was a great achievement, "of all the states created after 1945, Israel is one of the few that has maintained a democratic regime" (p. 179).

In 1950, large-scale immigration of Jews from Europe and the Islamic countries began. Unlike most countries where legal immigrants may move where they like, Israel's centralized socialist system believed that immigration must be managed. One director of an immigrant camp recalled "the immigrants were locked in, surrounded by barbed wire fences and guarded by armed police" (p. 225). The camps, called *ma'abara*, were nests of "shacks crowded together around the stinking latrines" (p. 229). Israelis, many of whom had only arrived in the country several years before, castigated the newcomers as a "motley crowd of human dust lacking language, education, roots, tradition, [or] national dreams" (p. 231). It is hard to read all this and wonder where the analysis is by the author. Why were immigrants treated like criminals by a state claiming to want to "ingather" Jewish exiles? Why were they forced into barbed wire camps and then settled in large towns, while European Jewish immigrants were subjected to a "selection process" (p. 233) and sent to build a bucolic Kibbutzim? The author suffices to stereotype the Arab-Jewish immigrants as people "compelled to get used to physical work, which in their countries of origin was considered demeaning" (p. 226) and claims the state was in fact burdened with "settling thousands of immigrants with neither experience nor inclination toward agriculture." The author suffices with these un-sourced sweeping generalizations and stereotypes, including claims that they deserved discrimination because "their level of education was very low" (p. 243). In many ways this reflects an orientalist mentality that everyone from the Arab world must necessarily have a "low education." In fact, many Jews from Iraq and North Arica were well educated; some had also studied at French schools and universities.

The stereotyping of non-European Jews runs throughout the book. Describing

Ethiopian immigrants, the author claims they had to "transition from the small village in the mountains of Ethiopia to the industrialized, achievement-oriented Israeli society" (p. 460). There is no source for this claim that Ethiopians came from a society that did not understand the concept of "achievement," but comments like this smack of a Eurocentric bias against people of color based on false notions that those from certain societies don't seek to "achieve." Many seeking a broad new survey of Israeli history will find these remarks jarring and ill-placed for a modern social history that is expected to provide a more broad-minded approach to Israel's diverse society whose origins are in many countries and cultures in the world. **SJF**

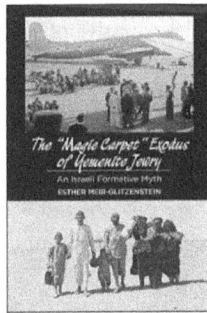

Esther Meir-Glitzenstein. *The 'Magic Carpet' Exodus of Yemenite Jewry.* Eastbourne, UK: Sussex Academic Press, 2014. 265 pp. $78.92. ISBN: 978-1845196165.

In 1949, they came from all over Yemen, from 1,000 villages, traveling often on foot on more than 77 roads to reach camp. "It was a desert place without any sign of vegetation. Refugees living in matted huts, like sardines, living a base, primitive life. The camp has 4,000 people and babies are born every day" (p. 61), recalled Ethel Slonim, a nurse who had arrived in Aden—now Yemen—in 1948. Many died en route and in the camp. Yet, even more than half a century later the traumatic immigration is thought of as a miracle. Why has the myth of the Yemenite migration not been fully understood for what it was, a massive tragedy in which a community was uprooted, the scars of the operation having never been healed? Esther Meir-Glitzenstein, an associate professor at Ben-Gurion University of the Negev seeks to set the record straight, and provide readers some nuance on this formative historical event in the founding of Israel.

Meir-Glitzenstein sets out to ask several important questions about the migration of Yemenite Jews in 1949. Who initiated it, what caused the Jews to suddenly leave en masse, why was there a humanitarian tragedy and was some of the tragedy underpinned by racism or bigotry among the officials charged with running the operation? She notes that the Yemenite immigration was part of the larger immigration of hundreds of thousands of Jews from both Europe and the Middle East who poured into Israel after the War of Independence. From December 1948 to March 1949 some 5,000 Yemenites arrived. Then an additional 45,000 were airlifted by 1950. Israeli representatives and the Joint Distribution Committee (JDC) played a key role in the operation.

The operation took on a Janus face in Israel's history. For years after the event, many Yemenite Jews claimed that their children had disappeared or been kidnapped. In 1994, Uzi Meshulam and some of his Yemenite followers became so enraged at what they saw as an official state cover-up, they barricaded themselves with weapons in a house in Yehud. In 2001, a commission of inquiry was still investigating what became of the children. Yet for the primarily European-born Israeli establishment, this was anathema to the national narrative of redemption. "This type of exodus story is also found in Golda Meir's autobiography…she describes how the life of suffering and despair led by the Jews of Yemen motivated them to leave, and she emphasizes that they fled spontaneously, clinging to their Hebrew biblical texts" (p. 5). Children in Israel learned in textbooks that claimed that "Yemen is a poor land, dry and barren. When the miracle occurred, and when Israel overcame her enemies and the State of Israel was established in perpetuity, the sound of *shofar* (ram's horn) announcing the coming of the Messiah was heard even by the Jews in far-away Yemen" (p. 6).

One of the reasons for the lack of an inquiry into what happened was that so few books on the subject were published. Yosef Zadok, an emissary of the Jewish Agency, who was born in Yemen, wrote a book about the events in 1956. But as the author notes, most research has only been done in the last two decades.

Yemenite Jews had lived in Yemen since the time of the Second Temple. Even Maimonides had intervened to save them. This was an ancient community, scattered in more than 1,000 villages—mostly in the highlands of the country. As the author notes, by the first half of the twentieth century there were some 50,000 Jews living among 3.5 million Muslims. In some areas they suffered great discrimination, being confined sometimes to collect human waste or animal carcasses. By 1914, some 5,000 Yemenites had already made their way to Palestine, where they played an integral role in the development of the Zionist economy; founding several communities.

During the Second World War, due to a famine and other issues, around 10,000 Jews fled from North Yemen to British administered Aden (South Yemen). The British interdicted these Jewish refugees who wanted to make it to the Holy Land. "The British wanted to expel these refugees to [North] Yemen, as they had done with the Muslim labor migrants, but they feared that the Jewish Agency would oppose such an expulsion" (p. 46). Later, the number of refugees would continue to swell. Then in December of 1947, a pogrom broke out in Aden in which Muslims, supposedly protesting the UN partition of Palestine, slaughtered 80 Jews.

The author argues the Jewish Agency and others did not do enough for these refugees. In one instance in Qa'tabah, the graves of hundreds of Jews were discovered.

"Why was insufficient help not sent to save these refugees…first and foremost because the Jewish Agency did not show any interest in their fate" (p. 57), she argues.
Other authors, such as Tudor Parfitt have linked this dismissive attitude to a "colonial" mindset among the European Jews of Palestine.

The text takes the reader through the tragic story of the deterioration of the situation in Yemen; the Muslim hostility, British indifference and the lack of organization by some Israeli officials. The author concludes that the inability of the state
authorities and others to admit that something had gone wrong led to years of denial
and lack of compassion or compensation for the hardships. Later in 1984, a repeat
of the disaster took place when more than 4,000 Ethiopian Jews died on the way
to Israel. "One is compelled to ask whether this tragedy might have been averted
had the lessons of the Yemenite immigration been learned, while the tragedy of
European migrant ships to Israel, like the Egoz and Sturma that sank, are commemorated, the suffering of the Yemenites is not part of the Israeli consciousness. It is an
important lesson raised by this book: the need for an Israeli society that can be both
introspective and acknowledge all its diverse communities. **SJF**

JUDAISM & JEWS

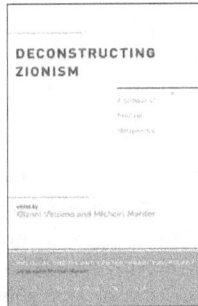

Gianni Vattimo and Michael Marder, editors. *Deconstructing Zionism: A Critique of Political Metaphysics.* New York, NY: Bloomsbury Academic, 2013. 208 pp. $100.00. ISBN: 978-1441143457.

A volume of 11 essays edited and introduced by a prominent Italian philosopher and public intellectual (Vattimo) and a polymathic young academic (Marder), Deconstructing Zionism is admirable for the revealing light through which it re-reads a phenomenon that, as the book's title aptly suggests, exemplifies the seemingly inextricability of politics from metaphysics—Zionism. Indeed, one of the volume's primarily stated aims is subjecting Zionism to a mode of critique indebted to the tradition of linguistic and textual interpretation, and philosophical inquiry associated with recent European thinkers like Martin Heidegger and Jacques Derrida. Looking back to ancient and biblical thought, Heidegger and Derrida had famously (and in the view of some, infamously) questioned whether there can "Be" any absolute reality whose essential qualities are accessible in a timeless form capable of grounding political, ethical, religious, and other varieties of human claim to universal truth and worldly order. Clearly, the contributors to Deconstructing Zionism participate in the general view that the modern assertion of a claim to territory demarcated as the State of Israel, on the basis of a supposed, millennia-long collective Jewish identity, and physical presence within (to say nothing of forced absence from) that territory, cannot be sustained, from a philosophical standpoint.

In tandem with the endeavor of peeling back and disassembling the metaphysical foundations of Zionism's notion that "the Jewish people... [share a] connection to the "Land of Israel"... [that is] trans historical and unitary, temporary exiles notwithstanding," the book seeks to engage in "a radical ideology critique" (p. xiii). The aim, therefore, is to expose concrete injustices wrought by Zionism upon Palestinians, and, as well, upon Jews who are ostracized by other Jews for the former's criticism of, or disengagement from prevailing paradigms of Jewish nationalism. As such, in the words of iconoclastic Jewish Studies scholar Marc Ellis, who in one of the collection's finest chapters, captures its animating spirit with singular clarity and concision: "Deconstructing Zionism is a philosophical act but it is also always a political act—with important consequences" (p. 100).

The interpretive and analytic strategies advocated by the book's contributors as necessary means for Deconstructing Zionism sometimes converge around the enterprise of hermeneutics; and to be sure, the close, attentive reading called for by a hermeneutical undertaking is required of one who encounters this decidedly challenging, but appropriately rewarding set of perspectives on Zionism and its multifarious, associated dilemmas. At the same time, a close reading demonstrates that Deconstructing Zionism's prime drawback is the uneven strength and pertinence of the essays comprising it—an unevenness that, curiously, corresponds in conflicting ways, with the considerable renown of some included writers. Roughly speaking, two categories of essay tend to present themselves in this particular connection: those that are outstanding and worthy, or even enhancing, of the author's reputation, and those that are notably disappointing. In addition, the book displays a third sort of essay, wherein there is something significant on offer, but the analysis is so recondite as to constrain, somewhat, the essay's immediate appeal. Welcome, then, that there are further inclusions, especially Marder's penultimate chapter, whose dense complexity, yet pointed relevance and insight allow them to serve as a place of confluence between continental philosophy and Middle East studies.

To begin with the most outstanding chapters: Ellis's evocative piece manages, within its brief span, to link the biblically grounded self-critique demanded by Judaism's prophetic tradition with the contemporary imperative for a distinction between "Progressive Jews" and "Jews of Conscience." While each group, he indicates, rightly "oppose[s] Israeli policies toward Palestinians," the former is characterized by its belief that "the fault line is the Israeli occupation and settlements following the 1967 Arab-Israeli war" (p. 108). By contrast, "Jews of Conscience," whose stance Ellis evidently finds more compelling, "have come," in a prophetic cast of mind, "to the end of Israel's innocence; that is, Jews of Conscience believe that Israel's state project is fundamentally flawed," and have arrived at the realization that "Zionism in its practical application in Palestine was and is a colonial and racist project" (p. 108). The political ramifications of Ellis's inquiry are manifest (while he does not mention such lobbying groups as J Street or AIPAC (American Israel Public Affairs Committee), one imagines that he would find the former a wholly inadequate rejoinder to the self-evident illegitimacy of the latter). In sum, Ellis's views place him in line with the volume's overall suggested sympathy for a "one-state" approach to the Israel/Palestine conflict—problematic though any nation-state-based model necessarily is—given the contributors' implication that the underpinnings, in philosophy and political theory, of an illusory "two-state solution" are precisely what demand thorough-going deconstruction.

Continuing in the intersecting vein of philosophy and political theory, Deconstructing Zionism includes a provocative and rigorous piece by Judith Butler. As it happens, the chapter is borrowed from, and representative of her recent book, Parting Ways: Jewishness and the Critique of Zionism (Columbia University Press, 2012); in Parting Ways..., Butler issues a profound and poignant call for the distancing of, on the one hand, Zionism and its inherent, politically sanctioned and executed violence from, on the other, a counterpoised, humane and self-reflective Jewish consciousness that makes itself aware of sharing with Palestinians a fundamentally Diasporic historical experience. That book, and the present essay, only enrich Butler's status as one of the most capacious and sensitive contemporary thinkers; within the latter, she lends to the volume a tone of searching humility, and courageous commitment, all the more compelling for its lack of stridency. Butler offers a painstaking meditation on Jewish identity, and ""religion" in public life" (p. 23) more broadly. At its heart is an unflinching critique, yet empathetic portrayal, of Hannah Arendt's struggling attempts to preserve some version of Jewish nationalism, even as Arendt foresaw the suffering and self-delusion characterizing Zionism's political fallout.

Parallel to Butler's incorporating of Arendt's "searing critique of the nation-state"—albeit a critique, Butler readily allows, that "[leaves us] with no sign of what the state or a polity might be that would be disjoined from the nation [and associated territory]" (p. 47)—Deconstructing Zionism presents a superb chapter from semiotician Walter Mignolo. With forceful elegance, a contextualization drawing upon broader forces of global history and unapologetic indeterminacy in terms of what one might propose as elusive political alternatives, Mignolo observes a paradoxical conundrum residing at the core of "the conflict of Palestine/Israel" (p. 57)—and implicit, for that matter, within numerous other postcolonial scenarios. Namely, because Zionism emerged as "a movement of liberation mounted on the model of the modern European nation-state,... entrenched [as the nation-state was] in European imperialism around the world," "to solve [the conflict] would require more than peace agreements—it would require decolonizing the form of the modern European nation-state" (p. 57). On Mignolo's interpretation, it remains uncertain (although dubious) whether the nation-state can be salvaged in this manner; whatever may come, though, the key lies in re-imagining political life in ways that meet "the needs of the people instead of the interests of the state" (p. 72).

Three less inspiring chapters, all by well-recognized figures, combine to begin and end the book. The first two, featuring, respectively, the prolific Slavoj Žižek, and Vattimo himself, broadly relate the tragic ironies of Jewish people who have been historically subjected to bigotry and dehumanization, and then become, themselves, responsible for imposing such misdeeds on others. However, the essays are quite loosely and polemically argued and edited, with Vattimo's, ironically, being marred by the misleadingly symbolic proofreading error of denoting the movie-producing Coen brothers as "Cohen" (p. 21). French feminist Luce Irigaray closes Deconstructing Zionism with a contribution whose call for strengthening "peaceful coexistence in difference" through a conscious integration of "sexuate identity" (p. 171), rather than a more neutral modeling of human subjects; this is not uninteresting, but remains somewhat vague and tangential with respect to the specific contexts at hand.

By comparison, essays within the volume's core by Artemy Magun, Christopher Wise, and Ranjana Khanna are carefully honed works proffering worthwhile insight on, sequentially, Karl Marx's and Arendt's understandings of how intertwining genealogies of Judaism and Christianity relate to what Carl Schmitt would recognize as the traditions' varying embodiments of political theology; Derrida's peculiar conception of Judaism's "exalted [messianic] status" (p. 113); and multivalent literary significations of asylum. The fact that these three chapters trace a sometimes obscure path through the not unexpected thickets of deconstructionist critique renders well-placed the subsequent markers lain down by Santiago Zabala, and Marder's "The Zionist Synecdoche." Zabala's brief but resonant essay demonstrates how hermeneutics compels the realization that "Palestinians and Jews" must be free to live in diverse modes of relation to ontological reality, unfettered by "political Zionism" ['s] (p. 151) superimposed regime of existence. Ultimately, Marder's intricate discussion of how Zionism's limited and exclusionary reading of the arrayed significances that might otherwise be intimated by "Zion, a hill in the city of Jerusalem" (p. 155) epitomizes the book's lofty and laudable vision—namely, contemplating how a disputed territory, and the ossified constructions of reality within which it has become appropriated and enwalled, might be reconceived as a site truly and openly "filled with justice and righteousness" (p. 166). **AMW**

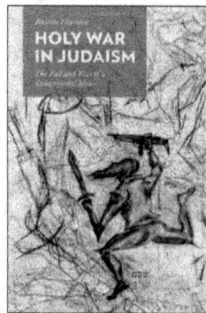

Reuven Firestone. *Holy War in Judaism: The Fall and Rise of a Controversial Idea*. New York, NY: Oxford University Press, 2012. 384 pp. $39.95. ISBN: 978-0199860302.

Reuven Firestone endeavors in this book to explain how the loaded concept of "holy war," that he defines as "organized mass violence directed against rival communities based on what is considered to be God's approval or authority" (p. viii), has fallen and then revived in Judaism. At the outset, Firestone states that "[a] mong the religious systems I have studied, Judaism has the least developed and least politicized ideology of holy war" (p. viii). This is a very strong statement for which the reader would expect systematic evidence.

Part I examines how "holy war" is institutionalized in the *Hebrew Bible* from Joshua's wars until the middle of the second century C.E., and waged, according to Deuteronomy, for the possession of the land promised by God to Israel, and ensuring that the people of Israel remain true to God. Last ancient success was that of the Maccabean revolt against the Greeks in the second century B.C.E., before the tide is turned with the defeat of the Zealots' revolt by the Romans in 70 C.E., resulting in the second destruction of the Temple and the Masada tragedy, and with the failure of the anti-Roman Bar-Kokhba rebellion in 135 C.E., that brought massive dislocation of the Jews. The author explains the defiance of the chief rabbinical interpretations, the Talmud and the Midrash, toward these events—assigning Maccabean success to divine, rather than human, action, and discrediting the Zealots and Bar-Kokhba in favor of their contemporary righteous sages—as a deliberate reaction to the calamitous failure of wars thought to be divinely-authorized, which required the encouragement of Jews to pious quietism rather than warring.

Part II analyzes the two constructs set by medieval rabbinical Judaism for that purpose: (a) a twofold typology of war—"Commanded War" which is "holy" but limited to the divinely-commanded Joshua's wars, and "Discretionary War," that could be understood as mercenary undertaking—that made "holy war" almost impossible to apply; and (b) Bible-based Three Vows, i.e., Jews should neither rebel against their ruling gentiles nor immigrate to the Land of Israel en masse, or otherwise it would amount to "forcing God's hand" to bring the messiah in return for divine prevention of severe persecution of the Jews by the gentiles. The Talmud required the approval of the king's request by a 71 sage court (Sanhedrin) to send fighters off to Discretionary War. Commenting on these, Rabbi Maimonides (d. 1204) generalized the categories of "Commanded War," to include defensive wars as well as an eternal order to destroy the Amalek and the Seven (Canaanite) Nations who are associated with any enemy of Israel, and "Discretionary War" to extend the borders of Israel, and the meaning of these borders by equalizing any legal Jewish conquest with Joshua's as long as the additional lands are conquered after the Land of Israel. Rabbi Nachmanides (d. 1270) rather considered God's command to his people to settle the land to be "equal to all of the commandments in the Torah" (p. 132).

Part III unfolds how "holy war" began to revive in the modern era through Zionism in the nineteenth century. Calling the Jews by secular Zionists to return to the Land of Israel, in contradiction with the Three Vows, caused a difference with Orthodox Jews though some of them supported the Zionist enterprise—in what became Religious Zionism—and started to settle Palestine in the early twentieth century in an actualization of Nachmanides' position. Moreover, Rabbi Abraham Isaac Kook (d. 1935) opined that World War I represents a divine sign for Israel redemption, and the Torah obliges the Jews to engage in conquering the Land of Israel even if this means going to war. During the Arab Revolt (1936–39), Religious Zionists' Rabbis, though occasionally condemning Jewish violence, referred to the struggle with the Palestinians as "holy war," and reminded, like Rabbi Bar-Ilan (d. 1949), of the Torah verse "do not let a single person [of the enemy] live" (pp. 195-196). Nonetheless, that it was not until two major miracles that "holy war" was fully re-established in Judaism. The first was Israel's victory in the 1948 war whose "holiness," and therefore the obligation on Orthodox Jews to join it, was based mainly on: (a) it was perceived, following Maimonides, as defensive; (b) saving Jewish lives takes precedence over all the Torah commandments; and (c) the will of the majority of the people of Israel is fit to replace the king's and the Sanhedrin's authority to call up troops.

Part IV discusses the effect of the 1948 victory in that it made Israel's rabbis connect the victory to the "beginning of the flowering of our Redemption" (p. 227) in their prayers, passing through the 1956 war after which the Israeli army's chief rabbi asserted the "sanctity" of the Land of Israel. This part then elaborates on the effect of the second miracle, Israel's shocking victory in 1967 war, which led the Religious Zionists to acknowledge for the first time the messianic, redemption mission of the State of Israel, and massively engaged in settlement as part of the "re-conquest" of the Land of Israel. Above all was the rabbis' cancellation of the Three Vows, citing that the Vows are deconstructed by the world powers' acceptance of the Jewish state and that the Vows were only against a conquest, not a defensive war as that of 1967 was perceived. Surprisingly, Israel's near-defeat at the 1973 war only reinforced this trend either by denial—"this is only a temporary delay" (p. 296), according to Rabbi Tzvi Yehuda Kook (d. 1982)—by rejecting any concessions of "God's offer" of territories to which it might lead.

Entering the early 1980s, where the book concludes, the views of Rabbi Tzvi Yehuda Kook dominated the thinking of the Religious Zionists, particularly the Settler Movement and the extremist group Gush Emunim. Though not explicitly instigating violence, he incited it through his prayers for God to "[b]ring vengeance on the gentiles" (p. 288), and his endorsement of the renewal of the Torah command to control the whole land—"[i]t is impossible to avoid this command" (p. 290). "Holy war" culminated in the anti-Palestinian terror committed by the Jewish Underground whose members were convinced that "virtually *any* war engaged by Jews is divinely sanctioned" (p. 310).

Firestone's historical journey through religious Jewish texts that begins with wars in the *Hebrew Bible*, and ends with the violence by Jewish settlers against the Palestinians in the 1980s constitutes a smoothly read, insightful historical and theological source. The book's major drawback is that Firestone falls short of corroborating his very strong statement at the outset. Not only the rich primary sources that the author employs attest to the fact that Judaism *does* have a quite developed ideology of holy war, but also a review of the history discussed reveals that this ideology has been highly politicized. Rather than religion, the power struggle with other Judean families primarily motivated the Maccabees to war, as much as taxation and unsatisfactory governors provoked the Zealots' rebellion. In the Diaspora, Jews under foreign domination had realistically no other option but quietism. Under the Zionist enterprise and the military power that the State of Israel amassed, rabbis resurrected evidence for a divinely-authorized war that their ancestors had strictly forbidden. Firestone oddly justifies the influence of politics over religious interpretations by stating that "[f]rom the perspective of the historian of religion … such creativity in the reading and 'management' of the authoritative sources is a given" (p. 233).

This drawback notwithstanding, *Holy War in Judaism* will be of significant interest to specialists of Israel and Middle East studies, and it will also appeal to scholars of comparative and religious studies. Especially if read in conjunction with Firestone's 1999 book, *Jihad: The Origin of Holy War in Islam*, this book has serious implications for the Arab–Israeli conflict whose peaceful solution, as Firestone stresses in the end, can only be reached when radicalism ceases on both, the Israeli and Arab sides. **AY**

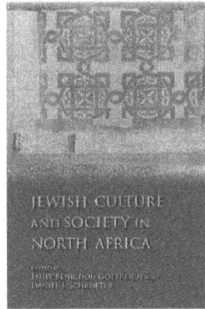

Emily Benichou Gottreich and Daniel J. Schroeter, Eds. *Jewish Culture and Society in North Africa.* **Indiana University Press, 2011. 373 pp. $29.00. ISBN: 978-0253222251.**

In 1948, there were 250,000 Jews in Morocco. Today there are less than 4,000. Across North Africa most ancient and important Jewish communities vanished in the years 1940–70 (p. 313). The upheavals and disappearance of Jewish communities in North Africa had a variety of causes, coming against the backdrop the Second World War, the creation of the State of Israel, and the end of the colonial regimes. In this important volume, the authors seek to shed light on that lost world from a variety of angles.

The origins of this volume lie in a 2004 conference of the American Institute for Maghrib Studies. The editors note that "the earliest attempt to write a comprehensive history of the Jews of the Maghrib dates to colonial Algeria in the nineteenth century" (p. 6). Yet, in Jewish studies "their culture had been assigned little value beyond the exotic by the dominant Ashkenazi ethos" (p. 9).

This book seeks to examine how Jews were part of the larger Muslim mosaic of North Africa. "There are practically no Muslims living in the Maghrib [North Africa] today who interact with Jews…the very notion of Jews as indigenous is an alien concept. Jews have become almost invisible" (p. 12). However, as late as 50 years ago this was not the case, and this volume attempts to provide a corrective, based on Muslim sources and Muslim scholarship on this important minority group.

Farid Benramdane, the dean of the Faculty of Letters at the University of Abdulhamid in Mostaganem, contributes an essay on the origin of place names in Western Algeria. He compiled a list of 20,060 names in the region (p. 35). He found, for instance, that 84 places had the name Musa or Moses. He shows how place name associated with Jews, Muslims and Christians came to influence the landscape and combine with local pre-Islamic terms. This essay is interesting but it doesn't seem to illustrate necessarily a Jewish origin for place names, merely a shared heritage of names relating to figures such as Moses who appear in both the *Torah* and *Qur'an*.

Mabrouk Mansouri presents an important essay on connections between Jews, Berbers, and Imazighen in North Africa. He argues that "the Arabs saw all North Africans, including the indigenous Imazighen and the Jews as inferior. Thus the Imazighen and the Jews found themselves in the same situation" (p. 49). Both groups, even though the latter embraced a form of Islam, were forced to pay the *jizya* tax levied on non-Muslims and "Ummayad governors of North Africa obliged them to give their daughters as a *jizya* tax" (p. 49). Abdallah Larhaid similarly examines the Sous region in Morocco in relation to Jewish access to land. Even though 90% of this region's Jews lived in rural villages "political leaders…conceptualized Jews as foreign migrants who therefore had fewer rights to land than the religious majority" (p. 59). Larhaid also sheds light on the role of Jewish and Muslims "saints" in the region. Some tombs of local Muslim saints became villages while "Jewish saints never fostered permanent settlement, even though their actions indicated an attachment to the land" (p. 65). Aumar Boum provides a very interesting essay on the need to reconsider the importance of European travel narratives in shedding light on Jewish history in the region. These narratives are "one of the key sources in the production of Jewish history in this part of the Islamic world" (p. 73). However, in recent years, many scholars rejected these narratives as being tainted with imperialism. "Skepticism surfaced about colonial sources of information regarding Moroccan Jews" (p. 87). In some Moroccan histories, such as that by Muhammad al-Mukhtar al-Susi, the Jews are not mentioned as being even a part of the social history of the region. This has the tragic impact of meaning that not only are Jews no longer present physically, but their history is removed. Boum argues for a re-evaluation of the European travel narratives, but doesn't seem to draw a clear conclusion on exactly how much weight to give them.

Albert Memmi was one of the most influential French writers of Tunisian origin. Born in 1920, he authored the critique of colonialism, *The Colonizer and the Colonized* in 1957. Yet, in later life, he became a strenuous critic of the Muslim treatment of Jews in his native land. He spoke of the "impossibility of being Jewish among Arabs" and argued that although many Jews like himself had preferred to be known as "Jewish-Arabs," this was impossible "because for centuries the Moslem Arabs have scornfully, cruelly and systematically prevented us from carrying on" (p. 111). Phillipe Barbe, assistant professor of sociology at Fatih University in Istanbul, notes that Memmi's statements should be put in perspective. "The Judeo-Arabic dialect, culinary traditions, or the type of clothing worn, the daily lives of the Jewish and Muslim communities in Tunic have borrowed a great deal from the culture of the Other" (p. 119). Babre accuses Memmi of orientalism in his description of his own mother, who Memmi had claimed was an "illiterate and superstitious 'Bedouin' woman" (p. 121). Barbe concludes that due to the conflict between Israel and the Arab world, an "idealized past where both communities cohabited harmoniously offers an optimistic model of Jewish-Muslim relations based on the recognition and respect for the Other" (p. 123). It isn't clear what exactly Memmi has to do with this, except that the author prefers that Memmi's comments should be critiqued.

Subsequent chapters examine the role of Jews in rebuilding Oran, and interactions between Jewish butchers and cultural figures in Morocco and Algeria. The last five chapters deal with the issue of Jewish women in North Africa. Two chapters examine the importance of the Alliance Israelite Universelle, an educational institution, in educating Jewish women. Three chapters deal with the issue of the tragic figure, Sol Hachuel in Morocco. Hachuel was born to a Jewish family in 1834 in Tangier. Seventeen years later, after some flirtations got her into trouble, she was beheaded at the order of the Muslim governor for being a Muslim apostate.

Yaelle Azagury argues that "the heroic figure of Solika (Sol) Hachuel fascinates like no other historical figure from this community." Since she is said to figure so prominently in Moroccan Jewish collective memory, the author accepts the logic that this story must be harshly critiqued. The story doesn't have enough exact historical details. "Did Sol have a mother or a stepmother? Are there any male figures to be taken into account" (p. 192)? One wonders, if Sol was a historic Muslim figure of great importance, such as Saladin, or a Christian—such as the victims of the Salem Witch trials—if such probing questions about the exact number of relatives they might have had, would be used to cast aspersions on his historical authenticity? Azagury argues that the secret reason that she is remembered is not because she was beheaded, and supposedly declared "I was born a Jew and will die a Jew" (p. 191), but because her story is a "means by which to think the unthinkable, in this case to imagine a specific type of sexual collusion—otherwise strictly forbidden—between two communities, the Muslim and the Jewish" (p. 192). This is an interesting academic sleight of hand. The scholar argues that Sol is of primary importance in Moroccan collective memory, without providing evidence of this, then claims that in fact, the story is a secret attack on her for having engaged in relations with Muslims, without any evidence of this either. Yet, she concludes that the story is a "cautionary tale that puts readers on alert against temptations of other worlds" (p. 195). This seems more what Azagury wants the story to be, so she can critique it, than how the story is necessarily interpreted by Moroccan Jews. After all, is not the beheading of a teenage girl for apostasy enough of a reason for her to be considered a sort of martyr?

Sharon Vance provides another essay, critiquing the memory of Sol for being a tool in the hands of colonizing Europeans or a means for Europeans to critique one another, part of a "liberal political struggle against absolutism and the Inquisition" (p. 202). In an essay that is more fiction than academic, Ruth Knafo Setton, makes fun of the Sol story, calling her "Joan of Arc for the Jews" and compares her death to a game show, "play the game and see what you would choose if the price was right for you" (p. 230). This essay is altogether offensive and has no place in an otherwise insightful and important volume, and paired with Vance and Azagury, it seems that the real story of Sol is not how Moroccan Jews think of her, but how Europeans and modern academics have transformed her into a caricature. It would be worthwhile to wonder that, if Vance, Azagury and Setton were confronted with a Muslim folk tale about a teenage Muslim girl beheaded by a capricious legal system, would their line of inquiry and mocking be similar? Except for the section devoted to Sol, this collection goes a long way to increasing our understanding of North African Jewish history and encourages new lines of inquiry into the subject. **SJF**

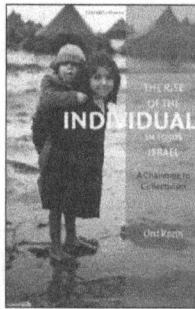

Orit Rozin. The Rise of the Individual in 1950s Israel. Waltham, MA: Brandeis University Press, 2011. 276 pp. Pbk. $35.00. ISBN: 1611680816.

In the early 1950s, Israeli reporters and newspapers were fascinated by the arrival of new Jewish immigrants to the newly created Jewish state. "The veteran Israelis were also aghast when they saw Mizrahi [Jews from North Africa and the Middle East] families packed together, parents and children, in a single room-or even more than one family in a single room-without any attempt to screen off the area where the parents slept" (p. 177). In another description "two native-born Israeli girls" went to visit an immigrant camp. There they found a "foreign country" full of people who were "naked from the waist down, with mucus dripping from their noses onto their upper lips and flies buzzing around their eyes." Writers at the daily Ha'aretz described the camps as a "wound in living flesh" (p. 177). These vignettes quotes in the rise of the Individual provide a fascinating glimpse into a struggle that was taking place in Israel between the socialist European Jewish elite, and the Jews who had arrived from Muslim countries. It is a struggle, full of racism, Eurocentrism, paternalism and outright hatred, which in many respects has defined Israel and continues to mark Israeli society today.

Orit Rozen, a lecturer in the Department of Jewish History at Tel Aviv University, sets out to understand how an Israeli society founded by "veteran Israelis" who were "ideologically committed to the national collective" confront changes that challenges this mentality (p. 192). In a sense, she sets out that "the achievement of statehood created a burden that threatened to overwhelm the state's own apparatus and the civil society" (p. xiii). Rozin posits that the 1950s marked a transition to individualism, rebellion against the state and the recognition of individuals. "Society became more individualistic, as Israelis became less inclined to sacrifice their personal preferences and health-and less willing to volunteer their energies, money, and time-for the good of the collective" (p. xv).

Ozin creates a picture of a society of "old timers"—what Israelis frequently refer to as sabras or native-born Israelis—and the newcomers. She claims that since the "Yishuv elite was overwhelmingly Ashkenazi...new Ashkenazi immigrants faced few obstacles to integration" (p. xvii). According to her figures, the pre-state Jewish population was only 11% Mizrahi. Furthermore she argues that "the adherence to religious, ethnic, and family tradition that characterized the immigrants from the Maghreb [North Africa] and Mashrek [Middle East] ran up against the ethic of enlisting in the service of the collective" (p. xvii). These sweeping generalizations will irk readers who will wonder whether the author agrees with this statement or is parroting the elitist's views. It is a problematic argument to note that the elite society was made up of one ethnic group, in this case Ashkenazi Jews from Europe, and then to claim that because of the minority population's "adherence" to their ethnic group that they could not become part of the collective? If a collective is Eurocentric and ethnicity based, then how can another ethnicity be castigated for not joining a group it is physically barred from joining? It would be like claiming that African Americans failed to join the white slave owning elite of the American South and therefore, didn't successfully integrate into the white collective.

The first section of the book examines the austerity regime enacted in the early years of the state. The socialist leaders of 1950s Israel, who were mostly members of one political party, the Mapai, intended to impose government controls from above. "They sought to direct and restrain consumption so as to make it possible for the country to absorb Jewish immigration" (p. 7). Women bore the brunt of this regime which Rozin argues limited the housewives' choices of food and other products.

Women resorted to the black market, and in retaliation, the government inspectors to search houses. Although "rationing sought to standardize behavior" (p. 45), the reality was that those connected to the government or elite families on the Kibbutz received lavish parties and profited from selling produce on the black market. Here would be an opportunity for the author to wonder about the collectivist claims and the reality that those who were ordering the austerity were, at the same time engaging in breaking the very laws they imposed. While the poor were ordered to be "standardized" and castigated for using the black market, the governing elite were also in the black market. At the same time, the judicial system actively worked to impose slight sentences on those accused of breaking the rules, apparently representing a judicial protest against the imposition of state socialism. This question of myth versus reality in the 1950s is an interesting one, and yet it is glossed over in favor of a factual telling of the story.

The book spends two chapters analyzing the politics of the early state before getting to the main chapters, which deal with the arrival of mass immigration and the transmit camps the state set up to house them. This is the most interesting portion of the book, for it sheds light on the contradictions of the state's goal of ingathering Jews, and how the state and its elite subsequently treated those immigrants. An early idea could be gleaned from journalist Amos Elon's visit to North Africa in 1953. "Elon portrayed the mellah (Jewish quarter) of Casablanca as a place of stench, degeneracy, disease, and perversity" (p. 150). He worried about the effects that "uncontrolled fertility would have on the Jewish people's genetic robustness" (p. 150). As Rozin illustrates, the "old-timers" claimed that the immigrants arrived with venereal diseases and had "a high proportion of mentally ill persons" (p. 151) as well as having diseases that "could spread from transit camps to kibbutzim" (p. 152). Supposedly, the transit camps were "plagued by prostitution" and the women were "sold for miserable pennies to men who are liable to destroy them" (p. 173)."

The numerous primary sources that this book includes, showing the stereotyping and racism employed by the elite in Israel against the immigrants, makes this book a major asset and important work for understanding Israeli society. Yet, at every instance where the author might have added analysis, the monograph falls short. Even though Rozin notes that some of these claims are stereotypes, she does not bother to probe deeper. Who was Dr. Erich Nassau, director of HaEmek Hospital in Afula, who claimed that the immigrants possessed such potent diseases that they might be carried airborne to affect the diseases? Who was Amos Elon who claimed that the people of North Africa were "degenerates?" What world view informed this racist eugenic pseudo-scientific mumbo-jumbo that would have had a better fit in the recently defeated Nazi Germany than in the newly created State of Israel? When these "old-timers" claimed to be shocked by prostitution, isn't it important to question how many brothels there were in the "old timers" part of Tel Aviv, and what sort of sexual mores the observers had? And why does the author employ the term "old timers" to refer to many of the Ashkenazi writers who, in fact were recent immigrants to the country, having only arrived in the 1930s and 1940s? There are many unanswered questions in this book that have to deal with analysis of the Eurocentrism that it so brilliantly uncovers from the primary sources. The author seeks to prove that the shock employed by the elite undermined their sense of a collective, but this seems to contradict the title, which claims to speak of the "rise of the individual." Very little evidence is provided to show that the new immigrants valued individualism, and in fact very few, if any, voices from the immigrant community are provided as sources. That the elite looked down on the new immigrant community is clearly illustrated, but whether that represents the rise of individualism is not clear. Orit Rozin's book represents a significant and important scholarly contribution, but it must be left to another scholar to synthesize and tease out conclusions from what she has revealed. **SJF**

LEBANON

❋

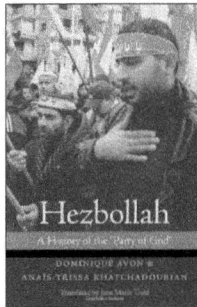

Dominique Avon and Anaïs-Trissa Khatchadourian. Translated by Jane Marie Todd. *Hezbollah: A History of the "Party of God"*. **Cambridge, MA: Harvard University Press, 2012. 244 pp. $24.95 ISBN: 0674066510.**

This volume addresses a timely and relevant topic: what—or who—is the Hezbollah? Is this, as many in the West might assume, merely a terrorist organization bent on taking over Lebanon and, thereafter, pursuing Israel's destruction? Or is there more to it than this? Taking an historical approach, these authors set out to answer (more or less) these questions.

The book is divided into two main sections. In the first 89 pages the authors present "An Itinerary," in which they offer the development of the Hezbollah over time, beginning in the early 1980s and concluding in 2009. In the second part of the book, which is much lengthier, a variety of documents and other unanalyzed raw materials are presented.

Much as I would like to provide an overview of the general argument of the first section, it is difficult to do so. Essentially, one encounters here a lengthy narrative or chronicle of events strung together with hardly any source citations. There is some analysis here, but it is largely speculative, based, it appears, more upon the authors' opinions than anything else.

For example, the reader is informed that the Lebanese people "believe" or prefer certain things (e.g., Do Lebanese Shi'a support the establishment of an Islamic regime? p. 41) and must take on faith the authors' word for the answers (in this case, "No"). The reader is told that the authors have no opinions of their own and are only reporting the facts—but it is unclear from where the "facts" originated.

Moreover, there is no doubt that there is a perspective here, one that suggests, for example, that the Israelis act in a "repressive" manner (p. 52), all the while enjoying "almost unconditional support" from the United States (p. 70) including, at one point, "diplomatic efforts to delay a cease-fire agreement with Hezbollah [in 2006 while providing] munitions to the Israeli air force, thus demonstrating Washington's desire to cooperate with a significant weakening, if not, complete destruction, of the Hezbollah military apparatus" (p. 83). Such claims are highly charged; the lack of any sort of evidence to prove such claims is quite puzzling.

As for the Hezbollah, one can't but help but sense a certain degree of affection for this group based upon the way they are portrayed by the authors. This is not said outright, but while we are learning of the Israelis' duplicity and repeatedly informed of their "failed" policies, Hezbollah, meantime, is quietly praised for "liberating" southern Lebanon (p. 55), and is referred to as an "impressive force" (p. 64) whose successes were due in part to "great internal effectiveness" (p. 65) within the party infrastructure.

Indeed, the tone of the narrative suggests that the authors seem to have an insider's intimate knowledge and familiarity with who knew what when. They offer—again, without explanation or source—that Hezbollah was privy to Syrian–Israeli peace talks in the early 1990s, but were politically savvy enough to know that it was wise not to challenge Damascus's actions at that time (p. 50). Again, this may be true, but if so, why not explain how the authors came to have this information?

In short, what is presented here amounts to page after page of undocumented innuendo and speculation. This, when combined with the fact that the book, at times reads as if it has not been fully translated from the original French, makes for a rather difficult read. As a source book, however, the numerous Hezbollah documents at the back of the book are quite interesting in their own right, and may prove useful to the casual reader. **SD**

William Harris. *Lebanon: A History 600–2011*. Oxford: Oxford University Press, 2012. 360 pp. £22.50. ISBN: 978-0195181111.

William Harris has written an expansive political and institutional history of Lebanon. Part One (pp. 29-143) traces the formation and development of the country's sects and communities from late antiquity. It marches smartly through the centuries of caliphs, crusaders, and Mamluks, and then decelerates to narrate and analyze the emergence of the recognizable precursors in Ottoman times of today's Lebanon. Part Two (pp. 147-283) encompasses the post-World War I establishment of the Lebanese Republic, and carries the story up to the present. Harris, a professor of Politics at New Zealand's University of Otago, is aware of the pitfalls of primordialist readings of Lebanon's history. Today's Lebanese sects, he says, are indeed historically rooted, but they are also culturally constructed; and there was nothing inevitable about the emergence of Lebanon as an Ottoman entity in the nineteenth century and as a formally sovereign republic in the twentieth. Harris's narrative takes care to highlight the various historical contingencies that shaped eventual outcomes.

The book is well sourced. Harris has consulted an impressive array of primary sources and memoirs, along with a wide selection of newspapers and secondary sources in Arabic, French, and English. The writing is clear and crisp. For this reader the narrative bogged down only when Harris attempted to track the dizzying and kaleidoscopic trajectories of factions and families in the seventeenth and eighteenth centuries, material which even readers familiar with Lebanon might find a hard slog. However, to Harris's credit a reader never loses track of the narrative's thread. Each chapter is introduced by a synopsis of the material to follow, an arrangement that allows Harris to move back and forth between detailed exposition and broader themes.

If Lebanon today is characterized by a sectarian structure deeply rooted in the state machinery, and by the emergence of the formerly marginalized Shi'a as a dominant sect and political actor, Harris puts these developments into their historical context. He does not challenge the well-established narrative regarding the central role of Maronite–Druze interaction in the emergence of Ottoman-era proto-Lebanon (i.e., the Shihabi emirate and its administrative successors). But Harris does explain how the nineteenth century politicization of Maronite Christian communal feeling created a template for other Lebanese sects, a template that the Shi'a have been the most recent to embrace. Moreover, it is clear that the consolidation of the eighteenth century Shihabi emirate came at the expense of Shi'a notables who formerly had played a significant role in the politics of the Mountain. Thus readers gain a historically informed appreciation of the accelerated emergence, post-1979, of Lebanon's Shi'a and the challenge that Shi'a assertion has represented to an earlier notion or idea of Lebanon.

This is an interpretive history, so Harris makes arguments or judgments that not all will embrace. His theses are, for the most part, internally consistent and well constructed so his intervention into debates about Lebanese history is invigorating and provides material for study and discussion. One major point (p. 142) is that European meddling or intervention was not the fundamental cause of the Druze-Maronite split in the nineteenth century. Rather, Harris sees the origins of this split in the manner of the Shihabi emirate's consolidation under Bashir II.

Another major point is that France's creation of Greater Lebanon in 1920 at the behest of Maronite Patriarch Ilyas Huwayyik amounted to "Maronite overreach" (pp. 178ff.), and in retrospect this overreach doomed the dream of a "Christian Lebanon" at the very moment when Huwayyik's partisans thought they had achieved it. Harris has little respect for the politics and politicians of the Lebanese Republic, characterizing the political elite as engaged in "a free-for-all under a venal government machine disregarding the interests of the bulk of the population" (p. 184). The vaunted National Pact power-sharing agreement of 1943 was but an agreement among cross-confessional business interests (p. 193), and these interests' devotion to unfettered free trade in the independence era led to dolorous social and economic consequences (pp. 194-195).

On one issue Harris's views appear not to be entirely consistent. On the one hand, he emphasizes the futility of Lebanese nation-building: "Neither [President Fuad] Shihab nor anyone else could make the Lebanese a conventional "nation," implying fundamental agreement on the meaning and orientation of their homeland" (p. 218). Harris characterizes the reformist but militarized presidency of Fuad Shihab (1958–64) as having raised expectations it could not fulfill, and setting in motion forces (Shia communal politicization) that the Lebanese state could not contain (p. 216). But Harris also sees Lebanon of the late 1960s as having had a potential for national coexistence and a "relative coherence" (p. 232) that was fatally destroyed by the regional fallout of the 1967 Arab–Israeli war. In any event, when Syrian tutelage restored peace of a kind after 1990, the Lebanese state also returned with a vengeance as little more than a mechanism for divvying up sectarian shares (p. 234).

Whether one agrees with Harris's interpretations and judgments, he offers a historical context and a set of arguments for considering the past and present of this complex, divided and vulnerable country. Sandwiched as it is between the regional superpower (Israel) and the post-2011 Syrian volcano, Lebanon's survival may be due more to inertia than to any innate inner strength or coherence. Harris's account offers much food for thought, and his book is suitable for advanced students including its comprehensive chronology and bibliography. **JAR**

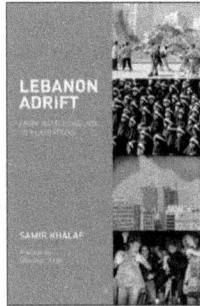

Samir Khalaf. *Lebanon Adrift: From Battleground to Playground.* **London: Saqi Books, 2012. 294 pp. $27.95. ISBN: 0863564348.**

Although the name "Lebanon" tends to be more readily associated with violence and chaos, in recent years it has become an increasingly attractive tourist destination. I remember travelling to Beirut in July 2006 on a plane full of rambunctious families and eager holiday-makers; a few days later, the country was engulfed once again in terrifying warfare. Despite episodes such as this, Lebanon is starting to evolve a new identity. But it is, as Samir Khalaf's latest book reveals, a complex and multi-faceted identity—on the one hand, a "hedonist's paradise" yet, on the other, the site of the widely respected Islamic resistance movement of Hizbullah, which succeeded in 2000 in defeating the region's most powerful army and forcing Israel to withdraw from all Lebanese territory. While Beirut has unexpectedly been transformed into the "party capital" of the Arab world, it is mired in contradictions, and it is these contradictions that Khalaf's book explores in fascinating and highly scholarly detail. His style is a rich mixture of anecdote and theoretical exposition.

Khalaf focuses on the "duality" of Lebanon, reflected in its image 'as a proxy battlefield for unresolved regional rivalries and breeding ground for Islamic militants and resistance groups, but also as a permissive playground and tourist destination for pleasure-seekers and itinerant tycoons' (p. 231). Having experienced a decade and a half of ferocious and apparently "meaningless" conflict, Khalaf argues, the Lebanese have been unable or unwilling to engage in necessary processes of "truth and reconciliation," as occurred in South Africa and elsewhere. As a result, the country finds itself "adrift," subject to the whims and priorities of selfish individuals; it is, as he says, "at a fateful crossroads in its political and socio-cultural history' and 'continues to be imperiled by a set of overwhelming predicaments and unsettling transformations" (p. 77).

In some ways, this book appears to be a culmination of the many strands of scholarship Khalaf has been investigating over the years: the transformation of urban space, the dangers of "uncivil" violence, and the role of collective memory and nostalgia. He mourns the loss of the convivial and democratic space of the centre of Beirut, the Bourj, taken over now by megalomaniac development schemes and a frantic and apparently uncaring quest for pleasure. It is as if the Lebanese, in their desire to "forget" the violence of war and the insecurity of "peace," are throwing themselves into untrammeled consumerism. But he is also looking ahead and assessing more positive developments and initiatives.

The book is structured around the concept of "being adrift" and how this affects both the Lebanese and their country. It begins with a discussion of violence. The "savagery of violence," as Khalaf notes, was "compounded by its randomness. In this sense, there is hardly a Lebanese today who is exempt from these atrocities either directly or vicariously" (p. 35). Such extremities of violence, inevitably, shape individual and collective identity, and lead to particular forms of behaviour. In Lebanon, these are characterized by an "unprecedented surge in mass consumerism, particularly its stylized, sensational and hedonistic features" (p. 27). Khalaf draws a stark contrast between the beauty of the country and its artistic heritage and the tacky, profit-driven developments that have sprung up since the ending of the civil war, particularly in Beirut, and also the casual indifference shown toward the environment, for example the reckless driving and ubiquitous smoking. He is critical of the excesses of consumerism and the evident abandon with which many Lebanese embrace it; these, he argues, are manifested in "two extreme by-products of excessive commodification and global consumerism: the spectacle and kitsch" (p. 29).

A final chapter considers "the prospects for transforming the consumer into a citizen." Although evidently gloomy about Lebanon's future prospects, Khalaf describes some more promising recent developments, such as the creation of organizations dedicated to preserving the environment, creating greater social awareness among young people, and improving the country's architecture and public spaces. He has faith in the resilience of the Lebanese public.

Clearly, times are changing. Four events in recent years have had a profound effect on the Lebanese collective identity and modes of coping. The first was the assassination in February 2005 of Rafik Hariri, a towering figure in post-war Lebanese history, elected several times as prime minister; neighbouring Syria was implicated in his murder. The second event, following on the first, has been called the "Cedars Revolution," a spontaneous uprising, described by Khalaf as "one of the most momentous and spontaneous collective demonstrations in Lebanon's recent history" (p. 44); people from all walks of life poured into the center of Beirut to call for the removal of Syrian forces from their territory; this is interpreted by Khalaf as a positive development and one which detracts from individual narcissism and disinterest in the general polity.

In July 2006, the third defining event took place; in response to the capture by Hizbullah of several of its soldiers on the Lebanese-Israeli border, Israel launched a large-scale air, sea and land invasion of Lebanon. In an assault that lasted for 34 days, the Israelis succeeded in causing massive material damage and killing over 1,000 people, mainly civilians; their objective was to "get rid of" Hizbullah once and for all but, in this respect, the invasion was a failure and, far from being defeated, Hizbullah proclaimed a "divine victory." Shortly afterwards came the fourth momentous occurrence; following the defeat of Israel, Hizbullah and its supporters, in Khalaf's words, "took hostage of the historic center of Beirut" (p. 216), constructing a "tent city" that lasted for the next 18 months and succeeded in paralyzing all governmental and parliamentary activity. Khalaf suggests that this "sit-in made a mockery of collective acts of public protest and civil disobedience" (p. 217); yet one could argue that it was just as much an expression of popular feeling as the "Cedars Revolution." However, it highlights "the difficult, even ungovernable character of the Lebanese polity" (p. 260) and the gulf between opposing national tendencies.

In an Epilogue, Khalaf reflects on what he calls Lebanon's "double failure," in the sense that 'movements of cultural resistance and civil disobedience' have both failed to 'meet their desired expectations' and also failed to "instill within the public any genuine enthusiasm in support of their role in cultivating social awareness to transcend their private or parochial interest" (p. 267). However, he sees a number of causes for cautious optimism, signs of what he calls "third spaces" or "in-between cultures of hybridity, mixture and tolerance" (p. 268). As a result of its enterprising and creative population and the growth of various organizations supportive of human rights, preservation of heritage and maintenance of civilized public spaces. It is his hope, he concludes, and that his book will inspire "self-reflection on how ordinary Lebanese citizens can shelter themselves from being colonized by global markets or reduced to clients" (p. 272). One can only share this hope that Lebanon will emerge from its post-war insecurities as a stronger and more self-confident nation—neither a battleground nor a playground. **MA**

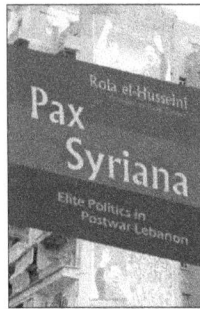

Rola el-Husseini. *Pax Syriana: Elite Politics in Postwar Lebanon.* **Syracuse, NY: Syracuse University Press, 2012. 319 pp. $45.00. ISBN: 978-0815633044.**

Rola el-Husseini, assistant professor in research at the City University of New York Graduate Center, has made a valuable contribution to the field of study of Lebanese politics based on fieldwork and interviews conducted in Lebanon in 2001–03, and 2006. El-Husseini interviewed 56 political elite and had "twenty-two informal discussions with journalists, academics, and other observers of the Lebanese political scene" (p. xviii). One is tempted to see el-Husseini's work as historical, given that the Syrian regime withdrew its armed forces from Lebanon in 2005. However, as el-Husseini states, the political order that the Syrian regime built is more or less still in place, and the Syrian regime still retains an "extensive network of agents and allies"—therefore "the legacy of Pax Syriana remains" (p. 22).

It is not possible to understand the Second Lebanese Republic (the Taif Republic) without understanding the political order that the Syrian regime engineered. El-Husseini's thesis is that the Second Republic did not develop Lebanon's democracy due largely to Syria's negative influence: "The Taif Agreement attempted to institute a new formula of power sharing among the various segments of Lebanese society, but this agreement was undermined by Syrian interference in the political process, and by Syrian clientelism in the recruitment of new elites" (p. 22).

El-Husseini's book consists of: a Foreword by Ryan Crocker; an Acknowledgments section; a Note on Transliteration; an Introduction; seven chapters; a Conclusion; Who's Who of Lebanese Politics; a Lebanese Political Timeline (1989–2005); Notes; a Glossary of Arabic Terms; a Bibliography and Index. Chapter 1, The Lebanese Political System: the Elite Pacts of 1943 and 1989 begins with the two words "Arend Lijphart" indicating that el-Husseini's work is grounded in theory and is not merely descriptive. Indeed, el-Husseini engages the theory of consociationalism and examines whether Lebanon's polity is consociational (she agrees with others that it is a "consociational oligarchy") and concludes that Lebanon's consociational democracy is neither stable nor a democracy (p. 6). El-Husseini blames the First Republic's breakdown on political sectarianism. Scholars have attributed this failure to internal or external factors, or a mix of both. She believes that "the refusal of traditional elites to incorporate emerging groups into their cartels undermined the political system from within" (p. 11). However, going beyond the Lebanon case, the focus on internal and external factors, and examining the Confrontation States—in addition to Lebanon, Syria, Jordan, Iraq, and Egypt—one notes that none of these countries has been a beacon of democracy or stability due to the regional turmoil of the Arab–Israeli conflict and the challenges of political and economic development. Taking the regional context into account, it is doubtful that Lebanon, consociational democracy or any other system, could have withstood the regional turmoil.

In Chapter 2, Postwar Elite Interaction, the author studies post-Taif elite interactions using the "notion of elite settlements" (p. 23). She conceives of this elite interaction between 1989 and 2005 in three stages, the third of which involved a "realignment of members of previously excluded groups and their co-option by other political forces, a process I call 'factionalization'" (p. 23). El-Husseini writes "the dissident [Christian] elites... came to recognize that participating in the settlement would be the most direct route to empowerment" (p. 31). Perhaps, but it is also plausible that at the time, the realization began to sink in that the Syrian presence was a stubborn reality to which they needed to adjust. The work of the strategic media elite, allied with Syria, promoted the Syrian presence as a guarantee against further erosion of Christian political power and as a check on Lebanese Muslims—especially the Shi'a—and political ambition undoubtedly had some influence in shaping the reality.

Chapter 3, Political Parties, is a particularly welcome addition to the literature due to the dearth of writing on Lebanese political parties. This relative lack of attention is perhaps grounded in the reality that these "parties are mostly organized around the charisma and patronage networks of individual leaders" which makes, in "most cases, the examination of individual elites... of greater significance than is the examination of party organizations" (p. 39). One of the parties she focuses on is Hezbollah, a group which she claims was born "in response to 1982 Israeli invasion of Lebanon" (p. 65). This assertion is inaccurate. Hezbollah emerged in the context of the Iranian attempt to export its revolution, as Wright's *Sacred Rage: the Wrath of Militant Islam* (1985), and Shaery-Eisenlohr's *Shi'ite Lebanon: Transnational Religion and the making of National Identities* (2008) make clear.

In Chapter 4, State Elites and the Legacy of Corruption, el-Husseini presents useful information about the well-known corruption of the Lebanese political elite. The weakness of this chapter is the weak connection between "corruption," "youth emigration" and "brain drain" (p. 119). In exactly two pages and with seven end notes, the author indicts the Lebanese political elite stating that "the phenomena [youth emigration and brain drain] did not seem to bother the political elites" she interviewed (p. 120). El-Husseini simply does not marshal enough evidence to warrant this broad assertion and the concomitant unsubtle indignation.

Chapter 5, Strategic Elite, is an examination of the "strategic elite" that include "military commanders, religious leaders, and important journalists" (p. 122). The focus of the book is on Pax Syriana, the period that began with the Taif Agreement and ended in 2005; yet, much of the focus is on leaders from the First Republic period. There is a focus on Imam Musa Sadr who disappeared in Libya in 1978. There is no mention of the deputy president of the Shi'ite Higher Council, Mufti Abdul Ameer Qabalan, a leader of the Shi'ite community who played an important role during Pax Syriana. Mufti Qabalan has been an ally of Speaker Nabih Berri who would make declarations about "numerical democracy" seemingly timed to increase the anxiety of Christian leaders when the issue of Taif-mandated Syrian redeployment was brought up. These statements helped the Syrian regime sell its presence as a guarantee to parity in the division of power between Christians and Muslims. As to the personalities from the press, she chose two anti-Syrian regime personalities—Samir Qassir and Gebran Tueni. But weren't pro-Syrian regime journalists as important as the anti-Syrian regime in shaping and perpetuating Pax Syriana?

In Chapter 6, Emerging Elites and the Absence of Women From Politics, el-Husseini provides an insightful discussion of the reasons for the "quasi absence" of Lebanese women from politics: (1) "The patriarchal and personalized structure of the

Lebanese political system;" (2) "The traditionally masculine connotations of pa-tron-client relations;" (3)"The contempt that many women have acquired for pol-itics in general;" and (4)"Women's lack of experience and confidence in the polit-ical realm" (p. 169). She develops a useful typology of "emerging elite:" The "civil servant activist," "the technocrat," "the academic," "the local representative," "the heir," "young elites within the primary Lebanese political party, Hezbollah" and "the nationalist militant" (p. 171).

In the last chapter of the book, Elite Attitudes on Syria and Sectarianism, el-Hus-seini discusses the "two central topics of concern" that emerged from her elite inter-views: "Lebanese-Syrian relations" and "deconfessionalization" (p. 187). Asking the elite about their attitude toward Syria as such is not the best way to ask the question about the Syrian regime intervention in Lebanon—about Pax Syriana. It is not a shock finding that there is a convergence on Syria between the two divided camps (p. 197). Syria is not Israel. The proper balance and how to deal with the imbalance was the divisive issue. As to the second part of the chapter, the future of political system, she finds that there is no convergence on "the future of Lebanon's system of confessional power sharing" (p. 197). The author reports that the Shi'a elite are the biggest supporters of deconfessionalizing the political system. El-Hussieni, un-fortunately, uncritically agrees with her Shi'a informants' demographic supremacy claim, thus helping to perpetuate the myth that the Shi'a are the "majority" of the population of Lebanon (p. 208). The Shi'a of Lebanon are neither the majority of the population, nor even the largest demographic group. In the absence of a national census, the most reliable data are the government voter lists that show that the Sun-nis are the largest community in Lebanon.

I strongly recommend this book because it fills a gap in the literature on Leba-non's elite politics. In a relatively small book, el-Husseini manages to give the reader a nuanced understanding of the Lebanon elite's political past, present and possible future direction. Given the fact that the Taif Agreement is the founding document of the Second Republic, if this book were to go into a second printing, this reviewer recommends that it include the Taif Agreement in the Appendix. Overall, this book is useful as a secondary book on Middle East politics, or as a primary book on Leb-anese politics. Some of the chapters are useful for other classes as well, including the chapter on women and politics which would be helpful in a class on international relations or women and politics. **IAA**

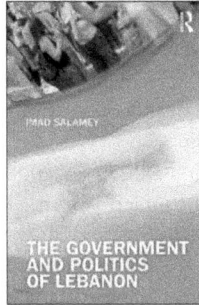

Imad Salamey. *The Government and Politics of Lebanon*. New York, NY: Rout-ledge, 2013. 256 pp. $136.03. ISBN: 0415636876. Pbk: 256 pp. $50.95. ISBN: 978-0415636889. Ebk: $40.76. 3847 KB.

A concise university textbook on the government and politics of Lebanon seems to be a laudable, timely, and surely challenging project. The existing literature lacks a systematically organized monograph that adequately copes with the complex and diverse nature of Lebanon's political, societal, and economic system. Imad Salamey, Associate Professor of Political Science and International Affairs at the Lebanese American University (LAU) in Beirut, aims with his recent book titled *The Government and Politics of Lebanon* at being "the first comprehensive scholarly based exam-ination of contemporary Lebanese politics and government" (p. xiii). Unfortunately, Salamey's book misses its target for several reasons.

First, although the title promises a presentation and evaluation of Lebanon's po-litical system, the author makes it clear from the beginning that the book's topic is restricted to the study of Lebanese consociationalism: its "origin, development, and institutionalization" (as stated on the first but unnumbered page). By reducing the politics of Lebanon to consociationalism, the book lacks sufficient analysis of many essential key concepts, such as the question of Lebanese national identity, state sovereignty, the economic system, clientelism, Palestinian refugees, Islamism, the "resistance" movement, and gender issues.

Second, the book is mostly descriptive and gives more information of Lebanon's historical development than the promised evaluation of *contemporary* politics and government. Even the chapter on the international affairs of Lebanon is purely his-torical. This, however, can be explained, and maybe even excused, by the notion that Lebanon's modern history is still a highly controversial and politicized issue. For example, school books sidestep the Lebanese Civil War and there is no consensus on a unified history book.

Third, the presentation of three consecutive political systems in modern Leb-anon—Salamey calls them "sectarian republics"—is inappropriate. The author distinguishes three historical phases of independent Lebanon which he calls the

"National Pact Republic" (1943–75), the "Taef Republic" (1989–2008), and the "Doha Republic" (2008–11). Whereas the National Pact and the Taef Agreement have set up the principles and rules of Lebanon's political system, including some foreign affairs norms, the Doha Agreement to which the Doha Republic refers, has only been a temporary package deal between two opposing political camps under the auspices of the Emir of Qatar.

As in most of Qatar's mediation efforts, the 2008 agreement was short-lived and failed to tackle the roots of the conflict. Nevertheless, Doha did lead to the election of a new president and the 2008 state crisis was solved by an interim deal and compromise. Although neither the political system nor the constitution has been changed in any respect, the author interprets the Doha Agreement as a kind of a new social contract that changed the nature of Lebanon's consociationalism. This is mainly explained by stating that the rival camps agreed to elect a *consensus candidate* as president and that the electoral law pertaining to the legislature was amended. However, anyone familiar with Lebanese politics knows that it is an ongoing tradition of Lebanese parties to discuss and eventually amend the electoral law and the constituencies prior to every new election.

It is therefore not plausible to place the Doha Agreement on the same level as the National Pact and the Taef Accord. Instead, it would have made more sense to identify the dynamic developments of 2005 as such a decisive historic moment of change. Triggered by the so-called "Cedar Revolution" in response to the assassination of former Prime Minister Rafiq Hariri in February 2005, Syria was at that time forced to end its thirty years of military control and political tutelage of Lebanon. For the first time since 1972, the Lebanese could elect their parliament without significant foreign intervention and manipulations. Also in 2005, anti-Syrian Christian parties were reactivated and former Christian political leaders (Michel Aoun, Amin Gemayel) returned to Lebanon, or were released from jail (Samir Geagea). The anti-Syrian March 14 and the pro-Syrian March 8 alliances were formed, and are still dominating Lebanese politics. Major new parties were created as well, most prominently Saad Hariri's Future Movement and Michel Aoun's Free Patriotic Movement.

The proposed Doha Republic, on the other hand, leads inevitably to further conceptual trouble. Since Salamey's Doha Republic ceased to exist in 2011, one wonders which republic has replaced it. In other words, what is the current Lebanese republic called? If we assume that no new republic came into existence in 2011, there are only two feasible options: either Lebanon switched back to the former Taef Republic, or Lebanon has entered a form of republic-less state order. The confused reader will not find an answer to this puzzle in Salamey's book.

Fourth, the May 2008 crisis itself is not adequately explained. All that is mentioned about this issue is that the government's decision to shut down Hezbollah's telecommunication network at Beirut's airport and relieve the airport's pro-Hezbollah security chief from his duties "were causing massive riots that would turn into an outright civil strife and armed clashes between factions" (p. 73). No word about the real importance of the May 2008 crisis, namely, Hezbollah's use of its weapons against their Lebanese rivals as an instrument of power as well as the related question of Lebanon's sovereignty. The phenomenon of an influential political party possessing a private quasi-army, controlling territory, and reserving the right to use its weapons against external and internal adversaries to seek its political goals is not addressed at all. Knowing that the issue is highly controversial in Lebanon and that many Lebanese regard Hezbollah's arms as a legitimate element of the "resistance" against Israel (and lately against so-called *takfiris* in Syria), a textbook on Lebanon's political system cannot avoid addressing the issue of a violated national sovereignty.

Fifth, a further weakness of the book is the insufficient conceptual and theoretical underpinnings. This is seen by inadequate, and, at times, misleading graphs. For example, in Chapter 7 (From Politics to Government), the author intends to conceptualize the political process of democracies. To illustrate "the political process," Salamey presents a graph which contains three circles, corresponding respectively to government, policies, and politics (p. 83). The circles are connected to each other by arrows indicating that government leads to policies, policies to politics, and politics to government. A single sentence provides the reader with the explanation: "In the ideal democratic society, government is formed by the people to express the popular will" (p. 83). The graph, however, does not clarify anything in this regard, but rather, confuses the reader. One wonders why Salamey disregarded David Easton's famous and vivid model of a political system, according to which a government responds ("output") to demands and support from the people ("input"), filtered and expressed via interest groups, parties, media, etc. ("gate keepers"). Unfortunately, Salamey's own graphs, including "the structure of the political mobilization" (p. 84) and the "branches of government" (p. 85) lack any tangible explanatory value.

Sixth, and most importantly, the author violates academic standards of integrity. Several complete pages of Chapter 4 on "The Lebanese Civil War 1975–90" (pp. 38-53) and Chapter 5 on 'Consociationalism Reformed I: The Taef Republic (1989–2008)' (pp. 54-72) are taken almost word-for-word from a paper written by Hassan Krayem—former professor at the American University of Beirut (AUB). Krayem's precious paper from 1998, titled "The Lebanese Civil War and the Taif Agreement" is not even cited as a reference; it only appears at the end of the book under "helpful websites." As the whole book is frugally referenced, one wonders how much of the book Salamey's own work is. As a matter of fact, Imad Salamey has done a huge disservice to the majority of university teachers in Lebanon who continuously insist that their students avoid plagiarism and uphold the principles of academic honesty.

In short, besides being mainly a historical documentation that lacks sound political analysis, Salamey's book misses important issues of Lebanese politics. Its few innovative and analytical parts (Doha Republic; typology of democratic regimes) are not convincing. And finally, the plagiarism is unacceptable and inexcusable, and disqualifies the whole work from being used as a textbook in classrooms. The book is a complete disappointment. Routledge should never have agreed to publish it. **MF**

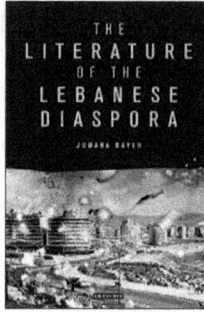

Jumana Bayeh. *The Literature of the Lebanese Diaspora: Representation of Place and Transnational Identity, Volume: 2. Issue: 12.* New York, NY: I. B. Tauris, 2015. 277 pp. $99.00. ISBN: 978-1780769981.

This book was mostly written at Macquarie University in Australia, where the author is a Fellow in the Department of Modern History, Politics and International Relations. Her approach to literature is sociological and, as such, offers a uniquely original contribution by concentrating on the representation of place and transnational identity in the literary writings of the Lebanese Diaspora. By using the theories and findings of Diaspora studies, she sheds new light on the literature of some Lebanese writers of fiction living in various countries, and brings to them a new understanding not fully possible otherwise.

Displacement and double consciousness constitute the main concept that concerns the author of this book. In other words, it is the ambivalence of the Lebanese writer in the Diaspora who feels he is neither completely at harmony with the setting of the new country in which he lives, nor fully free from that of the old one he left. To him, writing becomes a "place" in which to live. His diasporic condition incites him to reconstruct place and to contest essentialist definitions of it; and this book studies the ways he represents it and creates a "transnational" identity.

Apart from references to other writings, the Lebanese novels that are dealt with in detail are the following, in the order they are studied in the book: (1) *Unreal City* [1999] by Tony Hanania; (2) *De Niro's Game* [2006] by Rawi Hage; (3) *Somewhere, Home* [2003] by Nada Awar Jarrar; (4) *The Night Counter* [2009] by Alia Yunis; and (5) *Ports of Call* [1999] by Amin Maalouf.

The book has three parts, each being divided into chapters. Part I is entitled "War and the City" and focuses on Beirut in the Civil War, during which time it was divided into West Beirut (the Muslim sector) and East Beirut (the Christian one). Part II is entitled "Home, Mobility, Immobility" and focuses on women writing on domesticity and movement. Part III is entitled "Contesting the Nation-State," focusing on land as a place for the nation.

In Part I, Tony Hanania's *Unreal City* [shows the destruction of West Beirut, alienating his protagonist and inducing his recruitment into a militant Islamic movement in South Lebanon. Rawi Hage's *De Niro's Game* shows the isolated world of East Beirut's Christians and the fact that the city is what its inhabitants make it to be. In Part II, Nada Awar Jarrar's *Somewhere, Home* has a rural setting in the Lebanese mountains and reflects conservative domesticity and a static image of home. This is not so in the similar rural setting of Alia Yunis's *The Night Counter*, which shows that domesticity is inherently mobile. In Part III, Amin Maalouf's *Ports of Call*, the nation is the focus and its relationship with the Diaspora is examined; the notion of territoriality is emphasized, land being necessary in the formation of the nation-state and of identity. The novel deals with the years in Palestine before the establishment of Israel in 1948, and with the tireless effort of the narrator to keep Jews and Arabs together in productive coexistence in the same land. While these novels are not all equal in their attempt to represent place and identity, they all attempt to promote an idea of place that is pluralistic and open to diversity, exchange, and mobility.

Jumana Bayeh's analysis of the novels in light of Diaspora studies directs attention to a new perspective of Lebanese literature. In the meantime, her reading of the literary texts themselves is deep and informative. Her concentration on three themes in her analysis—namely: (a) the civil war and the city; (b) home; and (c) the nation-state—helps the reader understand the relationship of place and identity as represented in the Diaspora fiction she studies. Her book is a good read. **IJB**

LITERATURE

❧

Mahmoud Saeed. Translated by Kay Heikkinen. *Ben Barka Lane*. Northampton, MA: Interlink Books, 2013. 276 pp. Pbk.: $15.00. ISBN 9781566569262.

Mahmoud Saeed is a well-known Iraqi novelist and short-story writer with more than 20 books to his name. A political dissident, he was imprisoned several times in his homeland and some of his writings were banned. He left Iraq in 1985 for the United States, where he is now an Arabic language instructor and author-in-residence at DePaul University in Chicago.

His novel, *Ben Barka Lane*, originally published in Arabic in 1970 as *Zanqat Bin Barakah*, was immediately banned in Iraq, but it was later published in Cairo, Amman, and Beirut. It won the Iraqi Ministry of Information Award in 1994 after Iraq underwent regime change; and it is now translated into English by Kay Heikkinen, who teaches Arabic at the University of Chicago and is the translator of Naguib Mahfouz's *In the Time of Love*.

It may not be Mahmoud Saeed's best novel, or as gripping as his autobiographical novel *Saddam City*-about an Iraqi teacher tortured in Saddam Hussein's prisons, but it is certainly one of the most poetic of his novels in describing the feelings of the fictional characters and their reactions to events and to each other. To be noted particularly is his account, in the passionate words of this novel's narrator Sharqi, of the beautiful and enchanting Ruqayya with whom Sharqi is enamored—not ignoring the charming effect on him of her melodious voice, her elegant movements and glances, her intelligent conversation, her very presence that elevates his soul and transports him to heavenly existence.

Sharqi is a political refugee from Iraq in Morocco of the late 1960s and works as a high-school teacher in the small town of Mohammadiyya, not far from Casablanca. He becomes acquainted with several young Moroccans of both sexes, among whom Habib is his special friend, a comrade of Mahdi Ben Barka, the leader of the leftist opposition to King Hassan's government which is cracking down on all opponents. Sharqi lives in an apartment in the same building where Ruqayya lives, and both he and Habib admire the beautiful woman without either of them telling her so, until one day she expresses her friendship to Sharqi in the form of embraces and kisses with no commitment, still guarding her overpowering independence.

Sharqi gets to know Si Idris, a very rich and pompous man of poor origins, and he visits him in his sumptuous palace where he has maidens he calls "insects." Si Idris, who is also a gambler, thinks that money can achieve anything one wants and that all women are easy to possess, including Ruqayya. He boasts of his generous treatment of his farm workers and his servants, and believes they like him when, in fact, they hate his presumptuousness and live in poverty. When he is found murdered in Sharqi's building, the police conduct investigations with Sharqi after reading his diary that mentions his love and admiration for Ruqayya. He is not arrested, but Ruqayya thinks he killed Si Idris for her sake, which he continues to deny.

The novel's action becomes fast toward the end, but is very slow in the earlier chapters where the reader is made to follow Sharqi and his young friends, men and women, in their various activities where alcoholic drinks and permissive behavior are abundant in a manner not usual in Morocco. The plot of the novel is obfuscated and may confuse readers until the end is reached. The translation is very good except that, in reporting conversations where the Arabic text says: he said or she said, the translator invariably says: he cried or she cried. But on the whole, it is good to have this novel of Mahmoud Saeed in English translation. **IJB**

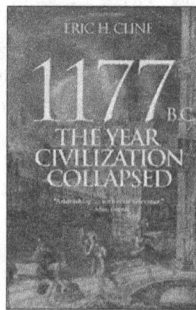

Eric H. Cline. *1177 B.C.: The Year Civilization Collapsed*. Princeton, NJ: Princeton University Press, 2014. 237 pp. $29.95. ISBN: 978-0691140896.

The Late Bronze Age saw the rise of the world's first truly international civilization.

City-states from Greece to Mesopotamia and Egypt became increasingly closely linked by trade, diplomacy, and artistic and cultural styles. In his intriguing new book, Eric Cline makes a strong case that "the politics, trade, and diplomacy of thirty-five centuries ago, especially during the fourteenth century B.C., were not all that dissimilar to those practiced as part and parcel of the globalized economy of our world today, complete with economic embargoes, diplomatic embassies, and both gifts and power plays at the highest diplomatic levels" (p. 72). In the twelfth century B.C. that civilization collapsed, plunging the entire region into the darkness of the Iron Age, which would last over six hundred years. In his book, Cline examines both the flourishing of the Late Bronze Age civilization—from about 1500 B.C. to about 1200 B.C.—and its collapse. He chose the year 1177 B.C. as "the most representative of the entire collapse" (p. 172), because it was in that year, according to Egyptian records, that a confederation of foreign peoples invaded Egypt, some arriving by land and others by sea. They had already overcome the forces of the Hittite empire, as well as several other kingdoms, possibly including the island of Cyprus. Although the Egyptians called the invading peoples by six different names, modern scholars have collectively termed them "the Sea Peoples." Their places of origin remain mysterious. The only one of these peoples that scholars have managed to identify with a degree of certainty is the Peleset, or Philistines. Ramses III was the only monarch who managed to defeat them, but Egyptian civilization never fully recovered from the onslaught. Within less than a century, all the great powers had fallen.

During most of the twentieth century, scholars tended to blame the Sea Peoples for all this destruction. More recent advances in archeology, however, have revealed that a number of additional causes—including climate change, drought, famine, earthquakes, and internal rebellions—contributed to the upheaval.

One of the more interesting theories Cline proposes is that the Israelites "may have taken advantage of the havoc caused by the Sea Peoples in Canaan to move in and take control of the region" (p. 95). Equally thought-provoking is his suggestion that the Assuwa rebellion against the Hittites (ca. 1430 B.C.), in which they were aided and abetted by the Mycenaeans, may have provided the inspiration for the later stories about the Trojan War.

Cline concludes that the collapse of the Late Bronze Age civilization, rather than resulting from any single cause, was brought about by a combination of disasters adding up to a "perfect storm." He further argues that "rather than envisioning an apocalyptic ending overall—although perhaps certain kingdoms and cities like Ugarit met a dramatic, blazing end—we might better imagine that the end of the Late Bronze Age was more a matter of a chaotic though gradual disintegration of areas and places that had once been major and in contact with each other, but were now diminished and isolated, like Mycenae, because of internal and/or external changes that affected one or more of the integral parts of the complex system" (p. 169).

This book is written in a lively, engaging style. There are 11 black-and-white illustrations, but some of these are so small that it is difficult to distinguish the features to which Cline refers in the text. The book is also accompanied by a lengthy (28 page) bibliography. **MM**

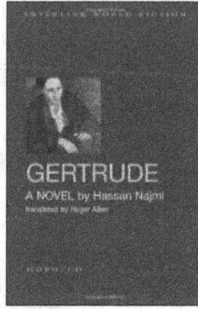

Hassan Najmi. Translated by Roger Allen. *Gertrude: A Novel by Hassan Najmi.* Northampton, MA: Interlink Books, 2014. Pbk.: 284 pp. $15.00. ISBN: 978-1566569712.

This is a beautifully written novel by a major writer of Morocco, masterfully translated from Arabic by Roger Allen, retired professor of Arabic and Comparative Literature at the University of Pennsylvania. A work of imagination as a novel, it is, nevertheless, based on historical facts relating to the writers Gertrude Stein (1874–1946) and Alice Toklas (1877–1967) who lived together in Paris as a married couple from 1907 to 1946. As is well known, Stein's home was a place where illustrious artists, writers, poets and other intellectuals of the day, including Picasso, Matisse, Braque, Modigliani, Jean Cocteau, Apollinaire, Hemingway, Francis Scott Fitzgerald, and dozens of others met in the famous salon. Hassan Najmi must have had access to an abundance of actual letters, diaries, and memoirs of relevant persons, as well as a plethora of books about Stein's salon and its luminaries—not to mention her writings and Toklas's—to make his novel a realistic and interesting representation of that renowned episode of Western culture.

His novel begins with an unnamed narrator visiting a friend of his, an old Moroccan man named Muhammad who is dying in hospital and who, as a young man with poetic pretensions, was a tour guide in Tangier who had guided Gertrude Stein and Alice Toklas during their visit to Morocco. Muhammad gives his papers to the narrator and begs him to write his life story. The narrator accepts, and the novel is his version of his research into those papers. It is from these papers that we learn that Muhammad once accepted Stein's invitation to visit her in Paris, and lived for several years in a rooftop room of her home as the man of the house who was in love with Gertrude, to the dismay of Alice Toklas. He attended Gertrude's salon and met the luminaries of her circle. He also visited the Parisian suburb where gypsies lived and had good relations with them.

Meanwhile, as the narrator becomes more engrossed in his research, he gets to know Lydia Altman, a diplomat at the U.S. Embassy in Morocco, who becomes interested in the story of Gertrude and Muhammad, and eventually in the narrator himself; and she has an affair with him. His research leads him to learn that Muhammad, one day, was rudely refused entry into Gertrude's home when he arrives at the door with writer Anaïs Nin. He had earlier noticed Gertrude's growing tepid response to him but did not do anything to deal with it. So he decides to leave, goes up to his rooftop room, collects his belongings, and leaves—forever to live on the memory of Gertrude.

In Gertrude's biography, *The Autobiography of Alice B. Toklas* (Paris: Gallimard, 1934), there is mention of a certain "Mohammed" (p. 173) as a guide in Tangier for 10 days who became a "pleasant companion" to Gertrude and Alice in their tour there. It is fascinating how Hassan Najmi has used this and other materials to construct a captivating novel with historical characters, including famous artists and writers, portrayed realistic scenes of Stein's salons, their conversations, and life in Paris and Tangier. **IB**

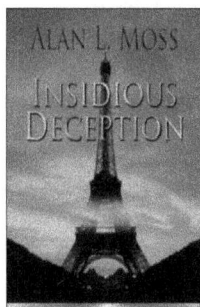

Alan L. Moss. *Insidious Deception.* **Casper, WY: Whiskey Creek Press, 2013. 460 pp. Pbk: $8.94. ISBN: 978-1611605488. Ebk: $4.99. 547 KB.**

This is a thriller, not an academic book. It is interesting to academics working on Middle Eastern studies only insofar as it pertains to issues of energy development and conflict resolution in the region. It was published by an amateur author through what appears to be a vanity press, and if we are to judge it by the standards of such works, it is above average. It is competently organized, its characters have reasonably plausible motivations, and it is free of grammatical and spelling errors. It also has a thought-provoking take on conflict resolution and its vulnerability to the efforts of those who profit from conflict to derail or subvert the process.

This is not to say that it is a good novel. It is not. While it retains the features of the genre, it fails to assemble its parts into a compelling sum. Moss has the novice fiction writer's habit of having a character say a line, then providing a paragraph of background prose explaining why that character would say such a thing. The novelist's mantra of

"Show, don't tell" is largely ignored throughout the text. Characters mostly exist to fulfill structural functions within the story rather than as psychologically realistic individuals. The prose, while competent, does not sing, nor does it reflect its subject matter or the themes of the novel.

Let us take a brief example. In the initial chapters, the young American man who is to become one of the protagonists is making extra money working as a deckhand on a luxury yacht where the corporate conspirators meet to hatch their plot. After the trip, he looks up the Italian woman who had lived in his house in the States as an exchange student years before: she is now an adult, remembers him quite fondly, and enthusiastically accepts his proposal to stow away on the yacht as it deadheads back whence it came. But on the voyage, the yacht explodes and sinks, presumably because the conspirators wish to erase any hint they ever met. The young woman dies; the young man's grief catalyzes his quest for revenge. This is not an unreasonable plot device for a thriller; but it's poorly executed. Moss describes the young woman entirely as a set of appealing physical attributes, not as a human with subjectivity; before the explosion, the evidence left behind by the conspirators is introduced very clumsily; after the explosion, the woman whose physical features have been so lovingly described is tossed away like a broken doll. A better thriller would give the woman a personality, would have the young man curious and wary about the passengers who just left (or enthusiastic about how great hobnobbing with the rich was), would have the young woman survive and then have the two young people evolve a relationship as they explore the conspiracy. But none of this occurs.

Moss has written a text that fits the description of "thriller," but is really something more like the treatment for a late-night movie on basic cable. It's a story, but not much of a novel. Academics who enjoy thrillers as a pastime might pick it up for airplane or before-bed reading, but there is a wide selection of much better material readily available. **IC**

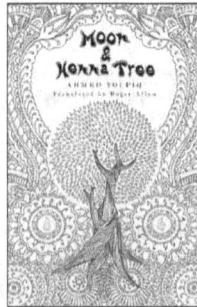

Ahmed Toufiq. Translated by Roger Allen. *Moon and Henna Tree*. Austin, TX: The University of Texas Press. The Center for Middle Eastern Studies, 2013. 276 pp. Pbk: $24.95. ISBN: 978-0292748248.

The author of this novel, Ahmed Toufiq, is the Minister of Religious Endowments and Islamic Affairs for Morocco, and former director of the National Library. He has published several works on pre-modern Moroccan history and edited many religious and historical texts in this field. As a novelist, he brings to his fiction a rich knowledge of pre-modern Moroccan society.

In this novel, he deals with the tribal society of the High Atlas region in pre-modern Morocco and particularly with Husn al-Suq in the mountains, its ruler Hmmu, and his adviser Ibn al-Zara. The main theme of the novel is the abuse of power. Hmmu (dialectal name for Muhammad) is the *qaid* or ruler of the tribal area and his adviser is Ibn al-Zara, a former slave trader, who manipulates him. Hmmu, like his father 'Ulla before him, was appointed qaid by the Sultan in Fez, the capital, and continued to keep his father's adviser Ibn al-Zara, a clever and crafty politician who was very knowledgeable about tribal affairs in the region with its several qaids competing with one another for the power, pleasure, and approval of the Sultan who appointed them.

The novel does not have a narrative plot as is usual in most novels, but it much plotting and intrigue in the service of political power and predominance. Ibn al-Zara's schemes include having his master marry al-Salima, the daughter of Shaykh Wald al-Shahba', the qaid of the plains in order to bring that competing area into the orbit of Hmmu's power as qaid of the mountains. But al-Salima gives birth to a girl, not the male heir that Hmmu hoped for; so Ibn al-Zara has his master marry Kima, the daughter of Shaykh Ahmad Nayit Ibrayim, qaid of a resisting area in the mountains. The two wives become good friends until Kima dies, bringing their relatives from the mountains and the plains together in concord. This state of affairs makes the tribes of the two areas organize and eventually succeed in assassinating Hmmu—now abandoned by Ibn al-Zara—and removing his tyrannical rule.

Ahmed Toufiq enriches this simple sequence of events with elaborate accounts of the circumstances, the motivations, and the consequences. In so doing, he shows the interactions between characters and describes their feelings and thoughts. As the translator, Roger Allen, says in his Afterword, the reader is given "an incredibly rich picture of the customs and rituals in traditional Moroccan society" (p. 273). This reviewer is also amazed at the details Ahmed Toufiq gives of certain occurrences in the novel, such as the visits of the tribal leaders to the Sultan in Fez, or the detailed description of the jewelry offered for sale to al-Salima before her wedding, or the details given depicting the intricate tattooing at Kima's wedding. Roger Allen's translation has painstakingly rendered these scenes—as with the rest of the novel—in beautiful English, successfully accommodating a strangely different culture of pre-modern times. **IJB**

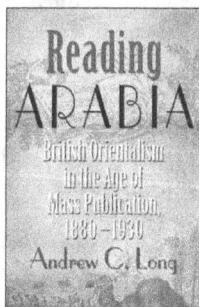

Andrew C. Long. *Reading Arabia: British Orientalism in the Age of Mass Publication 1880–1930*. Syracuse, NY: Syracuse University Press, 2014. 269 pp. $34.95. ISBN: 978-0815633235.

Nearly four decades after the publication of Edward Said's monumental *Orientalism*, his central thesis continues to be debated, elaborated, and expanded. "Said-ian" authors have taken the arguments of *Orientalism* far beyond the limitations Said set for himself when he set out to examine great works of literature, art, and other great contributions to European material culture. Today, one can find Said-ian critiques of books that are decidedly *not* high literature—media studies, popular movies, and cartoons. Said's critiques continue to be applied, and in the post 9/11 world there appears to be no shortage of material toward which his arguments can be directed.

Andrew Long's *Reading Arabia* is another conversation generated by Said's *Orientalism*, but unlike some of the more recent material scholars have begun to evaluate, Long returns to classical authors of the nineteenth and twentieth centuries, some of whom were covered by Said himself, such as T. E. Lawrence, Richard Burton, and others such as Edith Hull and Robert Cunningham Graham, who were not. Long prefers to focus on those authors who were considered to be "friends" of the Orient, and of Arabs and Muslims. There is a deliberateness to this task that we can appreciate: Long re-examines "classical" Orientalist authors, but also asks about how orientalism was reproduced en mass to audiences who were not necessarily reading Lawrence and Doughty. This leads to interesting citations of advertisements and popular literature from the nineteenth century. This presence of orientalism in the everyday embeds it in our unconscious. Long seeks to look for orientalism in places that Said, with his focus on high culture, and in some respects, on the obvious, did not. Long also conducts his investigation in a manner that leaves Said's polemicist net behind. Despite his returning to the nineteenth century for most of the analysis, the questions that motivate Long's study are thoroughly twenty-first century. He is concerned, for example, with the resilience of orientalism and with those texts which Said considered to be central to the problem of orientalism as he constructed it (for example, in the past five years, there have been a handful of new books published on T.E. Lawrence). But thoroughly steeped in contemporary continental philosophy, Long brings to his questioning of these works a touch of Lacan and Zižek and a concern—commonplace in the Occident—with the Orient as a place of fantasy.

For scholars of Said, Long's book is a valuable addition to the field of Orientalist studies. There are several points that a scholar of Said can greatly appreciate. First is Long's nuanced analysis of writers such as Marmaduke Pickthall, who deserve a comprehensive report of their work and projects in the study of orientalism. Long's discussion of Pickthall is thorough and looks at his conversion to Islam with respect to how he wielded it in an effort to criticize the West. That is, Pickthall's praise of Islam flowed out of his criticisms of Christianity (as well as British culture), which he saw as failing to live up to its potential. Long emphasizes Pickthall's use of his own British culture as a means to undoing the prejudices toward the Orient, which were by then an integral part of British culture and thought. Second, Long's discussion of orientalism includes discussion of those authors who are seen as resisting it, such as the Robert Cunningham Graham group. His discussion of Cunningham Graham—a now largely-forgotten figure—illustrates the vastly underemphasized fact that even in the nineteenth century there were figures who resisted orientalism in their writings and attempted to subvert its key components. Long cites Cunningham Graham's introduction to his *Arabia Deserta*, the opening lines of which are "I fear I have no theory of empires, destiny of the Anglo-Saxon race, spread of the Christian faith, of trade extension, or of hinterlands; no nostrum, by means of which I hope to turn Arabs to Christians…" Cunningham Graham proceeded to criticize British culture and its imperial projects, always maintaining that a "bad" national government was better than any one imposed by imperialism.

Finally, Long focuses on the question of why orientalist ideas found a ready audience in Victorian England, and continue to be attractive today. This allows him to use his critique of nineteenth century writers to refer to contemporary writers who continue perpetuating orientalist ideas (Thomas Friedman is one example). His concluding remarks of Chapter 4 in the book speak to the import of continuing to look for orientalism in places other than the "front door" of the orientalist storehouse and in places not less frequently encountered, but less obvious because of their frequency. Though *Reading Arabia* can at times seem disjointed, it is an important book that references both rare gems and new ways of understanding some old ones. **CF**

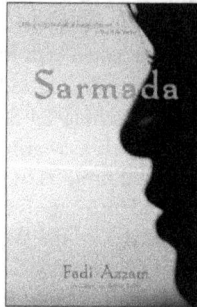

Fadi Azzam. *Sarmada*. UK: Arabia Books, 2012. 192 pp. $25.00. ISBN: 1566568722. Pbk.: 216 pp. $15.00. ISBN: 1566568625.

Sarmada is a remarkable book, a story that draws readers' attention, not simply to a plot, but more importantly into a society that might otherwise be deemed too alien to enter, let alone to understand. Fadi Azzam has crafted a brilliant narrative rendered beautifully into English by Adam Talib. It should be required reading for all trying to become familiar with the Middle East because *Sarmada* is one of those books that contains the history of an epoch. The novel opens in Paris. "And now, by the banks of the Seine, something new was flickering inside of me, bringing Sarmada back...," says Rafi, the narrator, whose travels give this story its energy (p. 3). Sarmada's return to Rafi's memory is the beginning of a journey of self-discovery forcing him to account for who he has become by going back to the village he routinely describes, to himself more than to anyone else, as "a hollow shell.... [having spent his] bitterest days...there...saddled...with pain and fear and self-effacement.... [that]... had taken years to get... out of me" (p. 3).

Had Fadi Azzam plunged us immediately into Sarmada's disorienting otherness, he would not have been able to show how this story with all its violations of the laws of nature is also a faithful representation of reality. Presumably by accident at a reception, Rafi meets Azza Tawfiq, a Sorbonne science professor, who says she lived in Sarmada in a past life as Hela Mansour, a young Druze woman brutally murdered by her brothers for running away with her Algerian lover. Expressing concern for the brothers responsible for exporting the soul that now hovers over her thoughts and feelings, the scientist asks the narrator what he remembers of the place he thought he erased from his consciousness when he changed his home address. Although skeptical of the story and of the belief that souls can wonder from Druze body to Druze body while marking an identity that insures blood purity, Rafi is drawn back to Sarmada presumably to discover how and why Hela died. In fact, his trip teaches him much more about himself.

For this is a novel about someone who no longer considers himself bound by traditions, but, ironically, styles his documentaries as building bridges between East and West though questions must be raised about what someone who has deleted genuine knowledge of the former, and not acquired linguistic fluency in the latter can say about this intersection. At the outset, the narrator assumes a secular idiom is necessary to understand the world and to banish the power of religious beliefs. But as he is drawn back to a village, saturated with so much tradition and so many layers of his past, he begins to realize that even if he wishes to leave the space occupied by Sarmada, he cannot fully cast off what it has meant for the creative energy he possesses, but has yet been unable to express. Without a candid exploration of the culture and society that gave him life and shaped the evolution of his personality, Rafi knows he will not be able to produce anything of real value.

Until his fateful return to the place of his birth, Rafi's life had been a series of rebellions against what he believed was a closed, static society governed by fixed norms and traditions where men and women were simply conscripted into their roles and where they were locked into a static social structure that denied them opportunity and individuality. People, particularly women, seemed to take submission for granted. Yet, back in Sarmada, Rafi hears stories of a traditional order that does find ways to accommodate difference and even deviance. Drawing out the agony of Sarmada's women denied dignity or imprisoned in loneliness, the novel also gives them a basis for hope. Qualities of compassion, humility, and empathy can be uncovered in the experiences of the villagers, while the actions structured by the supposedly secular and rational political world are absolutely unforgiving and inflexible. There are no long deep discussions of politics in the novel, but politics exerts considerable gravitational pull, and is represented in all its ferocity; its grim realities intrude on the fantasies and generate significant action. For example, Hela's murder in 1968 follows Israel's conquest of the Golan Heights, one local register of the national disaster. But the juxtaposition of a traditional order providing at least the slim possibility for individual authenticity, and a political order totally denying it, is telling.

The villagers find a place for Farida, the prostitute, to dwell and work among them while the faithful Ba'ath teachers drive the troublesome student, Fayyad, out of school and village, and ultimately to his death in Lebanon only to be praised as a martyr when his coffin is brought back for burial. Traditional beliefs and superstitions may have been unscientific, but they helped people believe they could exercise a measure of control over their environment and lives. Ba'ath Party slogans simply destroyed lives. Traditional societies did not deprive people of their imagination and the ability to find elements of the sacred that crossed normally impenetrable religious and sectarian barriers. Again and again, holiness seemed theologically composite, and cruelty and love coexisted. Even deviance could be made to serve a purpose: sexual relations with children were interpreted as a coming of age ritual.

Presumably the narrator ingests these stories and leaves Sarmada with them in his bones and his mind. Rather than cutting himself off from tradition, he incorporates it. In so doing, he teaches us something important about the paradoxical connection between the assertions of the self and the integrity of tradition.

Sarmada was the site of a battle during the Crusades, and now it is one of the staging grounds of the war against the dictatorship of Bashar al-Asad. Fadi Azzam wants us to read his novel and think about what a so-called modern and rational political order has done to men and women who once found their own, albeit imperfect, ways to live together.

Sarmada does not come with a set of causal explanations about the way things happen in history, nor with a pragmatic plan for shaping the course of the future. And the fantastic fate Fadi Azzam invents for the people of Sarmada is a manifest violation of conventional notions of how things happen in the real world. What is deeply instructive but troubling is that they are no more grotesque than the actual course of events. It is in this sense that storytelling, with its linkages to tradition, becomes an authoritative way to challenge the political system and gives a vivid sense of why men and women in Syria are today risking all they possess to be allowed to return to themselves and search for their own shared humanity. **DD**

Ahmad Mahmoud. Translated by Nastaran Kherad. *The Neighbors*. Austin, TX: University of Texas Press, 2013 [1974]. 409 pp. $29.95. ISBN: 978-0292749054.

What is the human cost of oil production? After reading Ahmad Mahmoud's *The Neighbors*, this haunting question resonates in my mind when I drive by gas stations surrounding American suburban neighborhoods. Extremely well written and thought-provoking, *The Neighbors* depicts a pivotal time in the life of Khaled, an adolescent boy coming of age during the turmoil of Iran's struggle to nationalize its oil industry. Khaled's story represents the undocumented accounts of Iranians in the mid-twentieth century who endured social, political, and economic resistance to the West. Undoubtedly, much of Khaled's experiences echo that of the author.

Living in poverty under the shadows of the oil refineries in the small port town of Abadan, Khaled has a somewhat idyllic life amidst the lives of his neighbors, who all share the same latrine, drink from the same water source, and know all the intimate secrets about one another due to such close proximity living. Though Khaled possesses a desire to learn, his father believes that, "a real man is one that, when you pat him on the back, dust rises in the air" (p. 4). Therefore, Kahled's hunger for knowledge must be fed by his observation of the neighbors and his father's proverbial sayings about life. However, the deteriorating economy leaves Khaled's father no choice but to travel to Kuwait for work, creating a void that invites new authority figures to shape his adolescent perspectives.

Khaled seeks work at the local teahouse, owned by Aman Aqa, one of the neighbors who physically abuses his wife, Bolur, who in turn seduces Khaled into exploring his sexuality. His father gone, Khaled desires to help his impoverished family, yet is conflicted with sleeping with the wife of his employer, who becomes like a father figure. Khaled's daily adventures take a dramatic turn when his close friend, Ebrahim, leaves him to shoulder the blame for breaking a window with a rock, and Khaled is dragged to the local corrupt police station. During his brief confinement, he encounters Pendar, who is networked with those who will change Khaled's youthful idealization of government.

Working at the teahouse, strategically located on the main road between the town and the oil refineries, Khaled thrives on listening to the customers talk about the idea of nationalizing oil. Meanwhile, political revolutionaries use Khaled as a delivery boy for illegal pamphlets. Intertwined with his growing attraction to women, desire to be a man, and awakening of Iran's political situation, Khaled realizes.

Everything is new to me. I have opened my eyes to a new world. Now, from the sorts of things I hear, I can grasp why the lives of the destitute worsen each day, and why people like my father have to pack up their bundles and go from one foreign country to another in search of work so that they can earn a pretty sum of money (p. 143).

He begins to comprehend that the lives of his neighbors reveal the hardships of the common people of Iran, who are exploited due British control over the oil refineries. The effects on one tiny acre in one small neighborhood in one small town in Iran reveal the oppression; and the neighbors in Khaled's world echo the lives of those in the working class who are exploited, whether the monopolies involved are land, oil or power. Prayers to Allah at least give hope to some, such as Khaled's father, while others, such as Aman Aqa, embrace reality and revolt with anger toward loved ones. Meanwhile, a growing number of Iranians, in order to include Pendar, seek to take matters into their own hands and revolt against the government.

When Khaled falls in love with a woman with black enticing eyes, Pendar warns him that he must not develop close relationships, "You should learn, in the course of battle, not to allow your emotions to take over" (p. 237). Then, during a very secretive and dangerous mission, Khaled is caught carrying a suitcase full of propaganda material. Flashbacks echo the present, and remind the reader that Khaled is still a boy, for the novel takes a dramatic turn. The second half of the book depicts a new neighborhood—Khaled's cell block. Mahmoud details Khaled's torture and mental transformation extremely well, drawing from his own personal imprisonment.

Linking Khaled's two communities—his family home and the prison—is Rahim the Donkey Keeper, who is imprisoned for the murder of his wife. When Rahim is hauled to the gallows, Khaled recalls a frightening childhood memory when he saw the stiff bodies of three faceless men soon after a town square hanging. A boy's distant engraved memory now has a face to it, his neighbor Rahim, and suddenly everyone who hangs is no longer faceless, for they all have a name, a story.

The reader transforms with Khaled, from innocence to embracing the imparity of life; from embracing all the potential youth offers, to possibly believing death is better than life in solitary confinement. So much is taken away from Khaled—his father's being forced to seek employment in Kuwait, his mother's being denied jail visitations, and his first love's never being seen again once he is thrown into prison. In the remainder of the book, the community of the neighbors with whom he grows up becomes the community of the prisoners he befriends. This remains with him as he is released from prison only to witness his best friend from childhood, Ebrahim, being dragged into prison.

Every struggle for power affects people, but what about the communities affected who have neither say, nor power, nor economic advantage? As American-Iranian relations have yet to reconcile from the time period in which this story takes place, Americans would benefit from reading *The Neighbors*. Perspective is everything; for what if oil were nationalized in some small town in Texas and a foreign power toppled our government and pillaged the profits, resulting in poverty that affected generations? Eurocentric history books in America skip over the thousands of lives that were destroyed as a result of the British and American intervention in Iran's oil production. Ahmad Mahmoud dares to reveal the turmoil experienced by Iranians; and in some ways, this novel reminds me of the bold writing of Aleksandr Solzhenitsyn who used fiction to communicate reality. **CL**

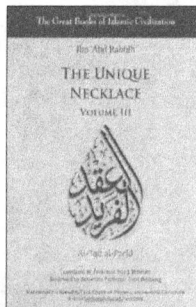

Ibn Abd Rabbih. Translated by Issa J. Boullata. *The Unique Necklace: Al-'Iqd al-Farid, Volume III* (*Great Books of Islamic Civilization*). Reading, UK: Garnet, 2011. (Center for Muslim Contribution to Civilization). 330 pp. $95.00. ISBN: 185964239X. Pbk.: 330 pp. $34.95. ISBN: 1859642403.

Professor Issa Boullata renders a great contribution to the study of Islamic civilization by translating the third volume of Ibn ʿAbd Rabbih's *al-ʿIqd al-farīd* . This volume is one the most important literary works that serves as a repository that comprises the main genres and themes in classical Arabic literature. The translated book, which is a continuation of the project that began in 2006, follows closely the thematic arrangement of the original text and is divided into four chapters: the Book of the Gem, the Book of the Emerald, the Book of the Mother of the Pearl, and the Book of the Unique Jewel. The translator relies on the three latest editions of the *ʿIqd*, but the translation follows, on the whole, the Beirut edition. (The Beirut edition was edited by Mufid Mue, the Beirut edition. (The Beirut edition was edited by Mufid Mu The translation has a general index of names and important terms.

The first chapter, which is entitled "On Proverbs" (pp. 1-49), contains collections of aphorisms, parables, and proverbs, their background and cultural implications. Since these sayings are arranged according to their importance, the author begins with proverbs adumbrated in the *Qurʾan* and the Hadith tradition and then moves on to dicta of learned and wise men. The author uses metaphors and traces the origin of these proverbs and sayings to offer a better understanding of life experiences, vicissitudes of time, and ingenious human interactions.

The second chapter, which is entitled "On Religious Exhortations and Asceticism" (pp. 51-149), is dedicated to exhortatory sayings and ethics and their place in the moralistic function in pietistic spaces. A significant part of this chapter, therefore, deals with asceticism and its ethical role in Islamic ethical tradition. The chapter begins with exhortatory examples recurring in the *Qurʾan* and the prophetic tradition to be followed by the exhortatory dicta of certain prophets (such as Jesus, John the Baptist, David, and Abraham) and wise men (Muslim and non-Muslim). This discussion includes pieces of advice given by fathers to their children. A section is also dedicated to encounters between exhorters and caliphs (Umayyad and ʿAbbasid) where the themes of injustice and piety figure prominently in their discussions. The chapter concludes with aphorisms of ascetics, which are arranged thematically, and their moral lessons.

The third chapter, entitled "On Women Mourners, Condolences, and Elegies" (pp. 151-226), focuses on elegies and mourning drawn from classical Islamic literature and the moral lessons that can be deduced from them. The author provides examples for these themes through the sayings of Mud non-Muslim). This discussion spans companions, caliphs, and prominent individuals. The chapter is full of elegies said by family members to their loved ones. An important section of this chapter is dedicated to elegies by prominent poets, such as al-Khansāʾ (died after 630), Abu Nuwās (d. 814), and Abu al-ʿAtāhiya (d. 828),). Interestingly, Ibn ʿAbd Rabbih shares his own elegies dedicated to his loved ones. The chapter concludes with condolences given by well-known individuals and their socio-religious context.

The fourth chapter, entitled "on lineage and the Virtues of the Arabs," (pp. 227-310) deals with genealogies and their socio-political significance. Examining the origins of Arab tribes, the author aims to emphasize the virtues of the Arabs. In doing so, he touches upon important themes in early Islamic literature, such as the contention between Northern and Southern Arabs and the Shu'ūbiyya controversy. The chapter begins with the genealogical origin of the Quraysh emphasizing its merits especially those of its two main clans—Banū Hāshim and Banū Umayya. Then he moves on to talk about the superiority of the Arabs in terms of genealogy, eloquence, and wisdom. This chapter also includes names of illustrious genealogists, such as Daghfal b. Ḥanẓala (d. 690), al-Haytham b. 'Adī (d. 821), and Muḥammad al-Kalbī (d. 723). The chapter also offers detailed information about the clans classified under the Northern and Southern Arabs, their genealogies, and famous persons that descended from them. The chapter ends with a discussion of the Shu'ūbiyya controversy and the arguments of the contended sides.

Again, by translating this volume of *al-'Iqd al-farīd*, professor Boullata makes an essential work on classical Arabic literature available to general readers and scholars of classical Arabic literature. However, the translator does not offer a critical comparison of the different editions (or manuscripts) he uses when variations in the text occur. For example, in the translated text, we are told that a drunken man was brought to 'Umar b. al-Khaṭṭāb (p. 16), whereas the name appears in the Beirut edition as 'Alī b, Abī Ṭālib. Second, the translator does not include biographical information about authors and well-known literary figures that Ibn 'Abd Rabbih mentions throughout his work. The translated text is also missing a commentary that can illuminate some of the difficult passages and place the text in a better historical setting. **ART**

MIDDLE EAST: HISTORY & LIFE

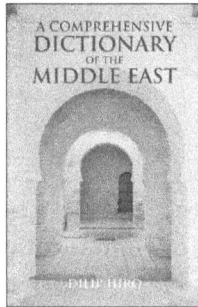

Dilip Hiro. *A Comprehensive Dictionary of the Middle East.* **Northampton, MA: Olive Branch Press, 2013. 756 pp. Pbk.: $29.95. ISBN: 978-1566569040.**

From "aal" and "Aal Saud" to "Zoroastrianism and Zoroastrians," this dictionary with over 1,000 alphabetically-arranged entries of various lengths offers up-to-date information on the Middle East that is as amazing for its wealth and accuracy as it is for its breadth and depth.

Its author, Dilip Hiro, is a well-known journalist, political writer, and historian specializing in South Asia, Central Asia, the Middle East, and Islamic affairs. He was born to Hindu parents in Larkana (about 400 km to the north-east of Karachi) when India was ruled by the British; but after the partition of the country in 1947, he moved to independent India and, since the mid-1960s, has been living in London. Educated in India, Britain, and the United States, he has published 33 books since 1969, including five literary works (a novel, poems, and plays—some of which were performed in London and Delhi), and he has contributed to 17 other books. He has written articles for *The Washington Post*, *The New York Times*, *Wall Street Journal*, *International Herald Tribune*, *The Guardian*, and *The Observer* and has often been a commentator on the BBC, CNN, and Sky News, as well as on various radio stations.

His *Dictionary...* is indispensable to students, scholars, journalists, politicians, and others dealing with this strategic and tumultuous region of the world that continues to be in the daily news. It is clearly written, with objective entries which cover political and military affairs, historical and societal matters, ethnic and religious groups, key concepts and important events, biographies of leading personalities of the region, and information about its languages and literatures.

Succinctly presented, its entries on each of the 15 modern countries of this ancient land give an account of its history, culture, people, government, and political and socioeconomic conditions. Whether dealing with Judaism, Christianity, Islam or with minor religions of the Middle East, the *Dictionary* ... is very helpful in giving their principal beliefs, theology, denominations, and sects; and, in an entry on "Titles," it even gives the titles of the various hierarchical positions in Christianity and Islam (but not in Judaism).

The *Dictionary* ... also contains good entries on noted literary writers such as Gibran, Naguib Mahfouz and Amos Oz, and poets such as Badr Shakir al-Sayyab, Adonis, Nazik al-Malaika, and Mahmoud Darwish. It also presents good biographies of noted intellectuals and activists such as Shirin Ebadi, Michel Aflaq, and George Antonius; but longer biographies of political leaders are given like those on Gamal Abdul Nasser, Levi Eshkol, Ariel Sharon, and Khomeini.

Eventful movements like the "Intifada" and the "Arab Spring" are well represented by long entries with detailed and evenhanded analysis. Political parties are also given a significant place such as the "Baath Socialist Party" in various Arab countries, "Shas" and "Likud" in Israel, the "National Progressive Unionist Party" in Egypt, the "Tudeh Party of Iran," and many others. Well represented also are matters of war in entries like: "Arab-Israeli War" (I, II, III, IV), "Gulf War" (I, II, III), "Iran-Iraq War" as well as matters of peace in entries like: "Peace Process" (1, 2, 3, 4, 5, 6, 7, 8, 9, and 10)—a process which is still evolving! And perhaps no dictionary on the Middle East can be complete without entries on "Oil" or more appropriately petroleum; this *Dictionary...* has several independent entries dealing with this industry in individual countries of the Middle East. Additionally, it has other entries dealing separately with oil's politics, embargoes, measurements, prices, and reserves.

But conspicuously absent from this comprehensive *Dictionary...* is an entry on Turkey. Except for a map of its Ottoman Empire, ca. 1800 placed after the book's Preface, Turkey is totally ignored when, in fact, it is part and parcel of the Middle East and has played an important role in its history. Be that as it may, the *Dictionary...* is an encyclopedic and well-researched work that will remain useful for many years to come. **IJB**

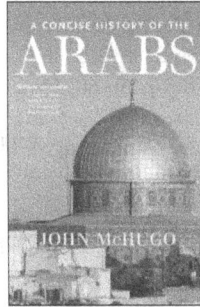

John McHugo. *A Concise History of the Arabs*. London, UK: Saqi Books, 2014. 352 pp. $26.95. ISBN: 978-1595589460.

This book is a well-written and useful resource, but it is mistitled. Its fourth through final chapters are concise and clear and explain in detail the geopolitical, economic, and cultural developments that led to the development of the autocratic Arab nation-states of the last century, as well as the Arab Spring protests and their aftermath. Especially cogent and worthwhile is McHugo's explanation of the details of the Israeli/Palestinian conflict and its roots in decisions made by Europeans in the late nineteenth and early twentieth centuries. An intelligent layperson who only understood the conflict through the lens of the Western corporate media would be well served by McHugo's work, which provides a nuanced, balanced treatment of the issue. This treatment would go a long way for the hypothetical layperson in understanding why the Arabs are often portrayed as the aggressors in the contemporary conflict; how this is often very misleading; and why the anger on the part of most Arabs has real justification not often fully explicated in the mainstream media.

McHugo's approach to twentieth and early twenty-first century Arab politics sticks closely to the core Middle Eastern states, giving comparatively short shrift to the periphery of the Arab world. Yet, he does an excellent job in explaining the economic and political developments that led to the standard pattern of autocratic presidents-for-life and monarchs that characterize the Arab world of our time. Furthermore, he describes the rise to power and the policies of well-known names such as Nasser, Sadat and Hafez al-Assad in such a manner as to lend real humanity to these names. The author also describes their drawbacks and failures in such a manner as to clarify the influence of Cold War superpower conflicts and Western financial institutions on the policies and aspirations of the Arab leaders. There's little in here that a well-read scholar of disciplines relating to Middle Eastern studies wouldn't already know, but again, for a layperson looking for a concise history of the Arab world—especially its core—in the last century, this is a valuable and worthwhile resource.

Had McHugo stuck to the last century, there would be little here to critique. It is in the initial three chapters, covering the history of the Middle East from pre-Islamic times to the nineteenth century, that issues arise. He presents the standard narrative of the founding of Islam, for example, without so much as mentioning the extent to which textual and critical scholarship of recent decades has problematized this narrative. The subsequent sections, while providing a concise and generally accurate description of the political history of the core Middle East is, if anything, perhaps too concise. But more importantly, his narrative very rapidly becomes a concise history of the (core) Muslim world. He doesn't address the factors that led to the comparative marginalization of ethnic Arabs during the high Abbasid period; an unwary layperson might not understand that the Abbasid culture was as much, or more Persian than Arab. This same problem applies to his discussion of the medieval period dominated by the Ottomans. The Arabs, as Arabs, aren't as present in the second and third chapters of the book as they could be. Also largely absent from the narrative is Arabic culture. McHugo sticks almost completely to political and economic aspects of Middle Eastern history, which are undeniably important, but to a layperson unfamiliar with the Arab world, an explanation of, for example, family life, gender roles, marriage patterns, the notion of "honor" that so often confuses Westerners, the role of poetry, etc., and the relation of these cultural aspects to orthodox Islam would have been a welcome addition to the text.

Again, insofar as the reader of *A Concise History of the Arabs* is interested in how and why the Arab states came to be dominated by autocracy, or the roots of the Israeli/Palestinian conflict, this is a valuable resource. But the background material leading up to McHugo's discussion is limited. This book is of comparatively limited use to scholars, though not at all without merit for the lay reader. **IC**

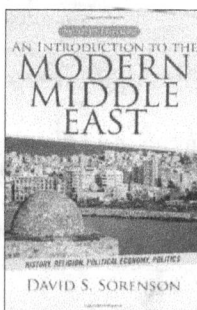

David S. Sorenson. *An Introduction to the Modern Middle East: History, Religion, Political Economy, Politics.* Boulder: CO: Westview Press, 2014. 2nd ed. 560 pp. Pbk.: $42.75. ISBN: 978-0813349220; Ebk: $16.49. ISBN: 978-0813349237.

This book should be required reading for all high school students, college undergraduates, nonprofit practitioners, and human rights' organizations. Sorenson's best contribution is the inclusion of anecdotes of places traveled in the Middle East. The author has a genius for insightful observations from personal experience in the Middle East and North African nations. Nonetheless, due to the multiple themes covered, this is not a definitive text. The author provides suggested readings to aid readers' additional opportunity(s) to acquire more in-depth knowledge.

An introduction to the country by country multifaceted politics of the Middle East presents a unique geopolitical and historical perspective. Sorenson briefly describes in each chapter a broad range in the literature of international relations, political science, public policy, and socio-cultural fields of study, which remains germane. The second edition includes recent events of the Arab Spring, Turkish politics, the Iranian power struggle with the West, and new developments in the Israeli–Palestinian impasse. Nonetheless, with the events in Iraq and Syria occurring in June 2014, the text is already outdated—an occupational hazard of writing history.

Has the author succeeded in writing an unbiased reasoned perspective of the New Middle East? I leave that judgment to each reader. Not an easy feat, as he includes the diverse politics and cultures of the Persian/Arabian Gulf, eastern Mediterranean countries, and North Africa. This unique book is relevant in that it enables the student to ground debates on the Middle East in a well-articulated, brief historical, and cultural perspective.

Conversely, what is absent from a balanced, objective, and rigorous scholarship, are issues of gender equity. Sorenson does a masterful job with the inclusion of a 'Status of Women' section in each chapter. However, they appear as an afterthought and not part of the author's cultural, and personal anecdotal stories. Surprisingly conspicuous by its absence is any reference to youth. The United Nations reports that population in the Middle East and North Africa is expected to reach 92.7,000,000 by 2040. This could be assumed to be a major contributing element in the Arab Spring and the politics of the region.

The United Nations also reported that Middle East and North African nations lack development of education for girls. This well-respected book could also similarly educate on the status of the education of girls by country. Sorenson's "Currency of History" value recalls major influences and contributions to literature, theology, science, philosophy, mathematics, architecture, astronomy, and language of Arabs—a few centuries before the credit of discovery was granted by Western civilization. Cultural and historical perspective of the Middle East is an effective contribution. This enables readers to ostensibly take off their Western lens and instead, examine the Middle East and North Africa on its own terms.

The book's topics, approach, historical, political, and cultural perspective is reason enough for adoption in schools. One caveat, Sorenson did not mean for this to be a comprehensive text. The subject topics are too complex. Therefore, I recommend readers pay close attention to suggested readings to expand their knowledge of the Middle East and North Africa.

The Preface, Glossary, and Introduction set the tone for "thinking about Middle

East politics." On a personal note, I would enjoy a dinner with Sorenson in order to hear more anecdotal stories. *An Introduction to the Modern Middle East...* is meaningful introductory exposure to the Middle East and North Africa for students. It should motivate all to want to learn more; what could be a better recommendation for a book? **DKW**

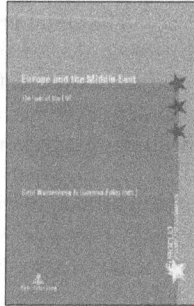

Birte Wassenberg and Giovanni Faleg, Eds. Europe and the Middle East: The Hour of the EU? Frankfort, DE: Peter Lang GmbH, 2012. 145 pp. Pbk. $36.95. ISBN: 978-9052018287.

The European Union publicizes its efforts to promote democracy and protect human rights in the Middle East, but these goals are secondary to Europe's security and economic interests.

Europe and the Middle East: The Hour of the EU? examines several strategic areas in the EU's relationship with the Near East and shows that, while Europe has provided more economic aid than any other great power, it has not made a significant political contribution to the region. This work, a collection of essays edited by Birte Wassenberg and Giovanni Faleg, does not examine future scenarios or propose a theory, but attempts to provide a simple portrait to illustrate some critical dimensions in the EU's approach to the Middle East.

The Arab-Israeli conflict is the first subject area addressed and Rory Miller and Amnon Aran contribute essays that look at the EU's economic and diplomatic efforts in the region. Europe made its first efforts in the Israeli–Palestinian conflict in the 1960s because its proximity to the conflict created risks, and these efforts provided an opportunity to craft a coherent foreign policy. The European Community offered its aid first to the Palestinians in 1971, but this effort never expanded into a political engagement. Europe has also signed economic treaties with Israel that have grown to include shared research and development, but when the Oslo Accords collapsed, the European Community was unable to convert its commercial policy to political influence, and ultimately had no impact on the Israeli government. Europe issued the 1980 Venice Declaration which stated that the Palestinian problem was political and endorsed self-determination for the Palestinian people. This statement did not reflect Europe's actual policy to the region and, unfortunately, Europe was not able to build a common policy toward the Arab–Israel conflict after the declaration. The United States is the only actor respected by both the Palestinians and the Israeli government; by deferring to the American position, the EU has not expanded its regional influence. The authors' conclusion is that Europe does not have a coherent position or strategy and has been unable to offer a significant contribution toward Arab–Israeli reconciliation.

The next section focuses on the European energy trade with Iran and shows how Tehran uses the proceeds from this commerce to fund its atomic research. Amir Kamel and Antonio Dai Pra provide essays that consider the consequences resulting from the EU energy shortage and its reliance on Iran to secure natural gas for European consumers. Two pipelines are being constructed that will transport Iranian natural gas through Turkey into European markets. Although Europe was unwilling to directly provide nuclear technology to Iran, it was prepared to do so indirectly by providing the income Tehran used to subsidize its capacity to refine uranium. Since the EU has no common energy policy, individual countries have an incentive to work with Iran to acquire resources for their domestic market. While the United States prevents all American investment in Iran, European firms are able to operate in that market without facing sanctions from Washington. The energy shortage requires the EU states to engage Tehran and prevents Europe from mounting any serious opposition to Iranian nuclear development.

The European Union claims to maintain unequivocal support for democracy, but this rhetoric is not supported in its policies toward individual states. Silvia Colombo and Benedetta Voltolino present two case studies that examine democracy promotion efforts in Lebanon and Morocco. These chapters illustrate that the EU cares more about the appearance of democracy than the institutional reality. The studies show that Europe champions democratic reform only when it does not conflict with its other interests. A more activist approach would create temporary disarray that could lead to more immigration and weaken local security. The EU only provided minimal aid to democracy promotion in Lebanon, and did not offer adequate resources to programs designed to improve the government. Likewise, Europe has a friendly regime in Morocco willing to hold show elections that work to further institutionalize and legitimize authoritarianism. The EU avoids supporting any program that would address the democratic weakness, as this would undermine its trade, security, and immigration policies. Europe's policies toward Middle Eastern states promote stability and trade while democratic support is secondary to its material interests.

The European Union must re-assess its relationships and policies toward Middle Eastern states to account for Turkey's reorientation toward the East. Giovanni Faleg and Sebastiano Sali's essays examine the consequences of Turkey's new foreign policy which emerged when the Justice and Development Party (AKP) came to power. Turkey held a pro-Western foreign policy throughout the Cold War, but its focus changed following the 9/11 terror attacks that saw its government adopt a new

Turkish-centered policy. Ankara lessened its emphasis on secular nationalism and sought multiple alliances to avoid any dependence on the West. The AKP sought a new "strategic depth" and wished for "zero problems with its neighbors" that led it to seek new relations with Iran, Syria, and other neighboring states. Turkey's relationship with Israel has been significantly weakened since the Mavi Marmara incident, where Israel fired upon a vessel in international waters, killing nine Turkish citizens. While Turkey was committed to the Western alliance, it enjoyed strong relations with Israel and was the first Muslim majority state to formally recognize the Jewish state. As Turkey seeks to engage Iran and Syria, Israel views this change with mistrust and this has resulted in a weakening of their relations. Europe is no longer able to count on Turkey to subordinate its policies to Western interests and must now contend with another strategic actor. This further complicates and weakens the EU's influence in the Middle East.

Overall, the book examines four dimensions of the relationship between the EU and the Middle East all showing that Europe's impact is limited to economic aid and trade policy, and this influence is weakening. The book reads like a journalistic narrative that neither accounts for the historical factors that have led to the events it chronicles, nor adequately deals with the long-term consequences of the European Union's inability to respond to the political reality in the Middle East. The one serious weakness in this work is its failure to examine the role the European Union institutions play in its inability to form a coherent foreign policy, or even act in its interests. The book has simple ambitions, as it does not seek to address theoretical problems and, as a result, it accomplishes its modest task.

Europe and the Middle East: The Hour of the EU? is a work that should be examined by scholars who wish to look at the recent history of European policy toward the Near East. **GDD**

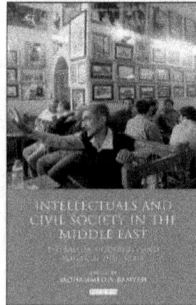

Mohammed A. Bamyeh, Ed. *Intellectuals and Civil Society in the Middle East, Liberalism, Modernity and Political Discourse.* **London, UK: Tauris Academic Studies. 320 pp. $99.00. ISBN: 978-1848856288.**

Mohammed A. Bamyeh's *Intellectuals and Civil Society in the Middle East, Liberalism, Modernity and Political Discourse,* centers on the subject of the social role of intellectuals in the Middle East and the manner in which intellectuals influence public life. This book collects essays from a wide range of perspectives on the issue of intellectuals and their role in civil society, including, historical, sociological, empirical, and contemporary treatments. It emerged out of a workshop entitled "The Social Role of intellectuals in the Middle East", organized in 2008, at the European University Institute in Florence, Italy. Contributors to this volume were asked to identify one intellectual or a group of intellectuals who have had a role in social life.

In the introductory chapter, Mohammed A. Bamyeh, outlines four central questions that this volume attempts to address. The first question is how does intellectual activity involve seeing society from a distance? The second question centers on whether alienation is only part of the experience of the intellectual in society, the other part being the intellectual's "organic" nature? The third question focuses on how is the duality of alienation and organicism connected to the dialectics of innovation? And finally, from what locations do intellectuals come to exercise a considerable influence on social life and civil society? Bamyeh suggests various modes of exploring these questions, which are addressed in subsequent chapters.

This book is organized into three segments. The first segment is titled "Intellectuals as Modern Vanguard." The first article in this section is by Elizabeth Williams. By examining the life of Nazik al-'Abid, an intellectual and founder of the *Nur al-Fayha* society, Williams explains that al-'Abid urged women to mobilize in defense of the nation. Williams' study reveals that the society's ideas concerning modernity complemented both the religious and social traditions of Syria; and that negotiating between the two when it comes to understanding women's status in society was what eventually led to the construction of the Syrian Arab national community. One can see parallels between the pragmatic approachs the women of the *Nur al-Fayha'* employed during the twentieth century, and the contemporary Muslim women preachers and leaders in Syria, such as Houda al-Habash.

An article by Lital Levy on the edification between sect and nation, introduces Murad Farag as a paradigmatic example of the modern Arab intellectual. Here, Farag appears as an organic intellectual at the peak of *al-nahda*, the modern Arab renaissance. This chapter revisits al-nahda through the perspective of Farag, to determine what the case of a Karaite Jew might be able to reveal about the Arab intellectual as a social reformer. A reading of Farag's journal, *al-Tahdhib*, shows how he adapted al-nahda discourse to a Karaite context, while also illuminating the void between those sublime al-nahda ideals and the social realities they intended to change. Levy illustrates how the *Tahdhib's* appeal to the language of rationalism and progress, and message of tolerance among religions, marked it as a al-nahda periodical.

The last article in this section, by Sanaa Makhlouf, presents Abd al-Rahman al-Kawakibi's legacy. In his book, *Tabai' al-Istibdad*, al-Kawakibi had been searching for an answer to the question of what went wrong? The author argues that al-Kawakibi's writings, enthused the Egyptian influenced Arab awakening and the dissemination of an anti-Ottoman Islamism in the Muslim world. By looking into the secret societies operating in Egypt, Makhlouf argues that the principles and structures of the Muslim Brotherhood and Tablighi Jamaat societies owe much to his ideas. Although the author accurately illustrates al-Kawakibi's influence on subsequent generations, she does not mention the significant impact Jamal al-Din al-Afghani—as well as his disciple Muhammad Abduh—had on al-Kawakibi's views.

The second section of the book is titled "Intellectuals as Defender of Heritage." The first article in this segment is by Steve Tamari, who focuses on the Damascene 'alim 'Abd al-Ghani al-Nabulusi. The author provides a much-needed critique of the excessive modernism in the study of Muslim intellectual history. Tamari suggests scholars should suspend their perception of the "modern" as exceptional and without precedent, in order to recognize that many of the modern features existed among Muslim intellectual in pre-modern times. By exemplifying the life of al-Nabulusi, Tamari challenges scholarship that exhibit bleak image of the intellectual life of the ulama. When analyzing the role of ulama in the contemporary society, there still exists a dismal picture of their intellectual contributions. Tamari's work provides scholars with the essential tools to identify the contemporary modernist binary modes of thought, which constructs modernity against tradition.

An article by Michelangelo Guida examines the founders of Islamism in Republican Turkey. The author argues that while the political and social context of Islamism has changed, its main figures in Turkey today come from conservative religious and political circles that trace their origins to Nacip Fazil Kisakurek and Nurettin Topcu. Guida argues that nowadays, Islamists in Turkey have become powerful elites in the media, politics, and society at large. Their discourse is much more moderate on capitalism, democracy, and relations with minorities. By gradually incorporating nationalism in their Islamist discourse, Kisakurek and Topcu have profoundly contributed to shaping contemporary Islamism in Turkey. Indeed, with the rise of a new generation of Islamist thinkers in the Muslim world, nationalism has became a new component of Islamist political thought, as the Muslim Brotherhood's appeal to the Egyptian national sentiment in the current election illustrates.

The last article in the section comes from Fatma Tutuncu, who discusses Islamist intellectuals and women in Turkey. The author states that Islamist women in Turkey—religiously committed individuals, once marginalized by the state—are now rising as organic intellectuals, involved in sociopolitical matters, shaping public opinion. Tutuncu explains that in Turkey, where political activism and intellectualism have been expressed on the left, and while religion has been articulated on the right, these women navigate the terrain where the principles of egalitarianism, and justice advocated in leftist discourse are articulated in the language of a faith that had been aligned with conservatism. By exploding the binary of the Islamist and the secular, Tutuncu's work demonstrates the fluidity and complexity among the left and the right discourse, where, at times their identities intertwine and at other times are inadvertently, purposefully, or artificially forced apart.

The third and concluding segment of this book is titled "Intellectuals as Migrants," and includes two essays that address how exilic locations could offer opportunities to new possibilities and perspectives. Thomas Brisson examines leading Arab intellectuals in the West. The two figures that are the focus of this chapter, Mohamed Arkoun and Edward Said are used to exemplify Arab intellectuals in exile, and to illustrate how such intellectual positions were shaped. The objective of this chapter is to show that sociological factors such as field structures must be taken into account if one intends to understand how Arab scholars shaped their positions as public intellectuals. Similarly, Nedal al-Mousa's article sheds light on some of the distinctive features of *Mahjar* Arab intellectuals, such as Hisham Sharabi and Halim Barakat. The author suggests that Barakat and Sharabi's common attraction to modernism, especially in its celebration of freedom, independent thinking, and human progress is due to their paramount concern for an Arab modernity. Most intellectuals in exile also share Sharabi and Barakat's vision that citizens in the East and the West should transcend binary thought and reductionist cultural categorizations as a way toward attaining better human understanding, and tolerance. However, the question which remains unaddressed is to what extent can a Muslim intellectual living in exile be a tool for the reform which they are advocating?

Overall, this book is a welcome contribution to the subject, and particularly to the current debates about the role of intellectuals in the Arab Spring. This book is a good source for both graduate and undergraduate students who are interested in understanding the social role of Middle Eastern intellectuals. It is important to consider that Muslim populations have undergone tremendous change since the Arab Spring, which occurred after the publication of this book. The lack of leaders and intellectuals to spearhead the Arab Spring raises the question of whether Muslim societies have reached a post-ideological era in which there is less need for unifying doctrines or the intellectual figures that provide them. **SOG**

Suleyman Elik. Iran-Turkey Relations 1979–2011: Conceptualizing the Dynamics of Politics, Religion and Security in the Middle-Power States. New York, NY: Routledge, 2012. 251 pp. $168.00. ISBN: 978-0415680875. Ebk.: $134.50. ISBN: 978-0203803028.

Suleyman Elik's scholarly research and analysis of Iran–Turkey relations during 1979–2011 is indispensable in understanding the politics, security, regional ambitions and agendas, and respective domestic issues involving these two "middle-power" states. Anoush Ehteshami writes the Foreword, in which he explains how Elik articulates Iran and Turkey's bilateral relations—in essence, describing and analyzing "how and why Tehran and Ankara interact." Elik effectively and analytically explains their use of soft power in the Middle East and North Africa (MENA).

The Introduction provides the historical background of the "Asia Minor and Persia rivalry," while at the same time providing an "Arab buffer" in the region. Elik begins with the 1926 Turkish–Iranian Friendship Agreement, and then he describes the post-1979 Islamic Revolution relations between the two countries. Elik mentions that Iran's current Supreme Leader, Ayatollah Ali Khamenei, is an Azeri Turk, something surely many people do not know. He also highlights historical bilateral economic relations, including the natural gas pipeline and mutual energy cooperation, which have been mutually exclusive to other concerns and issues in each domestic context.

Elik utilizes the theoretical framework of "Middle Power States," comprising domestic, regional, and systemic levels of analysis, emphasizing that this study "contributes to a new definition of middle-power states and also identifies the boundaries of middle-power statecraft in international politics." He further expands on the theoretical framework and the foundations of Iranian–Turkish relations in Chapter 1; and then in Chapter 2, he discusses the two countries' diplomatic crises over the last few decades; Chapter 3 focuses on terrorism in both countries, including the Turkish Hezbollah, the PKK, and respective counter-terrorism efforts and strategies; Chapter 4 talks about post-Cold War Turkish–Iranian security relations, particularly concerning the Kurdish problem. Elik explains the levels of autonomy of both countries' militaries (Turkey's military and Iran's IRGC), and similarities between

Turkey's National Security Council and Iran's Guardian Council. He explains both countries' use of the Palestinian card in domestic and regional politics, but emphasizes that both powers' regional influence is still limited.

Chapter 5 talks about post-Cold War ethno-religious conflicts involving Iran and Turkey; Chapter 6 analyzes post-Cold War Turkish–Iranian energy relations in the Black and the Caspian Sea regions; and Chapter 7 examines both countries' mutual economic relations from 1979 to 2011. These include gas deals, import/export, Turkey's invitation to the G20, and "Turkey's strategic economic opening towards the Middle East, especially Iran." Elik also addresses the impact of economic sanctions on Iran, as well as Turkish–Iranian economic relations; and Chapter 8 re-articulates the theoretical framework of Middle Power-States, explaining the findings of the study, which can be summarized as peaceful coexistence between the two middle power-states—Iran and Turkey. According to Elik, Iranian–Turkish bureaucratic politics have been conducted with "a détente and cordial relationship since 1639." In sum, Turkey and Iran "have all types of multi-balancing and multi-directional capacities."

This book is extremely resourceful for anyone interested in Turkish–Iranian relations, and especially for students, scholars, and researchers who focus on the MENA region. The next edition, if there is one, might consider addressing the complications of Turkish–Iranian relations due to the civil war in Syria.

In the Introduction, Elik reminds us that, "this study is the first comprehensive attempt at exploring Iranian-Turkish relations since 1979." He has done an outstanding job. **HA**

Mohammed M. Aman and Mary Jo Aman, Eds. *Middle East Conflicts & Reforms Vol. 1* **(see review of Vol. 2 under the title** *New Directions in the Middle East.***) Washington, DC: Westphalia Press, 2014. 386 pp. Pbk.: $16.45. ISBN: 978-1941472002.**

The Middle East and Islam have received considerable attention by scholars and media, especially after the global and regional events of September 11, 2001 and the Arab Spring of 2011. This present monograph, edited by Mohammed M. Aman and Mary Jo Aman, is a timely and integrated scholarly work addressing the challenges confronting the Middle East, North Africa, and Islam. Thirty-eight scholars contributed studies investigating their varied topics in depth.

The monograph is based on edited papers presented at two conferences: one the Middle East Dialog (MED) held in Washington, DC on February 21, 2013; and the other, the AMEPPA—Association for Middle Eastern Public Policy and Administration, held at Al-Akhawayn University in Ifrane, Morocco in November, 2012. The monograph consists of two volumes divided into seven parts and is composed of twenty-nine papers. The first volume includes four parts consisting of nineteen papers, while the second volume includes three parts consisting of 10 papers. There is also an extensive bibliography.

The book identifies significant academic and public policy approaches as well as socioeconomic, cultural, and political paradigms that bind together such timely topics as the Arab Spring, democracy, Islam, Islamism, sectarianism, secularism, globalism, modernity, identity formation, social justice, social media, foreign policy, leadership, women's rights, and peace.

Six papers comprise part one, "Democracy, Reform, and the Arab Spring." In his paper, "Democracy and Islamist Violence: Lessons from Post-Mubarak Egypt," Jérôme Drevon argues that the large majority of former Islamist groups in Egypt rejected the use of violence during the post-Mubarak era. Most of the Islamist militants were engaged in the political process and accepted democratic practices. Those who promoted violence in Egypt were marginalized, and so they turned to support the armed violence in Syria.

In her discussion of the socio-political effects of the Arab Awakening/Spring in relation to Turkish identity, Bahar Çevik states that the Turkish experience of the co-existence of democracy, secularism, modernity, and Islam should serve as a model for the Arab Middle East. The collapse of authoritarian Arab regimes and the civil conflict in Syria have enhanced the image of Turkey as a supporter of freedom and democratic reforms.

Concerning the survival of Bashar al-Assad, the dictator of Syria, Radwan Ziadeh depicts the oppressive Syrian intelligence system as a "Wall of Fear" depriving people of their freedom and dignity. In the article, "Iran and the Syria Crisis: Policies, Problems, and Prospects," Maysam Behravesh depicts how Iran utilizes its diplomatic, financial, logistical, and military efforts to save the Syrian Baa'thist regime. Such support alienates Iran and stigmatizes its image in the region.

Addressing the evolution of protest in Jordan, Sarah Tobin discusses different phases of protest, including the failed Arab Spring, indicating the limitations of King Abdullah and the Hashemite rulers to serve as a sufficient "umbrella state," encompassing all populations as equal political, cultural, and economic citizens. Susmit Kumar predicts that the global economic depression and global Islamic fundamentalism will redefine human civilization in the same fashion as the Great Depression and the two World Wars redefined human civilization.

Four papers comprise part two, "Policy and Economic Challenges." Bessma Momani uses the argument of "built environments" to view the lavish buildings in poor

Arab countries, being part of the investment of the Arab Gulf States, as a contributing factor to the Arab Spring.

Kenneth Wise argues that the image of "UAE, Inc." as a successful company has saved it from financial collapse. However, the concept of the "UAE, Inc." implies a sort of reductionism of the society to a mere corporation.

Alan Moss suggests a proposal, akin to the 1950s Pan Arab Union and Arab Federation, to establish a Middle East Union (MEU) comparable in scope to the European Union (EU), modified to meet the needs and aspirations of the people of the Middle East.

Politically oriented ideology has played a negative role in American foreign policy in dealing with the Middle East and Islamic world since, according to Lawrence Davidson, the media and pro-Israel lobbies have managed to fallaciously convince the American public that their lobbying interests are in America's national interests.

Five papers comprise part three, "Civilizational and Sectarian Cooperation and Conflict." Within a positive perspective, Amitai Etzione posits a cross-cultural dialog on social justice as a promising starting point for initiating constructive dialog between the Muslim world and the West. Andrew Wender suggests that derogatory caricatures of sectarianism, especially between Sunni and Shi'a in a country such as Lebanon, should be avoided since sectarianism reflects basic differences in human identity with each demanding respect.

The relation between Egyptian Copts and Muslims, during and after the Arab Spring, is addressed by Paul Rowe. There has been a change from a stable elite partnership with the hierarchy of the Coptic Orthodox Church, established by the Mubarak regime, to a pluralist model of citizenship in which individual Copts represent their own interests.

Zia and Hameed focus on the violent conflict in tribal areas of Pakistan and suggest the establishment of democratic governance structures with indigenous representatives and civil society actors. In another article, Behravesh provides an historical analysis of Iranian–British relations, as they existed during the reigns of Margaret Thatcher and the Ayatollah Khomeini, emphasizing the impact of their chilled relations on present-day foreign policies.

Four papers comprise part four, "MENA Women's Rights: Triumphs and Setbacks." The paper by Malmström and Hellstrand explains how Egyptian feminists navigate between various players: the global donor community, "western feminism," Egyptians in general, and the new state/political Islam after the uprisings. Egyptian feminists view the problem as related to the new state's incorrect interpretations of Islam and the global donor community's or Western feminism's obsession with Islam. Alessandra Gonzále discusses a number of common points of interest between women in leadership in the Arab Gulf and Latin America. She concludes that in both settings there is a resurgence of "traditional values" rhetoric among younger feminist activists who attempt to incorporate their traditional-religious beliefs, along with the pragmatic concerns of economic independence for women and due process in civil legal proceedings.

It seems that extreme religious fundamentalism obstructs women's full emancipation. This theme is discussed by Michal Allon who focuses on the phenomenon of the exclusion of women from the public sphere in Israel due to the influence of Orthodox-Jewish communities. The paradox here is that Israel claims to be a democratic country. The author suggests that religion and state should be separate to improve the lives of women of all faiths and all ethnic groups.

Bremer and Al-Talliawi, in their study of gender and leadership style in the Middle East with a special focus on Egypt's civil service, conclude that there are no statistically significant differences between men and women in managerial positions and leadership styles.

All in all, the monograph is a unique and compelling effort in the assessment of the future of the Middle East. The book will enhance the scholarship of the Middle East and help in understanding the ability of political systems, government and nongovernment or civil society, in managing current challenges confronting the region. The book is a welcome contribution to Middle East studies, scholarship of Islam, political science, and conflict management inquiries. **ESA**

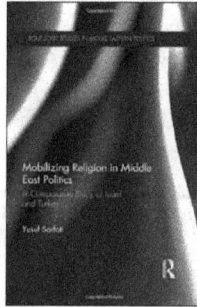

Yusuf Sarfati. *Mobilizing Religion in Middle East Politics: A Comparative Study of Israel and Turkey.* **New York, NY: Routledge, 2014. (Routledge Studies in Middle Eastern Politics) 241 pp. $145.00. ISBN: 978-0415540162.**

In this book, Yusuf Sarfati recounts the recent history of two religiopolitical parties in two Middle Eastern democracies: Israel and Turkey. Sarfati analyzes the electoral success of the movements, focusing on the social, economic, and political conditions which facilitated their rise, the growth of their electoral popular base, and their influence on the democratic governance of their respective countries.

It has long been recognized by scholars that religion plays a powerful role in politics. Social theorists, who had predicted an inevitable and irreversible process of secularization with the socioeconomic modernization of societies, have been proven wrong in recent decades by the emergence of religiopolitical movements in democracies worldwide. These developments have given rise to a myriad of scholarly attempts to identify the causes of these surges in religious political activity and their effect on modern democracies.

Sarfati's research is well within this tradition, but this book is unique in its comparative approach. The author compares and contrasts two countries whose political governance was founded on secular nationalist ideologies—Zionism in Israel and Kemalism in Turkey—in an attempt to understand the parallel electoral success of religious parties in them. The two parties which Sarfati studies are the *Shas* movement in Israel, and the *National Outlook Movement* (NOM) in Turkey. Both have become influential social movements that were able to mobilize great multitudes. Moreover, they have emerged as significant political players, which have to be reckoned with by any coalition government.

The author defines a religious party as "a political party that takes religion as a reference point for its policy proposals to address the major political problems of its country." This definition is flexible enough to allow the inclusion of the parties in question, both in Turkey, which is constitutionally defined as a secular republic, and in the State of Israel, which allows explicitly religious parties to operate and act in the political arena.

In the Introduction, the author lays the historical and theoretical foundation of his research, and lists the questions he aims to address, namely: Why does the electoral strength of religiopolitical actors increase in democratic settings? What are the mechanisms of political mobilization used by religiopolitical actors? What factors facilitate the success of religious parties in democratic politics? And finally: What is the effect of the increasing power of religiopolitical actors on democratic governance and stability? In Chapter Two, the author defines key terms used in the study, and lays out the rationale for a comparative research design. The subsequent chapters tell the history of the socio-cultural schism between Ashkenazim (Jews of European origin) and Sepharadim (Jews from the Middle East and North Africa) in Israel, and between the urban center and the periphery in Turkey. This is followed by an in depth description of the rise to political power of the Shas party in Israel and the National Outlook Movement in Turkey. The author explains how the Shas expanded its popular base in Israel through its message of empowerment of underprivileged sectors of the population. Similarly, the National Outlook Movement activists in Turkey employed various strategies to garner the support of marginalized and excluded sectors around a message of religious unity. The concluding chapter discusses the ways in which the religious movements in the two countries have utilized the education systems in their respective countries to mobilize party activists and broaden their political popular base. The book ends with an extensive bibliography and an index of names, terms, tables and figures, and foreign words.

Sarfati explains the rationale behind choosing these two particular movements and these two particular countries for his research. He argues that Israel and Turkey are dramatically different on several political, cultural, economic, and institutional levels. Opting for a comparative analysis rather than the more common single case study model allows him to control for alternative explanations and make causal inferences which would be impossible in a treatment of each case as an "exceptional case." Moreover, by comparing political Islam with a Judaic movement, the author strives to counter essentialist and Orientalist theorization, and to study religion and culture in a political context.

Sarfati draws on insight from the Social Movement Theory (SMT) to explain the religiopolitical mobilization in both Israel and Turkey. The political opportunity structure (POS) model frames the religious mobilization as a consequence of a historical sociocultural divide in these two Middle Eastern countries, which enhanced the grievances of Sepharadim and pious Muslims, respectively.

Sarfati parallels the schism between the Ashkenazi and Sepharadi population in Israel to that between the center and the periphery in Turkey. These divides became politicized by processes of socioeconomic change, which in turn heightened the frustrations of the lower classes. The incorporation of religious parties into coalition governments in both countries gave these parties access to state cultural and material resources, and enabled them to create patronage networks and employment opportunities for their activists. Sarfati's main conclusion is that the interaction between political opportunity structures, framing processes and social networks explains the successful religiopolitical mobilization in Israel and in Turkey over the past two decades.

The author discusses at length complex relationships between religion and democracy. On the one hand, religiopolitical actors contribute to the empowerment of marginalized segments of the population; but on the other hand, their practice sometimes undermines liberal-democratic political culture. In both democracies in question there has been an erosion of civil discourse and an undermining of liberal-democratic political culture, as a result of the exclusionary and abrasive language used by some religious leaders, especially toward "nonbelievers." One oversight in Sarfati's analyses is the gender-related impact of the rise of religiopolitical parties. The exclusionary effect of the rise of such parties on women is largely overlooked. Some religious parties (e.g., the Shas in Israel) officially exclude women from candidacy to the legislature, thereby denying them equal representation. The rise to power of such parties can hardly be said to advance democracy. It seems to me that ignoring the effect of any social development on half the population is an unfortunate omission. The author may have considered this issue to be outside the scope of his research.

The author bases his thesis on extensive field work in both Israel and Turkey. In his long visits to these countries, he interviewed numerous political activists, government officials, and graduates and educators of religious institutions. He also studied and analyzed newspaper archives as well as ample secondary literature on both countries.

The author's deep familiarity with both countries and the languages spoken in them afforded him first-hand access to sources and people whose opinions, information, and insights enrich this research and make it an interesting read as well as an impressive scholarly edition to the literature on the Middle East. Sarfati demonstrates impressive knowledge and scholarship of the political and historical subject of his research. This book is an important step forward in understanding one of the most prominent and influential socio-political phenomena today. The ongoing rise of religious parties and social movements worldwide makes Sarfati's analysis especially pertinent, as there is little doubt that the future of human society depends on how these developments play out. **MLA**

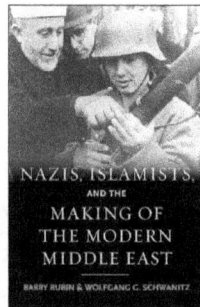

Barry Rubin and Wolfgang G. Schwanitz. *Nazis, Islamists and the Making of the Modern Middle East.* **New Haven, CT: Yale University Press, 2014. 360 pp. $24.26. ISBN: 978-0300140903. Ebk: 10593 KB. 361 pp. $16.99.**

Analysts of the career of the late Palestinian Mufti, Hajj Amin al-Hussaini, are divided into two groups about one of the most important parts of his legacy—his cooperation with Nazi Germany during World War II. Supporters of the Mufti claim that this was merely a matter of "the enemy of my enemy is my friend"—such as U.S. cooperation with the Soviet Union during World War II—since Nazi Germany was an enemy of Britain, as well as holding the League of Nations Mandate over Palestine and the Jews. Scholars taking a negative view of the Mufti's collaboration with the Nazis argue that he was an active and willing participant in the Nazi genocide against the Jews. In his basically positive, though not uncritical study of the Mufti *The Mufti of Jerusalem* (New York: Columbia University Press, 1988), Philip Mattar concludes his chapter on this controversial question, with the following assertion:

Neither Zionist accusations nor Arab Justifications have enhanced our understanding of the extent of the Mufti's cooperation with the Nazis, largely because the apparent purpose for studies about his years in Germany are an extension of the Arab-Israeli propaganda war. Only a thorough and nonpartisan study, based on captured German documents, could elucidate the role of the Mufti in Germany (p. 107).

It is just such a study, written by the late Barry Rubin and Wolfgang G. Schwanitz that provides an answer to Mattar's call for an archive-based study of the Mufti's role in Germany, and the book is a damning indictment of the Mufti's collaboration with the Nazis. Drawing heavily on the German archives, and the Mufti's archives captured by the United States at the end of World War II, the book goes into great detail about the Mufti's work with the Nazis, from recruiting Muslims in the Balkans and Soviet Union for service in the German Army (including SS units), to serving as a major Nazi propaganda agent to try to get the Arabs of the Middle East to rise up against the British, to urging the Nazis not to allow any Jews, including Jewish children, to leave German-controlled Europe, thus ensuring their deaths in Nazi extermination camps.

There are a number of new insights that the authors bring to light. The first is the continuity of the German academics and diplomats who worked on the Middle East in World Wars I and II—and they also point out that many of the World War II diplomats, a large number of whom were Nazis, served in the West German diplomatic service after the war, to say nothing of Kurt Kiesinger who became West German Chancellor in 1966 and served until 1969. The authors also have a chapter in their book titled "The Arab States' Useful Nazis" which gives a detailed list of the Nazi war criminals who escaped to the Middle East and served in Egypt and Syria after the war, highlighting the post-war careers of Alois Brunner and Johann von Leers. Second, the authors also note a number of parallels in German policy regarding the Middle East during both wars. Thus, there was an effort in both wars to stir up Muslim/Arab revolts against the British and French (although in World War II, the Germans were more sensitive to the needs of Vichy France in the early stages of the war); in both wars Germany supported a racist policy against ethnic minorities. Thus in World War I, Germany supported a Jihad against the British, French and Russians that led to the murder of a million Armenians by the Ottoman Turks, while in World War II, Germany carried out its own extermination of the Jews. Other parallels include the use of charismatic Muslim personalities such as the Mufti to stir up revolt in the Arab and Muslim worlds; a misunderstanding of the nature of Muslim and Arab politics by minimizing the differences among the various Muslim and Arab groups, and a lack of appreciation of the fact that only battlefield success would convince most Arabs to join Germany (King Ibn-Saud of Saudi Arabia being one of the fence-sitters waiting to see who would win the war) (p. 126). Third, the authors go into detail in describing the convoluted politics in the Middle East in the aftermath of World War I, noting how al-Hussaini served both the British and the French at a time when relations between them were strained. Indeed, the authors argue that the reason for al-Hussaini's appointment as Mufti of the Palestinian Arabs was due to his service to the British during World War I, raising Arab troops for the anti-Ottoman revolt (p. 66). The authors also cite the efforts of the French to undermine the position of the British among Middle East Muslims noting that Francois Picot (of Sykes-Picot fame—or infamy—depending on your point of view) told a group of Muslims in Jerusalem in 1919 that the British "had promised Palestine to Zionism," but staunchly Catholic France "would not let the land of Jesus go to those who crucified Him" (p. 62).

Perhaps the major strength of the book is its detailed description of the Mufti's aid to the Nazis during World War II. The authors list the groups of Central Asian and Balkan Muslims who served the Nazis during the war (p. 149), a number of whom participated in the genocide of Jewish communities in Eastern Europe. According to the authors, 53,000 men (equal to four German divisions) had been recruited, and the Mufti established institutes in Dresden and Goben to train Muslim chaplains for these units, with the graduates given the rank of captain in the SS (p. 149). Hatred of the Jews was a central part of the curriculum of the two institutes and a major theme of the al-Hussaini-controlled radio station, The Voice of the Free Arabs, which regularly broadcast to the Middle East calling on Arabs to kill the Jews. Evidence is also presented of the close relationship between the Mufti and Heinrich Himmler, the leader of the SS, and an architect of the Holocaust. Indeed, the Mufti, after visiting a concentration camp and being told by Himmler that the Germans had already exterminated three million Jews, noted that Himmler was "an understanding, generous and energetic man." The Mufti also had close ties with Hitler and Adolph Eichmann, and, following the war when Eichmann had escaped to Argentina, the Mufti gave money to Eichmann's wife, so she and their three children could join him in Argentina (p. 207).

One of the Mufti's aides, who was with him with the Nazis, was Abd al-Rahman Azzam, who became the first secretary general of the Arab league. When, at the start of the fighting between Arabs and Jews in Palestine in the late 1947, Azzam told a news conference, "This will be a war of extermination, and a momentous massacre, which will be spoken of like the Mongolian massacres and the Crusades" (p. 246). What he no doubt had in mind were the massacres perpetrated upon the Jews by the Nazis.

While I am in agreement with much of what was written in the book, I think the authors go a bit too far when they argue:

"The Middle East's future was thus determined starting in the 1930s when radicals set guidelines, and was made inevitable by their taking power in the 1950s and holding onto it in one form or another down to the present day. The basic approach of al-Hussaini and his comrades continued through the careers of such leaders as Abd an-Nasir, Arafat, the al-Assad family, al-Qaddafi, Saddam Hussain, and bin-Laden, as well as with Iranian Islamists like Khomeini and Mahmud Ahmadinejad." (p. 92)

Essentially, the authors argue that the combination of radicalism and unwillingness to compromise established by the Mufti remained the path of governance and opposition until today. One could argue, however, that the differences among the leaders mentioned outweigh their similarities. In addition, Hafiz al-Assad, and the Ayatollah Khomeini were indeed ready to make compromises when the situation dictated, and so were, to a lesser degree, al-Qaddafi and Arafat. This disagreement aside, I think the authors have written an excellent book and I think it will become the basic reference for students of the Mufti's policies during World War II. **ROF**

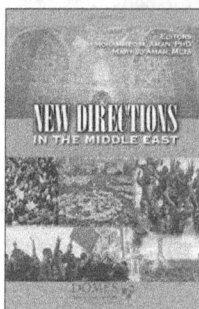

Mohammed M. Aman and Mary Jo Aman, Eds. *New Directions in the Middle East Vol. 2* **(see Vol. 1 under the title** *Middle East Conflicts & Reforms***). Washington, DC: Westphalia Press, 2014. 264 pp. Pbk.: $14.75. ISBN: 978-1941472019.**

The Middle East and Islam have received considerable attention by scholars and media especially after the global and regional events of September 11, 2001 and the Arab Spring of 2011. This present monograph, edited by Mohammed M. Aman and Mary Jo Aman, is a timely and integrated scholarly work addressing the challenges confronting the Middle East, North Africa and Islam. Thirty-eight scholars contributed studies investigating their varied topics in depth.

The monograph is based on edited papers presented at two conferences: one the Middle East Dialog (MED) held in Washington, D.C. on February 21, 2013; and the other, the AMEPPA (Association for Middle Eastern Public Policy and Administration), held at Al-Akhawayn University in Ifrane, Morocco in November, 2012. The monograph consists of two volumes divided into seven parts and is composed of 29 papers. The first volume includes four parts consisting of 19 papers, while the second volume includes three parts consisting of 10 papers. There is also an extensive bibliography.

The book identifies significant academic and public policy approaches as well as socioeconomic, cultural, and political paradigms that bind together such timely topics as the Arab Spring, democracy, Islam, Islamism, sectarianism, secularism, globalism, modernity, identity formation, social justice, social media, foreign policy, leadership, women's rights, and peace.

The three papers dealing with part five "Israel/Palestine Divide" do not offer any insight regarding Israel's opposition to peace negotiations with the Palestinians. Three studies constitute part six, "Communication, Media, and the Arab Awakening." Aman and Jayroe examine the impact of the new information, the Internet, telecommunication, and social media on events preceding and following the Arab

Spring. These new technologies have been effective means in mobilizing and organizing grassroots' protests against oppressive dictators and their regimes. Dina Wafa also highlights the crucial role played by the media in Egypt after the January 25th Revolution and how the state-controlled media, supporting the Mubarak regime, failed to gain public trust. The role of social media in the Arab Spring has been effectively discussed, but the broader impact of cyber-media in defining and redefining Middle East identities needs more ethnographic research.

Ivan Sheehan's study of an Iranian opposition group (Mujahedin-e Khalq) sheds light on the complex relationship between activists, the government, and the media; and how the opposition group promoted its frames in the opinion sections of major world news publications during the period of 2003–12.

Five articles appear in part seven, "Management and Conflict Resolution." Peter Mameli shows how the current effects of the Arab Spring highlight the significance of leadership, and management and public administration in MENA countries. He posits that continuous training in leadership and public administration is needed to help achieve change, learn new technologies, and remain active in engaging the public as honest players.

Slaoui-Zirpins discusses theories of decentralization and interest mediation aimed at addressing the issue of decentralization in the MENA region with a specific example illustrating economic policy for the promotion of offshore services in Fez, Morocco. He attempts to explain the management of formal and informal processes in the interactions within the bureaucracy and between the state, civil society, the market, and citizens.

Focusing on the nation-state of Iraq, Alexander Dawoody discusses the impact of external forces on the structure of government administration. For instance, during the Baa'th regime, Sunni Arab tribes dominated the government apparatus, but after the U.S. occupation (2013), Shi'a and Kurds dominated the government at the expense of the Sunni. The state collapsed due to the lack of administrative experience in the new governing groups.

El-Ghandour, Hatem, Bissat, and Rihan, in their discussion of building capacities in public financial management in a post-conflict country, highlight the positive role that a leading training institution can play in post-conflict reconstruction.

Finally, Dawoody and Marks suggest adapting complexity paradigms in observing the complex nature of the Middle East. They argue that prediction and a subsequent public policy bent on control do not yield good solutions.

All in all, the monograph is a unique and compelling effort in the assessment of the future of the Middle East. The book will enhance the scholarship of the Middle East and help in understanding the ability of political systems, government and nongovernment or civil society, in managing current challenges confronting the region. The book is a welcome contribution to Middle East studies, scholarship of Islam, political science, and conflict management inquiries. **ESA**

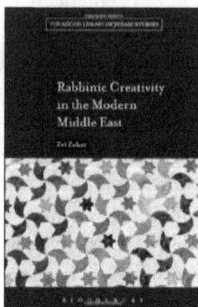

Zvi Zohar. *Rabbinic Creativity in the Modern Middle East.* New York, NY: Bloomsbury Academic, 2013. 399 pp. $42.95. ISBN: 978-1441133298.

The following article will attest to the author's thesis in which, it is argued, that Sephardi Judaism's challenge of modernity was not only a Western phenomenon, but was also found in the Middle East. The countries in which Zvi Zohar focuses on are Iraq, Syria, and Egypt, and as such, the book is divided into those three sections, respectively, as well as a fourth part which is the conclusion. It is recommended that anyone who begins to read this book be familiar with Judaic terms such as *Ashkenaz*, *Hassidim*, *Misnagdim*, *Halakha*, and other Judaic terms which deal with the respective religious thought and ideologies.

This book was originally written in Hebrew over a decade ago and has now been translated by the author and his appointed reviewers. Dr. Zohar himself states in the Introduction of the book that while translating his book, he had to re-frame his questions and responses since once translated, they made no sense in English. This translated and reviewed version of *Rabbinic Creativity...*, however, is certainly an intriguing work which sheds light on the oriental aspect of Judaism beginning in the late nineteenth century and up until the mid-twentieth century.

In his argument, Dr. Zohar poses the issue that much of what is known of rabbinical responses to modernism is based on the European Ashkeanzic point of focus. In his work, Dr. Zohar introduces a variety of responses to the issue of modernity in the Judaic Sephardi communities of the Middle East, thus introducing the fact that Judaic communities of Europe and the Middle East were divided by thought and ideology based on their responses to the rising issues of the modern world.

The book is divided into three major sections: Iraq, Syria, and Egypt. Dr. Zohar notes that in the "Egypt" section he includes information on rabbinical responses in Jerusalem. Dr. Zohar also states he plans to write a book primarily focused on the rabbinical responses to modernism from Jerusalem.

Dr. Zohar begins his first chapter with a discussion of the respected Iraqi Rabbi, 'Abdallah Somekh. During the time in which Rabbi Somekh was living in Iraq, it was known as Babylon and so it must be noted that Dr. Zohar uses Babylon and

Iraq interchangeably throughout the entire section. Dr. Zohar believes that Rabbi Somekh had the greatest impact on Babylonian Jewry in and out of Iraq; another country was India. As Dr. Zohar develops the chapter he begins to note a few of the areas in which Somekh has influence. Zohar attributes this influence on India based on the fact that Iraqi Jews immigrated to the country, but keept in contact with Rabbi Somekh.

Now, on the question of modernity in the Middle East, Dr. Zohar begins to give information on questions that were raised by Babylonian Jews in both Iraq and India. Modernity—in as much as it relates to technology and so on—began to be introduced under the Ottoman Empire during the *Tanzimat* (Reformation) period. These changes in society continued as the European powers such as England begin to make their way through India.

The rapidly changing Judaic societies in Iraq and India quickly began to seem stagnant as the ideologies of Ashkeanzic Jews began to threaten the loss of Judaism through these reforms and the rise of modernity. Ashkeanzic Jews of Europe had taken a critical approach to modernity as they adopted the idea of "The New is forbidden by the Torah." This stagnated Judaic society in a growing modern world in Europe and it seemed that it might reach the Middle East. Unlike the Ashkeanzic Jews of Europe, the Jews in the Middle East or the Orient were Sephardic Jews. The Sephardic Jews differed in practice and tradition to the Ashkeanzic and most importantly they had a different experience.

With all of this in mind, Dr. Zohar gives Rabbi Somekh's standpoint on the rise of modernity in both Iraq and India. The question of modernity arose due to Jews wanting to keep *Halakhic* traditions, some of the issues that arose dealt with *Shabbat* and its implications on travel and distance, water for *mikveh*, and so on. Along with a few other issues, Dr. Zohar is able to give a synopsis of Rabbi Somekh's answers and reasoning on the issues that arose.

The rest of the section on Iraq presents a new issue based on how Sephardic Jews were influenced by Ashkeanzic Rabbinical literature and its extent on the influence of Sephardi Rabbis. The idea arises that if a Sephardi reads of the Ashkeanzic literature, the Rabbi can no longer be a Sephardi; however, Dr. Zohar makes the simple statement that reading of Ashkeanzic literature did not keep a Rabbi from being Sephardi, it simply gave him a second glance at the *Torah*. At the end of Chapter 3, he says "…such acquaintance makes possible exposure to a variety of halakhic opinions, exposure to 'something new, or a new deduction that had escaped the attention' of the current decisor and an increased depth of understanding of the issues under discussion ('for thanks to this perusal, his understanding of the issue at hand would increase')" (p. 89).

The following section is devoted to Syria. Dr. Zohar opens the chapter by presenting the fourth chapter as the extremism of the Sephardi Halakhic communities, particularly in Aleppo. Dr. Zohar quotes Eli Penso's 1938 letter to the director of AIU, "…the city of Aleppo… lacked the opportunity to be exposed to the treasures of European culture... Egoism, indifference, greed, superstitions of various types, outdated customs and religious fanaticism—all these are alive and well in this community" (pp. 93-94). While the Jews of Aleppo saw themselves as being a "Holy Community" that withstood the pressures of modernity, others saw them as backwards, i.e., Eli Penso.

Zohar does agree that the case of Aleppo Jewry is one of extremism and radical religiosity; however the final two chapters of the section include two Syrian Rabbis who are the exception to this idea of radical religiosity. The fifth chapter of the book is dedicated to Rabbi Yitzhak Dayyan and the sixth to Rabbi Shaul-Matloub 'Abadi and their respective views of modernity in the Syrian context.

The third section of the book, Egypt, is opened by the seventh chapter which is an introduction to Rabbi Israel Moshe Hazan and his work, *Sheerit ha-Hahala*. The issue arises in that European Jews saw themselves as superior to Oriental Jews because they saw the Orient as undeveloped and lacking in technology. The seventh chapter presents Rabbi Hazan's defense for Oriental Jewry and his defense of the issue of language, especially Arabic.

The eighth chapter of the book deals with the overarching transformation of Egyptian society, both Arabic and Jewish, after the eighteenth century occupation by the French. This began, according to Dr. Zohar, the rise of secularization in Egyptian Jewry, which followed the example of secularization form German Jewry.

The ninth chapter of the book presents one of the responses to the development of secularization in Egypt, the role of the Synagogue. Dr. Zohar presents two challenges that arose: (1) "dealing with the challenge posed by customs and popular religious activities common among the indigenous Jews of Egypt;" and (2) "[a] mode of action [that] was to expand the range of religious activities performed in the synagogue" (p. 270). Dr. Zohar concludes this chapter by stating:

The political-social situation that included modern-secular influence on life in Egypt and that subsequently caused a dilution of the sacral dimension of in the daily lives of members of the Jewish community was also that which led the rabbis of the community to restructure the role of the synagogue in order to fill the 'sacral vacuum' created by the secularization of daily life. (p. 299)

As secularization and other challenges arose in Egypt, other Rabbis rose to fill the sacral vacuum. In Chapter 10, Dr. Zohar discusses Rabbi Refael Aharon Ben-Shim'on and his response to a suicide epidemic primarily in the city of Cairo. Chapter 11 deals with rabbinical responses to marriage, particularly the marriage between Karaites and Rabbanite Jews.

The twelfth and final chapter is the most interesting of all. The final sentence brings together the entire book and the basic understanding of modernity in oriental Sephardi Jewry:

The Sephardic classical cultural tradition—for which the ideal Jew is one who integrates a knowledge of the Jewish Torah literature with knowledge of the best of general culture and who reads the Torah in light of insights drawn from his holistic understanding of reality—is what enable Sephardic halakhic scholars to distinguish among different levels of permanence within halakah. (p. 368)

This book is intriguing and brings to light the oriental Sephardic thought and ideologies of the eighteenth through early twentieth centuries. To any reader who is interested in an Oriental or a Sephardic point of view in Judaism and modernism, this is a valuable resource that opens a window to the past and a simple and interesting read for all readers. **MS**

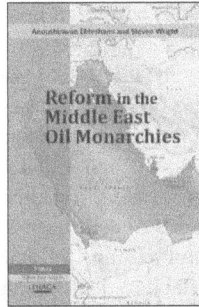

Anoushiravan Ehteshami and Steven Wright, Eds. *Reform in the Middle East Oil Monarchies.* **Reading, UK: Ithaca Press, 2008. 320pp. $66.45. ISBN: 978-0863723230. Pbk: 2011. 320 pp. $19.18. ISBN: 978-0863724145. Ebk: 2011. 320pp. 1872 KB. $8.99.**

We are encouraged to avoid judging a book by its cover. This dictum is no more apt than with *Reform in the Middle East Oil Monarchies*. The work is broadly concerned with contemporary economic and political liberalization in the monarchies of the Arabian/Persian Gulf. But the map on the front cover of the book erroneously includes Iraq in this category, despite the fact that Iraq has not been a monarchy since the 1950s and, even though it is frequently mentioned, no chapter in the volume is devoted to it. Even so, the contents of this book—the result of a conference held at Durham University in 2005—represent a cogent and serious attempt to tackle the issues of reform in the Gulf, and, although recent events have overtaken some of the discussion in the text, the analysis remains relevant.

The book is divided into three sections. Part one consists of three chapters and aims to place reform in its theoretical and historical context. In Chapter 1, Gerd Nonnerman reminds us that liberalization and democratization are distinct, and one need not follow the other. He notes that economic growth and the development of civil society are unlikely to be sufficient to promote democratization in the Gulf. He concludes that the immense capacity of the Gulf States to distribute rents to their populations is likely to work against democratization; this despite the emergence of constraints to rentierism such as the rules of World Trade Organization (WTO), to which all Gulf monarchies now belong. In Chapter 2, and with the backdrop of the UK/US invasion of Iraq, former UK government minister Baroness Symons attempts to reconcile two potentially contradictory positions, namely, that human rights are fundamental and universal, and preferably authentic and indigenous rather than Western impositions. In Chapter 3, Behgat Korany tackles the issue of Islam and democracy. The chapter is surprisingly incoherent: it begins with a comparison of the "democratic deficit" between Egypt and Iraq and abruptly transitions to a brief, under-developed treatment—more an assertion than a demonstration—of the basic compatibility of democracy and Islam. The approach marginalizes pertinent scholarship and evidence that could have been used to convincingly illustrate this crucial point.

Part 2 of the book presents individual case studies and consists of seven chapters. In Chapter 4, Neil Quilliam posits that the aim of political liberalization in Bahrain has been to consolidate the power of the ruling family, and (interestingly, given the events since his writing) he argues that the reforms have raised expectation to such an extent that a retreat is virtually unimaginable without a serious rupture. Along similar lines, Ahmed Abdelkareem Saif, in Chapter 5, predicts that limited, U.S.-championed political reforms in Qatar (and the region generally) are unlikely to deliver the regional stability that the United States seeks. Saif makes a compelling point about Islam and democracy; he argues that it is not Islam that is incompatible with democratization, but the extant tribal social structure, where the "mode of production" is associated with an oil-exporting economy and the "mode of consumption" connected to oil-funded imports. In Chapter 6, Sayyid Badr Bin Sa'ud Al-Busaidi, Oman's Deputy Foreign Minister, explains that the course of his country's democratic development is not pre-determined by a Western blueprint but is to be shaped by homegrown needs and priorities, echoing Symons.

The theme of local specificity stands in contrast to Rodney Wilson's analysis of economic reform in Saudi Arabia in Chapter 7, which illustrates how Saudi Arabia implemented the key Washington Consensus precepts that were required for it to join the WTO, eroding the state's capacity to allocate largesse in the process. On the other hand, Wilson also shows in this highly instructive chapter how Saudi Arabia has resisted International Monetary Fund (IMF) calls to diversify revenues through taxation. In Chapter 8, Christopher Davidson argues that economic reforms in Dubai, including the setting up of free trade zones and real estate restructurings, have facilitated economic diversification away from oil and encouraged foreign investment. This is a bold statement, even if one considers the euphoria that use to surround Dubai's economic development strategy and especially as Davidson does not consider other strategies that might have had similar, if not better, results. In Chapter 9, Emma Murphy presents a nuanced study of the effects of information technology on political transformation. In contrast to the sometimes exaggerated narrative concerning the role of technology in the Arab Spring, Murphy, writing well before the recent events, offers us a sober reminder that that new technology in the hands of the state might work to strengthen authoritarianism. In general, however, she tends to view new technologies as a small net positive for democratization. In Chapter 10, Mohammad Al Rumaihi attempts to anticipate the types of reform that might occur in the region.

Part 3 of the book contains two chapters that place reform in the Gulf monarchies in its geopolitical and international context. As of the mid-2000s, Steven Wright, in Chapter 11, detects a change in U.S. policy toward the Gulf, away from upholding the *status quo* and in the direction of political reform, a synthesis of *Wilsonian and Jacksonian* trends in U.S. foreign policy. Wright does not consider that the new policy might be an essentially Jacksonian defense of U.S. interests presented in a more appealing Wilsonian narrative of rights and freedoms, without which the policy could not be implemented. Finally, in Chapter 12, Mahjoob Zweiri, critically contrasts the reforms of Khatami's Iran with those in Saudi Arabia.

A number of themes run through the various articles in this book. There is a generally guarded view of reform and deep skepticism that it provides a clear or reliable roadmap to democracy. Indeed, Quilliam's article implies that the limited liberalization in Bahrain was designed to buttress the ruling autocracy.

There is also repeated reference in many of the articles of the book to the rentier state theory to explain authoritarianism: oil revenues provide the resources to buy off or repress social opposition and reduce the need to tax, enhancing the autonomy of the state. However, the line of causation that is invoked is essentially unidirectional and does not allow for the possibility that oil revenues have the opposite effect; for example, that they generate expectations (reasonable or otherwise) that constrain the state in its dealings with society.

The topic of unemployment (or underemployment) of local labor, which a number of articles talk about, underlines how oil wealth can warp expectations and arguably reduce state autonomy. The issue, fundamentally, in these oil monarchies is not stagnant labor demand (there are millions of expatriate workers in these countries) and (less and less) the low skills set of indigenous labor force, but that oil wealth has created a strong preference, on the part of the local population, for comfortable, well-paid, and prestigious jobs. Quotas, state subsidies (designed to encourage the private sector to hire more expensive local labor) and (or) expanded government employment are then pursued by the state in response to the public demand for more (and high-status) jobs.

Be that as it may, we are left to wonder how precisely the Washington Consensus reforms that have been applied in the Gulf (and the subject of a considerable part of the book) might enhance employment creation for indigenous labor, without radical and destabilizing departures from established aspirations (that are implied in wage cuts). Given the importance, vis-à-vis social stability, which is often attached to employment creation, the omission is an important one. **BY**

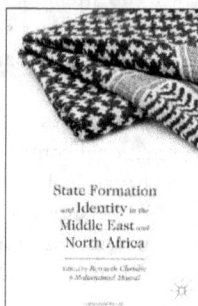

Kenneth Christie and Mohammad Masad, Eds. *State Formation and Identity in the Middle East and North Africa*. New York, NY: Palgrave Macmillan, 2013. 212 pp. ISBN: 978-1137369598.

A region as volatile and unstable as the Middle East is fertile ground for books dealing with questions such as state formation, identity, and stability. The book at hand is a compilation of papers presented at the Thirteenth Mediterranean meeting in Montecatini Terme, Italy, between March 21 and 24, 2012. The conference was held in the shadow of the Arab Spring and its inevitable implications over the question of state formation and identity in the Middle East. It is surprising, and somewhat disappointing, that countries such as Syria and Libya, which at the time of the conference, were engulfed in civil wars which threatened their continuing unity, were not covered, nor was Yemen, or Iraq, a country struggling with exactly the same questions which form the basis of this book. This is a notable editorial omission, yet not one which, in itself, is enough to depreciate the value of the book and its eight chapters.

On February 27, 2013, the veteran American diplomat and peace negotiator, Aaron David Miller published an article in the online edition of *Foreign Policy*, which dealt with these exact questions, a piece questioning the stability of the institution of the Arab State, a piece which triggered ferocious reactions. Strong reaction followed, examples being that of the blog Karl reMarks on February 28, 2013, and Issandr el-Amrani, in the noted blog the Arabist, who attacked Miller. There was a tone of anger and insult in these comments which was more than a reminder of Edward Sa'id's attack on Orientalism, which he also displayed when debating Samuel Huntington's theory of the "Clash of Civilizations."

The Arab Spring brought to the fore the question of statehood in the Middle East, in a way which cannot be dismissed with expressions of high emotions. When hundreds of thousands of people are killed in sectarian wars, when states disintegrate along sectarian lines, when Arab writers refer to the Sushi War (Sunnis vs. Shi'a) in the Middle East (Hassaballa, *The American Conservative*, 2011), it is inevitable that a serious question is raised over long-held perceptions regarding political stability in the Arab world, or lack thereof.

Another criticism of this book is the fact that there is no real debate about the issues involving sectarianism, tribalism, state existence, and stability. The book concludes that, while there are difficulties, the overall picture indicates that the institution of the Arab state prevails over the divisive forces of sectarianism and tribalism. It may prove to be the case, but a serious discussion about this point of contention is lacking.

Tribalism is one of the terms that the disciples of Sa'id liked to hate. The question was well covered in a book published 21 years ago titled *Tribes and State Formation in the Middle East* (Khoury and Kostiner, Eds, 1991). At least one article in this book under review deals with it, referring to Saudi Arabia, and the role of the Ikhwan Movement, and the conclusion is that "if the taming of tribalism, has been the winning element of Middle Eastern monarchies" (p. 105), then Saudi Arabia has to be considered a story of success. That is a plausible explanation, but it is also plausible to suggest another explanation—that tribal loyalty is a formidable source of identity, and when augmented by religious ideology (Wahhabism) and so much oil money, it creates conditions conducive for internal stability.

But then, what about those countries, where there are deep sectarian cleavages? The book deals with one of them, Lebanon, referring to the political alliance between the Maronite faction led by General Michel Awn and the Shi'a Hezbollah, and it seems to offer a somewhat optimistic view about the weakened sectarian tensions in Lebanon. When the conference took place, it became clear that sectarian tensions in Lebanon were on the rise, though more between the Sunnis and the Shi'a, constituting another manifestation of the Sushi War. Was this paper about Lebanon motivated by the overall sense one gets when reading this book—that Arab statehood has weathered the storm of the Arab Spring—or was it just an exaggerated assessment of a temporary alliance between two political parties, something that has always existed in Lebanon, but proved on so many occasions, as insufficient to prevent the sectarian tensions from developing into full-scale sectarian civil wars.

So, when passing final judgment on this book, it is imperative to note that the reader cannot get a fully realistic sense of the subject at hand, when there is no mention of some of the most dramatic examples of the failure of some key Middle East countries to maintain a common sense of identity, one which can prevent sectarian and tribal civil wars. What we have in this book is important, but more is needed. Perhaps a follow up conference, and a book focusing on Iraq, Yemen, Syria, Libya and Lebanon. **JO**

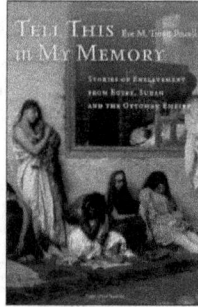

Eve M. Troutt Powell. *Tell This in My Memory.* **Stanford, CA: Stanford University Press, 2012. 246pp. $40.00. ISBN: 9780804782333.**

In the late nineteenth century, slave trade in Sudan, Egypt, and the Ottoman Empire was still very active. There is a huge silence surrounding slavery and its legacy in these regions. Eve Troutt Powell in *Tell This in My Memory* aims at presenting narratives of slaves and slave owners in order to show how slaves told their stories, and how the experience of slavery affected those involved. The narratives selected show how slaves travelled thousands of miles from their places of origin, how they changed, learned languages, and converted to new religions. Slave owners' narratives, on the other hand, show how slavery was considered a normal experience from childhood and how, for some it proved difficult to make the transition to a world without slavery. Eve Troutt Powell should certainly be commended, as she has been able to show slavery from an interesting perspective: the memory of those who experienced slavery, as slaves or slave owners. As this work relies, for the most part on memoirs, the feeling is that there should have been an introductory chapter problematizing sources. The author critically discussed the narratives presented and sources in every chapter; however, the book would have certainly benefited from a general methodological overview.

The book is divided into five chapters, well connected and written in a fresh style that allow the reader to appreciate the analysis of the narratives presented, and at the same time, become more curious about the lives of the characters under scrutiny. It is the variety of narratives and the diversity of the case studies presented that indeed constitute one of the strengths of this book. Chapter 1 is centered on the textual map of Cairo written by 'Ali Mubarak between 1886 and 1889. Troutt Powell, relying on the famous topography known as *Al-Khitat al-Jadidah al-Tawfiqiyah li Misr al-Qahirah*, explores the understanding of slavery in Egypt through the eyes of its author. In the analysis presented, 'Ali Mubarak openly talks about slaves and slavery; Troutt Powell has noted how he used the terms *'abid* defining black African slaves and *mamluk* to define white slaves. However, she points out that this dichotomy does not really tell us more about these slaves. The successful attempt made by the author to look at *Al-Khitat* focusing on the participation of slaves in Egyptian society shows that, though the identities of those men and women were often oversimplified, they were not silent and did possess a voice that was often translated into an active agency.

In Chapter 2, it is the narrative of Babikr Bedri which is under scrutiny. Babikr Bedri was a Sudanese trader, a previous fighter in the Mahdi's army, deeply religious and later interested in girls' education; and last but not least, slave owner. At the age of 94, in 1944, Babikr Bedri wrote his memoirs in Arabic, and shows that slaves were part of his life from childhood. An analysis of his memoirs takes the reader through the life of Babikr Bedri, showing how slaves were always in the background and formed an order that he considered natural. It is not a surprise, then, that the arrival of the British at the end of the nineteenth century was perceived by Babikr as a threat to his traditional way of life. Though the British for two decades did little to interfere with slavery, it was clear that this system was coming to an end. Babikr owned slaves well after the end of the First World War and never dropped his prejudices about 'Blacks' and 'Negroes'. In his life, he matured and acquired an appreciation for the difficulties experienced by women; he was a pious Muslim believing that treating women fairly and providing them with an education was a moral duty. Troutt Powell has noted that Babikr Bedri honored slavery and he always treated his own slaves as children, patronizing them but never giving them a choice. Though this narrative is revealing, it does not really say much about what slaves talked about, or gives insight into their personal histories.

With Chapter 3, the attention of the author switches to the narratives produced by slaves in order to find out more about the struggles of slaves narrated in their own terms. Through this chapter, the author shows how Salim Charles Wilson, a Dinka man enslaved in Southern Sudan, wrote of his own enslavement and how he struggled telling his story. Salim—the name was given to him by his first owner—was a contemporary of Babikr Bedri, but unlike him, he was a slave who eventually became a free man and worked as a lecturer in England looking at slavery with contempt rather than with nostalgia. Freed by an English missionary, Salim reached London in 1881, and while becoming proficient in English, he also converted to Christianity. Troutt Powell suggests that the narrative by Salim, *I Was a Slave,* produced in 1939 was meant to teach the reader about the Dinka, making Salim an anthropologist of his own people, exposing the audience to a history of slavery told by a former slave.

The following chapter explores the memoirs of two important women in Egypt and Turkey: Huda Sha'rawi and Halide Edib Adivar. This chapter compares these memoirs in relation to what these women heard, or from the slaves in their households. Likely the weakest chapter, the discussion of these memoirs should have been placed earlier in the book after the narrative of Babikr Bedri as a transition to the memories of Salim C. Wilson. The focus of this analysis is on domestic life in an attempt to establish the place of slaves in their relationships with the families who owned them. Though many details are revealed about the slaves that surrounded Huda and Halide—and it is clear that the slaves influenced the political views of these two outspoken national figures—the comparison of their memoirs fails to catch the voices of those slaves.

Chapter 5, on the other hand, sheds light on the yet relatively unknown work of Italian Catholic missionaries who trained former slaves to become missionaries themselves. Father Daniele Comboni, together with other Italian missionaries, purchased slaves in Sudan, liberated them, and sent some to Italy or Egypt. The stories of Caterina Zenab, Sister Bakhita Fortunata Kwashe, Sister Josephine Zenab, and Father Daniel Sorur Pharim not only reveal the meaning of slavery, but they also reveal the meaning of the transition from slavery to freedom, and from Sudan to Italy. They all fought against racism, but they also commanded respect. The most interesting aspect of this chapter is that it paves the way to look at the missionary work of the Comboni missionaries from another perspective—one that scrutinizes the narratives and voices of those who were the focus of the missionary work.

The last chapter is dedicated to one of the most famous former slaves: Saint Josephine Bakhita. Canonized in 2000 by Pope John Paul II, she was originally from Sudan, sold to an Italian consul, and reached Italy in the mid-1880s to become a nun. Saint Josephine is able to make her history known, though she was barely educated and never fluent in Italian. Bakhita's life was dictated by her to another nun, but it is with *Storia Meravigliosa* (Tale of Wonder) published in 1931 that Bakhita came to embody the history of slavery while showing the physical marks of slavery. Troutt Powell argues that the legacies of Bakhita's narrative had world-wide repercussions: "Bakhita is the first Sudanese to have history" a group of refugees told her, but Bakhita also had an impact on Black Catholics in the United States, not to mention her impact on Italians.

The author, in *Tell This in My Memory* successfully tried to tell readers that there are ways in which we can change how we read and tell the history of slavery. The stories told in the book show the voyages undertaken by slaves in their path to freedom. Though a lengthier discussion on slavery and the historiography on slavery should have been added, this is a welcome addition to a field that requires more research and analysis. *Tell This in My Memory* would be an excellent work to be used in a variety of classes in order to expose students to stories too often neglected. **RM**[2]

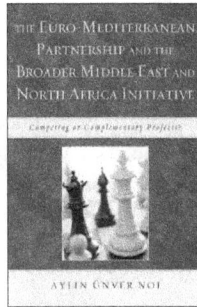

Aylin Ünver Noi. *The Euro-Mediterranean Partnership and the Broader Middle East and North Africa Initiative: Competing or Complementary Projects?* Lanham, MD: University Press of America, 2011. 280 pp. $70.00. ISBN: 978-0761855682.

This book's title sums up its major question and hints at its major conclusion. The author analyzes in depth the two post-Cold War projects advanced by the European Union and the United States in the Southern and Eastern Mediterranean, namely, the Euro-Mediterranean Partnership (EMP), and the Broader Middle East and North Africa Initiative (BMENA). The two projects by and large have similar objectives, but they also embody the competing interests and divergent approaches held by the EU and U.S. policymakers. In short, the answer to the question posed in the book's subtitle is that BMENA and EMP are both complementary and competing projects. Yet, the changing international as well as domestic dynamics have a transformative impact on the two projects and pose an interesting test for the future of the transatlantic relationship in general.

In reaching this conclusion, the author reviews the two projects with respect to their common objectives (specifically, political, and security; economic/financial; and social/cultural/human) and discusses each project's weaknesses and strengths. Her analysis is woven with an historical overview of the region's post-1945 geopolitics. She points out that EMP and BMENA illustrate the major difference between the EU and U.S. foreign policy: Civilian power, practiced by the European Union, emphasizes gradual transformation through regional cooperation and partnership. In contrast, military power, exerted by the United States, relies on rapid transformation through military pre-emption and unilateral action. The author argues that the difference stems from the two actors' respective geographical proximity and their respective historical, economic, and demographical links to the region, as well as their respective military capabilities. She notes that the Obama Presidency represents a policy shift from military power to smart power in the U.S. foreign policy. Moreover, the emergence of Brazil, Russia, India, and China as strong global actors, she argues, compels the United States and the European Union to align their policies in the Southern and Eastern Mediterranean and thereby highlights the complementary aspects of EMP and BMENA.

The book presents an extensive overview of EMP and BMENA, supported by aggregated statistics and detailed appendices (pp. 195-254). It also provides an extensive overview of the existing literature on the topic. Specialists will greatly enjoy finding in this book lengthy quotations from, and detailed summaries of the existing primary and secondary sources on the EU and U.S. policy in the region. Nonspecialists may however get easily lost in the rich detail and abbreviation-loaded narrative. Yet, the highly structured nature of the analysis makes it easier for the average reader to follow the major argument.

The book's major weakness is its heavy focus on high politics. This is particularly problematic when the author discusses the reception of EMP and BMENA and limits her analysis to the views expressed by policymakers or scholars. The reader does not hear the voices of those on the ground such as actual administrators or recipients of the EMP or BMENA projects. Nor does the reader get a detailed account of how these policies were interpreted by different audiences in the European Union or the United States. A discussion of these views may further substantiate the author's discussion of the two projects' weaknesses and strengths and may also help better assess the future of the transatlantic relationship.

This book may be of interest to policymakers, policy analysts, scholars of international relations, and foreign policy enthusiasts. It is a good introductory and reference book for those who are interested in deciphering the EU and U.S. policies in the Southern and Eastern Mediterranean. **BKK**

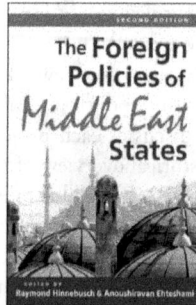

Raymond Hinnebusch and Anoushiravan Ehteshami. *The Foreign Policies of Middle East States,* **2nd ed. Boulder, CO: Lynne Rienner, 2014. 400 pp. $28.98. ISBN: 978-1626370296.**

It is arguably the case that Middle East politics have undergone a sea of change since the first edition of this book was published after the September 11, 2001 terror attack on the United States. It is timely, relevant, and useful to students, journalists, policymakers and not least, experts whose professional careers are devoted to this region of the world.

The authors have presented a panoramic picture composed of a sound theoretical framework, augmented by a very detailed, nuanced and illuminating review of the foreign policies of key Middle Eastern countries. The Arab Spring and its aftermath rightly sheds light on issues such as state stability, sectarianism and political legitimacy of regimes affected by the tidal wave that has been unfolding since the early 2011, and so there has been a natural tendency to somewhat neglect a discussion of foreign policy issues in favor of the inevitable focus on the questions cited above.

This book certainly redresses the balance, and offers us another important prism through which to look at the region with all the crises affecting it, and thus form a more comprehensive outlook on the domestic events and their regional implications. Raymond Hinnebusch, a veteran observer of the region gives us a very concise description of the key determinants of foreign policy in the MENA region and the Middle East regional system (pp. 1-72), and I found it to be clear and most coherent.

The reference to Israel and the Arab–Palestinian–Israeli conflict is one of the brighter sides of this book. Clearly, the conflict enjoys attention both in the theoretical chapters written by Hinnebusch and in discussing the foreign policies of specific countries, but it does not feature as the most important aspect of these countries' policies, nor as the most important key to understanding regional politics. This is in line with a growing tendency in recent publications about these subjects. The conflict has been downgraded in importance, both in the eyes of local people, as well as outsiders, whether experts or politicians. That seems to be a realistic outlook of those in the Middle East. If any evidence was needed to prove this point, and also the relevance of the book on hand, it has been amply demonstrated by the events of summer 2014, when Israel and Hamas were engaged in the third—and regretfully, not the last—round of fighting between them, and the Arab world was passive, if not outright disinterested.

It is one of the many pluses of the book, that both the theoretical discussion and that of particular countries address the changing environment; this goes to prove the relevance of the book. And so, referring to Egypt, Hinnebusch & Shama write, that "Morsi's fall marked a certain restoration of Mubarakism without Mubarak... [as] Egypt-first discourse became pervasive" (p. 101). While the writers do not predict the sustainability of this Egypt-first approach, they definitely leave us with the distinct impression that this is not going to be an insignificant chapter in Egypt's foreign policy. (pp. 101-103).

The chapter on Jordan is one of the best in the book, and I find myself in complete agreement with the clear cut conclusion of Professor Curtis R. Ryan, who wrote about Jordan that the key point regarding Jordan's foreign policy is "that regime survival is paramount" (p. 142). So, here too the line taken by Ryan is that it is about "Jordan First" (p. 153), something that the post-Arab Spring situation dramatized in a big way.

Hinnebusch gives us another great chapter, referring to his prime country of expertise, Syria. I was greatly impressed with the reference to Hafiz al-Assad's personal impact, as "under Hafiz [al-]Assad, Syria was widely seen to punch above it's weight" (p. 217). What is missing in this chapter is an analysis of the role of both al-Assads—father and son—to Iran, in the overall regional policy of Syria; but in particular, the Iranian veto over peace between Israel and Syria—something which fits into the Alawite sectarian nature of the regime—which even in the heydays of Hafiz al-Assad was very short on domestic legitimacy.

Professor Clive Jones, who wrote about Israel rightly refers to domestic Israeli concerns and deep-seated debates about interpretations of Zionism as significant determinants of foreign policy, and he may be following Henry Kissinger in arguing that Israel has a domestic policy, not foreign, but… much more attention should be given to the role of historic legacy in Israel's calculations, and the Israeli talk about "existential" threat deserves Israeli, not just Arab clarifications… (p. 312).

Other chapters, such as the ones about Turkey and Iran are sound and concise, in line with the overall strength of the book, but as an Israeli citizen, I find it astonishing that there is no chapter on the Palestinians and their foreign policy. It is a regrettable omission, one in the very few in a must-read, well-written, highly illuminating book. **JO**

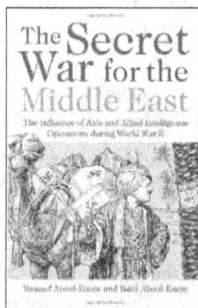

Youssef Aboul-Enein and Basil Aboul-Enein. *The Secret War for the Middle East: The Influence of Axis and Allied Intelligence Operations during World War II.* **Naval Institute Press, Annapolis, MD, 2013. 256 pp. $32.43. ISBN: 978-1612513096. Ebk: $30.21.**

Wars are a catalyst to changes, as big wars are to big changes. Clearly a truism in general, not without exceptions though, but not in the case of the Middle East, where the two world wars brought momentous changes, the effects of which have been felt, not just in the region itself, but rather throughout the entire world, and in many cases continue to be felt until our days.

Youssef and Basil Aboul-Enein are not professional historians; they are American military persons. Judging by their recently published book, however, they definitely are going to have a place of distinction among historians of the modern Middle East. They deal with a subject which has been somewhat neglected by other historians, who—generally speaking—referred to the Middle East in the Second World War by describing the main military moves. They also referred to the political designs planned in London—the capital of the most important colonial power—chief among them, the establishment of the League of Arab Nations, as well as the plans to solve the ever-escalating "Palestine problem."

What was lacking was the local input, that of the local people—mostly the Arab population of the region—and with it, the synthesis between their activities, aspirations and expectations and the actions and policies of the powers involved, and in that context, barely any attention was given to the connections between them and the Axis powers, Nazi Germany and Fascist Italy.

The authors have done a good job of setting the record straight, and they are absolutely right when referring to "the most important lesson to be learned is ...[that] it is vital to know the region, the area of operation... get inside the history of the region; walk around between perception, conspiracy, and fact" (p. 190). And sure enough, there was a lot of all of that in the Middle East during WWII, and the authors dutifully deal with it. In particular, they are referring to the element of conspiracy.

Conspiracy (*Muamara*) is a key word when analyzing the Middle East. This is the part of the world, where deep-seated mistrust of rulers has created a sense of disbelief in almost anything official, and so the authors rightly refer to one, Captain Anwar Sadat, who was jailed by the British during the war for his pro-Nazi activities, a man who, after the end of the war, wrote a letter congratulating Adolph Hitler, calling him "the real victor"... (p. 1). This is the same Anwar Sadat, who made the famous peace visit to Jerusalem, in 1979, ending the historic conflict between Egypt, the largest Arab state, and Israel, the state established by the people that Adolph Hitler worked so hard to completely annihilate.

Another plotter, much more important than Sadat, was the Grand Mufti of Jerusalem, Hajj Amin al-Husseini, whose infamous meeting with Adolf Hitler on November 28, 1941 receives its due attention in the book. This was clearly a dark page in the annals of the Palestinian National Movement, of which Husseini was its undisputed leader at that time. The two leaders definitely shared the same vision—to kill all the Jews; and the Grand Mufti helped recruit an SS Muslim division, mainly composed of Bosnians. (There were also Turkistani soldiers in the Red Army, who were taken prisoners by the Nazis and then were recruited by them to the SS). An interesting book about these details is Stephen L. Crane's *The life of Isakjan Narzikul, Survivor from an Unknown War* (Diane Publishing, Upland, PA, 1999). According to a new book by Edy Cohen on Nazi influence in the Middle East, in May 1943, the Mufti torpedoed a German–British plan to trade 4,000 Jewish children for 20,000 German civilians held by the British. This and many other episodes like this shed light on the role of the Mufti and with it, about Nazi activities. But then, what was this role? How did it fit into the grand scheme of things?

The authors do not shy away from this question, and they rightly put it in proper context. They refer to the Italian Bruno De Cordier and some "extremist Zionists," who "have attempted to present the existence of Muslim units in the Wehrmacht and the SS... as proof that Islam and Muslims have a weakness for Fascism" (p. 186). No, Islam and Muslims have NO particular weakness for Fascism and Nazism, and the authors are absolutely right about that.

In fact, this is a fundamental theme of the book as it deals with "perception, conspiracy and fact," and as such, deserves to be presented as part of a bigger context. The great historian, Bernard Lewis, referred to the 1930s in the Middle East as being the "era of the shirts," the era when many in the region—Ahmad Hussein and the Green Shirts in Egypt, the Phalange Christians in Lebanon, the Syrian Social Nationalist Party of Antun Sa'ada in Lebanon and Syria, and many others—seemed so fascinated with the rising power of the Axis, mainly in Germany. The parades, the youthful spirit so much on display, the discipline and order—all were captivating to so many young Arabs, among them many intellectuals, army officers and would-be influential politicians—and sure enough, also the anti-Jewish Nazi propaganda; but above all, it was the sense in the Arab Middle East that the real enemy were the Western Colonial powers, Britain and France, and the burning desire to rid the Middle East of their yoke. It was NOT racism, as Islam's sense of solidarity is strictly religious, not ethnic, racial, or linguistic. And there are so many other differences, but in a world of misguided perceptions, so many were attracted to support the Nazi cause, much less so the Fascist one. "In the war itself, whenever the pathetic Italian army was defeated in the Western Dessert, the newspaper boys in Cairo screamed *"inkasara al-makaruni,"* the makaruni was broken." Rommel and Hitler were considered the modern-day incarnations of Abu Ali, the mythological Arab hero. The authors refer to these manifestations of Arab pro-Nazi tendencies as "sound bites," and they are right, though some of these sound bites caused a hell of a headache to the British during the war.

Such was the case with Aziz Ali al-Masri, who founded the Arab Nationalist societies Al-Qahtaniyya and Al-'Ahd who worked with the Hashemite in WW1, but defected to the Nazis in WW2, not an inconsequential episode, but it is not covered by the authors. Also the Iraqi situation in the 1930s and early years of WW2 caused the British a lot of trouble. It was in Iraq, where the influence of the Grand Mufti was significant, particularly after 1937, when he fled from Palestine. The Iraqi Golden Square, the group of four officers, led by Salah al-Din al-Sabbagh, were the plotters who made possible the revolt of Rashid Ali in May 1941. The revolt is widely and adequately covered in the book, but not the Golden Square. This revolt, a dramatic indication of the anti-British in Iraq as well as the pro-Nazi sentiments, was also a dramatic indication of the Arab misunderstanding of Nazi foreign policy.

It was Bismarck who famously said that he would not the risk the bones of one Pomeranian soldier for the sake of the "Eastern Question," and Adolf Hitler simply adhered to this policy. For him, the East was the vast lands of Russia, where the "Jewish-Bolshevik" connection could be destroyed, and the German race would have its living space, the much-coveted *Lebensraum*. How could young, agitated, enthusiastic and less educated Arab officers and plotters know and understand all that? They could not, nor could they know that the German Luftwaffe was preparing to attack the Soviet Union in June 1941, and hardly had anything to spare for the Iraqi rebels.

The authors refer to the actual complexities of Nazi Middle East policy, relying on Francis Nicosia's writings, as well as others. They also cover the activities of Fritz Grobba, but they failed to mention Werner Otto Von Hentig's activities, and his opposition to the line advocated by the former, supporting more Nazi involvement in the Middle East. This and other omissions may be related to the scarcity of primary sources, but even this weakness cannot take away from the importance of the book, its usefulness and the desire it leaves with the reader to have more from these promising authors. **JO**

Jillian Schwedler, Ed. *Understanding the Contemporary Middle East.* **Boulder, CO: Lynne Rienner, 2013. 4th ed. 487 pp. $27.50. ISBN: 978-1588269102.**

This fourth edition of *Understanding the Contemporary Middle East*, edited by Jillian Schwedler, offers a detailed overview of the region. As Schwedler states in her introduction, the book is intended for Western scholars to challenge their perceptions and misconceptions through an exploration of Middle East history, geography, culture, politics, economics, religion, and people. However, its detailed presentation also makes it quite useful in supplementing introductory studies of Middle Eastern scholars as well.

This book has 14 chapters written by 15 authors with diverse disciplines. It offers a well-balanced approach, in addition to varied expertise and disciplines which present a study of historical and contemporary impact of the world on the region, and vice versa. The authors are all specialists in their fields, including several who have first-hand experience in the region. An element that distinguishes the book is its unimpeded flow of information and material, which creates a clear link between the various chapters and topics.

Understanding the Contemporary Middle East has four features that are distinctively different from past editions. The first is that it includes a new chapter on the "Role of Women," by Lisa Pollard, which enriches the edition with its description of how the status of women was used to define states' agendas. Pollard portrays how women were used as vehicles to advocate modernity and secularism, on the one hand, and also how they were the main targets of repression, on the other. The second unique feature is that two authors provide an analysis of the Israeli–Palestinian conflict. The chapter is co-authored by an Israeli Jew and a Palestinian citizen of Israel, Simona Sharoni, and Mohamed Abu-Nimer. Third is that this is the first edition to be published after the death of the series' original editor, Deborah J. Gerner. Schwedler, who co-edited the past two editions with Gerner, includes Gerner's co-authored chapter on "Middle Eastern Politics," one of the most informative and longest chapters, at 50 pages, in the edition. The final distinct feature is that it naturally contains updates on the still unfolding impact of more recent events in the Middle East, such as the "War on Terror" and the Arab Spring. The updates and their analyses are brief, which is quite understandable since the current outcomes are still unfolding and their implications regarding the region and the world remain unclear.

The Middle East portrays a diverse culture, varied economies, and an influence over two continents. Yet, Schwedler distinguishes three shared common historical experiences, which have had an impact on the region: the rise of Islam, the Ottoman Empire, and European colonialism. Although there have been earlier invasions in the Middle East, including the Greeks, Romans, and Semites, it is the more recent ones that have had a greater impact. Earlier invaders tended to absorb rather than disseminate their dogmas. It was through the Roman Empire that Christianity spread from the Middle East to the majority of the Western world.

Throughout the book, the authors outline the impact of the Ottoman Empire and European colonialism on the modern states' geography, politics and international relations, economies, and even literature. Territories were formed or divided mainly to satisfy their colonizers; this led to several contemporary struggles and grievances. The authors have adopted valid arguments to attribute the outcome of the current state to the influence of the colonial past and the present, indirect influence. However, one may also attribute current grievances to local leadership as well, as the world has recently witnessed a domino effect of uprisings in the region. Other parts of the world, such as the Americas, have experienced external influence and rule during the course of their history, yet several have managed to fashion their independence and development. The Middle East states' strategic and economic resources merit a more developed region of the world, yet most of the states continue to rely on external influences. Perhaps expanding on the five-page chapter on "Trends and Prospects" to explore the challenges of governing modern states and political reforms would have further enriched the manuscript. The Arab Spring calls for freedom and equity; the questioning of governments' legitimacy warrants a further analysis of the developments in the region, and the impact of such developments on other areas of the world.

Understanding the Contemporary Middle East is recommended primarily for undergraduate studies on a detailed overview of the region. The book has a clear thematic structure, and is further enriched with an appendix of basic political data on the Middle Eastern states, and three pages of acronyms. Additionally, an appendix on the contributing authors' affiliations is included. This title is a well-balanced introduction to the Middle East. **DW**

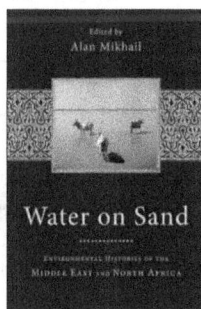

Alan Mikhail, Ed. *Water on Sand: Environmental Histories of the Middle East and North Africa*. New York, NY: Oxford University Press, 2013. 326 pp. $22.46. ISBN: 978-0199768660.

This volume, written by multiple authors, attempts to bridge the gap between Middle Eastern studies and environmental studies. Its editor argues that environmental studies have heretofore lacked a focus on the Middle East and North Africa (MENA), while MENA studies have lacked a focus on the environment. Most notably, this volume does not concentrate on the presumed inherent fragility of Middle Eastern ecosystems, as do earlier works on the topic; nor on their inherent unsuitability for human settlement. Its focus remains on the transformative nature of human effects on the environment, especially within the relatively short term of decades or centuries rather than millennia. Also, its chapters take pains to include not only geological, geographical or meteorological data, but also the "mass of human observations, anecdotes, poetry, narratives, bureaucratic records, and chronicles recorded on paper about relationships between humans and other parts of the environment" (p. 5). Insofar as the book's chapters exhibit continuity, it certainly accomplishes this goal, in addition to providing a great deal of material to reflect upon for scholars of other disciplines within MENA studies.

The volume's first chapter is its most general, and in many ways its most compelling. J. R. McNeil of Georgetown University enumerates the various geographical, environmental, and climactic "eccentricities," (p. 29) that characterize the MENA region. Notably, this is the volume's one chapter that does not pay tremendous heed to documentable human sources. Rather, it focuses on the physical sciences, making the argument that the eccentricities of the region prohibit broad expanses of continual settlement. Furthermore, because the expanses of arable land and grassland were not broad swaths with long, continuous borders, but rather small regions with fractal and often changing borders, McNeil calls this the "mosaic" of grassland and arable land: "This fragmented pattern maximized the interaction between pastoralists and farmers, between tribal confederations and agrarian states" (p. 34). This interaction led in turn to lactose tolerance among adults—an example of the environment's modifying humanity rather than the other way round. The rewards of exchange between pastoralists and farmers, "combined with the good transport opportunities afforded by the interpenetration of sea and land, and with the abundance of pack animals... encouraged commercial development very early in the region's history" (p. 36). Large agrarian empires were simply unable to form as they could in many other parts of the world.

In the subsequent chapter, Richard W. Bulliet of Columbia University goes into great detail with documented human sources in order to explain why the number of large mills for grinding grain, as well as the status of the miller, was so much higher in Western Europe during the medieval period than it was in the Middle East. Because Western Europe essentially lacked marginal lands suitable only for pastoralism, increased animal husbandry of necessity decreased the plant food available for human consumption; thus, Western Europeans turned to water power and wind power to grind their grain. By contrast, the essentially zero cost of fodder in the MENA made it more economical to use animal power for the same purpose. Bulliet includes documents from thirteenth century England detailing the relative costs of maintaining working animals, as well as modern name registries, in order to buttress his conclusions. Whereas Smith and Miller, in their various translations, are both extremely common surnames in nearly all populations derived from Western European origins, the word for "Miller" in Arabic is much, much less common than the equivalent for "Smith." Bulliet argues that this speaks to the comparatively low status of the miller in the MENA, given that milling with animal power did not require the technical expertise necessary to maintain and operate complicated machinery. Bulliet then goes on to use modern documentation of the increasing populations of camels and donkeys in Pakistan to illustrate how animal power in the larger MENA region can still serve as an economical substitute for machine power. This is the sort of well-sourced, comparative analysis that makes *Water on Sand* a valuable addition to the library of any scholar of the MENA interested in how environmental studies might pertain to their particular subfield.

In the following chapter, Sam White of Oberlin College addresses the "Little Ice Age" of the early seventeenth century and the disastrous effects even a very small climactic shift could have upon marginal regions—in this case, the economic and political stability of the Ottoman Empire. Subsequent chapters examine fishing techniques in Ottoman Istanbul; the cyclical effect of plague on the population of Cairo in the eighteenth century; the equestrian culture of Central Asia; ecological and political changes wrought by the construction of the Aswan Dam in Egypt; the environmentalist movement in Lebanon; the role of water as at least as important as oil in the making of the modern Saudi State; and the history and politics of land reclamation in Egypt. Of note among these chapters is the work of Diana K. Davis of the University of California. Davis, who explores the means by which a superficial concern for the natural environment was used by French colonists in North Africa for political purposes, to deprive native pastoralists of their land rights. Davis provides repeated examples of colonial authorities' framing the traditional activities of pastoral peoples as disruptive to the natural environment: "Such environmental disruption, the French story claimed, had been occurring since the Arab nomad 'invasions' of the eleventh century, the so-called Hilalian invasion. This claim was based on a combination of observation of the landscape, unfamiliarity with traditional Algerian land-use practices, and a highly selective reading of certain medieval era texts like the work of Ibn Khaldun… what the French never understood during the colonial period was that traditional North African land-use practices were largely ecologically appropriate and thus 'sustainable' for the population levels of the early to mid-nineteenth century" (pp. 164-165).

Davis is perhaps too generous to the French, but nevertheless, successfully makes her point that environmentalism, as in so many other regions and eras, was intimately tied to politics.

Water on Sand… will aid most any scholar interested in expanding the scope with which they view their particular sub-field. Many of the chapters may be too specific for direct relevance, but they are all well-sourced, well-written, well-argued, and often quite interesting. The scholars, editor and publishers are to be commended. **IAC**

PALESTINE

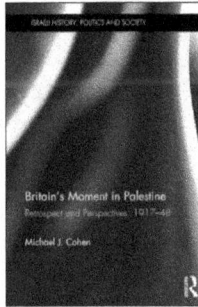

Michael J. Cohen. *Britain's Moment in Palestine: Retrospect and Perspectives, 1917–1948.* New York, NY: Routledge, 2014. 518 pp. $150.00. ISBN: 978-0415729857.

In December of 1937, at the height of the Palestinian Arab revolt in Palestine, one soldier wrote home "If you run over an Arab make sure you kill him, even if you have to reverse over him" (p. 272). At the same time, the Committee of Imperial Defense in England created a sub-committee tasked with bribing Arab officials in neighboring states into supporting partition of the country. King Abdullah in Jordan and some of his sheikhs would get around £10,000, while Ibn Saud in Saudi Arabia would get £200,000. These two examples—one of them from the lower level ranks of the British forces in Palestine, and one representing the elite policy—represent a colonial and bigoted policy, directed toward the Middle East, to prop up a Palestine policy that many officials knew was failing. They are symptomatic of a larger picture relating to the Palestine problem—the need to negotiate between promises made to the Jewish community under the Balfour Declaration and the increasing anger of the Arab community.

Britain's Moment in Palestine… joins a long list of good studies on the Mandate period in the country, such as Naomi Shepherd's *Plowing Sand* (2000), and Roza I. M. el-Eini's *Mandated Landscape* (2004). In a sense, the Mandate period of 1917 to 1948 is the best researched in all of Palestine or Israel's history. This is because of the accessibility of English sources in the UK and Israel, and the copious amount of documents the British civil servants produced. It is also due to the fact that many researchers see this period as formative and transitional—the period where Palestine, in a sense, became Israel. Under the Ottomans, it had been a slowly burgeoning province in the nineteenth century, home to a diverse group of residents, from German Templers to Syriac Christians. By 1950, two thirds of it had become Israel; and some 750,000 of its Arab residents had become refugees, their 420 villages abandoned.

Michael Cohen, a professor emeritus of history at Bar-Ilan University in Israel brings a long career of study of the British mandate to bear on this opus. Cohen earned his Ph.D. under the well known historian Elie Kedourie at the London School of Economics. He sets out to answer seven questions in his study—many of them obvious, such as "why did the British government issue the Balfour declaration in 1917" or "why did the British scuttle from [sic] Palestine in 1948?" (p. 2) Unfortunately, Cohen does not relate to previous studies or situate his book within the historiography. Since some of the chapters rely chiefly on primary sources, it might seem natural not to discuss all the secondary material. But there are chapters that rely on other scholars; and to rarely discuss the relative importance of these historical works on the period that has come before (references to Kenneth Stein in chapter six are a rare exception), or that have just been published seems self-centered in the extreme, as if this book exists in a vacuum, which it does not.

The first chapters are tied up with the context of the Balfour Declaration, in which England undertook to support the creation of a Jewish state, and challenges to it. Cohen provides an incisive look at the degree of anti-Semitism in Britain in the period in which support for a Mandate was official policy. The author takes issue with the notion that many English politicians or aristocrats were "Gentile Zionists." He claims "no Gentile ever subscribed to the Zionist thesis that Palestine should, much less could provide a shelter for the ingathering of all, or even of a majority of Diaspora Jews" (p. 22). He argues that ascribing one type of Zionism to disparate politicians such as Winston Churchill and Josiah Wedgewood, is not historically viable. For instance, Churchill's support for Zionism ended in 1944, when his friend Lord Moyne was assassinated by Jewish extremists in Cairo. Cohen even asserts that "Churchill feared Jewish influence in Washington and believed that Britain's sponsorship of Zionism would help secure American support [for England]" (p. 23). This is an interesting claim, but no source is provided for it.

Cohen provides an interesting account of how the British, once they were saddled with actually running a Mandate that was supposed to produce a Jewish state, systematically backtracked on the goal. It wasn't all cut and dried however. In the Mandatory civil service, the author notes, that Jewish representation ran to 32% by 1929, even though they were 15% of the population. Cohen asserts that "the Jewish who migrated to Palestine from Europe were frequently better educated than the British officials they negotiated with. They were too clever and too stubborn by far for the liking of the average colonial official" (p. 102). This sounds like a gratuitous stereotype and was hardly accurate, for the diverse population of Palestine's Jews, some of whom were from Yemen or Orthodox shtetls in Russia. He argues that the

"Yishuv was quite aware of the official's preference for the Arabs." Maybe it wasn't so much that the Jews were more "clever;" there was simply a competition between them and the Arab population for favors from the Mandate.

The middle chapters are interesting for their examination of the economic position of Palestine within the empire, and of the local economy in the country. One of the most interesting developments was the decision to grant concessions to commercial interests to develop the country. Pinhas Rutenberg received rights to produce electricity, and Moshe Novomeysky began developing methods to extract salts and minerals from the Dead Sea. Some of this produced apparent anti-Semitic backlash. Viscount Templeton claimed in parliament that "the Rutenberg concession, which gave a Russian Jew a stranglehold on the economic life of Palestine and Transjordan for 70 years…, indicates the undue influence of Zionists and international financiers." Templeton claimed also that the Dead Sea was the "key of the Middle East" in its "vast wealthy and power" (p. 204). He exaggerated the importance of the, at that time, nonexistent development of both these resources; but what is important is to note how much the British helped facilitate the groundwork for the subsequent self-sufficient economy of Israel after 1948.

The last chapters of the book provide interesting discussions on the influence and role of Nazism in the Middle East. Even though this is not a book on Egypt, Cohen provides an interesting discussion about modern "revisionist" history of Egypt in the 1930s. He references scholars Gershoni and Jankowski and challenges their claim that Egyptians were not influenced by Fascism. He claims these scholars "play down the contacts between Egyptian leaders and Nazi Germany" (p. 391). This is interesting, but then Cohen changes course and notes Egypt's case was *sui generis*, unique to Egypt; so why include it? The author returns to Palestine and argues that one of the major leaders influenced by Nazism was the Mufti, Hajj Amin al-Husayni. The German consul Wolff sent a telegram in 1933 that "the Mufti explained to me today at length that Moslems [sic]both within Palestine and without welcome the new regime in Germany" (p. 407). Except, this was in 1933, when Hitler had first been appointed Chancellor, before the truly evil nature of the Nazi regime was apparent. Isn't it logical that the Mufti, opposing England, might welcome a "new regime" in Germany; one whose future he could not predict? Cohen goes on to include a whole chapter on the Mufti's role in Germany in the 1940s after he fled Palestine. This role has been studied before and is not entirely clear how much effect it had on Britain's policy in Palestine, so it seems slightly beyond the scope of the book.

In the end, *Britain's Moment…* is an interesting read that brings together a wealth of primary sources and contributes to our understanding of the British role. It supports a more Zionist reading of this material and challenges modern historians who have attempted to argue that the British did not abandon their promises during the Mandate. The reader would do well to balance this research with one from the other side; but either way, Cohen has produced an insightful, if sometimes disjointed, book on the Mandate period. **SJF**

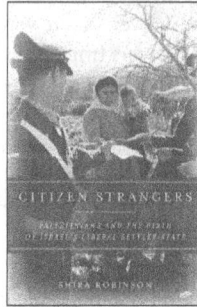

Shira Robinson. *Citizen Strangers: Palestinians and the Birth of Israel's Liberal Settler State.* **Redwood City, CA: Stanford University Press, 2013. 352 pp. $76.50. ISBN: 978-0804786546. Pbk: $14.97. ISBN: 978-0804786546. Ebk: 351 pp. $14.72. ISBN: 0804788006.**

In April of 1950, Arabs in villages across Israel celebrated the country's first Independence Day. As scholar Shira Robinson describes it in *Citizen Strangers...,* "local residents [came out] to greet the governor, observe a formal military ceremony, raise the flag and listen to speeches by teachers" (p. 118). Alongside traditional Palestinian folk dancing, students honored the Israeli flag in ceremonies that sometimes lasted five hours, according to Jewish officials present. This is a far cry from the situation in those villages, such as Taibe or Qalansuwa today, where residents mark the day as the Nakba—the disaster that befell Palestinians in 1948.

Robinson's pioneering work on the life of Arab citizens of Israel in the first decade of the state seeks to examine how the state sought to incorporate them, and in what ways they suffered severe discrimination, expulsions and racism. The author, an associate Professor of History and International Affairs at George Washington University, sets out to understand the contradiction between Israel's liberal democratic foundations and the way in which those foundations operated in practice. She argues that in fact, the country was founded as "a modern colonial polity whose procedural democracy was established by forcibly removing most of the indigenous majority from within its borders" (p. 3). Robinson argues, as have other scholars in the last decades, that Zionism is a "movement within a broader context of European imperialism and settler nationalism" (p. 4). But where she seeks to innovate is in noting the paucity of research on Israel's early state period which has received only "cursory and static coverage" (p. 5). She asserts that to ignore this period "flouts basic methods of historical reasoning by perpetuating an image of the post-1967 settlement enterprise as emerging in a vacuum" (p. 5). It is important that Robinson draws this out, reversing the tendency, especially among Israeli scholars, to present the 1950s as an egalitarian utopia of equality in order to justify present political arguments over the nature of the occupation. That she critiques the ideology of the "small and beautiful Israel" of the 1950s, to challenge how that period treated the Arab minority, is an important contribution in itself (p. 6).

However where Robinson strays from her massing of primary sources to provide insight into the analysis, there often appears to be an inordinate axe to grind against Israel, and a lack of investigation. In discussing how Zionism came to power in 1948, the monograph states "the Yishuv's efforts to pit Palestine's Arabs against one another bore substantial fruit, facilitating clandestine land purchases and contributing to the crushing defeat of their anti-colonial revolt in 1939" (p. 20). This dog-eared analysis takes any burden of responsibility and agency from the Palestinian Arabs in the 1930s and places all mechanisms of action in the hands of the Jewish minority in Mandate Palestine. To argue that every conflict and tension between the various Arab factions, such as the Husseini and Nashashibi families in Jerusalem, or between Druze and Muslims, was part of a conspiracy of machinations, inflates the role of the Zionists and turns the Arab leaders into mere pawns; which other scholarship and primary sources clearly show they were not. Their failure in the 1936-1939 revolt wasn't related to the Zionists, but to their inability to defeat the massive power of the British Empire. Similar revolts were crushed in Iraq, where there were no Zionists. Another weakness is the decision to use the term "collaborator" without questioning its overtones. Writing about the village of Abu Ghosh, the author claimed "...due to their notoriety as collaborators" (p. 113). This is a fundamental mistake, for the villagers were only "notorious" as "collaborators" in the Palestinian nationalist narrative. This is not an objective view; as if the village's very soul is tainted and the author knows it to be. Collaborator is a charged term and to use it without qualification, as in "viewed as collaborators by," applies acceptance of a highly political issue.

After tracing the way in which the Zionist movement came to power, in Chapter 2 the book examines the way in which the newly established Israeli democracy sought to govern a minority with whom it had just been at war. The Arab community was restricted to certain areas and a military regime of curfews placed on top of it. "The nightly curfews and blackouts imposed on them were not imposed on their Jewish neighbours, even where they lived on the same street" (p. 31). However, the relationship between government and minority was not similar to one of colonizer and colonized. "Israeli officials generally avoided the word natives, as well as other charged terms that might have implied a colonial relationship" (p. 50). Robinson asserts that "they never referred to the Arabs who remained after 1948 as Palestinians; doing so could serve as an unwanted reminder of their collective history" (p. 50). This theory goes too far, for there isn't evidence that the Palestinians referred to themselves this way at the time; it was an identity that was still in transformation, in the Benedict Anderson sense of an imagined community. For instance, Jordan didn't refer to the residents of the West Bank as Palestinians in this period either, rather as the "Palestine refugees," "Arabs," or "Palestine people."

What is important is that from the moment peace came in late 1948, Israel set about making sure the Palestinian Arabs who had fled would not return. In addition, the authorities wanted to make it so that Jewish immigrants could move to the country. The author argues "that the juridical and social content of Israeli citizenship was determined not by an ideal vision of whom to include but rather by the stark imperative of whom to keep out" (p. 72). For instance the authorities chose not to register thousands of Bedouin as citizens, in the opinion of the author, because then it would be easier to expel them. This overall project of keeping more Arabs from becoming citizens of the nascent state is termed "the war on return" (p. 75).

The most interesting part of the book illustrates the way in which the authorities attempted to cultivate a veneer of coexistence among the Arab citizens. As described above, one of the key components was certain ceremonies, such as Independence Day. They sought to work with local Arab elites or dignitaries, such as the Catholic Archbishop of the Galilee George Hakim, who they believed could be made to reconcile themselves with a Jewish state. Hakim wanted help reunite families, and a working relationship was developed. In describing some of the impact of the Israeli administration of Arab villages in the 1950s, some conclusions seem exaggerated. For instance, Robinson argues that villagers were impoverished providing food and hospitality to Jewish officials who visited them. "Today few recognize the role that military rule played in fostering the tradition of Jewish consumption and tourism in Palestinian villages and towns...an industry that boomed in the 1990s" (p. 93). This is beyond far-fetched—that a few hundred or a thousand military officials responsible for dealing with different villagers influenced a tourism industry forty years later? Perhaps numerous other economic forces helped foster that industry? In another instance, the narrative claims that after a massacre of Arabs in Kafr Qassem in 1956, Israel arranged a reconciliation ceremony "orchestrated to normalize the subordination of Palestinian citizens for the sake of Jewish privilege" (p. 155). This is a strong assertion—namely that the whole ceremony was a conspiracy, rather than an honest attempt to reconcile after a terrible event. The notion of "normalizing subordination" is not explained, and the assertion is not referenced, leaving the reader skeptical about the claim. The author herself notes that Israeli citizens were outraged on both sides, at the prosecution of the soldiers involved, and at the inhumane massacre; and the Knesset held a special session; it was more than just a simple story obviously. The theory of privilege is not borne out in the texts long discussion of the massacre.

There was dissent by the Arab minority, not only from the Arab communist members of the Knesset, but also from Arabs who ran on Labor affiliated lists. One Communist MK argued against the Israeli citizenship law of 1952 "the people will never agree to allow the state to be controlled by laws like the kind of racist laws in South Africa or anti-Negro laws in the American 'democracy'" (p. 107). Examining the relationship, the book concludes that there was an "existential conflict that characterized the relationship of the Jewish state to the small minority of Palestinians who had managed to stay" (p. 164). She tries briefly to examine how the problems of the 1950s reverberate today, noting that "the instability of the liberal settler state is greater than ever" (p. 198).

Citizen Strangers… is an interesting and important book. However, parts of it have been covered by other schools and historians, such as Tom Segev and Hillel Cohen and it delves too deeply into issues such as the Kafr Kassem massacre, ignoring developments between 1960 and 1966, when military rule ended. In many ways, the attempt to shed light on the profound inequalities of 1950s Israel is an important corrective, and this book should serve to kindle interest in this period. **SJF**

Madelaine Adelman, and Miriam Fendius Elman, Eds. *Jerusalem: Conflict and Cooperation in a Contested City.* **Syracuse, NY: Syracuse University Press, 2014. 364 pp. $39.95. ISBN: 978-0815633396.**

Madelaine Adelman (an anthropologist) and Miriam Fendius Elman (a political scientist) have assembled in this book 10 good studies about Jerusalem. The editors do not advocate the use of different disciplines in order to bring to the subject a better and more comprehensive understanding of it, but they believe that different disciplines do have the capability of presenting a variety of insights, and the contributors to their book have been chosen from multiple disciplines. These studies originally were papers read at a conference entitled "Jerusalem across the Disciplines" held at the Arizona State University campus in Tempe on February 19–20, 2007.

As is well-known, Jerusalem is central to the Israeli–Palestinian conflict, and it is eye-opening to see this centrality through the lens of many disciplines, and not only the political one that is usually adopted. Other disciplines offering other insights include: the religious; the historical; the social; the literary; the economic; the legal; the international; the anthropological; and so on. And this book attempts to offer a combination of them in 10 chapters and succeeds in affording readers various new insights.

In a chapter written by Arieh Saposnik entitled "Contested Ignominies and Conflicting Sacralities: The Changing Faces of Zionism's Jerusalem," it is shown that Jerusalem was not always viewed by all Jews in the same light historically. The

Orthodox "Old Yishuv" in the city who claimed to represent the sacred and the authentic in Judaism was challenged by the upcoming modernizing Zionists who hoped to take the leadership into their own hands. It was not merely the usual fight between tradition and modernity, but a struggle on the part of the Zionists for a new modernity in which secularization and re-sacralization were both engaged—however uneasily—to bring about a modern Israel.

In another chapter written by Shai Ginsburg entitled "The City and the Body: Jerusalem in Uri Tsvi Greenberg's …," Jerusalem as a literary topos is shown to be problematic in this poetic work published in 1928. Greenberg, who called himself "the poet of Jerusalem" is deemed to express an anxiety about the city, an anxiety that Shai Ginsburg believes undercuts the discourse of dominion over it; he offers a close reading of this poetic work and a literary comparison with other Greenberg writings, and shows that "Jerusalem fades away from the poem" (pp. 170-171), and what remains are images anticipating those of the Jewish Holocaust in Europe.

Madelaine Adelman offers another insight into Jerusalem in her chapter entitled "Sex and the City: The Politics of Gay Pride in Jerusalem." She says that Israel's first gay pride parade was held in 1998 in Tel Aviv, considered to be "the modern and secular face of Israel." It was not until 2002 that Jerusalem's first "Pride March" took place and it drew some protesters prompted by the sanctity of the city. However, it took place almost annually after that, in 2005 with an interfaith coalition against it and three participants stabbed, and in 2007 with 10,000 security personnel lining the parade route. Today, Pride events are held in many Israeli cities, including Haifa, Ashdod and other smaller locales (p. 257).

"Jerusalem in Java" is the title of a chapter by Mark Woodward, and it speaks about the city of Kudus, founded in the sixteenth century on the Island of Java (in today's Indonesia) by a Sufi saint called Sunan Kudus. The city's name is a Javanese transliteration of al-Quds, the Arabic name for Jerusalem which means "holiness." Woodward's article gives an account of the saint who founded the city that now has his venerated tomb and shrine; and he discusses the symbolism and the theology of founding Kudus as an *axis mundi* (in Mircea Eliade's understanding) mediating between the sacred and the profane—much as the real al-Quds and Mecca for all Muslims.

Other chapters of the book offer contributions that show how the distinction between politics and religion has been blurred, particularly in the conflict over Jerusalem's holy places on the Temple Mount/al-Haram al-Sharif. But they all show, each in their own way, that a solution to this conflict is absolutely necessary in order to achieve a viable peace between the Israelis and the Palestinians.

Valuable as all contributions to this book are, one has the feeling that on the whole, they tend to represent Israeli and Zionist insights—and not in any significant way—that Palestinian and Arab insights as a parallel would make the book academically fair and impartial. For example, there is no chapter that considers Jerusalem as a literary topos in Palestinian and Arabic literature similar to Shai Ginsburg's mentioned above. In their bibliography, the editors mention Ami Elad-Bouskila's good 1999 book, *Modern Palestinian Literature and Culture*; they even mention Ahmad Harb's 2004 article "Representations of Jerusalem in the Modern Palestinian Novel," and Farouq Muwassi's 1996 Arabic book, *Jerusalem in Modern Palestinian Poetry*.

At any rate, this book is a good addition to the recently growing number of books on Jerusalem and is particularly interesting because it embraces various disciplines in its 10 chapters in order to give a variety of insights, thus acknowledging that each discipline has different expectations, since no single one can claim to offer a full account of the subject studied. **IJB**

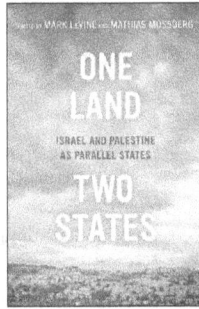

Mark LeVine and Mathias Mossberg, Eds. *One Land, Two States: Israel and Palestine as Parallel States*. Oakland, CA: University of California Press, 2014. 273 pp. $29.95. ISBN: 978-0520279131.

Especially when read in the wake of this year's latest, tragically dispiriting developments in the thus-far interminable Israel–Palestine struggle—above all, the devastating Gaza-centered Summer war—*One Land, Two States* ... offers an innovative and sympathetic, if by its own seeming admission, a somewhat quixotic new "vision for an end [to occupation and] of conflict" (p. 2). As introduced by the editors, the core concept elaborated by the book's various contributors has been germinating for around a decade now (interestingly, the specific research endeavor culminating in this volume was undertaken with support from the Swedish Government, which in a further, Fall 2014 occurrence, has extended diplomatic recognition to a Palestinian state), and is signified by the term "Parallel States Project (PSP)" (p. xiii). The Parallel States model sets forth from the assertion, shared with myriad scholars, activists, and political actors operating from an incommensurable array of intellectual and ideological standpoints (if not, withal, pre-eminent global power brokers like the United States), that there no longer is, if ever there was, a viable "peace process" leading toward a "two-state solution." As well, the idea stands on the claimed unfeasibility of "one-state" approaches ranging from Israel's current de facto domination, to binational or multicultural versions that would require Zionists and Palestinian nationalists alike to cede much, if not all, of their raison d'être. By contrast, *One Land, Two States* ... seeks "to envisage a new kind of two-state structure that could meet some of the basic demands and desires from both sides"—this, by positioning "two parallel state structures, both covering the whole territory [of historic Palestine/Eretz Yisrael, i.e., the whole area between the Mediterranean and the Jordan River], with one answering to Palestinians and one to Israelis regardless of where they live" (pp. 1-2).

In terms of its overall arrangement, and inclusion of thematic motifs and contributors, the book suggests itself as trying to be compelling to a fairly broad spectrum of potential readers, critics, and implementing stakeholders. It would seem that, in the editors' eyes, this inference is quite appropriate, as PSP—to invoke the sometimes rhetorically-deployed acronym—is presented, to be sure, as a "hope"-inducing theoretical principle, but no less as a practicable policy paradigm, "even as a complement to other alternatives" (p. 27). Thus, *One Land, Two States* ...opens with a provocative yet cautious statement of intent: "our goal is to stimulate new thinking in a situation of deadlock,...[but we] make no pretense of offering a new "definitive" solution to a century-old conflict" (p. xii). Next appears a supporting Foreword from a United Nations diplomat, and then a lucid project overview from the editors (the first of whom, Mark Levine, is well-known for his frequent *al-Jazeera* columns, and the cutting-edge contemporary cultural observations of his book *Heavy Metal Islam*, among further diverse outputs in Middle East studies, and the other, Mathias Mossberg, a Swedish diplomat as well as a knowledgeable Middle East analyst).

Following, thereafter, come two foundational chapters on the theory of political sovereignty by, respectively, a political scientist and a peace and conflict studies scholar. The fundamental reimagining of "the notion of indivisibility in the early modern accounts of sovereignty by Jean Bodin, Hugo Grotius, and Thomas Hobbes" (p. 31) proves axial to the book's overall thesis; as such, this proposed revision to the conceptual architecture underlying the Westphalian nation-state demands a singular degree of reflection and critique. The core argument running through this portion of *One Land, Two States* ... is that, given the globalized conditions of economic, socio-cultural, and geo-strategic interdependency under which the Israel–Palestine conflict today necessarily proceeds, the time is ripe for addressing the conflict through new mechanisms of political authority moving beyond the outmodedness of a seventeenth-century version of sovereignty. On this line of reasoning, the notion "that sovereignty lies exclusively in the hands of states, is inherently indivisible and inherently territorial" (p. 9) has been amply demonstrated as a present-day fiction—from worldwide trans-boundary capital flows, to Michel Foucault's emblematic insight that we must recognize the real, contending currents of power coursing beneath the illusory sovereign. So, why not follow the path of political evolution where it already seems to be leading?

In this manner, Israel and Palestine could reposition themselves ahead of the historical curve, as it were, by relinquishing the notion that existing, or aspirational states can any longer hope to maintain a centralized monopoly of power and control over their discrete territories. Instead, the long-time antagonists could build on "the present close integration between Israel and the Palestinian Authority" (p. 49), by agreeing to share an international boundary and some crucial dimensions of sovereignty, like the protection of that boundary from external security threats, and further "human security" needs "includ[ing] matters of health, transportation, water resources, and environmental matters, as well as possibilities for reconciliation" (p. 63). At the same time, each of the two sovereign entities, comprising—in an embodiment of genuine democracy—only those citizens who wish to fall under its mandate, would provide them with the expected public goods of an independent state, from constitutional protections, to education, to essential political identity.

There seems little doubt that, even when tempered by well-placed humility ("if [this book demonstrates] one thing, it's that at least we are not hallucinating") (p. 252), the volume's ambitious proposal manages to position itself directly at the nexus of two of the most vexing political conundrums of the current historical epoch—not merely the Israel–Palestine conflict, but the problem of sovereignty, itself. The latter persists amidst a split-consciousness political universe that tenaciously, violently, clings to nation-state forms of power, and identity, together with the modernist understandings of individual personhood that these forms embody and uphold, even (indeed, especially) as transnational forces threaten all their effacement.

Ironically, the region that *One Land, Two States...* tends to emphasize as a workable template for PSP, the European Union, has been experiencing acute pains over attempted divisions of sovereignty of late, from the Eurozone crises to the Ukrainian frontier. Yet, the irony intensifies; as Wendy Brown has influentially emphasized, nowhere are the stubborn boundaries of nation-state sovereignty being more fiercely re-inscribed, over and against their would-be "post-Westphalian" dissolution, than along the literal wall that Israel has raced to erect between itself and Palestine (*Walled States, Waning Sovereignty*, Zone Books, 2010). Continuing in this vein, the classic theoretician of sovereignty most conspicuously absent from *One Land, Two States...*, neo-Hobbesian Carl Schmitt, exemplifies the uncomfortable fact that sovereign power truly reveals itself, in its quasi-divine immensity, only under conditions of emergency. Given that Israel personifies a Leviathan whose conflation of sacred with secular power is perpetuated by the notion of perpetual emergency conditions, it is difficult, indeed, to conceive of this Leviathan as willingly consenting to be divided.

From here forward, there follows a series of chapters detailing institutional elements of the Parallel States vision whose intricacy and commitment sits, nonetheless, in something of a tension with the omnipresent question of whether the vision rests on a realizable basis. Therefore, there are a couple of paralleling chapters on Israeli and Palestinian security interests: the first by two self-proclaimed "old-fashioned, left-leaning Zionists" (p. 68); and the next by prominent scholars of Palestinian affairs, Hussein Agha and Ahmad Samih Khalidi. All four authors must grapple with the "basic assumption that Israel will [both] maintain its overwhelming military superiority" (p. 112), and also seek exceptionally tight controls on people entering the shared territory—not least, returning Palestinian refugees—even as the Palestinian state strives, at minimum, not to "be denied the right to self-defense" (p. 107). A similarly alternating approach of a Palestinian and then Israeli-written chapter strikes a notably hopeful tone on the possible mutual benefits of economic cooperation in such sectors as technology, agriculture, and tourism, subject to the need for integration to confront such obstacles as a vast disparity between the two economies. Two culminating team-written chapters feature, first, "Judicial Dimensions of a Parallel States Structure" (p. 175), impressive for its integration of contemporary legal theory's emphasis on legal pluralism as a deep-rooted historical phenomenon allowing varied legal traditions to effectively overlap with one another, including "within historic Palestine" (p. 185). Explored, next, are laudable possibilities for overcoming religious divides, by "Jewish, Christian, and Muslim" collaboration drawing on "[the] Abrahamic faiths'…deep ethical framework…centered on notions of justice and the common good" (pp. 206, 225).

It is abundantly clear that *One Land, One States…* is admirable and sincere in its objective to "think outside the box" (pp. 233-243)—albeit in ways that might gain an actual hearing from policymakers, and members of extraordinarily fractious Israeli and Palestinian civil societies. One wonders whether the Israel–Palestine conflict, intractably bound as it is—in the authors' own indicated acknowledgement—within a quintessentially modern struggle centering on the linkage between identity and sovereign control over territory, may ultimately demand even more radical means of disassembling and reimagining statehood itself; this, together with such of statehood's basic premises as modernist, ethno-national conceptions of personhood and citizenship (viz., Israeli and Palestinian). **AMW**

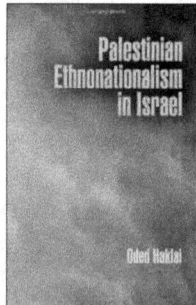

Oded Haklai. *Palestinian Ethnonationalism in Israel.* Philadelphia, PA: University of Pennsylvania Press, 2011. 256 pp. $59.95. ISBN: 978-0812243475.

Oded Haklai is said to have had written the first book investigating the manifestation of Palestinian claims and challenges to the Israeli state; however, having read books such as *Palestinian Identity* by Rashid Khalidi, and *The Origins of Palestinian Nationalism,* by Muhammad Muslih, we can see that it is an untrue statement. What Haklai does is simply reinforce the arguments of both Muslih and Khalidi. Although it cannot be said that Haklai offers any new evidence to the cause of Palestinian Nationalism, his arguments on the growth and expansion of ethnonationalism is intriguing.

Within the Introduction, Haklai coins the term, "Palestinian Arab Citizens of Israel" (PAI) and introduces them as the minority political entity. He describes the PAI as quiescent up until the 1970s and 1980s, and then he begins to introduce the PAI's political activism through the Communist regime. He goes on to state "I argue that the increase in vociferous PAI ethnonational mobilization is a result of changes in the institutional structure of the Israeli state... the fragmentation of political authority in Israel, coupled with the sustained lack of state autonomy from Jewish nationalism, have engendered conditions conductive to ethnonationalist minority political activism by multiple organizations claiming to speak on behalf of the minority" (p. 7).

In the first chapter of his book titled "Transition in Minority Political Activism, Grievances, and Institutional Configurations," Haklai begins to give underlying theories for the growth and transitions of political activism in Israel by Palestinian minority. Throughout the chapter, Haklai gives various arguments for the reasons for Palestinian political activism. These include, but are not limited to the lack of Israeli state autonomy, lack of minority representation within the Israeli government, segmentation of the majority and the minority in Israel, as well as the ethnic conflict between Palestinians and Jewish-Israelis.

In the second chapter of his book titled "The Formation and the Creation of National Boundries," Haklai begins a comparative study to the rise of the Israeli state and other small nations. In a conference Shlomo Sand, the author of *The Invention of the Jewish People*, states that nations do not create nationalism, instead, nationalism creates nations.[1] In the case of the Israelis, the nationalistic Zionist movement was a leading factor in the creation and implementation of the Jewish state of Israel. Haklai argues throughout his book that the Zionist movement continues to control the Israeli state, and because of this fact, the state of Israel is not autonomous. The Zionist movement itself can be considered an ethnonationalist political movement. Zionism's aim is to have a homogeneous Jewish state and in order to reach its aim, it has marginalized the PAIs.

In this chapter, Haklai speaks on the creation of the Jewish state through the World Zionist Organization (WZO). Haklai does a decent job in giving a brief history of how the WZO lobbied in the European countries and in the United States in order to get control over British Mandate Palestine. Britain recognized and treated the Jews and the Arabs of Palestine as two distinct communities and understood that the land of Palestine could not be controlled in a joint rule. Through the lobbies the Zionists were able to request and obtain a bi-national state. Haklai goes on to state that although the Israelis accepted the offer, the Arab leaders did not. He registers a few encounters between the Jews and the Arabs in this chapter, and concludes by acknowledging the Jewish victory over the land of Palestine, now known as Israel.

The third chapter of the book discusses how the PAIs took to their new Jewish dominated government. As was previously mentioned, Haklai argues that Israel did not have, and continues to lack, state autonomy because it is under the control of the ethnonationalist Zionist movement. Although the state lacked autonomy, it does not mean that it was weak. The Israeli state was strong enough to continue it sporadic growth through the immigration of Jews from various countries. It was also able to create a stable military force and begin to secure its own borders. This process, however, not only strengthened the Jewish state, but it also began to marginalize its Arab population.

The Jewish state, though being a bi-ethnic state was treated as a uni-ethnic state by almost completely ignoring its Muslim-Arab inhabitants. A complex relationship began between the Jewish religion and the secular Zionist based state. Although the majority of the elites were secular, the state began to function as religious. Judaism was adopted as the official religion of the new nation. Jewish holidays were made national holidays and the Sabbath was made into an official day of rest. "The state formed a government ministry for religious affairs and integrated religious courts into its judicial system to deal with matters of personal status" (p. 61). In essence, the Muslims and their holydays were ignored. The only Arab-Muslim practice that was integrated into the new Jewish system was that which was similar to that of the religious courts that the Jews had.

In essence, the PAIs were now marginalized in the new Jewish state. To an extent, they did not exist and they were not a part of the Israeli communities. For years they were quiescent, but that was to change all too soon.

During the years that all of this was taking place, the Cold War began. The capitalist country of the United States and the Communist Soviet Union were at odds with each other, constantly seeking countries to join their cause. In the fourth chapter of the book, Haklai shows the end of Palestinian quiescence and the rise of the Communist movement of the Palestinian-Arabs. Haklai tells us that the first Communist Party arrived with Jews from Russia. This backfired, as the Palestinian Communist Party, Rakah, came onto the scene. Haklai argues that Rakah was the first organized voice of the PAIs and a direct front to Zionism. Haklai also argues that although Rakah was not challenged at the beginning, it did not always have the best interests of the PAIs at heart. No other organization could challenge them because all other organizations lacked organizational infrastructure, resources, and support from the PAIs. There was no challenge until the 1990s, as ethnonational organizations began to be based on the same organizational model as Rakah. This was brought about in part by the *Intifada* which began in 1987, and brought with it the rise of other groups, such as Hamas.

The fifth chapter covers many small details which cannot be explained in bulk. Haklai in this chapter discusses "The Vision Documents" in some detail. He also adds charts to explain the ethnonationalist political turn in Israel. It must be noted that this is a confusing chapter, and that, although it is a fountain of information, it is bland and not woven into the body of the text. What Haklai writes in the conclusion of the chapter, however gives the reader the key to the chapter's argument. In its most basic terms, Haklai reveals how the Jewish majority were able to oppress the Palestinians; thus causing the rise of ethnonationalist organizations.

The sixth chapter of the book then gives us a look at how the Israeli state has changed in the last two decades. Haklai argues that there is a growing fragmentation within Israeli politics; and because of this, the Jewish Israelis are beginning to lose their effective control over the political spectrum and, therefore cannot completely control the state as they once had. Haklai states, "...while the state is still relatively well institutionalized, its extensiveness has declined considerably... It has withdrawn from large portions of economic activity and social service provision, it no longer monopolizes the media, or controls public discourse, and its military no longer governs PAI areas" (p. 171).

Oded Haklai has done an incredible job in presenting an ethnography of the political challenges of Palestinians within the state of Israel. This is an excellent source for any reader studying the Arab–Israeli conflict or the rise of the Palestinian activism in politics. Combined with books such as *The Origins of Palestinian Nationalism* by Muhammad Muslih, and *Palestinian Identity*, by Rashid Khalidi, any author can have a strong background for a good argument. A unique argument in his work is that Haklai states that, due to the lack of a Palestinian national state, Palestinians have an ethnonationalist movement within the Jewish Israeli state.

1. Sofia University. "Shlomo Sand—The Invention of the Jewish People." YouTube. Flash Video File. https://www.youtube.com/watch?v=TX_xXMsg9BI (accessed April 7, 2014). **MS**

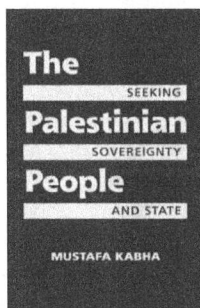

Mustafa Kabha. *The Palestinian People: Seeking Sovereignty and State*. Boulder, CO: Lynne Rienner Publishers, 2014. 399 pp. $68.50. ISBN: 978-1588268822.

Mustafa Kabha's *The Palestinian People: Seeking Sovereignty and State* is the latest addition to a number of studies on the historical development of the modern Palestinian nationalist movement and its struggle for independence and statehood. The book is a revised and updated version of an earlier manuscript, *The Palestinians: A People Dispersed*. In this revised edition, the author states that the history of the Palestinian people in the twentieth century was shaped by three triangles: an external one involving Britain and the other superpowers; pre-1948 Zionism, the state of Israel, and the Arab world; the second includes aspects of national identity (Arab, Palestinian, and Islamic); and the third is a social and deeply rooted in the culture of the veteran, traditional family-based elite, the intellectual middle class, and working class groups with armed representatives (p. 6). The main body of this book provides a wealth of details on the effort of different Palestinian entities for independence and statehood, and the internal factors that have foiled them. The author draws from a long list of primary and secondary sources in Arabic, Hebrew, and English to elaborate the representation of Palestinian national identity from the 1930s to the present.

The book consists of 15 chapters. The first chapter deals with the 1936–39 Arab Palestinian revolt that, according to Kabha, was the first event to demonstrate the relationship between the three triangles. Chapters 2–6 move the narrative through a chronology of subsequent events beginning with the decade following the end of the Arab Revolt in 1939 to the post-1967 War. Chapters 7–13 chronicle the successful and failed attempts toward a unified national strategy. These chapters provide vivid details of critical transitions ranging from the Palestinian–Jordanian fighting in 1970, the first Intifada (uprising), to the Oslo Peace Accords in 1993. The last two chapters discuss the inter-Palestinian conflict between the Palestinian Authority (PA) in the West Bank, Hamas in the Gaza Strip, and many Palestinians in diaspora, and the impact of the Arab uprisings (the Arab Spring). Kabha is inclined to attribute the emergence of Palestinian modern national identity to unique problems involving Palestine and the growing conflict with the Zionist movement (p. 2). While this is true, equally true is what other studies (for example, Muhammad Muslih's *The Origins of Palestinian Nationalism*, and Rashid Khalidi's *Palestinian Identity: The Construction of Modern National Consciousness*) have concluded: that modern Palestinian nationalism, while inextricably intertwined with that of Zionism, the pre-Zionism Palestinian history reflects a range of patriotic feelings, local loyalties, Arabism, and religious sentiment that defined the earlier development of Palestinian identity that date back to the late Ottoman period.

The author does not devote much time to discussing the genesis of Palestinian nationalism. Instead, he begins the first chapter by contextualizes the evolution of Palestinian identity during the 1936–39 Arab Palestinian Revolt. The revolt, while inspirational, did not succeed in derailing the influx of Jewish immigration or gaining British support to stop it. The Palestinian leadership that led the revolt was unable to avoid sectarian conflicts and incapable of mobilizing and uniting the general public against British and Zionist presence in Palestine. Once the revolt ended, the author argues persuasively, the Palestinian national movement emerged morally wounded and its leadership fractured and forced into exile (pp. 20-21). The departure of one

of the main leaders of the revolt, Hajj Amin al-Husayni (Mufti of Jerusalem), in October 1937 to Lebanon and then to Iraq, British troop reinforcement, and increasing Jewish reprisal attacks signaled a setback to the Palestinian drive for self-determination. The failure of the revolt was further evidenced by Arab acts of retribution
against those who were suspected as traitors—a pattern that continued persistently
into the twenty-first century. Nevertheless, it is clear that the revolt eventually forced
the British government to reassess its policies in Palestine and develop different plans
to administer it more effectively. The proposed partition plan recommended by the
Peel Commission in 1937, and the 1939 White Paper to limit Jewish immigration
indicated the need to recognize and address urgent Palestinian concerns.

With the advent of World War II, many Palestinians recognized their limited
resources and hence, the difficulty in fighting both the British and the Zionist Jews.
Despite their disappointment with the failed 1936–39 rebellion, the Palestinians
continued to seek British support for their cause. This necessitated, in return, their
support of the British war effort. Kabha indicates that the Palestinians supported
the war effort on two levels: enlistment of young men for active service, and recruitment of skilled men to work in army camps. He also states that the newly found
employment to serve the British war effort also contributed to slowly alleviating the
economic hardships that followed the Arab revolt (pp. 31-32).

The continuous absence of an effective local leadership to lead the Palestinian
movement toward independence made it possible for the newly formed Arab League
(1945) to play a direct role in Palestinian affairs. The League provided a major plat-
form for activists from all divisions and levels of the Palestinian national movement.
Kabha states that the League became the undisputed patron of the Palestinian. It
virtually became the only entity in a position to select which organizations would
represent Palestinian national interests (p. 36). Prior to the establishment of the
Arab League, a number of Palestinian entities with different political agendas surfaced, for example, the National Liberation League that called for the termination of
British presence in Palestine and the establishment of a democratic Palestinian state
in which Arabs and Jews would equally coexist. Also, labor movements and trade
unions were instrumental in improving employment conditions for Arab workers
(pp. 45-59).

As the British Mandate approached its end in 1947, the United Nations became
the only credible arbiter to determine the future of Palestine. The UN Special Commission on Palestine was formed to evaluate the volatility of Arab–Jewish relations
and to recommend a solution. The commission recommended the creation of two
states in Palestine, one for the Jews and the other for the Arabs. Despite their consistent opposition to partition, the Arabs were unable to prevent the recommendation
proposal from being drafted into a UN Resolution in November 1947 that formally
partitioned Palestine. Kabha argues that the resolution "had a critical impact on the
history of the two nations fighting for the country and on their respective evolution"
(p. 79). Indeed, the resolution made possible the creation of the state of Israel on

May 15, 1948, a day the Palestinians refer to as *Nakba* (Disaster). Additionally, the Arab world rejected the existence of Israel and resorted to armed struggle against it. On behalf of the Palestinians, the Arabs declared war on Israel in June 1948. The war ended with a devastating Arab defeat and, as Kabha states, "the Palestinian nation underwent a complete transition. From a nation endeavoring to become united on its own land, it became a nation scattered among many countries" (p. 80). The war resulted in the dispersal of half of the Palestinian people as refugees in neighboring Arab countries. Meanwhile, the inability of the Arab armies to effectively confront Israel led the Palestine Liberation Organization (PLO) and its armed groups to engage in guerrilla warfare in the occupied territories with operational bases in Jordan and Syria. Kahba indicates that such a tactic was only partially successful. Israel arrested and killed many fighters and neutralized many others (p. 234). Moreover, 1967 witnessed the Israeli capture of what was left of Palestinian territories, forcing the Palestinians to rethink their national goals and strategies. Additionally, the 1970 Jordanian civil war in Jordan and the 1982 Israeli invasion of Lebanon that led to the expulsion of the PLO from those countries, further deepening Palestinian and Arab inter-fighting.

Kabha concludes that the external triangle began to lose its significance in the early 1920s. The influence of the superpowers and their direct intervention in Palestinian affairs gradually diminished, beginning with the end of the British mandate and the collapse of the Soviet Union. Only the United States and the European Union appear to have some influence, but mostly in matters related to peace negotiations. The Arab world is no longer in control of Palestinian affairs, particularly after the establishment of the Palestinian Authority in 1994. As for Israel, its continuous building of Jewish settlements in the West Bank and East Jerusalem has complicated the two-state solution equation, and deepened the rift between the PLO and Hamas. Kabha writes that the second triangle has seen many changes over the years. While the PLO's commitment to the creation of a secular Palestinian state has been steadfast, its approach has shifted from armed movement with guerrilla warfare to an institution of governing in the West Bank with pragmatism and statesmanship. The inner-Palestinian conflict between the PLO, represented by the PA, and Hamas in the Gaza Strip has underlined an intense debate on whether a secular or a religious political ideology can best achieve the goal of independence and statehood. Finally, the third triangle has seen many changes, too. The traditional elite and representatives of leading families, such as Haj Amin al-Husayni, are all but gone from the Palestinian national scene. The intellectual and liberal professionals have been an important element in in the Palestinian national movement. However, the working classes and youth have also emerged in importance, particularly after the first and second intifadas (pp. 361-362).

In short, both student and general reader may find this book challenging. The scholar of the Arab–Israeli conflict may find its valuable analysis key to historical understanding of Palestinian nationalism. **AHI**

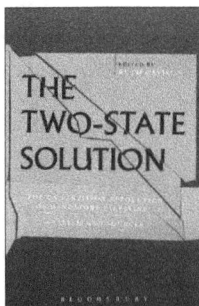

Ruth Gavison, Ed. *The Two-State Solution: The UN Partition Resolution of Mandatory Palestine-Analysis and Sources.* **New York, NY: Bloomsbury Academic, 2013. 330 pp. $39.95. ISBN: 978-1623566074.**

It is arguably the case, that when dealing with the Palestinian–Israeli conflict, Questions of definition and context are of paramount importance. To start with, what conflict? Is it really only a Palestinian–Israeli conflict, or is it an Arab–Israeli conflict? And then, is it a religious or ethnic struggle, or a combination of the two? Beyond that, what is the time frame of the problem? Did it start with the Balfour Declaration, the beginning of "Zionist invasion," as is so blatantly formulated in the now moribund [or is it?] Palestinian National Covenant of the Palestine Liberation Organization [PLO], or did it start when Zionist idealists began the return home to the Promised Land in the 1880s?

These and other questions are of the essence, not a sophisticated ploy used in order to confuse the Western reader of literature about the conflict; thus making it seem unsolvable. Rather, it is relevant to the understanding of the current positions of the parties involved—hence, what could be possible solutions to this on-going conflict? And this is so, because the parties cling strongly to historic narratives, not just as a basis for an academic debate, but as the justification for current political/ diplomatic positions. The term "two–state solution," which is the theme of the book discussed is another indication of the state of affairs described above. What two states? Where? And is this the solution?

A personal confession on my part is in place here. I do support the creation of two states in the historic land of Eretz Israel/Palestine, one which will be the nation-state of the Jewish people, and one which will give satisfaction to the unassailable right of the Palestinian people for self-determination. Clear? Not so—what boundaries for the respective states? What Palestinians? Only those who currently live within the territories known as Judea-Samaria/West Bank and Gaza, or those who live within the Hashimite Kingdom of Jordan (a majority of the population there), which occupies the lion's share of Mandatory Palestine? Perhaps also those citizens of Israel, who define themselves now as Palestinian citizens of the state, thus, laying the ground–work for a demand for a national solution for them outside of, or in separation from Israel? Just to clarify, I do not profess here to suggest an end of Jordan; rather, to shed light on the undisputed historic, geographic and demographic fact, that Jordan is part of the problem; therefore, it could be part of the solution.

I, for one, believe that the two-state solution should encompass most of the territories of Judea-Samaria/West Bank, Gaza, and Jordan as an expression of the Palestinian–Arab aspiration for statehood and then be in some kind of connection with Jordan, but not any territory included in pre-1967 Israel. I realize though that this is just my observation/belief/solution, and there are so many others who use the very term "two-state solution," still come to different, even contradictory conclusions about territory and statehood.

And with that, I raise my first reservation about the combination of essays and documents which is the book on hand. While the book exclusively deals with the UN 1947 Partition Plan, it has to do with a subject which is at the very core of every current discussion about Israel/Palestine. I, for one, expected to see an introduction putting the question on hand in an historic context, stretching from the 1930s when partition was first raised as a possible solution. It may seem too presumptuous to include so much in an introduction, and this is exactly where the role of the editor is so significant, how to present the issue discussed without losing the interest of the readers. Ruth Gavison is a brilliant legal mind, and her own personal journey from past positions to her current strong Zionist convictions is a fascinating subject in itself, but I miss the hand of an historian in the introduction. Still, Gavison's words of introduction about the uniqueness of the Zionist enterprise were important and even moving. I feel that a similar introduction by a Palestinian writer, whether legal expert or an historian was in order, at least in order to present the reader with the basic ideological perspectives which are so significant in dealing with the conflict.

Then I detected a problem with the essay of Professor Galnoor where the discussion about Zionist attitudes regarding two states omits any reference to two important issues of the Zionist movement, i.e., the historic revisionist movement, the mother movement of the current Likud Party, which for most of the period since the 1967 war, was the dominant political movement in Israel, and the religious Zionist camp. P. M. Netanyahu does speak about his support for the two-state solution, but there are serious doubts whether rhetoric in this case is matched by actions. Yet, whenever he appears in meetings, the pictures of the founding fathers of the movement, Jabotinsky and Begin are hung over his head. The two objected to the creation of a full-fledged Palestinian–Arab state, so if Likud today—and it is a very big "if" indeed—supports the creation of such a state, this is definitely a development of significance—one that deserves to be analyzed in a book about the two-state solution, but it is not. The same goes for the religious Zionist movement, a somewhat marginal force for many years, but a highly significant and influential one in post-1967 Israel. The inclusion of such an analysis could be very useful as a tool in understanding the process of evolution of deeply-held political convictions, something which is essential in dealing with the Jewish–Zionist as well as the Palestinian–Arab positions.

In this context, both the contributions of Kabha and Magally are of importance, are useful and even somewhat innovative. Kabha breaks the myth, traditionally promoted and upheld by Zionists, and pro-Israel writers, that all Palestinians objected to the initial partition plans. He gives us a political map of the Palestinian side—a very detailed and illuminating one—in which we discover those who supported partition. I wish Galnoor did the same. Still, the historic record clearly shows that Palestinian rejectionists had the upper hand, but there were others as well, and the importance of these others is to be evaluated properly, not mainly due their small numbers, but to their very existence. Magally makes an important contribution to the discussion by criticizing Palestinian rejectionism. There are very few essays in the book, and there should be more, also on the expense of some of the documents. Two many of those were given, and some are repetitive, so more analysis was in place.

Altogether, this book is a good basis, a beginning to a discussion about the two-state solution, past, present, and future. Here is a challenge to Professor Gavison and her think-tank—give us another volume, one that will be more relevant to current realities, and prospects, one that will bind past and future. **JO**

POLITICS

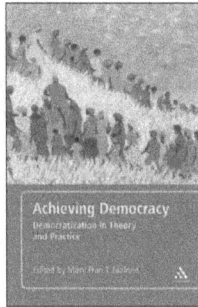

Mary F. T. Malone, Ed. *Achieving Democracy: Democratization in Theory and Practice.* **New York, NY: Continuum Books, 2011. 394 pp. $114.00. ISBN: 1441191798. Pbk: $39.95. ISBN: 1441181822.**

Mitchell A. Seligson, in the Introduction to this interesting and important volume, asks "Why should we care about democracy" (p. xvii). Indeed this is a worthwhile question in a world that has come to accept that democracy is the most preferable form of government and, in the absence of the old Marxist view of a linear history, there is a view that most societies are progressing toward democracy. Seligson, a professor at Vanderbilt University, argues that "democracy continues to evolve and spread throughout the world. However, one wonders if there are parts of the world where democracy will not take hold, and whether things can be done to nudge along the process of democratization" (p. xix). This is particularly pertinent in light of the Arab Spring and the seeming march toward democratic reform in Egypt, Tunisia, Libya, and elsewhere in the Middle East.

Achieving Democracy... is a monumental monograph that seeks to examine democratic reform and history throughout the world. Mary Fran T. Malone, an assistant professor in the Department of Political Science at the University New Hampshire, examines in her first chapter how democracy has come to the world in waves—first in Greece, then in the English speaking world after 1776, and then after the Second World War. "Several watershed moments sustained this [democratic] optimism. Democracy had spread to the most unlikely places" (p. 3). This included South Africa in 1994 and Eastern Europe after 1989.

In Chapter 2, authors Alynna Lyon and Jonathan Hiskey argue that it is important to understand to what degree democracy plays a major role in economic development and peace. They focus on why "third wave" democracies have not seemingly benefited economically. "The uneven democratization process experienced by many democracies in the developing world can potentially have a curvilinear impact on development" (p. 43). The confusing chapter posits primarily that the results are unclear and the jargon-laced explanation does not leave the reader with a clear understanding of what the data show. In examining the democratic peace model, that argues that democracies are more peaceful and do not go to war with each other, the authors also note that "the causal mechanisms of this relationship remain unclear" (p. 53).

The succeeding dozen chapters deal with efforts at democratization in such disparate places as Switzerland, England, India, Poland, and South Africa. While interesting, this does not speak to an audience involved in Middle Eastern or Islamic studies. One must skip forward to Chapter 13 to find an important and interesting examining of "authoritarian regimes and democratic demands in the Middle East" (p. 335). The author, Jeannie Sowers is an assistant professor in political science at the University of New Hampshire. She is primarily an expert on the environment and the Middle East. She connects the sudden outbreak of protest and departure of dictators in Egypt and Tunisia to the velvet revolutions in Eastern Europe. However "it is much too early to say whether the recent largely peaceful mass protest movements will bring substantive democratization to the Middle East" (p. 338). The author notes that several other countries, such as Turkey, Israel, Iraq, and Lebanon either are democracies, or have moved in that direction since 1950. This begs the question, why another chapter was not devoted to democratization processes in one of these countries. Iran is mentioned in the context of American meddling over oil. "The cold war policies, however, produced a number of internal contradictions… the Iranian revolution ushered in a new form of authoritarian rule for the Middle East" (p. 349). But this misses a central point: Iran has had a tradition of democracy dating back to 1906. Even under the Shah, and later under the Ayatollahs, Iran still had both structures and a yearning for greater democracy; this has manifested itself in major street demonstrations and circumscribed elections.

Instead of analyzing the historical aspects of democracy that do exist in three countries, such as parliaments in Jordan and Egypt and the presence of old historical parties such as the Wafd or Muslim Brothers, Sowers argues that "to explain the persistence of authoritarian rule in the Middle East and understand prospects for democratization, this chapter argues that we must examine international influence, patters of economic development and state-society relations" (p. 357). In other chapters, the authors have analyzed elites, institutions and electoral structures. This analysis is totally absent from the examination of the Middle East. It is unfortunate, for the Middle East not only has important prospects for democratization, but also has some important institutions and electoral structures that might pave the way for democratization in certain states and not in others. Sowers leaves the reader with the claim "clear movement toward more institutionalized, robust forms of democratic practice often become apparent only in hindsight" (p. 358). If this is the case, then what can one say about democratization? Evidently and unfortunately, not much in the section of this monograph dealing with the Middle East, even as important events continue to occur throughout the region. **SJF**

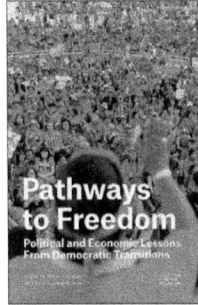

Isabel Coleman and Terra Lawson-Remer, Eds. *Pathways to Freedom: Political and Economic Lessons from Democratic Transitions*. New York, NY: Council on Foreign Relations. 2013. 264 pp. $14.99. ISBN: 978-0876095669.

This excellent volume makes a valuable contribution to the debate on democratization, not by introducing new concepts or evidence, as such, but by bringing together the key arguments and evidence with eight well-written country case studies that clearly lay out several relatively successful democratic transitions in the developing world. The authors stated that their aim is not to advance a "new, one-size-fits-all theory of democratization," but instead to take a long view of progress made over the past 25 years in order to "distill practical lessons for reformers in transitioning countries and policymakers in supportive outside states." This is a useful purpose and the book accomplishes it admirably.

The summary is particularly useful. It is presented as two chapters. The first structures the issues to be addressed in the country cases and presents the main conclusions derived from the case. A second chapter briefly reviews the statistical evidence from the literature on this same set of issues.

The case studies include two from Latin America (Brazil and Mexico), two from Europe (Poland and Ukraine), two from Africa (Nigeria and South Africa), and two from Asia (Indonesia and Thailand), all selected based on their credible and sustained progress toward democratization.

This criterion explains the absence of cases from the Middle East. The authors express their hope, however, that success in the nascent democratization processes underway in several Middle Eastern, African, and Asian countries will contribute to reversing the past seven year's regression in democracy, documented by Freedom House. At the same time, the authors freely acknowledge that several of the cases chosen remain works in progress—witness the recent nondemocratic changes of government in Thailand and Ukraine and Nigeria's rising insurgency.

The summary chapter is arguably the most useful. A brief but valuable concluding chapter aimed at decision makers, which highlights key messages for democratization programming, is somewhat less convincing.

A common framework of six issues organizes the statistical evidence chapter and the case studies: (1) socioeconomic inclusion and exclusion; (2) economic structure and policies; (3) civil society and media; 4) legal system and rule of law; (5) government structure and division of powers; and (6) education and demography. This disciplined approach facilitates comparison of the different country stories and calls attention to key similarities and differences among them.

The summary chapter, written by editors Isobel Coleman and Terra Lawson-Remer, deviates from this structure slightly to focus on insights regarding seven major differences found to matter most in determining the course of democratization. Four of these relate to a country's initial circumstances, including economic growth and crises before or during the transition; experience with elections, whether legitimate or less-so; whether dissent takes the form of violent uprisings or generally peaceful civil society engagement; and neighborhood effects. Recognizing that these factors are not necessarily under the effective control of the government, the authors argue persuasively that the way in which governments and their partners deal with these circumstances will nonetheless shape success at democratization.

Each of the country cases is cited throughout the summary to illustrate points made, illustrating the range of experience and outcomes. For example, the economic crises suffered by Indonesia, Brazil, and Mexico are identified as precipitating factors to all three democratic transitions. Coleman and Lawson-Remer argue that, although economic growth does not lead ineluctably to democracy, the growth of a middle class is both a core requirement and a driving force for change, particularly when crisis causes its members to reconsider the "authoritarian bargain" of passivity for prosperity and demand a greater role in decision making.

A valuable insight from their review is that even crooked elections generate pressure for democratization over time, building an expectation that governments must be sanctioned by the ballot box, generating pressure toward more legitimate electoral processes over time. Even where elections have been rigged or even symbolic for decades, as in pre-2000 Mexico, the opposition parties gradually built up credibility and effective electoral machinery; impelled by repeated economic crises, they were eventually able to force a real opening and to take power. Two decades elapsed between the economic crisis of the early 1980s and Vicente Fox's victory in 2000, a pattern repeated in several case studies.

Teorell's review of the statistical evidence on democratic transitions further enriches this discussion. He finds a preponderance of evidence that neither inequality nor economic growth, as such, has been confirmed as a driver of democratization; indeed, an autocrat who can turn in a solid economic growth performance tends to strengthen his hold on power. Conversely, economic crises trigger a drive for democratization. Nonviolent mass mobilizations whether set in motion by economic crises or other concerns, also are likely to lead toward greater democracy, whereas violent movements have the opposite effect.

Of particular relevance to the current developments in the Middle East, Coleman and Lawson-Remer argue that violent uprisings very rarely lead to lasting democratization. Conversely, countries that have strong but essentially peaceful civil society organizations capable of mass mobilizations stand at a real advantage in the democratic transition process. The author's cite Poland's Solidarity and South Africa's civil society organizations as cases in point. One might also cite as a confirming Middle East example Tunisia's powerful labor union federation, the UGTT, which navigated that country through the Arab Spring with its vision of democracy largely intact (at least at this writing).

The second sets of key choices discussed in the summary are those made during the transition itself. Coleman and Lawson-Remer cite three as the most important: (1) delivering on economic and social expectations; (2) rule of law and economic governance; and (3) decentralization of government power. These requirements, more than any of the others, represent areas where Arab countries have seriously lagged by many measures. If one accepts the book's conclusion that successful adoption of policies to advance these areas is vital to success in democratization, one cannot be optimistic for the near-term prospects of the Arab Spring countries.

The summary closes with a set of valuable comments on sequencing, which emphasize the need for economic reforms to build a middle class; support of a "vibrant civil society," transparency, and the rule of law, and prioritization of reforms that can deliver social and economic opportunity. Although the authors do not put it in these terms, the conclusion one takes from this discussion and the case studies is that the transition to democracy takes a good quarter-century, once the key requirements are sufficiently advanced to start the ball rolling. This is not a hopeful conclusion for the Middle East, where almost none of the boxes can be checked. **JB**

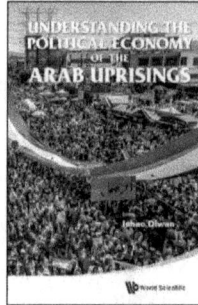

Ishac Diwan, Ed. *Understanding the Political Economy of the Arab Uprisings.* **Singapore: World Scientific Co., 2014. 300 pp. $56.00. ISBN: 978-9814596008. Ebk: $29.39. 6055 KB. ASIN: B00LF3VPYG**

This volume makes a valuable contribution to the growing literature on the Arab Uprisings (arguably a more appropriate term than "Arab Spring"). As suggested by the title, most of the pieces fall within the trend toward applying a political economy lens to Middle Eastern development. Clearly influenced by North's concept of "limited access orders," several of these studies examine how rulers and the economic elite have, together, created rents and then shared the benefits. This often-successful collaboration creates a system that is both deeply unequal and depressingly resistant to change. With a limited access order in place, reforms that would open up competition or distribute resource rents more equally expose the ruling class to overthrow by the elite, giving both sides strong incentives to maintain the status quo.

The volume opens with three pieces exploring the genesis of the uprisings. Owen's piece summarizes the developments in the region and the dynamics that enabled autocratic regimes to maintain power. His essay will be of most interest to readers looking for a general overview of the political antecedents of the Arab uprisings and their immediate aftermath. Kadoub provides an insightful discussion of the uprising in Tunisia, the country that has thus far proven the most successful in sustaining political reform. His analysis brings together the most important dynamics underlining the uprising, including increasing centralization of corruption, the resulting dissatisfaction of the elite, the breakdown of the longstanding social contract based on government employment, and the emergence of political Islam as both an effective opposition force and a real factor in pro-reform coalitions.

Diwan uses data from the World Value Survey (WVS) and the stock market to underpin his analysis of why Egypt's uprising occurred and why the opposing forces of privilege and reaction have proven so determined to prevail. His analysis addresses two main questions with broader relevance across the region: (1) what have been the roles of the middle class and political Islam in popular support for democracy; and (2) how has the three-way coalition of autocratic rulers, elite, and security sector been able to capture the benefit of market-opening reforms?

These complex questions cannot be fully addressed in an essay, but Diwan provides convincing evidence on both. He draws on the WVS to document an important shift in attitudes toward democracy between the WVS "waves" of 2000 and 2008. In Egypt, as in Tunisia, this period saw deep erosion in the social contract that had ensured the educated middle class a good standard of living through government employment. Although market-opening reforms started in the 1980s, it was not until the latter period that the full impact of government hiring freezes and the shift toward rent-based strategies (real estate, oil, gas, etc.) really began to bite. In Egypt, as in Turkey, a group of small business entrepreneurs arose in response to the reform's new openings, but in Egypt they found growth blocked by informality and closed crony networks.

Whereas the young and the leftists (measured by their pro-equity stance on the WVS) supported democratization in both periods, the middle class's weak support for democracy in the early period gave way to majority support by 2008. Conversely, the rich—never as supportive of democracy as the middle class—had become even more anti-democracy by 2008, while older generations joined the youth in supporting democracy. Although adherents of political Islam generally did not hold strong democratic values in either period, by 2008, the middle-class Islamists (but not the poor) had also shifted to support democracy.

Diwan argues that this shift is partially explained by the surge of the crony elite, positioned to capture reform benefits through "networks of privilege." He provides statistical support for this link by demonstrating, first, that network members benefited from their privileged status through higher market shares and better access to capital, and, second, that their share values fell more than did those of less-connected firms following Mubarak's overthrow. Together, these findings provide important insight into the dynamic of the Arab Uprising in Egypt.

Several essays in addition to Diwan's extend standard political economy analysis through what might be called the "political economy of Islamism," particularly Kaboub (Tunisia), Esfahani and Gurakar (Iran), and Ersel (Turkey). This analysis generally identifies the rise of Islamism with the exclusion of a rising entrepreneurial class and its educated (but often unemployed) offspring from the closed circle of economic privilege created by the limited access order. From Turkey to Egypt to Tunisia, this group has formed the core of Islamist leadership. The failure of the Arab Uprising (if such it is) stems in large part from this group's inability to form a broad coalition with either other elites or the excluded.

A potential weakness of the volume is that, despite the title, only four of the 10 pieces provide an analysis directly focused on the Arab Uprising countries (Owen, Diwan, Kaboub, and Schwedler). The remainder falls into two categories: those that address specific political economy issues in a broad comparative framework, and those that analyze experiences elsewhere in the Muslim world.

In the first category, Nugent writes on mechanisms to control corruption, Freund and Jaud analyze the determinants of democratic transition using a database of 90 attempted transitions over the past 50 years, and Atiyas examines Turkey's experience for insights on the use of regulatory reform to build a more competitive marketplace. Both Atiyas and Nugent provide a useful summary of their topic with relevance both within the Middle East and beyond it. To this reviewer, Nugent's piece would have been strengthened by complementing the comprehensive (if necessarily brief) review of sanction-based approaches for corruption control (the "push" side) with a discussion of "pull" measures, including efforts to strengthen ethical support systems in the public service, such as codes of conduct and the OECD's integrity frameworks. Both are needed to erode the "culture of corruption" and replace it over time with a "culture of compliance."

Freund and Jaud's piece contribute to our understanding of the factors that favor a country's transition to democracy and the transition's ultimate success. They begin with an analysis of global transition experience between 1965 and 2005, documenting that MENA countries have indeed been much less likely to begin a transition than countries in any other regions, with an average probability in any year of only 0.6%, one fifth the global average of 3.0%. Only four attempts were recorded among the 19 MENA countries during this period, of which only one can be counted a success (Lebanon) and three failed (Iran, Djibouti, and Algeria).

They find that, while economic growth is associated with democracy in general, a comparatively high GDP may actually stand in the way of transition: autocracies with high GDP per capita are less likely to experience a transition. Heavy reliance on natural resources also makes a transition less likely to occur (as expected) or to succeed, if one occurs. Urbanization, by contrast, increases the chances of a transition, as does military rule and the presence of low-level conflict (but not high conflict).

Perhaps their most interesting finding is that the size of the gap between male and female literacy is a strong determinant of whether a transition will start and whether it will succeed. This does not augur well for the Arab Uprising, of course, given the comparatively high female literacy gaps in many of these countries (Egypt: 66% of adult females (F) literate versus 81% of adult males (M); Algeria: 64% F versus 81% M; Morocco: 58% F versus 76% M; Yemen: 49% F versus 82% M). They find that a smaller literacy gap favors both a transition to democracy's being launched and its chance of near-term success, giving added impetus to those advocating greater equality for women and girls in the Middle East.

World Economic Forum. 2013. The Global Gender Gap Report 2013, p. 53. Retrieved from http://www3.weforum.org/docs/WEF_GenderGap_Report_2013.pdf. A rate for Tunisia is not reported and other sources differ widely. **JB**

SYRIA

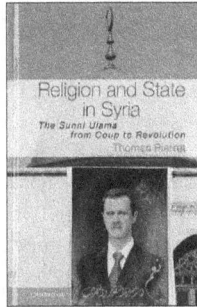

Thomas Pierret. *Religion and State in Syria: The Sunni Ulama from Coup to Revolution*. Cambridge, UK: Cambridge University Press, 2013. 276 pp. $85.50. ISBN: 978-1107026414. Pbk.: $29.99 ISBN: 978-1107609907.

Syria is a country of many contrasts. It is one of the most heterogeneous countries in the Middle East. It is comprised of a rich myriad of religious groups. It includes Sunni Muslims, the Alawis, Isma'ilis, Shi'a, Druze, and Christian groups. However, Syria has been dominated and ruled since the 1960s by a determinedly secular regime, whose rule involved brutal military methods as well as "soft" approaches to win hearts and minds. The uprising that began in Syria in 2011 has raised many questions and speculations about the role of religion in the country's politics. This recent study of Thomas Pierret is a welcome addition to the existing literature on the subject, and is a comprehensive study of Syria's little known religious scene. It sketches the complexity of the relationship between the Baa'th regime and Muslim scholars—the *ulama*. The book is based on Pierret's extensive fieldwork in Syrian schools and mosques, and interviews with local Muslim scholars. Although the book focuses on the religious elite, it provides new insight regarding the political system in Syria as well. The range of topics explored makes it a worthwhile addition to any library of religion, politics, anthropology, or sociology. The book is divided into six chapters. The division itself suggests the complexity of issues involved in this book.

The first chapter discusses the religious scenes of Aleppo and Damascus, and how the significant development of secular schooling and the impact of Westernization changed the ulama's identification. In the face of secularization, the Syrian ulama reaffirmed their identity and modes of preaching in a changing society. The second chapter examines the role of the ulama in the 197282 insurgency, and the strategies followed by the Syrian regime to promote loyal religious partners, such as Mohamed Said Ramadan al-Bouti who portrayed himself as a mediator rather than a mere apologist for power. The third chapter shows how the clergy, with the help of the state, overcame the challenges posited by the Salafis. The chapter also illustrates the conflict between old orthodoxy and Salafism. The Salafi trend continued to exert a growing influence, thanks, in particular, to new information technologies.

The fourth chapter examines the economic resources available to the traditionalist ulama. These resources enabled them to strengthen their dominance over religion. The economic transformations and liberalization that Syria experienced financially benefited the ulama and strengthened their position in Syria. Through their deft handling of merchant networks, the ulama increased their influence, and overcame the challenges of social change and Ba'thist authoritarianism.

The fifth chapter deals with the involvement of the ulama in politics. Due to the ulama's influence, the Ba'athist regime was compelled to bring them into the political fold. While some ulama tended to focus on sectorial interests rather than on regime change, others saw it otherwise. This ambiguous relationship was exposed in 2011 with the split of the ulama between regime supporters and opponents. The sixth chapter talks about the reforms that Syria witnessed, and how the ulama played a major role in the uprising that began in 2011.

Although the chapters are readable and accurate, they differ in length and complexity. Some chapters are longer and more densely footnoted than the others. Pierret's strongest chapter is Chapter 6, where he clearly outlines the role of the ulama during the uprising. However, many of the topics discussed are weakly argued or insufficiently developed. The shortcoming of this chapter could have been remedied if the author had updated the book to reflect the current political situation in Syria. For example, the late scholar Al-Bouti is frequently brought into the discussion in many chapters as a vocal supporter of the Ba'athist regime, but his murder unveiled many mysteries that need more investigation. Also important is the discussion of the new clerics who have recently emerged as a result of ongoing uprising.

It is unquestionable that this book affords a new perspective on Syrian society as it stands at the crossroads of political, social, and religious fragmentation. However, the events reported in the book are very condensed and confusing to the reader. It would have been helpful if the author had arranged the events in a chronology table.

Of course, the minor objections raised in this review are not meant to undermine or question the merits of the book under review. Pierrett's book is a thought provoking, complex and engaging work. It is well written and includes useful explanations that help the reader navigate through a complex and very condensed history. The author's arguments are also enriched by an impressive list of references. **AZ**

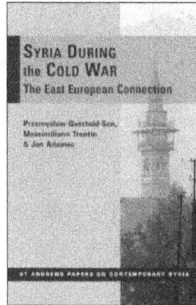

Przemyslaw Gasztold-Seń, Massimiliano Trentin and Jan Adamec. *Syria during the Cold War: The East European Connection.* **Fife, Scotland: University of St. Andrews Centre for Studies, School of International Relations, 2014. $13.95. ISBN: 978-0956873224.**

Syria during the Cold War: The East European Connection is a monograph within the St. Andrews Papers on Contemporary Syria series, in collaboration with Lynne Rienner Publishers. The goal of the series is to publish brief (30,000 words or less) research on aspects of modern Syrian politics that are often overlooked by journals and larger publishers. *Syria during the Cold War...* fits within this framework.

Generally speaking, the strength of analysis presented by Gasztold-Seń, Trentin, and Adamec in their respective chapters is solid. All three writers benefited from access to the archives of Poland, and former East Germany and Czechoslovak that opened following the collapse of communism in Eastern Europe. It is clear from an examination of the endnotes for each chapter that the authors have a strong command of the archival materials.

Gasztold-Seń examines Polish–Syrian relations during the Cold War. The chapter is concerned with party level political relations (Baa'th-Polish United Worker's Party), trade, government-to-government interaction, and the nature of international relations for Warsaw and Damascus. For example, Baa'th-PUWP connections were influenced by domestic events in both countries. The PUWP was, at times, suspicious of the Baa'th regime due to the latter's occasional suppression of the Syrian Communist Party.

In contrast, the Baa'th Party was very hostile to the Solidarity trade union movement, viewing it as "provoked by the Zionists and imperialists supported by the White House" (p. 12). Zionism and imperialism were always the standing "bogeyman" for any actions by Warsaw that Damascus might view as hostile. Syria failed to understand that Poland was motivated more by economic considerations than ideology, especially as the Cold War came to an end, leaving Syria with a declining circle of East European contacts.

Syrian–German Democratic Republic (GDR or East Germany) relations as presented by Trentin were at first influenced as much by events in Bonn and Jerusalem as in Berlin and Damascus. The "German Cold War" (p. 43), between Bonn and

Berlin as represented in part by the Hallstein Doctrine* slowed the establishment of full diplomatic relations between Syria and East Germany until 1969. Once relations were establish, East Germany became a significant trade partner for Damascus. Military and nonmilitary trade, as well as economic assistance in heavy industry, served as the cornerstone of the relationship. This partnership grew when Hafiz al-Assad came to power and remained in place until the East German regime collapsed in 1990.

Like East Germany, Czechoslovakia and Syria developed important economic and political connections during the Cold War. Military equipment and industrial machinery were Prague's main exports to Syria. In return, agricultural products were the primary item imported by Czechoslovak. Political relations were strong except between 1958 and 1961, during Syria's brief membership in the Egyptian dominated United Arab Republic (UAR). After Syria left the UAR in 1961, the relationship between Damascus and Prague returned to a previous level of normality as trade and political connections rebounded. This pattern maintained itself until the 1967 Arab–Israeli War.

Syria's defeat in the 1967 Arab–Israeli War weakened Syrian–Czechoslovakian relations. Prague felt the defeat was the result of problems within the Syrian regime. Militarily, Syria was lacking in the areas of intelligence, preparedness, morale, planning, and the technical competence necessary to operate the weapons supplied by the Eastern Bloc. Following Moscow's lead prior to the war, Prague believed that Syria and Egypt had unnecessarily escalated tensions, resulting in Israel's preemptive attack. Syria resented these assessments but still returned to Czechoslovakia for weapons and training prior to the 1973 War.

Improvements in political relations and nonmilitary trade issues continued between Prague and Damascus throughout the 1970s and 1980s. Czechoslovakia extended credits to Syria to stimulate trade, and the Czechoslovakian Communist Party (CCP) and the Baa'th Party signed agreements of understanding. These measures led to President Hafez al-Assad's visiting Prague in 1975.

In the 1980s, Syria's failure to pay back the credits Czechoslovakia had provided soured the relationship. Prague also tired of Syria's anti-imperialist rhetoric and obstructionist orientation toward Middle East peace efforts. Syria may have been an important partner but it was still expected to pay its bills in a timely manner. With Czechoslovakia's Velvet Revolution in 1989, communist rule in Prague ended and Syria's importance was reduced to that of a debtor state. Not until 2008 did the separate Czech and Slovak republics reach an agreement with Syria to repay its loans.

Despite the points above, this reviewer considers the work to have both editorial and thematic weaknesses. It is clear that the three chapters are separate and distinct papers cobbled together into a single volume without proper editorial oversight. For example, concerning money, Gasztold-Seń states "960,000$" and then "100 million dollars," Trentin uses "900 million US$," and Adamec "100 million USD." The proper form is "$100 million." There are also inconsistencies in reference to Syria's Baa'th Party. Gasztold-Seń and Trentin use "Baa'th Party," whereas Adamec writes "Baa'th party" without capitalization of the last word. Perhaps these are minor issues to some, but for this reviewer they are a sign that the work was rushed to publication, and that little editorial review occurred.

A restructuring of this work around common themes would provide the reader with a more sophisticated and nuanced analysis. The U.S.–Soviet competition during the Cold War is an essential part of the story these writers present, but is only examined as a part of bilateral (e.g., Syria–Poland) relations, not as a part of regional (Council for Mutual Economic Assistance or Warsaw Pact) policy. Party to party relations (Baa'th Party to Communist Party) are discussed in each chapter, but not analyzed from a regional perspective. Trade connections are also presented on a state-to-state basis, without any thought to whether Syria attempted to develop a common trade policy toward East European states. The importance of the 1967 and 1973 Arab–Israeli Wars also exists in a bilateral vacuum. Finally, the issue of relations between Israel, Poland, and East Germany are discussed in the individual chapters with little comparative analysis.

There is a brief Foreword written by Tina Zintl (Political Science, University of Tubingen), but it is not sufficient to tie these three chapters together. A concluding chapter written by all three authors would have overcome this sense of disconnection. Finally, a bibliography (beyond the chapter endnotes) and an index are missing, but needed. In conclusion, despite the above concerns, this reviewer does recommend Syria during the Cold War for library but not individual adoption. **WLR**

*The Hallstein Doctrine was developed by West German Chancellor Konrad Adenauer and State Secretary for Foreign Affairs Walter Hallstein in 1955. The doctrine stated that countries which recognized the German Democratic Republic would lose their diplomatic relations with the Federal Republic.

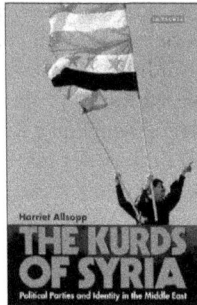

Harriet Allsop. *The Kurds of Syria: Political Parties and Identity in the Middle East*. London, UK: I. B. Tauris, 2014. 299 pp. $87.89. ISBN: 978-1780765631.

The Kurdish minority in Syria comprises nearly three million people, about 12% of the entire population—by far the largest ethnic minority in the fragmented country.

Yet, much of the literature relating to the Kurds in Syria refers to them as the "silent minority," the "newly discovered minority," the "forgotten people,"—terms which tend to downgrade their significance in the political history of the country, as well as their future in it.

Harriet Allsop definitely puts it all in the right context, and this is clearly the greatest virtue of this important book. She tells us the story of the Kurds in Syria with the largest collection of data and reading material ever to be included in any other book about the subject. The abundance of material is significant, as it gives a comprehensive picture of the current state of affairs among the Kurds of Syria— something which will serve for a long while as the blueprint of any reference to this population.

Allsop gives us an historic context, when she relates to the birth of a Syrian Kurdish Polity, 1920–57, but I believe that she should have expanded on this little known chapter in history, by referring more to the role of people like the Bedirkhan brothers, the Barazi family, Husni Za'im, Sami Hinawi, Adib Shishakli (who acted against Kurdish distinctiveness), and Khalid Bakdash in the modern history of Syria. Many of them may not have acted as representatives of their community, as they presented themselves as Syrian patriots; still many Sunni Arabs referred to them as Kurds, whose actions and policies were attributed to their different ethnicity, and this is a feature of the Syrian sectarian issue that ought to be given its proper attention in any book about the Syrian Kurds. It is a methodical question of how to relate to the role of individual Kurds in Syrian political movements, were they representatives of their community or acting according to their individual political conviction. This is a question relevant also to the political behavior of members of other minority communities, such as the Alawites, and also the Druze, Christians, Turkmens, and others.

Allsop is aware of this problem, so she rightly refers to questions of definitions (p. 416). That is helpful in the review of Kurdish political parties in Syria, a subject not so easily researched, since Kurdish political activity in Syria has always been illegal (p. 28), and the first organized Kurdish political party was established as late as 1957 (p. 69). This was the Partiya Demokrat a Kurd Li Suriye, which is the party to which nearly all of today's political parties trace their origin (p. 73). This party was established a year before the institution of the United Arab Republic, a period of almost four years (from February 1958 to September 1961), which hardly gets any mention by Allsop—probably because of lack of sources, although she relates to the ban on Kurdish language publications (p. 125), an indication of a policy of Arabization which came to a head under the Baa'th regime, particularly in the 1960s. This problem was mentioned by Allsop that by the beginning of the Syrian uprising in 2011, about 300,000 Kurds were stateless, and deprived of the basic civil rights of ordinary citizens (p. 24).

Allsop expands on the development of the Kurdish parties, their factionalism, the ideology and the role of personalities (pp. 81-90), and the description of the parties on the eve of the uprising (pp. 193-194). This is very useful and informative, especially as it comes after a fascinating chapter on the role of political parties in the overall tribal Kurdish society of the Jazira of northeast Syria, the region where most of the Kurds reside. (pp.121-148). She could however further the discussion (pp. 90-94) on external influences—a subject of great import, as the Syrian civil war has evolved into a regional crisis.

In analyzing the role of the Kurdish parties in the civil war, Allsop rightly emphasizes the need for the parties to maintain a precarious balance in relationship with the Kurdish population, the Arab Sunni opposition and the Baa'th Alawite regime, and concludes that none of these bore fruit. (p. 195), although she rightly notes that the circumstances of the conflict make it inevitable that Kurds will have to have a special, distinct status in the future, federal Syria; but if that is the case, it is doubly significant to relate to the regional context—something which, hopefully, will be covered more in a future edition of this book.

Altogether, Allsop has written a master book, the standard of reference from now onwards, about the Kurds of Syria and their role in the future of this tormented country. A highly readable, highly important, and highly recommended book. **JO**

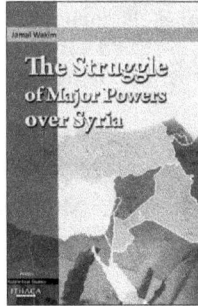

Jamal Wakim. *The Struggle of Major Powers over Syria*. Reading, UK: Ithaca Press. 238 pp. $69.95. ISBN: 978-0863725111.

Discussions on the Middle East and the Arab World tend to focus on topics of religion, oil exploitation, and terrorism. Debates on Syria, in particular, draw from these topics in order to explain the state's modern geopolitical significance and recent government dysfunction. Yet, scholar Jamal Wakim goes deeper by emphasizing centuries of interplay between geography, society, and economy to clarify Syria's unique place in Middle East and global history.

According to Wakim's work, Syria has a multilayered and complicated history. First, Syria possesses a delicate societal structure where multiple religious communities and people groups vie for political and economic power. More importantly, however, Syria also sits atop the world's overland crossroads. Inside Syria's borders rest vital way points along century old trade routes linking Europe and Asia. Imperial powers had for centuries coveted the lucrative, geostrategic position leading to a long history of foreign occupation. Moreover, its location—sandwiched between Egypt and Turkey—linked Syria to other regional events. In essence, Syria's situation directly impacted those nations around it. Wakim contends that this culturally fragmented nation served as a global intersection of economy, geopolitics, and cultural exchange. From the second millennium BCE, Syria was the major junction for international economy, culture, and politics, he argues, representing the first "instance of globalization in history" (p. 7). His global angle sets his thesis apart from previous analyses attempting to explain Syria's modern dysfunction. The approach is an interesting change of pace to an otherwise predictable topic.

Wakim segments the treatise into 11 chapters, organized chronologically. Although the content is somewhat dry, the encyclopedic style works well in retracing Syria's evolution from tribal land to Arab nation state. The textbook style offers a digestible overview of Syria's history and is well-suited for novices and educated nonspecialists alike. Wakim is not challenging long-standing arguments in the field or posing a new, path-breaking analysis. Rather, he is taking a comprehensive approach in a retelling of Syria's lengthy history, in order to demonstrate geographical and cultural importance in the course of world civilizations.

In Chapter 1, Wakim establishes the foundation to his thesis, exploring Syria's early history before the start of the Middle Ages proving that, even in these early years, the area was already a center for international trade and commerce. Such an important economic center naturally became the target of foreign empires seeking to expand their kingdoms. The region witnessed a cavalcade of successive occupiers to include the Greeks, the Romans, and the Arabs. Here, Wakim should be lauded for his extensive use of maps, as they offer critical assistance to an otherwise convoluted period of frequent turnover and ease the task of recalling names and places over time and space. Chapter 2 is a rather basic retelling of Syrian history from the eleventh through sixteenth centuries that recalls multiple Crusades and the eventual takeover by the Ottomans. In Chapter 3, Wakim makes a keen observation arguing that the critical transition for Syria came with the Portuguese establishment of sea-based trade lanes reaching Asia. With new trade lanes, Wakim writes in Chapter 4, Syria's chief significance shifted from economic to a central seat for imperial powers to maximize their reach into far-flung corners of their empire. Colonial empires, especially the French, "assigned special importance to Syria, and throughout the nineteenth century tried to impose their influence on this highly important geostrategic region" (p. 61).

Chapters 5 and 6 retrace the mandate period and national independence, in which Wakim claims that the European's planned for the endorsement of Israel's nationhood, more or less, to undermine future Arab domination of the Levant. In essence, imperialism continued under new strategies after the mandates collapsed. Chapters 7 and 8 bring readers into a modern period with a recounting that begins with the reign of the Assads up through the 1990s. In these periods, Wakim contends, Syria's history of societal fracturing became painfully evident. The volatile mix of competing religions and ethnicities, which has historically undermined Syrian cohesion, Wakim writes in Chapter 9, led to Assad's "delicate equilibrium" to hold the nation together. Yet, "chronic Syrian-Iraqi disagreements," normalizing relations with Israel, and U.S. meddling all continued to threaten regional stability (p. 49). In Chapters 10 and 11, Wakim veers off his otherwise logical progression of Syria's history into some rather startling conclusions. First, without a single reference to primary evidence, he claims that the United States used the September 11 attacks as an excuse to invade Afghanistan and Iraq, much like Nazi Germany used the "Polish attacks on its eastern frontier in 1939" (p. 157). He goes on to argue that the invasions were "decided upon" long before September 11 (p. 158). Wakim wants readers to believe the U.S. government purposefully staged the attacks much like the Nazis did on the Polish border. Unfortunately, he offers no evidence to support his conclusions. Such a major development without any evidence appears as an egregious deviation from quality scholarship. In the final Chapter, Wakim contends that the Arab Spring highlighted Syria's regional importance as its own instability went on to negatively impact Turkey, Iraq, Jordan, and Egypt. The Arab Spring reminds readers that the consequences of Syria's ongoing internal dysfunction reach far beyond its borders. The recent revolutions remind us that the nation plays a vital role in regional and international stability.

Wakim's approach is refreshing. Syria's geostrategic position goes further in explaining why the area has been the frequent target of occupation in spite of weak nature resources. His basic argument will surely change the way readers view Syria's role in international affairs. However, Wakim's use of sources is a glaring drawback. Firstly, Wakim relies heavily on secondary materials, which alone is not a problem. The issues rest with the large amount of secondary material, coupled with his infrequent endnotes. In fact, there are times when several pages go by without any reference. For example, in Chapter 5, Wakim makes the fascinating observation that Europe's case for Israel had to do with preventing "the creation of an alliance between Mesopotamia and Egypt" (p. 86). Yet, there is no reference within 50 sentences of the information. Together, it left this reader wondering if certain information is derived from a published source or his own previous research. This weakness looms especially large in Chapter 10 with his assertions that equate the United States and September 11 to premeditated Nazi actions. Here again, Wakim offers no reference or evidence to support his rather incredible conclusion. An unsubstantiated claim that the U.S. government orchestrated these attacks is bizarre. It appears cavalier and it mars an otherwise interesting monograph.

Taken together, source usage and notation needs some serious revision and reorganization, but the overall narrative offers a fantastic overview of Syria's historical evolution. The book is a good tool for those seeking a readable rehashing of Syria's history. **DAG**

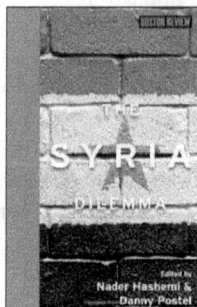

Nader Hashemi and Danny Postel, Eds. *The Syria Dilemma*. Cambridge, MA: Massachusetts Institute of Technology, 2013. 285 pp. $14.95. ISBN: 978-0262026833.

On January 31, 2011, the President of Syria, Bashar al-Assad, already aware of the political upheaval in Tunisia and Egypt, granted an interview to the *Wall Street Journal*. An interview? Well, it reads more like a sermon, pontification from the young leader for both, the American public, and more importantly, for his fellow Arab leaders. In it, al-Assad praised the internal stability in Syria, and expressed confidence that the riots (at the time) in some Arab countries would not spread to Syria. The main reason for that was the "fact" that the Syrian people liked their great leader, because of his firm resistance to the machinations of American and Israeli imperialism. Six weeks later, the streets of Syria started to explode. After almost three years, the fallout has surpassed anything that has already happened in the Middle East, and a lot of bad—even beyond-belief—tragedies occurred in that volatile region before the eruption in Syria.

So, if the "reformist" (Secretary of State Hillary Clinton referred to al-Assad as the "reformist" on March 27, 2011 on CBS) President of Syria himself, as well as so many of his well-wishers did not know what was really happening in Syria, no wonder it took so long for many scholars to form an opinion of a situation that had not been predicted by most of them.

But then, in the late 2013s, it was not so difficult anymore to relate to the roots of the conflict—not necessarily to agree on all of them, and surely not to have one fully agreed upon opinion on how to terminate the carnage and achieve a lasting solution. Therefore, it was with great anticipation that I read this book, intrigued especially by the list of contributors. As great as my expectation was, so also was my disappointment. Let us start with the name: *The Syria Dilemma*. Well, at the end of the book, I was really confused as to what really is the Syrian dilemma. The book does not answer this pivotal question, and if the book's emphasis is on the question of foreign intervention, whether it is military or only humanitarian, and then it should have another name.

But the name is the least of the problems here. The bigger problem is the reference by the editors, Hashemi and Postel to the root of the crisis. In their view, "while the conflict in Syria has its origins in domestic politics rooted in the corruption, nepotism, cronyism, and repression of 42 years of Assad family rule, its regional and international dimensions are manifold" (p. 6). First, I read this with disbelief, then with a deep sense of bewilderment, but finally it dawned on me that there are those in the academic community, who somehow refuse to understand some basics about the Middle East in general, and Syria in particular. Among these basics is the problem that sectarianism is at the root of so many conflicts. To relate to the Syrian civil war without an analysis of the sectarian struggle and its deep-seated historical roots is really to nullify a great deal of the interest in this book.

Rafif Jouejati [spokeswoman for the Local Coordinating Committees in Syria, a network of activists, and Director of FREE-Syria, a nonprofit humanitarian organization that focuses on women's empowerment] does refer to this aspect, claiming that the atrocities "committed without any specific sectarian agenda in mind, as they are solely the desire of one clan to dominate, and in the process, to do whatever it takes to survive (pp. 175-176). This is a legitimate but wrong description of the problem. The Syrian civil war is a multi-faceted dispute, and there can be a debate as to whether it is an "anomalous conflict," or a more conventional, though extremely complicated case of protracted political and social conflict.

Azar and Haddad* discussed this question in relation to the Lebanese civil war, but their article could and should be a good basis for a similar discussion about Syria. So, when two distinguished writers relate to the Syrian dilemma in a way that ignores the domestic Syrian roots of the problem, and pin the blame on foreign actors or one clan, as important as it is, one is left to wonder at the sincerity behind dedicating the book "to the Syrian people." The Syrian people surely suffer, and their suffering is unacceptable and should stop, but they are fighting each other. It shows no disrespect to them if any serious reference to their plight also deals with the element of not blaming others, whether they are foreigners or a clan. The al-Assads alone can fight no one, but the Alawites, Druze, and the many Christians who support them know why; this is not to justify, by any stretch of the imagination, the atrocities of the regime, buy simply to put them in context.

Do the writers really believe that the Syrian people's main concern is the fact that "Syria has morphed into a key battleground between Saudi Arabia and Iran for regional hegemony" (p. 6)? For that matter, I wonder if too many Syrians share the concerns of Richard Falk, the UN Special Rapporteur to monitor alleged violations by Israel of human rights in the occupied territories. This rapporteur, who is one of those who subscribe to the 9/11 conspiracy theories—a fact, that in itself, should have disqualified him for any UN job—found the Israeli connection to it all. The solution to the Syrian "dilemma," is for the US "to join with other governments in the region, including Iran, to sponsor a comprehensive security framework for the Middle East that features a nuclear weapons free zone, with an insistence that Israel join in the process [rather than being engaged] in a permanent struggle to maintain

Israeli military dominance" (pp. 74-75). So, now the readers know how the Syrian "dilemma" was created and should be solved.

It is to the credit of the editors that they insisted on supplying a divergence of opinions in the book, so in the interest of free speech, Falk can vent his hatred of Israel, but the Syrian people, what about them? Do they really believe that their redemption will come from what is suggested by Falk? I doubt it, and apparently many other Syrians—surely those who flock by the hundreds to the Zefat hospital in Northern Israel for treatment—doubt it.

In the department of free debate over intervention, there are some interesting chapters by Hamid, Ignatieff, Roth, and Zakaria which present the entire gamut of arguments, both in favor and against military intervention; these articles save the entire book from being totally irrelevant and misleading.

Still, it is my firm recommendation that, on the bookshelf where we put our books on the Syrian civil war, its background and possible solutions, this book should be pushed to the rear. There are so many better books on the subject, written by Arab and Western authors. **JO**

*Azar, E. E., & Haddad, R F. (1986, Oct.). "Lebanon: An anomalous conflict?" *Third World Quarterly, 8*(4), 1337-1350.

TERRORISM

Abdel Bari Atwan. *After bin Laden: Al-Qa'ida, The Next Generation*. London: SAQI Books, 2012. 300 pp. Pbk.: $14.20. ISBN: 0863564194. New York, NY: The New Press, 2013 (reprint). 304 pp. ISBN: 159558899X.

The death of Osama bin Laden was a setback for al-Qa'ida , but the organization was able to survive this loss through the strategic and institutional changes enacted in response to the 2001 NATO intervention in Afghanistan that had reduced bin Laden to a mascot and had transformed the group into a jihadi franchise where local units could operate independently of the central leadership. Abdel Bari Atwan offers an account of this transformation and its present geographic expansion in *After bin Laden: Al-Qa'ida , The Next Generation*. The author is a journalist who interviewed bin Laden in the 1990s and has reported on Sunni terrorist networks for decades. Atwan's work deserves serious reading as he describes how al-Qa'ida survived the War on Terror and is now expanding globally in Libya, Yemen, Pakistan, Afghanistan, Syria, Somalia, and Nigeria.

The book opens with an introduction that looks at the role of bin Laden within al-Qa'ida and the organizational changes that allowed the group to survive the NATO intervention in Afghanistan in 2001. This incursion could have destroyed al-Qa'ida had bin Laden perished, but this was not the case. Additionally, the 2003 Iraq War allowed it to reemerge through the volunteers who sought to oppose the unpopular invasion where American troops occupied an Arab state. The jihadi groups underwent institutional changes that saw the regional affiliates become independent from central leadership, and al-Qa'ida transformed from an organization into a broader movement. Al-Qa'ida 's long-term goal continues to be the establishment of an Islamic Caliphate; and it wishes to carry this out by provoking the United States to enter Arab lands. It believes this effort will bankrupt the American government and allow jihadi groups to overthrow individual Arab regimes. Al-Zawahiri emerged as the leader replacing bin Laden, and his goal has been to establish cells in every country, and to structure al-Qa'ida to survive the death of individual leaders who have a high probability of being assassinated. The movement has expanded through allied groups in Yemen, Iraq, Afghanistan, Pakistan, Africa, the Caucasus, Indonesia, Thailand, China, and Uzbekistan and through 'lone-wolf' activity in the United States and Europe. The largest threat to the organizational leadership is American drones which routinely target and kill regional commanders. Atwan observes that even this threat may be counter-productive as "drones can target leaders, but not a mind-set" (p. 33), and lead to increased anti-Western violence in the long-run. Ironically, the West's short-term response to these terror networks may hurt its future security by driving more individuals to embrace terrorist violence.

The next major topic discussed in the book is the Arab Spring that saw peaceful protests facilitate regime change; thereby presenting an alternative to the al-Qa'ida strategy that targeted Arab governments with violence. While bin Laden and al-Zawahiri publically celebrated these secular revolutions, the al-Qa'ida jihadists were only present in Libya where 200 armed fighters recruited and trained rebels. Nevertheless, Atwan believes that al-Qa'ida will likely become further entrenched through the uprisings as the weakening central governments will create a power gap that jihadists will be quick to fill. The resultant elections have seen Islamist parties win; and this works to strengthen extremists if they are denied a place in government. In addition, the Arab Spring is likely to worsen the Sunni-Shi'a division and has compromised local intelligence networks. Both outcomes are likely to strengthen al-Qa'ida allied groups. The NATO intervention in Libya saw the West inadvertently arm al-Qa'ida affiliated groups who participated in the overthrow of Gaddafi and profited by raiding Libya's advanced weapons which were smuggled outside the country and used to support other jihadi groups. The Arab Spring is creating conditions that appear to help jihadi organizations strengthen their social position and weaken moderates and individuals supporting liberal democracy.

The Arabian Peninsula is the next focus of this work and Atwan shows how al-Qa'ida is growing in Saudi Arabia and Yemen. Al-Qa'ida in the Arab Peninsula (AQAP) emerged in 2009 when the Saudi and Yemeni groups united to form the largest regional terrorist threat. The Saudi government had a problem with thousands of returning fighters who targeted the state and has tried over 11,000 of its citizens for membership in al-Qa'ida. The crackdown was effective and caused jihadists to relocate to Yemen where the central government's inability to control its territory has allowed the terrorist network to re-organize. AQAP is independent from the central al-Qa'ida leadership and is a typical example of the organization's new strategic alliance with regional groups.

Al-Qaʻida used the franchise strategy to move into Africa, as al-Shabaab formally swore allegiance in 2007 and was accepted into the organization in February 2012. The author discusses how Somalia, a failed state, has been home to jihadi fighters since the early 1990s and how the global implications of this group were evident in the West when 700 fighters traveled to help Hezbollah in 2006 during the Israeli invasion of Lebanon. Somali pirates have a relationship with al-Shabaab and provide them with 20% of all funds raised through ransoms. Al-Qaʻida has expanded geographically by forming associations with like-minded groups in Nigeria, Iraq, Indonesia, and in the Palestinian refugee camps in Lebanon, and this growth is linked to al-Zawhiri's plan to expand the organization globally.

In the following sections, Atwan examines how Afghanistan and Pakistan have provided al-Qaʻida with protection and support from the Taliban and from the Inter-Services Intelligence (ISI), Pakistan's intelligence organization. The Taliban are the key regional allied movement and have regained their popularity in Afghanistan where they now control two thirds of the territory. When jihadists fled Iraq during the Sunni Awakening, many returned to Afghanistan and Pakistan and shared their knowledge with the Taliban, leading to an increase in anti-NATO IED and suicide attacks. The ISI arms and finances some of the most dangerous terrorist groups; and Pakistan has been the source of more Western terrorist attacks than any other country. There is enhanced cooperation between the Afghan and Pakistani Taliban who provided aid to al-Qaʻida fighters and allowed the terrorist organization to move the majority of its training camps to Pakistan. The NATO effort has failed as the Taliban fighters it removed from power in the late 2001 are now returning and re-taking much of the country.

Atwan provides accounts of al-Qaʻida's expansion in Algeria, Morocco, Tunisia, Libya, and its new alliances in other regions. There are now 40 organizations with links to al-Qaʻida and this has given the terrorists an expanded presence in the Middle East, North Africa, Sub-Saharan Africa, and East Asia. The last substantive chapter discusses the efforts al-Qaʻida and its associated groups have made in marketing themselves through websites and how many have established a press office and film production staff. Al- Qaʻida is using the Internet and popular media defend its ideology and to recruit.

The work suffers from two major weaknesses. First, despite the fact that Atwan is a journalist and is effective at providing narratives, this work is purely descriptive and not systematic. In presenting information about al-Qaʻida's strategy since bin Laden's death, Atwan offers a summary explanation and then proceeds to the stories detailing how it was carried out in several states. The problem is that all regions are presented as equally important, and this leads the author to supply significant details on minor events while presenting weaker accounts of areas that are more fundamental to al-Qaʻida's global strategy, such as Pakistan and Afghanistan. Atwan's work is informed by journalism rather than social science, and this left the final product with significant content gaps. The second principal shortcoming concerns the author's pessimism regarding efforts to counter al-Qa'ida and his implicit projection of the organization's continued menace to Arab governments and the West. While Atwan correctly states that al-Qa'ida has changed its methods in response to the Afghanistan invasion and the global war on terror and has positioned itself to survive similar attacks in the future, the mere survival and ability to thrive in failed-state environment does not mean that it will accomplish its goals. The West has also learned from its confrontation with al-Qa'ida and is likewise adapting its methods to counter the network. Terrorist groups can kill or wound the innocent and inflict economic damage, but this alone will never be sufficient to allow al-Qa'ida to grow into a real threat the West, to overthrow Arab leaders, or to enable it to re-establish the caliphate.

Overall, Atwan's work provides an important account of the contemporary changes that have occurred within al-Qa'ida since the killing of bin Laden. Since it focuses on the jihadi network, this book is a good compliment to Seth Jones' *Hunting in the Shadows: The Pursuit of Al-Qa'ida since 9/11* (Norton, 2010) which offers a description of the West's action against bin Laden and his organization and fills in some of the content holes in Atwan's valuable contribution. **GDD**

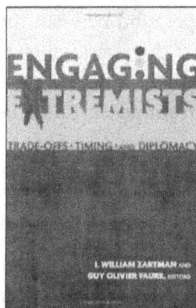

I.W. Zartman and G.O. Gaure, Eds. *Engaging Extremists: Trade-offs, Timing and Diplomacy*. Washington. United States Institute of Peace, 2011. 311 pp. $24.95. ISBN: 978-1601270740.

As a new decade has dawned under the leadership of U.S. President Barack Obama, there has been some hope that the acrimony of the Bush years and the War on Terror would recede. However, the number of terrorist incidents has not greatly declined; in Nigeria and elsewhere, random and complex terrorist attacks continue to take numerous lives. In this volume, editors I. William Zartman of Johns Hopkins University and Olivier Faure of the Sorbonne, seek to examine strategies and trade-offs associated with negotiating with terrorist organization and extremist groups.

The most important hurdle the Zartman and Faure identify is how a state can overcome the knee-jerk feeling that negotiating is a type of concession, a failure. "Negotiating with terrorist organizations is not talking with the devil. It is not soul-selling or evil pacting [sic], nor does it require surrender of goals and values that the parties have held dear" (p. 1). They note that "without such movement on *both* sides, the horror of terrorism will stay with us" (emphasis in original, p. 1). This paradigm is important. Not only can negotiating not be seen as a weakness, but it is important that the onus also be on the terrorists, not just the state.

The authors and succeeding essays view terrorism as part of a longer process. "It is more useful to see terrorism as a phase in a conflict waged by ethnic, religious, ideological, and other groups than as a distinctly separate phenomenon" (p. 3). The editors also note in their introduction that the state must be clear on what is the goal of engagement with the extremists. Is it merely trying to save lives in a hostage situation, or is it also providing legitimacy and status to a terrorist organization. "Engagement with terrorists can be seen as both admitting compromise on policy… and accepting unconventional violence as terms of trade" (p. 7). What is surprising about this book is that it is from a hard-nosed realistic perspective. There is no coddling of the means terrorists employ here. "It is irresponsible to let terrorists shoot their way through civilian casualties into policy decisions; rewarding their blackmail" (p. 9). Nevertheless Zartman and Faure conclude that "if one is to draw them away from their tactics and change their ways, they must be given something in exchange" (p. 287).

In the first chapter, Zartman and Maha Khan, an M.A. student at Johns Hopkins, examine how people become terrorists, since ideally one prevents terrorism before it happens. "What was it in the general perception of grievances that moved individuals from passive to active?" (p. 32). They note that scholars have long debated whether terrorists come from a humble and poor background or are middle class professionals. They then note that in fact the terrorist might have both backgrounds, since he or she might grow up poor and later become middle class. This however avoids a third alternative; that terrorists come from the upper class. Many of the members of the Red Brigades, and the German Beider-Meinhoff gang were born into wealth. In addition Osama Bin-Laden, the arch-terrorist, was extremely wealthy. These are not the only ones. There is a long list of wealthy terrorists, some who became wealthy due to terrorism, or some who were wealthy and became wealthier, such as Che Guevara. That most of the terrorists killed in suicide bombing attacks were poor may be true, but the 9/11 hijackers, by contrast, came from the wealthiest Arab state, not the poorest.

Khan and Zartman acknowledge this slightly by noting that "they are not just poor, alienated slum dwellers but also educated, frustrated middle class members" (p. 41). They argue that the state can pre-empt the turn to terrorist through intervention and affirmative action to target groups that are susceptible. They also note that spiritual leaders, such as Jonas Savimbi and Abimael Guzman, can be weaned away from terrorist movements.

In Chapter 2, William Donohue and Moty Cristal, of Michigan State and Nest Consulting respectively analyze how terrorist organizations function. They argue that rather than having static structures, many organizations have a "dune-like organization [that] shifts with the wind" (p. 59). For instance they argue that the Palestinian Fatah "bounced back and forth between its terrorist and political missions" (p. 69). This begs the question as to whether the organization "bounced back and forth" or simply employed multiple methodologies.

Robert Lambert, co-director of the European Muslim Research Center, uses a case study of police interaction with the Muslim community in Brixton in the UK to provide a positive analysis of engagement. He argues that "paradoxically, one of the most effective groups from the small list of Muslim Londoners identified [by the police] as having a track record of confronting al-Qaeda propagandists were themselves as vilified dangerous extremists" (p. 88). He identifies work with young Salafi men in helping to wean people from terrorist propaganda. The police injected money and resources in supporting football, boxing and encouraging Salafi outreach. The author seems to think that the Salafi movement is often derided as a Wahhabi extremist movement, whereas it is similar to mainstream Catholicism. "A correct Salafi interpretation that exposes the paucity of religious understanding in al-Qaeda's propaganda" (p. 101). The solution that Lambert proposes in engaging extremists is to employ members of local Muslim communities "with the needed street skills to counter al-Qaida" (p. 100). This is an interesting theory, but it ignores one problem. One way that Salafis were able to "counter" al-Qaida was by outflanking radical preachers on the right, by showing that one could be extreme and also peaceful. However, Salafism embraces numerous ideologies that are antithetical to the progressive liberal state. When a state works with a movement that preaches peace but also discrimination and anti-liberal values, then it becomes problematic. It needlessly entangles the state in supporting "a correct interpretation" of religion, which is a problem in a secular system.

In Chapter 5, Stacie Pettyjohn proposes a theory for understanding when the United States will engage with nationalist terrorist organizations. She argues that the United States was able to work with the Irish Sinn Fein and the African National Congress because America was not deeply opposed to the groups, and therefore did not force the groups to modify their goals. However, the United States "stipulated that the PLO and Hamas must limit their aims before it would even consider beginning a dialogue with either group" (p. 148). Thus, she places the onus on the terrorist group to signal its moderation, in contrast to Lambert who saw it as the state's obligation to work with local religious elements.

Chapter 6 is one of the most fascinating chapters in that it tries to provide a "what happened to terrorism" lesson in understanding why terrorism has seemingly become more brutal (p. 169). Camille Pecastaing, an assistant professor at Johns Hopkins University, traces how terrorism lost its romance from the period prior to the 1970s through the 1979 overthrow of the Shah. "Ayatollah Khomeini...was no romantic figure" (p. 175). The author claims that one cannot look for reasons for terror in psychological problems or a "flawed personal disposition." Therefore if the terrorist is not a psychopath or criminal, then his or her motives must be understood. Oddly Pecastaing references "deradicalization programs for Jihadists… [where they are held] in relative comfort and engaged in dialogue about Islam." He mentions that Egypt and Libya are among the countries that employ these programs. This clearly marks this essay as having been written before the Arab Spring, when regimes in Libya and Egypt were still able to propagandize Western academics with the idea that they were doing something progressive. Most of those who survived prisons in Libya and Egypt testify to the opposite of "relative comfort."

Engaging Extremists… is an important and interesting book, even if some of its chapters are already out of date due to fast moving events. It posits an important and muscular way to engage with terrorists, and provides a variety of perspectives. In one of its last chapters, the author examines Egypt's radical Islamist fringe and how it was successfully moderated and encouraged to embrace politics. Now, with the Muslim Brothers in power and Salafis forming a significant percentage of parliament, one can see how this comes to fruition. **SJF**

Tunisia: Politics & History

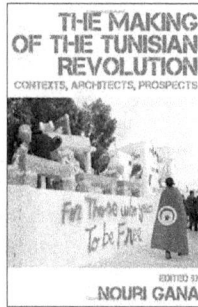

Nouri Gana, Ed. *The Making of the Tunisian Revolution: Contexts, Architects, Prospects.* Edinburgh, UK: Edinburgh University Press, 2013. 352 pp. $118.00. ISBN: 978-0748691036. Pbk: 352 pp. $29.95. ISBN: 978-0748691043.

The Making of the Tunisian Revolution... is what an edited volume about Tunisia should be: holistic, polemic, and strategically incendiary. Each chapter is placed to bring into question much of what the media has presented as truth. Herein lays the opportunity to be guided by experts who lead us through the Tunisian revolution into the post-revolution present. Reading this volume compels us to reconsider the standard Tunisia we are often provided: a progressive oasis in "the region," a liberal and neoliberal economic success story for international lending institutions and their cronies to hold up as proof that (so-called) free market capitalism works.

Part 1, Chapter 1 by Emma C. Murphy is an authoritative, albeit less abashed than might seem appropriate for the circumstances: reification of the hegemony of neoliberalism. Murphy jumps back on the neoliberal horse of *neoliberalism-as-progress*: had Tunisia's infitah been brought about by scrupulous capitalist leaders, then the revolution would not have been necessary. The savagery of structural adjustment, its crushing structural violence on Tunisians' everyday lives, is absent in Murphy's estimation. Murphy's chapter functions to set up an intense structural dialecticism that characterizes this volume.

In Part 1, Chapters 2–4, Kenneth Perkins, Lotfi Ben Rejeb, and Amy Aisen Kallander situate Tunisia in cosmologies of power. In Chapter 2, Perkins takes on the international and Tunisian national misrepresentations of Islam, exposing the ways in which secular Tunisian politicians manipulate Western Islamophobia and elite Tunisian Islamophobia. In Chapter 3, Ben Rejeb counters Murphy, primarily by analyzing her neoliberal arguments as part of a system of power situated in a region strategic to United States' and European interests. Ben Rejeb explains the United States' government's view of Ben Ali as "precious" because of the security he could enforce via autocracy.

In Chapter 4, Kallander scrutinizes French support of Tunisian authoritarianism. Kallander elucidates the impacts of both the European Union Trade Agreements with Tunisia and the stipulations of the International Monetary Fund, and particularly the French government's willingness to help Ben Ali counter the revolution demonstrations. In considering her analysis, it becomes necessary to consider if the term "globalization" is a euphemism for "neocolonialism."

In Part 2, Chapters 5–8, we come to understand the nuances of Tunisian dissent. In Chapter 5, Sami Zemni challenges media depictions of Tunisian revolution as a product of social media-savvy youths, instead describing the vital part played by trades unions and syndicalist organizations that have had a protracted conflict with the crony capitalists. Zemni's piece is important for moving analyses of the revolutions in the MENA (Middle East and North Africa) toward a focus on political economy, away from the facile conclusions drawn from reports on "new media." With attention to stratification within the unions, he describes the tensions between leadership (more loyal to the Ben Ali government) and the rank and file members who were often swift in their support of the protests.

In Chapter 6, Tarek Kahlaoui, himself a key social media activist during the Tunisian Revolution, takes issue with U.S. and French coverage in particular for ignoring the importance of Tunisian cyber-activism since the early 1990s. While Kahlaoui makes important connections between the over-emphasis of U.S. media on what it termed early on to be a "Facebook Revolution," Kahlaoui also elucidates exactly what was so important about Facebook activism in the creation of the Tunisian Revolution.

In Chapter 7, Rikke Hostrup Haugbolle provides a historiography of Tunisian "old" media. The United States pressured Arab dictatorships to privatize the state-run media outlets, and when Ben Ali did so, the close relationships between these moguls and Ben Ali's personal interests is a case in point on how media liberalization inhibited democracy.

In Chapter 8, Nouri Gana describes how Tunisian filmmakers disrupt the veneer of "good governance" under dictatorship and neoliberalism. Gana's chapter will also be important for those interested in scholarship on hip hop. He discusses the stark vulnerability expressed in Tunisian rap, contrasted with apolitical *mizwid* music, whose decadent esthetic belies a politics of domination. However, in his comparison of Tunisian hip hop with U.S. hip hop, Gana does discuss misogyny. In his description of rapper Balti's song "Passe Partout," he describes Balti's use of photographs of partying Tunisian women as "unflattering," stopping far short of condemning this as a violation of women's privacy (the photographs were used without permission), much less of what it means to humiliate women for expressing their sexuality in ways that are not socially sanctioned (the Tunisian men who are partying in the photographs are not the object of scrutiny). Hip hop, in the United States, as well as in Tunisia, holds great counter-hegemonic promise, but the genre has yet to reckon with its celebration of entitled masculinity.

In Part 3 of the volume, a holistic analysis of Tunisia's prospects in the "post-revolutionary moment" are laid out. These chapters compel readers to confront the shallows of media coverage. In Chapter 9, Nadia Marzouki explores Tunisian Islamist political theory. She critiques the romanticization of "the people's will" prevailing. She traces the genealogy of Ennahda leader Rachid Ghannouchi's theory of Islamism and democracy, and locates Ghannouchi's politics, rooted not so much in Islamism as in a de-colonization ideology, a pedagogy of the oppressed, designed to liberate Tunisian masses, and to have a state that serves its people, rather than the other way around. However, Ennahda remains, "eloquently vague" when it comes to how they plan to moderate the freedom of the people's will with the need to protect minority rights, and here Marzouki elucidates Ennahda's weakness, a weakness that harms Tunisia's prospects.

In Chapter 10, Monica Marks, like Marzouki, insists on treating Ennahda to a factual, fair assessment, remedying the Islamist-phobic hysteria promoted both by dominant corporate Media (Western and Tunisian) and opportunistic politicians, particularly when it comes to Tunisian women's rights. She clarifies the media frenzy over Article 28 of the Constitution, which states that, "men and women complement one another," not that women are the complements of men, an error that went viral. She emphasizes that which is often ignored in media coverage and political rhetoric, that a consequence of Ennahda's being in power is that many women have been elected; more, in fact, than many Western countries. However, most Ennahda women also promote a conservative agenda that keeps marginalized women, like single mothers (and their children) without rights. Marks insists that the real threats to Tunisian women's equality are a deeply ingrained (but not Islamic) patriarchal cultural habitus. While it is important to drive the discussion away from a focus on Islam itself as the culprit for women's unequal rights, it is also reprehensible to deny that Islamic ideology is patriarchal, so a necessary component of this analysis is missing. Women's rights are estimated by Marks primarily in terms of the constitution, the government's institutions, and by social custom. However, women's rights must also be considered through analysis of their labor participation. Social class must be part of this assessment of women's rights.

In Chapter 11, Fabio Merone and Francesco Cavatorta employ a skillfully understated political economic analysis to explain Tunisian *salafism*. They argue that salafism is a product of the social, economic, and political circumstances of Tunisia itself, rejecting the popular notion that salafism is an import from other Muslim countries. Jihadis as a youth movement are symptomatic of the lumpenization of proletariat youth. These youths are conceptualized by Merone and Cavatorta as without class consciousness, and easily manipulated. Tunisian salafists are an internally diverse group; some represent themselves as defenders of the Revolution of Freedom and Dignity, and are reticent to wage violent conflict, while other salafists seem to be aligned with al-Qaeda and are adamant on the need for shari'a law to be the law of Tunisia. Merone and Cavatorta's analysis would be augmented by a focus on gender as well as class. It is glaringly obvious that salafism holds most appeal to lumpenized boys. What about the lumpenized girls? What does Tunisian working class masculinity (and what it has had to endure during decades of neoliberalism) have to do with the appeal of salafism?

In Chapter 12, Lise Storm's assessment of the fragility of Tunisian democracy's prospects for the future is especially apropos considering the successes of the January 2014 constitution. This chapter brings readers back toward a macro-level assessment of the Tunisian Revolution. Storm also points to the ineptitude of U.S. political analysts, who initially dismissed the Arab uprisings as the beginning of a new era of Islamic fundamentalism. Storm argues that the main inhibitors to democracy in Tunisia are to be found in the parties that are filled with relics from the *ancien regime*. At this point in Storm's analysis, there is a missed opportunity to engage with questions of Tunisian labor organizations' political participation. Storm sees the internal conflicts transpiring in the Troika as vital because they compel the diverse interests to consult, coordinate, and bargain to make the constitution, rather than concede to the will of the most powerful. Storm gives us a detailed account of power struggles within the government, giving credit to President Moncef Marzouki for his stabilizing, democratic actions. The plodding rate of progress is necessary in building a consolidation of democracy. **COP**

TURKEY: POLITICS & HISTORY

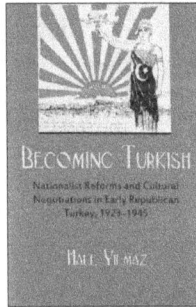

Hale Yılmaz. *Becoming Turkish: Nationalist Reforms and Cultural Negotiations in Early Republican Turkey, 1923–1945.* Syracuse, NY: Syracuse University Press, 2013. 328 pp. $39.95. ISBN: 978-0815633174.

In standard narratives, the processes of modernization in the Ottoman Empire and early Republican Turkey have often been explained from the perspectives of the elite in their top-to-bottom reformist trajectories. This study by Hale Yılmaz is a welcome attempt to challenge this dominant state-centric narrative of modernization by examining how the larger social segments came to negotiate the terms of the Kemalist reforms in Turkey between 1925 and 1945. Hale Yılmaz is particularly interested in men's and women's clothing, language, and national celebrations—that is, sites of reform where she uncovers a set of societal responses to the reformist trajectories, ranging from passive acceptance to sustained rejection. In doing so, Yılmaz sees the Kemalist reforms and the reactions they brewed in the social sphere as part of twin processes of nationalization and modernization whose terms were negotiated by a larger segment of the population. With her emphasis on societal responses to the political visions imposed from above, her study certainly complements the recent focus in the field of the Middle Eastern studies toward writing histories of modernization from below, as processes of negotiation and compromise in state and society relations.

Framing clothing reform as part of a wider revolutionary push in introducing new socioeconomic arrangements, the first chapter of the book starts off by discussing the Ottoman origins of men's clothing reform as a background to the (in)famous clothing reforms of the early Republican Turkey. As Yılmaz traces the Ottoman age of reform during the nineteenth century with her discussion of the introduction of the fez in the late 1820s and its gradual negotiation as the official Ottoman gear, the Hat Reform of 1925 which came to designate European hats as the official national headgear of Turkey reflected a clear desire to do away with the Ottoman past with the coming of the Republican arrangements. While the initial public reaction to the Hat Law was readily suppressed by the government, Yılmaz examines what James Scott has called everyday modes of resistance which, for instance, included the evasion of public sphere in order not to wear hats. Motivations in everyday resistance certainly varied, as the author notes. Some had culture- and religion-specific reasons, while those in the textile industry were affected by the changing market conditions. At times, the poor could not afford buying a hat. In some villages, there were formed community chests of hats and European clothing, made available to those going into the town. Thus, while the Turkish state's attempts to impose uniformity of clothing often resorted to the reliable and extensive networks of mosques and schools, reactions to, and negotiations of clothing changes not only varied greatly, but also reflected class distinctions, since peasants and workers came to wear caps, and bureaucrats the European hats.

In the second chapter, the author explores women's clothing reforms in the early Turkish Republic. While what women wore and its implications informed ideological and administrative debates in the late Ottoman Empire, positions vis-à-vis women's clothing in general and veiling in particular remained varied. With the gradual emergence of the Republican arrangements, women's clothing such as *peçe, çarşaf, yaşmak*, and *peştemal* (a picture on page 89 illustrates their differences) began to be labeled as backward and uncivilized pieces of clothing, unfit for the modern Turkish women. Yet, women's clothing reform lacked a hat law of its own, partially because, as the author suggests, the popular backlash to the unveiling campaigns in places such as Uzbekistan and Afghanistan was part of the lesson learned for the republican elites. Instead, regulations toward women's clothing were often articulated by the local councils. As for negotiations of such local-level reforms, different attire (e.g., overcoats and umbrellas) started replacing the banned pieces of clothing. Just as the harassment of "the new woman" on the streets by those who took moral positions was not unheard of, the evasion of the public sphere by women also took place. The lack of a centralized initiative for reforming women's clothing, however, leads the author to conclude that the state's coercive capacity also varied greatly in the early Republican era in contrast to the conventional wisdom that neatly attributes a greater coercive capacity to the republican state apparatus.

Yılmaz's third chapter examines the Alphabet Reform of 1928, another site of modernization, which aimed to improve literacy rates, fight ignorance, and unify the nation. Accordingly, the Republican elite embarked upon teaching the new alphabet to the masses through multiple channels such as schools and barracks. While literacy rates increased in the decades that followed, different provinces showcased uneven levels of progress. While Yılmaz observes that the resistance to the alphabet reform was minimal, she skillfully notes the persistent usage of Arabic letters, not only in private lives, but also in public transactions—an admittedly blurry distinction since most continued to write in Arabic letters, which were to be transliterated for public consumption. The author has also found instances when official correspondence came to feature continued use of Arabic letters such as the correspondence about the Menemen Incident in the late 1930 "when the state was particularly worried about the forces of reaction[aries]" (p. 174).

The last chapter of this book addresses the issue of national celebrations in early Republican Turkey where the vision of creating a modern and secular nation-state came to multiply the number of secular celebrations. While each national holiday certainly reflected an ideological desire to remember certain historical episodes as well as forgetting others, Yılmaz is particularly interested in the 23rd of April celebrations that not only commemorated the gathering of the National Assembly in Ankara in 1920, but also evolved into Children's Day which certainly became laden with notions of national renewal, regeneration, and optimism for the future. The author describes in length some of these celebrations by utilizing provincial reports. As these celebrations certainly provided some level of nationalist sociability for the participants, whether in public festivities or evening balls, the remembrance of the Ottoman past, as in the Ertuğrul Gazi commemorations, began to develop after the late 1940s, paving way for the re-imagination of the Ottoman past.

Yılmaz's study provides a mine of information, with plenty of examples that contribute to a multi-layered narrative, which bears significant comparative relevance to places such as Uzbekistan, Iran, Afghanistan, the interwar states in the Middle East, and well beyond. The book boasts of a very accessible language and style, but I think it could have benefited from a short historical background to the transition period from the late Ottoman to the early Republican era—a consideration particularly for the nonspecialist. Furthermore, even though Yılmaz has purposefully gone against historicizing the acts of the centre in an attempt to draw attention to the negotiation of the reforms in the provinces, such a thematic focus by the author often forces her to make constant chronological jumps from the mid-1920s to late 1930s, which amounts to a characteristic problem in the first two chapters. Some readers may also find long discussions of reports and oral histories a bit redundant. One minor correction for the future editions: on page 87, it should read "post-1922 shift."

Minor suggestions and criticisms aside, Yılmaz's study provides a much needed revision of the reformist trajectories in the early Republican Turkey where she successfully illustrates the co-existence of the old and the new, the variation in the state's coercive capacity, and the bottom-up reformist push, as observed in women's clothing changes. Differing from the existing studies that had so far focused on the organized opposition in Turkey, Yılmaz's study captures the everyday negotiations of diverse nonelite sectors of the populations, including but not limited to peasants, women, men, and children vis-à-vis the Kemalist reforms. For this monograph, the author has sifted through a plethora of untapped primary source material and made use of extensive oral interviews. The result is a nuanced narrative that complicates our otherwise neat understanding of top-to-bottom reformist trajectories in its early Republican Turkish setting. **RHO**

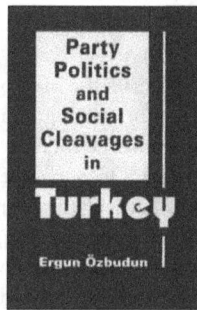

Ergun Özbudun. *Party Politics and Social Cleavages in Turkey.* **Boulder, CO: Lynne Rienner, 2013. 155 pp. $49.95. ISBN: 978-1588269003.**

Ergun Özbudun's *Party Politics and Social Cleavages in Turkey* offers concise and clear analyses of the origin of the Turkish party system, the relationship between social cleavages and political parties, the patterns of voting behavior, and the problems of the electoral system. Özbudun applies a variety of approaches to political parties, elections, and party politics such as Lipset and Rokkan's social cleavage theory, Sartori's party system categorization, and Duverger's law to shed light on different aspects of Turkey's political and electoral systems throughout this book. As he emphasizes, this book is about how Turkey's party system has evolved over time rather than how individual political parties have worked (p. 3).

This book has six chapters. In Chapter 1, Özbudun presents his main theoretical framework to explain the continuity and change of the party system in Turkey. Adopting Seymour Martin Lipset and Stein Rokkans' analysis of social cleavages and party formation, Özbudun argues that the Turkish case can be meaningfully studied through this cleavage model. In Turkey, important cleavages include the center–periphery cleavage and the church-state cleavage, and the party system has evolved around these divisions of society.

The center–periphery cleavage in Turkey, however, is not a geographical division as originally presented by Lipset and Rokkan. Instead, the center–periphery relations in Turkey refer to the antagonistic relationship between the rulers and the ruled. Agreeing with Serif Mardin who first introduced the center–periphery framework to the study of Turkish politics more than 40 years ago, Özbudun argues that this cleavage has caused the electoral strength of the conservative center-right parties (p. 3). Chapters 2 and 3 trace the impact of the center–periphery cleavage on national politics in the late Ottoman period and in contemporary Turkish party politics. Although the late 1960s and the 1970s witnessed a shift from the traditional center–periphery cleavage to a functional left–right, Özbudun contends that the current party system under the Justice and Development Party (AKP) is based on the old center–periphery cleavage. What is new about the current cleavage is that the periphery is now divided into two camps, including the religious-conservative opposition represented by the AKP and the Kurdish peripheral opposition represented by the pro-Kurdish Peace and Democracy Party (BDP) (p. 55). Both parties compete with the Republican People's Party that has maintained the secular centrist orientations.

Chapter 4 is probably the most important part of this book. Özbudun analyzes what is called "three maladies" of the Turkish party system including fragmentation, volatility, and polarization. Using Giovanni Sartori's categorization of party systems, Özbudun describes the evolution of Turkey's party systems ranging from a two-party system to moderate multipartism and to today's predominant party system in which the AKP has won the absolute majority in Parliament in three consecutive elections. Özbudun notes that Turkish democracy was damaged by both the presence of anti-system minor parties in the 1970s using their bargaining power vis-à-vis major coalition partners to gain disproportional political influence and what Juan Linz called "semiloyal" behavior of major parties. The second malady of Turkish democracy is electoral volatility, the level of change in voting behavior from one election to another. Turkey' elections have been famous for their high electoral volatility, but it is "interparty volatility" rather than "interbloc volatility" that affects party politics. Özbudun identifies three causes of volatility in Turkey: the military's intervention dissolving political parties, party splits and dissolution, and floating voters. Also, Özbudun claims that polarization is the "most serious and persistent" malady of the Turkish party system (p. 87). For Özbudun, the term "polarization" does not refer to an increase in the ideological distance between the left and the right as many Turkish political scientists have meant. Instead, polarization should be understood as cultural and psychological alienation between the center and the periphery, as well as ethnic and sectarian cleavages. Presenting a pessimistic forecast, Özbudun notes that it is difficult to resolve socio-cultural conflicts evolving around intangible interests—such as identity—in the near future in Turkey (p. 94).

In Chapter 5, the author shifts his focus to the effects of electoral systems upon party systems in Turkey. Özbudun provides a succinct summary of the frequent changes of electoral systems and the role of governing political parties that have attempted to change electoral systems to maximize their representation in legislature. Theoretically, it is well known that the electoral system shapes the party system as Duverger's law hypothesizes that proportional representation encourages multipartism and a plurality rule of elections leads to a two-party system. In practice, however, Özbudun argues that the relationship between electoral systems and party systems is "reciprocal instead of unidirectional" (p. 117) in Turkey because all of the changes in the electoral systems in Turkey were made by the governing parties of the time to solidify its dominant position in Parliament. This observation suggests that the politicization of the electoral systems for political gain negatively affects popular perception about the legitimacy and fairness of elections.

The electoral system plays a central role in political competition among political parties in the distribution of power in Parliament. Therefore, it is very natural that it has been a major source of debates in Turkey's public sphere. In the final chapter, Özbudun discusses main political parties' preferences regarding the electoral system, various proposals for new electoral systems made by individuals and civil society organizations, and public opinion about issues related to elections.

Özbudun's *Party Politics and Social Cleavages in Turkey* nicely presents the current state of empirical studies on Turkey's party system and electoral system. Although brief and concise, this book greatly helps us understand how Turkey's electoral systems have changed since its transition to multiparty politics in the 1940s. Furthermore, the book theoretically contributes to the study of party politics in general by examining how the existing theories and approaches can be usefully applied to study the Turkish case. The current reviewer believes that this book will appeal to those who are interested in democratic consolidation and party institutionalization of new democracies with a comparative perspective. Experts on Turkish party politics will also find this book useful because it reviews important previous research on electoral systems and the relationship between social cleavages and voting behavior. **MK**[1]

U.S. MILITARY INTERVENTION

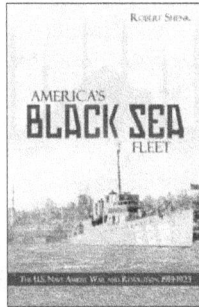

Robert Shenk. *America's Black Sea Fleet: The U.S. Navy Amidst War and Revolution, 1919–1923.* **Annapolis, MD: Naval Institute Press, 2012. 366 pp. $34.95. ISBN: 978-1612510538.**

In January 1921, a U.S. sailor aboard the ship *Scorpion* in what was then Constantinople shot an Italian, evidently while drunk. Several days later, another naval man shot a Japanese man under similar circumstances. At the same time, men aboard the *St. Louis* were debating whether to marry Russian girls they had met in the city. Against the backdrop of what seemed like times mixed with joy and too much carousing, the U.S. Navy was stationed amidst cataclysmic events.

Robert Shenk is a retired U.S. Naval captain and professor at the University of New Orleans. He hit upon the idea of writing a book on the U.S. Navy's experience in Constantinople because it seemed interesting that so many U.S. servicemen had been station in the region. To what end? He notes "it was in several ways similar to that of the Yangtze Patrol that America had maintained in China for decades, this in roughly the same period, though on the other side of the globe" (p. XIV). Shenk used both secondary sources to provide a picture of the general events in Turkey and also searched through national archives and met with descendants of the navy men who had served.

America did not declare war on the Ottoman Empire in the First World War, only on her ally Germany, and therefore American assets in Turkey remained largely untouched during the great conflict. American schools in Anatolia enrolled as many as 25,000 students, usually under the auspices of various Protestant missions. American

399

diplomats, businessmen, travelers and journalists often visited the country. In the aftermath of the Great War, with European powers attempting to lay claim to parts of the empire, the United States found it imperative to have a larger naval presence in the area. Toward that end, in 1920, three destroyers were dispatched to the Hellespont. They received a good welcome. "Almost every visitor from the States after World War I was struck by the admiration shown widely by Turkish and other Near Eastern people for Americans" (p. 39).

The admiral of this squadron was Mark Bristol. A veteran of some 30 years in the navy, he had served on other foreign missions, off China and in the travels of the "Great White Fleet" around the world. His task was to deal with the squadron, but he also shouldered political responsibilities and spent a great deal of time working with visiting dignitaries and attending official events. For instance, some 45 U.S. naval ships called at his station during in just one year of his service there. He was appointed a sort of "high commissioner" to Turkey and thus also had a political role in working with the Turks and Europeans (p. 44). As Shenk tells it, the Europeans were not impressed with him, apparently due to his strict neutrality in dealing as liaison between them and the Turks. "For example, he ordered his ships' crews not to render the traditional honors to the yachts of the Allied high commissioners" (p. 45).

The author castigates Bristol primarily for what he views as pro-Turkish sympathy in his dispatches and work. This was the period of the aftermath of the Armenian genocide, and it was a period in which Greek minorities were forced to flee Turkey. "Not only was Bristol always blaming the Armenians for bringing upon themselves their massacres and deportations...but by his typical analogies, he was, of course, also excusing the Turks" (p. 53). Shenk blames this on the fraternization in Istanbul. "The admiral's staff members were invited to follow the admiral's lead, and many made good friends among the Turkish elite in Constantinople" (p. 65).

However, the admiral's view of the Turkish role was not exactly sympathy, but more an orientalist and dismal view of their "character." In one dispatch quoted he notes "the Turks, during the fighting, had their usual brutal instincts aroused and resorted to massacres of the Armenians" (p. 59). He argued that often reports of massacres were part of a cycle of violence of "indiscriminate killing of each other" (p. 59). Whether he was "pro-Turkish" or rather simply thought all the peoples of Anatolia were simply full of "brutal instincts" is not entirely clear. It seems that his attitude was in line with other U.S. commentators at the time. Another officer named Robert Dunn had accompanied Armenian fighters in the Caucasus. He noted "the Tartars of Azarbaijan...are hereditary enemies of the Armenians wherever found, whom they massacre, and who retaliate in kind when possible" (p. 61). The Americans viewed themselves as having entered a sort of slaughterhouse inhabited by foreigners whose behavior and character they were not keen on. This was the typical style of travel writing one would have found at the time, in descriptions of the "East" or even of parts of the Balkans.

The U.S. fleet found itself serving at a time of numerous crises. In November 1920, some 140,000 Russian refugees from the civil war in Russia between communists and "white Russians" came pouring into the city. They had embarked from ports on the Black Sea, particularly Odessa. Some American vessels were employed in bringing out the refugees. These people changed the demographics of the city. They opened nightclubs and restaurants, and sang songs at beer halls and in the theater. Many Americans were taken with the Russian women. At a restaurant called the Moscovite, Americans reported being waited on by a granddaughter of a former Prime Minister. A survey claimed there were 200 brothels in the Christian part of the city, with some 4,000 prostitutes.

At the same time that navy men were getting venereal disease in their port of call, they also witnessed the devastating exodus of Greek Christians from northern Turkey and the port of Smyrna. In northern Turkey in the area known as Pontus, hostilities that had simmered during the First World War boiled over into massacres and expulsion of Christian minorities. In western and southern Turkey, the Greek decision to invade the country and try to carve out a Greek empire and its subsequent defeat by Turkish nationalist forces resulted in a mass exodus of Greeks, many of them via the port of Smyrna. In this evacuation, Shenk applauds admiral Bristol. "To his credit Bristol had sent several Constantinople relief people to Smyrna very early on; from the beginning of his conversations about the events there, he was adamant the Greeks and Allies should take the initiative and bear the main evacuation responsibilities, because they had caused the refugee problems in the first place" (p. 229). U.S. Embassy officials ignored the issue and did not dispatch ships to help out. It fell on YMCA official Asa Jennings to help coordinate the American efforts to help. Around 200,000 Greeks fled through the port, some of them assisted by Jennings and some U.S. naval personnel.

However, as with the Pontus story and the goings on in the Crimea, it was never clear where the U.S. Navy was exactly in these events. Shenk paints a picture of an uncaring and biased Bristol, sitting in Constantinople, purposely playing down reports of massacres. The role of the navy seems to have been always as a side element in the larger story of other Americans, such as missionary workers at Marsovan College, the YMCA, or other groups. This perhaps jives with the title, the U.S. Navy "amidst war and revolution," since the U.S. Navy does not seem to have placed much of a role. The reality is that the book focuses much more on these other side stories that took place. His research about the navy men's perceptions is often richest in describing what they did in Constantinople. When the narrative leaves that area, the story is primarily about other Americans and events. This makes for a compelling and interesting view of events, just one that is surely beyond the scope of a book about America's Black Sea fleet. **SJF**

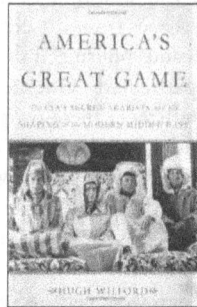

Hugh Wilford. *America's Great Game, The CIA's Secret Arabists and the Shaping of the Modern Middle East.* **New York, NY: Basic Books, 2013. 342 pp. $29.99. ISBN: 978-0465019656.**

While American diplomatic history has exhaustively explored the effect of U.S. foreign policy on the Arab Middle East, a missing dimension has been a close examination of the role of the intelligence community, and in particular, the CIA's secret pro-Arabists in the early years of the Cold War. Hugh Wilford admirably fills this gap with an examination of U.S. diplomacy based on group biographies of key players in America's version of Britain's Great Game. The result is a fascinating story of how the CIA shifted from being supportive of Arab nationalists to condoning covert missions designed to contain Arab nationalism.

His methodology includes first, drawing on the personal files of the three leading CIA Arabists, Kim and Archie Roosevelt, Miles Copeland, and their published memoirs, as well as oral history interviews, and personal correspondence with family members. Kim Roosevelt, Jr. was Chief of CIA covert operations in the Middle East; his lieutenant was Miles Copeland, Jr., and Archibald Roosevelt, Jr. (Kim's cousin) was an intelligence officer stationed in the region, involved in coup plotting in Syria, and an enthusiastic champion of Nasser until the Suez crisis. Second, in addition to the official records at the U.S. National Archives, presidential libraries, and the State Department, he mines the archives of the domestic anti-Zionist citizen network, which was covertly funded by Kim Roosevelt, Jr. (grandson of President Theodore Roosevelt). Third, he incorporates narrations of adventure fiction writing, which had a powerful influence on the perceptions and actions of the CIA Arabists.

The book is divided into three chronological sections that trace the childhood and family background, and OSS roots of the CIA's principal Arabists; their attempt to effect a coup in Syria in 1949; their support for Nasser's rise to power, and the successful coup effort in 1953 Iran; and lastly, the decline in their influence as the Cold War's Eisenhower Doctrine, which conflated pro-Arabism with pro-communism, came to be implemented. Through this chronology, the author essentially tells two intersecting stories in great detail: that of the organizing of a coordinated and committed anti-Zionist civilian network, which was first mobilized to prevent U.S. recognition of Israel in 1948; and that of the Arabist "game players" in the CIA who, for roughly a decade, briefly dominated the activities of the CIA in the Middle East.

Wilford depicts the CIA Arabists as initially embracing anti-colonial, pro-nationalist goals; however over time, they ceded their moral high ground as the original intelligence-gathering mission of the CIA slowly shifted toward a preoccupation with covert operations. They compromised their ideals, for example, when they supported regime change in both Syria and Egypt, sacrificing backing for democratic rule in favor of supporting Arab nationalist military leaders taking power. In Iran, they toppled one of the region's leading nationalists overestimating Mossadegh's vulnerability to Communism and being strongly influenced by MI-6's Orientalist lens through which it viewed Iran. The final coup de grâce to their moral luster was their plotting to reduce Nasser's influence in the Arab world in favor of more reliable pro-Western leaders (like Chamoun in Lebanon).

The author tells a balanced story. On the plus side, the CIA Arabists had firsthand knowledge and experience of the Middle East unlike earlier U.S. prior involvement in the region. They had unprecedented access to, and influence on Arab leaders (like Nasser), and they made a sincere (albeit, a failed) effort to resolve the Arab–Israeli conflict. On the other hand, they were not able to contain the nefarious imperialist scheming of their British counterparts in the Middle East, nor were they able to rein in the anti-nationalist sentiments of Secretary of State John Foster Dulles. Moreover, they were not immune from imperialist and Orientalist modes of thinking themselves. **MJP**

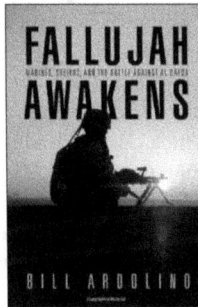

Bill Ardolino. *Fallujah Awakens: Marines, Sheikhs, and the Battle Against Al Qaeda.* **Annapolis, MD: Naval Institute Press, 2013. 290 pp. $ 36.95. ISBN: 978-1612511283. Ebk.: $19.99. ISBN: 978-1612511290.**

Bill Ardolino, an associate editor and overseas correspondent for the *Long War Journal* has written a book that many would be tempted to dismiss as a long version of the embedded journalism he did in 2006, 2007, and 2008 in Iraq. That would be a mistake. Mr. Ardolino has, perhaps unintentionally, written two books in one.

The first book is the one that Ardolino intended, that is the story of the success of United States' counterinsurgency strategy in Fallujah and the lessons that can be drawn from it. The second book that Ardolino perhaps inadvertently wrote is about the Sunni Iraqi community and the challenges and hardships they faced in the aftermath of the 2003 invasion.

Ardolino's book is based exclusively on 120 interviews, primarily with U.S. Marines and officers, as well as Sunni Iraqis that cooperated with the U.S. military. The book consists of a List of Maps, Introduction, 17 chapters, Afterword, a note on research methodology, Acknowledgements, and Index. In 17 chapters, Ardolino, as expected from a good writer and a seasoned reporter, engagingly tells the story of how U.S. Marines succeeded in fighting al-Qaeda and other terrorists in Fallujah. This was done by working with willing and able Sunni Iraqis who were caught between a new "democratic" order that treated them as a defeated and vilified community to be marginalized and a motley-crew insurgency of foreign and domestic elements that was getting bloodier and more savage by the day.

The book captures the struggle of the American military in dealing with a full-blown insurgency that it was not prepared to fight. The 2003 war was sold as an invasion that would be welcomed by Iraqis and would have very limited costs imposed on the United States. The reality turned out differently. The United States faced an indigenous insurgency that attracted foreign militants and radicals with their own agendas for fighting the United States and the new regime in Iraq.

Ardolino, through those who implemented policy on the ground, describes how the Marines were able to build bridges and relationships with influential Sunni Iraqis in order to gain valuable intelligence about the insurgency as well as to enlist Sunni Iraqis to fight the insurgents. A limitation of the book is that it does not draw on scholarly knowledge on Islam and the Middle East. Therefore, Ardolino, the reporter writing a book, makes generalizations that are commonly encountered in news reporting. For example, in Chapter 1, in telling the story of an Iraqi who cooperated with the Americans he states: "Such double-dealing is a common characteristic of Middle Eastern politics and tribal relations" (p. 11). Wouldn't hedging one's bets be as valid an explanation of the behavior of a party in a situation with low trust capital or lack of trust? As to Islamic religiosity, he writes that "the everyday tribesmen weren't particularly radical in their practice of Islam" (p. 11). It is unclear how the practice of one's religion could be "radical." Writing about an accidental shooting, Ardolino states that in addition to the fact that the killing was not intentional, "two elements of local culture might also help explain the tribe's willingness to forgive the tragedy. The first, stressed in Dark's entreaties to the justifiably angry mob, is the concept of fatalism symbolized by the Arabic expression *insh'allah* 'It is as Allah wills' or 'God willing'" (p. 82). In Islam the usage of insh'allah/God willing is not a cultural phenomenon, it is mandated in the *Qur'an* for believers: "And never say of anything, I shall do such and such thing tomorrow? Except (with the saying) if Allah wills" (Sura Al-Kahf 18:23).

In telling the story of a successful counterinsurgency strategy, one learns of the importance of personalities and empathy with the target population, an empathy that Ardolino mischaracterizes as "sympathy" (p. 30). In Chapter 3, COIN (counter insurgency), "Whether it was bravery, Arab world fatalism, or something else that drove the Iraqis to carry on, Kopera admired and sympathized with them. His men tried to show respect in their dealings with the locals and executed what he thought of as well-considered rules of engagement and detainee-handling procedures. But no good intentions and careful execution could blunt the terror of war and the disruption to their way of life, perhaps especially for Iraqi's politically displaced Sunni minority. Kopera thought Americans should try to imagine how they would feel "if a superpower invaded the United States and dismantled the government, directly or indirectly causing deaths of tens of thousands of fellow citizens" (p. 30). Here in telling the story of a successful counterinsurgency undertaking, Ardolino is telling the story of the struggles and hardships of the Sunni Iraqi community in the aftermath of an occupation which produced violence that was mischaracterized by many Iraq observers, such as Fouad Ajami (*The Foreigner's Gift*, Free Press, 2006) and Vali Nasr (*The Shi'a Revival*, Norton, 2006), as solely a Sunni Arab fight to deny the Iraqi Shi'a "majority" the political power that the 2003 invasion handed it.

In *The Foreigner's Gift*, Ajami sees the turbulence in Fallujah as a result of the Arab Sunnis not accepting defeat and their obsession with keeping the Shi'a Iraqi "majority" from ruling Iraq: "No victorious American tanks had rolled through the streets of Fallujah and Ramadi. Defeat has not been visited on Fallujah; the city has not been forced to acknowledge that its political regime had been overwhelmed. This reprieve played into the Fallujah insurgency, fed its sense of defiance" (2006, 143). As Ardolino's book shows, indiscriminate and blunt force against the Sunni Arab community only helped further alienate the Arab Sunnis and strengthened the insurgency. Successful counterinsurgency required an empathetic reading of the situation of the Iraqi Sunnis and the myriad reasons for the violence: "On top of that, the tempo of rougher operations, including raids and mass detentions of military age males, had been especially high in the early years of the war, as the U.S. military reacted forcefully to the growing insurgency. If an American unit had reared locals with disrespect—and some had—it made Kopel's job exponentially harder. This was especially true in the context of a tribal society that demanded restitution, or revenge, for an insult. The challenges could be depressing, but they were simply the products of culture and human nature. These were facts Kopera understood, even as he struggled with them" (p. 37).

An important counterinsurgency tactic was splitting the insurgency and peeling off those who were redeemable. In Chapter 4, Ardolino tells of the American classification of the insurgents into "Bad Bad Guys"/ "BBGs" and "Good Bad Guys"/"G-BGs:" "BBGs were irreconcilable. They were wholly out for themselves to kill Americans in their quest for religious purity, power, or both; they would eliminate anyone who got in their way. GBGs were also out for themselves, and they might never come to work hand-in-hand with the nascent Iraqi government or water any seeds of democracy, but they had interests that could align with United States' interests.... The hard truth was that the Americans needed to work with them [the GBGs]. That was the nature of COIN" (p. 58).

Despite the above-mentioned shortfalls that result from a lack of specialization and expertise in Middle East politics and Islam, I strongly recommend this book. Ardolino has managed to write two important stories of the Iraq war in one book. One is of the heroic American Marines who were capable of empathy and working with a population traumatized by war. The second is about the Sunni Iraqi community, a community demonized by what the exiled Vice President of Iraq, Tareq Al-Hashimi—the top Sunni Arab in Iraqi government convicted of murder and sentenced to death in absentia—calls the sectarian pro-Iran regime that emerged in post-2003 Iraq. Ardolino's book also tells the Iraqi Sunni Arabs' story through their own voices. This book is a valuable addition to the literature on Iraq, the Middle East and naturally, terrorism/counter-terrorism. Ardolino tells the story of successful counterinsurgency in Iraq, drawing lessons for other conflicts; and he manages to tell the story very well in a relatively small book. It will not be hard to get the students to read this well-written and engaging book. *Fallujah Awakens...* is useful as a secondary book in Middle East Politics, Iraqi Politics, Terrorism/Counter Terrorism, and Community Policing. **IAA**

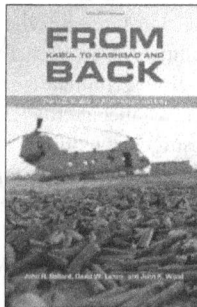

John R. Ballard, David W. Lamm, and John K. Wood. *From Kabul to Baghdad and Back: The U.S. at War in Afghanistan and Iraq.* **Annapolis, MD: Naval Institute Press, 2012. 369 pp. 2012. $32.64. ISBN: 978-1612510224.**

From Kabul to Baghdad and Back: The U.S. at War in Afghanistan and Iraq, by John Ballard, David Lamm, and John Wood, is a detailed military history of the wars in Iraq and Afghanistan from 2000 to the summer of 2012. The book covers the major military decisions and actions of these two wars in great detail. The central argument of the book is that a country cannot fight two wars simultaneously. By choosing to fight wars in both Iraq and Afghanistan at the same time, the United

States essentially guaranteed that one of those wars would go badly. And the one that went badly was the Afghanistan conflict.

The war in Afghanistan, entitled Enduring Freedom, was a direct and rapid response to the 9/11 attacks on the World Trade Towers and the Pentagon. Its fundamental purpose was to find, apprehend, and punish those responsible for the 9/11 attack, largely Al-Qaeda and, by association, the Taliban. The war, at least initially, was unconventional in many ways. Within weeks of 9/11, CIA operatives had connected with Northern Alliance fighters in Mazar-e Sharif and in the Panjshir Valley. By October 7th air strikes were launched against Taliban targets. Mazar-i Sharif was captured on November 10th, and Kabul surrendered on November 14th. Although pockets of Taliban fighters remained, the initial phase of the war in Afghanistan was won in just a little over two months after 9/11 and with very little direct involvement of U.S. military ground forces.

Events continued to go well. In December 2001, an Afghan Interim Authority was created at the Bonn Conference with a six-month mandate; Hamid Karzai was named chairman. In June 2002 the Afghan Interim Authority convened a loya jirga to bless the interim government; a second loya jirga in October 2003 approved the new Afghan constitution. In October 2004, the first successful presidential elections were held in which nearly 12 million registered voters participated, electing President Karzai with over 70% of the votes. And in 1985 Afghan parliamentary elections successfully took place and the first Afghan parliament of the new era opened.

In 2005, from the United States' point of view, events seemed to have gone extremely well in Afghanistan, with little direct involvement of U.S. troops. The authors attribute this to a combination of fortuitous events, but give much of the credit to Zalmay Khalilzad, who was named ambassador to Afghanistan in November 2003, and to General David Barno who assumed command of forces in October 2003. The authors credit these two leaders for working together closely in developing a new strategy for Afghanistan that focused on counter insurgency measures that synchronized coalition military, civilian, and Afghan government activities and the development of a strong national government. By 2005, with less than 20,000 coalition troops in Afghanistan, it appeared that al-Qaeda and the Taliban had been defeated and that a fairly elected functioning government was in place. What could go wrong?

The war in Iraq had a different trajectory. Although it was clear behind the scenes in Washington D.C. that an invasion in Iraq would soon follow the operations in Afghanistan, the actual invasion, called Iraqi Freedom, did not occur until March 2003, 19 months after the beginning of the conflict in Afghanistan. Iraqi Freedom was a more conventional war than Enduring Freedom. Led by General Frank, two military divisions, one marine and one army, rolled out of Kuwait toward Baghdad on the night of March 19, 2003. Although they faced greater resistance than expected (the American soldiers had expected to be greeted by exultant Iraqis throwing flowers at them), the marines entered Baghdad on April 9, 20 days after the invasion had begun.

It was at this point that things began to go badly. Riots broke out in many areas of Iraq as looting began, and the U.S. troops could do little to stop the looting. And at this time a national insurgency against the coalition troops began in earnest. The insurgency was an unexpected surprise to the U.S. troops who had expected to be greeted as liberators, but were instead seen as occupiers. When U.S. troops finally left Iraq on December 18, 2011, 4,485 American soldiers had died and over 31,000 had been wounded by hostile fire. Even more devastating was the death of over 100,000 Iraqis. The war cost the American taxpayers over $805 billion. Whether Iraq is better off today, the authors suggest, is an open question.

This book tells these two stories well and, although the book is filled with technical military jargon and acronyms that can bog down the average reader, the book is a must read for those who want to know more about the military side of these two campaigns. Two of the authors are faculty members at the National War College and this book will be, and should be, required reading for future military officers. This is a sad period in American history—a period of great cost in lives and money, and a period in which the international reputation of the United States has been greatly damaged.

However, despite the book's strengths, a military history of war does not tell the entire story. By focusing on military decisions, tactics, and personnel, much of the cultural and historical richness of these two wars is missing. This is particularly true of the Afghan front, where the authors seem unaware of the ethnic, sectarian, regional, and tribal complexities of the country, and its history of foreign invasions. Taking the struggle to form an Afghan National Army as an example, the authors focus on the difficulties of military and technical training. However, the real struggle to recruit and train an Afghan National Army has been thwarted by the ethnic and tribal nature of Afghan society. To put it differently, you can't create a national army when the ethnic and tribal differences are stronger than national identity. Because of ethnic and tribal animosities, Afghanistan cannot recruit, for example, Tajik soldiers and send them to the Pushtun areas, where the Taliban stronghold is.

In addition, the book presents an oversimplified picture of the Taliban, what their motivations are, and how they have evolved and changed since 9/11. Many of the insurgents in Afghanistan are not Taliban fighters at all, but belong to groups only loosely connected to the Taliban. These groups include especially the Haqqani network, which is briefly noted in the book. But the role of the Haqqani network, which is closely connected to the Pakistani military, in attacking the Kabul region is not discussed. The same could be said of the Hezb-e Islami insurgents of Gulbuddin Hekmatyar. Both the Hezb-e Islami and the Haqqani insurgents pose a serious threat to the government in Kabul, but are not members of the Taliban. Even in the so-called Taliban areas in Kandahar and Helmond provinces, many of the insurgents are local farmers concerned with local issues and only loosely connect to the Taliban leaders in Quetta.

By focusing on military aspects of these two conflicts, the authors do not present a good picture of who the Iraqi or the Afghan people actually are and how they think. The military term *COIN*, counter insurgency, is often used to indicate a military strategy that takes into account the welfare and concerns of the local citizens, but in fact much of the opposition that arose to the occupation of Afghanistan and Iraq came from average citizens who opposed the occupation of their countries by foreign troops. This opposition is not ideological—the citizens of these countries just resent the presents of tens of thousands of troops in their country.

Finally, it is not clear that the book's basic point that United States lost the war in Afghanistan because it was also fighting a war in Iraq is true. In fact, the United States lost the war in Afghanistan for multiple reasons, many of them not related to military decisions. Although the United States met its original goals in Afghanistan, it long overstayed its welcome, supports a corrupt and ineffective government in Afghanistan, and has long since lost the support of the Afghan people by becoming an occupier instead of a liberator. The question now is how to get out.

In summary, this is a well-research and well-written book on the Afghan and Iraqi wars. Written from a military perspective, the book covers most of the important military decisions regarding the strategies and tactics of these two wars. Yet, unlike some military historians, the authors are realistic about the ultimate outcomes of these two conflicts and the mistakes made in them. The book is a must read for those who are interested in understanding these two conflicts. **GF**

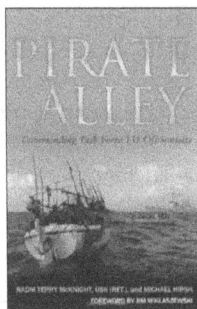

Terry McKnight and Michael Hirsh. *Pirate Alley: Commanding Task Force 151 Off Somalia.* **Annapolis, MD: Naval Institute Press, 2012. 233 pp. $24.95. ISBN: 978-1612511344.**

In 2011, the fourth edition of *Best Management Practices for Protection against Somali Based Piracy* was released. It described a number of methods with which ships should familiarize themselves to defend against pirate hijackings in the Indian Ocean. "Masters on some Chinese merchant ships have prepared barrels of Molotov cocktails" (p. 64). Authors Terry McKnight and Michael Hirsh refer to another "beer bottle" defense where cases of beer bottles are brought aboard, drunk by the crew and then smashed on the deck to keep pirates away from the bridge. These inventive means have all been developed to deter a very specific form of piracy that has come to plague the shipping lanes off of Somalia, but which also affects ships up to 1,200 miles away from the coast of Somalia. Around 200 ships have been hijacked, many millions of dollars paid in ransom and some crews held hostage for years.

Rear Admiral Terry McKnight was chosen in 2009 as the first commander of Combined Task Force (CTF) for 151, a special multi-national unit assigned to combat Somali piracy. His co-author Michael Hirsh is a professional journalist. The main contribution of McKnight's book is that it sheds light on the navy's response to Somali piracy. In addition, McKnight spent time after leaving CTF 151 speaking with experts in the field to provide an introduction to Somali piracy. This gives the reader a multi-faceted look into the subject. He organizes his read by theme, beginning with his appointment in 2009, and concluding with some observations and recommendations.

McKnight has some grudging respect for the pirates. "It does take guts. Most of these pirates come from the hill country of Somalia; they've never been to sea. A lot of them can't even swim...I suspect they see it as the only way you break away from generations of hopelessness and poverty" (p. xiii). He saves many of his frustrations for the complicated and inconceivable bureaucracy that has enabled piracy to flourish. For instance, in 2007, the *Danica White*, a 200 foot bulk carrier hauling cargo from Dubai was hijacked. The *USS Carter Hall* was in the vicinity and was able to come upon the hijacked ship just before it crossed into Somalia's territorial waters. When it crossed the line, the captain of the *Carter Hall* asked permission to follow it, but was denied. "From where I sit—from where I sat—that troubled me...they got past the line without being tagged. They are free to go. Who was going to get angry with us if we went into territorial waters to try to save the hostages? The nonexistent government of a failed state?" (p. xviii).

As McKnight describes it, the attempt to combat piracy is littered with these types of no-win scenarios. Since Somalia is a failed state, it can't be asked to stop the pirates. Yet in many cases, the foreign ships sent to protect the shipping lanes will not violate Somalia's waters, even though the pirates are free to come and go as they please. McKnight felt that the pirates knew the rules of engagement only too well. "The pirate mantra goes like this: 'they will not shoot me. I will get their money. And no one will arrest me. It's a good job'" (p. 3). Because the owners of the ships often pay the ransom, there is no real deterrent to the piracy. In another incident he documents, a ship captures more pirates then it was capable of holding in a specially lined room and was faced with legal ramifications. Even the captured pirates often cannot be prosecuted. So "they take them into shore...somewhere on the Somali coast where they can put them in the water and make sure the pirates can walk to shore. They just say 'don't do it again' and turn them loose" (p. 30).

In such circumstances, it makes sense why manuals are issued explaining to ships' crews how to defend themselves. The beer bottle defense may help combat piracy more than relying on all the highly equipped naval forces that are hampered by policies back home. In the case where pirates get aboard a ship, the ships are encouraged to outfit themselves with a "citadel" where the crew can hide and from which the ship can be controlled. The idea is that the crew can hide behind locked doors and wait for rescue. "Before a naval or military force will attempt to retake a ship from pirate control, 100 percent of the crew must be secured" (p. 65). Before writing his book, McKnight interviewed several experts on Somali piracy, including Martin Murphy, J. Peter Pham, and Jatin Dua. They paint a picture of pirates who are relatively incompetent and in it for the quick money; and who prefer being captured to remaining with no prospects in Somalia. "There is a sense that anything, especially prison in Europe, would be a great idea" (p. 41). McKnight attempts to debunk the theory that Somali piracy was just a local reaction to foreign fishing off the Somali coast. "The Somalis actually disdain fish and fishing" (p. 49). He quotes Pham, "the idea that Somali fishermen went out of business because of foreign trawlers is laughable, because any Somali fisherman would've been out of business year ago for want of customers" (p. 49). He sees it as merely a good storyline or narrative that fits the foreign press' need to have a simple narrative of disenfranchised people forced into a life of crime. McKnight also estimates that there are only several thousand Somalis actively engaged in piracy.

McKnight provides several chapters analyzing and describing the rescue of Captain Richard Phillips of the MV *Mearsk Alabama*. Mcknight notes that "Yes, Capt. Richard Phillips wrote a book about his rescue, but he was in the hijacked lifeboat" (p. 119). He then proceeds to provide a blow-by-blow account of the rescue of Phillips and the killing of several pirates who had captured him. This story is interesting, but for those wanting to learn about the larger issues of Somali piracy it doesn't provide that many lessons, since the odd circumstances that ended up with Phillips in a lifeboat and Navy SEALS flying in to rescue him probably won't be repeated.

McKnight sheds light on the cooperation between the United States, China, and other navies on the high seas. He forecasts that "we expect the Chinese people's popular support for the mission will be high" in the future (p. 179). However, his conclusions are not optimistic. He notes that the hunt for pirates is like "a game of whack-a-mole on steroids, played out over 2.6 million square miles of ocean" (p. 184). It pits the most sophisticated military equipment against men in shoddy skiffs. He notes that we are not "any closer to a coherent strategy to fight them than we were at the start of this scourge" (p. 184). In describing various legislative efforts, he notes that some have suggested a more active U.S. congressional role that would allow the creation of a "pirate exclusion zone" and the boarding or "skinning" of vessels engaged in piracy. However, the law of the sea already allows for the arrest and detention and suppression of piracy. The real issue is finding nations willing to prosecute the pirates. It is a significant investment; in one UN study to establish a court in Somalia it was found to cost some $24 million as an initial investment. How does one fly the witnesses back and forth when they have departed on their vessels? It is a perplexing and complicated issue. Rear Admiral McKnight has provided an important insight into this issue; and his remains one of the only books by an ex-serviceman, and certainly the most senior naval officer to write on this subject. **SJF**

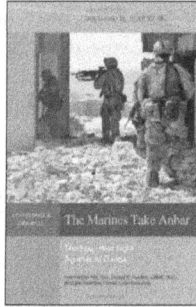

Richard H. Shultz Jr. *The Marines Take Anbar: The Four Year Fight against Al Qaeda.* **Annapolis, MD: Naval Institute Press, 2013. 293 pp. $39.95. ISBN: 978-1612511405. Ebk.: 288 pp. 1953KB. $19.99.**

The Marines Take Anbar: The Four Year Fight against Al Qaeda is a well-written volume on Marines fighting insurgency in the al-Anbar governorate (province) in Western Iraq from 2004 to 2008. Al-Anbar is a dominant area of tribal Sunni Arabs.

The book describes and analyzes the fight against mainly foreign terrorist groups that infiltrated the area, and made it a front line fight by American troops in the aftermath of the fall of Saddam Hussein. The author considers the battle for al-Anbar among the best battles in the history of the Marines, and their success a major turning point in the Iraqi war which changed events and paved the way for fighting in Baghdad later in the year. The book highlights all the crucial details of how Marines adapted and improved as they applied lessons from past mistakes.

In March 2004, part of the 1ˢᵗ Marine Expeditionary Force (I MEF) was deployed to al-Anbar Province, and found itself in a bloody war with al-Qaeda. This campaign culminated in the spring of 2006, when the Marines were faced with a sharp rise in violence. When new counterinsurgency initiatives were adapted (with the help of local tribal sheiks), the Marines gained the upper hand, and two years later, victory was accomplished.

This book of seven chapters begins with an overview of Anbar Province. The author emphasizes that in order to fight successfully, Marines needed a cultural understanding of the native population. The early Marines deployed in March 2004 were not equipped with cultural knowledge, but in the following four years, they acquired an understanding of the province.

In Chapter 2, the author describes the post-conflict and the failed campaign to eliminate violent opposition to the American presence in the area where the opportunity for al-Qaeda was suitable. In the beginning, the Marines found themselves in "the fog of war" (p. 3), suffering from al-Qaeda's attacks. In 2005, the situation worsened, but the Marines were learning and becoming more knowledgeable, which prepared them for the 2006 campaign plan of counterinsurgency. The new strategy consisted of the phrase "clear, hold, build" (p. 119) to engage tribes, which changed the situation on the ground. In doing so, the Marines added a new entry—al-Anbar—to the long list of the "Corps' other historical triumphs at Belleau Woods, Guadalcanal, Tarawa, Peleliu, Iwo Jima, Okinawa, Inchon, Chosin, Khe Sanh, and Hue City" (p. 4).

The volume details the tribal engagement strategy of the Marines that was to: first, know the tribes' history and how important that history is to the Sunni tribes of Anbar. The author explains how overthrowing Saddam constituted a loss of their special status, and that the Shi'a would take revenge on the Sunni who had dominated the Baath regime.

Another lesson drawn from the conflict was to understand that "the Sunni tribes of the Dulaymi confederation are made up of proud people who demand respect" (p. 29), and should not be underestimated. To the Dulaymis, the United States was an invader and occupier that had to be resisted. Prior to the Marines moving into al-Anbar, the message coming from the Coalition Provisional Authority (CPA) in Baghdad was "hardly one of respect for the folkways and traditions of the tribesmen of the Sunni Triangle" (p. 29). They viewed them as backward and primitive and not to be part of the CPA's new Iraq.

The third lesson was to learn, accept, and emulate the code of values and beliefs that guide the tribes' behavior and ways of doing things. Most important to that system of principles was honor. The fourth lesson, according to the author was to "understand the system of prescribed methods used to bring to justice those who violate honor" (p. 30).

The fifth lesson was that it is a male-dominated society and that demonstrating manliness is another one of those enduring aspects of the tribes' code of values. Other important principles mentioned included hospitality, generosity, careful etiquette, and civility.

The sixth lesson was to know that religion is likewise very salient to the Sunni tribesmen of al-Anbar. They all follow the same two primary sources, the *Qur'an* and the Sunna. The seventh lesson was to know that the tribes of the Dulaym confederation are political actors and have a strong political identity. And the eighth lesson to understand that a core principle of these confederation affiliates is group solidarity that begins at the family level, and moves up through the clan and tribes to the confederation. The traditional Bedouin ways of fighting became important attributes of tribal and Arab culture that were passed on from one generation to the next.

The ninth learned lesson was for Marines to be open to working with tribal leaders, even though they would not conform to modern concepts. This resulted in the establishment of the Sunni Awakening that was a work with key members of the community specifically with the influential Sheikh Sattar who was able to encourage key tribal leaders to become engaged. Here, credit should be given also to the U.S. Army and Navy troops who contributed to the success in al-Anbar. The tenth guideline was to never think that the tribesmen of the Duraymi confederation want to adopt Western ways and become like the West.

The author concludes that in the twenty-first century's irregular conflict, "the center of the gravity is the population" (p. 236). Therefore, providing security to local people and protecting them from armed groups is crucial to winning the war. This is what America did when providing infrastructure to accompany fighting the insurgency.

The book idea came from a general who was the president of the Marine Corps University; the grant for the book was provided by the Marine Corp Heritage Foundation. The primary resources were provided by Marine affiliate institutions. This fact can make the book appear biased toward Marines by presenting only one side of the story, and possibly ignoring others. **SH**

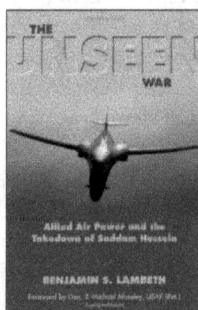

Benjamin S. Lambeth. *The Unseen War: Allied Air Power and the Takedown of Saddam Hussein*. Annapolis, MD: Naval Institute Press, 2013. 435 pp. $59.95. ISBN: 978-1612513119. Pbk: 480 pp. $39.99. ISBN: 978-1612513119. Ebk: 2359 KB. ASIN: B00EGWFLBQ.

The first Iraq Gulf War of 1991 included a prolonged air phase and has been studied thoroughly. However, the air power contribution to the second Gulf War of 2003 has largely been ignored. As Benjamin S. Lambeth notes in the opening to this important volume "the major combat phase of Operation Iraqi Freedom conducted in the spring of 2003 was a true joint and combined campaign by American, British, and Australian air, land, and maritime forces to bring about a decisive end to Hussein's regime" (p. 1). The author also argues that "the campaign that brought down Saddam Hussein was an all but flawless undertaking" (p. 2). The book seeks to shed light on the planning and execution of the air war, as well as providing insight into the major operations and what shortcomings can be identified.

On its surface, analyzing a war that was so one-sided, especially in the air, may seem superfluous. That it was conducted in a flawless manner is interesting, but it is like a professional boxer fighting a blind man—if he doesn't have a flawless fight, that would seem to be the only real news. CENCOM's air component commander was Lt. General T. Michael Moseley. When he presented his plan for air operations, the major difference with 1990 would not only be combining the attack with a land invasion, but also the increased efficiency and accuracy of targeting.

The initial plan called for allied attacks against 1,000 targets a day. Vice Admiral Timothy Keating, who headed the carrier groups involved, recalled "never before in history [had] one naval force projected such a concentrated amount of firepower" (p. 37). The logistical side of the buildup was astronomical. Approximately 32,000 combatants were flown to the region on some 475 missions. They also ran into trouble when Turkey denied the United States the use of its airspace on the eve of the war. In the end 1,800 aircraft would participate, 863 from the Air Force.

According to this account, the Iraqi air force was far from passive in the lead-up to the war. They "had continued to fly as many as a thousand training sorties a month in the airspace between the two no-fly zones" (p. 69). These no-fly zones were set up in the aftermath of the previous war, and in the later Clinton years. The first years of George W. Bush saw activity by the Iraqis aimed at interdicting this imposition on Iraq's sovereignty. The Iraqis still had some 60 SAM weapons and hundreds of combat aircraft. However, as with the first Gulf War, these forces seem to have performed miserably, if at all. This was always the big question about the Iraqi army; although on paper, it had large numbers of tanks and other supposedly advanced weaponry, it was totally defeated by the coalition forces in 1990 and 2003. Benjamin provides a narrative of these facts without asking to what extent resistance was expected from the Iraqi air force, or if allied planners exaggerated its abilities and numbers.

The air war opened early with the momentous decision by the United States to aim for a decapitation strike of Iraq's leader and his two sons, who, according to intelligence, were at a place called Doha Farms near Baghdad. Benjamin concludes that this attack "initially appeared to stiffen the regime's resolve" (p. 113). Two F-117's stealth aircraft were tasked with dropping bombs on the location. "Early reports that Hussein had been killed proved to be false" (p. 79). On the night of March 21, the main attack began with the "shock and awe" bombing of Iraqi commander centers in Baghdad (p. 83). As the author explains, some of these operations were "largely symbolic" while others sought to "attack specific nodes in or underneath government structures" (p. 89).

On March 24, a huge sandstorm enveloped Iraq, grounded aircraft and helicopters, and disrupted missile guidance systems. On March 26, the army's 173rd Airborne Brigade was dropped into an airfield near Tikrit. This was "the largest [drop] since the combat drop into Panama in 1989" (p. 111). As in the first Gulf War, friendly fire bedeviled the air force. In one instance, a Patriot missile downed a

British plane, and in another incident, an F-16 fired a missile into a patriot battery that had locked onto it. "We had no idea where the Patriots were and those guys were locking us up on a regular basis," commented one pilot (p. 115).

The commander sought to minimize civilian casualties among Iraqis. This decision to make the lack of "collateral damage" a priority resulted in a change in the type of weapons used. "The great availability of precision guided weapons and the heightened imperatives of collateral damage avoidance also drove a progressive trend toward the use of smaller munitions in Iraqi Freedom" (p. 231). This is an interesting observation, but as with much of the book, the jargon laced details on the munitions make it hard to distinguish them. For instance, the author discusses a "AGM-154A joint standoff weapon (JSOW), a gliding submunition dispenser carried exclusively by the F/A-18 that was intertially guided and GPS aided, and could, under ideal conditions, be released twenty miles away from the target" (p. 232). This is a fascinating description, but for most nonprofessionals or industry insiders, it doesn't convey the weapons' capabilities. What is a "submunition"? One might assume "intertially guided" means that it simply falls from the sky, guided by gravity, but actually the definition is "Inertial navigation is a self-contained navigation technique in which measurements provided by accelerometers and gyroscopes are used to track the position and orientation of an object relative to a known starting point, orientation and velocity" (Wikipedia). Readers get lost in the TLAM, JDAM, CENTCOM, JFCOM, and more than 200 acronyms for various ordinance and command structures. There is nothing wrong with this in a book published primarily for military or professional personally, but it makes some of it hard to penetrate even from an academic standpoint.

Nevertheless, this crisply written book will remain a standard in describing the air war in the second Gulf War for years to come. The author identifies some problems the pilots faced, such as the inability to receive good battle damage assessments of targets attacks, and difficulty in finding tankers to refuel at the end of mission. In one of the worst near disasters of the war, a contingent of 30 Apache helicopters attempted to fly 50 miles to attack a Republican Guard unit. Half of the helicopters were badly damaged, one was downed and the unit was put out of action for a month in order to repair their helicopters. Only a few Iraqi vehicles were damaged, one Iraq commander having used a cell phone in order to warn his comrades of the attack. This is one of the more interesting accounts of a fact filled, but colorless book on an important conflict. **SJF**

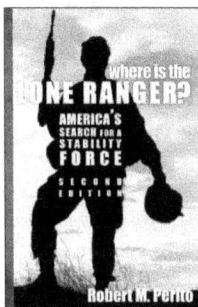

Robert M. Perito. *Where is the Lone Ranger? America's Search for a Stability Force.* 2nd ed. Washington, DC: United States Institute of Peace Press, 2013. 247 pp. $20.00. ISBN: 978-1601271532.

Over the course of its history, the United States has been involved in roughly a dozen wars, as well as many lesser conflicts. One common theme among these events has been the search for stability after armed conflict has ended. Robert Perito's book, *Where is the Lone Ranger? America's Search for a Stability Force*, looks at instances of United States' military intervention since the 1990s, arguing that the United States needs to organize and field a constabulary force, similar to our European allies, to carry out stability tasks that are beyond the capacity of civil police but that do not rise to the level of combat operations. He uses a case study approach, drawing examples from Bosnia, Kosovo, Iraq, and Afghanistan to illustrate the challenges of stability operations and to argue that conventional military forces are not organized, trained, or equipped to conduct stability operations successfully. His solution to this lack of capacity is to build a separate U.S. constabulary force with the training and equipment to fill the gap between conventional military forces and civil police.

Perito's text is well written and persuasively argued. His background as a Foreign Service officer and his experience in some of the areas from which his case studies are drawn certainly gives his argument weight. He buttresses contemporary case studies with historical examples of constabulary operations, including examples drawn from America's own history: the Texas Rangers, the Army in Cuba after the Spanish–American War, the Marines in several Central American republics, and others. He evaluates these experiences and acknowledges some were successful, others not.

If one accepts Perito's thesis that the United States requires a constabulary force-in-being, ready to deploy on short notice to a trouble spot, with experienced personnel trained in the skills of civil policing, but with the capabilities of light infantry to establish and enforce security, then the book is compelling.

On the other hand, if one is not automatically convinced of the need, but is willing to investigate the constabulary option, his argument has significant weaknesses. Perito focuses on the "what" and "why" of establishing a deployable constabulary force, but is relatively weak on the "who" and "how" of his proposal.

From both history and contemporary examples, some type of security force is clearly needed to bridge the period between the end of active conflict and the restoration of effective governance, including civil security. This is Perito's "what" and "why." He glosses over the significant questions of "who" and "how." He argues that the constabulary force should be made up of "experienced cadre" under the sponsorship of "some federal agency," but while an organization of cadre might provide a framework, it would not be a readily deployable force. The cadre framework would have to be filled out with additional personnel having necessary skills and experience. Once the personnel were on hand, the organization would be likely to require some training—if only at the refresher level—to make it ready for operations. Given sufficient lead time, fleshing out a cadre organization and providing sufficient training is within the realm of possibility, but if we examine Perito's case studies, lead time is one thing in very short supply.

Perito never addresses the question of government agency sponsorship adequately. He argues implicitly that the unspecified federal agency should not be the Department of Defense, or the constabulary force would become just another conventional military unit. Other possible federal sponsors might include the Department of Justice (but does Justice have the requisite budget or expertise beyond civil investigation and law enforcement?), or the Department of Homeland Security (analogous to the Coast Guard), but each possible sponsoring agency raises challenges as well as possibilities.

One can counter these objections by noting that if the American body politic determines that it is in our national interest to organize, train, and hold ready to deploy a constabulary force such as Perito describes, then the questions of who and how become irrelevant. Quite true, but given the contemporary challenges of getting political consensus on more fundamental issues of budget, it is unlikely that Perito's concept of a constabulary force separate from the already-existing conventional military will get even a polite hearing, let alone the resources needed. Which is a shame, as he has effectively demonstrated a need for such a force.

Perito's image of a constabulary force as the twenty-first century equivalent of the Lone Ranger, while vivid, may well be misleading. In the stories of the Lone Ranger from radio and television—the image that Perito invokes—the Masked Man and his Indian Friend, Tonto (if I remember the line correctly) arrived on the scene to investigate the bad guys and render justice, but rarely caused more damage than a few bruises from a fist fight or shooting the gun out of an outlaw's hand. Perito's proposed U.S. constabulary force would similarly be charged with investigating wrong-doing and enforcing civil law, but without risking the level of collateral damage of conventional military operations. It might be inconvenient to remember, however, that the Lone Ranger character originated as the survivor of a massacre. He was the Lone Ranger because he was the lone survivor. Not a very comforting image for a force meant to bridge the gap between conventional military operations and civil security. **GH**

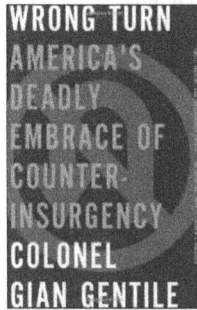

Gian Gentile. *Wrong Turn: America's Deadly Embrace of Counter-Insurgency.*
New York, NY: The New Press, 2013. 182 pp. $24.95. ISBN: 978-1595588746.

In 2005 Colonel Gian Gentile was serving in Southwestern Baghdad when the
Samarra shrine, a holy site for Shi'a Muslims, was blown up. Soon a civil war began
to develop between rival insurgent militias. "During those three weeks after the
bombing, my squadron pinged back and forth from Sunni mosque to Sunni mosque
under vicious attacks from roving Shi'a militias" (p. 103). In the year that followed,
America began to adopt a new counterinsurgency strategy that many have credited
with ending the violence there, and which has since been applied to Afghanistan.

In his unsparing narrative, Gentile seeks to overturn what he sees as a growing
myth about the defeat of the insurgents. Blending examples from his own command
in Iraq with military history, the author lays out a clear thesis against trusting the
myth that there was a silver bullet to defeat the insurgents. Gentile is excellently
placed to write a critique like this, as an army colonel, and as the director of military
history program at West Point, America's premier military academy.

The latest principle of counterinsurgency adopted by the Americans in Iraq has
been known in shorthand as COIN, military jargon for "counterinsurgency," and
it has numerous elements—one which is central is the protection of civilians. "This
new army doctrinal manual presented a simplistic set of actions to counter an insurgency that distorted what I had witnessed in 2006" (p. xvi). The manual, which was
rooted in the history of fighting insurgents in Malaya and Vietnam, was "a blend
of some history, a lot of myth and suppositions about roads not taken" (p. 12). The
operational observations encourage commanders to do such things as "listen and
adapt" and "live our values," as well as "focus on the security of the population"
(p. 32). What Gentile seeks to debunk is not so much the idea that the manual is
flawed, but that the myth that General David Patreaus "won" the Iraq war through
a "surge" is highly problematic. He sees Patreaus as a "savvy" political social climber
(p. 24). The notion is that Petraeus and others in the limelight, such as Colonel
John Nagle, Samantha Power and Victor Davis Hanson, present a narrative ark that
favors a simplistic story about insurgents being beaten in Iraq. As history has shown,

in Afghanistan, the myth has been dulled, and Gentile hopes readers will finally put it to rest.

To understand the problem with COIN and the lessons America learned, the author takes us back to Malaya. The Malayan Emergency of 1948–54 was a Communist insurgency against British colonial forces that was put down by the British. In the end, the British defeated the Communists, who were concentrated among Malaysia's Chinese minority. "At their peak, the Malayan Communist fighters numbered no more than 7,500" (p. 39). However, the defeat of this rag-tag Communist insurgency has been used as a model of the correct way to defeat insurgencies elsewhere. Most infamously, many have argued that the Malayan model could have been applied to Vietnam, a war that saw the United States confronting much larger forces and losing exponentially more men and material. For instance, only 470 British soldiers were killed in Malaya, whereas almost 60,000 Americans died in Vietnam. Gentile questions why there is anything in common between these two wars. Other factors Gentile highlights as reasons the British were successful in Malaya were large unit sweeps and the resettlement of 500,000 Chinese to prevent aid going to the insurgents. Could the United States have resettled millions of people in Vietnam or Iraq? As the author notes, "the COIN narrative in its current form relies heavily on superficial interpretation of events, so it is with its use of Malaya" (p. 51).

One of the main elements of the narrative is that a winning general has been a sort of godsend in each scenario. In Malaya, it was General Gerald Templer; in Vietnam, it was General Creighton Abrams; and in Iraq, it was Petreus. Each time, the narrative portrays a clean break between one command that is losing and another that is winning. "The improvement in the overall situation had much more to do with the effects of Templer's predecessors and the implementation of the Briggs [a former commander] plan" (p. 57). For Gentile, the lesson is clear: If the narrative of the "winning commander" is a fallacy, the the whole doctrine is problematic.

The author seeks to show that a bad reading of history is encouraging a new history of the Iraq war that is full of holes. "The idea that the surge turned the tide of war through a significant shift in operational method provided comfort and would act as a guidepost for the future" (p. 86). However, he points out that the "levels of sectarian violence [in Iraq] started to drop In December 2006, two months before the arrival of Petraeus and his purported change in strategy" (p. 90).

His central agenda has to do with the future of Afghanistan. "There was a better strategy in Afghanistan to Americans and military leaders from the start. Our leaders could have discerned early the folly of trying to build Afghanistan into a modern state overnight and would have concluded that the core policy goal of destroying al-Qaida could have been done by much smaller force" (p. 135). The failure to draw the right lessons is hampering the United States, as evidenced by recent initiatives to negotiate with the Taliban. Gentile was a Cassandra for a while, an outsider when Petraues was the hero. However, perhaps his views are finally showing that it is important to poke holes in clear narratives that offer us a "better war." **SJF**

WOMEN: RIGHTS, STATUS

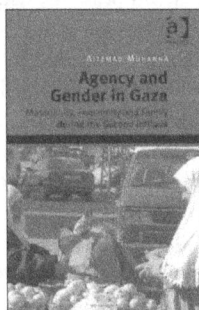

Aitemad Muhanna. *Agency and Gender in Gaza: Masculinity, Femininity and Family during the Second Intifada.* **Farnham, Surrey, UK: Ashgate, 2013 (published in hardback in 2012). 208 pp. $99.95. ISBN: 978-1409454533. Ebk: $87.96. 666 KB.**

This volume examines the effect upon two groups of impoverished Gazan women—one of refugee descent and the other native to Gaza—of the dramatic drop in living standards caused by the closing of Israel to Palestinian labor during the Second Intifada (2000–08). While retaining careful respect for the subjective experiences of the individual women she interviews, Muhanna is able to weave anecdotes together with data and the work of other scholars to create an impressive and moving impression of how women of different generations negotiate power with their husbands, children, and in-laws in order to make ends meet while maintaining their and their families' honor and dignity as best they can.

Muhanna begins by providing a great deal of welcome context to the issue by describing in very apt prose the history of the conflict within Gaza and the socioeconomic conditions under which very poor Gazans lived before and after the Second Intifada. She summarizes her thesis as follows:

Men and women use both the structure and ideology of gender to cope with the consequences of chronic personal and familial insecurity. Some coping mechanisms have enhanced the hierarchical structure of the Palestinian family, and some have transcended it, depending on which mechanism has the capacity to achieve the immediate goal of family survival and security from within the existing structure of household and local community gender relations. The Second Intifada has facilitated the fluidity of gender relations in which each gender is reconfigured to resist the threat to family stability. (p. 12)

But it is in providing the details of these reconfigurations—and more important-ly, in lucidly explaining their causes, especially their ideological ones—that Mu-hanna's text excels. After grounding her study in the methodology of her interviews and in a clear explanation of the applicability of intersectional feminist theory to her work, she opens her analysis by tracing women's agency within their family structure beginning with the mass arrival of refugees from other parts of Palestine after the 1967 conflict. Refugees, unlike Gazan peasants, had no land; the scarcity of hous-ing and especially of real estate among the refugees produced somewhat different patterns among them than among the peasants. Yet, a common traditional family pattern remained: a young married woman would live in the communal home of her in-laws' family, usually under the domination of her mother-in-law as well as her husband. Once her own sons grew to adolescence and her mother-in-law aged, the now-middle-aged woman was able to free herself from domination; once her sons grew and married, she could keep them in her own communal home, now the dominant matriarch. And all of this was done with a great deal of hard work among the women in maintaining the illusion of male supremacy and the seclusion of the family's women.

After 1967, the Israeli labor market was opened, and large numbers of Gazan men moved from the peasantry to the proletariat, becoming comparatively prosperous in the process. For the wives of these men, the additional income often provided the means to move out of the communal home and establish a nuclear family. Becoming the mistress of her own house a generation early was obviously appealing to these women; but Muhanna explains the ideological dimension of this and its compa-rable importance to considerations of autonomy and economics. She argues that women in Gazan society gained status within the patriarchal order by reproducing the patriarchal order; and being mistress of her own home while a high-earning and conveniently often absent husband enabled her to raise her children, removed from her in-laws, to keep her and gain the high status of a proper housewife—again, all while maintaining the illusion of male dominance. It's all explained so clearly (and with much reference to other scholars' work on the relevant subjects) that *Agency and Gender in Gaza* … does an excellent job of showing rather than telling us why it might make perfect sense for example, for a destitute woman to want 12 children.

With the establishment of the Palestinian National Authority in 1993, jobs in the public sector become available to Gazans. This throws an additional layer of complexity into the issue of gender dynamics within the family as educational at-tainment for her children enters the range of options that a woman might have in negotiating greater power and autonomy for herself or her children. That these women make choices that reify traditional patriarchy is for Muhanna an implicit critique of Bordieu's *habitus*; this is easily the weakest part of the text, in that the cri-tique is only touched upon. It would have been more effective to expand the critique and weave into the narrative an ongoing engagement with Bordieu and Bordieu scholarship; or perhaps better still, to leave mention of such a critique to footnotes and expand upon it in a separate journal article. But this is very much a minor issue in an otherwise excellent book.

With the beginning of the Second Intifada in 2000, the Gazan economy was progressively devastated by Israel's direct military response, its closure of the labor market, its seizure of previously productive Gazan agricultural land and fisheries, and the withdrawal of aid to Gaza by most Western governments and organizations after the Hamas electoral victory. This devastation was profoundly gendered, in that it was men who were left without any means of providing for their families, and women who were left to shoulder the burden; neither gender liked the idea of women going out to seek sustenance for their families, but aid agencies were much more likely to provide aid to women than to men. One primary consequence was that women who had been living in nuclear families were often compelled to move back into their in-laws' communal home, under the thumb of their mother-in-law. This section is where Muhanna makes the most use of her interviews, giving detailed and often heartbreaking stories of the suffering these women underwent, not only to sustain their families in the absence of any kind of suitable work for their husbands, but also in order, once again, to maintain the illusion of male dominance. The interviews enable Muhanna to demonstrate that the ideological need to maintain a plausible façade of male supremacy often outweighed purely socioeconomic concerns: many of the women actually preferred their husbands idle, angry, and dominant over, for example, taking over housework and childcare duties while their wives worked full-time in petty commerce, aid agency jobs or networking for access to aid coupons. She goes into much detail on the sheer fragility of Gazan masculinity and the efforts undertaken by women to maintain and support their men as dominant, all in the face of the near-total destruction of men's ability to provide for their families after the beginning of the Second Intifada. Muhanna also manages to pull off the very difficult trick of being personally invested in a subject—she herself is from a poor Gazan community and is the widow of a man killed in the uprising—and yet managing to convey its nuances lucidly and objectively.

This book is well worth the time even for the casual reader, but will be of especial interest to those studying intersectional feminism. As an example of allowing poor women of a marginalized group the opportunity to tell their stories, it would suit the efforts of scholars working on poverty, gender, and the effects of war and of modernity on traditional family structures. Muhanna is to be commended for a thoughtful, enlightening, and well-constructed work. **IC**

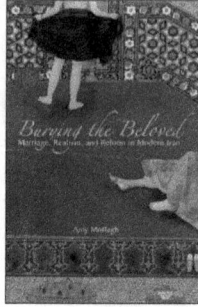

Amy Motlagh. *Burying the Beloved: Marriage, Realism, and Reform in Modern Iran.* **Stanford, CA: Stanford University Press, 2011. 200 pp. $55.00. ISBN: 978-0804775892.**

The field of gender studies in modern Iran has witnessed a sea change in the past decade. In the wake of the scholarship of Afsaneh Najmabadi, Ziba Mir-Hosseini, and Arzoo Osanloo, it is impossible to read Iranian civil and religious codes pertaining to marriage and domesticity as neutral tools for regulating social life. Until now, this florescence of scholarship dealing with the Iranian state's regulation of female and male sexuality has not been accompanied by a similar upsurge in the field of literary studies, which for the most part does not seriously consider the social construction of the Iranian self. Amy Motlagh's reading of Iranian modernist prose (both novels and short-stories) against the background of changes in normative gender roles aims to intervene in this impasse, and for the most part succeeds.

One of the most innovative aspects of Motlagh's study is the way she intersperses her chapters on literary texts with brilliant insights concerning the intimate—and largely unexamined—relation between dominant canons of literary representation and civil codes. "Although the law may disguise itself as a standardization of existing norms," Motlagh observes, "laws are more frequently…instruments of social reform" (p. 12). While on the surface, this argument many seem self-evident, the introduction of literature represents an innovation in a field that has historically shied away from literature. The dialectic between legal norms and literary form unfolds throughout this book with occasional flashes of brilliance, and is consistently stimulating and new.

Another strength of Motlagh's book is the author's fluency in multiple theoretical traditions and her ability to cross national boundaries, a tendency all too rare in scholarship oriented to single national traditions. From the introduction, which opens by invoking Jean Franco's work on the persistence of dead bodies in Latin American cultural memory, to the ensuing chapters, which engage Benedict Anderson and Ian Watt on the rise of the novel, Kwame Anthony Appiah's postrealism, and Fredric Jameson's concept of postmodernity (pp. 14, 64), Motlagh shines as a literary critic at the cutting edge of social scientific inquiry. Her capacity to speak at once to two distinct areas of inquiry enriches her social and historical contextualization of the Iranian novel.

From the perspective of comparative literature, *Burying the Beloved...* is arguably most provocative when it focuses its attention on Jameson's conceptualization of postmodernism as the defining characteristic of contemporary literature. Paraphrasing Appiah and contesting Jameson, Motlagh argues that in postcolonial societies such as Iran and Africa, where the idea of the novel has been "from the first imbricated and tainted in colonial discourses... care must be taken... not to subsume [contemporary literary productions] into metropolitan categorizations" (p. 14). The discipline of comparative literature needs more work like this: fully conversant with regnant understandings of literary signification, and yet sufficiently immersed in the local contexts that fall outside mainstream paradigms to show how postcolonial archives revise the discipline's normative understandings.

Motlagh's study ranges widely across the Persian literary canon. She is particularly effective at demonstrating parallels between classical and modern Persian texts, as when she argues that Iranian literary modernity transformed the female beloved (*macshuq*) of classical Persian poetry into a companionate wife, entrusted with the task of purifying the nation (p. 51). This book's guiding metaphor—burial of the female beloved—is similarly suggestive of an analogy between the female body and the nation state. In text after text, we are shown how male lovers who search for their female beloveds inevitably bring about these women's dismemberment.

When reviewing a book that is at once so provocative in its implications and so brief in its explications, the reader is inevitably left wishing for a fuller treatment of certain lines of inquiry. Motlagh focuses exclusively on the literature of modern Iran, leaving the Persianate literatures of Afghanistan, Tajikistan, and other Persophone borderlands to other scholars. Her empirical focus generates a desire for a break in the Iran centric account of Persian literary modernity. Such a desire is partially satisfied with the discussion of Zoya Pirzad's *I'll Turn off the Lights* (2001–02). Written by an Armenian fluent in Persian, Pirzad's novel provides refreshing respite from a long line of Iranian texts, which, against the evidence both of history and of contemporary ethnographic reality, assume full congruity between the Persian language and Iranian ethnic identity.

Motlagh's provocative discussion of Pirzad's text, including her innovative reading of Deleuze and Guattari's conception of "minor literatures" in connection with Pirzad's deployment of Armenian to estrange the Iranian reader, leaves this reader wishing for a more direct critical assault on the nationalistic aspects of Iranian literary modernity than is offered in this book. For, as the very term "Persophone" implies (see pp. 10, 120), the commonplace restriction of modern Iranian literature to the nation-state that bears that name is itself a trope worth calling into question.

For the social sciences, Iranocentrism may be justified on intellectual grounds, given the pervasive transformations wrought by the Iranian nation-state. But neither

Motlagh nor her scholarly peers—Najmabadi, Mir-Hosseini, and Osanloo—have reflected extensively on their self-selected empirical constrictions. It is as though, having set themselves the task of calling into question the category of the nation-state, due to the work it performs on women's bodies, these scholars nonetheless prefer to work within a national framework defined by the boundaries of modern Iran. And yet, Persian is the language of literary culture and daily life across much of Central Asia, including Afghanistan and Tajikistan, and was also relevant to the construction of South Asian modernity. These are criticisms of a field more than of this specific book. I raise them here only because Motlagh's literary acumen and conceptual powers make her perspective all the more needful and relevant to the entire Persianate ecumene. Her study of Iranian modernity ought to revise our conceptions of literary modernity generally.

In sum, this elegantly written work is necessary reading to scholars engaged in Islamic feminism, the history of modern Iran, and Persian literary culture. Only two errors were noted, the first on p. 135, which reproduces the same paragraph twice, and the second on p. 142 (endnote 7), where the publication date assigned to Tayyeb Salih's *Season of Migration to the North* is 1972. Salih's novel was first published in 1966. **RG**

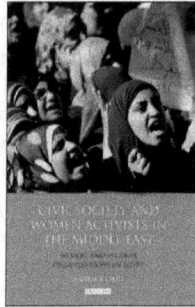

Wanda Krause. *Civil Society and Women Activists in the Middle East: Islamic and Secular Organizations in Egypt*. London: I. B. Tauris, 2012. 263 pp. $96.00. ISBN: 978-1848858855.

This book is based on 10 years of research on Islamic women's and secular feminist organizations in Egypt, from 2001 to 2011. Earlier researchers, she argues, have focused too much on the state and on secularism and have missed women's activism, which is instilling democratic principles at society's foundations. She argues that the Islamic discourse is often more effective than the secular discourse in expanding civil society. She explains that the law governing private voluntary organizations is very restrictive, enabling the government to proscribe the activities of any organization, prohibit foreign funding or fundraising, appoint temporary leadership, dissolve organizations, transfer funds from one organization to another of its choosing, and merge organizations despite the wishes of their members. Efforts to revise the law are on going, but most organizations work without official permission.

The author has selected the following five secular organizations for study: the Center for Egyptian Women's Legal Assistance (CEWLA); Alliance for Arab Women; Association for the Development and Enhancement of Women (ADEW); Women and Memory Forum; and the New Women Research Center. She has located five Islamic organizations for study—four that she does not name and the Zakah Committee of Salah al-Din Mosque. She interviewed 33 women with interviews lasting from twenty minutes to two hours. She gave her interviewees prepared questions, and over tea and sweets, explained her purposes. She agreed to the many requests that interviewee's names not be used. All the secular organizations agreed that the organization's names could be used. Two of the five Islamic organizations requested that their names not be used, and chose to omit the names of two more to preserve trust that had been established. A male or female research assistant usually accompanied her to help with the Arabic. She quotes often from the interview transcripts, but unfortunately does not give us information that would establish context, such as the date, place, organization, or name of the interviewee (not even a pseudonym).

She tells us that ADEW has helped around 2,500 women get birth certificates enabling them to access many rights. The Alliance for Arab Women has educated women about their role in water management. The Islamic organizations teach homemaking skills and also give women lessons in the study of the *Qur'an*, memorization, and recitation—all work to empower women through expansion of civil society. The author then turns to the many women who network as a means of confronting oppressive state.

For many years, women have participated in informal mutual savings associations. Many younger women blog and use Facebook and Twitter. The Internet was crucial during the revolution, and women were very active in calling for and coordinating protest activities. Readers familiar with the history of the revolution will cringe at the author's reference to many women being killed, with no citation. Sally Zahran is the only women thought to have died from repressive actions during the revolution; and the circumstances of her death are in dispute (see Walter Armbrust, *Cultural Anthropology*, http://www.culanth.org/?q=node/491).

The author concludes that the way forward lies in expanding civil society and democratic values. Given events since the revolution, this will be an uphill battle, but considering the courage and perseverance of these Egyptian women and men gender activists, it will be won, though with many ups and downs along the way. **NEG**

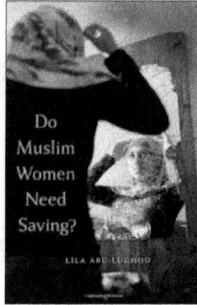

Lila Abu-Lughod. *Do Muslim Women Need Saving?* Cambridge, MA: Harvard University Press, 2013. 324 pp. ISBN: 978-0674725164. Ebk: $19.25. 839KB.

The titular question, "do Muslim women need saving?" leads to various answers: "No, Muslim women do not need saving by military interventions that result in unending devastation and destruction." Or: "How can tens of millions of individuals be lumped together in one term such as 'Muslim women?'" Or: "Yes, Muslim women and everyone else on the planet need saving from the unequal distribution of wealth and power, poor education, working conditions and healthcare, the lack of security, and environmental degradation. But we know that another answer is, "Yes, Muslim women need to be saved from their religion."

Abu-Lughod sets out to refute this last answer by asking Zaynab, a longtime Muslim friend of hers, if her religion was the source of her many problems. Zaynab is Egyptian, has a difficult marriage, and a precarious income, among other problems. Shocked by the question, Zaynab firmly blames the government, but certainly not her religion.

Abu-Lughod points out that there are many local NGOs that support Muslim women who are confronting domestic violence or social ills, yet we hear far more about the work of international institutions that may not understand local conditions. She points out, for example that certain high profile cases of rape in Bangladesh where women were forced to marry their rapists were actually consensual relations. Girlfriends brought charges in order to cover up a pregnancy or to force a recalcitrant boyfriend into marriage. On the other hand, I know of at least two cases in Morocco when victims of rape committed suicide when a judge forced them to marry their rapists. Abu-Lughod likes the term "portable seclusion" for the burqa and other forms of veiling. We all like our privacy and it is best to dress appropriately for any given occasion, but there is more than a hint of apologia in her arguments.

Still, I know what she means when she hesitates to sign petitions in defense of Afghan women circulated in the name of Hollywood celebrities knowing full well that these same celebrities have never shown much concern, say for Palestinian women who are subjected to daily harassment at Israeli checkpoints, not to mention dispossession of their homes and land. She further wonders how many of those who denounce the abuses of women under the Taliban are ready to sacrifice their own high level of consumption, so that less privileged women can have a better life.

She then argues that while women everywhere want their rights and justice, their ideas of rights and justice may vary. She states that in her 30 years doing research in Egypt, she cannot think of a single woman from any walk of life who has expressed envy of women in the United States. On the other hand, I too have been in Egypt off and on for 30 years (or more) and have heard such statements of envy, just yesterday in fact by a friend who wishes to emigrate to the United States.

The author reiterates that we need to stop trying to save Muslim women and try to make the world more just. Societies that have been torn apart and broken down by continued warfare and international drug trafficking are not safe for anyone. We would do better, the author suggests, addressing problems at home where women also suffer from high rates of domestic violence and other threats. She singles out Kristof and WuDunn's *Half the Sky* (Vintage, 2009) and Ayaan Hirsi Ali's *Infidel and Nomad* (Simon and Schuster, 2009), all of which feature victimized Muslim women and the language of international human rights without addressing the geopolitical forces that have degraded their and our societies.

She then turns to the burgeoning genre of literature in which women tell their horrific and sordid stories of victimization by Muslim men. These books sell well in the context of immigration anxieties and post 9/11 and 7/11 fears, but they are superficial, sensationalist, and often fictionalized. The author then takes up that icon of Muslim injustice: "honor crimes." She argues that the way honor crimes (and also polygamy and forced marriage) are dealt with in Western parlance oversimplifies morality, puts the West above the rest, and does not take into account rapid social change, neoliberal reforms, and on-going political conflict.

She observes that the concept of Muslim women's human rights has a long grassroots history, but has in recent years been taken over by international or local political interests, by Islamists, and by multinational corporations for their own purposes. Western-funded campaigns on behalf of Muslim women launched in the wake of the wars against Afghanistan, Iraq, and Gaza find it more convenient to locate local problems in local/Islamic culture/tradition then in wars or occupations, or in changing patterns of consumption that benefit Western interests.

Abu-Lughod concludes by asking us to ask who is really concerned with Muslim women's rights and why. Well-meaning rights advocates must analyze carefully their own motives and the societies they seek to aid. The place to start, she suggests, is the world of privilege and power in which we live our comfortable lives. We need critical self-reflection and an awareness of our common humanity. We need to challenge the unequal distribution of wealth and power in our own societies and everywhere else.

Yet, after almost every talk I give, someone in the audience asks, "But what can we do to help?" They want to donate money or goods. Some want to volunteer. They know there are no quick fixes, but they still want to DO something. I will now suggest that they read this book. It is a wonderful basis to begin the discussion. **NEG**

Suzanne E. Joseph. *Fertile Bonds: Bedouin Class, Kinship, and Gender in the Bekaa Valley.* **Gainesville, FL: University Press of Florida, 2013. 256 pp. $63.81. ISBN: 978-0813044613.**

Ethnographies about the changing lives of the Bedouin communities of the Middle East and North Africa have become relatively commonplace over the past few decades. Growing out of the Orientalist tradition of Patai, Musil, and Lawrence, the late twentieth century saw a spate of these works, including, most notably, Emanuel Marx's landmark monograph, *Bedouin of the Negev* (Praeger, 1967).

No work of note considered the Bedouin of Lebanon, however—until now. This volume seeks to fill a long standing void in the anthropological literature by analyzing the changes now occurring among the Bedouin communities of the Bekaa Valley. Specifically, Joseph seeks here to look at social change most especially, and to do so by analyzing the communities through the lenses of reproductive behaviors, fertility patterns, gender role change, and shifts in regional demographic growth and development.

For example, Joseph looks at the intersections of family size, levels of polygyny, and divorce rates in the evolving Bedouin community (pp. 87-88). In so doing, she seeks to find evidence here of the ways and means through which women are now exercising greater control over their bodies, their relationships with one another and further, their ability to leverage new aspects of their growing power and control vis-á vis their husbands and other men in the community.

Similarly, she looks at the role of social cohesion and kinship. Using consanguineal marriage as her primary area of discussion, Joseph addresses the ways and means through which kinship is repeatedly reiterated, forged, and maintained during a period of stress and change (p. 101). At the same time, however, Joseph also rightly notes that economic class (that is to say, wealth and poverty) also play a key role here; across the spectrum of Bedouin (and indeed, non-Bedouin) communities, it is the poor, in addition to women, who often serve as the vanguards of "traditional culture" (pp. 109-111).

She poses a discussion of the demographic-transition model of socioeconomic development to make this case. She writes: "Villagization and rural industrialization precipitated a decline in Bedouin pastoralism and an increase in agricultural share-cropping and wage labor. Once Bedouins [sic] lost access to the means of produc-tion (in terms of livestock and grazing lands), they became increasingly reliant on their labor for survival" (p. 127). Dependence upon monetary finances rose, while in turn, just as the model suggests, family size has slowly begun to shrink (p. 130).

Such conclusions in and of themselves are hardly unexpected. What is unex-pected, and what makes this volume worth reading and worth using as a brief but handy reference, is its effective usage of a critical feminist framework. For much too long, Western feminists have viewed women's concerns such as fertility, polygyny, hijab/modesty dress, and other aspects of Muslim/Middle Eastern life through an Orientalist's neo-colonial perspective. The "oppressed woman" narra-tive is strongly ingrained in the minds of many objective observers. And yet here, Joseph is one of very few to recognize this shortcoming in the literature (pp. 73-77), and it is here too that this volume is particularly strong.

That being said, the book does suffer from a few shortcomings of its own—most if not all of which I attribute to the editing process, if not to the author herself. The one issue which I feel is the most outstanding concerns the inclusion of Chapters 7 and 8. Virtually all of the material here is ideally suited to the in-terested demographer, but seems to go off on a tangent relative to the previous six chapters. For me at least, it reads like a literature review for a dissertation with little connection to Bedouin communities widely, or to the Bekaa specifically. One almost gets the sense that this material has been added on in order to lengthen the book. In my view at least, it adds little to the argument already constructed in the rest of the volume.

I have a few additional quibbles. For such a brief work, it seems strange that there would be repeated material, sometimes almost verbatim (pp. 85, 111, and so on). Further, the Index is incomplete. Terminology is inconsistent: For example I think that in 2013, it's safe and reasonable to refer to the "Zionist entity" (pp. 15, 21) by its actual name without suggesting any political bias, and that seems to be the case here too when the "Israelis" are also mentioned (p. 44). Lastly, for the popular media to add an "s" to "Bedouin" to make it plural may be excusable; but here, in an academic work?

Unfortunately, the list of distractions goes on. The Bekaa Bedouin are repeated-ly compared to the men and women of the Bible—a questionable methodological approach, in my view, which does not further the author's argument. Nor, for that matter, does it help to compare their condition to that of the Jews of Europe during the Nazi period (p. 68).

All of this being said, this volume has quite a bit of interesting information to offer. If one is willing to negotiate through some of its weaker areas, there is a wealth of worthwhile theoretical and empirical material to be found and mined.
SCD

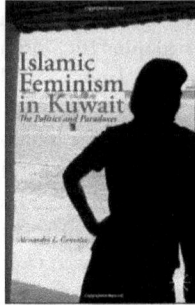

Alessandra L. González. *Islamic Feminism in Kuwait: The Politics and Paradoxes.*
New York: Palgrave Macmillan, 2013. 254 pp. $57.50. ISBN: 978-1137304735.

Gonzáles's *Islamic Feminism in Kuwait: The Politics and Paradoxes* is a case study of the complex phenomenon of a non-Western genre of feminism which is emerging in a majority Muslim society. The author, a research fellow at the Institute for the Studies of Religion at Baylor University and a Research Associate at John Jay College of Criminal Justice at CUNY, challenges the ubiquitous Western belief that Islam is inherently oppressive to women, through her research which consists of surveys and in-depth interviews.

Gonzáles is interested in her subjects' own views about their status, their personal and political aspirations vis-à-vis their traditional religious culture, and their attitudes toward their Muslim religion and their male-dominated culture. Among the intriguing questions that the author focuses on are why so many Kuwaiti women choose to wear the veil, and why Islamists are winning elections with the help and support of women. The author observes that Kuwaiti women are not jealous of Western women and their achievements, but are rather critical of the emphasis that Western feminism places on individual rights at the expense of communal values, and of the disregard for religious sensibilities. Her main conclusion is that Kuwaiti feminists strive to further their agenda of empowering women, granting them political rights, and improving their social and economic status, within the boundaries and constraints of their Islamic culture and religion.

Central to her thesis is the theory of legitimate authority, which stipulates that Islamic feminists strive to achieve progressive women's social and political rights by means of seeking sources of authority such as religious texts, the community, and religious or political leaders.

The rejection by Kuwaiti women of Western secular feminism is expressed in different forms throughout the book. The claim that Islamic feminism is an indigenous approach to women's rights, which is culturally and religiously compatible with the patriarchal culture, is voiced in many interviews. The author concludes that Kuwaiti women acknowledge the difference between the "real" Islam and patriarchal social practices, and strive to advance their political, social, and economic status, thereby challenging social customs, traditions, and practices, while respecting the core tenets of Islam. They generally accept the fact that social change takes time, and that women should be patient.

In the Introduction, the author defines *Islamic Feminism…*, outlines the sociological theory of legitimate authority, and summarizes the main contributions of her findings to the study of feminism in other conservative societies. She gives a brief history of social and political events since the emergence of Islam in the seventh century A.D., and their effect on the status of women in Kuwait, up to and after the election law of 2005, which granted women suffrage. She then proceeds to review the contemporary status of women's rights in Kuwait, and their roots in both the Islamist context and in Western political liberal movements.

The book has five chapters. In Chapter 1, the author explains why the Western model of feminism has not become popular among Kuwaiti women. Chapter 2 is a look at the political Islamists' resurgence and the rejection of the secular and individualistic model of Western feminism. Chapter 3 examines the intriguing phenomenon of the resurgence of the veil in the Muslim world, including Kuwait. Chapter 4 discusses the role of men in enabling what the author calls "Islamic Feminism," and Chapter 5 is a discussion of Arab youth, who are both modern and traditional.

The majority of the subjects in the research are young college students, mostly female, who represent the future political social and economic elite of Kuwait. However, the author did not restrict her research to this group. She interviewed Salafist members of parliament, university professors, and religious leaders. Some Islamist conservatives were opposed to women's suffrage altogether, while others agreed to granting women the right to vote, but were only opposed to women running for office in elections for the parliament. However, she observes that although Islamists had been originally more opposed to women suffrage than liberals, they were able to mobilize and attract more female candidates and voters once the election law was passed. Gonzáles quotes Salafist and other conservative Islamists who are generally opposed to women's suffrage and other political rights for women as they explain their views and their rationale for limitations on women's rights. According to some conservatives, these limitations are based on Islam, and on a sense of honor and respect toward women, and their biological, natural, and human abilities, which are different from those of men, and which should preclude them from running for political office.

The book contains several figures which summarize the popular surveys the author conducted, as well as sample interview responses to select interview questions. There is also a glossary of relevant Arabic religious and cultural terms, a selected bibliography, a much too short and incomplete index, and an appendix which describes the particular methodology which was used in the research. In the latter, the author explains and justifies her choice of sample. A survey of the particular subjects who are college students at a national university in an Islamic country, offers an opportunity to analyze the attitudes and behaviors of an elite in a majority Muslim context, which may become the next generation leaders of a society in the making, and are significant indicators of future social and political trends.

Gonzáles clearly empathizes with her subjects, their culture, and their choices, and her research highlights the similarities between the difficulties that are experienced by Islamic and Western feminists. One of the interesting observations she makes is that of an analogy between the men-only *diwaniyas* (male social gatherings) and male-only Western power structures (such as golf clubs and bars) that are strongholds of men in the West. Such institutions, albeit often informal, exclude females from social and political networks and sources of information, and serve as obstacles to women's advancement in society.

The book is replete with quotations from the author's interviews with Kuwaiti men and women, which illustrate her insightful analyses and her conclusions. These quotations make the book animated and interesting, as well as accessible to a wider readership, and not only to academic scholars.

Gonzáles exhibits impressive scholarship and familiarity of both theory and subject matter. It is unfortunate that there are grammatical errors and occasional awkward English constructions in the text, which could have been avoided if the manuscript had been edited more professionally. This shortcoming, however, does nothing to diminish or obscure the substance and purport of the book.

The importance of this book is in its contribution to the study of Muslim and other conservative societies and their attitudes toward women's rights and religion. The research outlined in this book can serve as a model for the understanding of women's rights in other modern Muslim societies. **MLA**

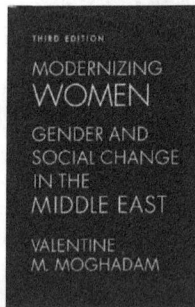

Valentine M. Moghadam. *Modernizing Women: Gender and Social Change in the Middle East.* **Lynne Reinner Publishers, 2013. 332pp. $26.50. ISBN: 9781588269331.**

This is a new edition of the author's work, updated to include events of the Arab Spring and subsequent revolts. Its comprehensiveness, its use of reams of real-world data to illustrate and support its conclusions, and its willingness to look at gender issues from a wide range of highly critical perspectives all combine with a limpid prose style to make this an invaluable resource for scholars in all manner of fields touching on gender studies and the MENA region.

Moghadam begins by emphasizing that the comparative lack of gender equality in the region, especially with respect to political and legal rights and participation is, contrary to stereotypes, not a result solely of Islam or of traditions dressed up as Islamic. She argues "why Muslim women lag behind Western women in legal rights, mobility, autonomy, and so forth as more to do with modernization and development—the extent of urbanization, industrialization, and proletarianization, as well as the political ploys of political elites—than with religious and cultural factors (p. 8).

The starting point for the book's analysis is "world-polity" or "world-systems" theory, a variant of modernization theory wherein a hegemonic (here, Western) order spreads at an unequal rate its own institutions, standards and organizations to other parts of the world. The spread of these institutions, which affect gender relations for better or worse (often both, but in the aggregate, generally better), in combination with regional and local material and cultural peculiarities, create differentials in the spread of more equal relations. Development, at least in the mid-twentieth century, often comes from the top down: the stronger the state and the greater its degree of Westernization, the generally higher is the level of improvement for women. It is notable that the book argues this point without in any meaningful way diminishing the importance of grass-roots women's activism; rather, the point it makes at convincing length and in detail is that strong and modern state institutions enable such activism to flourish and change societal patterns.

The second chapter provides an overview of late twentieth century developments across the region. In brief, the expansionary postwar period provided much more meaningful advances for gender equity then did the contractions of the 1980s and beyond, especially when challenges to Westernization arose, e.g., political movements using a concern with Islamic "legitimacy" in the form of an obsession with (re-) controlling women. In many ways, this significantly slowed women's progress in the region, all while most of the rest of the developing world surged ahead.

The third chapter addresses the changes in employment patterns that are part and parcel of changes in women's empowerment. The book goes into detail on choices in industrial economies that lead to differential outcomes for women: notable among them is the idea that "rentier" economies—those that rely primarily on tourism or resource exploitation—result for complex reasons relating to patterns of employment in much smaller advances for women than those countries that choose to develop domestic manufacturing industries. The argument also brings in the issue of Muslim family law: "Traditional gender norms codified in [Muslim family law] may discourage the adoption of policies and arrangements favorable to broad-based maternal employment, such as paid maternity leaves and childcare centers" (p. 99).

This leads to an analysis of what might be necessary for *women's economic citizenship*, i.e., as autonomous agents rather than as dependents on, and subjects to a larger, usually patriarchal, family unit. The fourth chapter continues this analysis, focusing on statistics relating to marriage, childbearing and education.

Chapter 5 addresses the effect of war and conflict on women's progress in Palestine, Afghanistan, and Iraq, where in each case armed conflict has weakened strong states and thus exposed women to both economic and personal insecurity. Such conflicts are typically "hypermasculine" affairs, and thus reduce women's economic as well as political citizenship. The bellicosity of the United States in the last decade comes off almost as badly as it ought to—both resistance movements and newly-formed governments in the latter two countries were all too willing to trade away women's rights for a sort of stability. This leads Moghadam to a larger argument about how including women in official peace talks and reconciliation movements cannot help but make things better: "Without idealizing women, one may plausibly postulate that an enhanced role for women in reconstruction could minimize corruption and cronyism—if only because women's absence from economic and political domains of power has prevented their involvement in patronage and clientelism" (p. 169).

The next chapter addresses Iran, where as political winds and demographics changed in the Islamic Republic, things grew worse, then better, for women, until growing much worse under Ahmadinejad. In all three periods, women's paid employment has remained well below that of comparable countries. The book teases out the overlap among cultural factors and choices and industrialization to elucidate this difference.

Chapter 7, the most relevant to the distinction between this new third edition and its predecessors, addresses feminism, women's issues and female participation in the Arab Spring of 2011 and subsequent protests and movements. The chapter begins by establishing the conditions necessary for democracy or pro-democracy movements to establish themselves: peaceful protests, already-strong women's movements, quotas for political representation. Moghadam goes into detail on the specifics of levels of involvement of women's groups in Tunisia, Egypt, and Morocco and how they influenced the comparative peacefulness of the protests and movements. The final chapter clears up what had, until then, been the book's only notable defec—its tendency to accept the existence of a formal women's group or meetings among women's groups as proof of their causing positive social change.

This book is an excellent resource for scholars in a wide variety of disciplines. It is very well organized, very well sourced and very well written, and its extensive bibliography provides scholars the opportunity to follow up on a host of different issues. Moghadam should be commended, not only for maintaining, but also for expanding the scope and quality of her work. **IAC**

❀

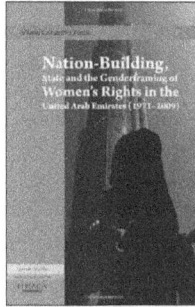

Vânia Carvalho Pinto. *Nation-Building, State and the Genderframing of Women's Rights in the United Arab Emirates (1971–2009)*. **Reading, UK: Ithaca Press, 2012. 134 pp. $74.95. ISBN: 978-0863724329.**

The book addresses the interconnected notions of gender, nation-building, and domestic socio-political dynamics in the newly established state of the United Arab Emirates (UAE) that, while aspiring to establish a modern country, is still searching for self-definition and empowerment. It presents two forms of analyses. On the one hand, it investigates the strategic plan of the UAE state in creating and re-configuring alterations to the genderframe. On the other hand, it examines the resonance or impact of such a genderframe on the society in general and Emirati women in particular.

The abstract term of "genderframing" is used by the author to refer to the dynamic and interactive process between the government or state and its population or society, which aims at reshaping or reinterpreting meanings connected to women-related policies. Such reinterpretations have been made by the UAE state revealing the changing roles of women as enviable and necessary for reasons related to nation-building objectives that include the promotion of family values and the maintenance of religious and cultural orientations. According to the author, this genderframing activity leads to the construction of a genderframe, a collective framework of interpretation that provides the population with constructive orientations with which to address women-related policies. The book provides a case study of the intersection of genderframing and nation-building in Gulf countries with a special focus on the UAE as the only successful experience of political union in the Arab world, notwithstanding its traditional polity as a tribal hereditary monarchy.

The author collected data based on Internet searches, personal connections, and interviews that were conducted across the seven Emirates, the majority of which came from the Emirates of Dubai and Sharjah. In addition, the author used content analysis of women-related speeches and statements made by state officials and members of the ruling families, obtained from a variety of sources, including official publications, websites, and online newspapers such as the *Gulf News* and *al-Khaleej*.

The author briefly reviewed previous studies, especially those of Suaad al-Oraimi and Wanda Krause that defined the UAE state's position toward women as part of the government's project of development accentuating the nation's unity and identity building. In her attempt to further develop these insights, the author focused on the theme of how Emirati women have been a central part of the process of nation-building in their country. She tackled the historical economic, social, and political conditions of the region showing how it has transformed from tribally organized trucial states—dominated by British colonialism that made very little effort to improve the living conditions of the population of that region—into a confederation of seven Emirates.

The book divided the temporal development of the state's involvement in women empowerment into three stages, discussed in three independent chapters. First, during the period from 1971 to the early 1980s, tasks of nation-building were undertaken by the newly established state of the Emirates locating women as crucial players in the realization of those tasks. During this period, the state was involved in the creation of a modern nation and was particularly eager to eliminate the image of the backwardness of the society and its women. In a word, Emirati women were in the process of modernization and having their rights expanded. Second, was the period from the late 1970s until 2009 during which the state focused on the religious and indigenous roots of national culture as well as on the policy of emiratization. The state was dealing with waves of traditionalism that swept the country, and reacted by promoting culturally authentic values and lifestyles. In this changing period of time, women were re-traditionalized, and their behavior and range of rights were seen as significant indicators of cultural authenticity. Third, was the period from the late 1990s until 2009 in which the state dealt with issues of nationalizing the labor force and opening up political participation aimed at renewing and empowering the Emirati nation. During this period women were viewed as central to the achievement of the national goals.

After addressing the effects of 40 years of genderframing as regards the education, employment, and political participation of Emirati women, the author provides judgmental statements saying that young women (especially those born in the 1980s and 1990s), unlike their predecessors, will not benefit from ample employment opportunities in the public sectors, and less so in gender-segregated environments. She also argues that the young generation cannot compete with the highly killed expats. The author depicts the young generation as showing little understanding of what it is to struggle for something as well as accentuates the imbalance and dilemma between tradition and modernity. Further, the next female generation, according to the author's view, "may be losing out employment-wise by spending all their formative years within a segregated educational system" (p. 96). Such a statement reflects a hidden Western model against which the Emirati youth is judged. Further, this statement is countered by the fact that the majority of students enrolled in universities in the UAE are women. Though the work force continues to be dominated by expatriates, Emirati nationals, including women, hold high-ranking positions, such as the cultural attaché in Washington DC, university professorship, doctors, etc. Furthermore, the UAE is unique in that employability or social activeness can be measured not necessarily by employability for salary, but on social-based activities. Women may well be using their education to participate in charitable organizations that are encouraged by the UAE's culture of philanthropy.

Overall, the book is dry and abstract. It focuses on women's issues as judged and evaluated by Western orientation. Furthermore, it lacks clarity and precision in using certain terms especially "genderframe," and its related forms (genderframing/s," "diagnostic genderframing," "prognostic genderframing," and "motivational genderframing"). For example, in page 103, the author writes "Although the genderframing of education seems to have been the most successful of all, women's employment and political participation are still genderframings in progress." If by this statement the author means that progress is being made for Emirati women's employment in professional arenas, I would agree. However, the author claims that one of the principles behind the UAE state's policy toward women concerns the recognition given by the international community to the conditions of women and women's issues within a given country as a reflection of the social advancement and civilization of that country. Thus, as the UAE has sought to attain respected statehood, the expansion of women's rights has been seen as a means to secure that recognition. Such a statement is objectionable as it depicts the UAE's plan as an instrumental tool for achieving international recognition, not as a genuine effort to empower Emirati women, socially, economically, or politically.

In addition, the book argues that there is no direct relationship between the state's policy that aims at empowering women and society's acceptance of them. In other words, Emirati society in general is still not ready to conceptualize women's rights and entitlements. In this regard, the book suffers from sweeping generalizations. For example, the author claims that in "many countries of the Middle East and North Africa, as many excellent collections have demonstrated the education, employment, and political participation of women have never really been that easily accepted by their own societies" (p. 5). But, the author does not mention a specific country or society to justify her statement. To support her claim, the author cites Abu-Lughod's book, *Remaking Women: Feminist and Modernity in the Middle East* (Princeton University Press, 1998).

However, within the same book Abu-Lughod, in her discussion of women in contemporary Egyptian society, states, "Urban women today, of a variety of classes, veiled and unveiled, are generally more radical than Qasim Amin was on issues of education, work, and participation in some aspects of the public sphere, such as politics" (Abu-Lughod 1998, 262). This societal acceptance of new roles of women was supported by the state where Nasser's "policies of mass education and guaranteed employment for graduates, regardless of sex, were based on a conception of women as worker and citizen whose participation was essential for national development"

(Abu-Lughod 1998, 262).

The book is limited by its restricted view and stereotyped expectations of Emirati culture. Though it calls for empowerment for women, it fails to acknowledge the progress made to date in the country's half decade of statehood. With its theoretical shortcomings discussed above, it is difficult to recommend this book to students in the field of Arab Gulf studies in general, and Emirati culture, in particular. **ESA**

Afsaneh Najmabadi. *Professing Selves: Transsexuality and Same-sex Desire in Contemporary Iran*. Durham, NC: Duke University Press, 2014. 418 pp. $77.18. ISBN: 978-0822355571. Pbk: 432 pp. $21.80. ISBN: 978-0822355571. Ebk: 4880 KB. 433 pp. $15.37. ISBN: 0822355574.

In November 2–14, 2014, BBC World News aired a documentary entitled "Iran's Sex Change Solution," in which several Iranians who had sought refuge in Turkey to escape forced sex change operations, were interviewed. In Iran, government officials deny the existence of homosexuality and offer subsidized gender reassignment surgery to bring those perceived as deviant in line with accepted norms. Often, however, those forced to transition are actually gay or lesbian and not transgender. According to those interviewed in the documentary, surgery is often followed by depression or even suicide. A 2008 BBC documentary, "Be Like Others," also called "Transsexual in Iran," followed the stories of patients at a gender reassignment clinic in Tehran. The patients insisted that they were not homosexual—which is illegal and perceived as immoral—and hoped that the surgery would enable them to live lives free of harassment. The results were positive in some cases, though families were ostracized in others. Female-to-male transsexuals were generally more successful in their new lives than male-to-female transsexuals, perhaps reflecting the prevailing gender hierarchy. The journalistic accounts were widely viewed in Europe and North America, but lacked historical context and scholarly analysis.

Afsaneh Najmabadi has answered this lack by writing a fascinating book that begins by challenging the Western media's depiction of transsexuality and sex reassignment surgery as coercive while ignoring the vibrant reform movement and history of progressive activism in Iran. She interrogates medicine, religion, psychology, criminology, trans activism, and everyday life with the tools of oral history, archival research, and ethnographic fieldwork. Chapter 1 shows how medical specialists attempt to determine if an applicant is indeed a candidate for transition and not homosexual or suffers from a classified psychological disorder. This process has opened new social spaces for "deviant" categories with applicants creatively using the system to answer their needs.

Chapter 2 surveys the history of sex-change surgery and how it became part of the discourse of scientific modernity and medical progress in Iran. The health of the nation, modern family norms, and progressive education led to the conviction that deviant sexuality was responsible for violent crimes. Chapter 3 addresses female homosexuality through a high profile case in 1973 that involved a lesbian "crime of passion." The alleged perpetrator had expressed a desire for sex reassignment surgery and the media projected this as a missed opportunity that, along with better parenting and education, could have prevented the crime. She then explains why male-to-female transitions differ from female-to-male transitions in the Iranian context.

Chapter 4 shows how males presenting as women were relatively accepted in certain walks of life before the 1979 revolution. After the revolution, however, they were stigmatized as homosexuals and as violators of new regulations against gender dressing. Ayatollah Khomeini had long held the view that sex change was permissible under Islamic law.

Chapter 5 shows how, in the decades that followed the revolution, Iranian legal, biomedical, psychiatric, and clerical authorities worked out procedures and financial and social support for the diagnosis and treatment of trans persons. Not only had the state supported this initiative.

Chapter 6 explains that trans activists themselves had challenged social and cultural norms and had contributed to changing state policies. The author emphasizes that the Iranian state is not static and monolithic; it is continually changing and reformulating itself like any other state formation. Chapter 7 builds on case studies of clients at a clinic in Tehran. The author is aware that her research questions reflected the legal and dominant understandings of sexuality in Iran. They were not however-er the dominant understandings of the persons she interviewed. Her case studies enable the reader to understand how trans lives are lived in difficult circumstances.

Sometimes, the struggle to decide if one is homosexual or trans results in a zone of undecidedness that makes a satisfactory life impossible. Chapter 8 concludes the book by asking if it is really necessary to ask if a person identifies as trans or lesbian, or gay or straight or something else. Identities could shift depending on circumstances, according to where one lived or worked, or according to the needs of families, spouses, and partners. Self-knowledge is a complex topic in contemporary Iran with roots in Islamic philosophical thought, Sufism, and modern psychology.

Conduct is more important than identity and a girl who acts like a boy may be nicknamed with a boy's name. The opposite does not happen, the author suggests, because nonnormative sex is received far more badly for adolescent males than it is for adolescent females. The author concludes this well-researched and important book by arguing for an alternative space where loving lives can be successfully lived. Identities would not have to be self-defined as trans or homo. Why not an ambiguous identity without categories imposed by modern science, medicine, religion, state, and society? **NEG**

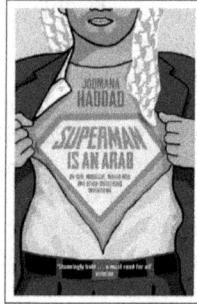

Joumana Haddad. *Superman is an Arab: On God, Marriage, Macho Men and Other Disastrous Inventions.* **London, UK: the Westbourne Press, 2012. 173 pp. £8.99. ISBN: 978-1908906090.**

Being brave is a high honor that a person can earn, and Haddad has earned it. Yet, not like a superhero, rather as an ordinary woman with an ordinary body, mind, desire, and reason. Being ordinary is a key concept for Haddad. It means real, as against a supernatural creature like superman: a macho man who fears to reveal his "clumsiness, timidity, flaws, slips and weak spots" (p. 12). Supermanism—the belief in superiority and invincibility—results in awful phenomena like despotism and terrorism. Casually put, it is a type of attitude: I am stronger, thus more suitable to solve any given problem; you are weaker, so step back and remain passive—I lead, you follow. Behind such mentality, Haddad says, "you'll find nothing but lies, falseness, cowardice, and hypocrisy. He may claim to be saving the world, but the world actually needs to be saved *from* him" (p. 15). Nevertheless, the blame cannot be put entirely on the supermen because women are also responsible for empowering them. For example, literature contains examples of women who enable supermen: "Lilith, quick to betray her sex Quick to betray, Whose thousand cuts Are more tender than a thousand kisses" (p. 24).

Metaphorically speaking, God created women for men to play with, but the project failed because women turned out to be independent and strong, and "took no bullshit from Man (nor from God, for that matter)" (p. 30). Haddad admits that there might be a woman, who may be "quick to betray her sex," but then she quickly points out that this woman is posited within a patriarchal society; therefore, it is critical firstly to understand the mannish environment capsulating her. In fulfilling her key objective, Haddad unmasks an aspect of identity, particularly of male Arabs, which is exaggerated and unwholesome by setting forth arguments on two levels—personal and institutional—although as a gifted writer she never separates these two so stridently.

Haddad openly acknowledges her intimate experiences with men. This is brave for a woman who lives in the Middle East where outspokenness is not a virtue, particularly for women.

First of all I'll peel that tender spot on the left side of your neck where my tears and your sweat run to hide Then I'll take your lips—that sugary fence between my hunger and you—and I'll lick then off slowly with mine Then I'll suck your tongue—that mouthwatering archer's bow crying out my name like a zesty dart [...] Then I'll drink three drops of your poisonous milk to sink my thirst under yours (pp. 111-112).

Haddad then proceeds to give 20 pieces of advice under the heading of "Penis: directions for use" (pp. 113-118). Knowing that her language may strike many readers, she asks why is it that what makes a man a "stud," makes a woman a "slut" (pp. 122-123)? And why should women be judged by men's standards, anyway? "What do ethics have to do with how frequently (or not) I use my vagina" (p. 123)? At the same time, Haddad does not dehumanize men, and brings to the equation the role of institutions in making supermen out of men.

The main institutions that Haddad targets are monotheist religions that sanctify patriarchal standards, that is, Judaism, Christianity, and Islam. "These three religions have the same attitude toward women: oppressive and misogynic" (p. 54). She further argues that they are in fact "racist, sexist, homophobic, merciless, bloody, and biased against humanity, freedom and human rights" (p. 55). More specifically, she defends Islamic feminism as an oxymoron because men and women are not equal in Islam.

There are also some suggestions made by Haddad that secularism is necessary (although it is not sufficient); women should participate in political affairs; their freedom is inseparable from their financial independence; men and women must avoid forging a patriarchal versus matriarchal world, and should rather collaborate to form a world for men *with* women in which they are equal. Although these suggestions are by no means new, their representation in the book does no harm. All in all, it can be easily said that Haddad is brave. But, it cannot be so easily said what *Superman is an Arab...* is. That is, the author is frank and gifted and the book is engaging, but what is this book attempting to accomplish?

If *Superman is an Arab...* is read as an academic text, the authenticity of its scholarship becomes questionable. She does speak about social institutions, and puts forth a solution, which is a full-fledged revolution that would result in total annihilation of the old system: "change cannot come from compromising with rotten system, but only by overthrowing it. So it is time to start fighting *against* the negotiator inside of us. The solution is to destroy. And destroy. And destroy. And re-build again" (p. 109). How theoretically and practically sound this suggestion is should be judged cautiously.

If *Superman is an Arab…* is read as a dialog with a woman (Haddad), and as a means to share some personal experiences, feelings and thoughts, the book is inspiring and entertaining. It is the voice of an Arab woman, in which a great number of women might hear their own life stories. Haddad is certainly testing the limits of freedom of speech in a region that is not known for tolerance and human (particularly women) rights. And it is indeed impressive.

Haddad illustrates the discrimination against women so lucidly that no reasonable person could remain indifferent to a women's life in a patriarchal Arab society after reading this book. **MMM**

Paul Amar. *The Security Archipelago: Human-Security States, Sexuality Politics, and the End of Neoliberalism.* **Durham, NC: Duke University Press, 2013. 310 pp. $94.95. ISBN: 978-0822353843. $25.95. Pbk.: ISBN: 978-0822353980.**

In the linked assemblage of essays that make up this study of the rise of a new kind of governance regime associated particularly with "hot spots" in the global semi-periphery, Paul Amar offers a series of case studies focusing on Brazil and Egypt to argue that "a grammar of humanitarian protection or securitized humanization" (p. 3) is increasingly the new discursive and material logic of state control and population management. Rather than seeing this as a strategy disseminated unilaterally to the Global South by the political–financial institutions in the capitals of the Global North, or "West," Amar argues persuasively that it is in sites—or "laboratories"—such as Rio de Janeiro and Cairo that such policies are formulated, put to the test, and refined, to be disseminated thereafter laterally to other semi-peripheral locations as well as to the strife-ridden urban landscapes of Europe, North America, China, and the like. Hence, the archipelago of the title: a series of physically and culturally disconnected sites and moments that nevertheless constitute a global system in formation. These are "laboratories" for socioeconomic and cultural management in which local but also international institutions (NGOs, UN bodies, multinational capitalist enterprises, and the like) come together in ways that are not always predictable, in the shape of what Amar calls "parastatal formations." Such clusters of institutions and individuals replace, consolidate, redefine, and occasionally contest the work of the state. In the name of "security" and "humanitarian rescue"—concepts previously linked to situations of war and natural disaster—international actors and state bodies (notably, police, and military cadres) secure social peace—at least temporarily—as they redefine population groups through new or revived deployments of gendered, racialized, and class-specific subjectifications. And they save the state from itself.

Trained in the disciplines of anthropology and politics, Amar spent considerable periods in Egypt and Brazil, and in addition to fieldwork, he draws on insight gained from employment in the UN Development Program. He thus brings together a wealth of on-site knowledge and familiarity with the workings of international development institutions as well as reliance on a wide array of scholarly and media sources in three languages.

The scheme that Amar traces is rooted in a displacement of the notion of the political subject, from being the rational-choice individual who produces and consumes, to a subject who is targeted as being in need of "protection" and moral training that will shape a culturally appropriate, sexually respectable, and spatially docile population. Notions of idealized masculinity and femininity, and their stigmatized contraries, are central to the kind of moral policing and spatial cordoning-off that characterizes this governance strategy. Amar maps the elaboration of this through a series of interlinked themes and strategies, beginning with the policing and spatial politics of the 1992 Earth Summit held in Rio, and the 1994 Cairo Population and Development Conference—both so important in registering the purchase of NGOs on the emerging, moralizing politics of security in the Global South. The dynamic, contentious encounters between independent oppositional formations and the apparatus of international development both challenged the agendas of development and security-focused players and led them to adapt certain labels associated with an anti-globalization and anti-capitalist outlook, a move that is all too familiar within the neo-liberal universe of "empowerment." In this case study, as throughout the book, Amar demonstrates how the notion of protecting "culture" became a channel through which to claim, reify, and attempt to impose naturalized notions of gendered respectability via the policing of sexuality. Moreover, one outcome of trans regional conferences such as these, coupled with other forms of collaboration, was the formation of new "cultural alliances" that drew on pre-existing fetishes of the Other: Brazil and Egypt as partners in a new world of "cultural-sovereignty enforcement" (p. 57) that could celebrate romantic notions of trans-global Arabness, in what Amar nicely calls a "theater of seduction and couplings" (p. 58).

Amar's chapters go on to consider the targeting of certain population categories—particularly young males—through vigorous repression of "aberrant" sexualities that also expressed subjectivities not regarded as "respectable" for a modern society visibilized as a middle-class-led, consumer-oriented participant in global (West-led) capitalism. In both Cairo and Rio, this entailed campaigns of harsh physical and discursive policing against alleged male sex workers. Similarly, the anti-sexual harassment and anti-trafficking campaigns in Cairo and Rio, respectively, aided by international and local feminist-oriented NGO efforts at getting local legislation passed, could easily have the effect of terrorizing and exploiting large groups of adolescent boys, through imprisonment or demands for bribes. Another elaboration of the human-security state has been in the realm of "heritage protection." Amar's tracing of the Egyptian government's attempt to separate the Egyptians living and working in the old city—what has come to be known as "Fatimid Cairo" amongst heritage developers—from the built heritage, on the premise that their work and their very presence "polluted" the area. Amar discusses the master's thesis of Muhammad ʿAtta, some years before his involvement in the 9/11 attack, which argued for a development policy that would place a moral-policing function in the hands of selected families known for piety, good money management and conservative family values, and would, in particular, segregate women in the purified inner cul-de-sacs of the neighborhood, while the public realm of production and tourism remained (or rather, became) a masculinized space.

A brief review cannot do justice to the complexity of these case studies, nor to the issues do they raise. Ethical messiness is not Amar's topic, but some of these issues are difficult ones. How to navigate, for example, between the coercive practices engendered in the name of "human security" and the very real threats posed to vulnerable people—whatever their sexual orientation or gender assignment—within the blighted landscapes wrought by modern capitalism, however "global" or "local?" The book would be even richer than it already is with the inclusion of more voices which might capture some of these dilemmas. The shift in the subject/target of governance from the individual ideally enjoying something called free choice, to what we might see as the protectable subject (in my words, not Amar's) of the human-security big-brother state with its parastatal apparatus offering both deniability and securitized expertise, is persuasive but it would be good to highlight the ways in which this may not be a smoothly implemented master narrative. And how new is it? Amar certainly gestures to earlier histories, but I think even more could be done to link those histories with present trajectories. These are perhaps future research projects that Amar's articulate, sophisticated discussion encourages.

As his book promises an "alternative political history of neoliberalism" (p. 30) through an analysis of these governance strategies, Amar ends with an excursus on the discredited premises of neoliberalism and yet the ways in which the phoenix of a new "post-neoliberal" outlook has been able to emerge, one that reclaims "investment" for an allegedly people-centered politics as it continues to secure the profits of "zombie finance" for the few. How such an articulation intersects with the processes and rhetoric of "human securitization" is at once obvious and elusive. And as Amar points out in what manages to be the slightly optimistic ending to a story that is somber indeed, the alliances and the resistances that the human-security state recognizes and provokes will always, in some measure, escape its control. **MB**

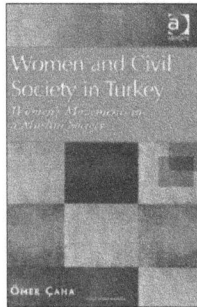

Omer Çaha. *Women and Civil Society in Turkey: Women's Movements in a Muslim Society*. Farnham, UK: Ashgate, 2013. 222 pp. $99.95. ISBN: 9781472410078.

This book discusses civil society and the role of women's movements within that society, particularly in Turkey. It argues that the feminist movement transformed the conceptual framework of civil society and the public sphere in Turkey. The book is divided into seven chapters, starting with a theoretical discussion of civil society and feminist movements; it then moves on to a chronological analysis of the development of civil society since the Ottoman period, and the feminist movement from the late Ottoman Empire into the 2000s. The chapters dedicated to the Islamic Women's movement and the Kurdish Women's movement focus on the diversity of the feminist movement in Turkey.

The first chapter focuses on political philosophers such as Hobbes, Locke, Rousseau, Hegel, Marx, and Gramsci, and shows how the early modern philosophers did not consider women as part of a civil society. However, the feminist movement challenged this perception. Caha defines feminism as "a political movement directed at changing existing power relations between men and women" (p. 12). He follows the division of the feminist movement into two periods: (1) the women's rights movement, which focused on gaining political and legal rights for women; and (2) the women's liberation movement, which included diverse feminist groups which began in the 1960s. The author discusses the radical feminists' criticism of the separation of public versus private domains as an extension of the patriarchal worldview. For Caha, all the demands of feminists toward change in women's role in public and private areas actually lead to "the development of a plural and heterogeneous public domain" (p. 25). The transformation of the public sphere into a plural and diverse environment, then, maintains the self-organization of feminist groups, their protection against oppression, and empowerment against threatening policies.

Caha next deals with the historical development of civil society and women in Turkey since the Ottoman Empire. Although he identifies the non-Muslim congregations, religious communities, guilds, and local notables as elements of civil society, he dismisses them for being highly dependent on the state and playing merely an administrative role. While his assessment is based on literature dealing with Ottoman history, I argue that these groups functioned beyond merely serving the interests of the Ottoman governance and acted in defense of their own interests as a class as well. The *Sened-i İttifak* (Deed of Agreement) of 1808 between the local notables and the state is a good example of how rival interests between these groups and state could lead to a redefinition of the roles of the institutions in the public arena. Similarly the *millets* (non-Muslim congregations) as well as the *ulama* (the class of scholars) could be viewed as self-aware classes which were in constant negotiation with the Ottoman administration. Therefore, dismissing these groups as mere administrative functionaries is an understatement of their role, and thus civil society, in the Ottoman social and political life.

The author correctly points out the problems with the way Kemalist reforms were implemented and how these in turn limited the liberation of women. The radical pace of the Kemalist modernization, the attempt to create a cohesive society, disregarding non-Turkish groups, and excluding veiled women from public led to the disengagement of women from that sphere.

Caha traces the origins of the feminist movement, especially among the leftist socialist women. Particularly during the 1980s, the feminist movement crystallized through publications and symposia and eventually turned into a liberal feminist movement focusing on equality with men in the workplace, in the house, and in social life. He also discusses radical feminists and social feminists explaining their ideologies reflected in their publications in the late 1980s. The radicals promoted "feminizing" men, while the socialists seem to be closer to the liberal feminists in promoting man-based values to emancipate women. He points out the numerous public activities by the feminist groups such as street protests, festivals, and the founding of shelter houses, and concludes that throughout the 1980s, feminism became an active part of the civil society.

Caha argues the feminist movement was institutionalized in the 1990s. The author describes in detail the various major feminist organizations and publications that focus on the education of women, the fight against domestic abuse, and the promotion of women's legal and political rights. After 2000, he points out, the issues of women's rights, especially pertaining to commonly accepted problems across social groups such as domestic abuse, honor killings, and equality in professional and social life have been upheld by groups beyond the feminist organizations. The feminist movement was transformed from the Kemalist and the socialist movement of the 1970s and 1980s into a widespread, grassroots, post-modern, and social movement in the 2000s.

The author properly devotes two chapters to specific groups of women's movements that have increasingly become a major phenomenon in Turkish civil society—Muslims and Kurds. This chapter on Islamic women's movement focuses—a bit excessively—on the headscarf issue. Muslim women faced discrimination, especially in universities due to their headscarf as a result of the Kemalist campaign against religious symbols in the public domain. However, with the spread of girls' schooling and the rise of a Muslim middle class throughout the 1980s, the visibility of the headscarf, and the challenges it faced, increased rapidly beyond the university campuses into every aspect of social life. The reaction of the assertive secular elite against the "threatening" spread of the headscarf culminated into the February 28, 1997 military memorandum—which is often referred to as a post-modern coup— eventually banned the headscarf on university campuses. This repression, Caha states, turned the headscarf into a mobilization symbol for the conservative masses. Following a detailed analysis of the various women's associations and various Islamic publications on women, he focuses on Islamic feminism and the Islamic feminist movement in Turkey. While many Muslim women agree with the fundamental aspects of feminism such as seeking legal, political, and social equality, fighting discrimination, and awareness of the feminine identity, they typically depart from the larger feminist movement on issues of family and sexuality.

On the issue of Islamic feminism—an interesting aspect dismissed in this book— the contribution of Islamic movements in general assisted in the rise of limited gender awareness and feminism. Starting especially in the 1980s, the rise of a middle class and expansion of educational institutions in Turkey by Islamic social movements has led to an increasing number of women, who are college-educated professionals, mobilized for a religious cause in female-dominant environments. By the 2000s, while working women justified their jobs as a religious duty, this experience also exposed their need for equal rights and shared family responsibility based on Islamic arguments. Thus, Islamic feminist rhetoric quickly spread among this group of professional Muslim women who practically, and then theoretically, found it necessary and appealing.

The Kurdish Women's movements, Caha argues, is likened to the African American Women's movement in America of the 1970s. He identifies the Kurdish, Islamic, and similar other women's movements as the third-wave feminism in Turkey. The historical and cultural context that is mostly dismissed in the first and second wave of feminisms is emphasized by the various ethnic and nationalist women's movements. Caha traces the origins of the Kurdish Women's movement back to the 1970s, and describes how their organizational experiences began in the socialist movement, and turned into an ethnic struggle through the rise of the PKK [The Kurdistan Workers' Party] and later the Kurdish political movement. The Kurdish Women's movements emerged as an autonomous movement, independent from the Kurdish ethnic movement or the Turkish feminists, after the mid-1990s. Caha at this point closely analyzes, compares, and contrasts the ideas expressed in leading Kurdish Women's journals, such as *Roza*, *Jujin*, and *Jin u Jiyan*. While there were differences among these journals in terms of their attitude toward the Kurdish nationalist movement and the larger feminist movements, they had numerous shared concerns, such as traditional Kurdish patriarchal values, women's problems in cities, and oppressive practices of the state.

The author's well-studied and well-nuanced work quite successfully presents a picture of the feminist movement in Turkey. He views the feminist movement as part of the rising Turkish civil society. The diversity within the feminist movement is handled in minute detail. The book reflects a deep comprehension of the various branches within the feminist movement as well the distinct characteristics of the various women's movements. Caha does a good job in focusing on the Islamic and Kurdish Women's movements in separate chapters. His methodology of providing historical and cultural context to the rise of feminism is very helpful in aiding the reader digest the complexity of the issue in a specific context. I would recommend this book to all scholars and students of feminism and civil society. More specifically, anyone with an interest in Turkish society, culture, and history would find this book useful in expanding their horizons. **MG**

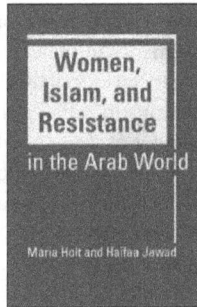

Maria Holt and Haifaa Jawad. *Women, Islam, and Resistance in the Arab World.* Boulder, CO & London, UK: Lynne Rienner. 2013. 211 pp. $55.00. ISBN: 978-1588269256.

Most previous research on Arab women in general, and Muslim women in particular, has focused on issues such as the constraints confronted by many of them in the context of highly patriarchal, male-dominated societies, and what has been singled out by many scholars—oftentimes in a simplistic and unquestioning fashion—as manifestations of this social suppression, such as the phenomenon of veiling or re-veiling, in the midst of contemporary Islamic resurgence movements. The problem with these studies has been their highly Orientalist inclination, and their focus on women's traditional roles, as wives, mothers, and caretakers in the private sphere, rather than their active engagement and multiple contributions in the public sphere.

It wasn't until the eruption of the Arab Spring movements that we started to witness a slight shift in this trend, as some scholars started to tackle the issue of Arab and Muslim women's political activism, and even heroism, as they became iconic figures and influential public opinion leaders in their respective countries and communities. Aside from these few recent studies, very little has been written about Arab and Muslim women who are actively involved in political activism, let alone those who are ideologically driven to join resistance movements in areas where political struggles and violent confrontations are a troubling reality.

In an attempt to fill this void and to break away from these predominantly stereotypical depictions and overly simplistic (mis)representations of Arab and Muslim women, Maria Holt and Haifaa Jawad in their book titled *Women, Islam, and Resistance in the Arab World* (Lynne Rienner, 2013) embark on a rich ethnographic journey, which allows the readers to explore three in-depth case studies exemplifying Arab women's different modes of resistance, in the context of several violent conflicts, namely: Shi'a women in Lebanon, Iraqi women, and Palestinian women in the West Bank and Gaza Strip.

By doing so, "this book invites new perspectives to existing literature on women and Islam and on women and conflict: it provides a comparative perspective; draws on firsthand accounts of women involved in conflict, whether as active participants, victims, or bystanders; places Islamic belief and ritual into a practical framework and considers how religious faith influences women's responses to crisis situations; and advances theoretical understanding of women's participation in violent conflict" (p. vii).

The fieldwork for this book was conducted in Lebanon, the West Bank, Syria, Jordan, and Yemen in the years 2002–03, 2006–07, and 2010–11. The authors relied on questionnaires and semi-structured interviews with a wide range of women from different backgrounds, occupations, ages, and social classes. The interviewees included "professional women (university lecturers, teachers, doctors, lawyers, etc.) and women who had no schooling at all; women living in towns, villages, and refugee camps; political activists; women involved in welfare activities; students; Islamist women and secular women; the widows and mothers of martyrs; and women who refer to themselves as 'feminists'" (p. 8).

The book consists of seven chapters. The first chapter titled "Women and Islamism in the Arab World" lays out some of the theoretical underpinnings which guide our understanding of how and why Arab women engage in various forms of resistance in situations of violent conflict. In doing so, the chapter exposes and challenges some of the misconceptions surrounding this notion, by revealing that "far from being excluded from the dominant discourse, many Arab women are finding their 'voice' through the modernizing processes of Islamic resistance" (p. 7). This chapter also discusses the used research methodology in this study. Chapter two titled "Islamic Discourses on Women and Violence" sheds light on the religious foundations of 'Islamic resistance' and women's role in it, as well as ways in which their activism and agency challenge patriarchy and other power structures. Chapter three titled "Expressions of Resistance: Women and the Arab Spring" presents an overview of different examples of women's activism and heroism in the context of the Arab revolutions which have swept the region since 2011, and which the authors argue parallel the case studies covered in this book. The following three chapters present the findings of the extensive fieldwork which was conducted in the three case studies in Lebanon, Iraq, and Palestine, with the aim of linking "the discourse on gender and national identity with discussions of women's role in national liberation and Islamic resistance movements" (p. 8). Finally, the last, concluding chapter attempts to chart the "Way Forward" in terms of the future of Islamic resistance movements and women's multiple roles and levels of participation in them, which remain as uncharted and influx as the complex and shifting realities of their own countries and societies.

In this book, the authors succeed in illustrating to the reader the profound influence which Islam—whether as a spiritual faith and a religion, a cultural system and a way of life, or an ideological orientation and a form of activism—has on the lived realities and experiences of Arab women. By allowing us to hear the voices of different Palestinian, Iraqi, Lebanese, and other Arab women telling their own stories in their own words, the authors manage to question some of the misleading and commonly held (mis)perceptions about "women and Islam," through exploring "the influence of Islamic teachings and practices on Muslim women caught up in situations of conflict, in terms both of their ability to participate in the conflict and of their private lives" (p. 27). In every case, the authors allowed us to find out how and why for the women participants in this study, "their religion is meaningful to them, whether as a source of spiritual comfort or an aid to activism" (p. 27).

In doing so, the book challenges, not only the false images and stereotypes of Arab and Muslim women as powerless, marginalized, oppressed, and victimized, it, most importantly, shakes the equally false association between "Islam" and "oppression," since many women who narrate their stories in this book attribute restrictive practices and control mechanisms in their societies to inherited traditions and cultural baggage, rather than to Islam itself, as a belief system, faith, and ideology.

The most important theoretical contributions of this book to the already existing literature on Arab and Muslim women could be summarized in the following key points. First, instead of simply buying into, or superficially negating, commonly held (mis)perceptions regarding Arab and Muslim women's powerlessness, victimization and/or marginalization, the book paints a rich and deep picture illustrating their contributions as active participants in resistance movements and as "agents" of change. Second, the book equally complicates the notions of feminism and resistance by enriching our understanding of their multifaceted and multilayered nature, as manifested in these women's complex roles, identities, lived realities, and various forms of activism. Instead of adopting a "one size fits all" outlook on these complex, and highly intertwined, phenomena, the authors illustrate, through these women's own narratives, how they exemplified new types of "Islamic feminism," through engaging in multiple forms of resistance, which could be obvious or subtle, violent or nonviolent, directed at internal or external forces, as well as directed against social forces, such as patriarchal structures, or political forces, such as Israel and the West. Third, by interviewing women from different countries, ages, backgrounds, experiences, and orientations, as well as including men's voices, the book provides us with a rich, deep, varied, and comprehensive understanding of how and why Islam affects the lives of these women, not just as a religious faith, but also as a day-to-day lived reality and as an ideological force which guides and shapes their various forms of resistance to different powers on many levels.

This book, which is truly valuable for anyone who is interested in learning more about Arab and Muslim women, in general, and their involvement in various forms, levels and manifestations of resistance, in particular, concludes by asserting that "the tension between inherited patriarchal patterns of thought and behavior, on the one hand, and freshly articulated Islamic norms and principles, on the other, looks set to intensify further. The way in which this tension plays out will determine the degree to which women's participation in political struggle will translate into the recognition and institutionalization of women's rights in society" (p. 181). **SK**

WEBSITES

MARA Foundation. *Modern Assyrian Research Archive (MARA).*
http://www.assyrianarchive.org/

Access to a reliable source of archival documents and other primary sources is essential for historians, social scientists, and for those studying the modern Assyrian community in the Middle East, the Modern Assyrian Research Archive (MARA) will provide an excellent source for both primary and secondary sources. Established in 2008, MARA is a web-based archive housed at the Faculty of Asian and Middle Eastern Studies at the University of Cambridge, and organized by scholars and doctoral students studying the Assyrian community of the Middle East. MARA administrators are in the process of collecting and digitizing a large number of historical documents, pictures, audio, and video recordings. They aim to make these sources digitally available for both researchers and the general public. In fact, half of the materials are now available for use by researchers. The administrators hope to make the entire collection digitally available during the early months of 2013.

MARA's webpage is well organized, and easily navigable. The home page has two distinct links: the first is for the archives, and the second is for the non-for-profit foundation that administers and manages the archives and research library. When visiting the archives, a photograph of General Agha Petros, and various other pictures of ordinary Assyrians greet the user. At the top of the page, tabs link the user to various important sections that include information about the organization, the mission statement of the archives, the advisory board, donors' lists, other relevant information, and most importantly, a tab dedicated to the archival collection.

The "archive" tab is organized like a library search engine, where the user can look for materials by title, author, keyword, publisher, ISBN, language, or call number. This section is available to all users, and it could potentially serve as a starting point for researchers looking to compile a bibliography of primary and secondary sources available on the modern Assyrian community. The type of publication, author, and year can also be sorted in the search menu, which allows researchers to quickly organize and sort search results. The search engine is linked to WorldCat, in which users can rapidly look for copies of any material not available digitally on the MARA website.

For researchers interested in using the already digitized material available at the archive, the process is very simple. A quick registration form must be completed, and the user is then able to login to the website, with the ability to view and utilize the available material. Once in the member section, the user is able to save searched results, navigate to external sites where some of the published materials can be found, tag certain publications to view and use in the future, and most importantly, view digitized materials, including but not limited to, memoirs, letters, and diaries of colonial officials, missionaries, and members of the Assyrian community. Another research tab is entitled "links;" this page offers a variety of external research websites that might be useful for researchers studying the Assyrian community and other important historical subjects.

The MARA search tools are very user friendly. One of the many benefits of the MARA website is that it provides a great venue in which researchers can navigate and compile large bibliographies. MARA also allows the user to access Assyrian produced primary sources, which, in the past were very to difficult to access; however, with material now being available online, researchers are now able to utilize those sources. This makes MARA a very important tool for scholars hoping to gain a better understanding of the modern Assyrian community, and the condition of minorities in the modern Middle East.

Finally the tab "MARA FAQs" provides detailed information on the research archives, the material available for researchers, the formats of documents, instructions on how to search the archives, and MARA account information. System administrators should consider placing this tab in a more prominent location on the website. An average user might not easily find this tab and this could hinder the user's ability to navigate the website. A name change for the tab might also be appropriate; the tab should be given a name that allows the reader to understand that this is in fact an instruction tab.

If the reader were to navigate to the "foundation" page, the home page includes a news blog, which Administrators use to regularly post news and information for researchers and visitors to the site. This section of the website provides useful updates that keep the visitor aware of any technical difficulties, updates to the database, and other organizational news and information. This blog is very useful, but a link should be posted at the research side of the website; this way, individuals not visiting the foundation's webpage could still read the latest news updates.

Administrators have also set up Facebook and Twitter accounts, which are frequently updated, and have become an integral part of the communication strategy for MARA. Frequent visitors should consider subscribing to one of the organization's social media pages in order to keep updated and informed. The administrators should consider copying the updates posted to the Facebook and Twitter pages to the foundation's blog; individuals without accounts with the social networks can still be updated of any important updates.

MARA could potentially change the way research is conducted into the Assyrian community. The digitization of historical materials will allow scholars to access personal and family collections quickly and efficiently. The organization and the digital database have the potential to expand even further, creating an environment where MARA could partner with larger archives and organization to further promote the documents that are housed in the online database. The administrators should also consider creating a community page. The page has the potential to create an online community of researchers where ideas can be exchanged, research advice can be given, and questions answered. MARA has the potential to help Middle East write histories through the perspective of the Assyrian community. MARA is a great organization that should continue to expand in order to help researchers and interested individuals access important materials and sources. **FD**

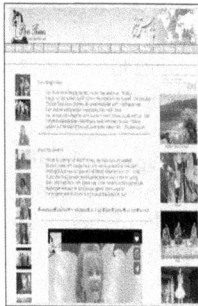

Pars Times. *Pars Times: Greater Iran and Beyond.* http://www.parstimes.com/

Pars Times is a nonprofit and independent website dedicated to collating news items and useful information from other Internet pages on the Middle East, but with almost exclusive focus on Iran and the Iranian community abroad, particularly in Southern California where many Iranians have settled. From its Home Page, articles are indexed under different tabs, which are in turn, organized by category: geography, news, business, culture, life and style, and weather. Each tab is further divided into subcategories for easier browsing. Besides written pieces, *Pars Times* also has a dedicated section on videos, featuring interviews and items on notable Persian individuals.

The News Section is a central feature. It attempts to gather all items of various issues affecting Iran, the Iranian community or even particular Iranian individuals, taken from other news agencies. This makes it a centralized site for those interested in news on Iran and Iranians scattered throughout the world. Furthermore, as *Pars Times* is aimed at researchers and analysts, it divides articles into categories that might be of interest to them; for instance, news stories related to oil and gas, or defense and proliferation are listed separately. Since it is updated regularly, it is convenient for the researcher to constantly keep abreast of developments in these areas. The News Section lists headlines and URL links to other major news websites, such as *The Economist*, *The BBC*, The *New York Times*, The *Guardian*, and *The Independent*. Additionally, more minor news agencies are also linked: such as those from the United Arab Emirates, Japan, Thailand, New Zealand, and Australia. Essentially, *Pars Times* gathers all kinds of news items from a wide variety of sources. However, this also means that there is no filter to what is posted, as the articles and websites are unverified by the webmasters for reliability.

Additionally, *Pars Times* is a reliable website for quick referencing for anything Iranian. This makes it a valuable first-stop introduction to those who are interested in Persian history and culture. The great eras, such as the Achaemenid and Sasanian periods, are conveniently listed from Ancient to Modern and everything in between. There is also some information on the archaeology and geography of Iran. However, it is not organized very systematically, which can make it difficult to find a specific topic or a related article. Like the News Section, the articles are sourced from elsewhere, such as the Library of Congress, *Encyclopaedia Iranica*, and various universities, museums, and institutes. For the professional or casual historian, *Pars Times* is suitable for looking for various articles on a general—albeit not in depth—snippet of Iranian history.

Pars Times has an impressive page on the Who's Who of and from Iran, in every possible field: academia, medicine, sports, the arts, fashion and modelling, music, journalism, literature, politics, activists, and film. Each of these individuals is listed alphabetically, together with the links to their professional pages or official profiles. As the list of Iranian individuals is so diverse and expansive, this could be a valuable database for anyone who needs to check on their credentials and background.

With the growing popularity of Iranian films, *Pars Times* has conveniently gathered news on Iranian cinema from elsewhere on the Internet. As it is up-to-date, this makes it a reliable source of information for those studying, or who are simply interested in Iranian cinema. Similarly, there has been an increasing fascination of Iranian books, especially novels, memoirs, and accounts of life under the Islamic Republic. There is a section dedicated to the popular best sellers with relevant links to their publishing houses, reviews, or interviews with the authors. Particularly for scholars or students working on Iran, there is also a useful sub-section that lists academic books and journals on a variety of topics in the field of Persian studies by different publishers.

The website is a good introduction in order to understand the structure and functioning of the Islamic Republic. In fact, there is also a dedicated section for this purpose. Besides links to the Constitution, it also has comprehensive sections in both English and Persian, on the different branches of the State, including its structure, executive, legislature, and judiciary. Under each section, there are various links to the official pages for those branches and useful information, sourced from other sites such as the BBC. As such, material regarding personalities and official activities are easily accessible.

The website is a useful and convenient resource showing the laws and regulations existing in Iran. Laws on narcotics, environment, citizenship, election, family, public health, labor, and the media are covered. As is the style of *Pars Times*, information regarding each subject area is taken from other websites and is merely collated. Those pertaining to trade, foreign investment, insurance, and intellectual property are helpful pointers for those interested in doing business in Iran. The laws and regulations section also provides the reader with up-to-date developments and changes to any international legal issues, including the U.S.-led sanctions. This makes it convenient for researchers, academics, and the general public to access legal information on the Islamic Republic. It also has a list of a number of law firms in Iran that deal with specific legal issues, from domestic to international.

Almost like a Twitter page for Iran, *Pars Times* essentially gathers articles and media sources from other Internet pages and organizes them according to category. It aims to be an alternative source of news and information for all things Iranian, and this seems to be the main and only purpose of the person behind it. The indiscriminate method of amassing anything on Iran, although useful in terms of convenience, makes it difficult to verify the reliability of a particular web link. This means that a lot is left to the discretion and discernment of the reader. Furthermore, as this website covers a whole range of topics, they and the corresponding links are listed in no particular order, thus making it somewhat difficult for a visitor to navigate. However, all in all, in addition to acting as a source of news and information for researchers, the website provides links to basic and varied online articles regarding Iranian history and culture. As such, *Pars Times* is a good introduction for those who are interested in, or are just beginning to study Iran. **RAR**

REVIEWERS

AERT = Abed el-RahmanTayyara, Ph.D., Department of Modern Languages Cleveland State University; Cleveland, OH, USA

AHI = Ahmed H. Ibrahim, Ph.D., Qatar University; Doha, Qatar

AHT = Alfons H. Teipen, Ph.D., Furman University; Greenville, SC, USA

ALG = Alessandra L. González, Ph.D., Princeton University; Princeton, NJ, USA

AM = Anne Meneley, Ph.D., Trent University; Peterborough, Ontario, Canada

AMW = Andrew M. Wender, JD, Ph.D., University of Victoria; Victoria, BC, Canada

ART = Abed el-Rahman Tayyara, Ph.D., Cleveland State University; OH, USA

AY = Amr Yossef, Ph.D., American University in Cairo, Cairo, Egypt

AZ = Abderrahman Zouhir, Ph.D., Wayne State University; Detroit, MI, USA

BKK = Burçak Keskin-Kozat, Ph.D., Stanford University; Stanford, CA, USA

BY = Bassam Yousif, Ph.D., Indiana State University; Terre Haute, IN, USA

CA = Coeli Fitzpatrick, Ph.D., Grand Valley State University; Allendale, MI, USA

CL = Cynthia Lindenmeyer, Rev. Dr., American Public University; Charles Town, WV, USA

CL¹ = Caroline Lancaster; Furman University, SC, USA

COP = Claire Oueslati-Porter, Ph.D., Florida International University; Miami, FL, USA

DAG = David A. Grantham, Texas Christian University; Ft. Worth, TX, USA

DD = Donna Divine, Ph.D., Smith College; Northampton, MA, USA

DHG = Douglas H. Garrison, MA, University of Denver; Denver, CO, USA

DKW = David Kenneth Waldman, Ph.D., Colorado State University Global Campus; Baltimore, MD, USA

DM = David Mason, Ph.D., Zayed University; Abu Dhabi, UAE

DW = Dina Wafa, Ph.D., The American University in Cairo; Cairo, EG

ESA = El-Sayed el-Aswad, Ph.D., United Arab Emirates University; Al-Ain, UAE

ET = Eren Tatari, Ph.D., Rollins College; Orlando, FL, USA

FD = Fadi Dawood, MA, University of London, London, UK

FK = Feras Klenk, MA, University of Arizona; Tucson, AZ, USA

FM = Francesco Melfi, Ph.D., Cleveland State University; Cleveland, OH, USA

FV = Fatih Varol, University of Illinois-Urbana Champaign; IL, USA

GDD = G. Doug Davis, Ph.D., Troy University, Troy, AL, USA

GF = Grant Farr, Ph.D., Portland State University; Portland, OR, USA

GH = Gary Hobin, Major (Ret.), US Army Command and General Staff College; Fort Leavenworth, KS, USA

HA = Hayat Alvi, Ph.D., Naval College; Annapolis, MD, USA

IAA = Ihsan Ali Alkhatib, Ph.D., Murray State University; Murray, KY, USA

IC = Ian Campbell, Ph.D., Georgia State University; Atlanta, GA, USA

IJB = Issa J. Boullata, Ph.D., McGill University; Montreal, Canada

JAR = James A. Reilly, Ph.D., University of Toronto; Canada

JB = Jennifer Bremer, Ph.D., American University in Cairo; Egypt; Association for Middle Eastern Public Policy and Administration; Washington, DC, USA

JBR = Jane Bristol-Rhys, Ph.D., Zayed University; Abu Dhabi, UAE

JCAR = James C. A. Redman, Ph.D., University of Utah; Salt Lake City, UT, USA

JEN = Jamal En-nehas, Ph.D., University of Saint Boniface; Manitoba, Canada

JJC = John J. Curry, Ph.D., University of Nevada; Las Vegas, NV, USA

JO = Josef Olmert, Ph.D., University of South Carolina; Columbia, SC, USA

KLW = Kenneth L. Wise, Ph.D., Creighton University; Omaha, NE, USA

KMC = Kenneth M. Cuno, Ph.D., University of Illinois at Urbana-Champaign; Champaign, IL, USA

MA = Maria Holt, Ph.D., University of Westminster; London, UK

MAT = Mary Ann Tétreault, Ph.D., Trinity University; San Antonio, TX, USA

MB = Marilyn Booth, Ph.D., University of Edinburgh; Edinburgh, UK

MF = Maximilian Felsch, Ph.D., Haigazian University; Beirut, Lebanon

MG = Mustafa Gokcek, Ph.D., Niagara University; Lewiston, NY, USA

MH = Mahmoud Haddad, Ph.D., University of Balamand; Koura, Lebanon

MJP = Marcie J. Patton, Ph.D., Fairfield University; Fairfield, CT, USA

MK = Muqtedar Khan, Ph.D., University of Delaware; Newark, DE, USA

MK¹ = Masaki Kakizaki, Ph.D., University of Utah; Salt Lake City, UT, USA

MLA = Michal L. Allon, Ph.D., Tel Aviv University; Tel Aviv, Israel

MM = Michael McGaha, Ph.D., Pomona College; Claremont, CA, USA

MMA = Mohammed M. Aman, Ph.D., University of Wisconsin; Milwaukee, WI, USA

MMD = M. Mizanur Rahman, South Asian University; New Delhi, India

MMF = Mateo M. Farzaneh, Ph.D., Northeastern Illinois University; Chicago, IL, USA

MMM = M. M. Mazinani, MA, University of Utah; Salt Lake City, UT, USA

MS = Mauro Sierra III, University of Texas—Pan-American; Edinburg, TX, USA

MSC = Martin Scott Catino, Ph.D., Henley Putnam University; Santa Clara, CA, USA

MY = Maya Yazigi, Ph.D., Simon Fraser University; Burnaby, BC, CA, USA

MZ = Mahjoob Zweiri, Ph.D., Qatar University; Doha, Qatar

NEG = Nancy E. Gallagher, Ph.D., University of California; Santa Barbara, CA, USA

NM = Nazan Maksudyan, Ph.D., Zentrum Moderner Orient; Berlin, Germany

PAS = Philip A. Schrodt, Ph.D., Pennsylvania State University; State College, PA, USA

PSR = Paul S. Rowe, Ph.D., Trinity Western University; Langley, British Columbia, Canada

RAR = Rowena Abdul Razak, ABD, St Antony's College; University of Oxford; Oxford, UK

RDM = Roxanne D. Marcotte, Ph.D., Université du Québec à Montréal (UQAM); Montréal, Canada

RF = Reuven Firestone, Ph.D., Hebrew Union College; Los Angeles, CA, USA

RG = Rebecca Gould, Ph.D., Yale-NUS College; New Haven, CT, USA

RHO = Ramazan Hakkı Öztan, University of Utah; Salt Lake City, UT, USA

RJH = Robert J. Haug, Ph.D., University of Cincinnati; Cincinnati, OH, USA

RM = Robert Mason, Ph.D., British University in Egypt; Cairo, Egypt

RM² = Roberto Mazzo, Ph.D., Western Illinois University; McComb, IL, USA

RM ¹ = Rolin Mainuddin, Ph.D., North Carolina Central University; Durham, NC, USA

ROF = Robert O. Freedman, Ph.D., Johns Hopkins University; Baltimore, MD, USA

RRW = Rebecca R. Williams, Ph.D., University of South Alabama Mobile; AL, USA

RS = Renat Shaykhutdinov, Ph.D., Florida Atlantic University; Boca Raton, FL, USA

SA = Salua Fawzi, MA, McGill University; Montreal, CA, USA

SCD = Steven C. Dinero, Ph.D., Philadelphia University; Philadelphia, PA, USA

SD = Steven Dinero, Ph.D., Philadelphia University; Philadelphia, PA, USA

SH = Shak Hanish, Ph.D., National University; San Diego, CA, USA

SJF = Seth J. Frantzman, Ph.D., Hebrew University of Jerusalem; Al-Quds University, Jerusalem, Israel

SK = Sahar Khamis, Ph.D., University of Maryland; College Park, MD, USA

SO = Susanne Olsson, Ph.D., Södertörn University; Flemingsberg, Sweden

SOG = Samaneh Oladi Ghadikolaei, Ph.D., University of California; Santa Barbara, CA, USA

SRS = Sanford R. Silverburg, Ph.D., Catawba College; Salisbury, NC, USA

SS = Stephen Sheehi, Ph.D., University of South Carolina; Columbia, SC, USA

WLR = W. Lynn Rigsbee II, Ph.D., Central State University; Wilberforce, OH, USA

YY = Youssef Yacoubi, Ph.D., Ohio State University; Columbus, OH, USA

www.ingramcontent.com/pod-product-compliance
Lightning Source LLC
Chambersburg PA
CBHW052118270326
41930CB00012B/2667